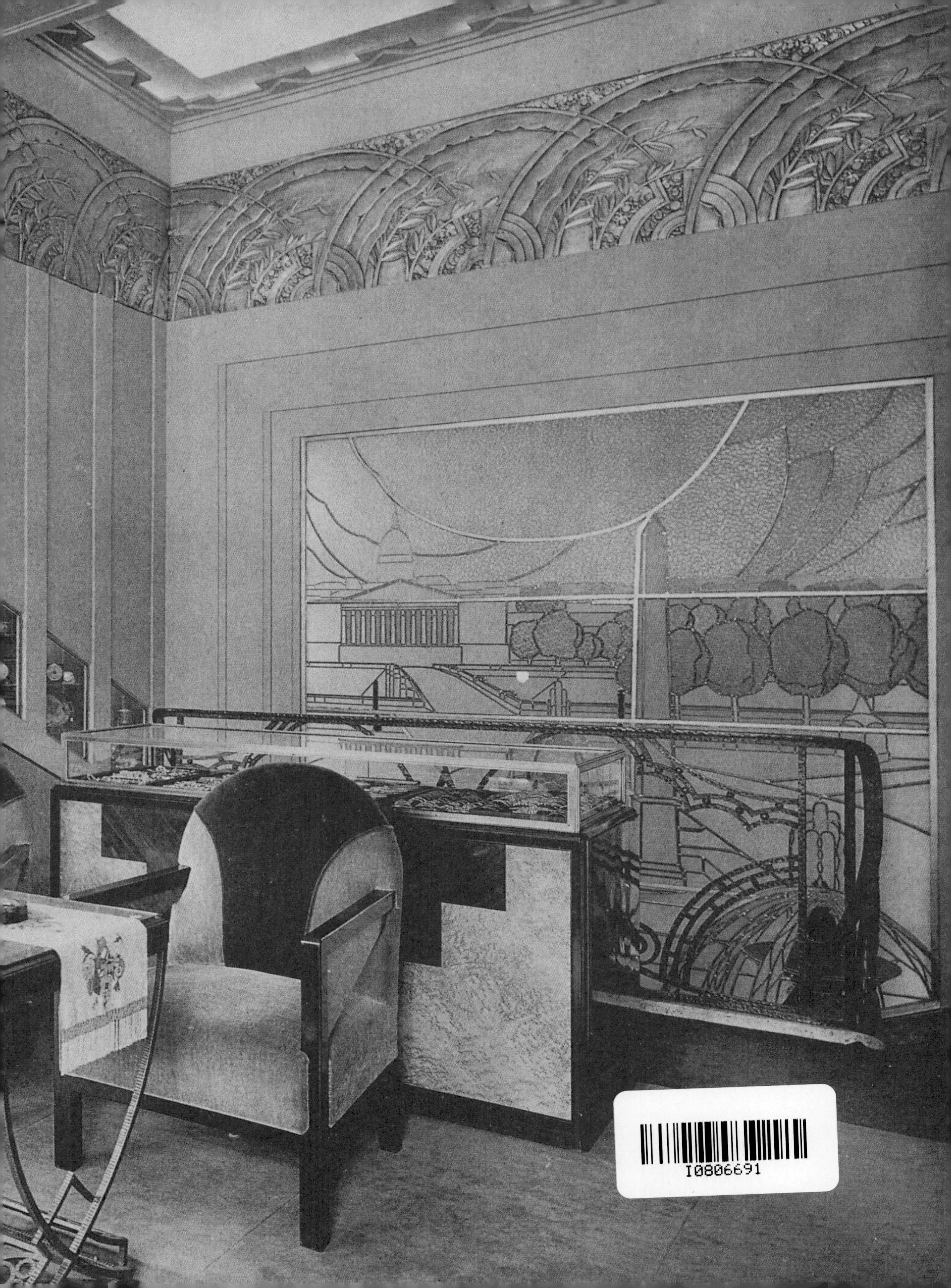

ART DECO

Ironwork & Sculpture

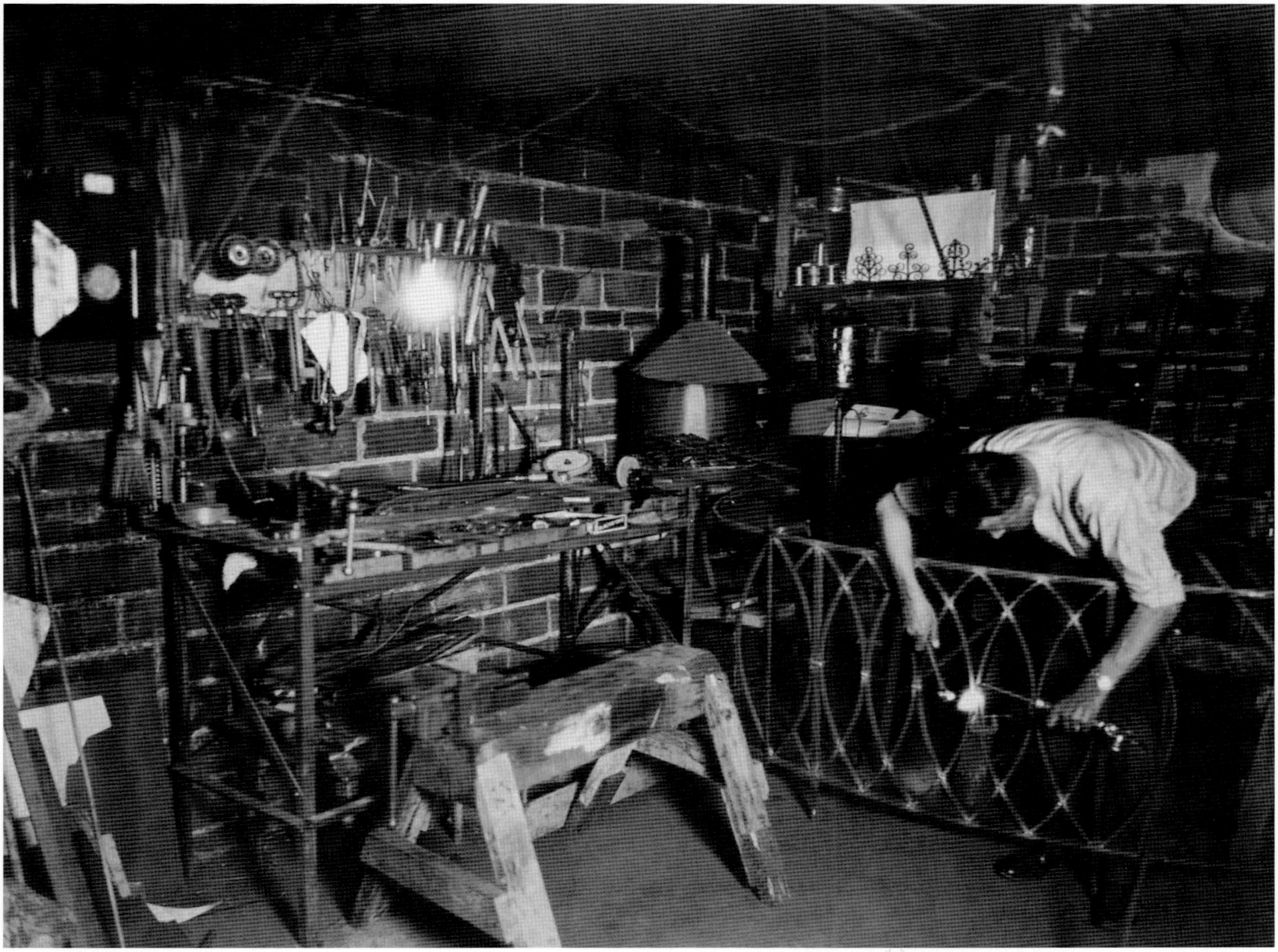

Tina Skinner

S. F. "Jerry" Cook III

Schiffer Publishing Ltd

4880 Lower Valley Road, Atglen, PA 19310 USA

Library of Congress Cataloging-in-Publication Data:

Skinner, Tina.
Art deco ironwork & sculpture / Tina Skinner, S.F. "Jerry" Cook III.
p. cm.
ISBN 0-7643-2292-3
1. Ironwork—History—20th century—Pictorial works. 2. Decoration and ornament, Architectural—Pictorial works. 3. Decoration and ornament—Art deco—Pictorial works. I. Title: Art deco ironwork and sculpture. II. Cook, S.F., 1951- III. Title.

NK8210.3.A78S55 2005
739.4—dc22

2005049919

Designed by John P. Cheek
Cover design by Bruce Waters
Type set in Zurich BT

ISBN: 0-7643-2292-3
Printed in China

Published by Schiffer Publishing Ltd.
4880 Lower Valley Road
Atglen, PA 19310
Phone: (610) 593-1777; Fax: (610) 593-2002
E-mail: Info@schifferbooks.com

For the largest selection of fine reference books on this and related subjects, please visit our web site at
www.schifferbooks.com
We are always looking for people to write books on new and related subjects. If you have an idea for a book please contact us at the above address.

This book may be purchased from the publisher.
Include $3.95 for shipping.
Please try your bookstore first.
You may write for a free catalog.

In Europe, Schiffer books are distributed by
Bushwood Books
6 Marksbury Ave.
Kew Gardens
Surrey TW9 4JF England
Phone: 44 (0) 20 8392-8585; Fax: 44 (0) 20 8392-9876
E-mail: info@bushwoodbooks.co.uk
Free postage in the U.K., Europe; air mail at cost.

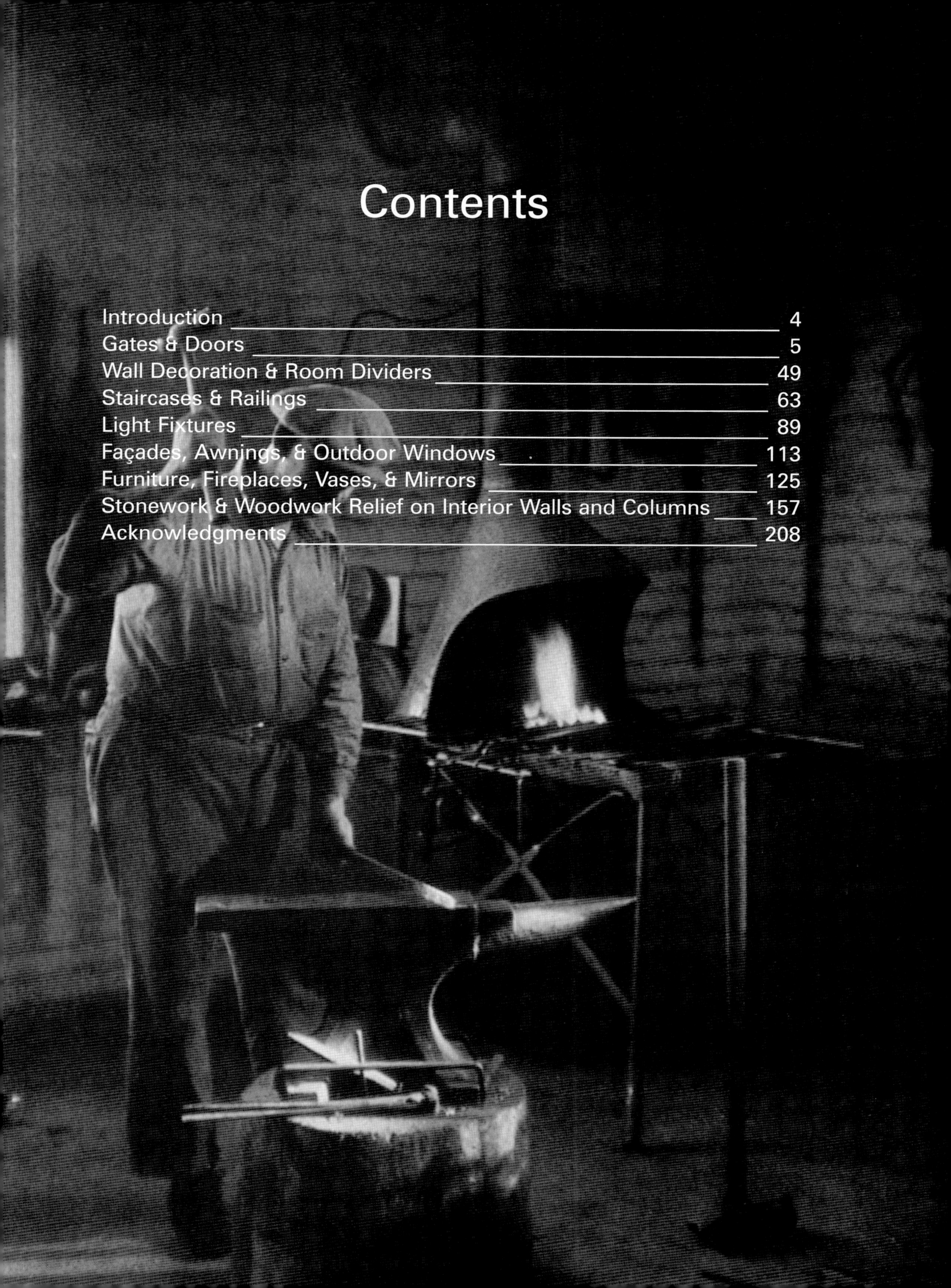

Contents

Introduction ____ 4
Gates & Doors ____ 5
Wall Decoration & Room Dividers ____ 49
Staircases & Railings ____ 63
Light Fixtures ____ 89
Façades, Awnings, & Outdoor Windows ____ 113
Furniture, Fireplaces, Vases, & Mirrors ____ 125
Stonework & Woodwork Relief on Interior Walls and Columns ____ 157
Acknowledgments ____ 208

Introduction

The Art Deco style was born in a time of modernization when new, fresh ideas and abstract designs encouraged people to look at decorative arts in a new light. Architects from all over Europe and the United States looking to achieve better design standards began breaking away from dictated styles of decoration and began using various forms of ironwork and sculpture in their interior and exterior designs to accent the décor of their new structures.

Influenced by the drive for modernization after the First World War, architects and artists worked together to align art with industry. Designers derived inspiration from the past and drew on Persian, Assyrian, Greek, Roman, Mayan, and Egyptian designs. Incorporating the distinct cultural designs from all around the globe and mixing them with modern elements from the industrialized era, designers began to develop something new. As the designs evolved, streamlined industrial architecture was tempered by natural, botanical elements that created Art Deco styling. Putting tradition aside, the Art Deco style that evolved was fresh, playful, and inviting with new forms of abstract designs.

The industrial age brought with it many new technologies that revolutionized the manufacturing processes of nearly every industry. Architects and builders began to replace the iron beams of the past with stronger, more durable steel, shifting their focus toward large skyscrapers. The new buildings were designed to be more than just structures; they were now intended to be beautiful statements of engineering. Incorporating the freshest designs for ornamentation, the designers took advantage of many forms of ironwork and sculpture to make buildings objects of great attention, inside and out.

For ironworkers and metal artists, new fabrication technologies, such as the advent of the oxyacetylene torch and electrolysis, opened new doors in what was technically possible. As the demand for iron ornamentation grew, companies began implementing prefabricated construction methods to keep up with the demand. Casting had become a less expensive option for mass production of more standard iron ornamentation, but the best examples of ironwork were from the craftsmen who used hand-worked wrought iron in the composition of one-of-a-kind designs. Competition in the decorative ironwork industry forced companies to look for new ways to differentiate their products; better designs were the answer. Creating gracefully flowing designs that were delicate yet striking in composition, the ironwork designers were daring and flexible, pioneering the Art Deco movement and leading the way in creating the styling that made these designs as appealing now as they were at their creation. Gates, doors, room dividers, staircases, railings, furniture, and many more objects were designed and created to ornament the new Art Deco structures.

The sculptors incorporated the aesthetics of Art Deco in their façades, joining the designs of the Far East and Roman Empire with those of the industrial age. Sculptors were instrumental in evoking passionate feelings through their powerful design, and architects strived to use these works in the ornamentation of their new structures. Sculptors used a number of mediums for their designs; stone, plaster, and wood were the most common and versatile for their purpose. Artists adorned the entranceways and exteriors of buildings with figural relief carvings, columns, and many detailed accent pieces. Some of the sculptures depict figures of many forms and tell of epic stories with great significance to their surroundings; other panels and sculptures are geometric designs with the purpose to inspire.

The Art Deco movement was in large part driven by the influences of the architects and designers that displayed the new forms in the buildings they created and through their daring pursuit for a modern, higher standard of design. Ironwork and sculpture are two areas that exemplify the diversity and genius of the Art Deco style.

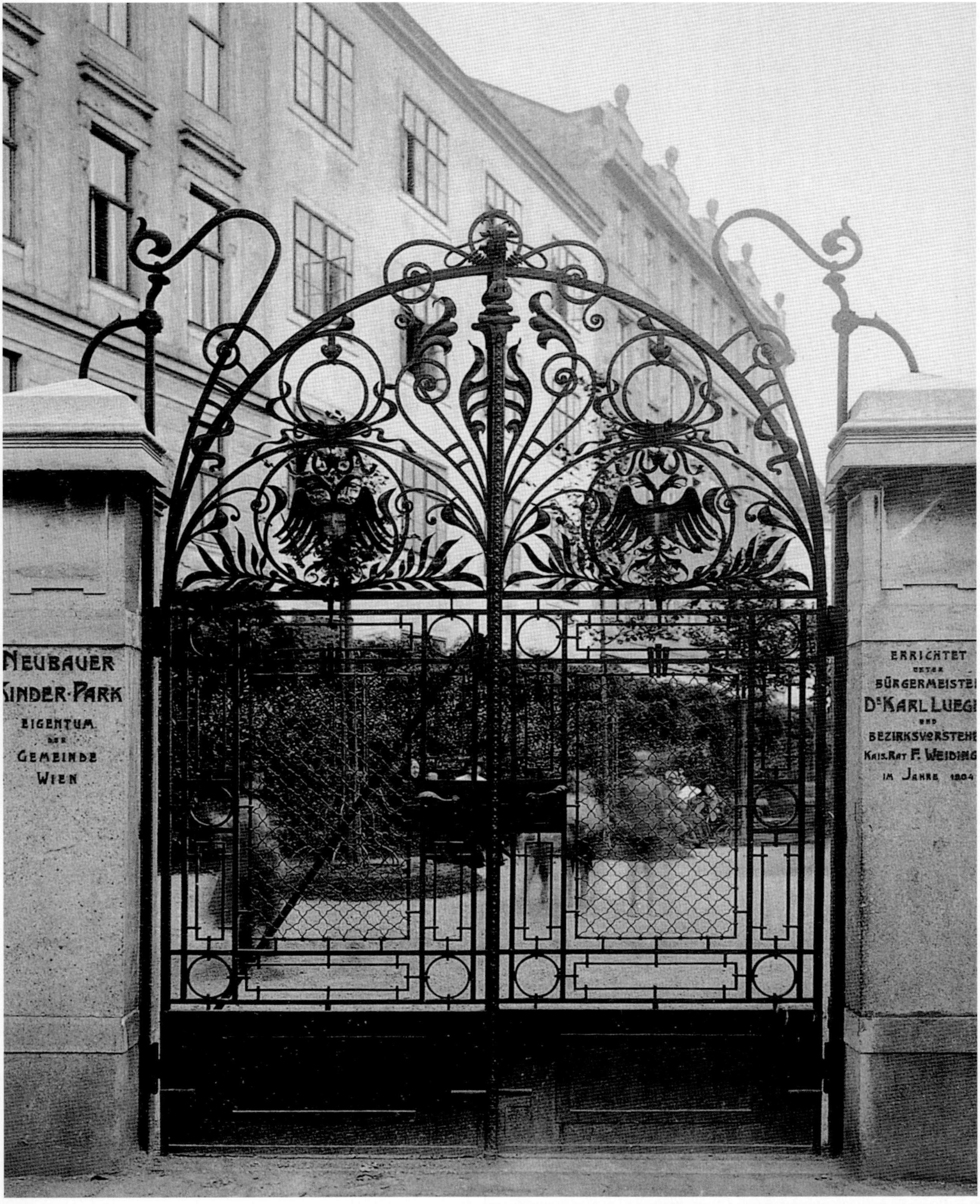
NEUBAUER
KINDER-PARK
EIGENTUM
DER
GEMEINDE
WIEN
ERRICHTET
UNTER
BÜRGERMEISTE
Dr KARL LUEG
UND
BEZIRKSVORSTEHE
KAIS. RAT F. WEIDING
IM JAHRE 1904

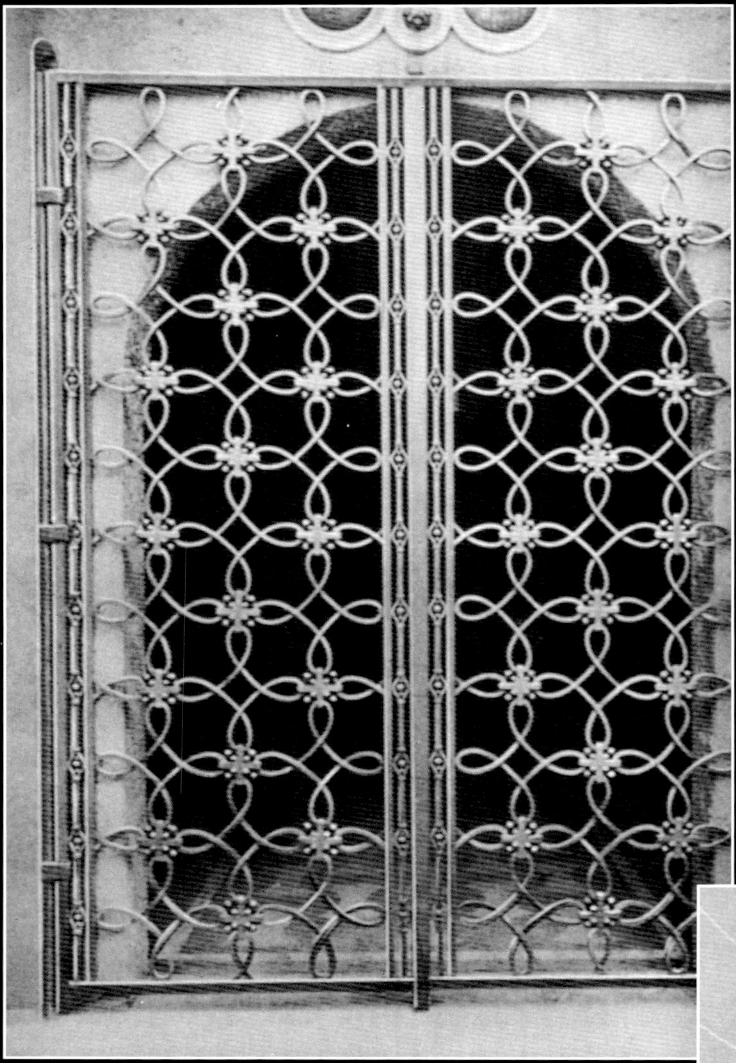

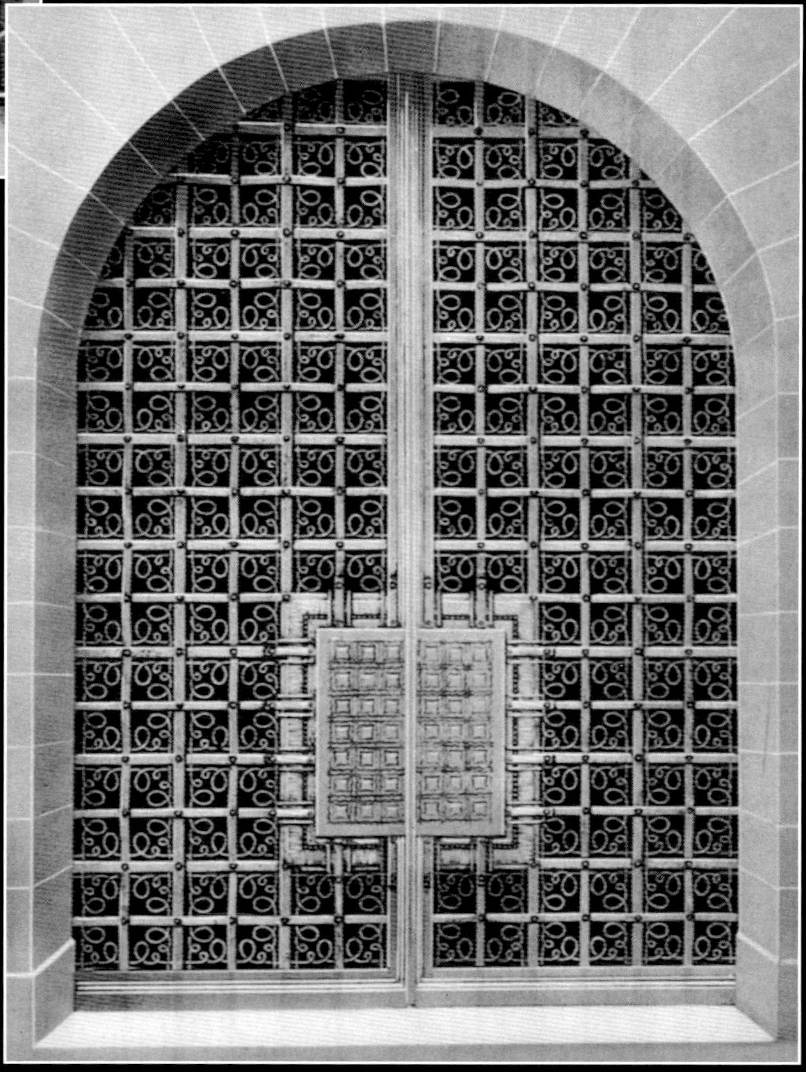

M. C. GENUYS, ARCH

M. SAUVAGE, ARCH.

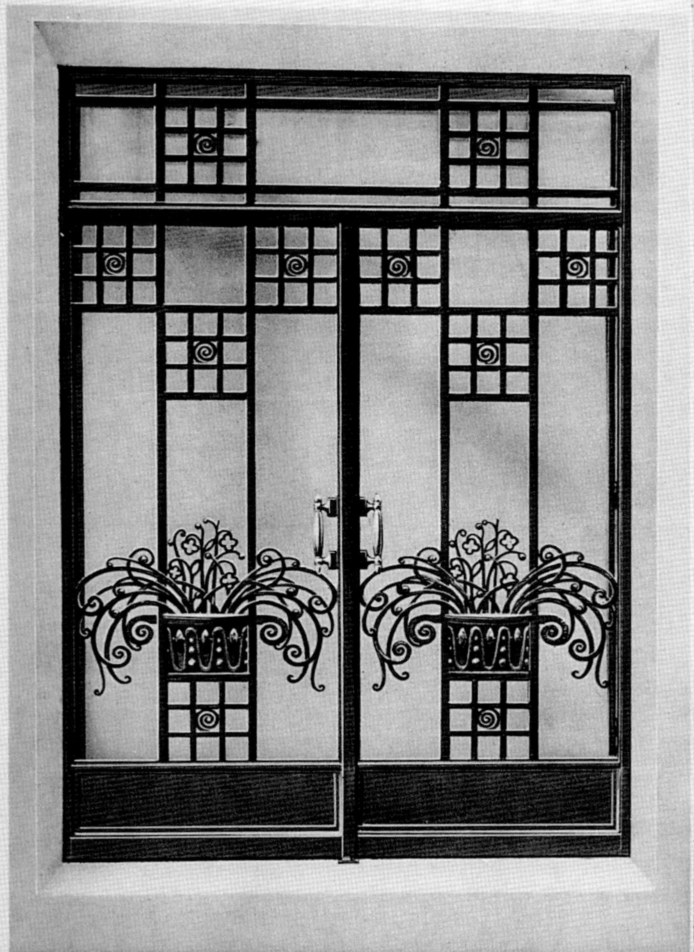

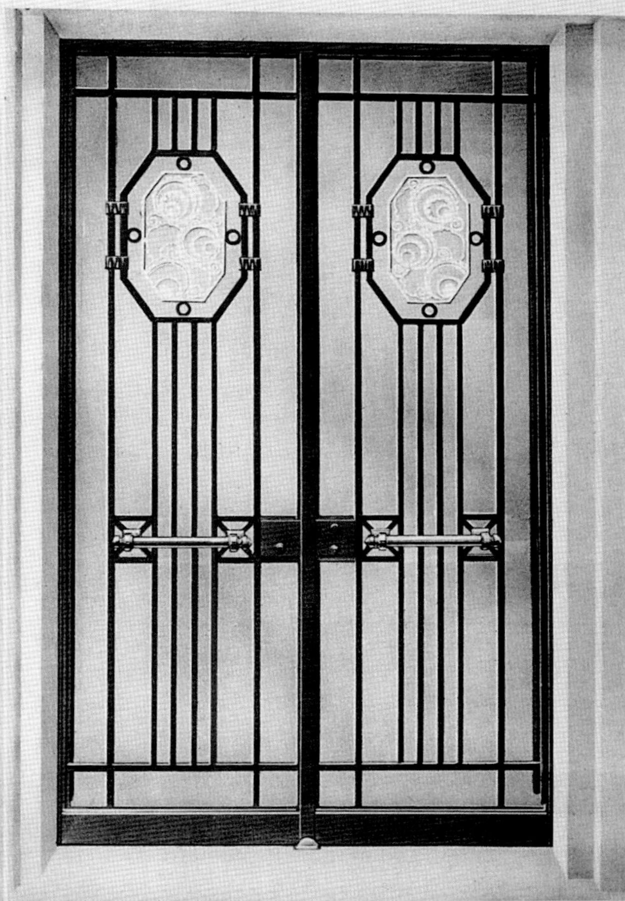

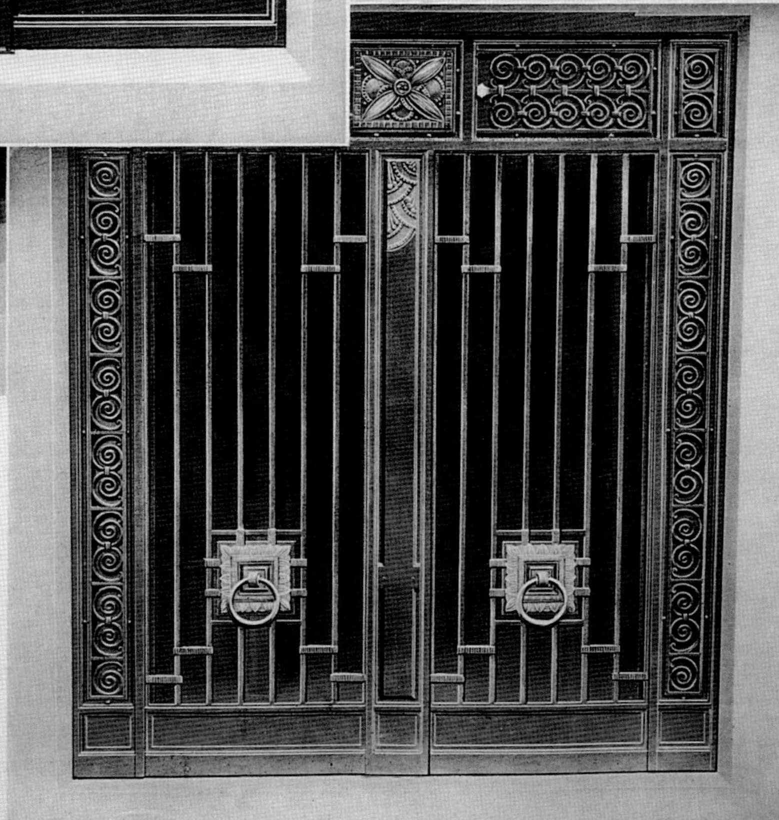

M. PATOUILLARD-DEMORIANE, ARCH.

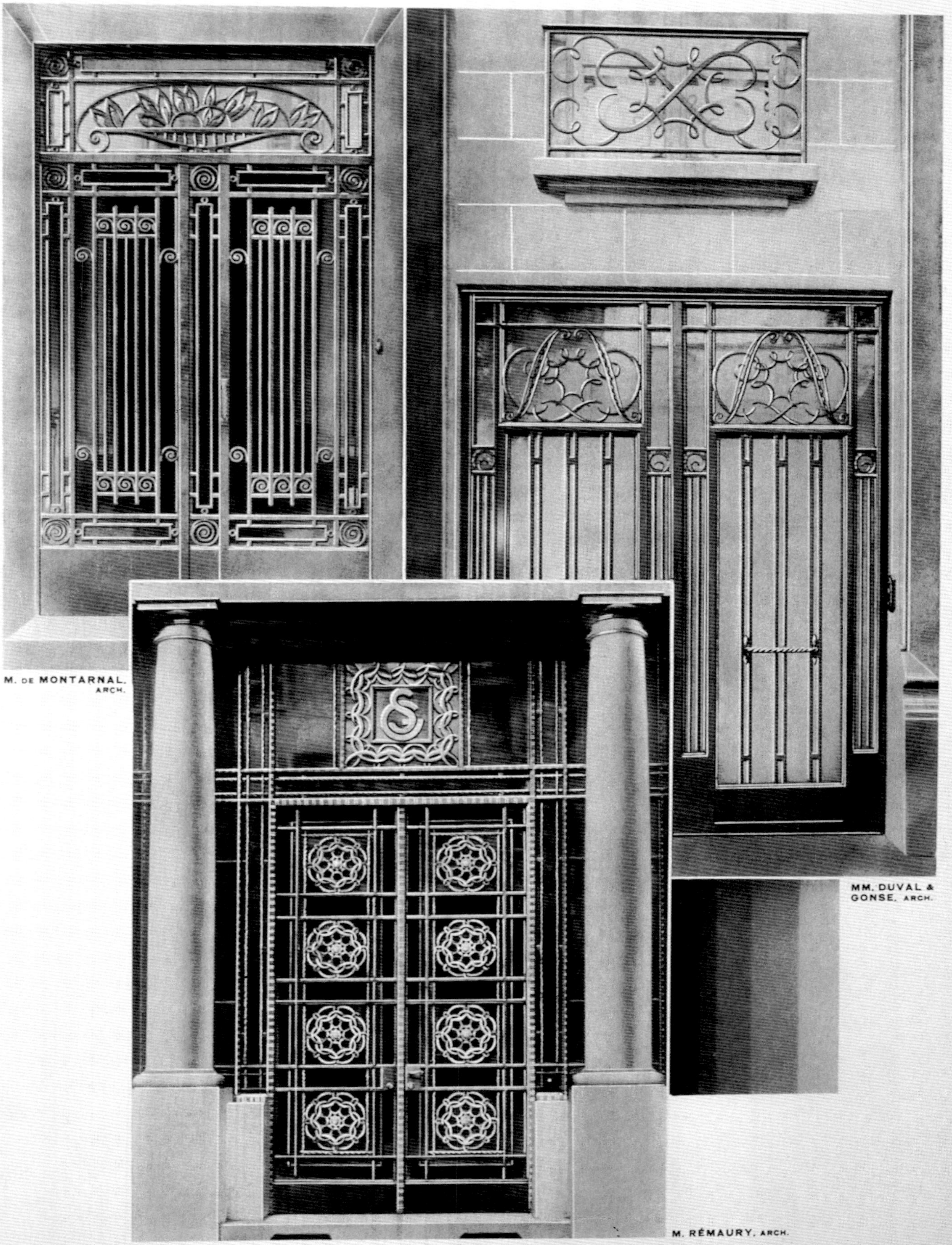

M. DE MONTARNAL, ARCH.

MM. DUVAL & GONSE, ARCH.

M. RÉMAURY, ARCH.

M. JEAN BERTRAND, ARCH.

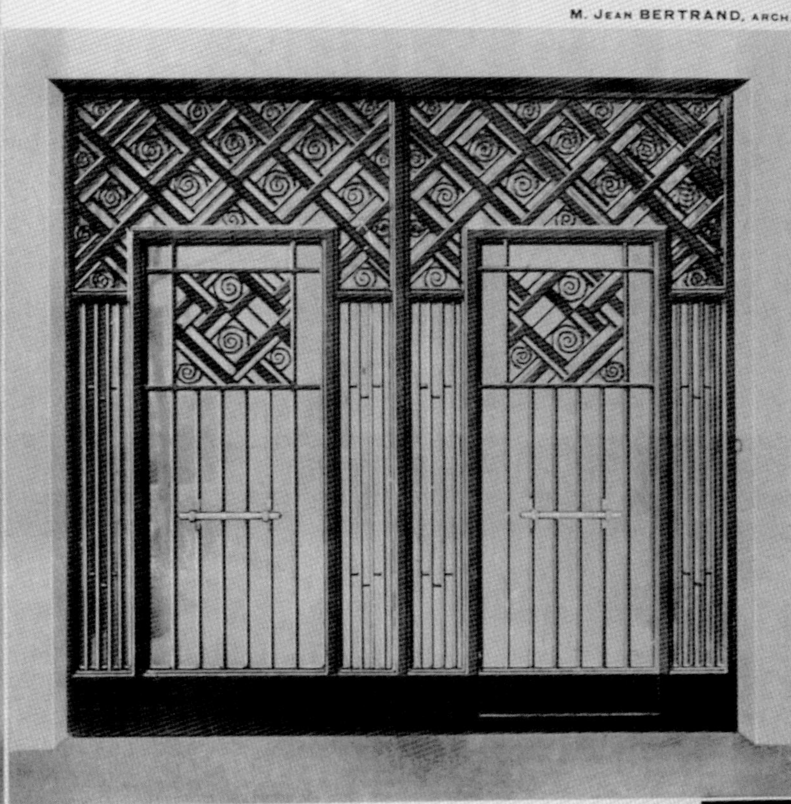

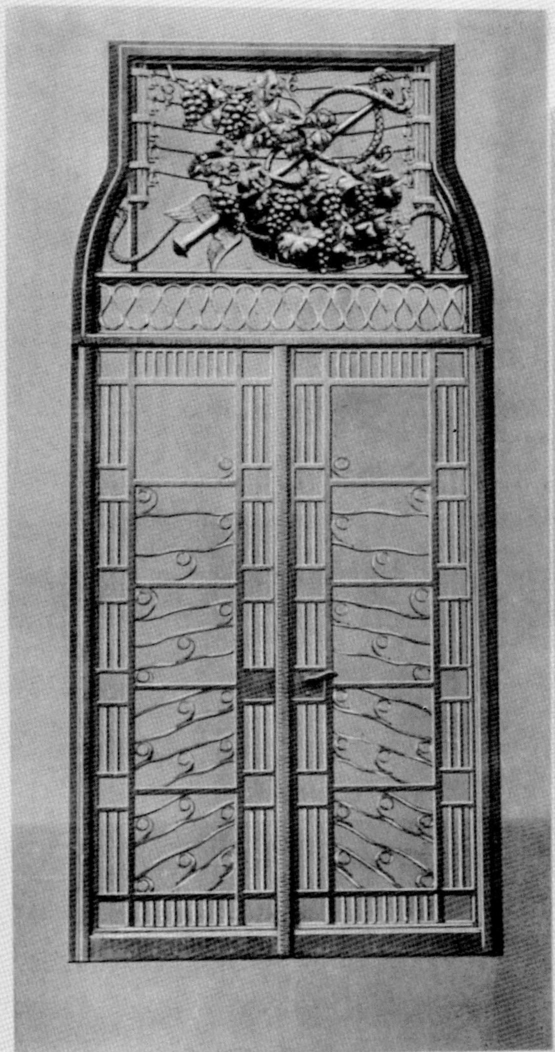

M. DERVAUX, ARCH.

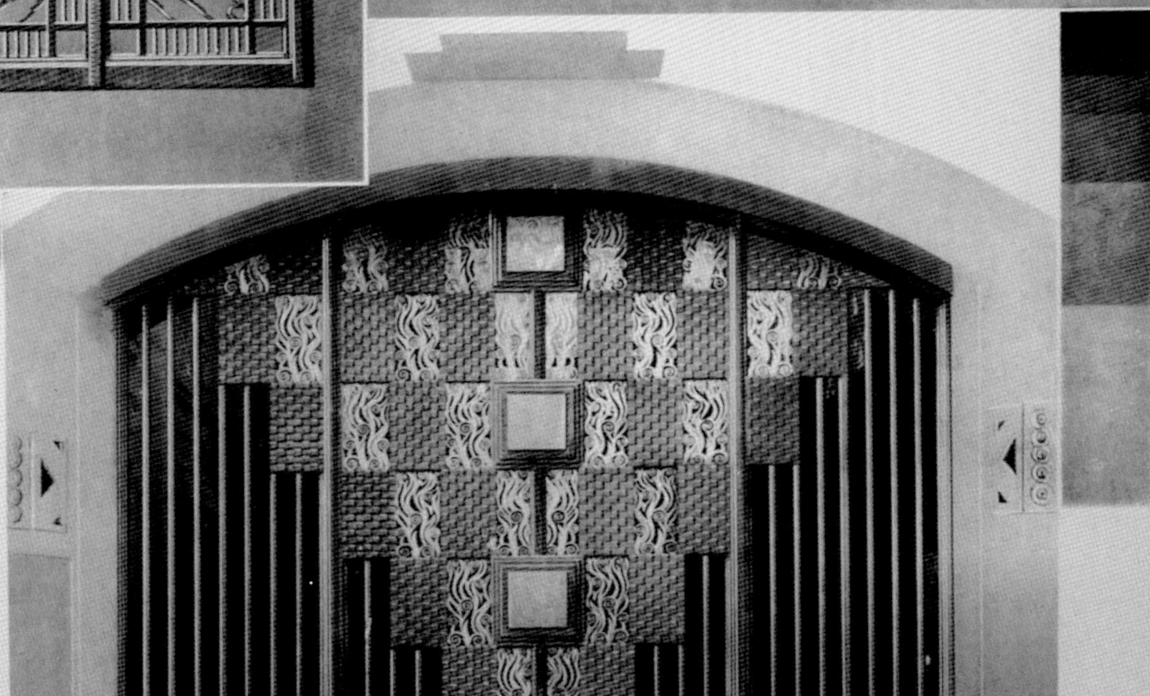

M. TOURNON, ARCH.

E. BORDEREL & ROBERT

I

M. EXPERT, ARCH.

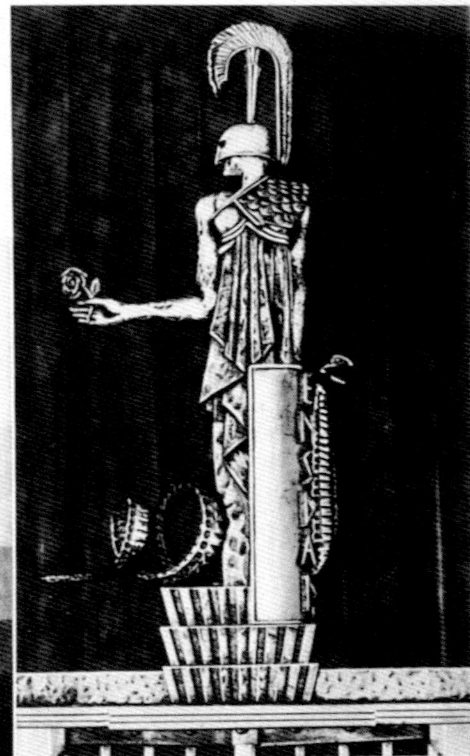

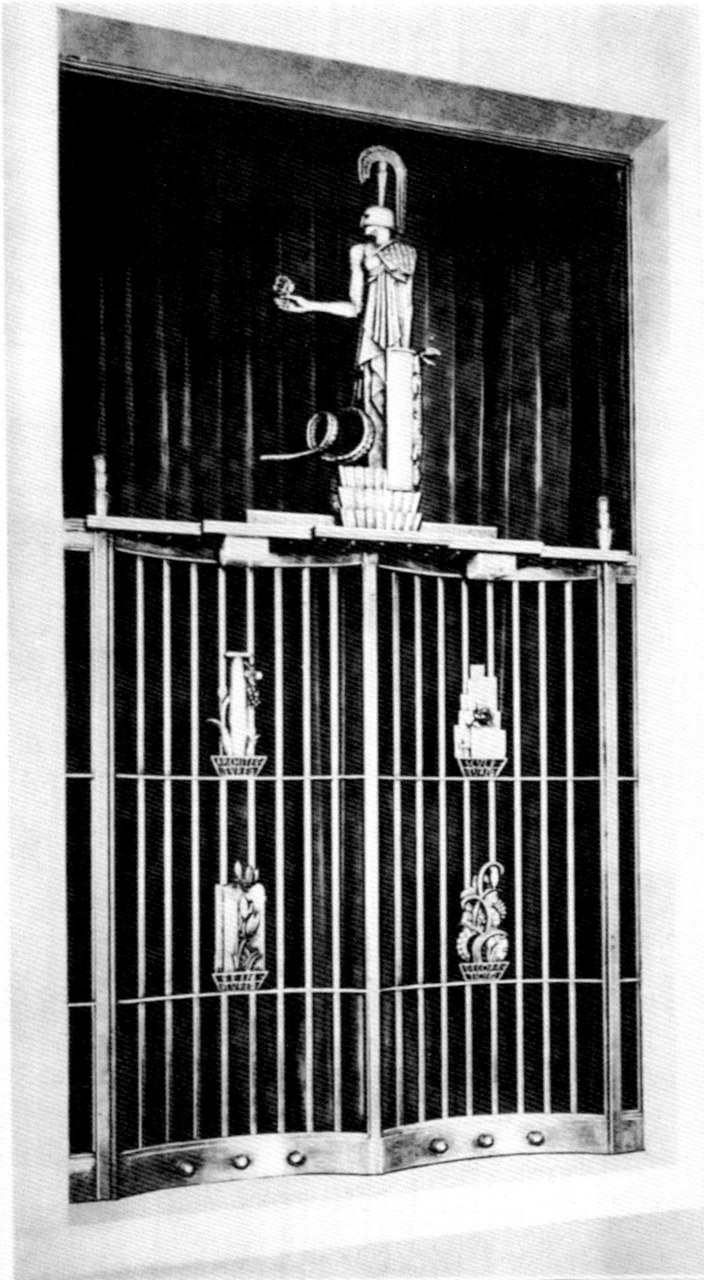

M. EXPERT, ARCH.

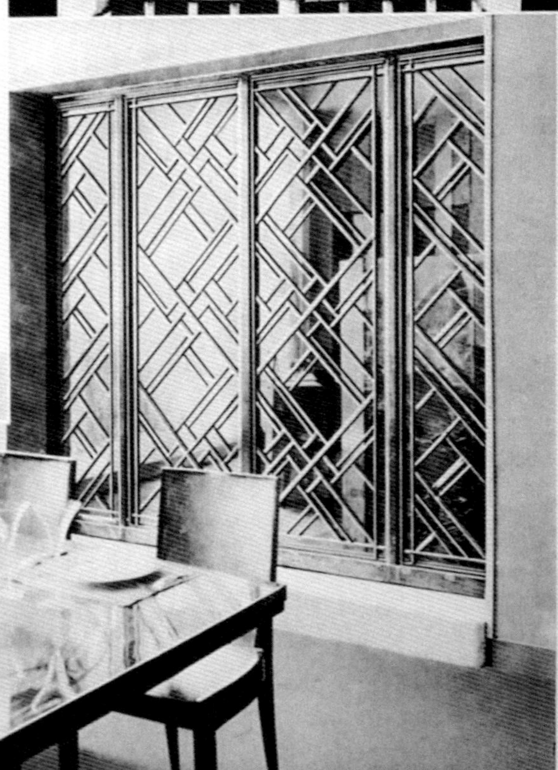

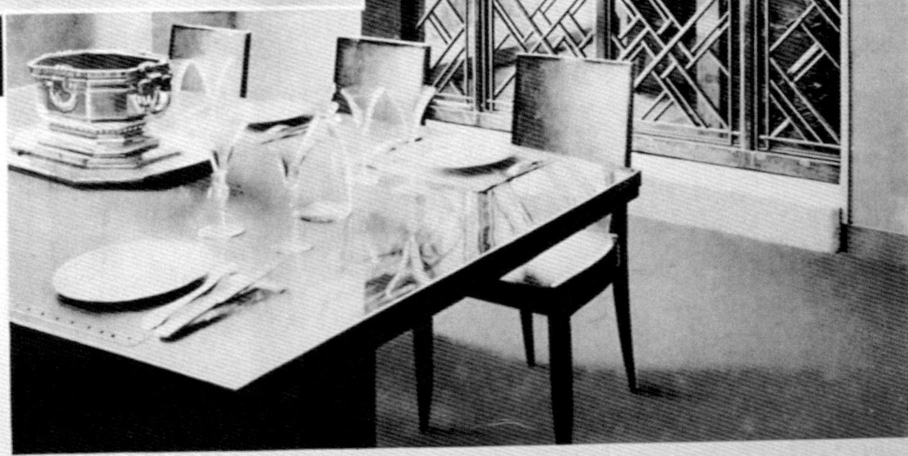

MM. JALLOT, DÉCORATEURS.

E. BORDEREL & ROBERT II

204

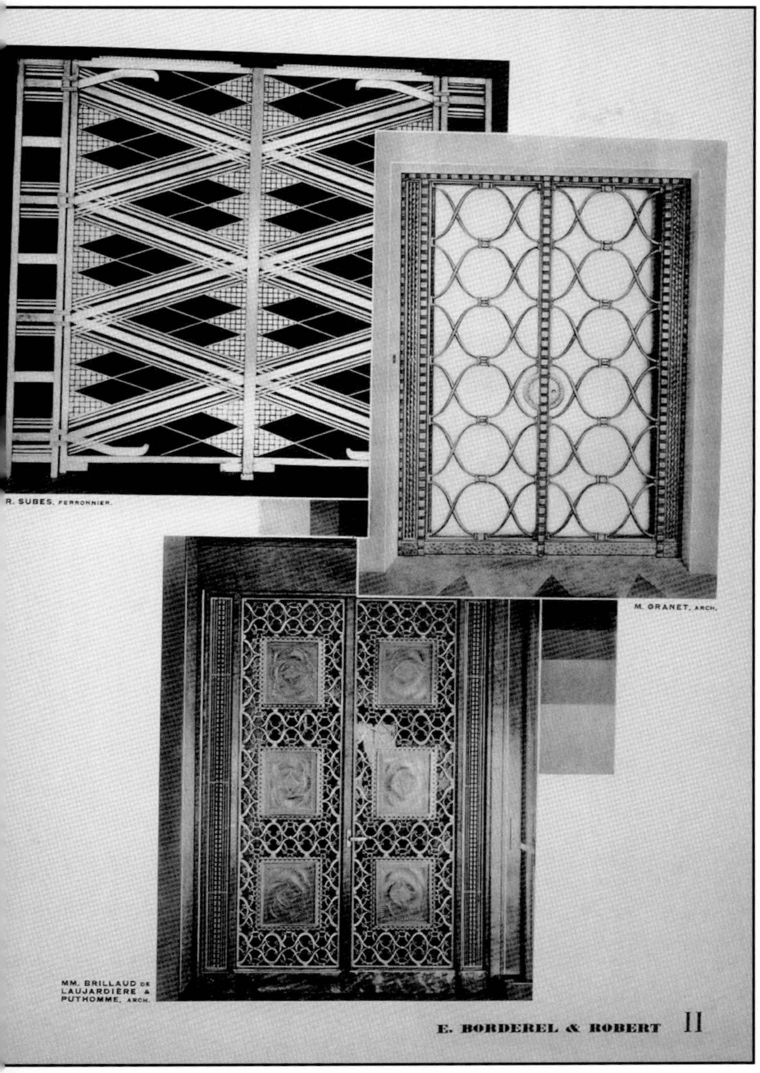
R. SUBES, FERRONNIER.
M. GRANET, ARCH.
MM. BRILLAUD DE LAUJARDIÈRE & PUTHOMME, ARCH.
E. BORDEREL & ROBERT
II

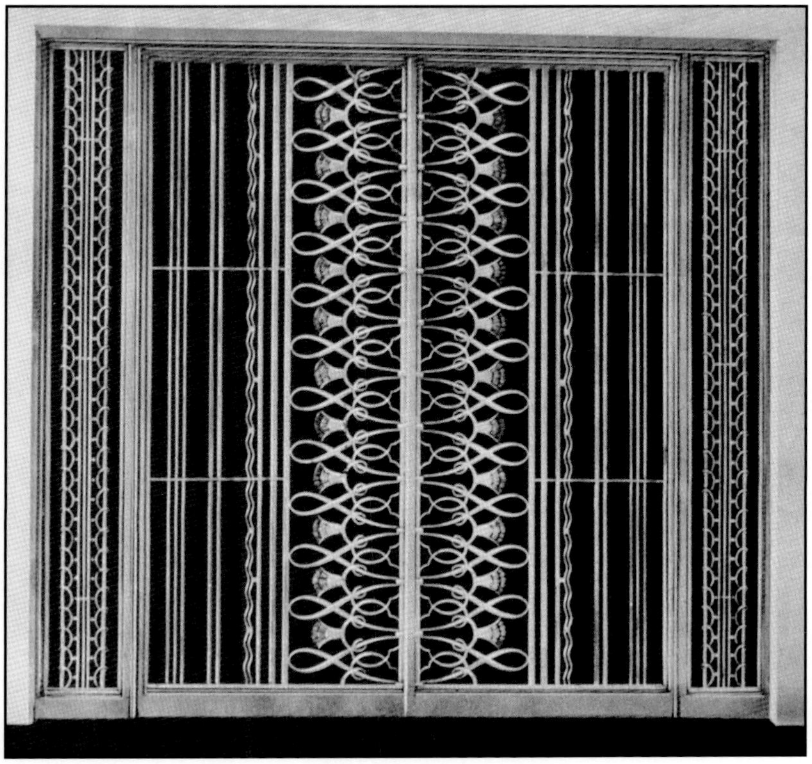

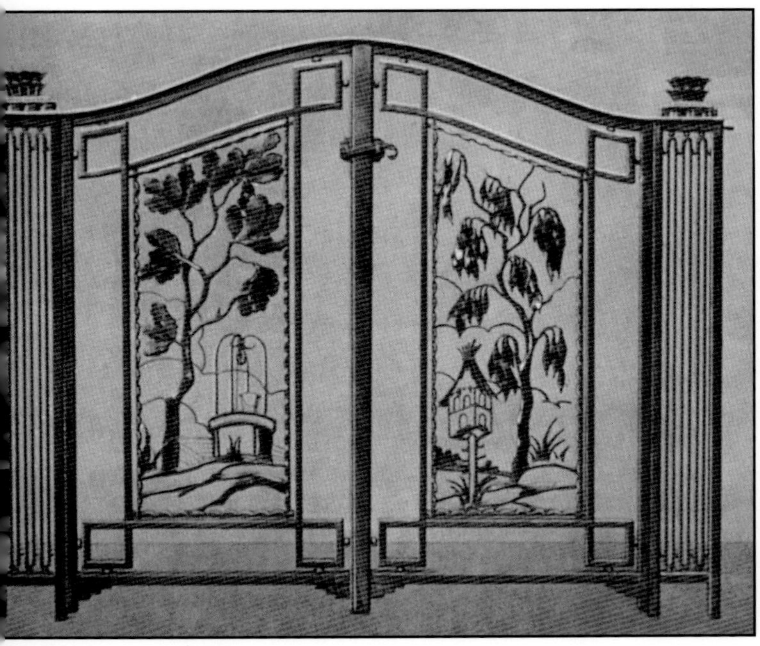

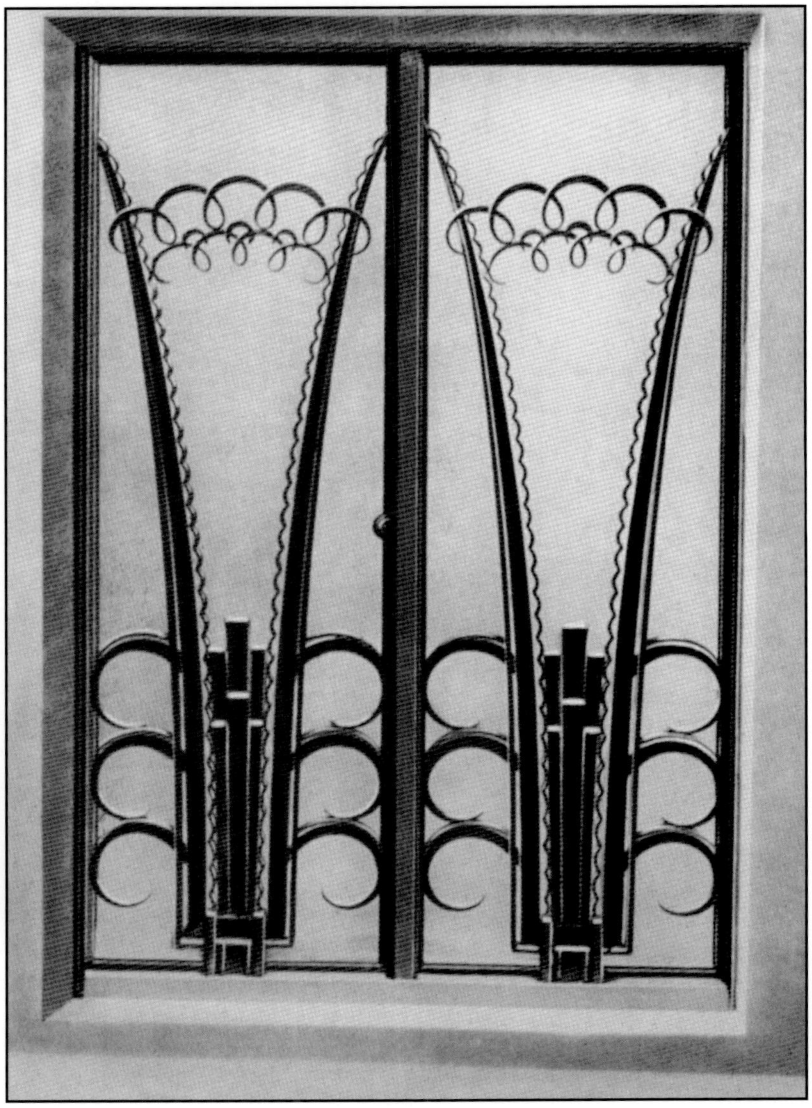

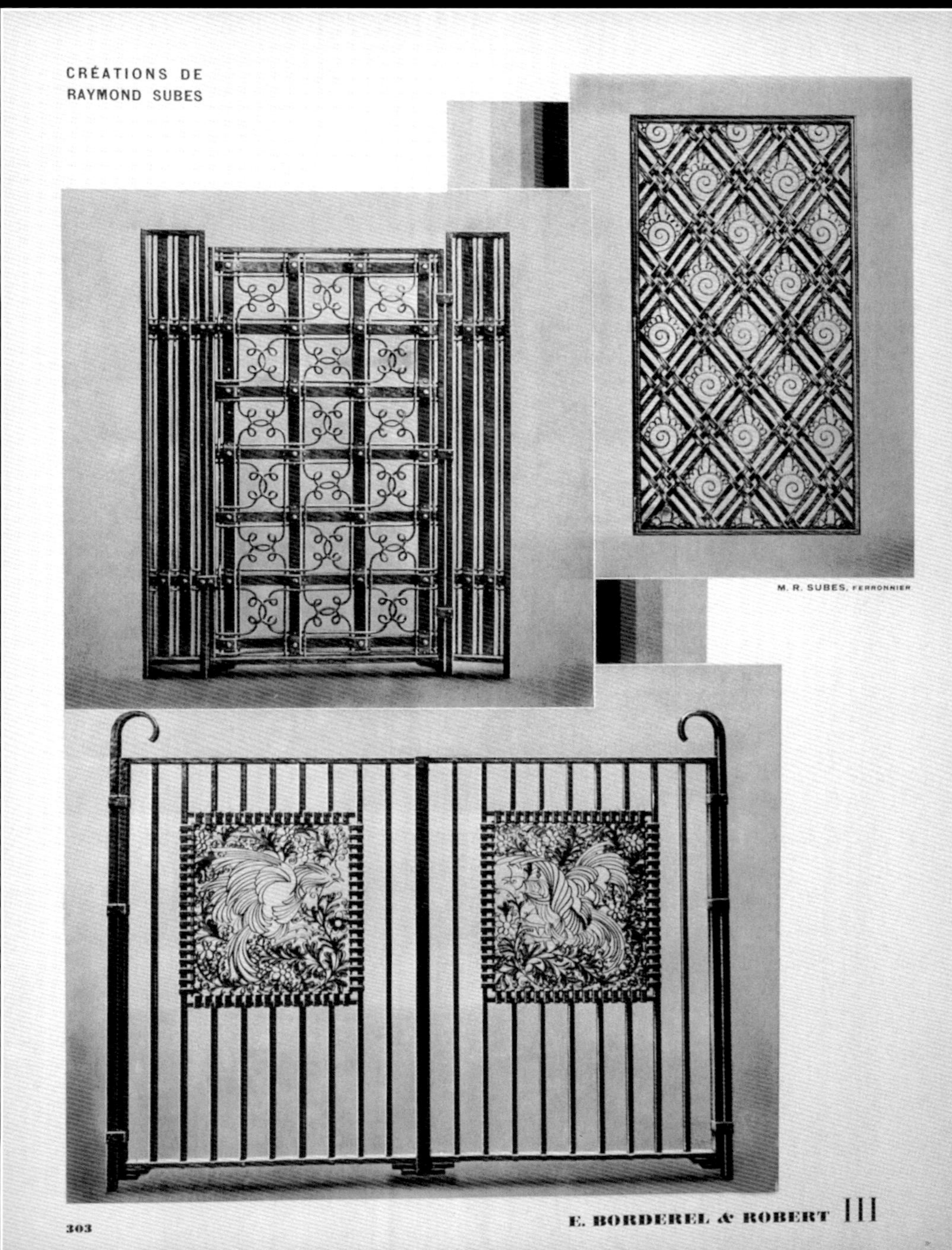
CRÉATIONS DE
RAYMOND SUBES
M. R. SUBES, FERRONNIER
303
E. BORDEREL & ROBERT III

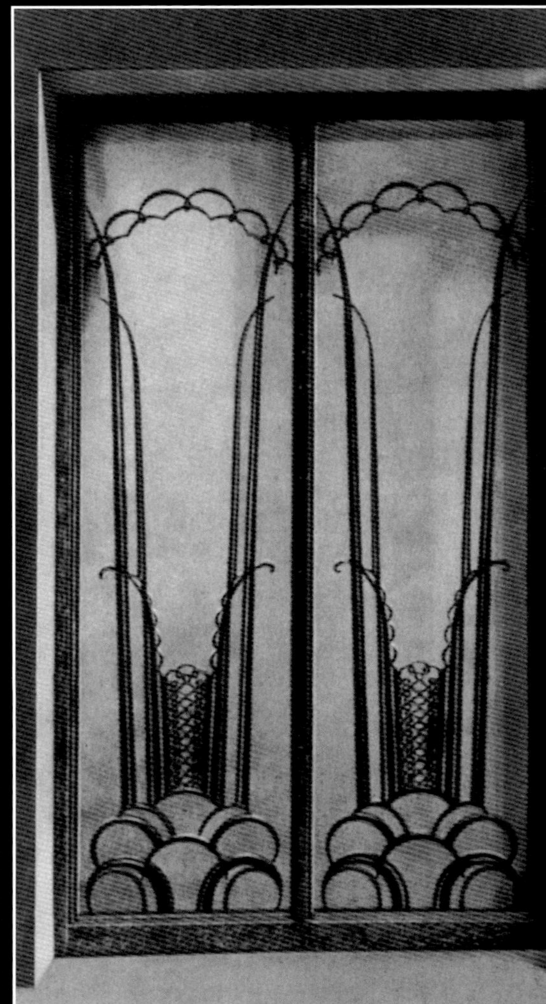

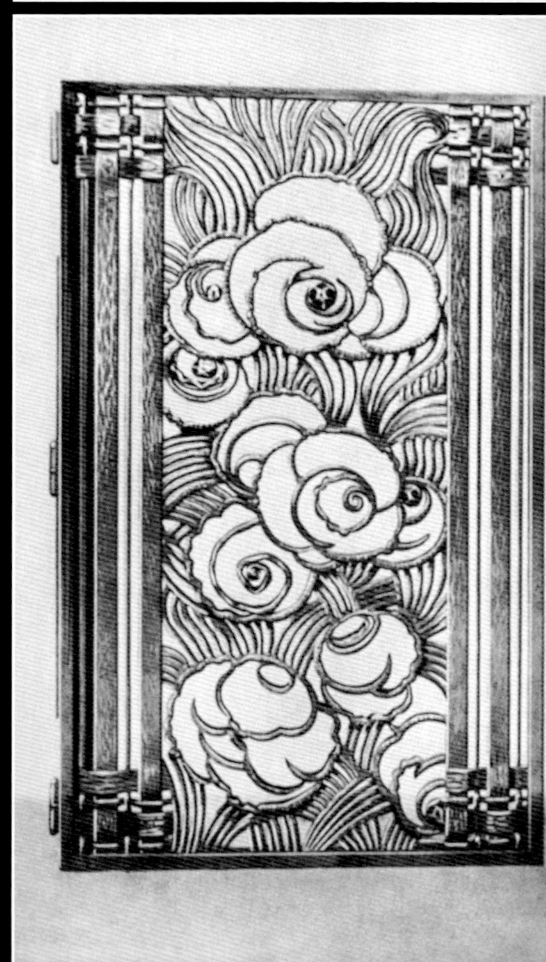

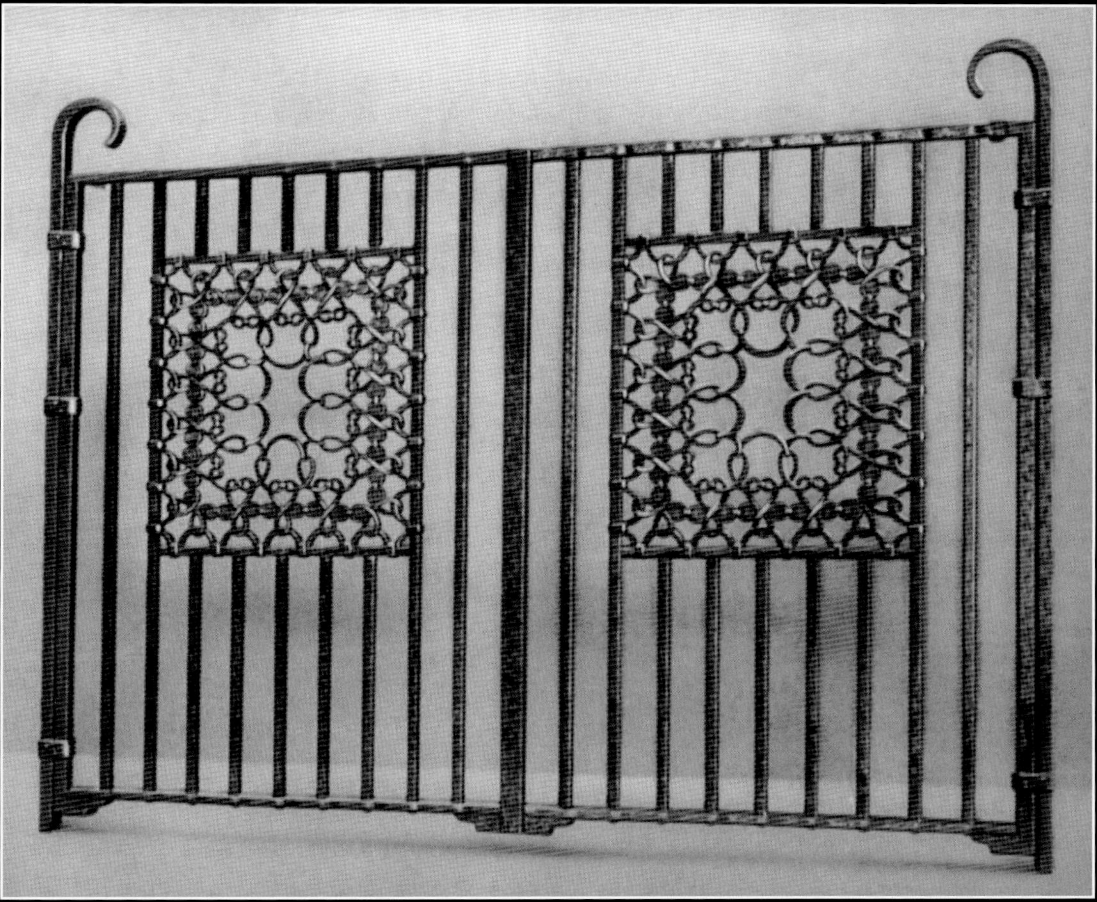

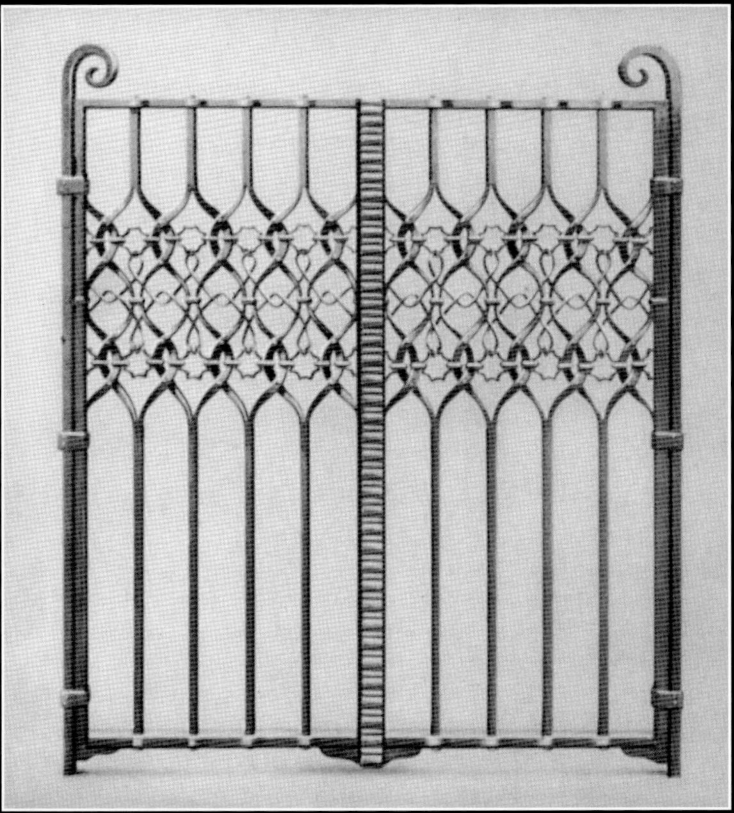

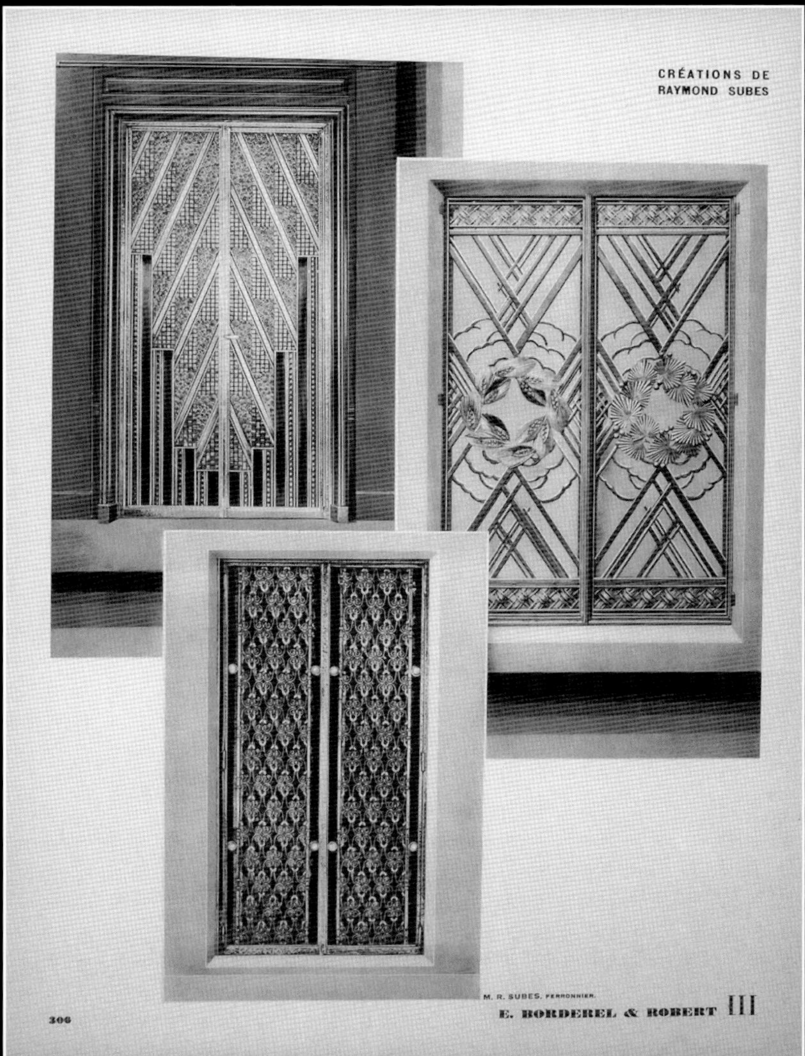
CRÉATIONS DE
RAYMOND SUBES
M. R. SUBES, FERRONNIER.
E. BORDEREL & ROBERT III
306

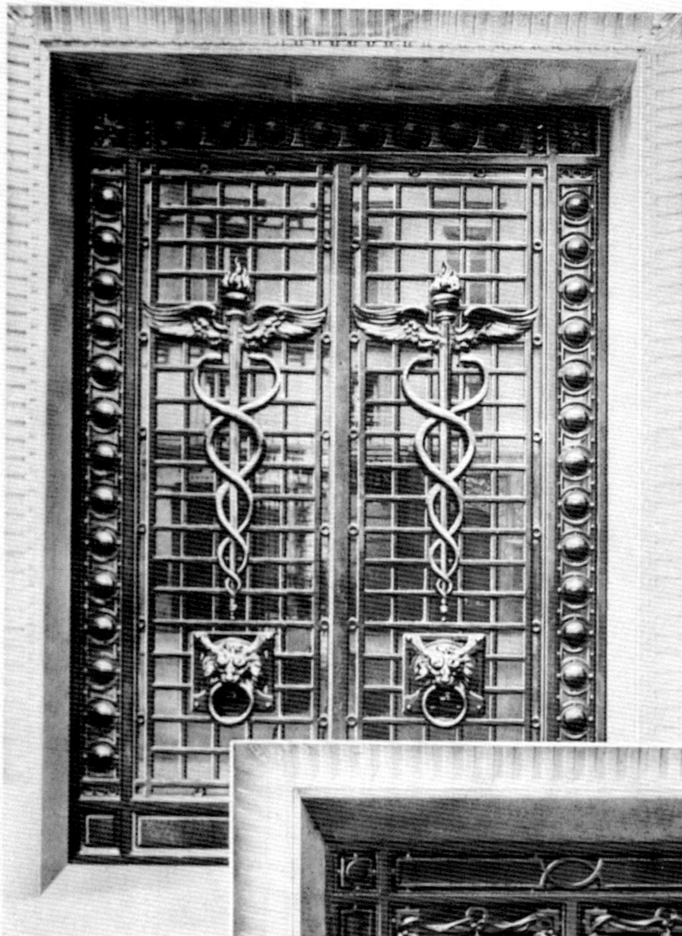

MM. LEFÈVRE, DUHAYON & JULIEN, ARCH.

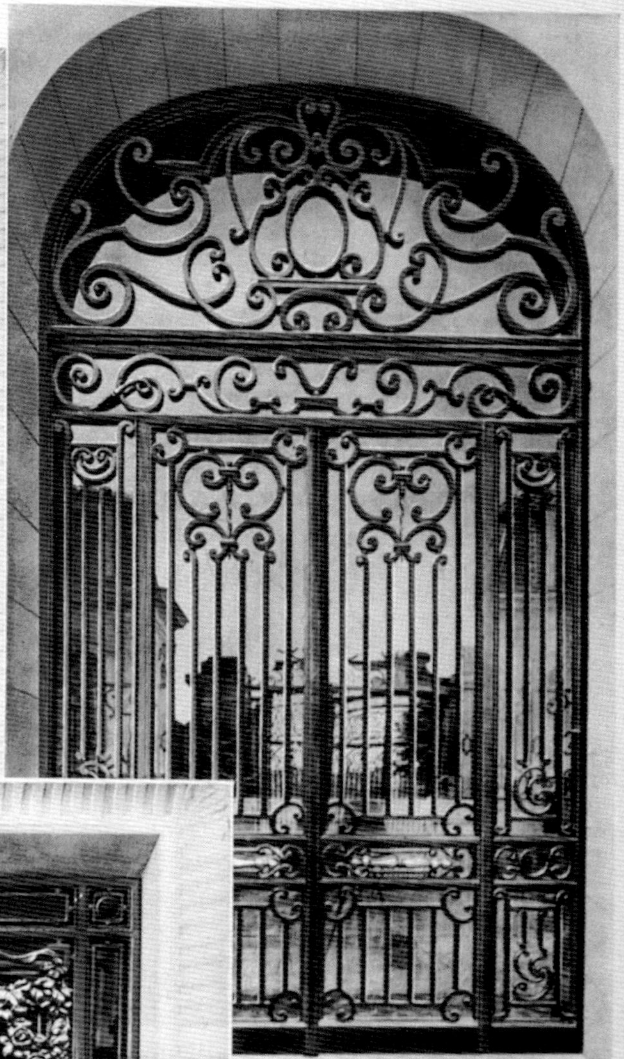

MM. DEFRASSE ET GUILLEMIN TARAYRE, ARCH.

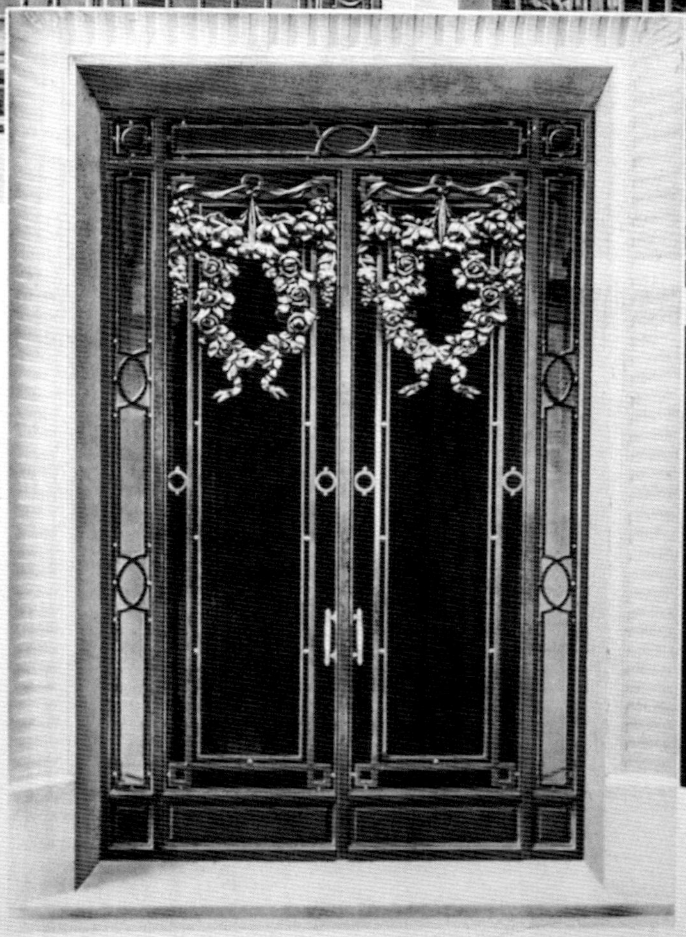

MM. LEFÈVRE, DUHAYON & JULIEN, ARCH.

401

E. BORDEREL & ROBERT IV

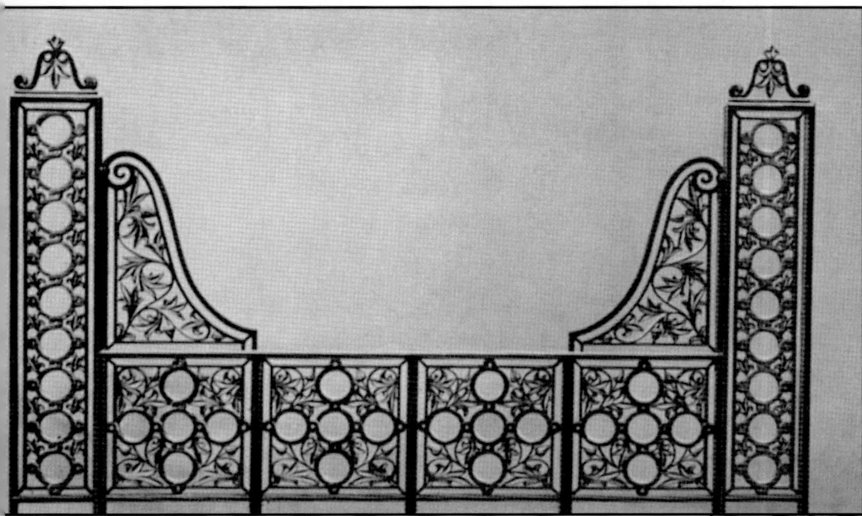

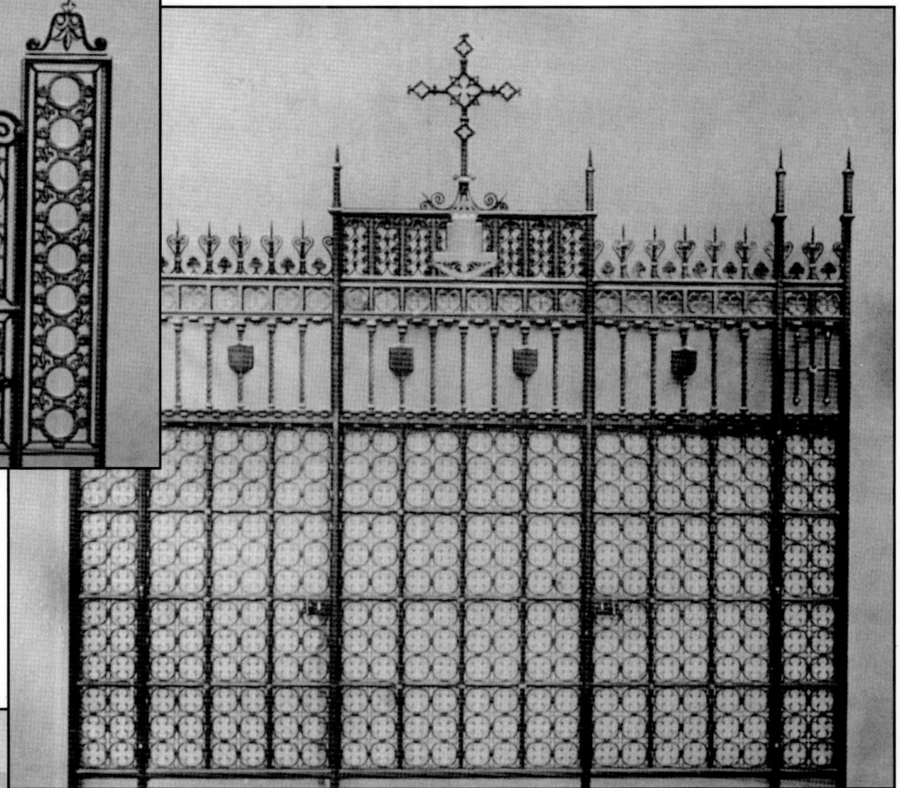

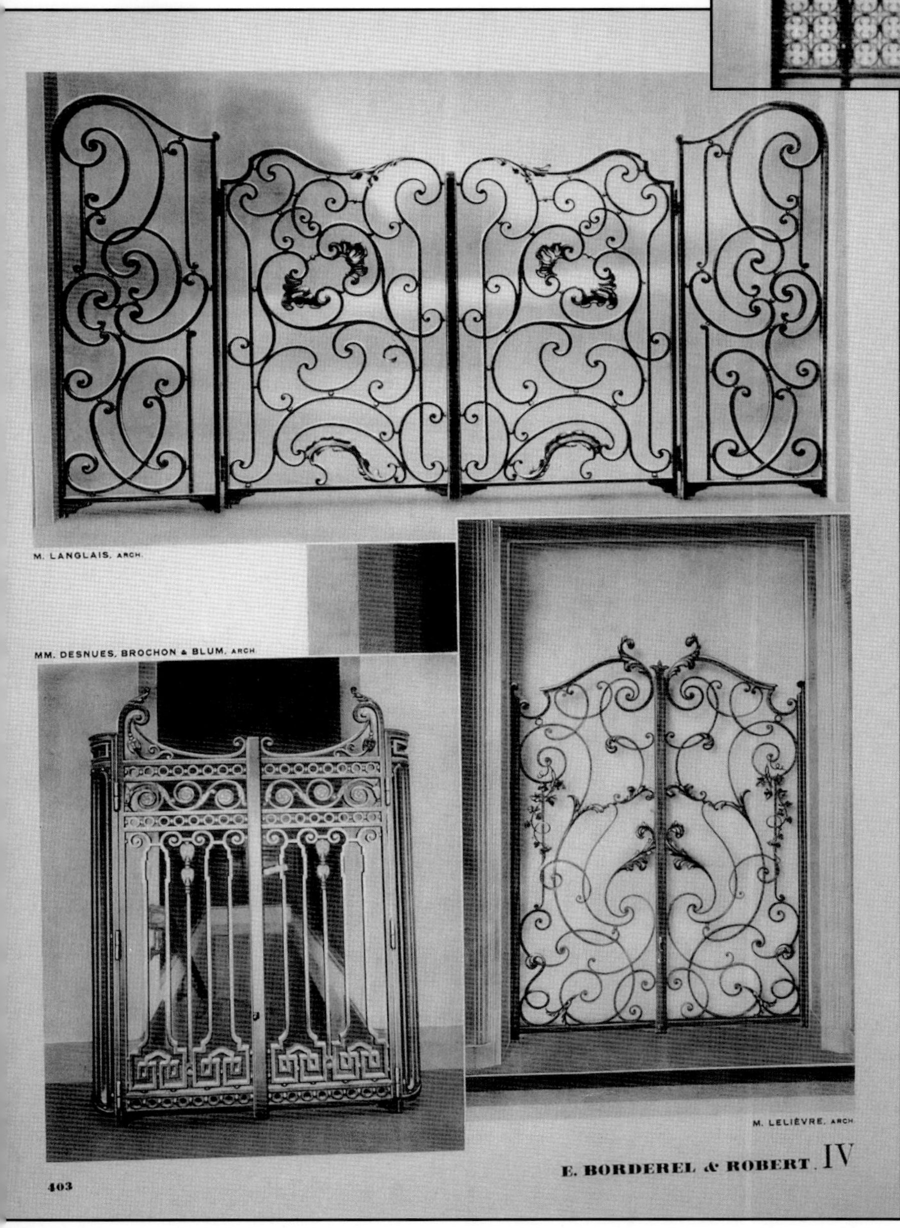
M. LANGLAIS, ARCH.
MM. DESNUES, BROCHON & BLUM, ARCH.
M. LELIÈVRE, ARCH.
403
E. BORDEREL & ROBERT. IV

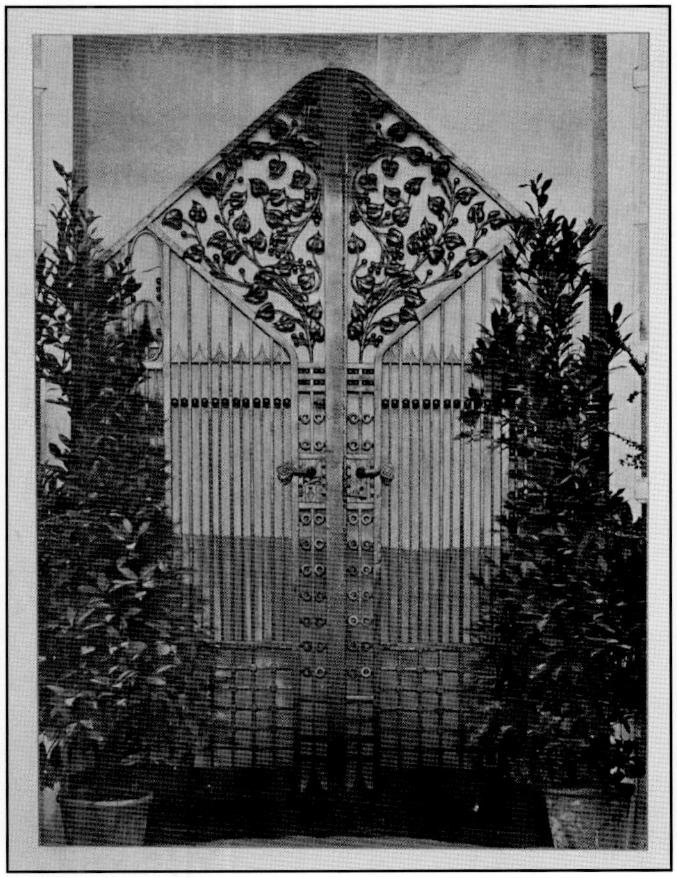

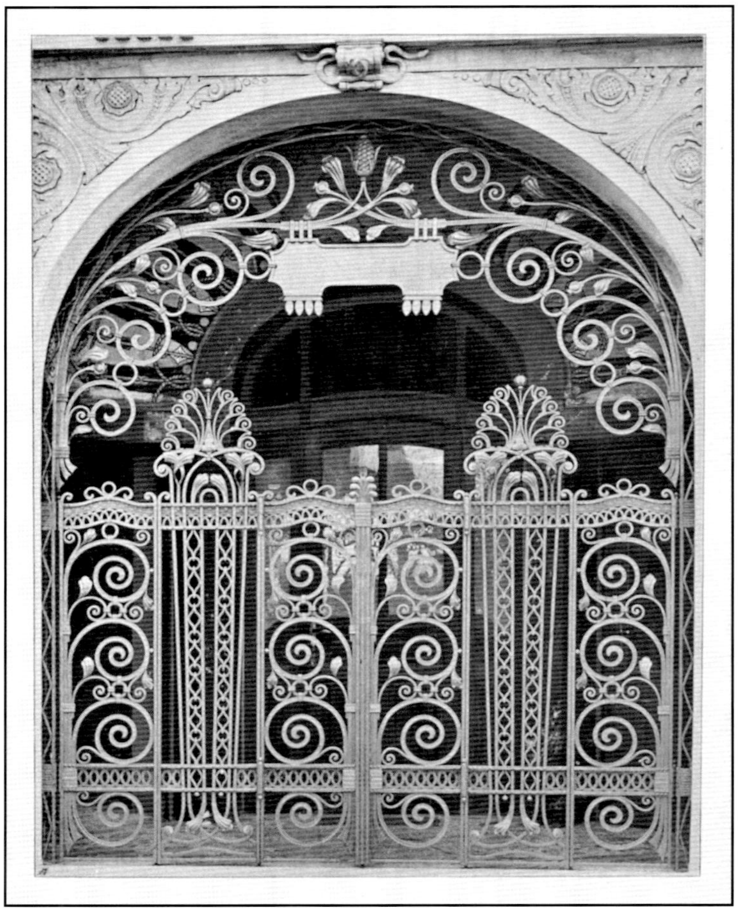

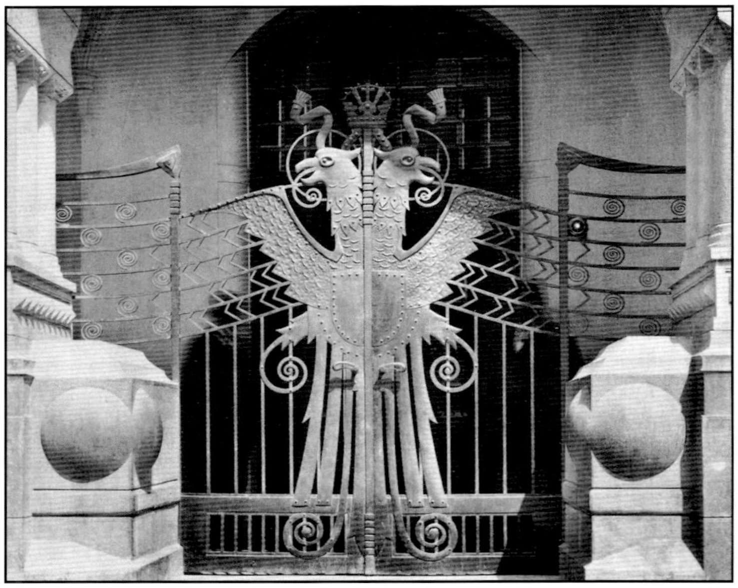

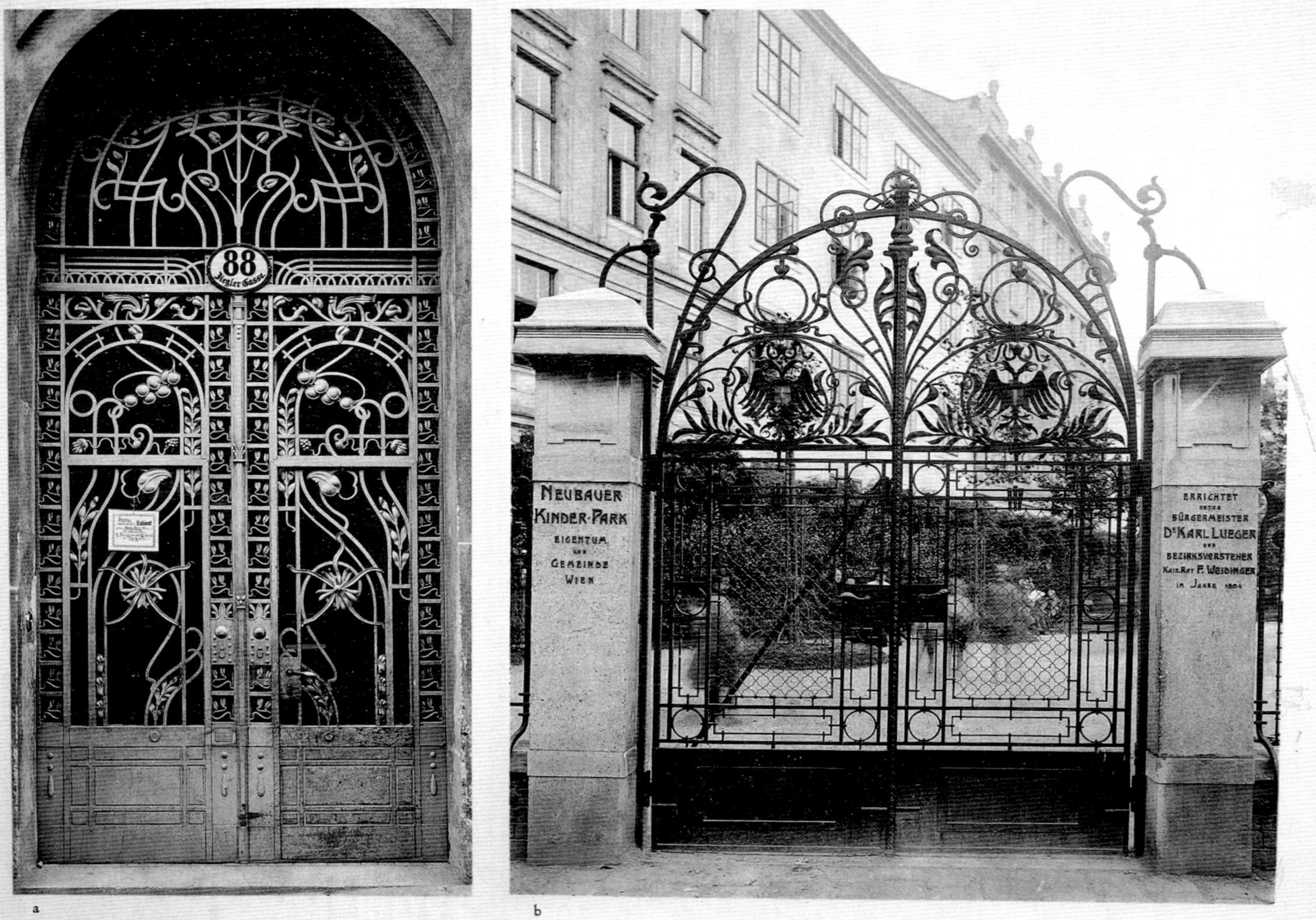
88
NEUBAUER
KINDER-PARK
EIGENTUM
GEMEINDE
WIEN
ERRICHTET
BÜRGERMEISTER
Dr KARL LUEGER
BEZIRKSVORSTEHER
KAIS. RAT F. WEIDINGER
IM JAHRE 1904

a

b

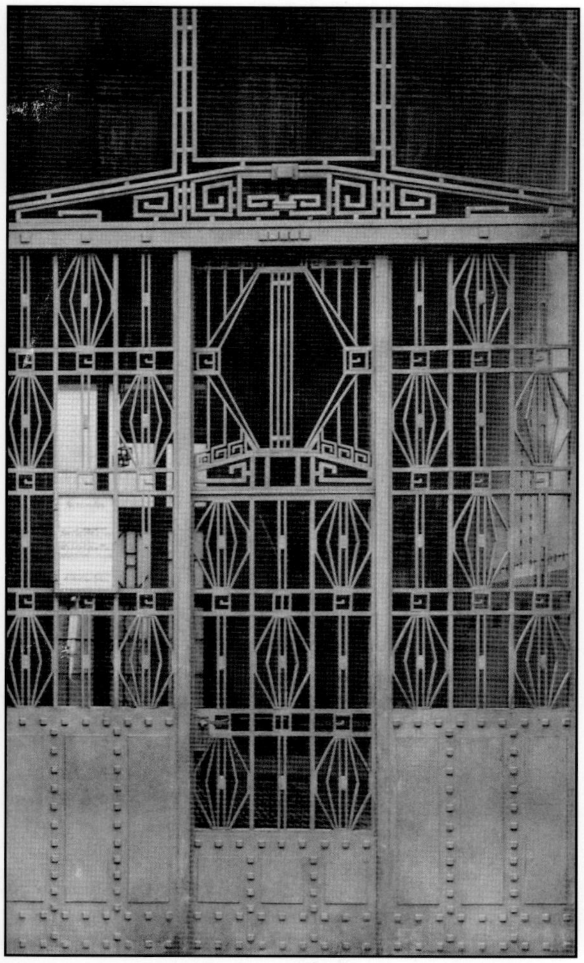

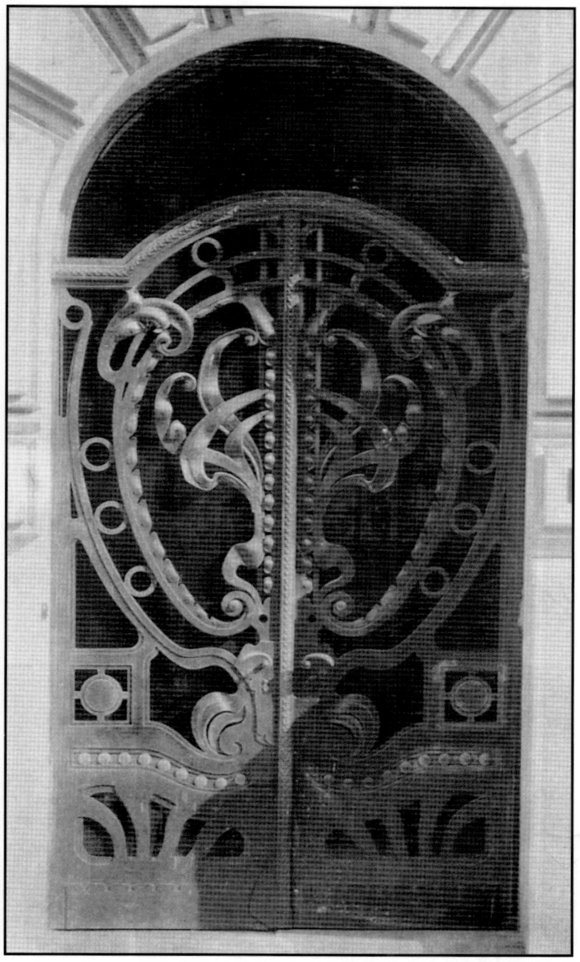

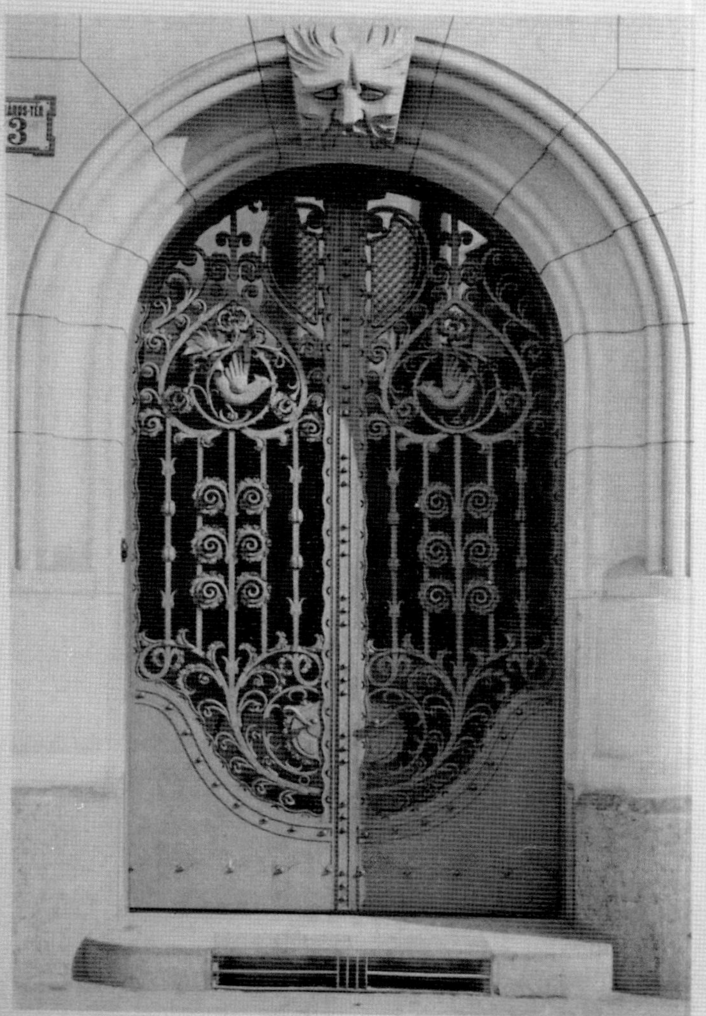

a

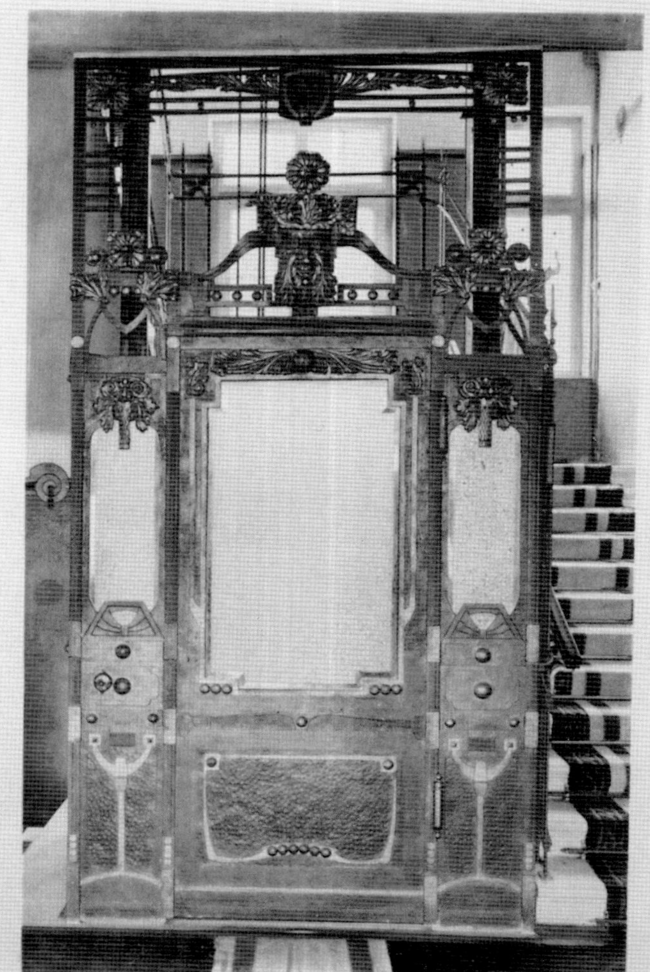

b

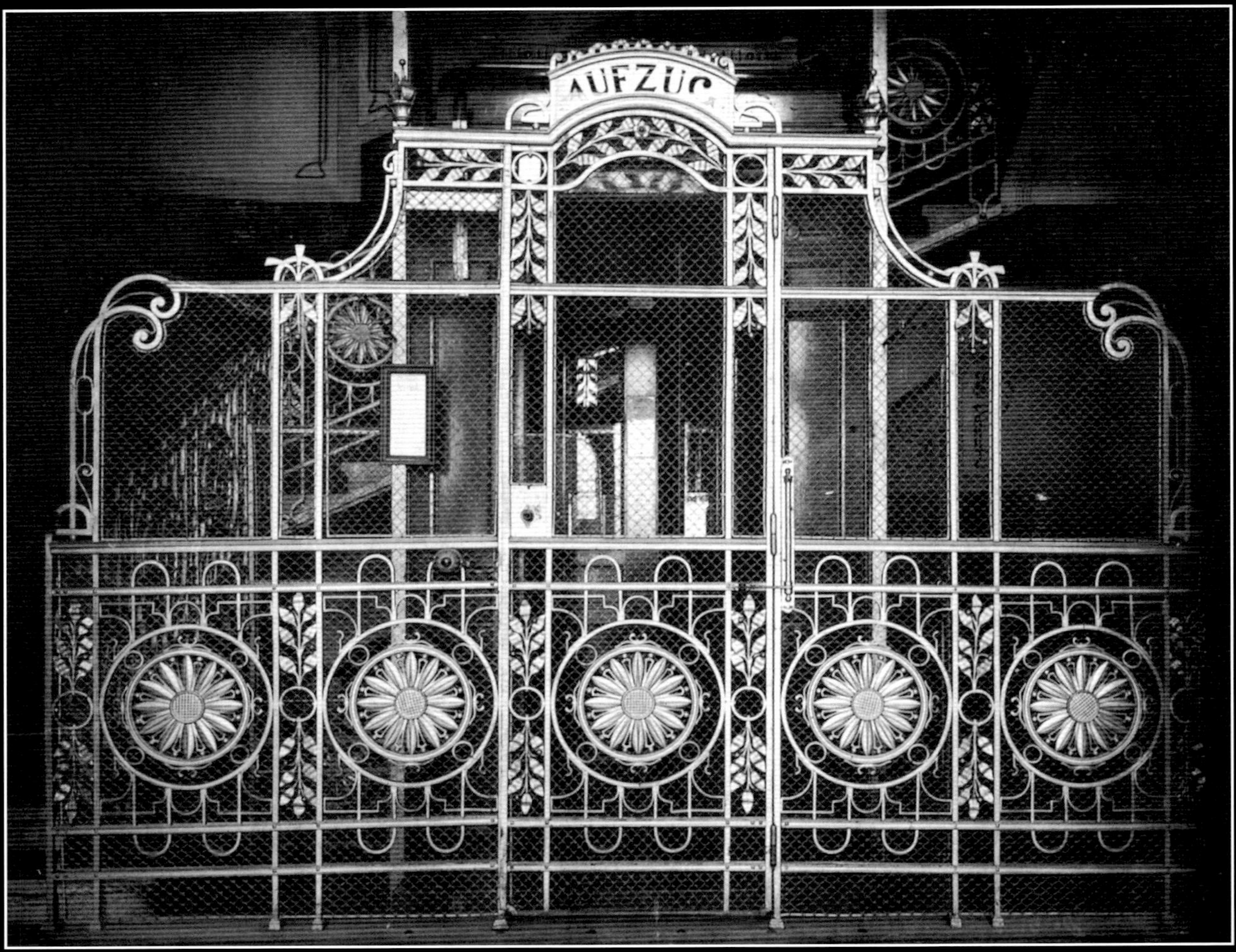
AUFZUG

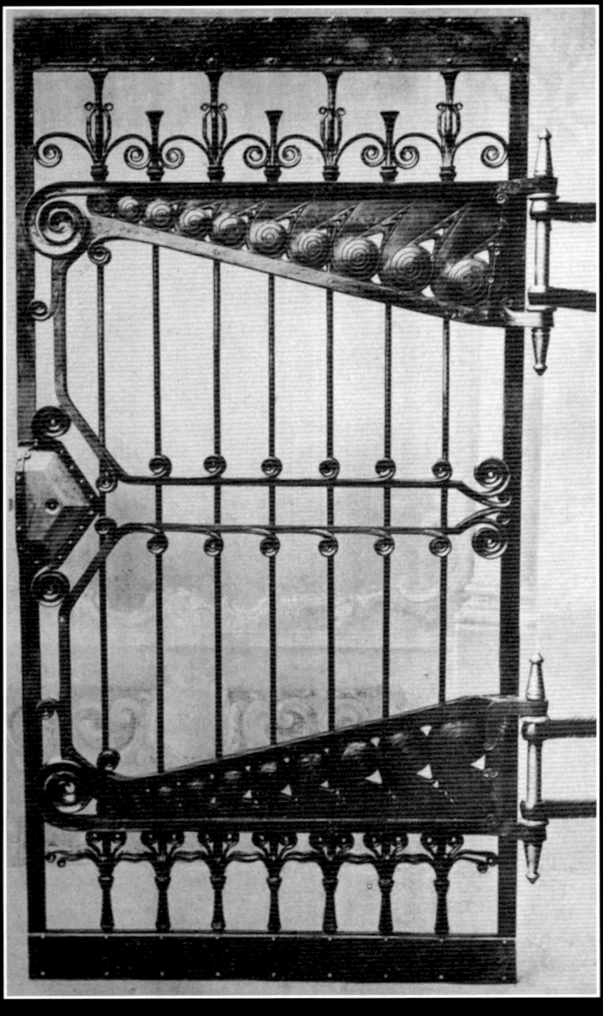

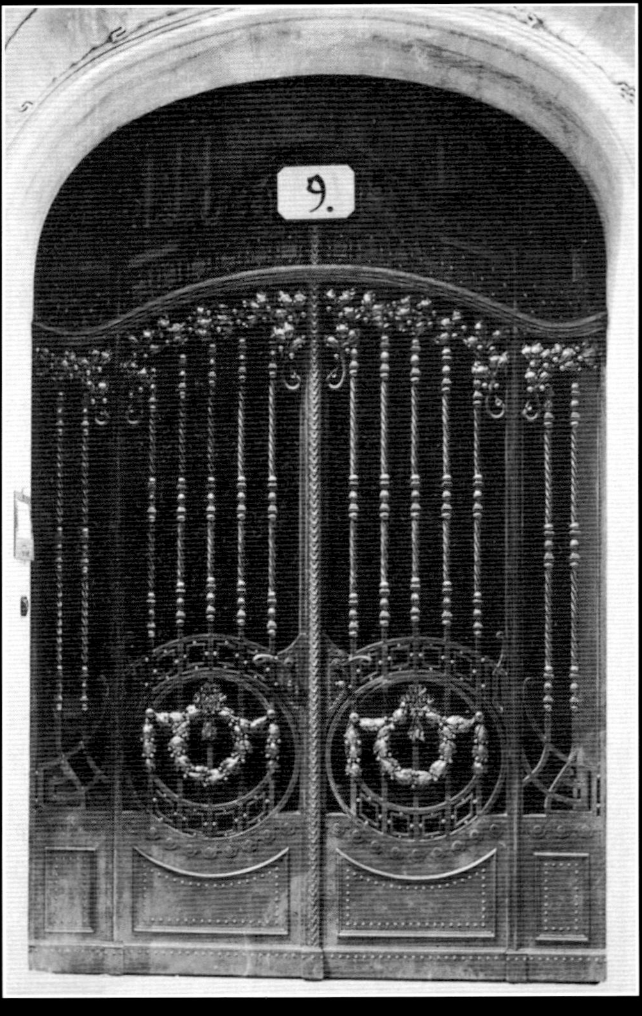
9.

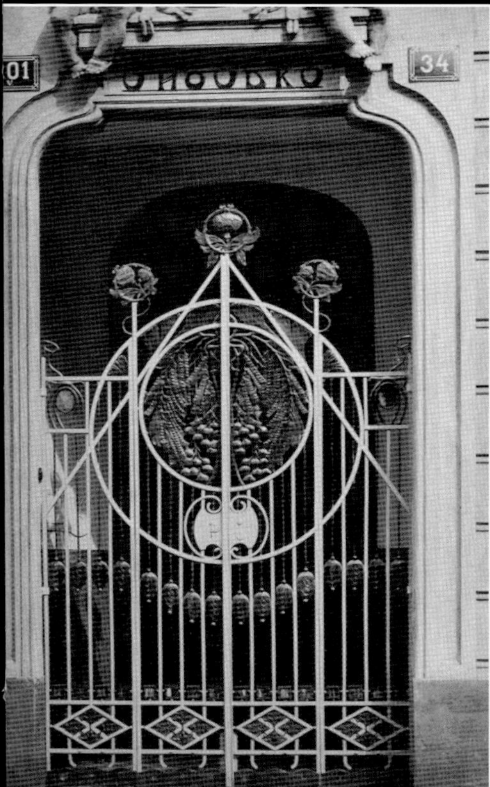

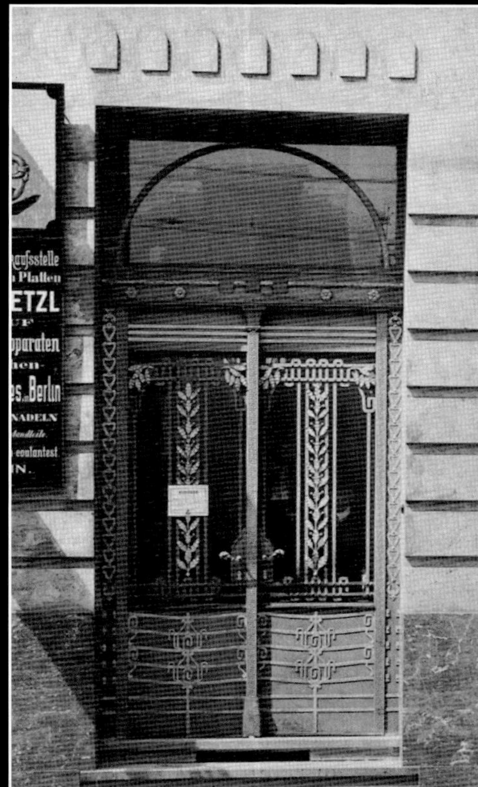

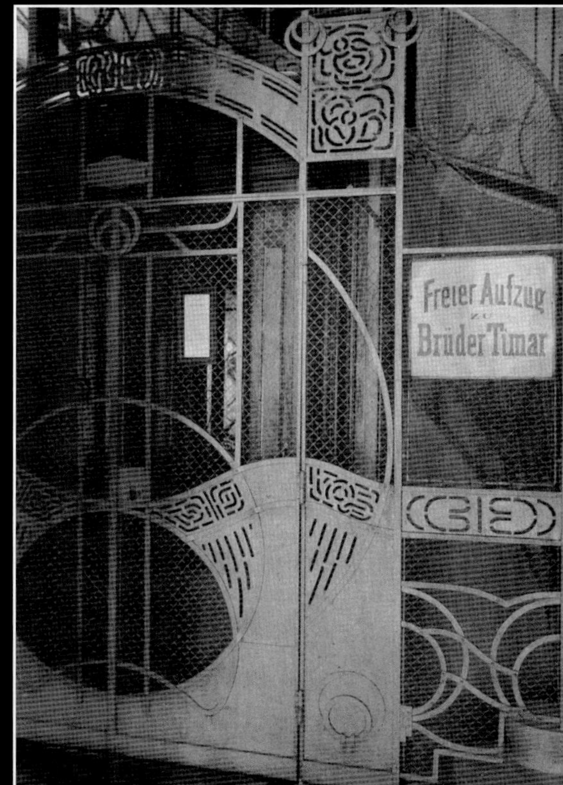

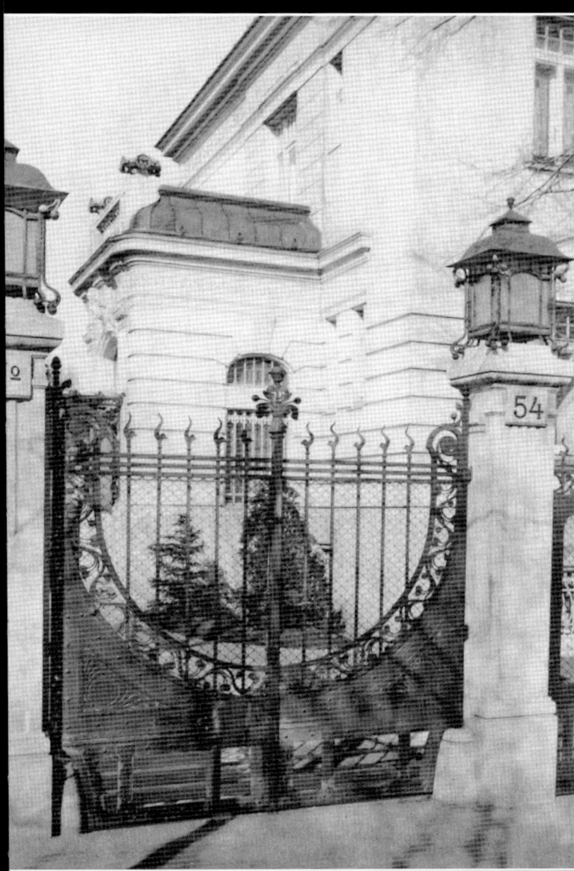

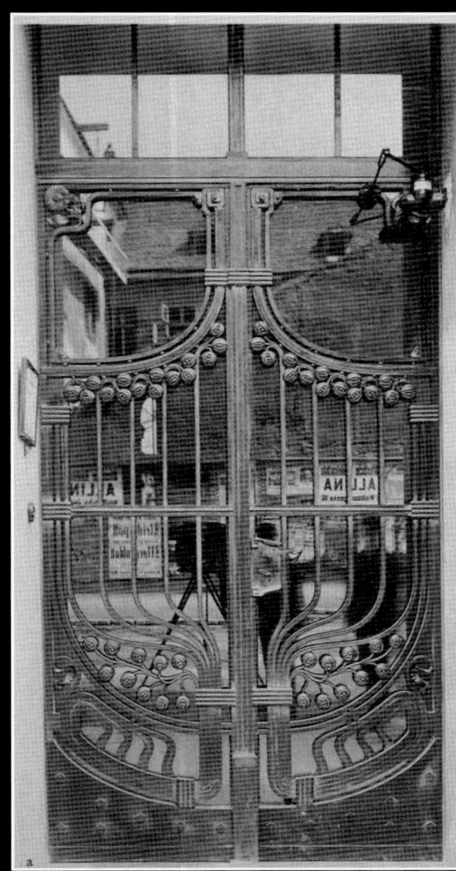

a

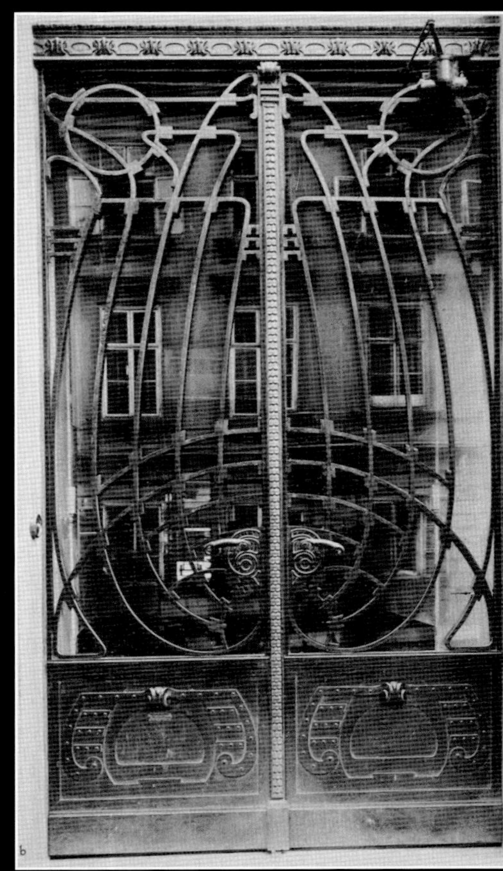

b

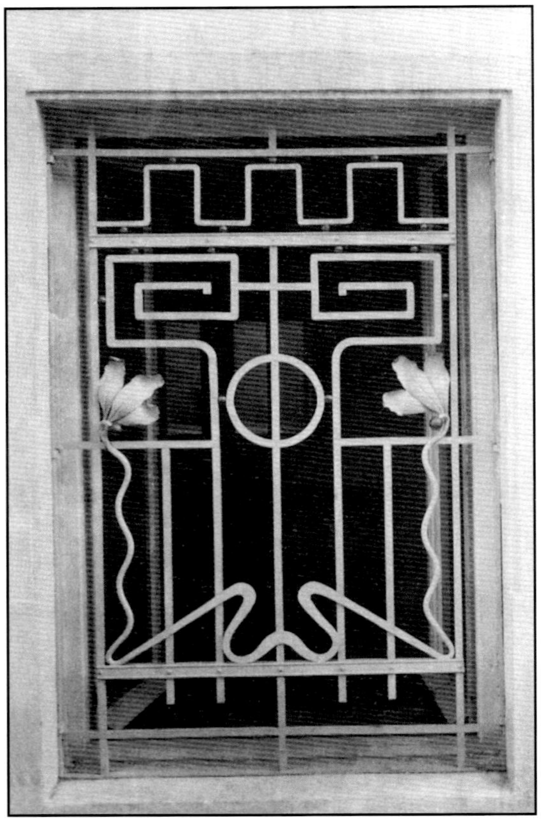

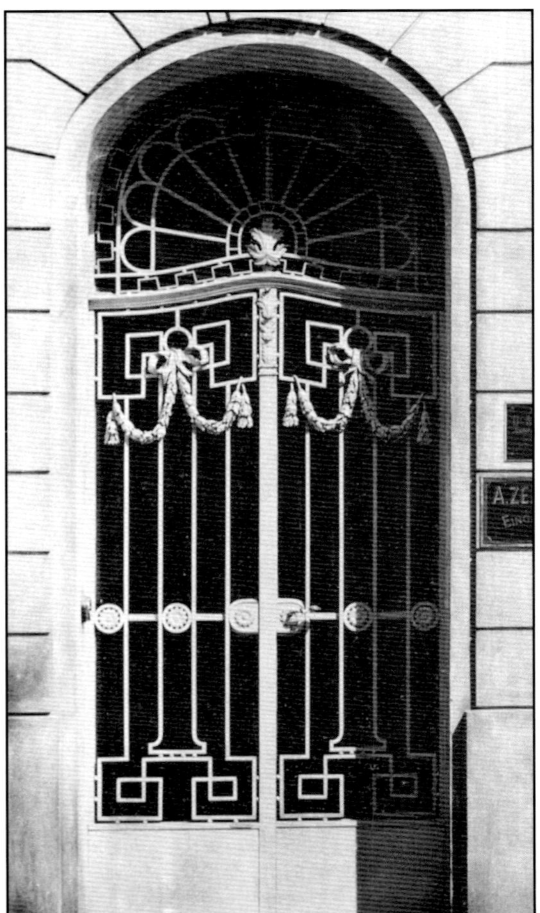

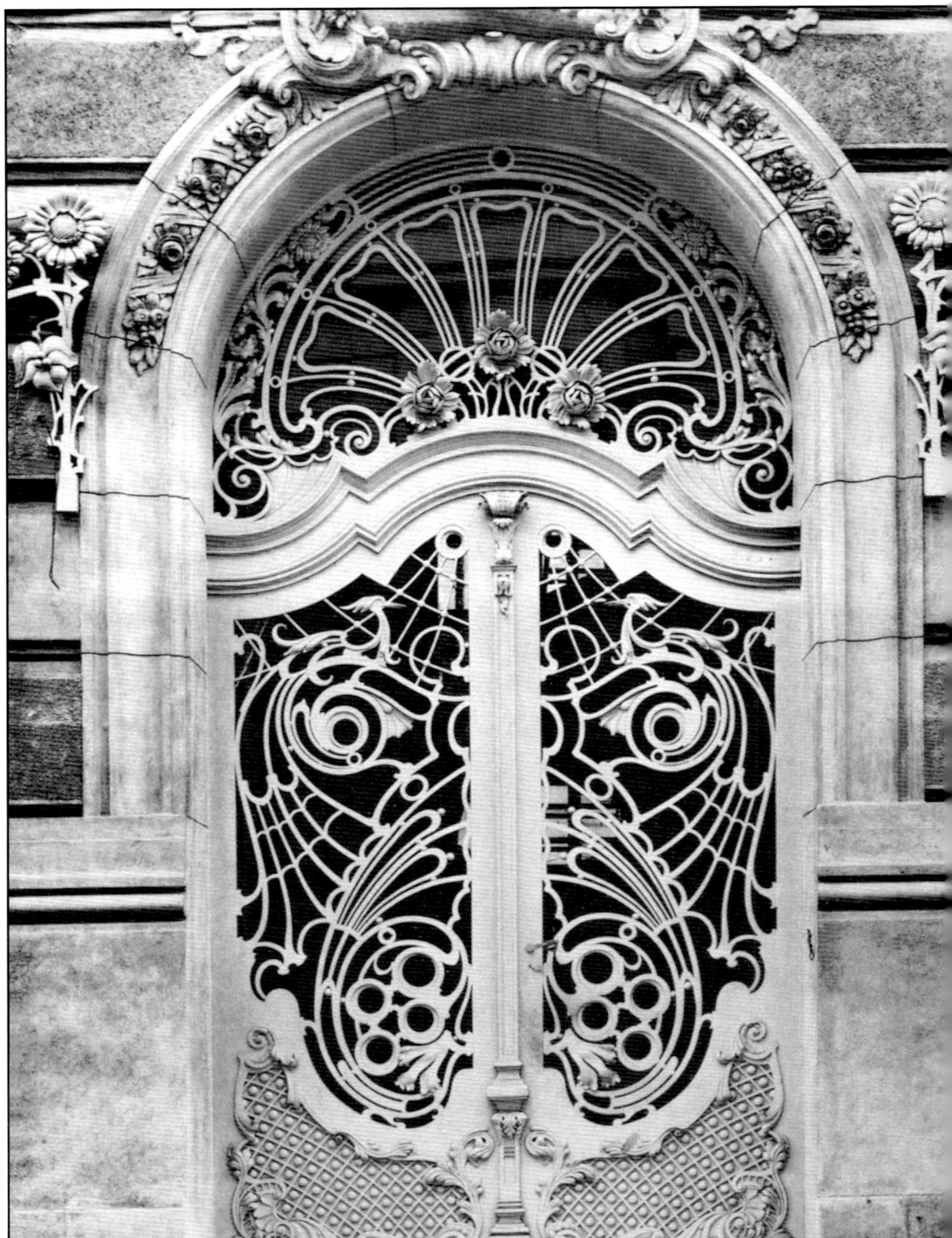

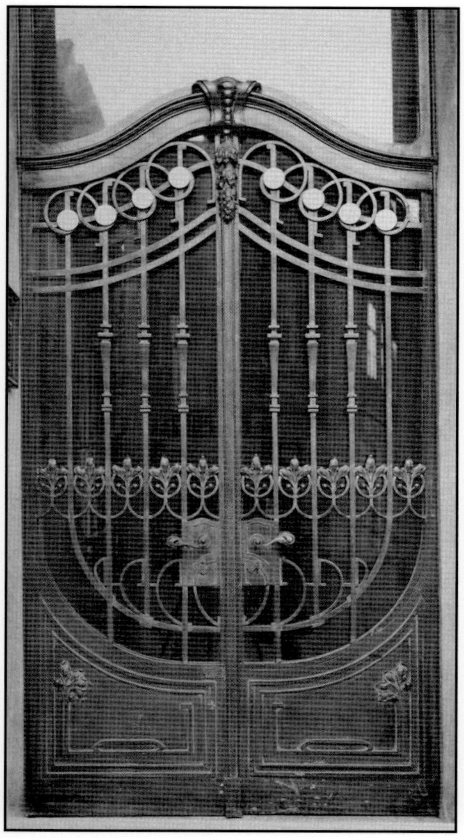

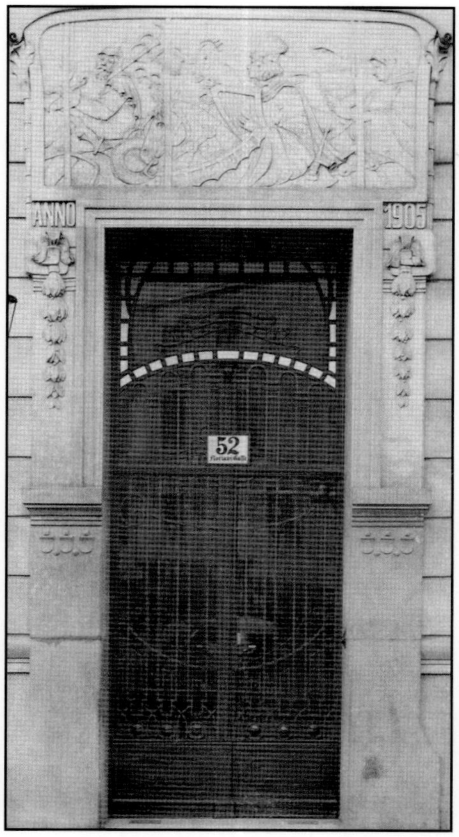
ANNO
1905
52

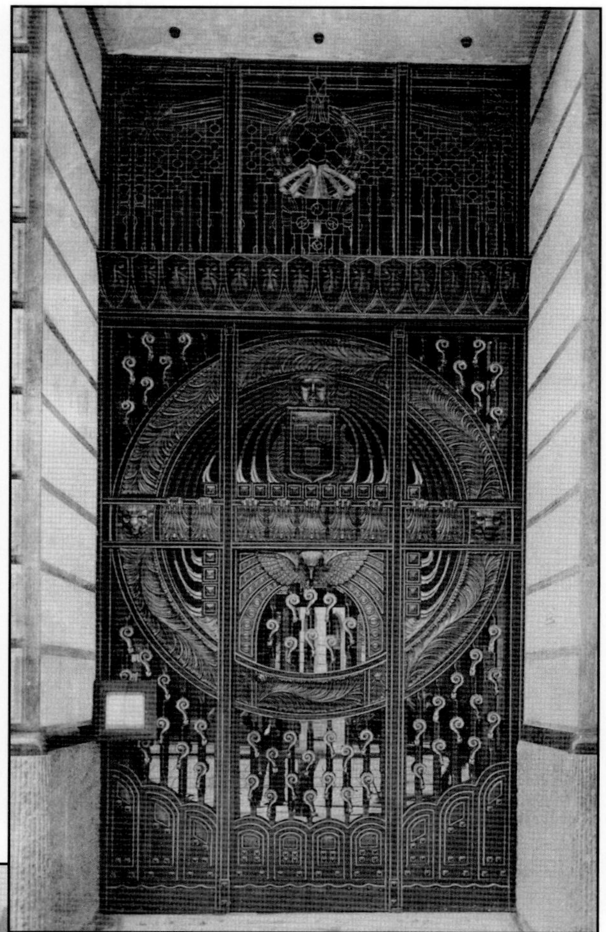

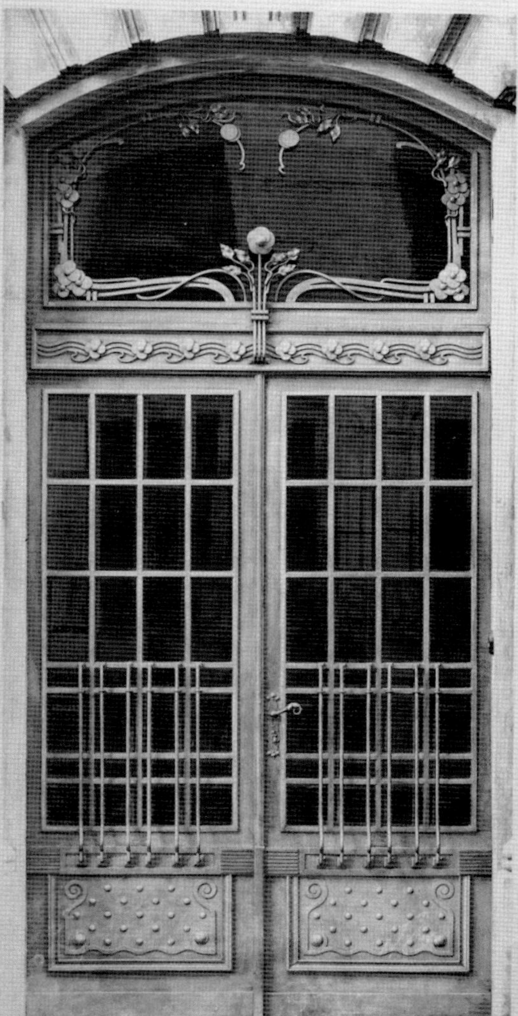

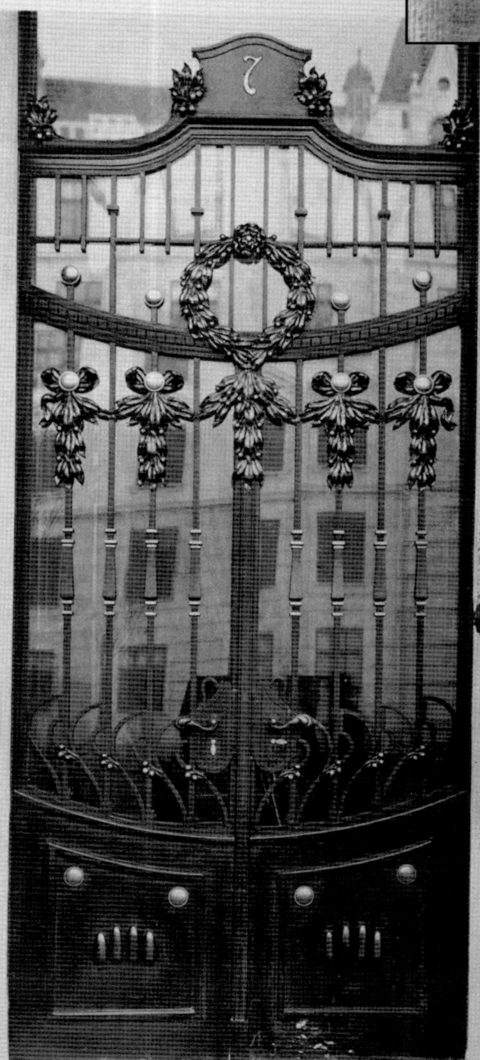
7

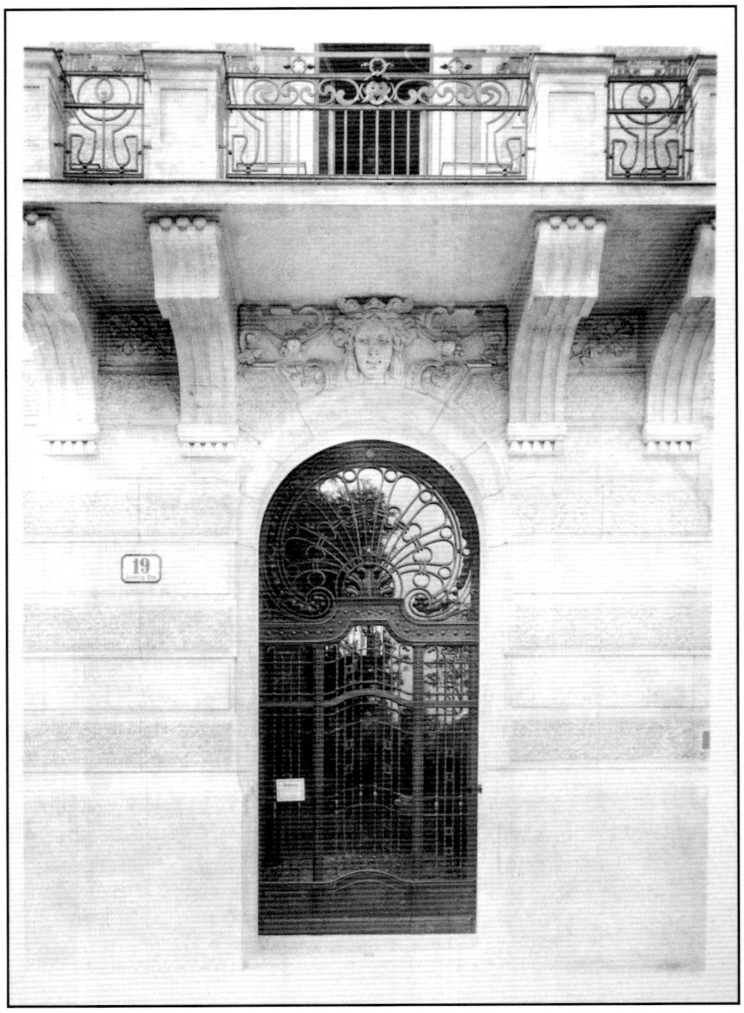
19

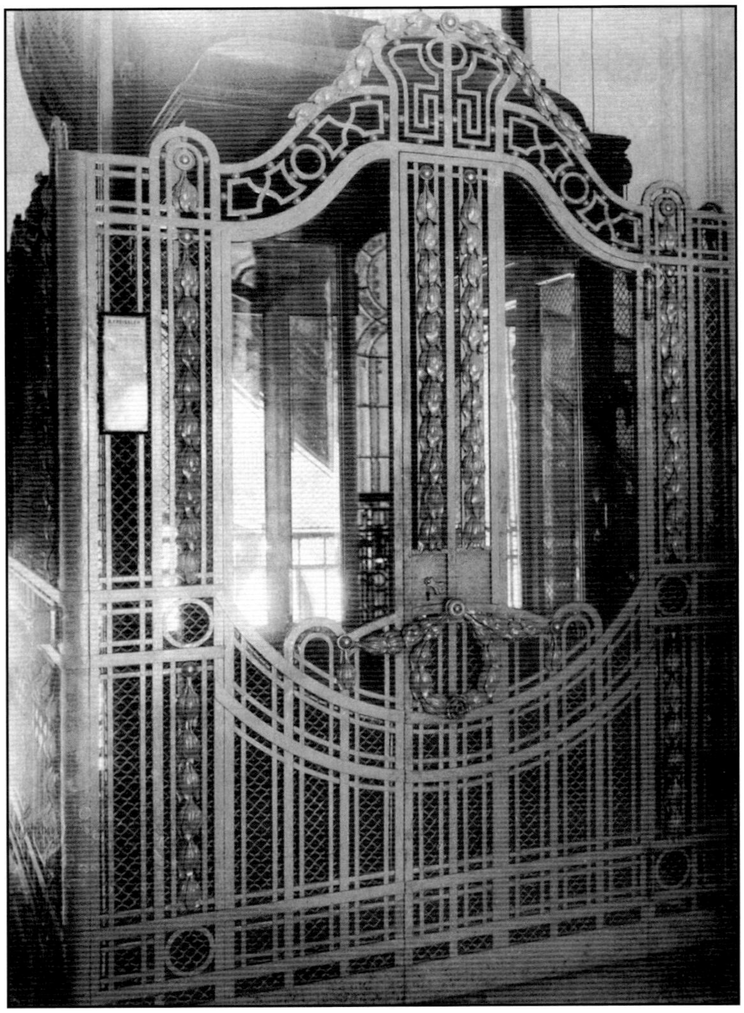

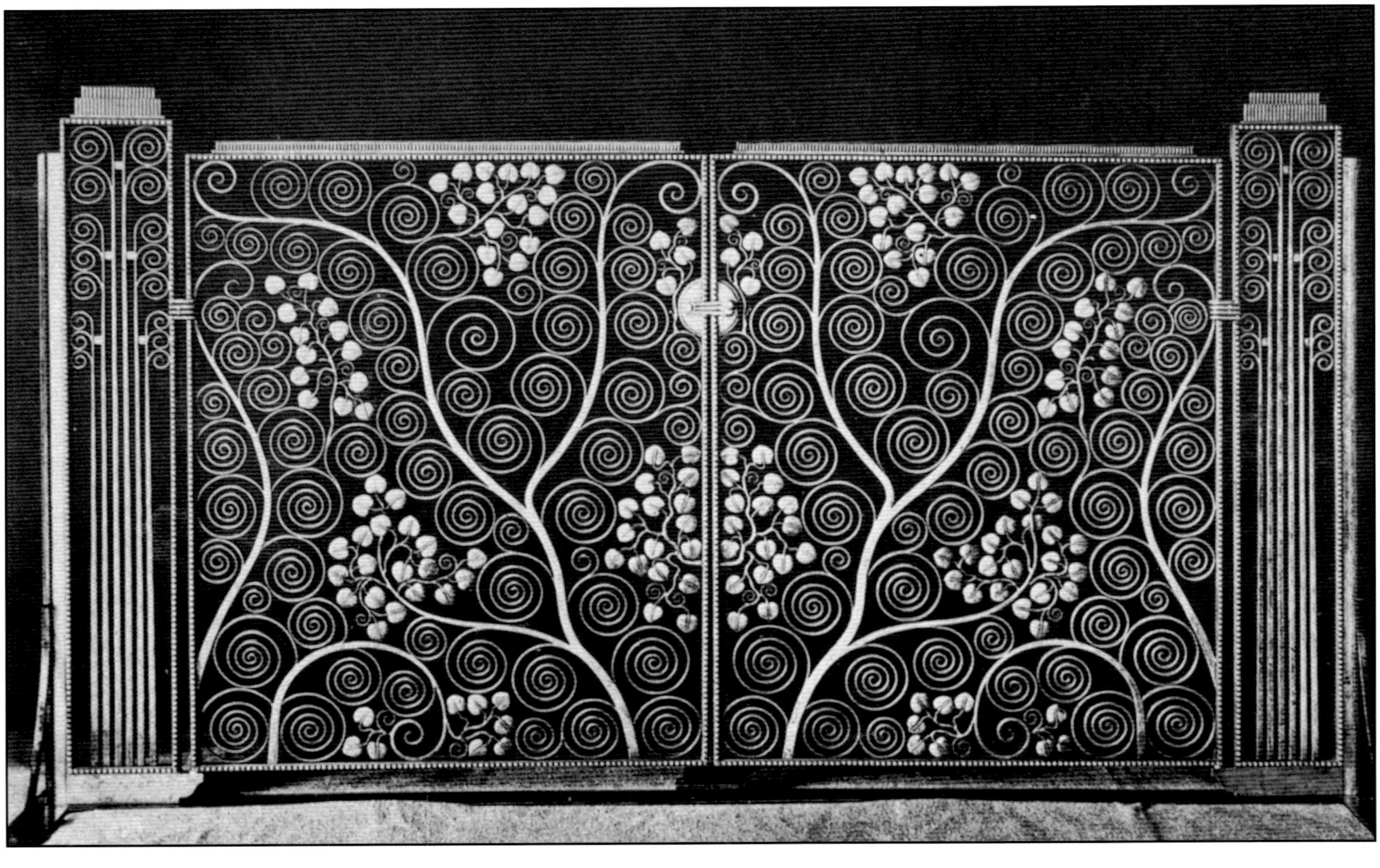

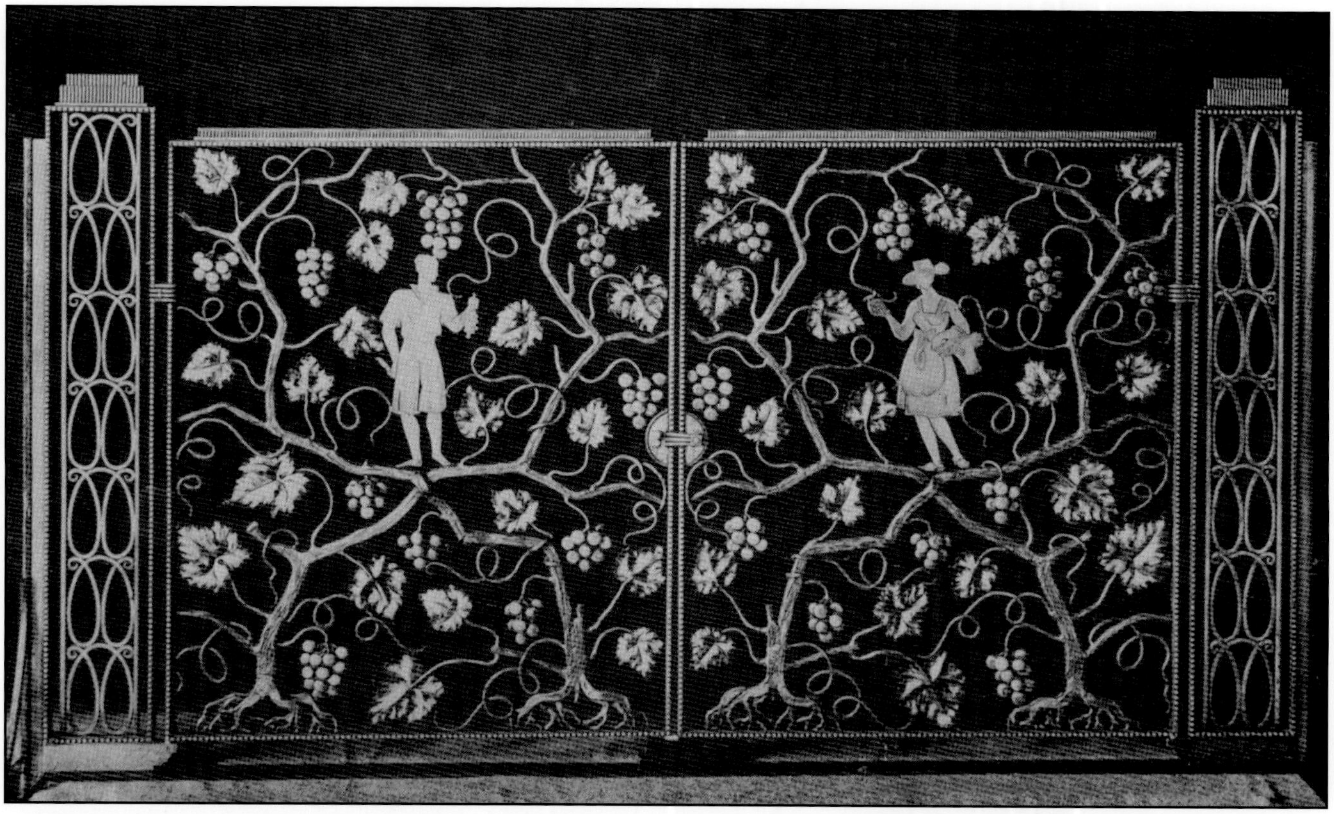

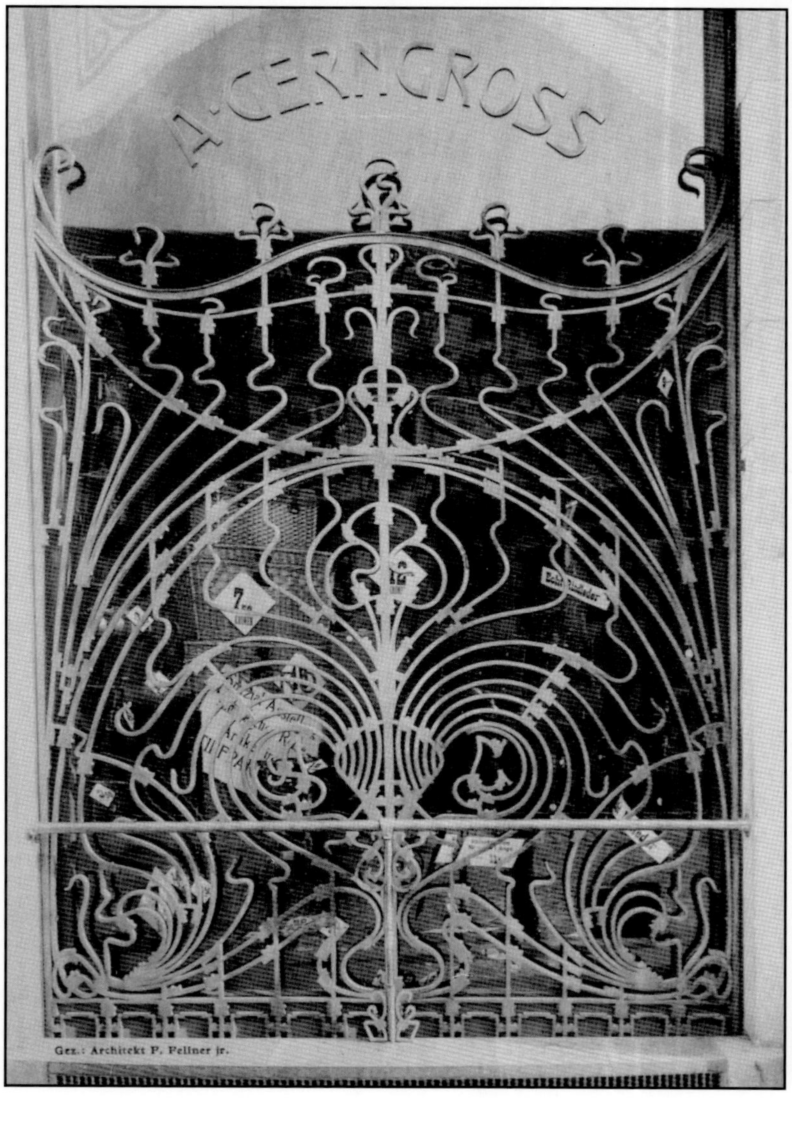
A·GERNGROSS
Gez.: Architekt F. Fellner jr.

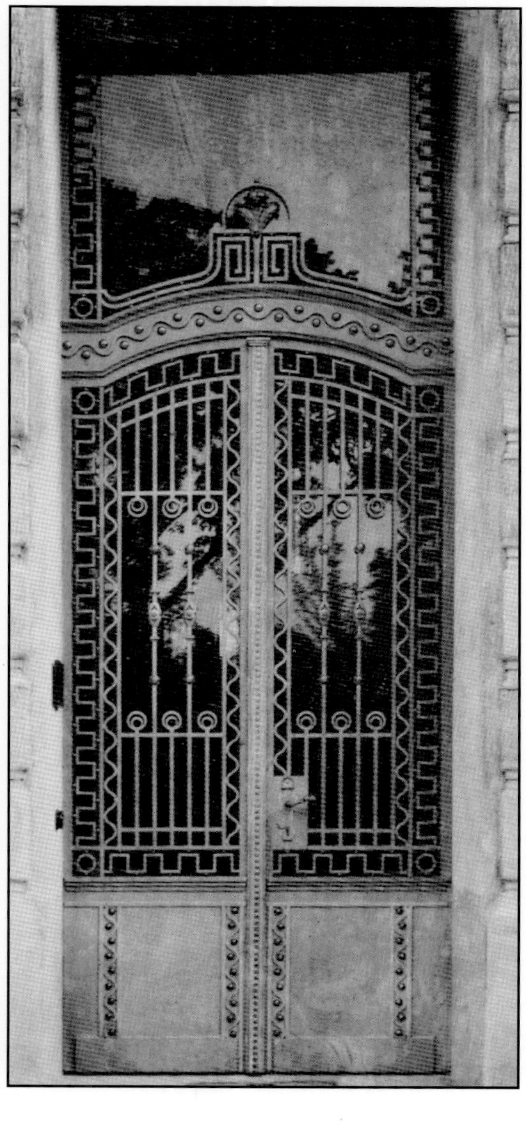

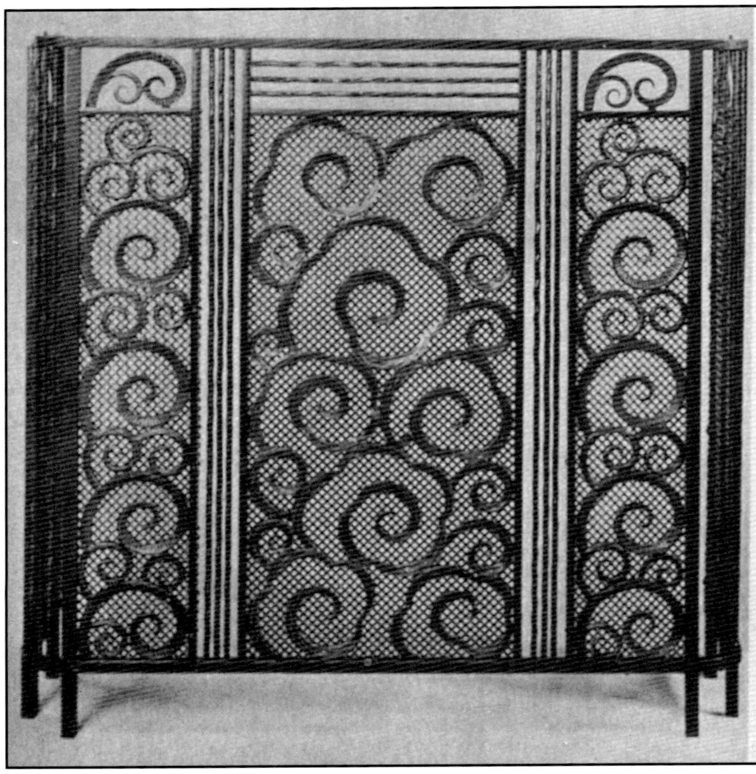

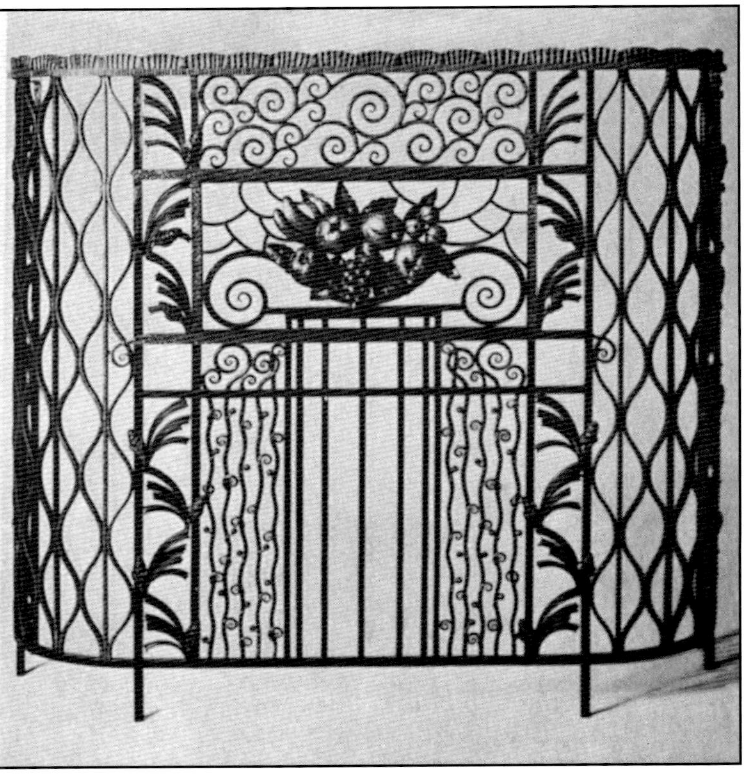

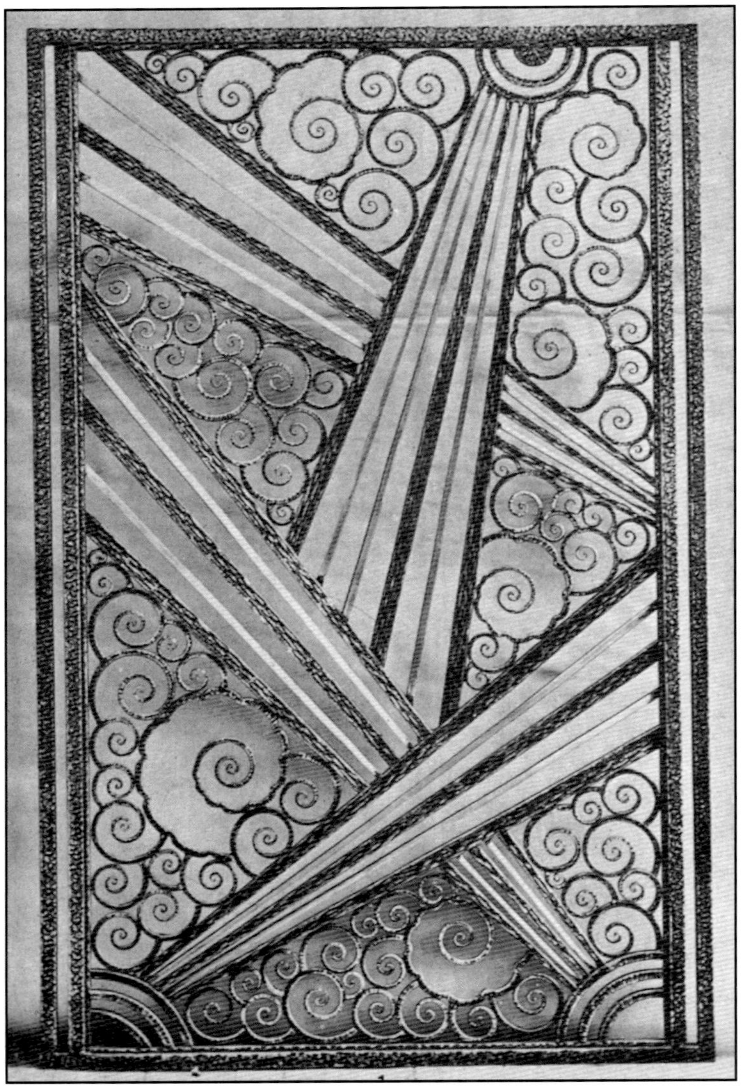

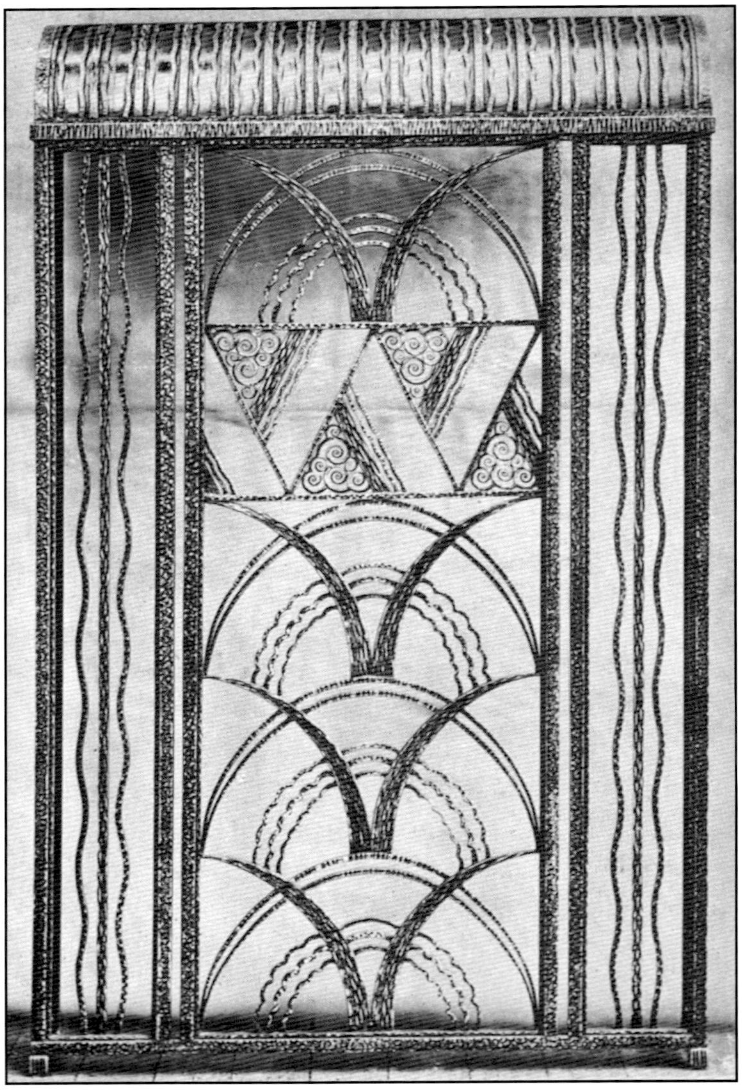

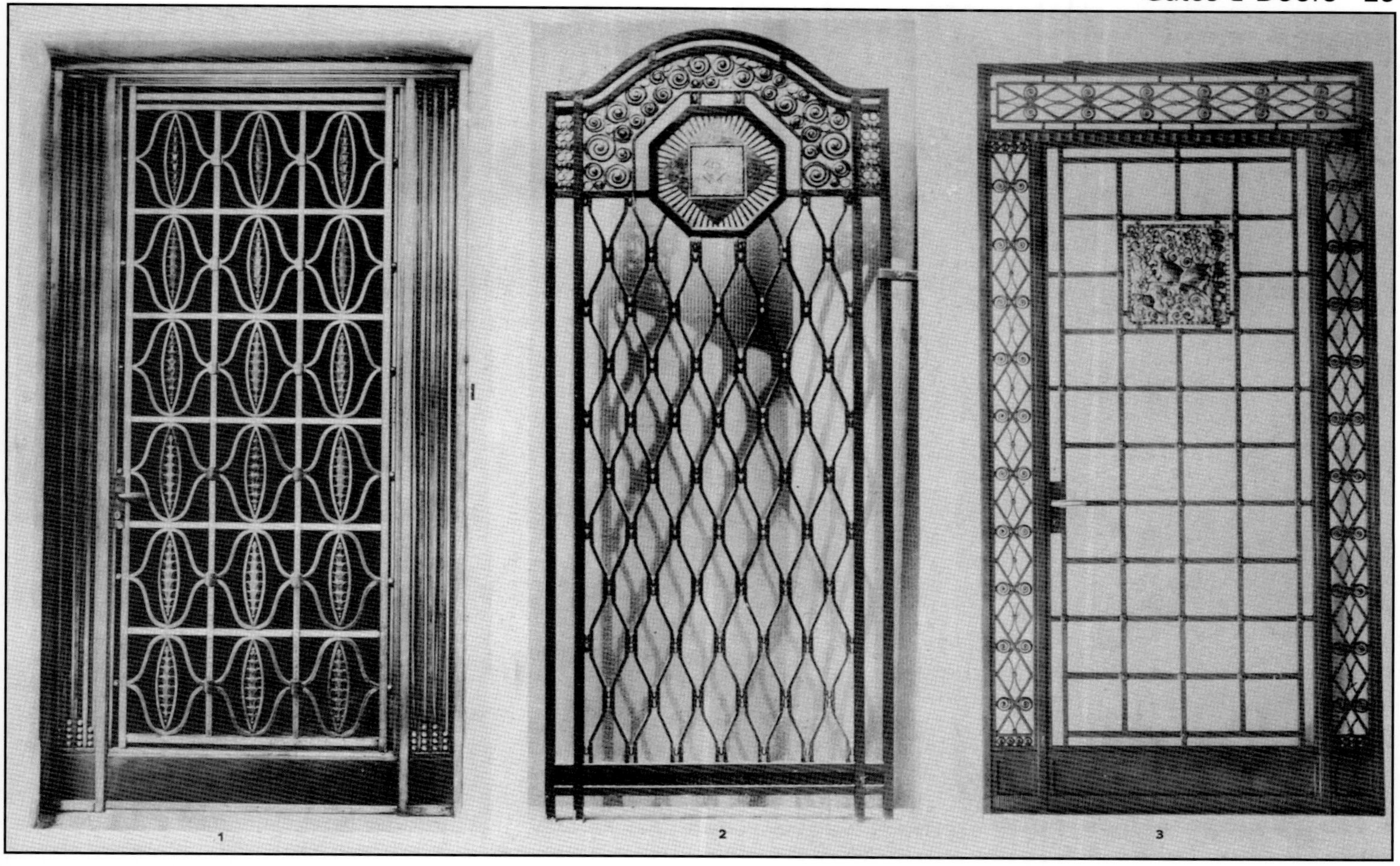
1
2
3

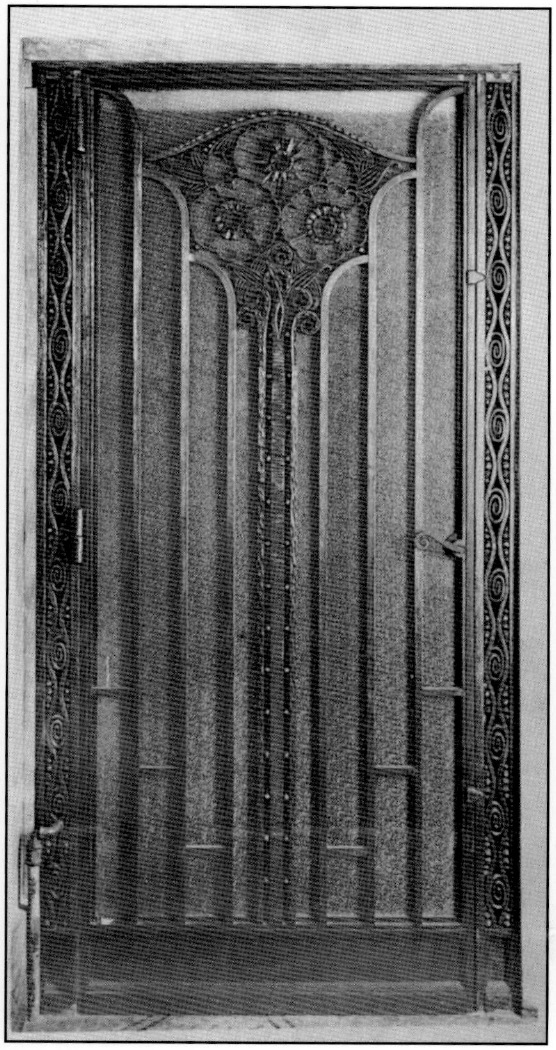

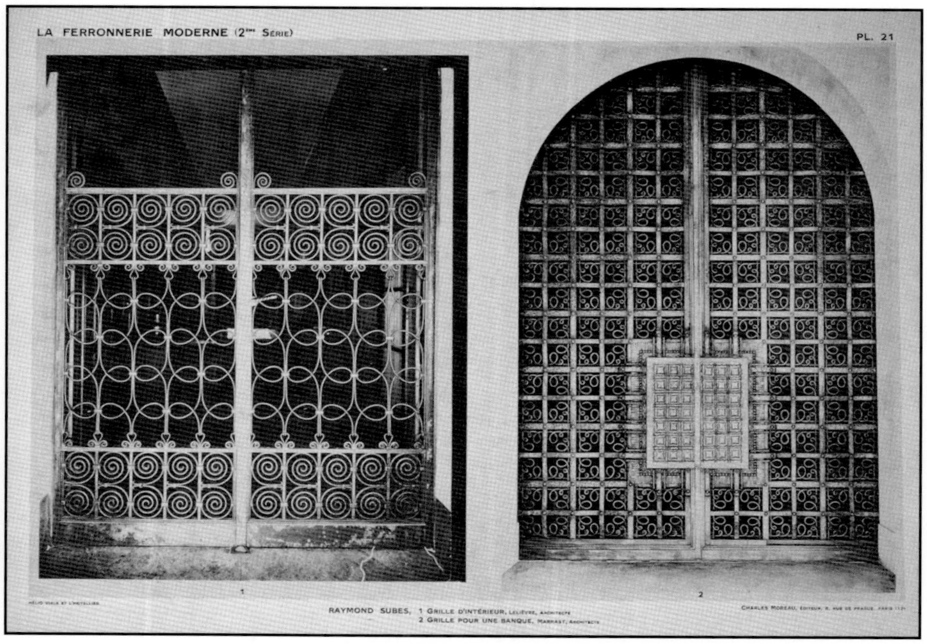
LA FERRONNERIE MODERNE (2me SÉRIE)
PL. 21
1
2
RAYMOND SUBES, 1 GRILLE D'INTÉRIEUR, LELIÈVRE, ARCHITECTE
2 GRILLE POUR UNE BANQUE, MARRAST, ARCHITECTE
CHARLES MOREAU, ÉDITEUR, 8, RUE DE PRAGUE, PARIS

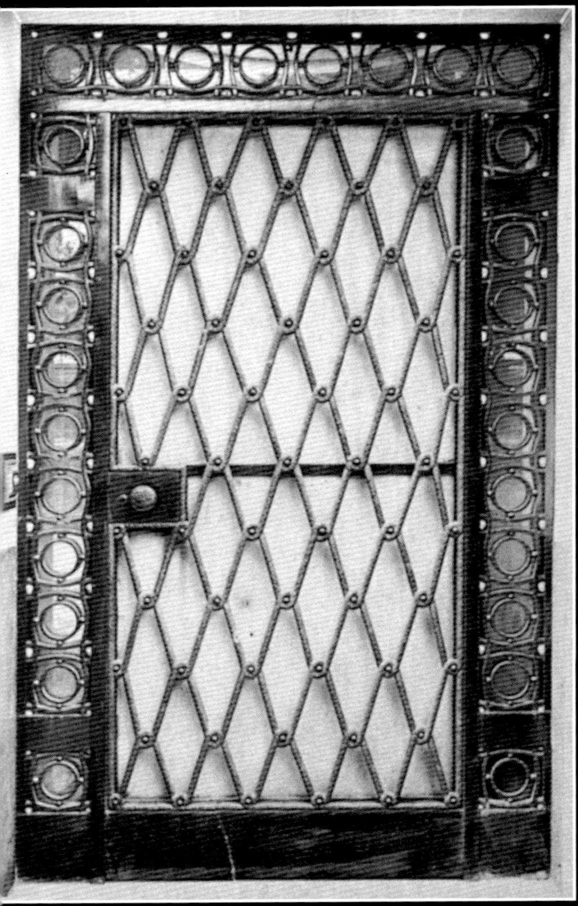

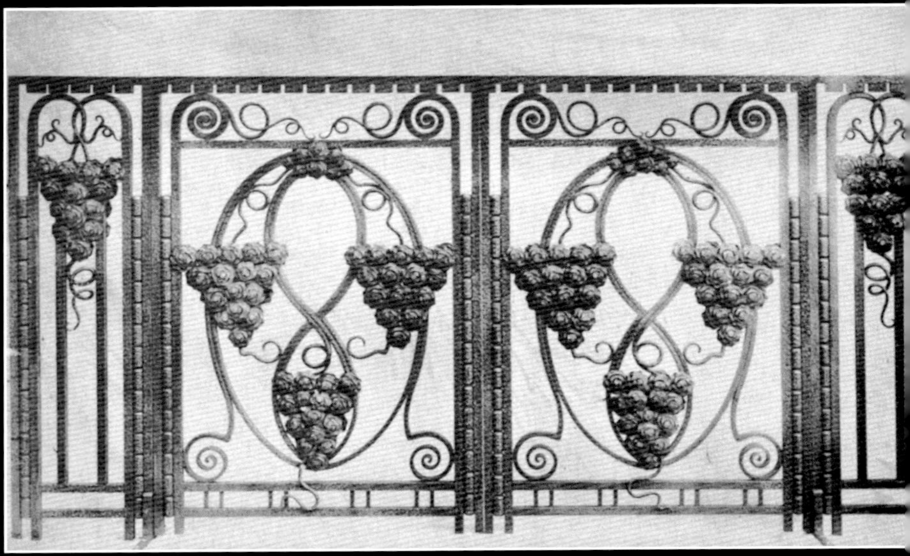

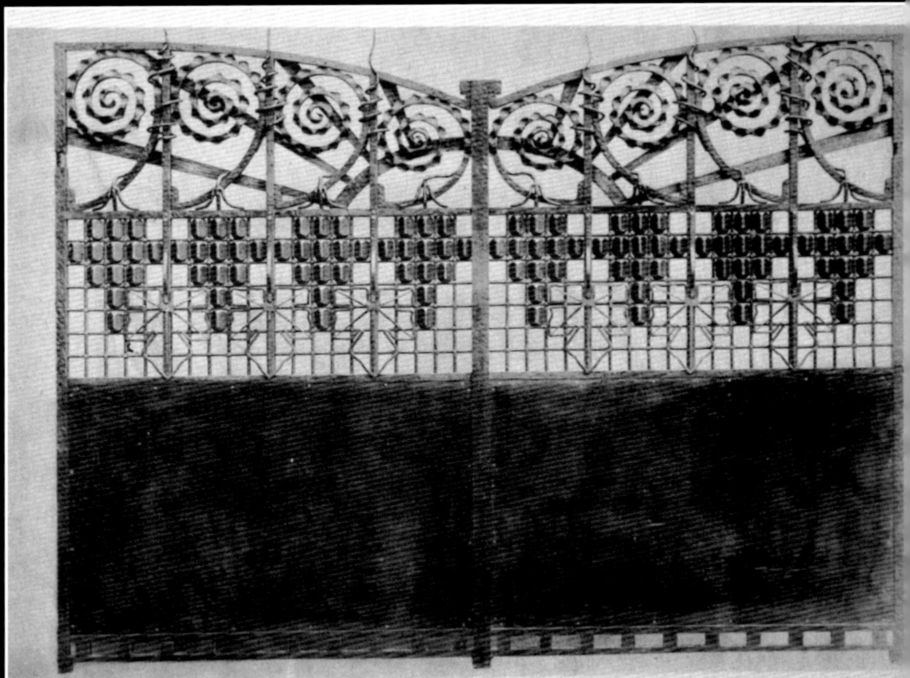

2

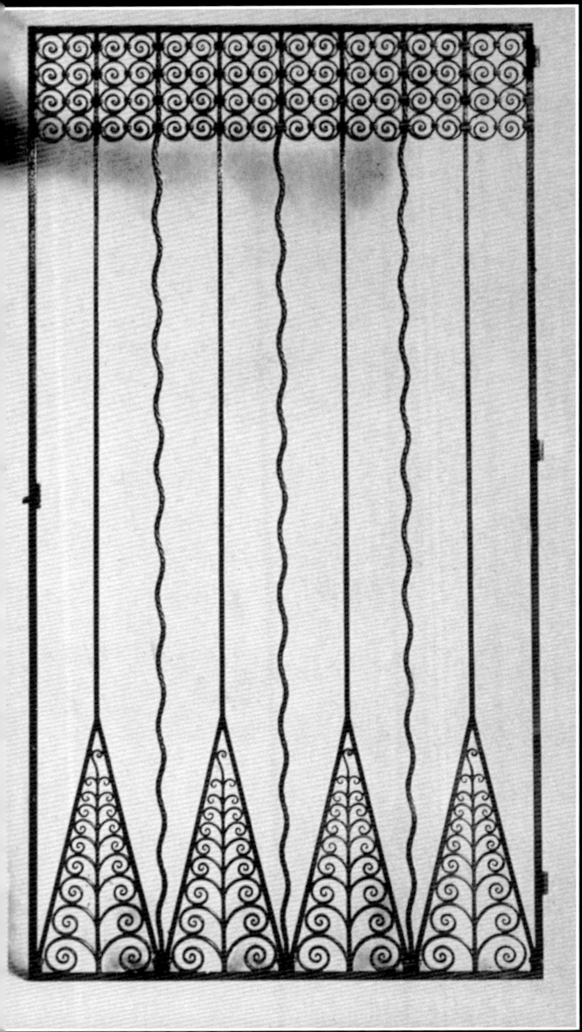

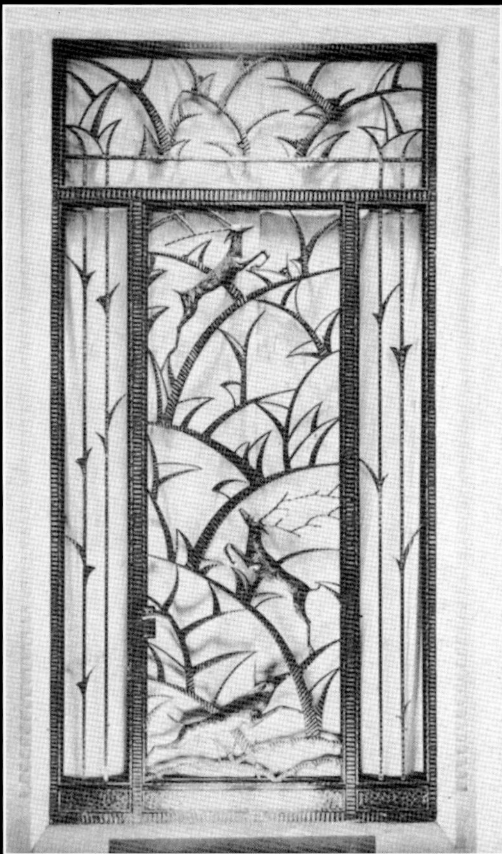

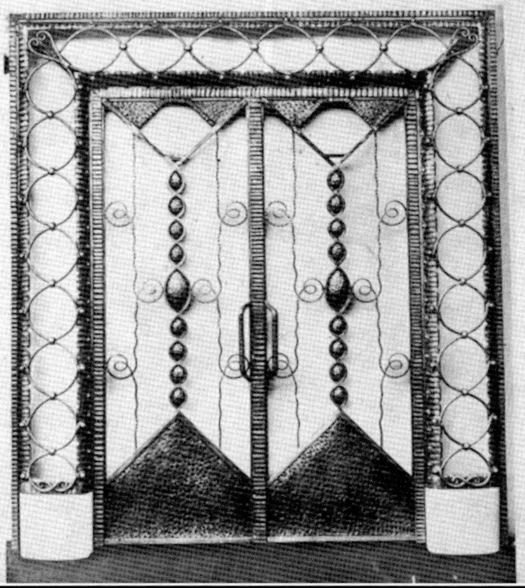

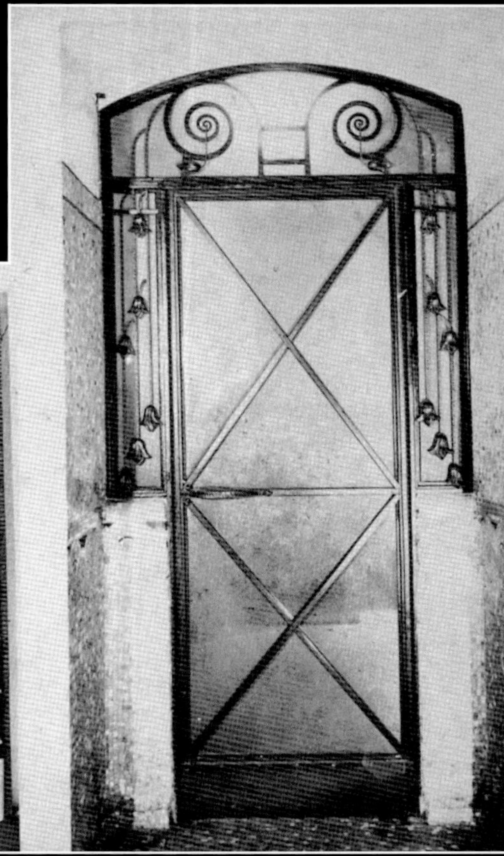

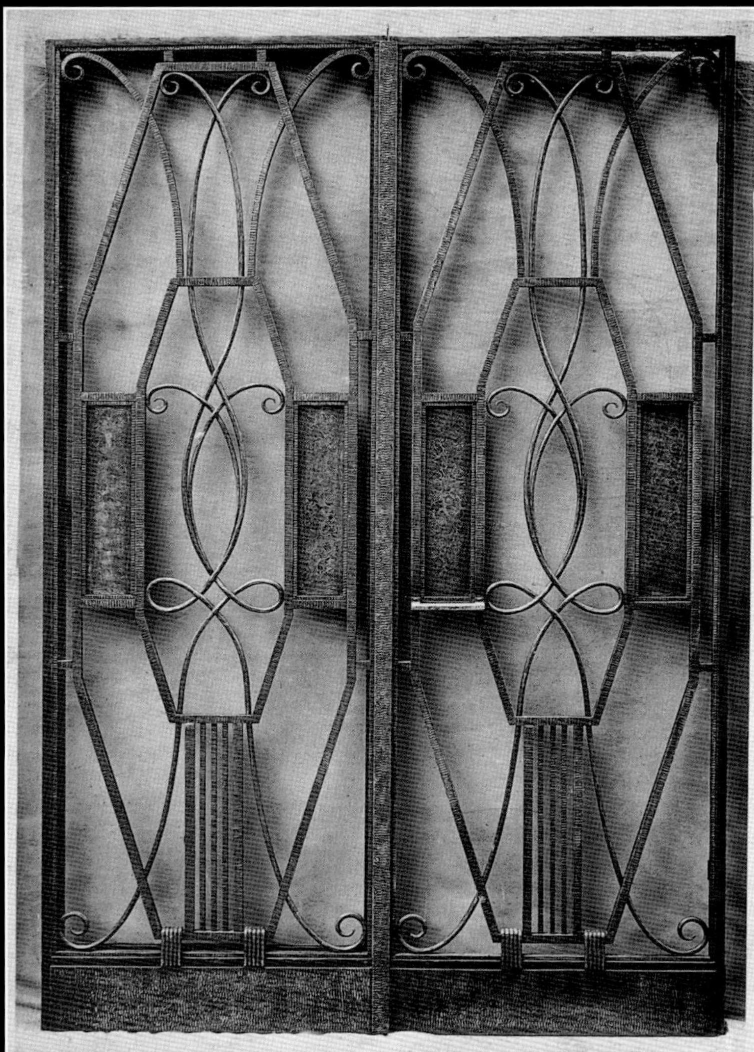

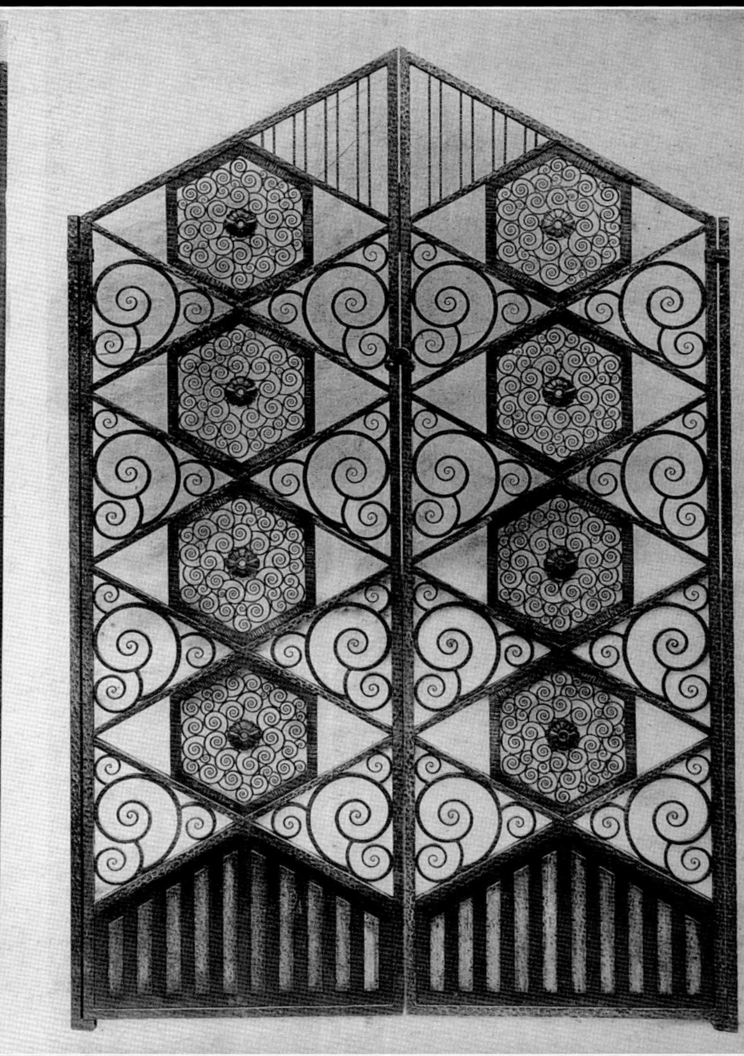

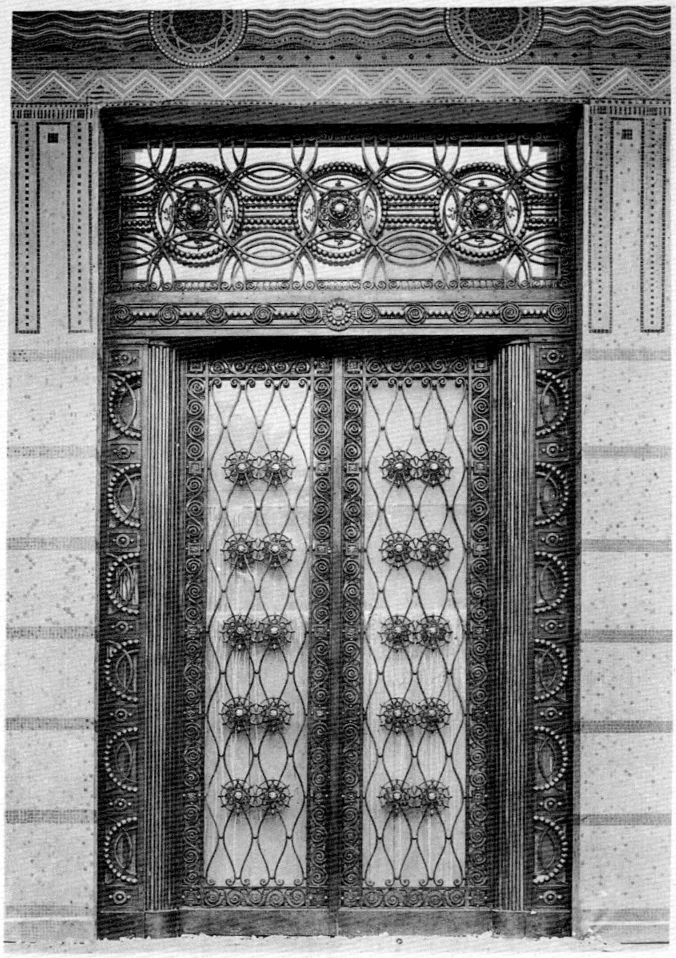

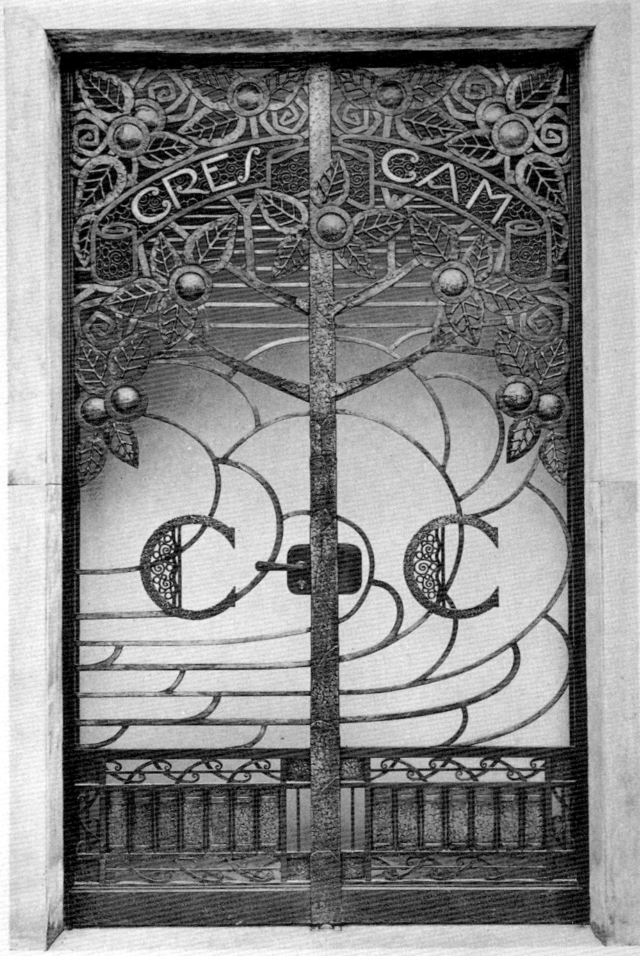
CRES CAM

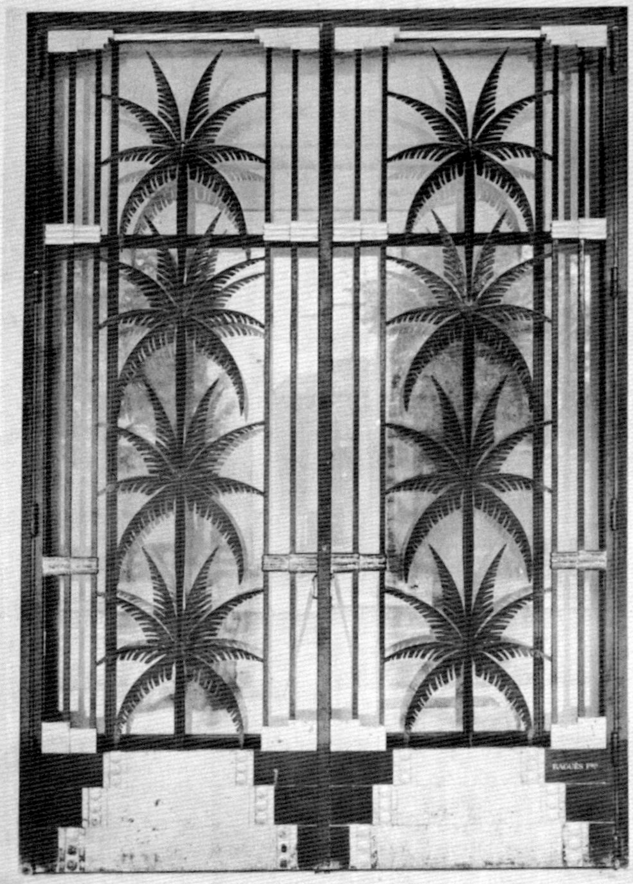

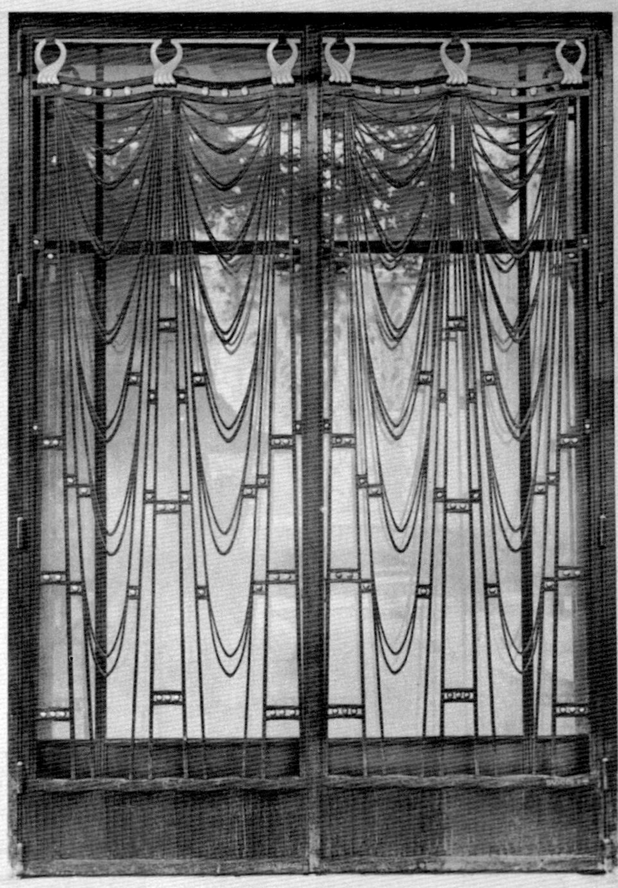

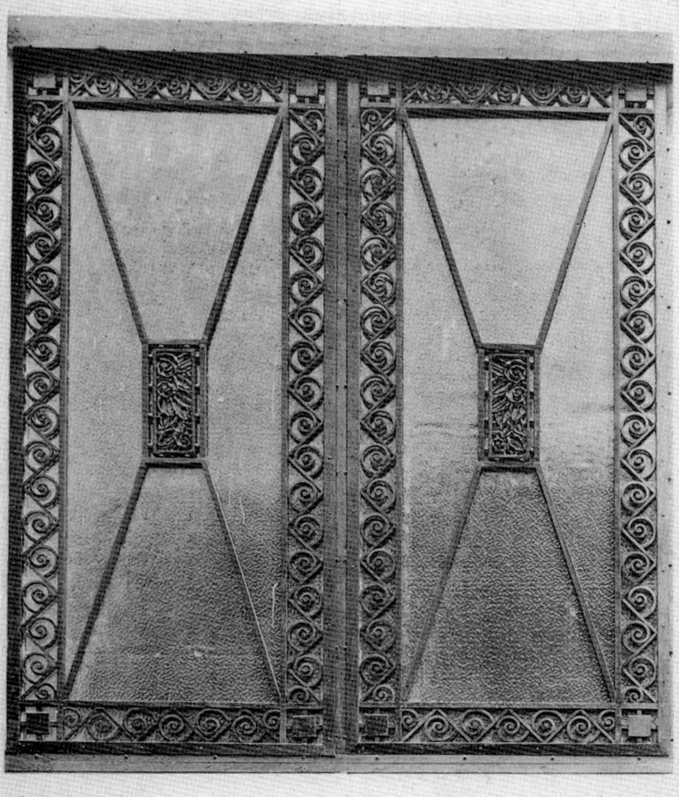

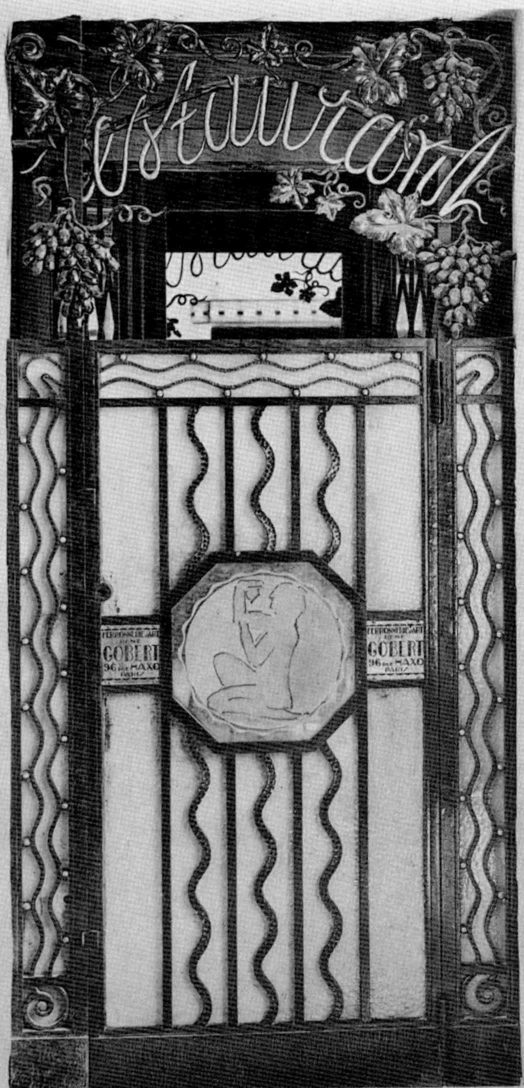

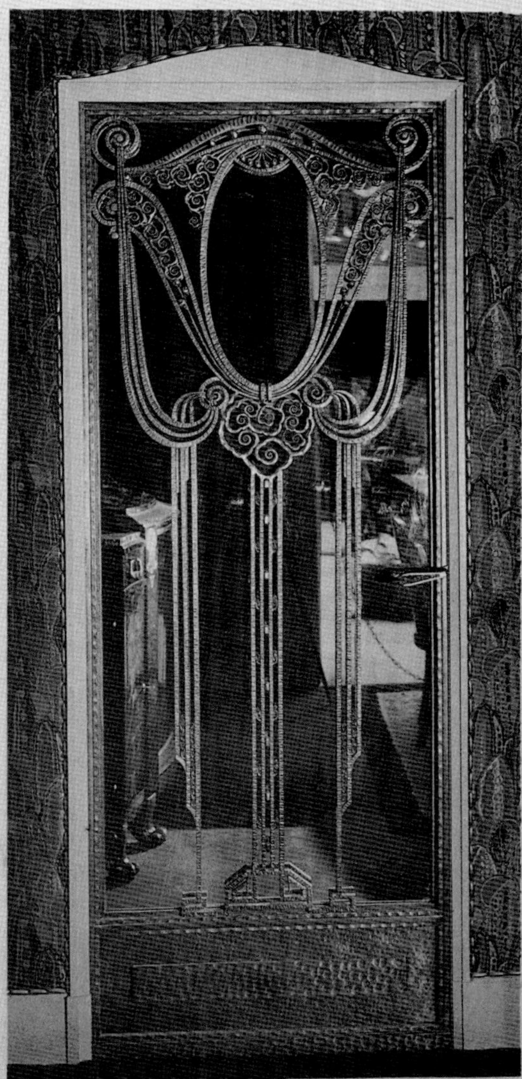

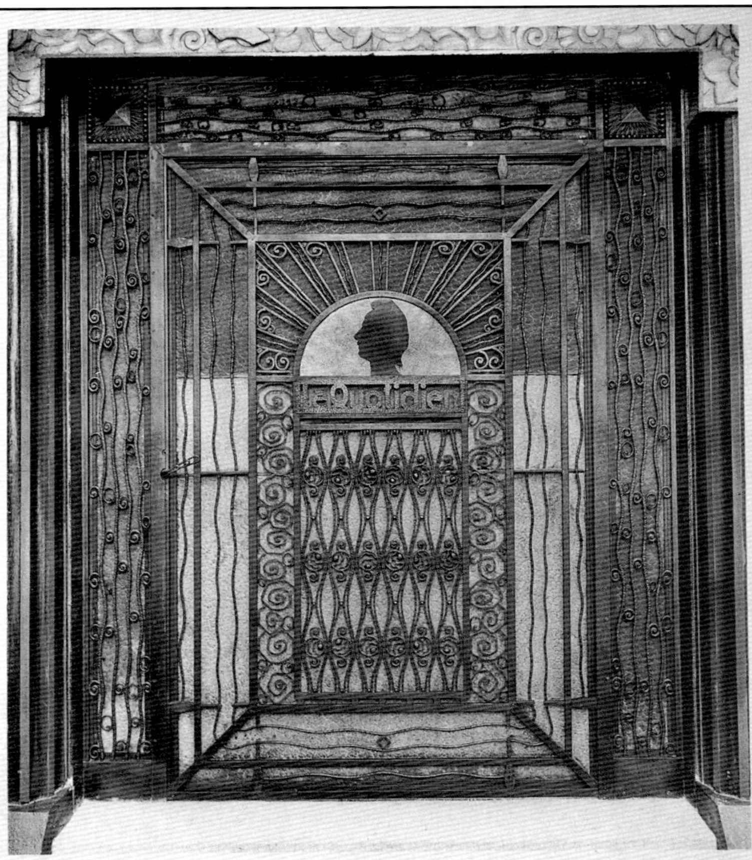
Le Quotidien

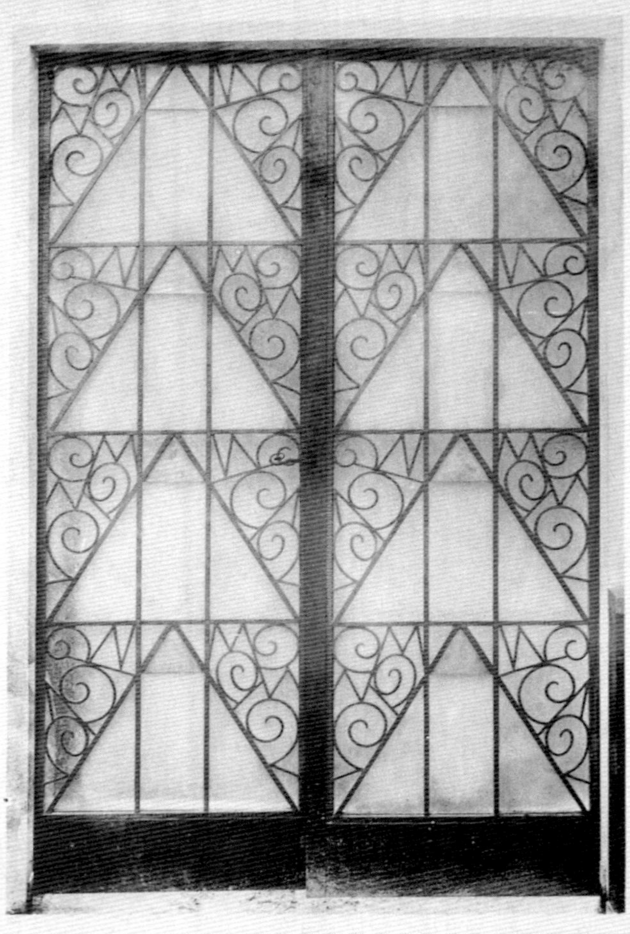

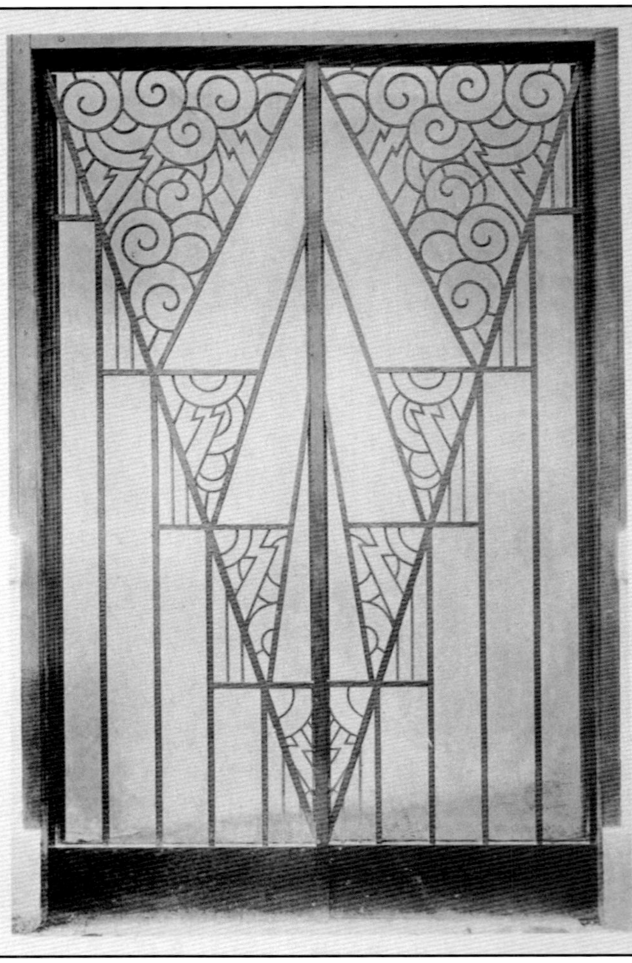

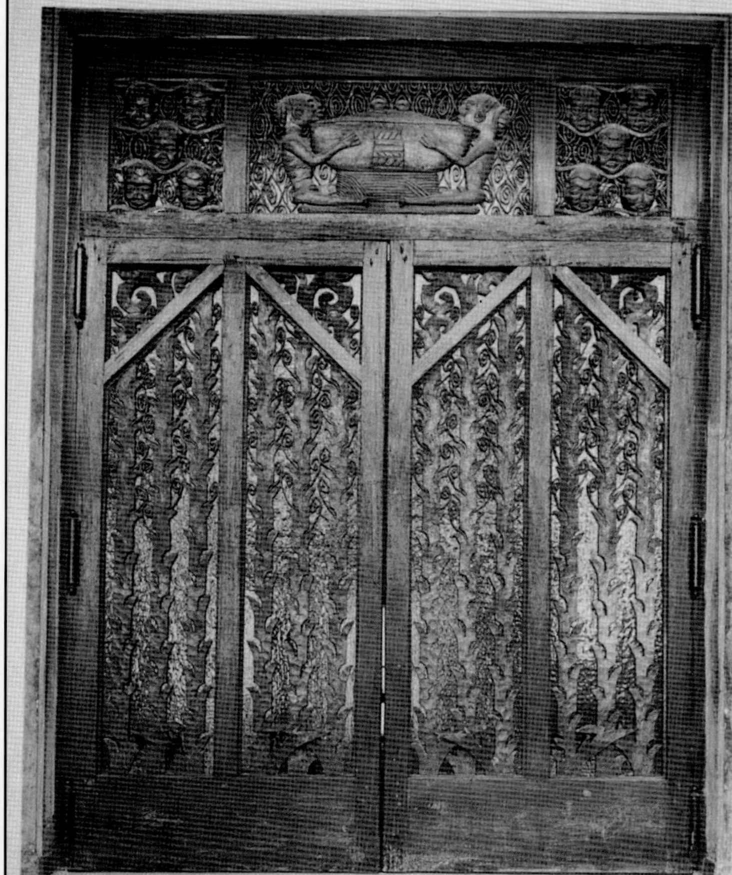

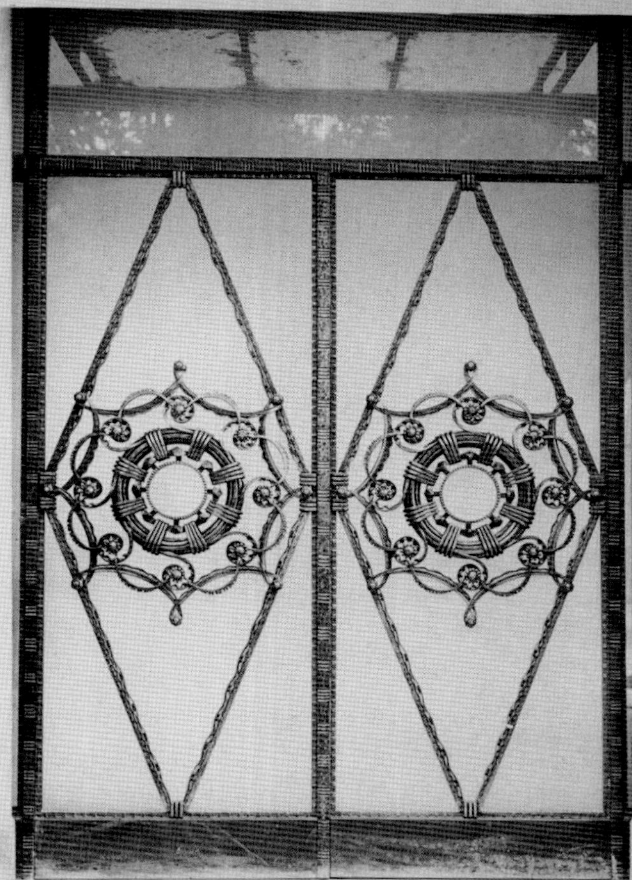

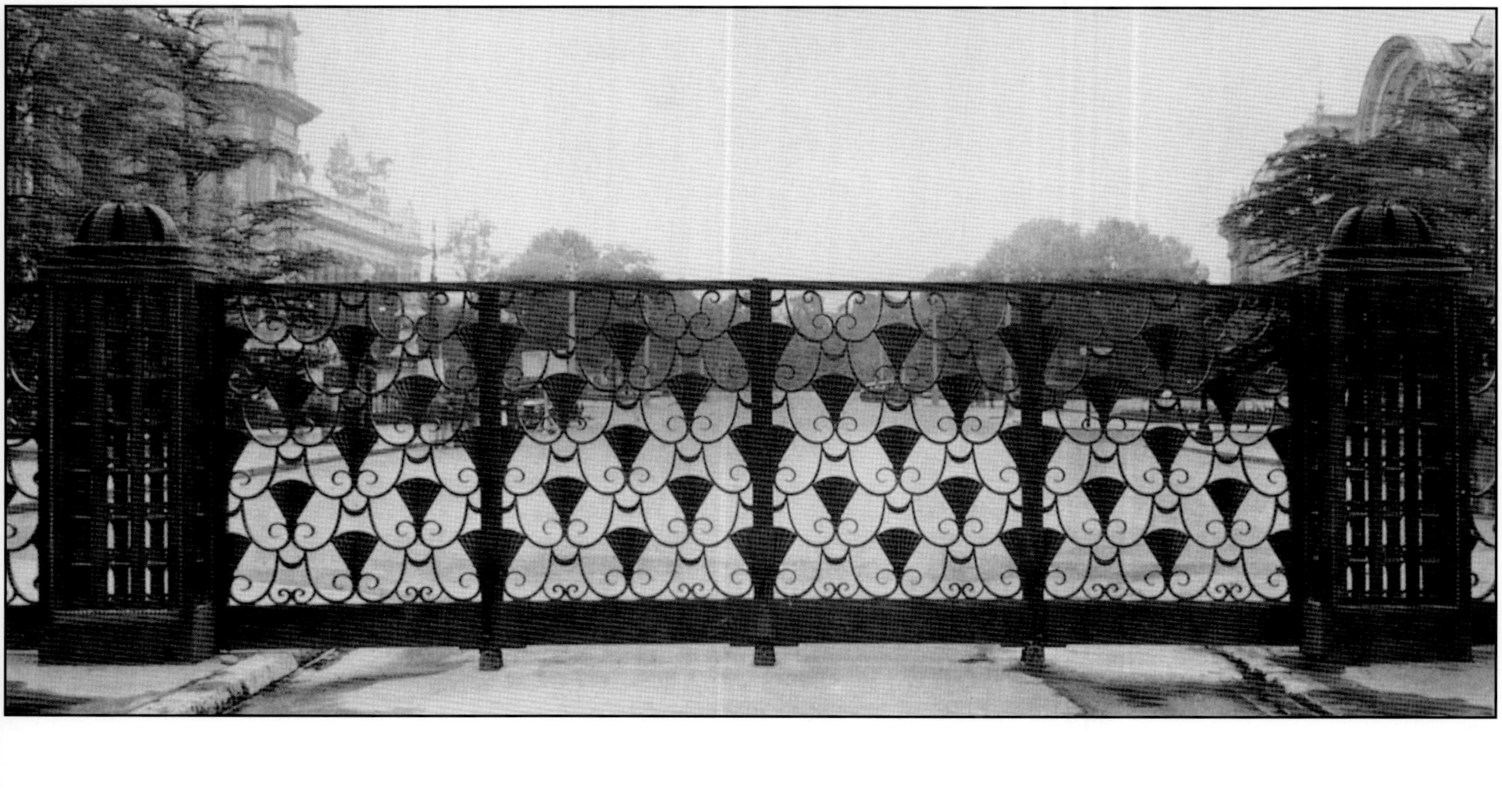

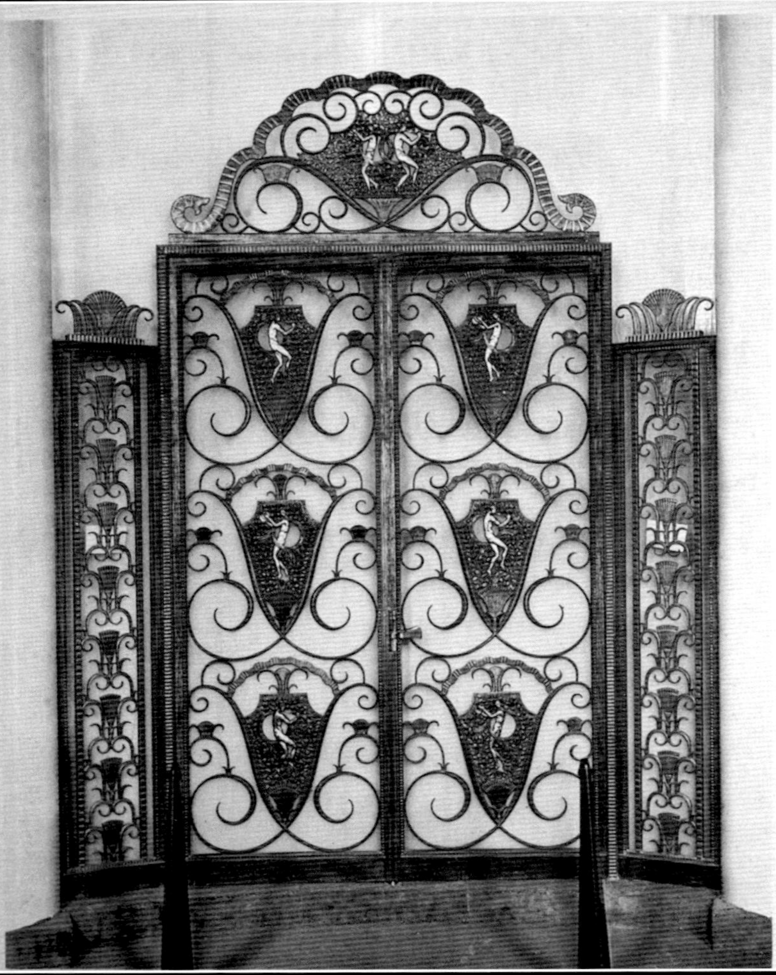

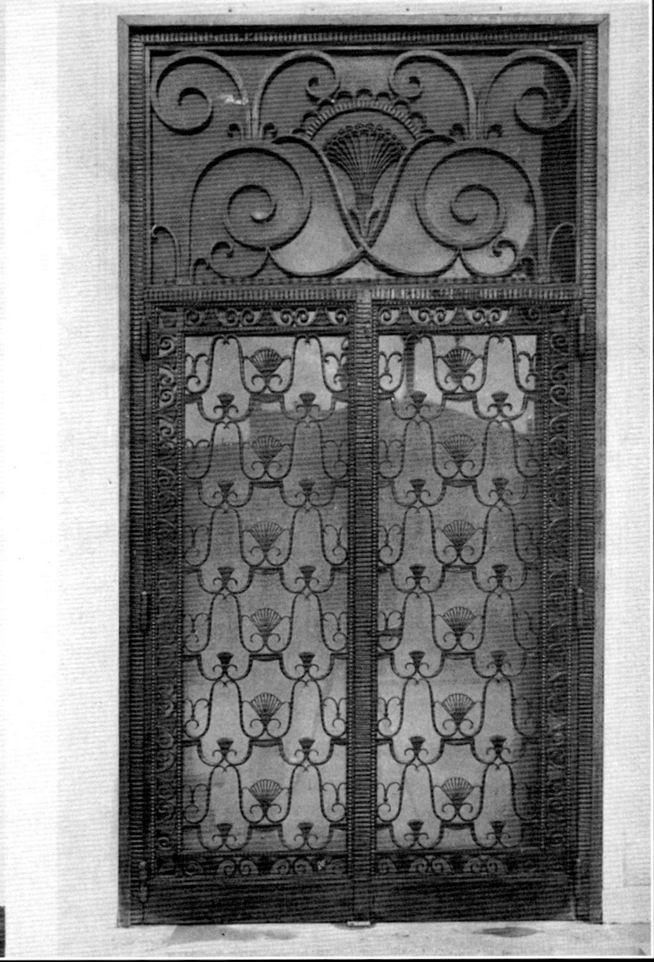

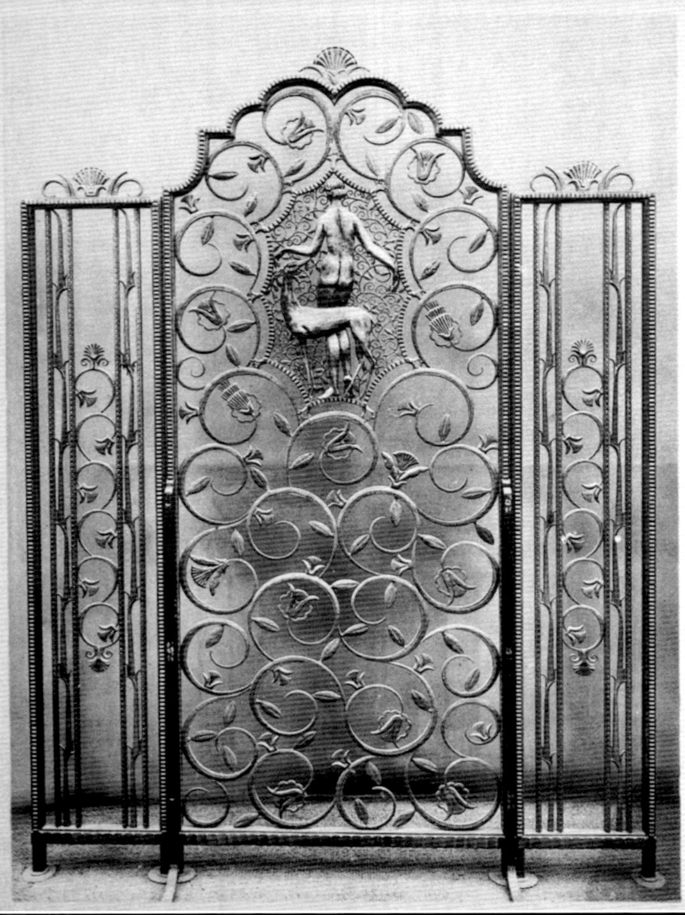

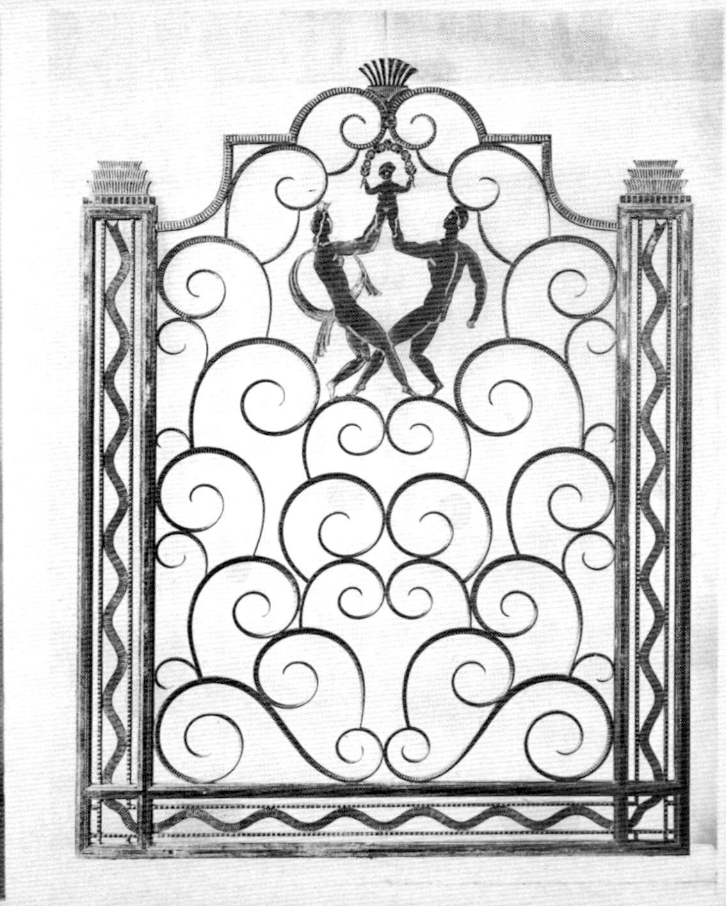

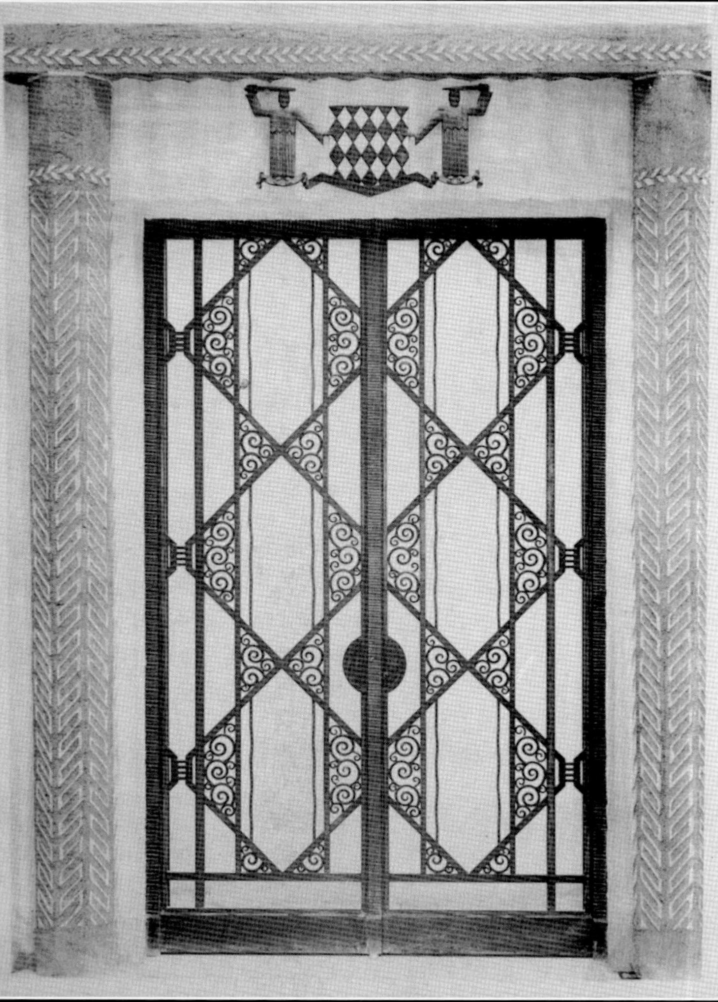

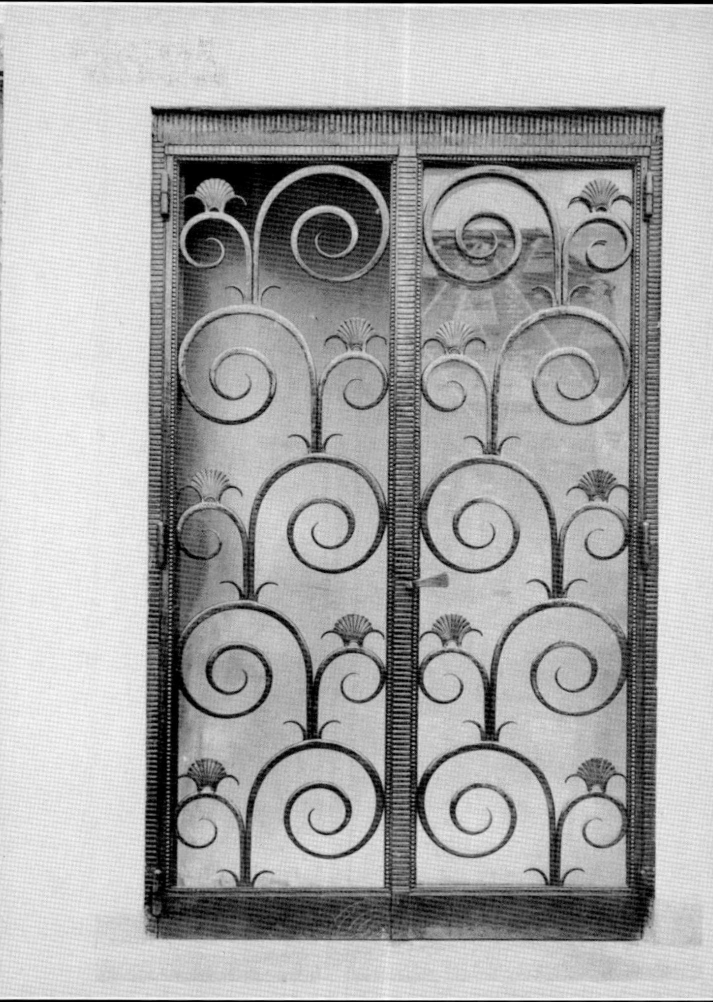

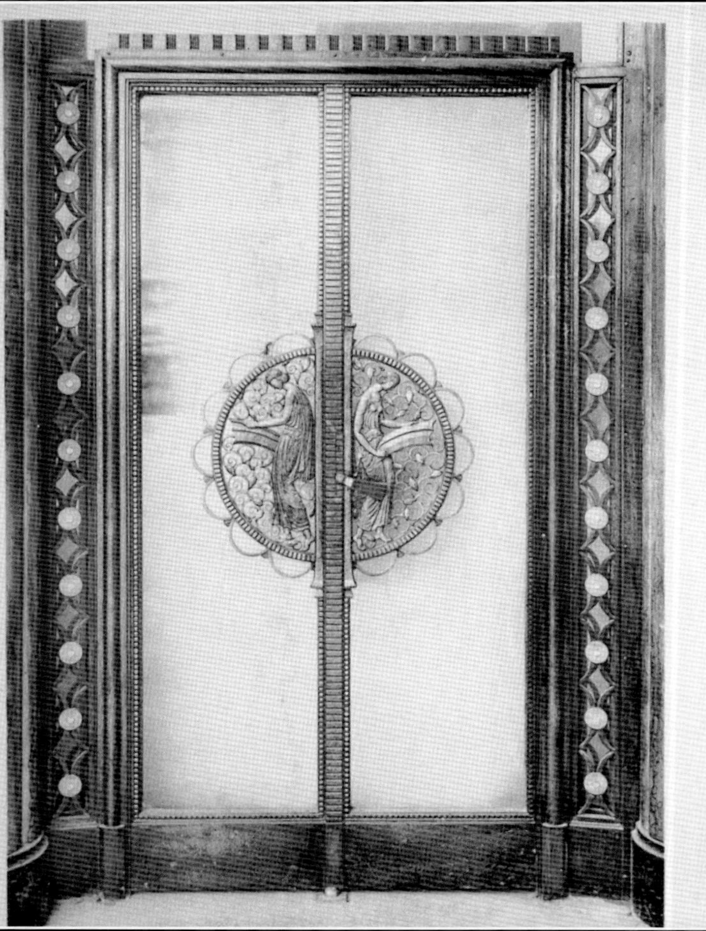

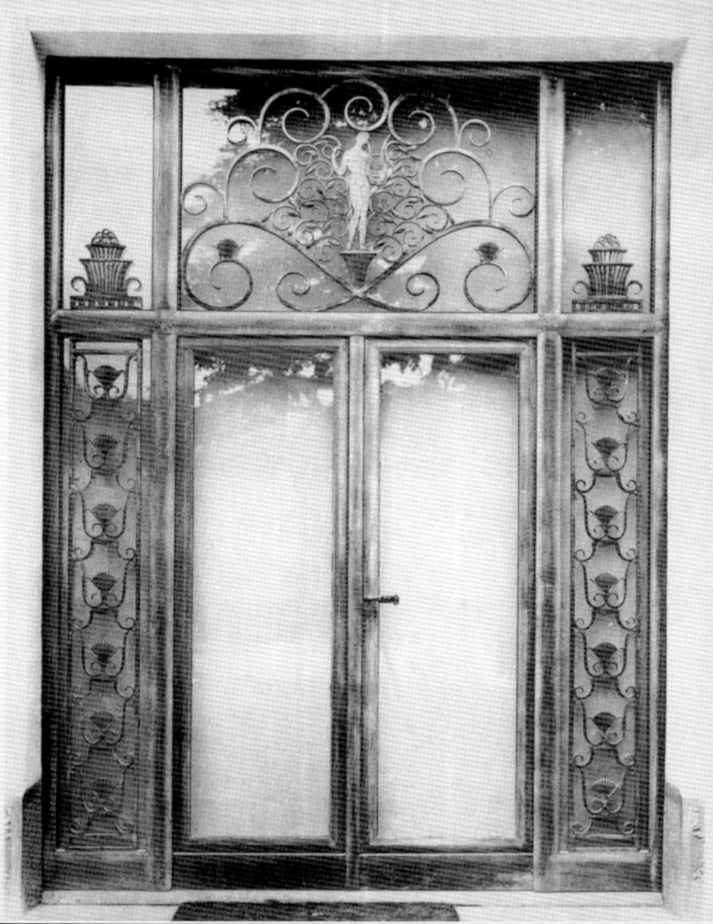

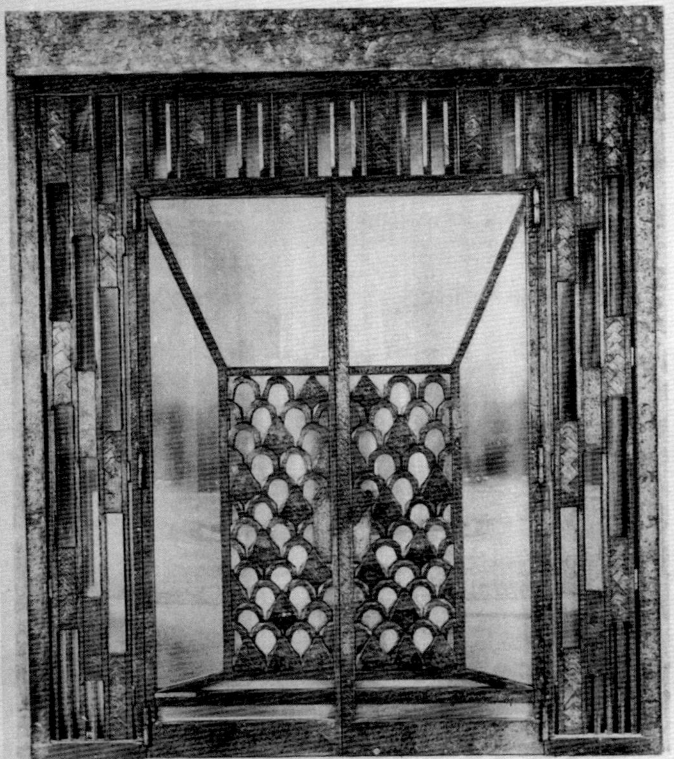

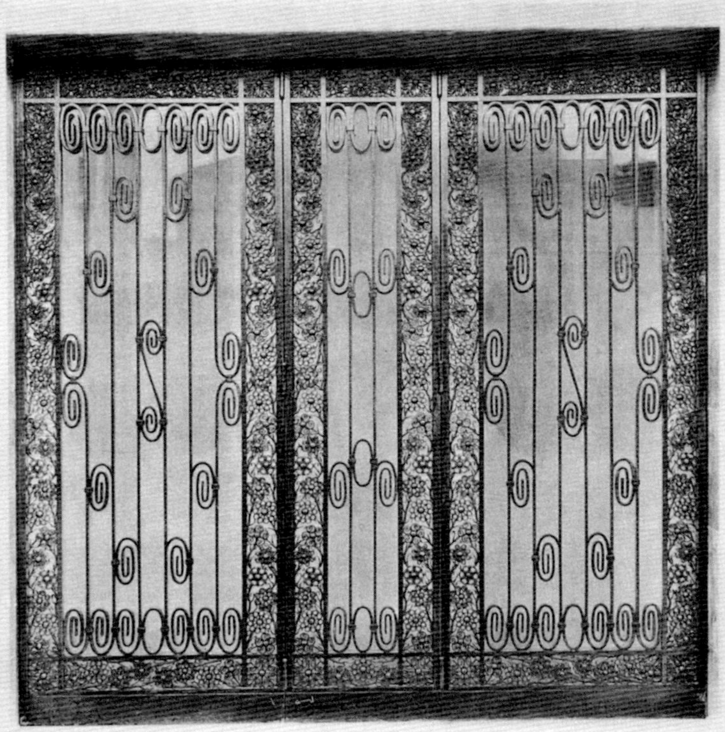

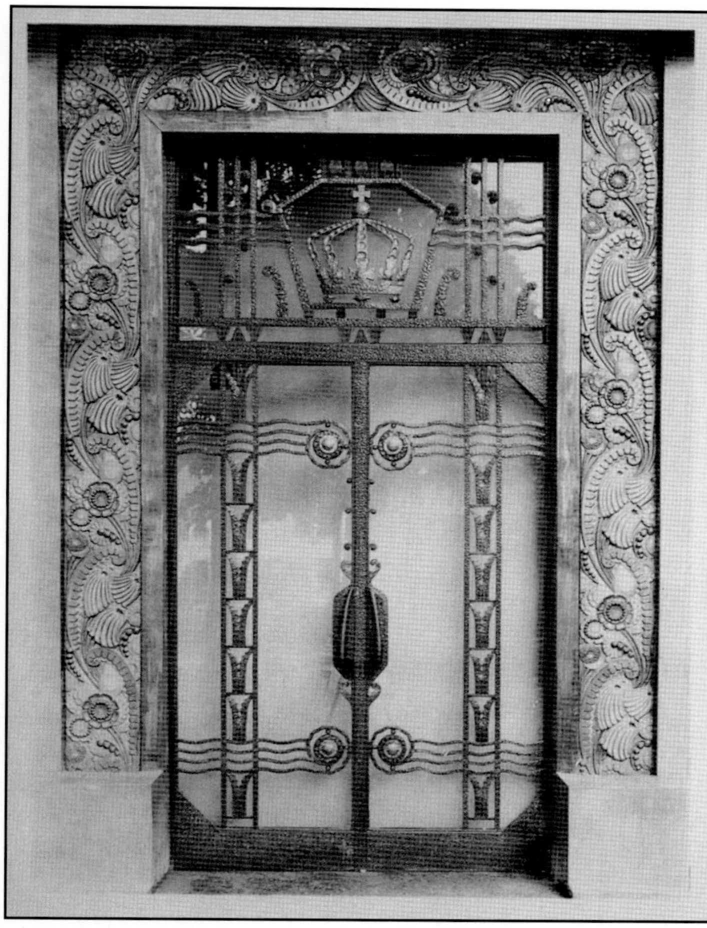

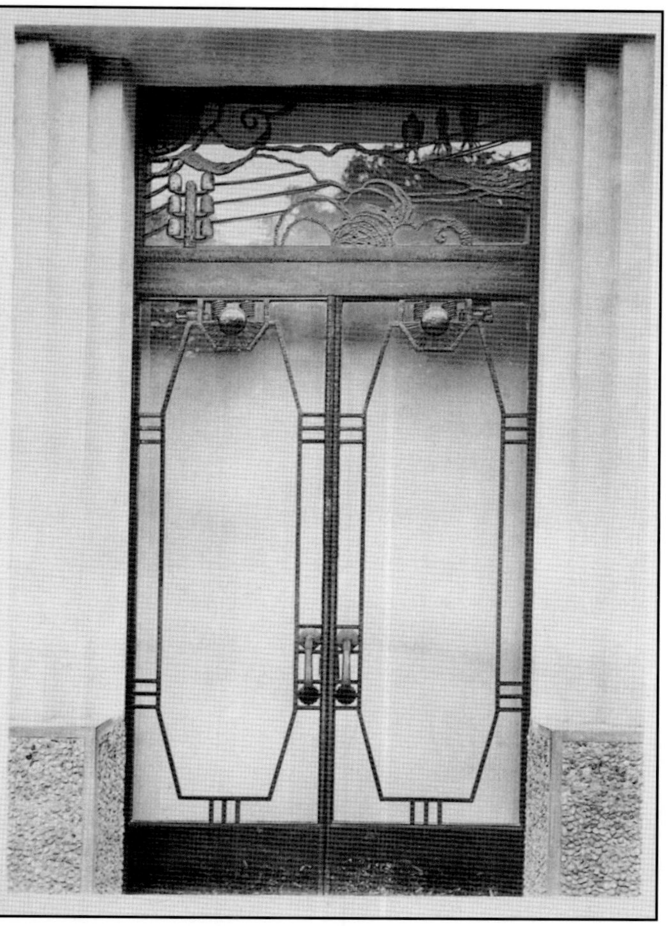

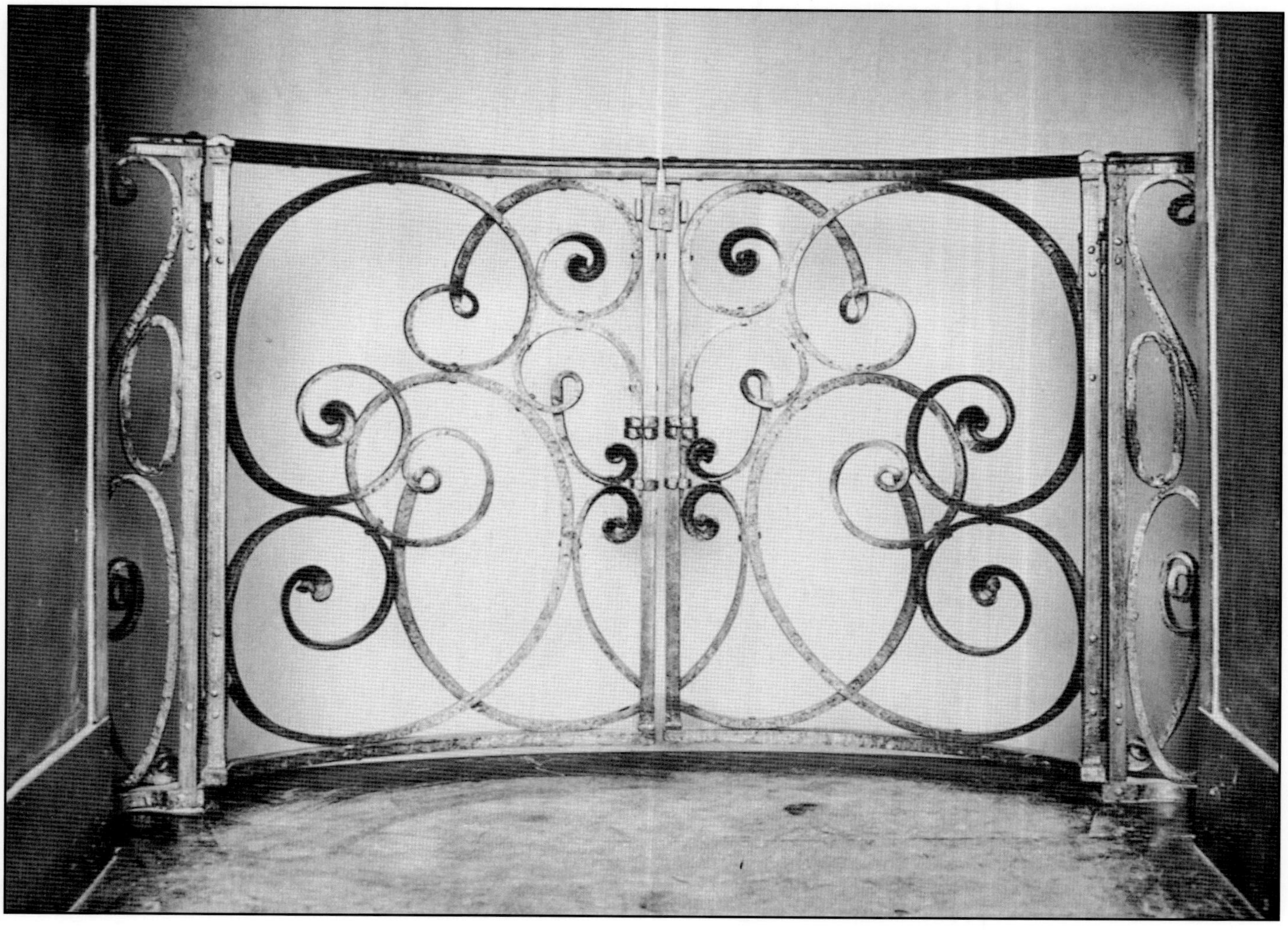

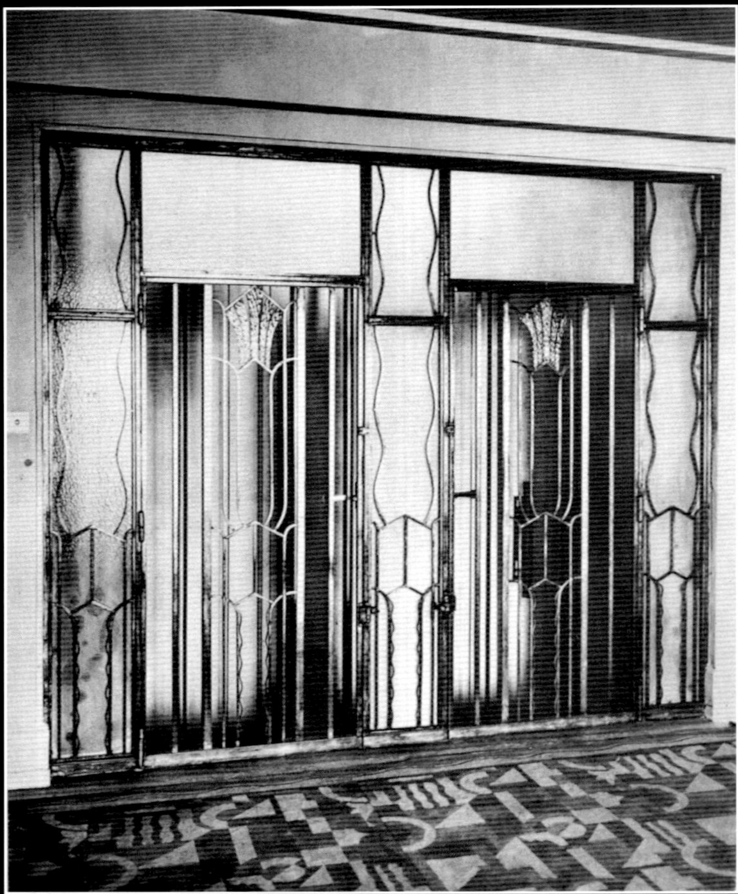

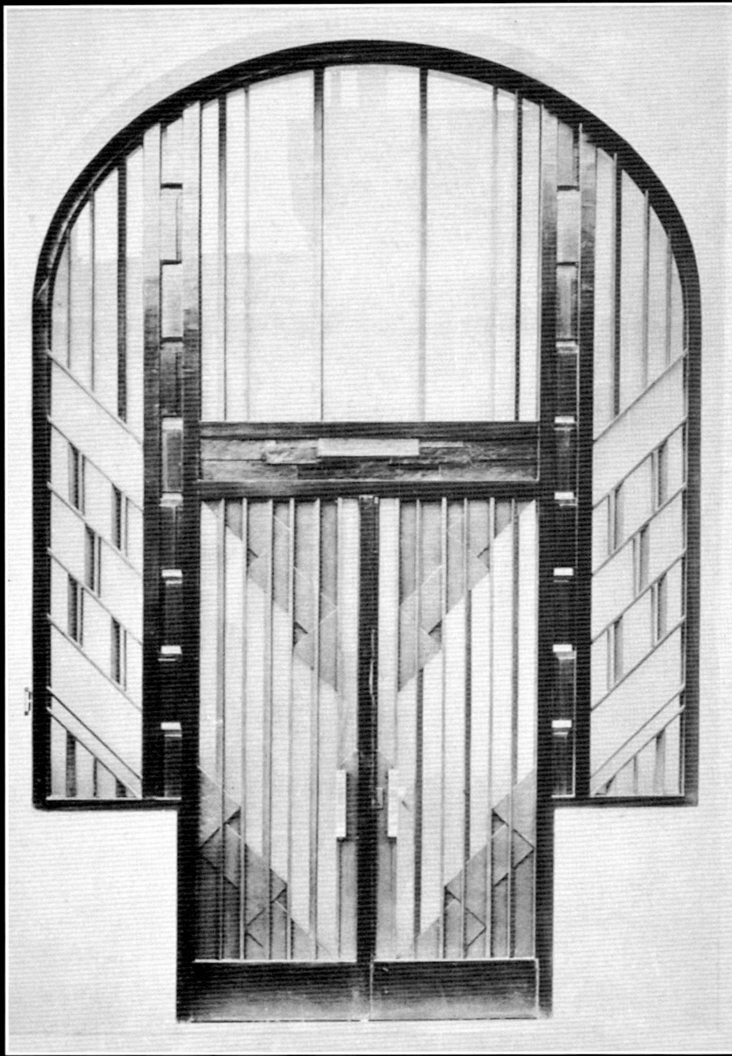

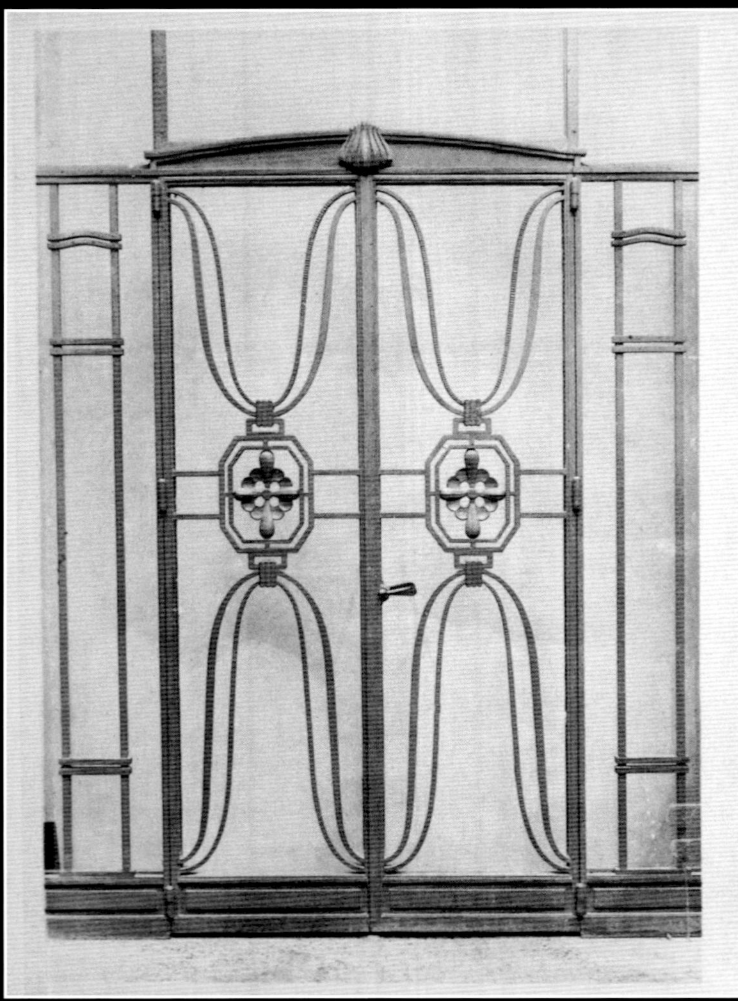

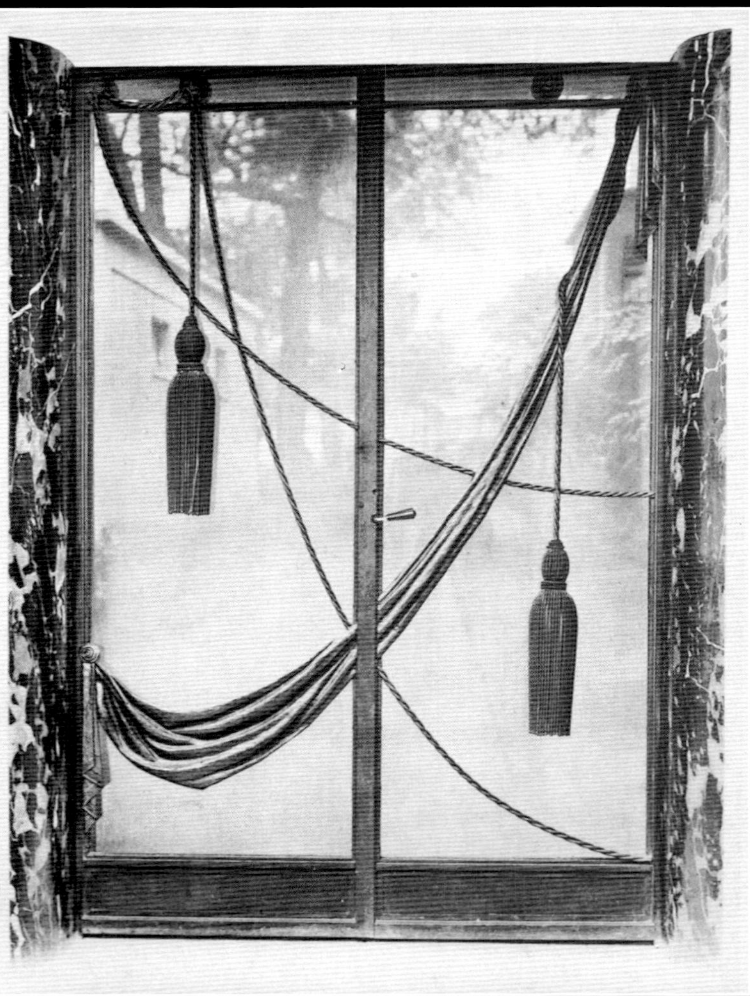

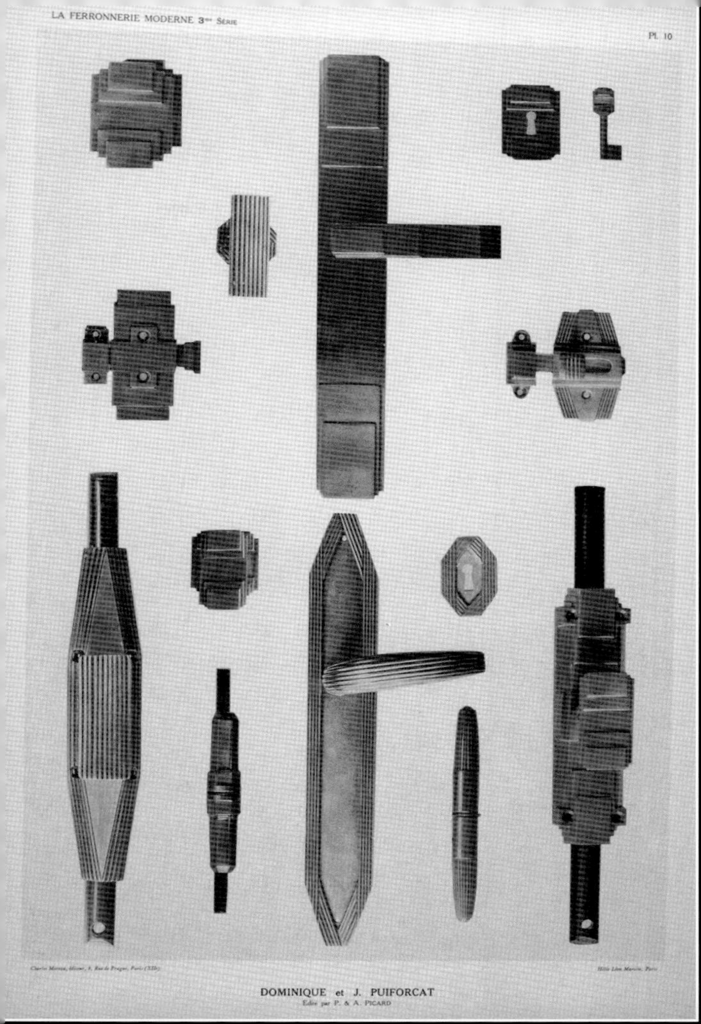

LA FERRONNERIE MODERNE 3me Série
Pl. 10
DOMINIQUE et J. PUIFORCAT
Edité par P. & A. PICARD

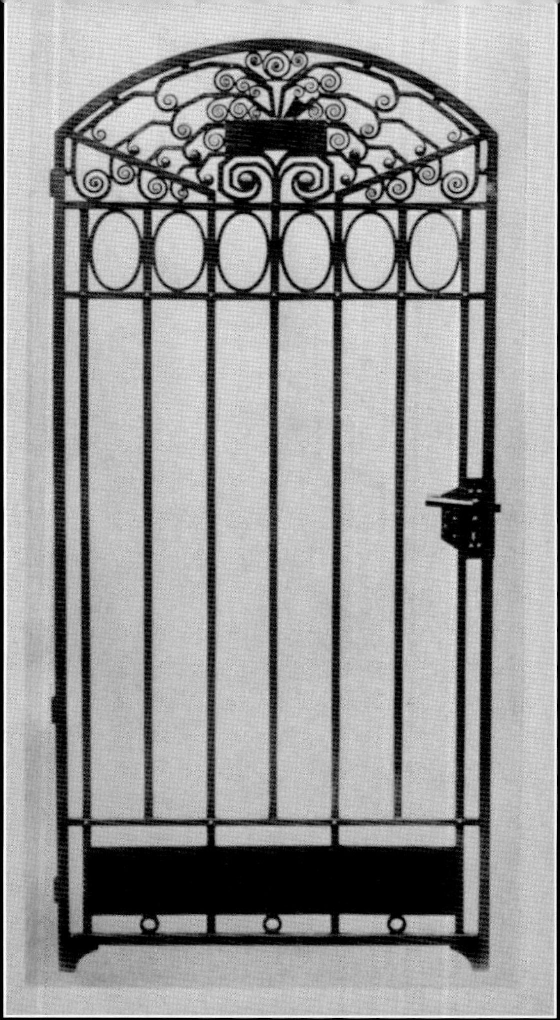

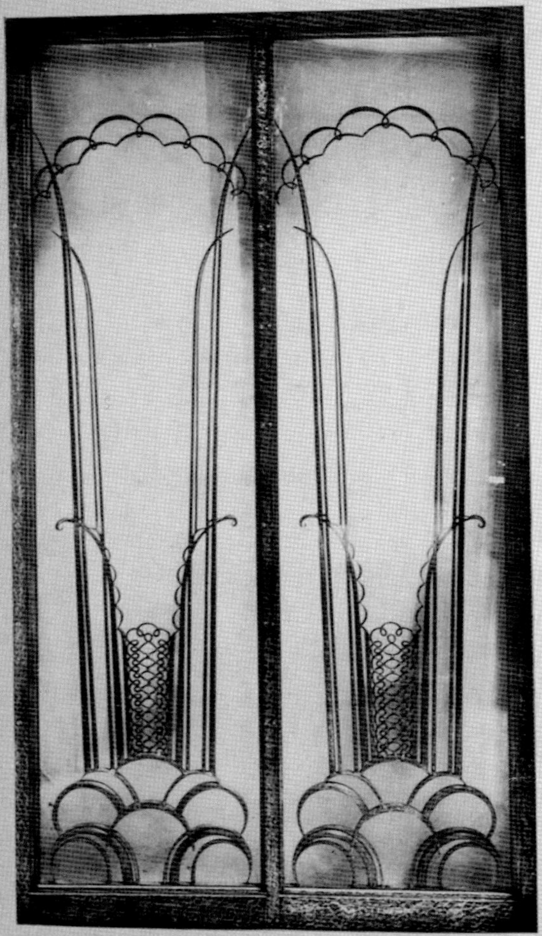

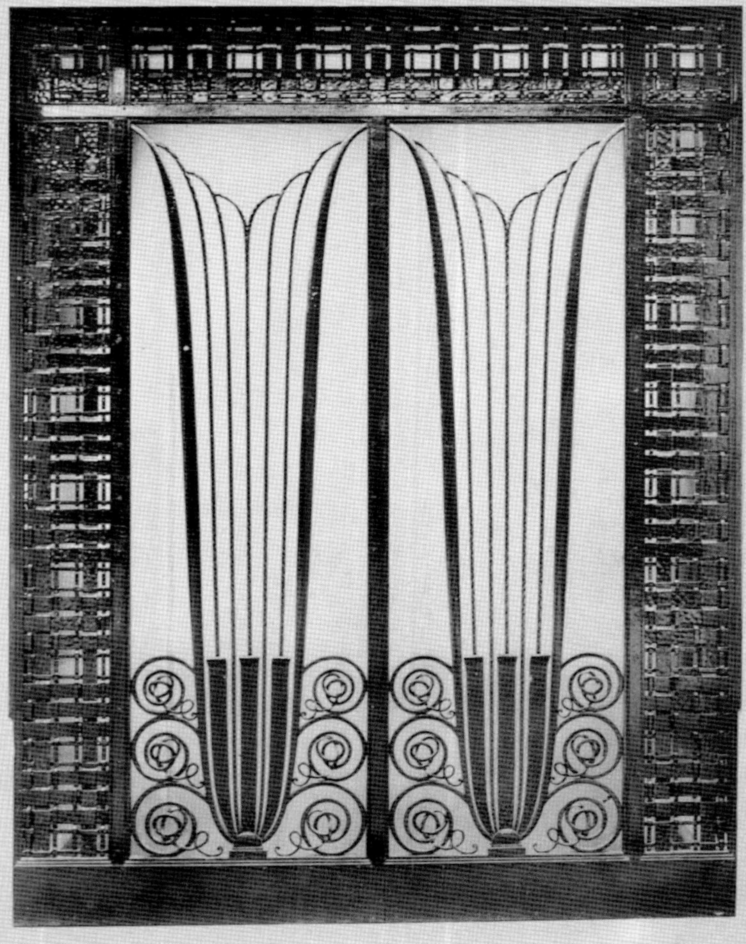

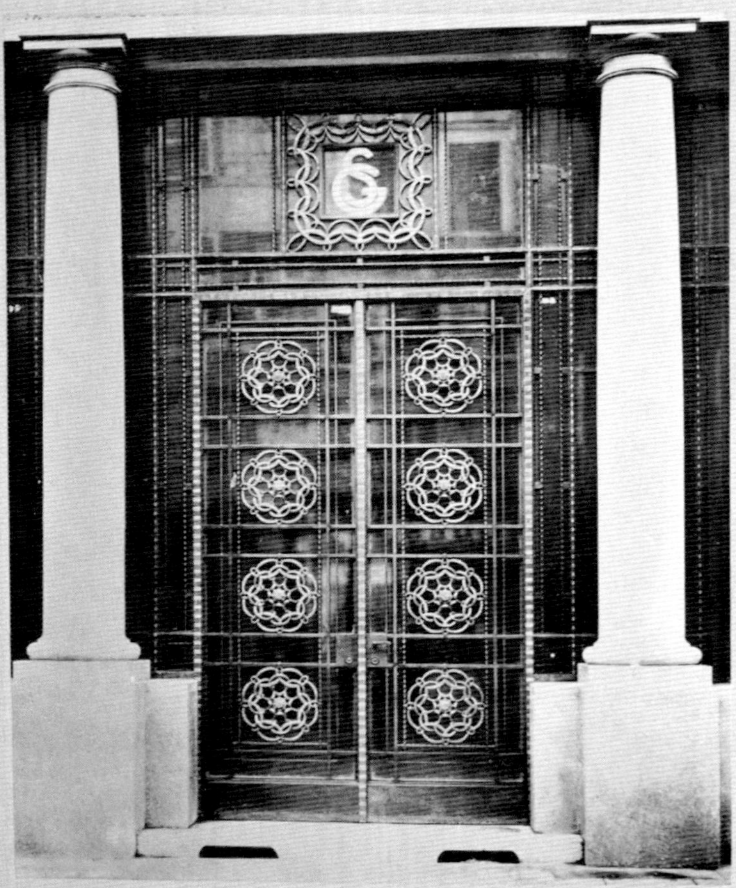

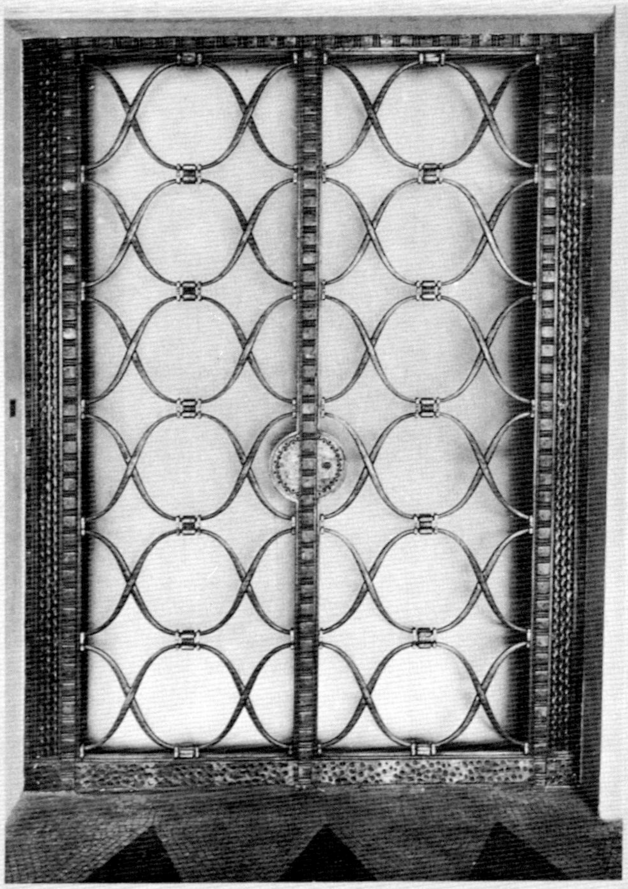

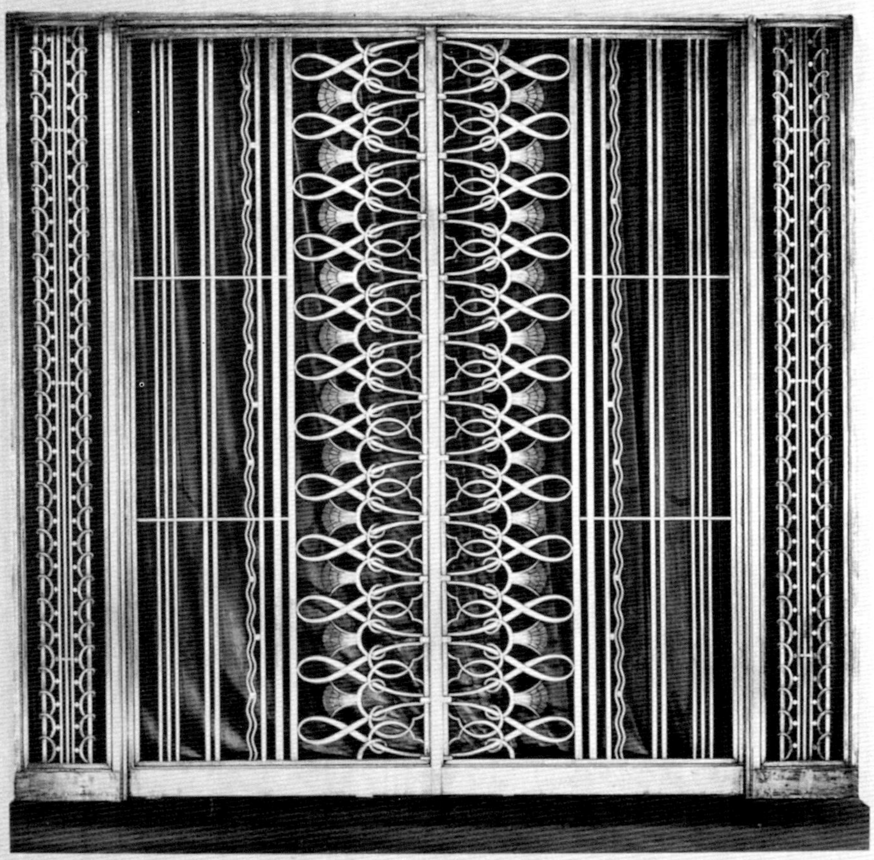

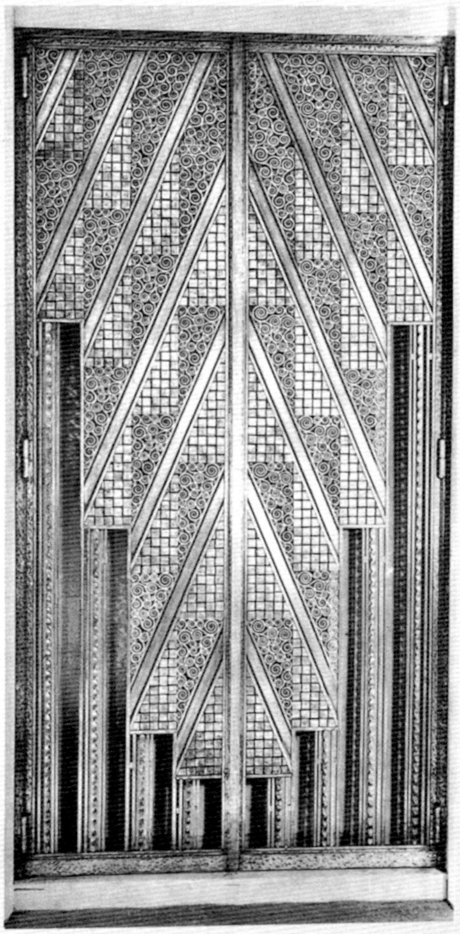

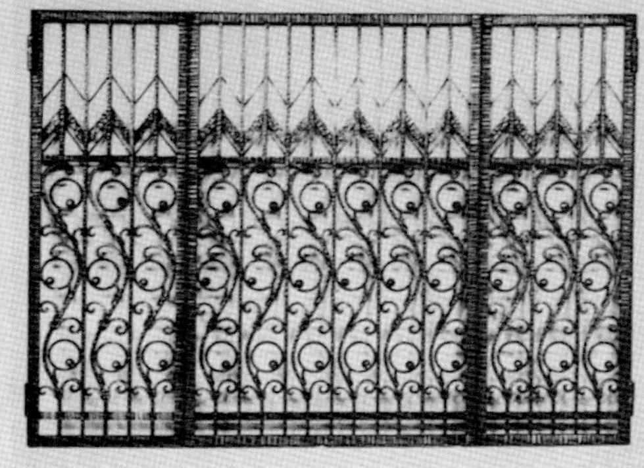

2

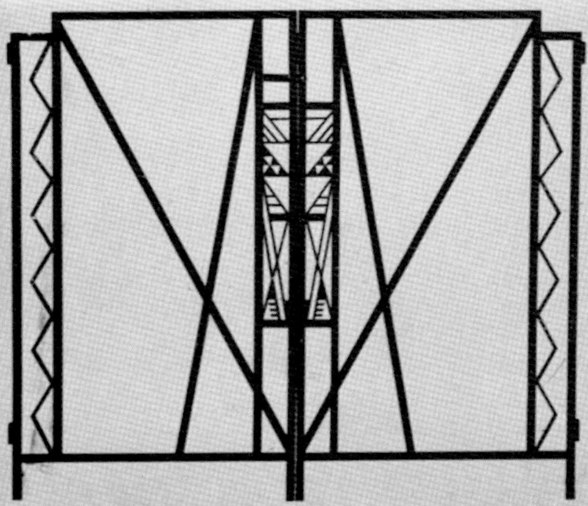

5

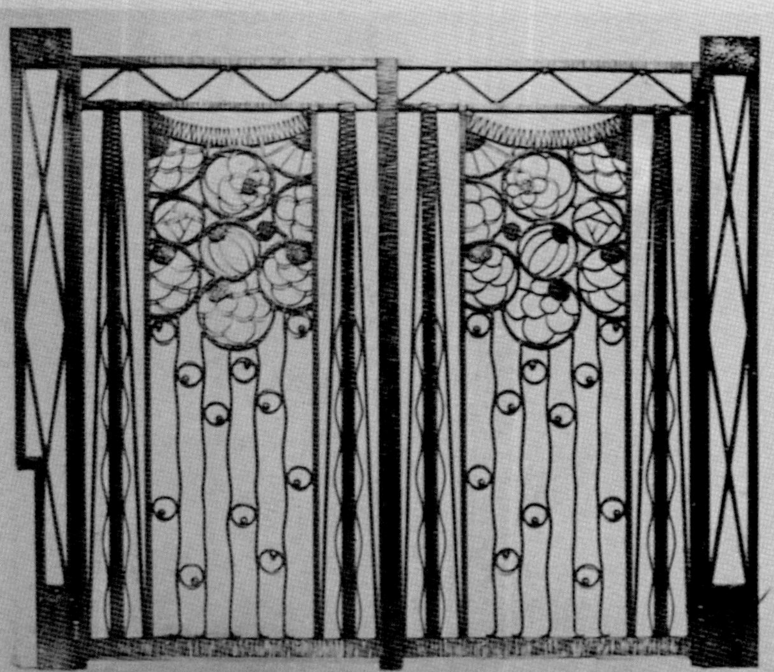

3

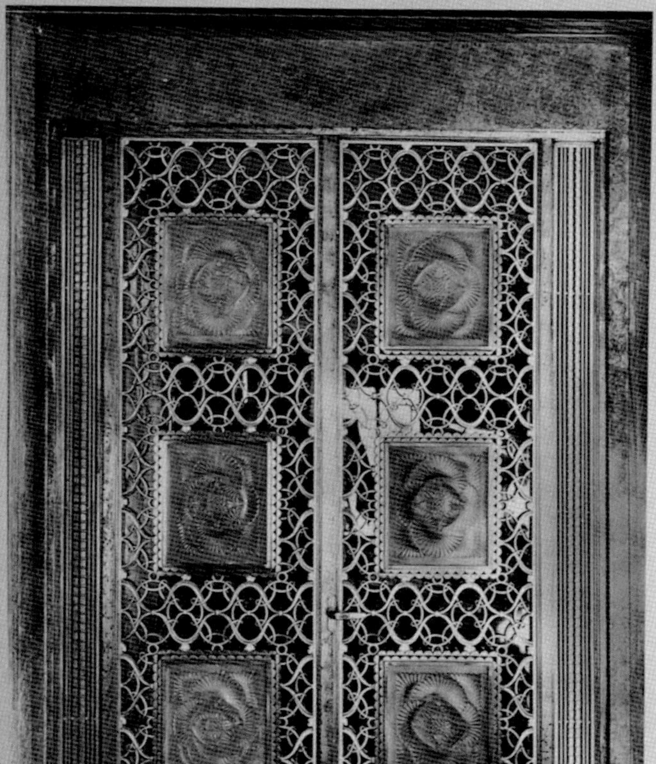

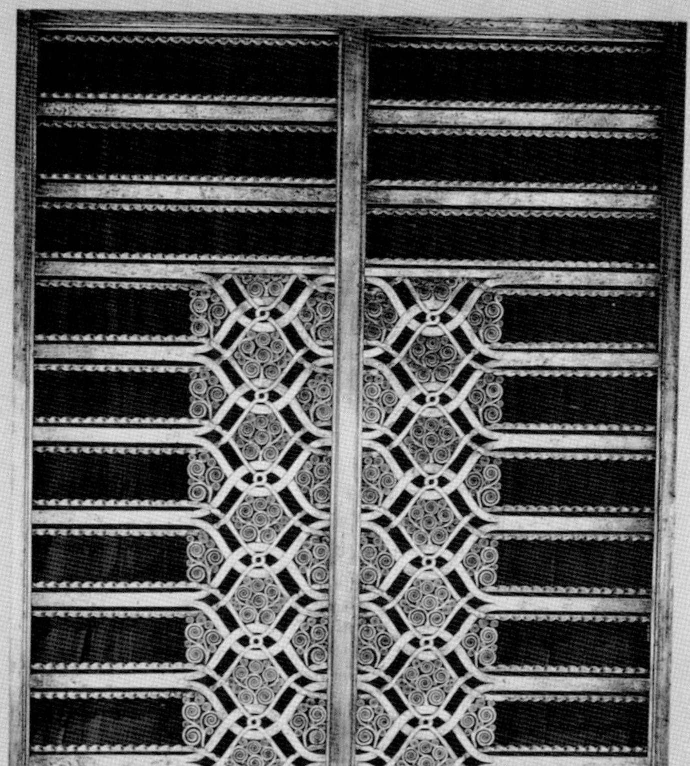

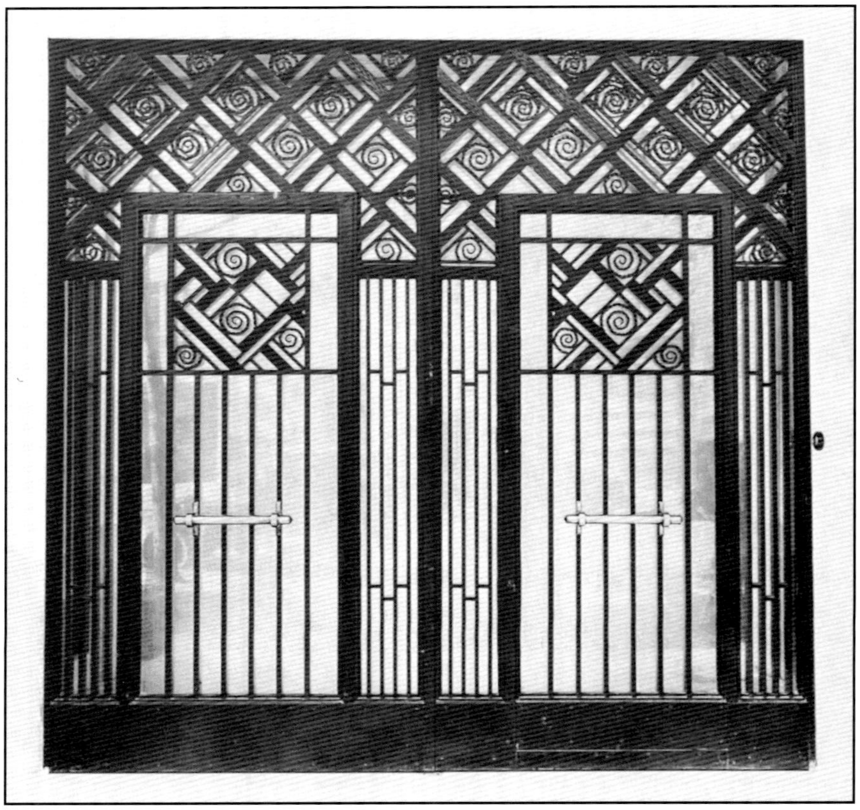

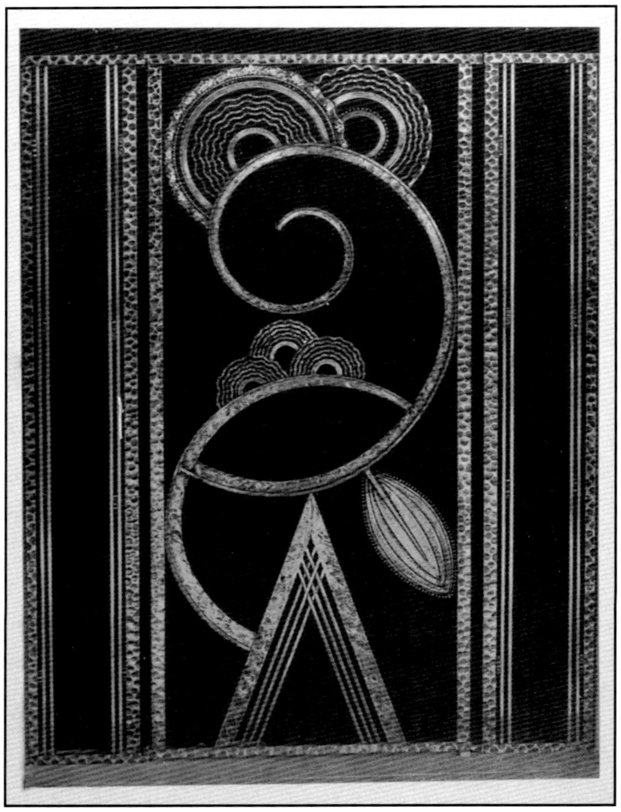

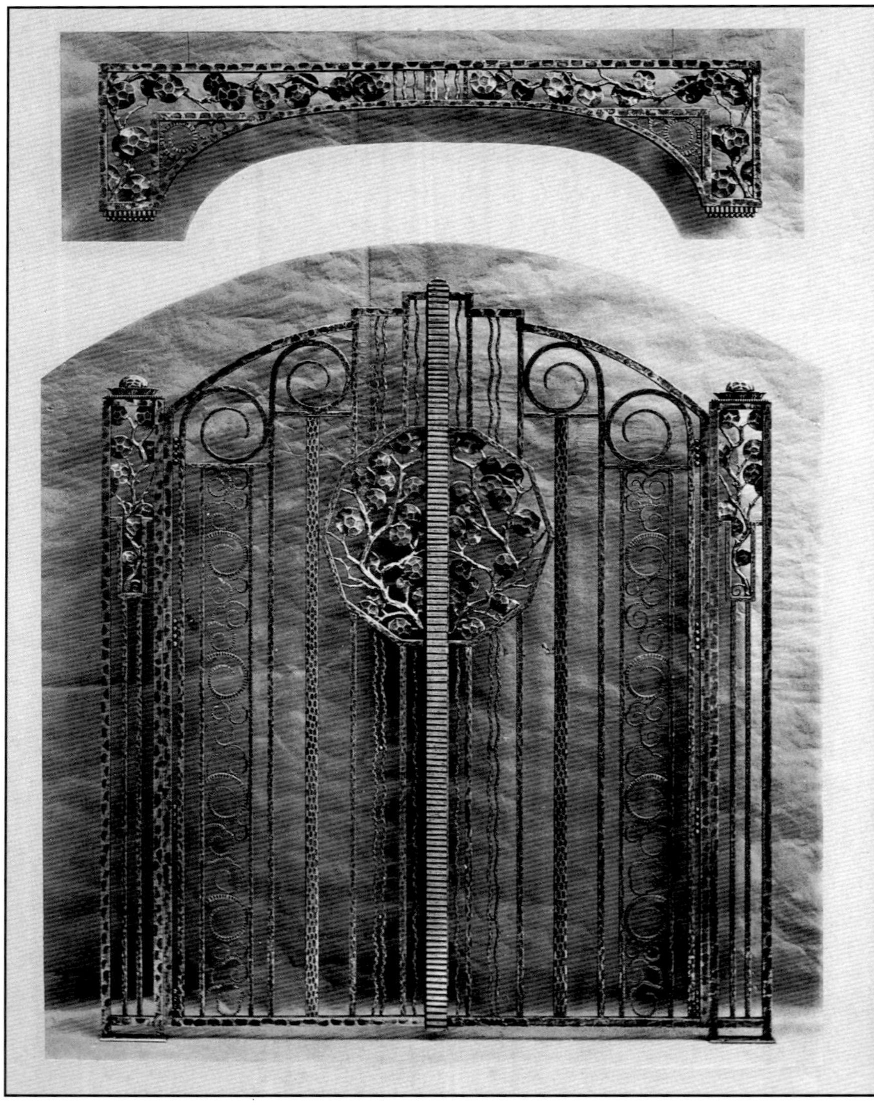

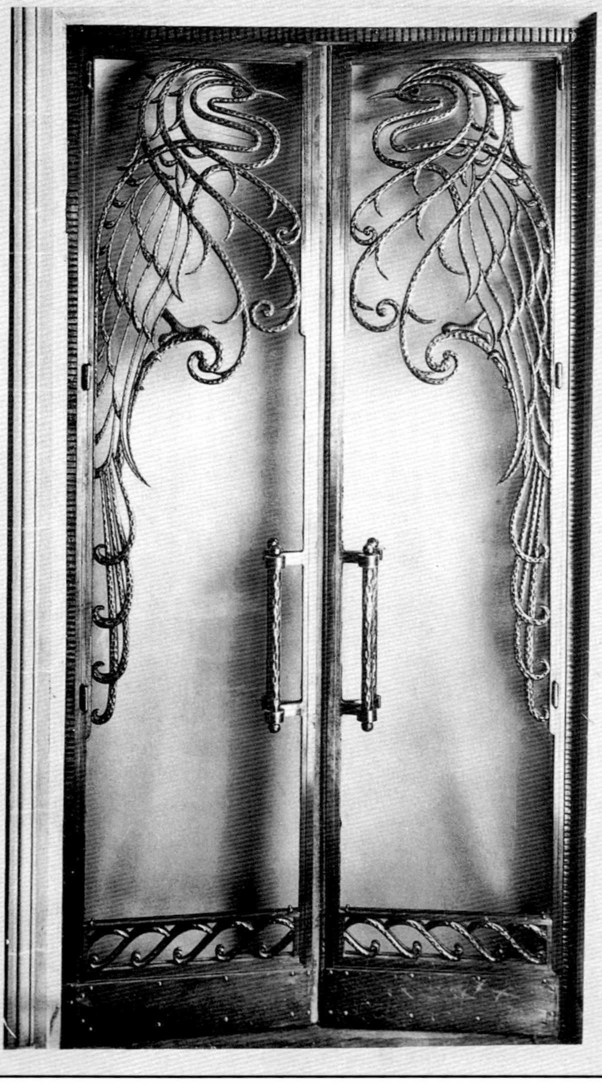

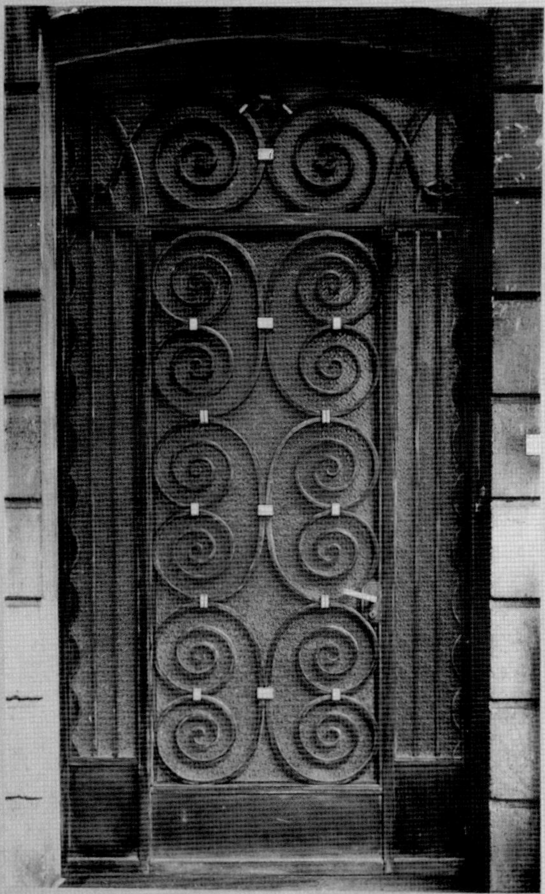

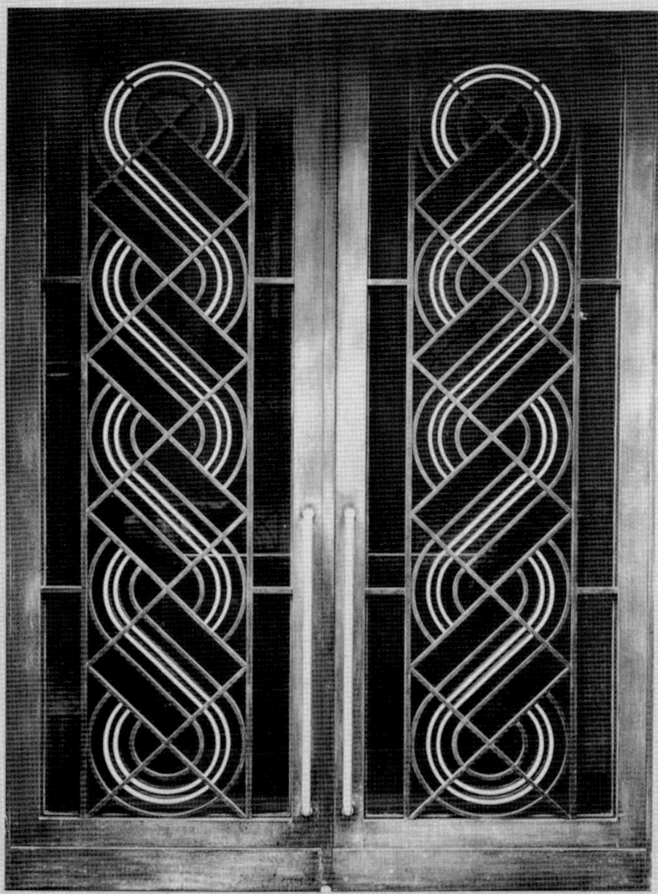

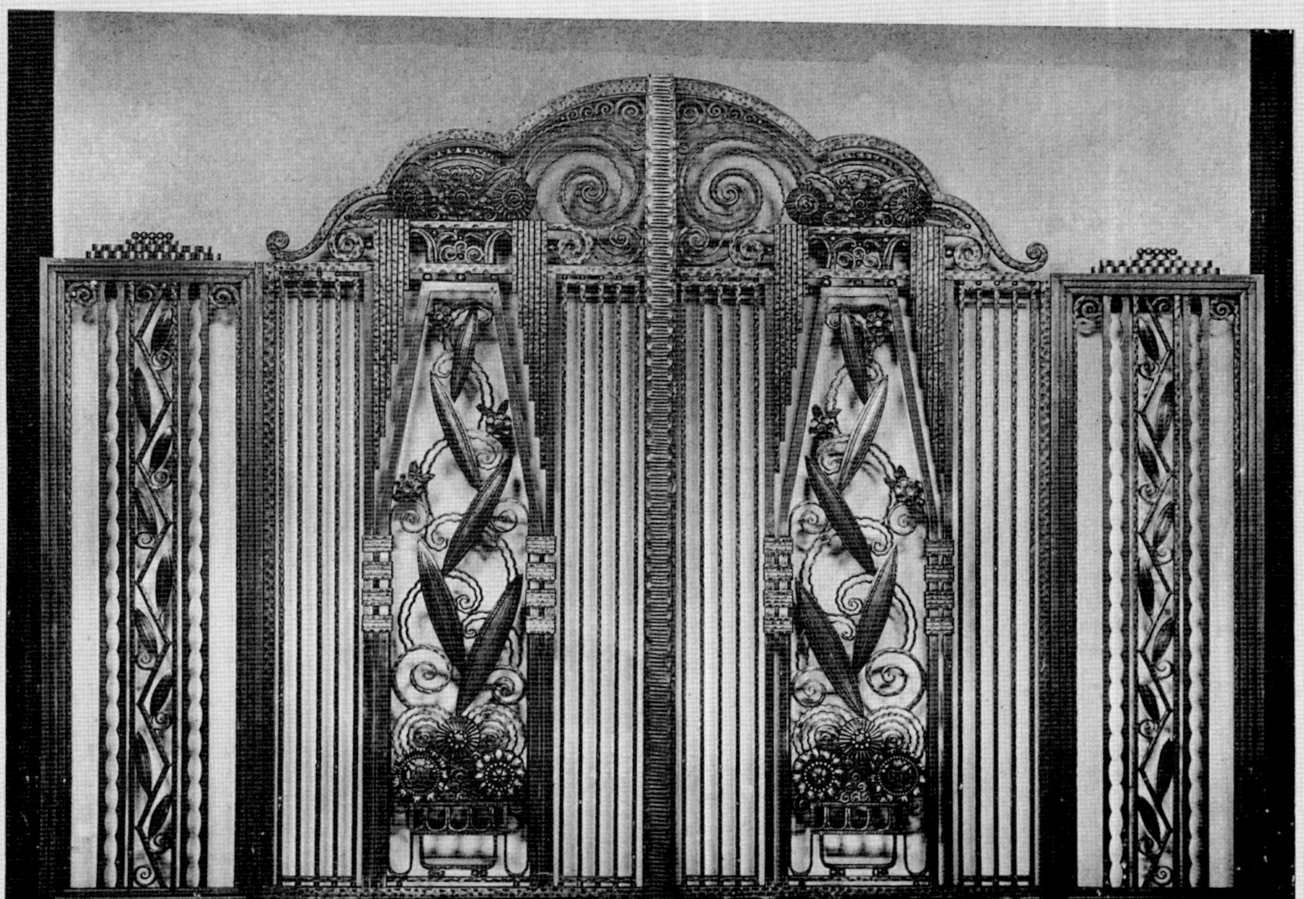

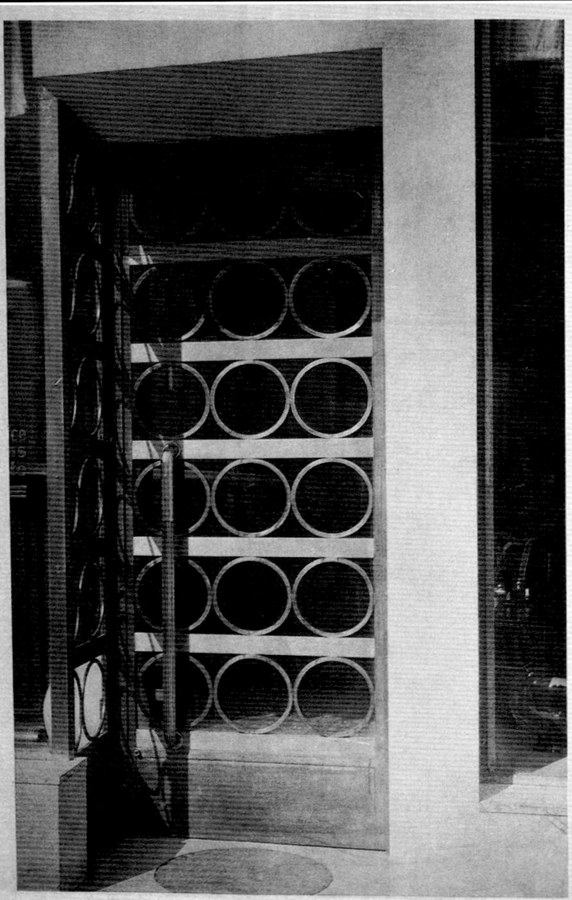

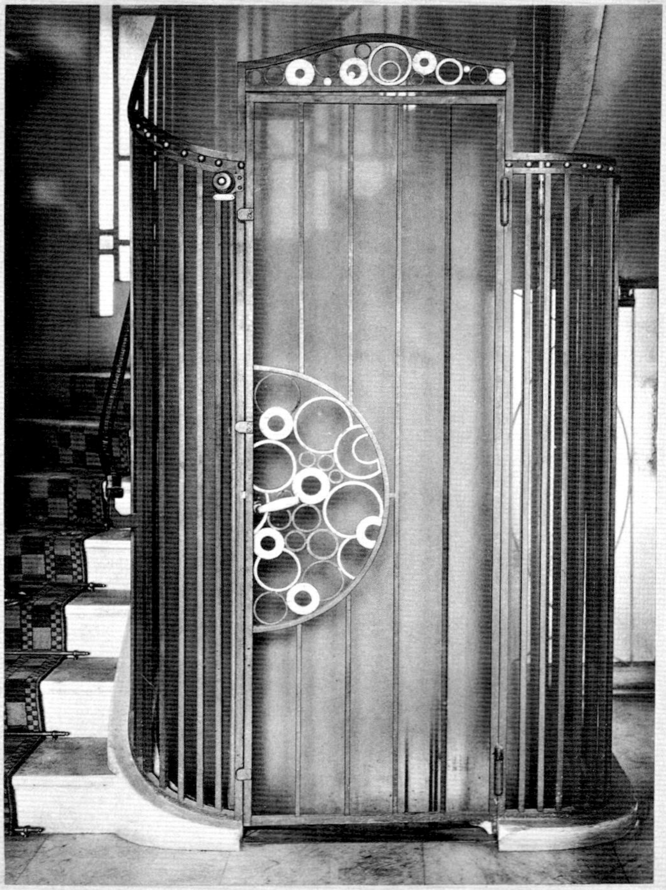

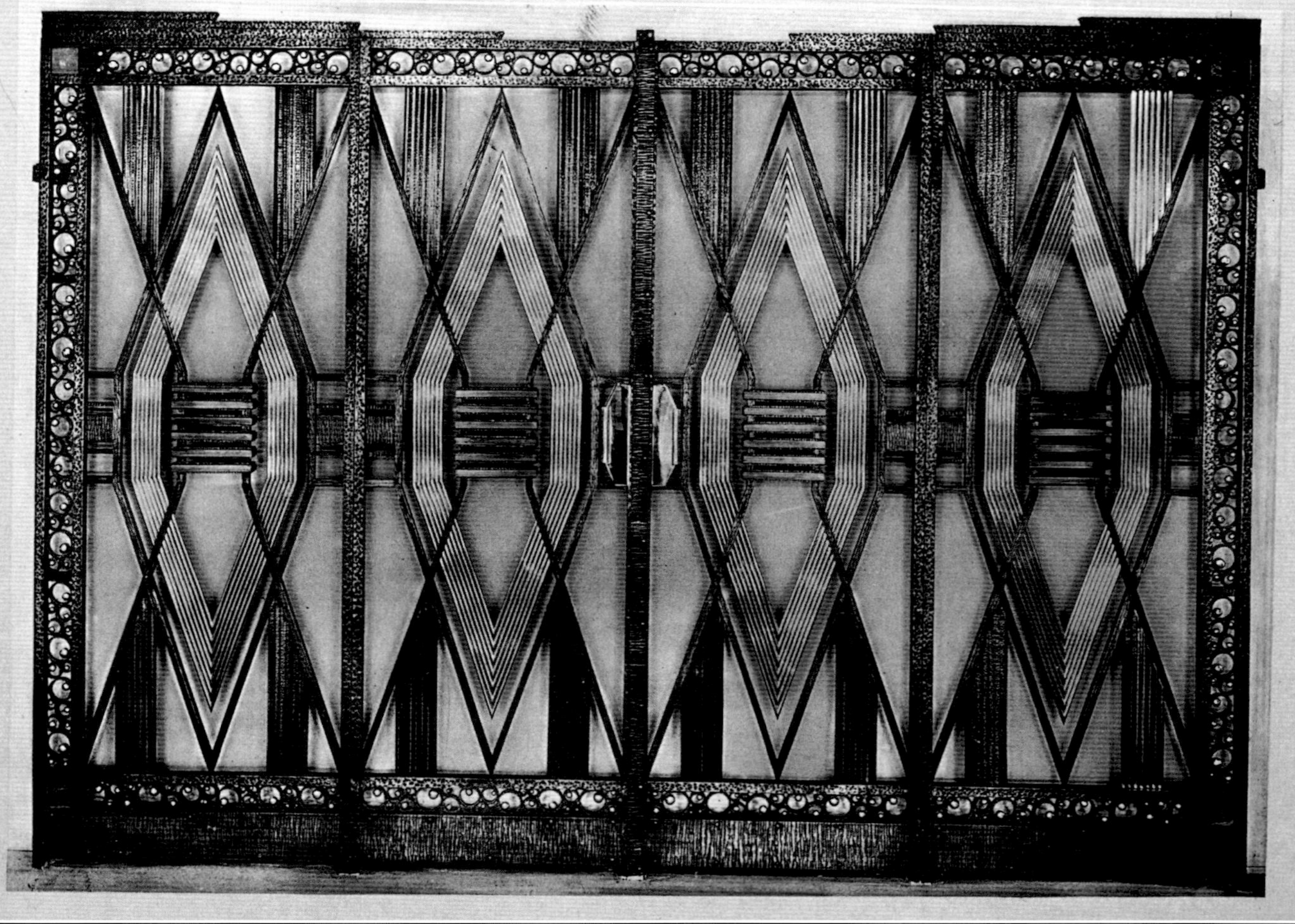

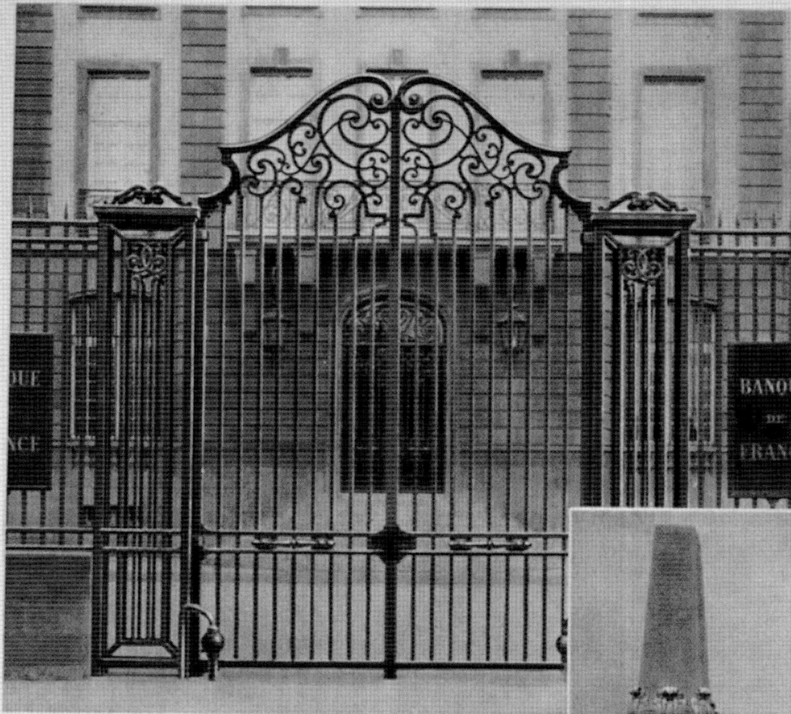

MM. DEFRASSE & DEDUN, ARCH.

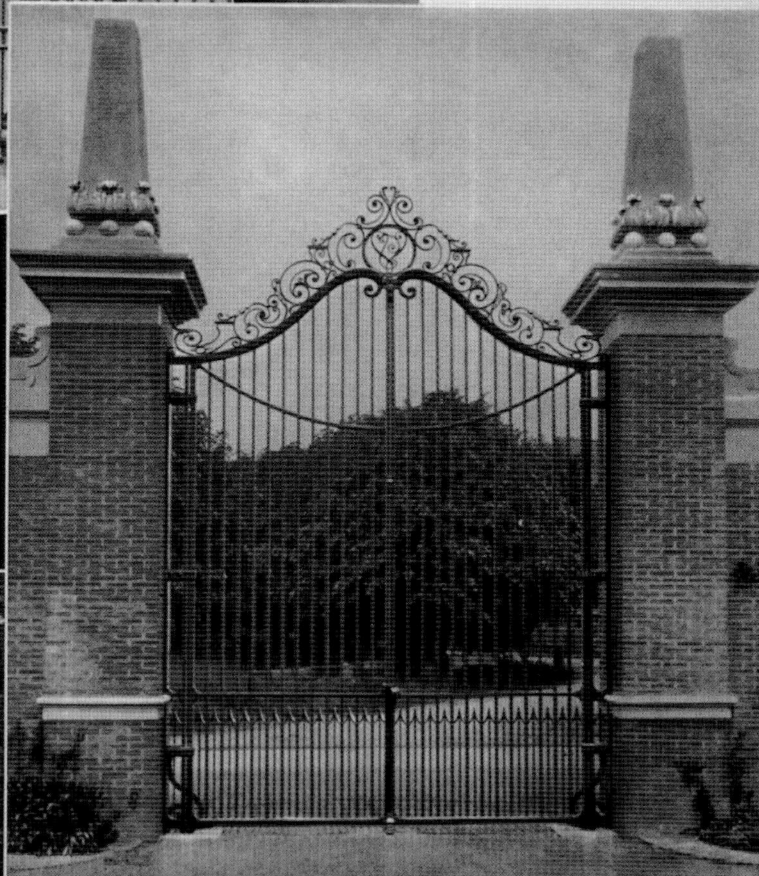

M. FORESTIER, PAYSAGISTE ARCH.

M. GREBER, ARCH.

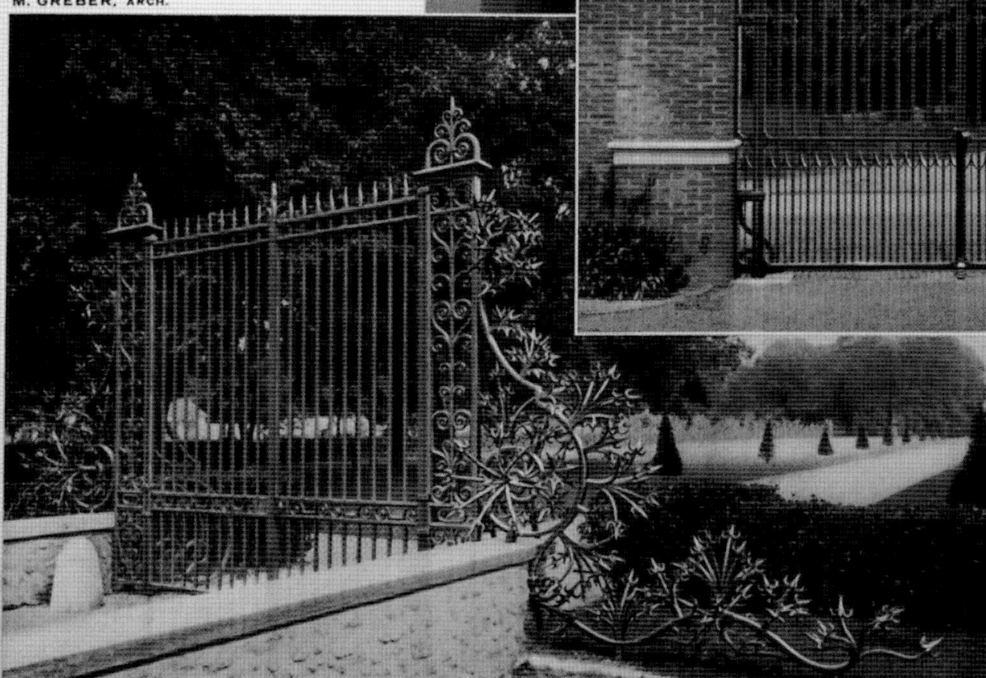

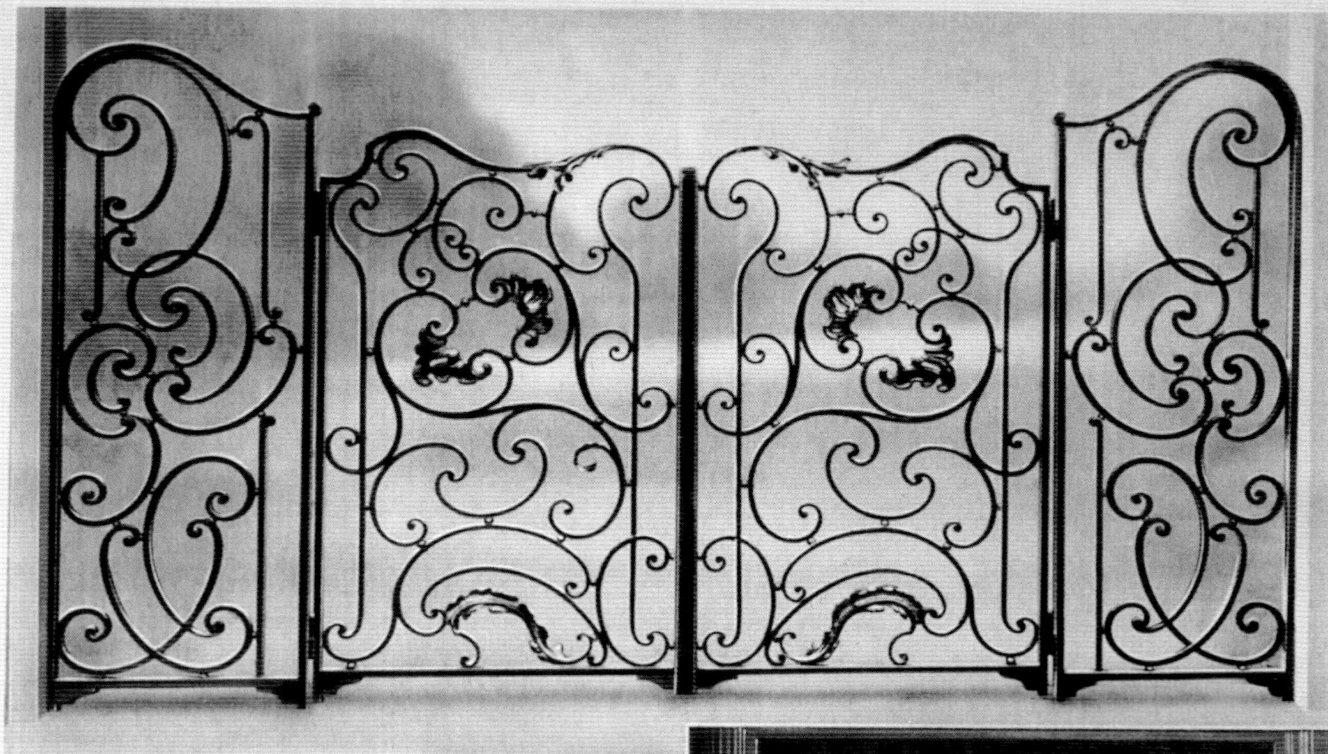

M. LANGLAIS, ARCH.

MM. DESNUES, BROCHON & BLUM, ARCH.

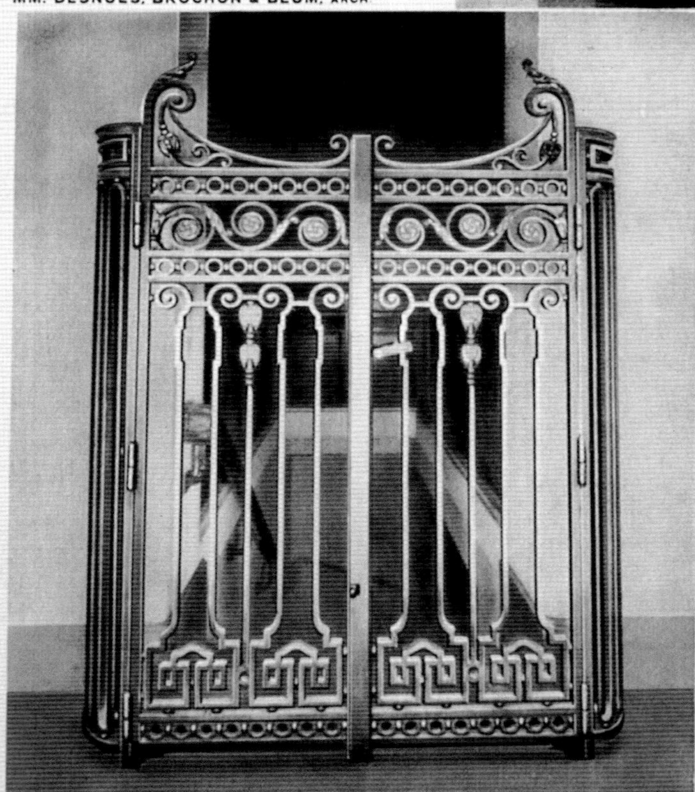

M. LELIÈVRE, ARCH.

403

E. BORDEREL & ROBERT. IV

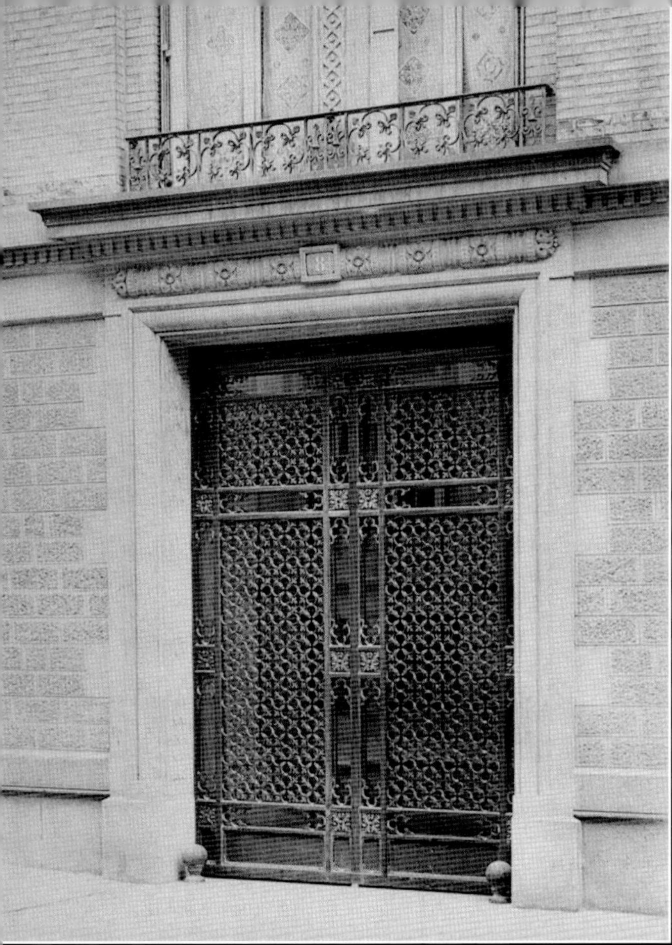
8

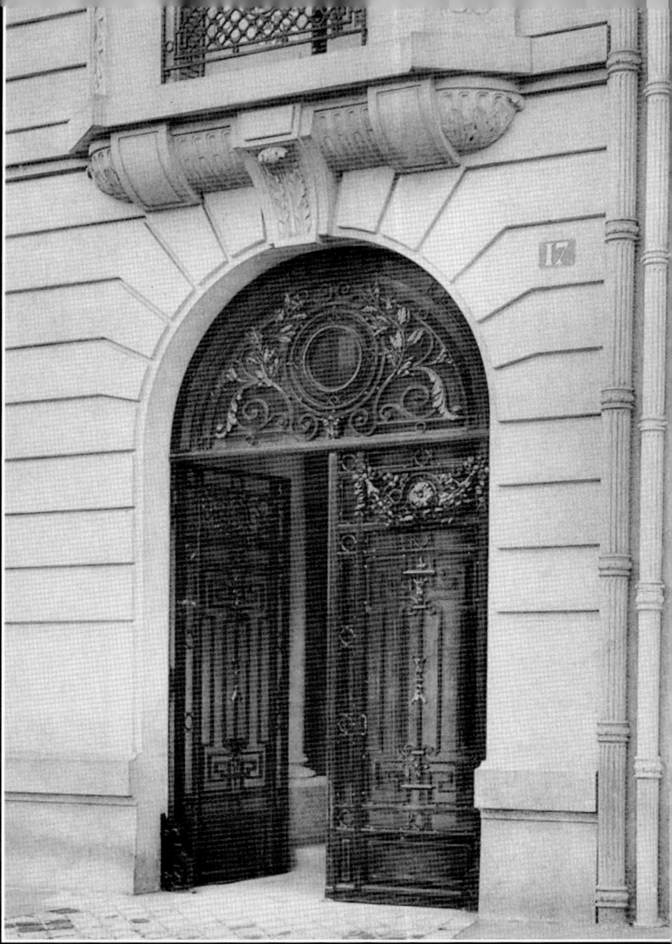
17

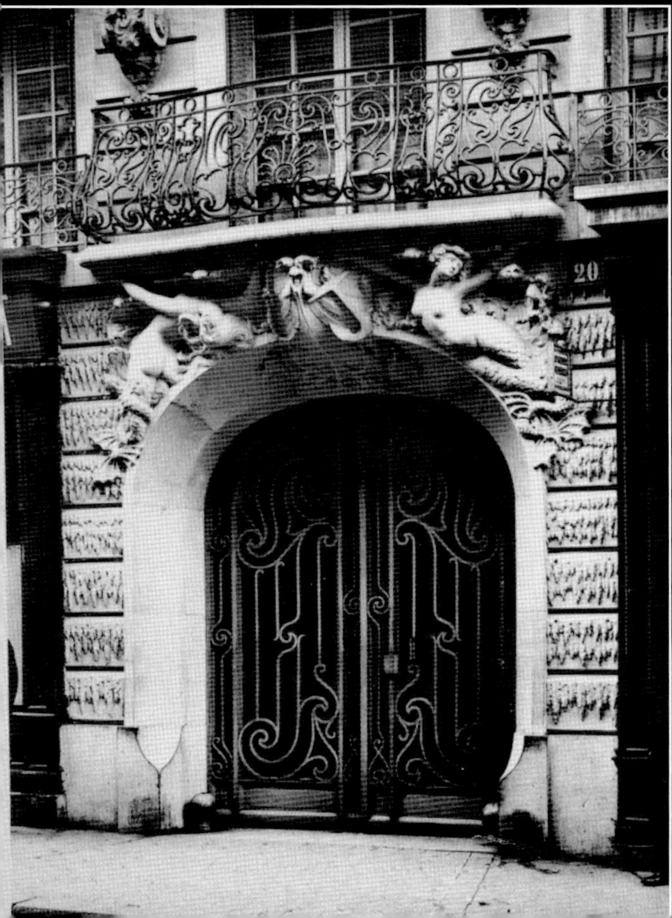
20

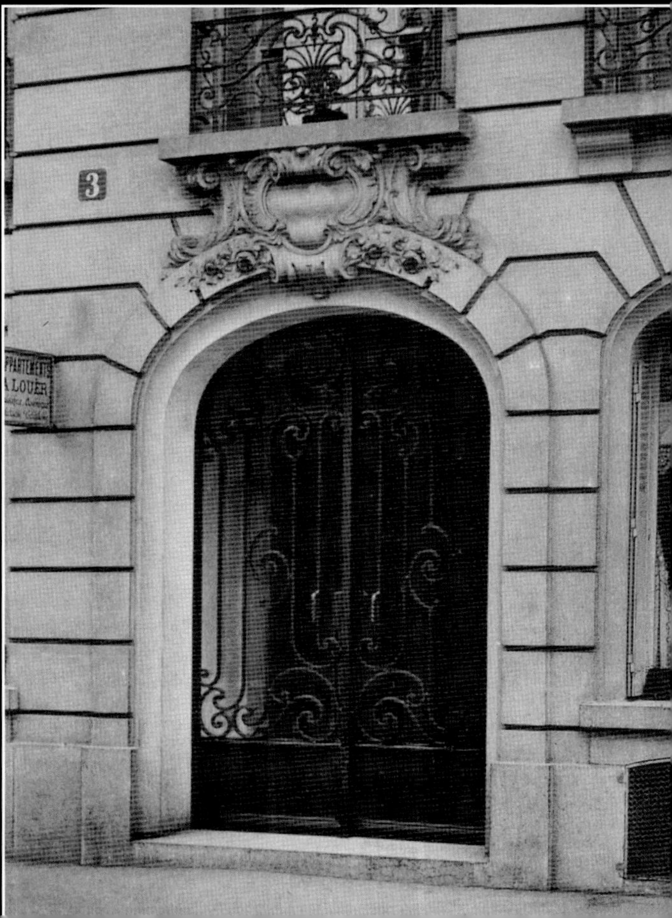
3
A LOUER

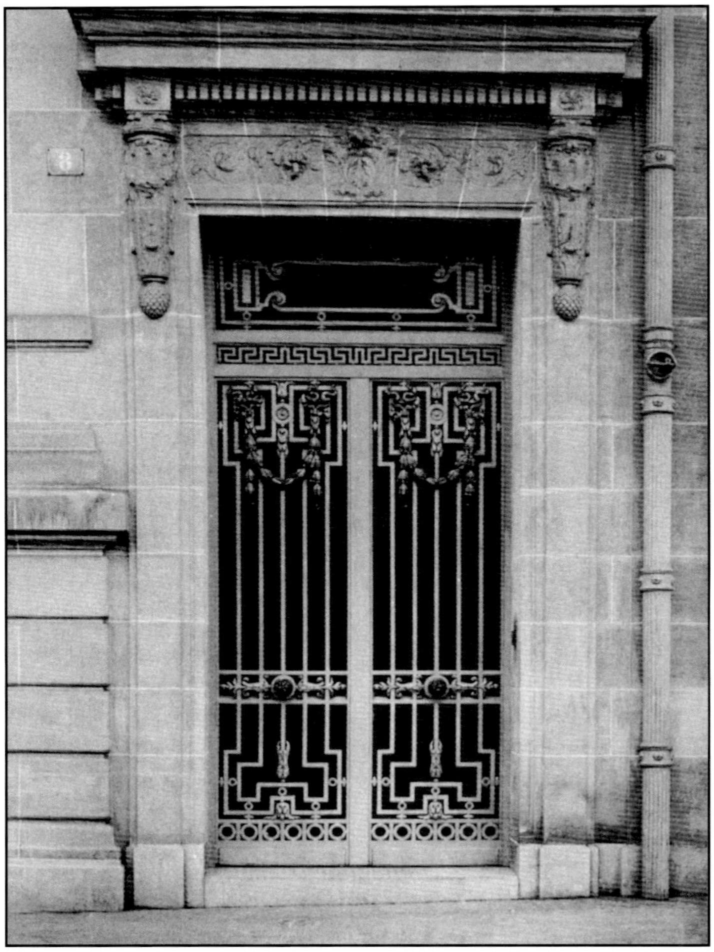
8

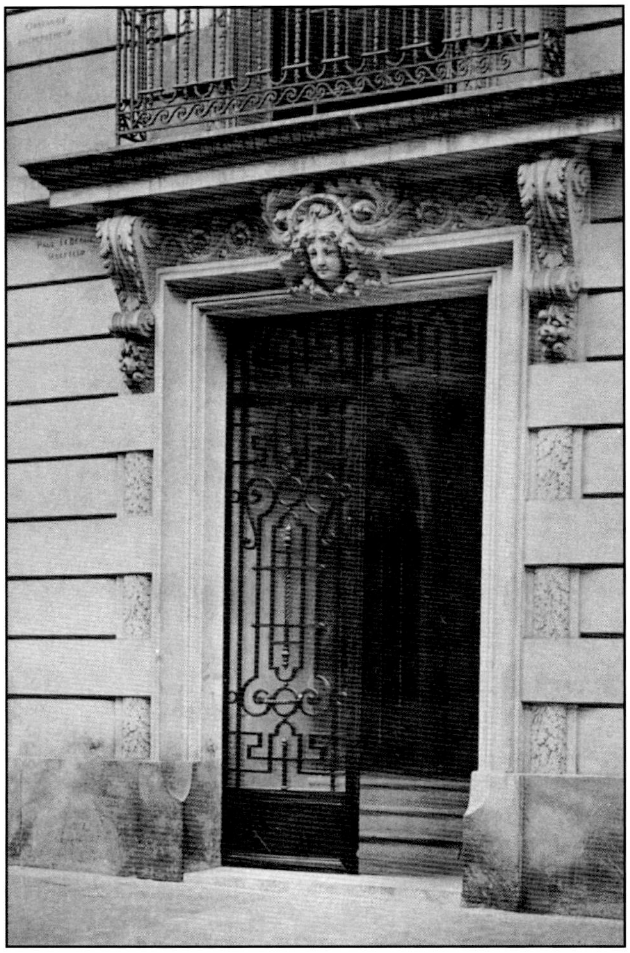

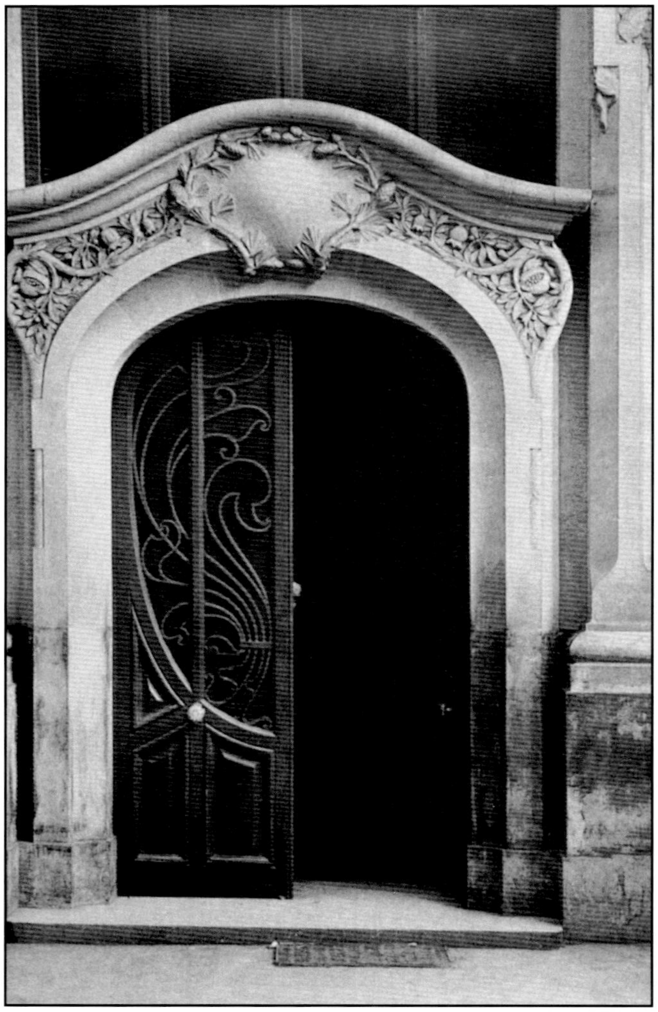

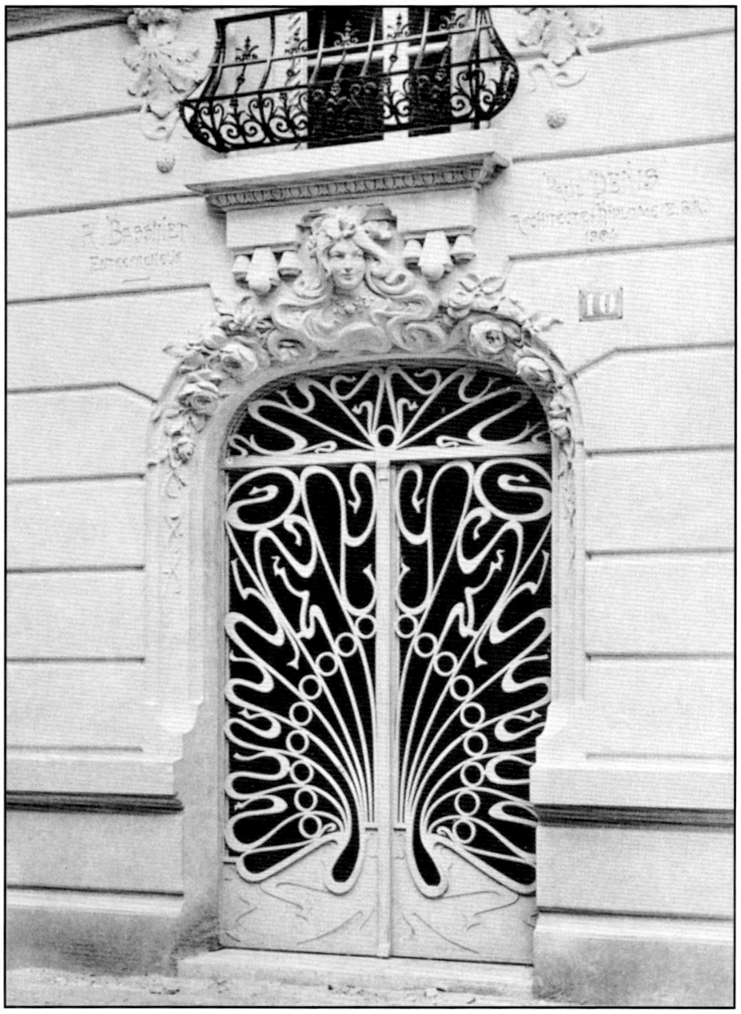
10

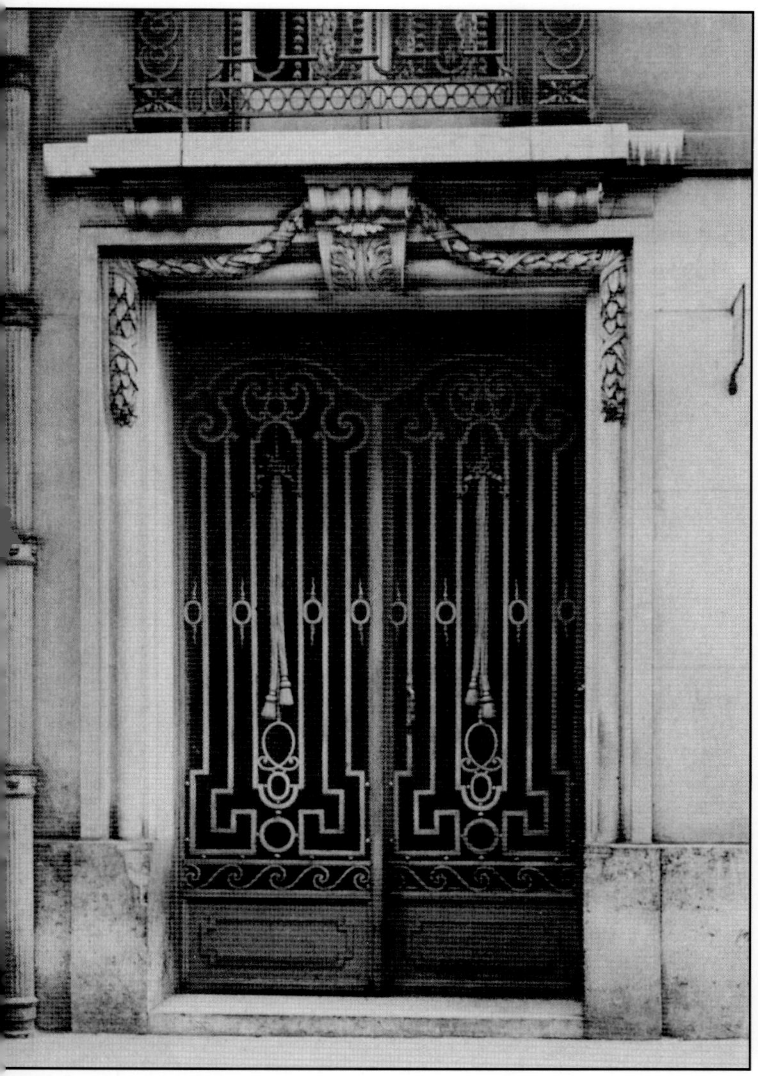

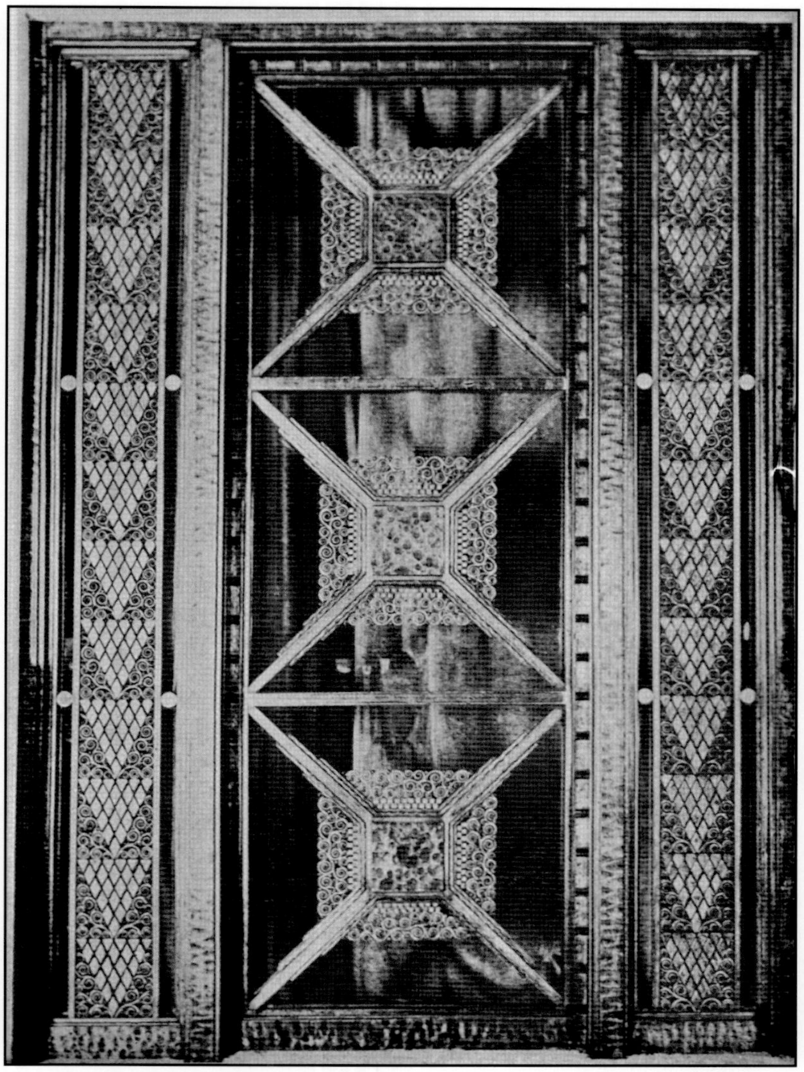

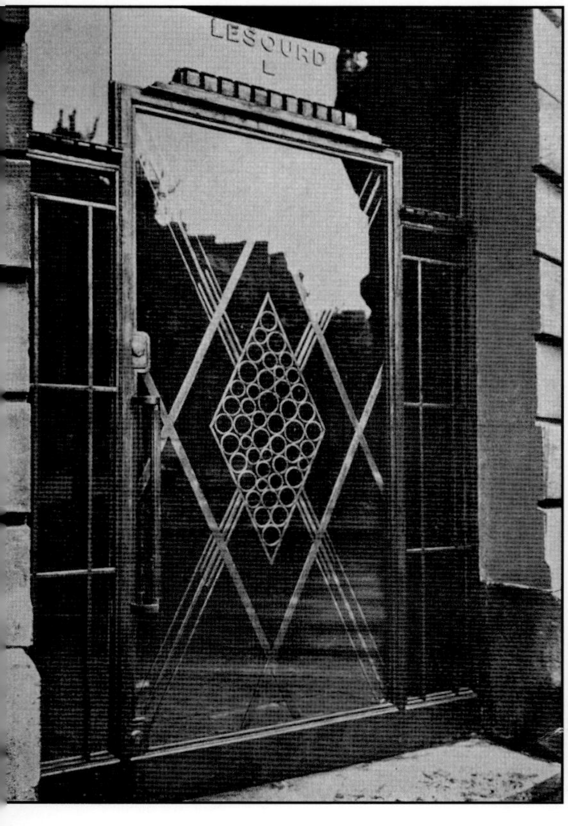

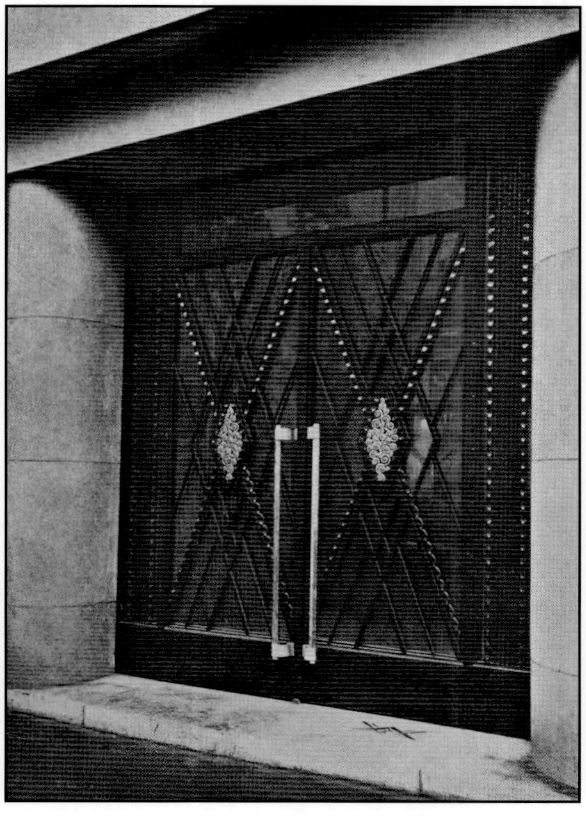

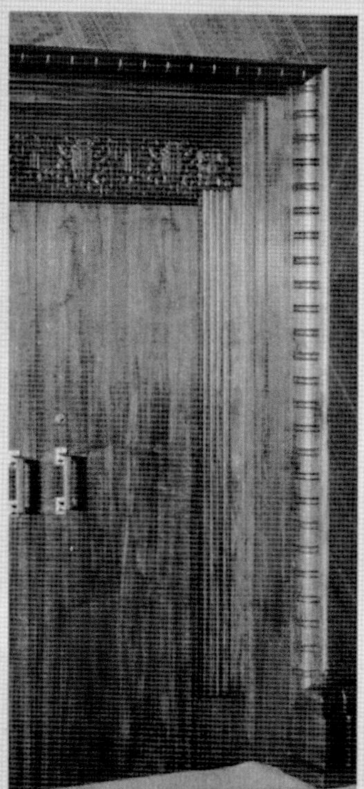

Samuel Lunden ; John and Donald

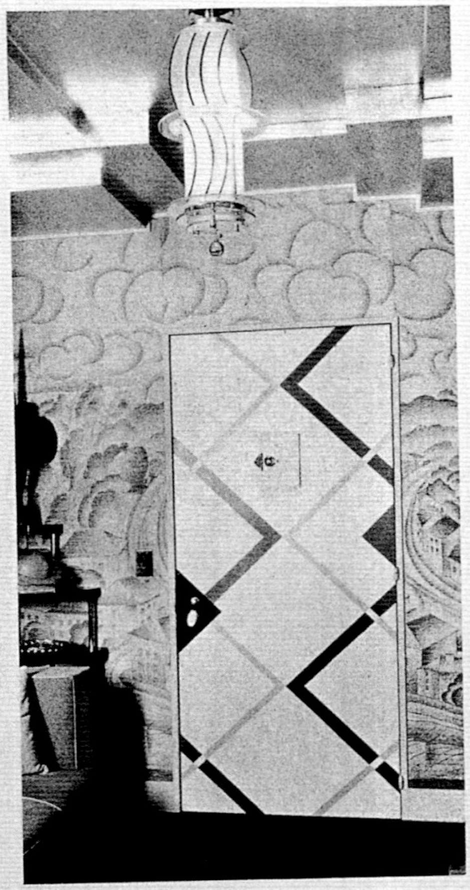

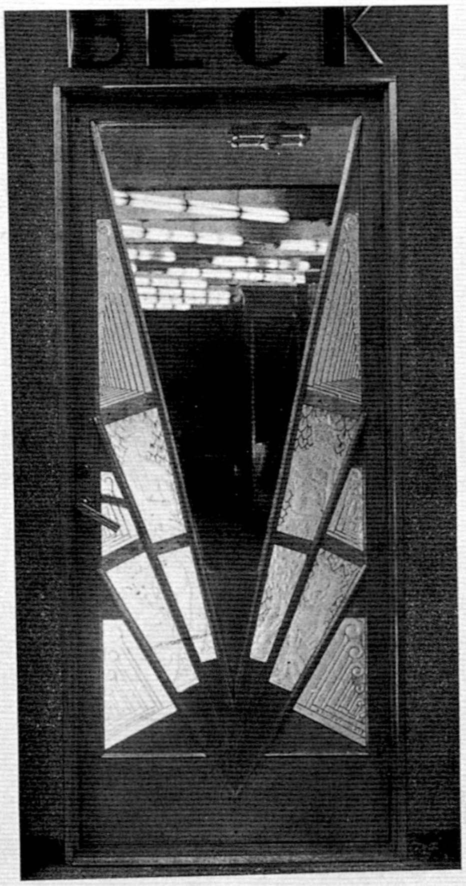

© Amemya

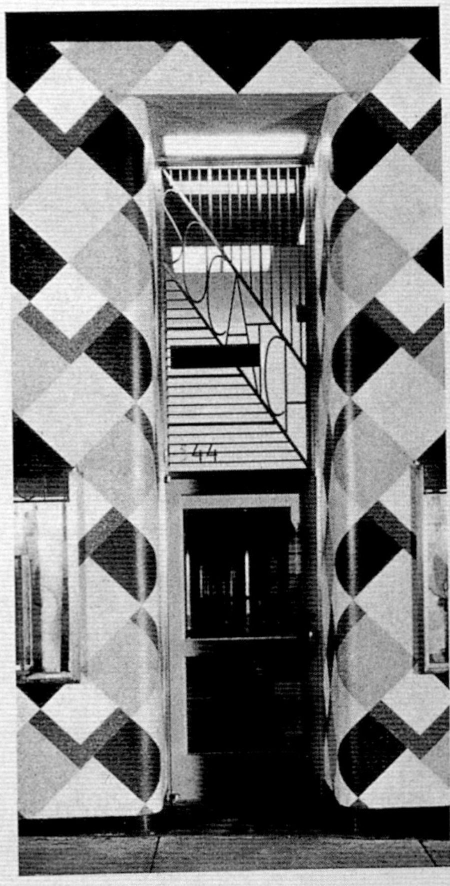

Holabird && Root

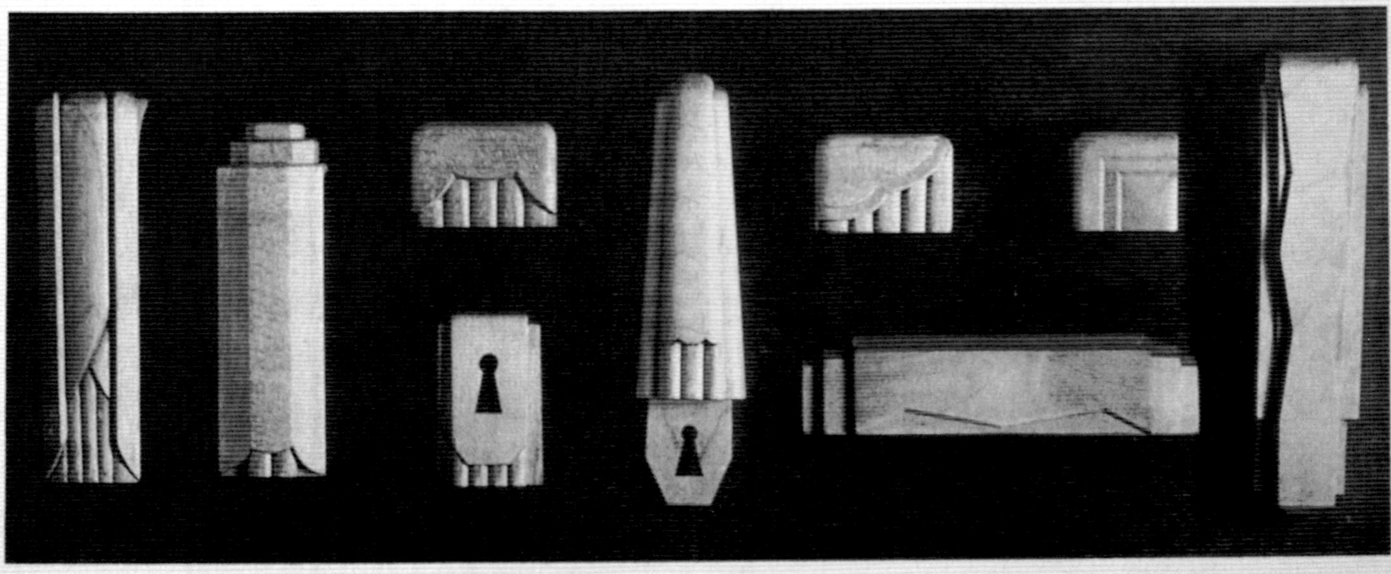

5

Wall Decoration & Room Dividers

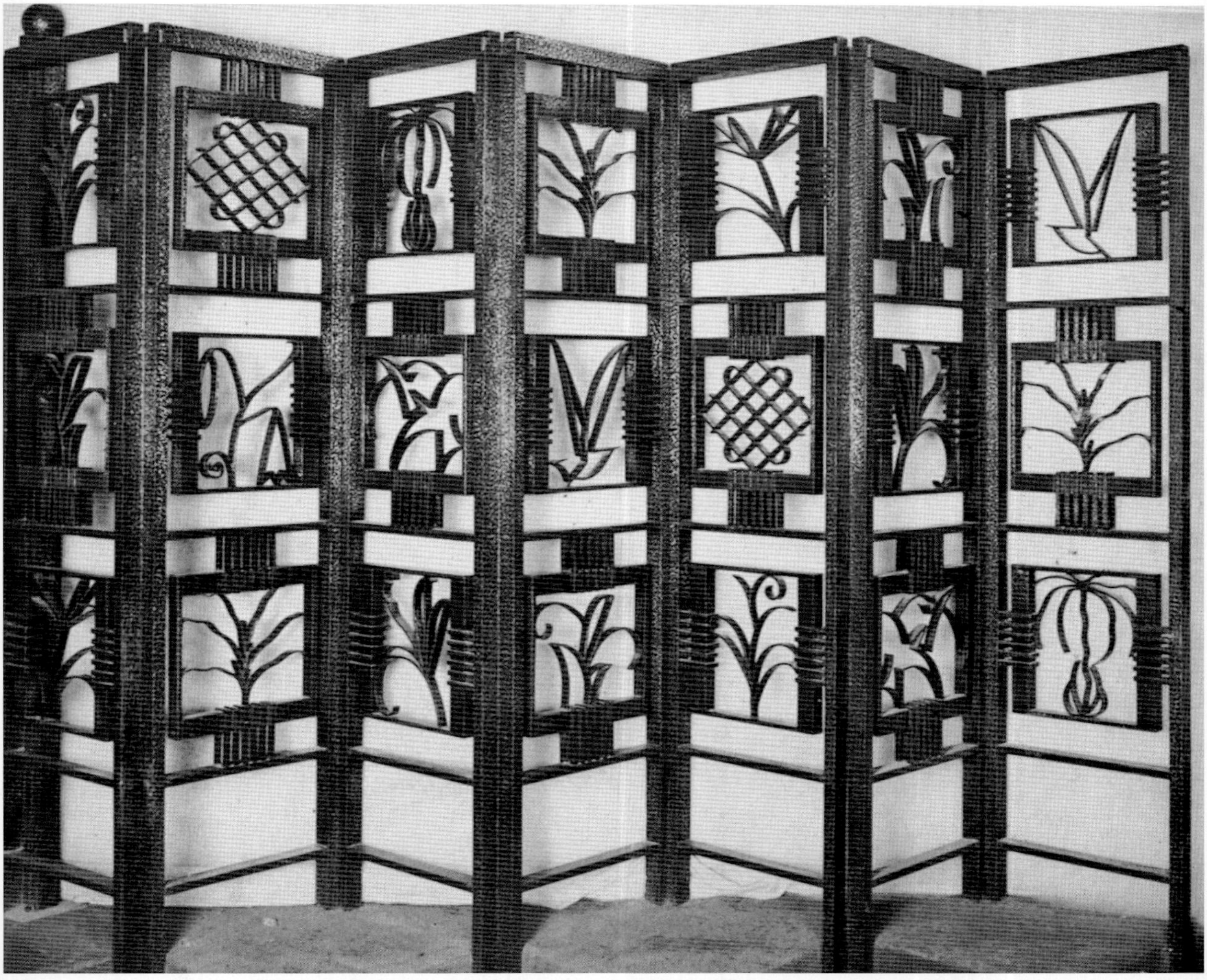

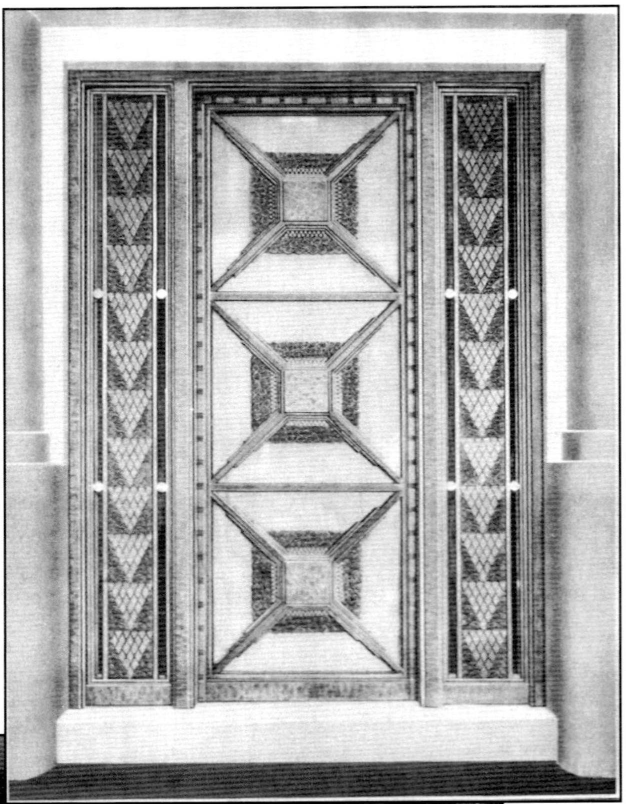

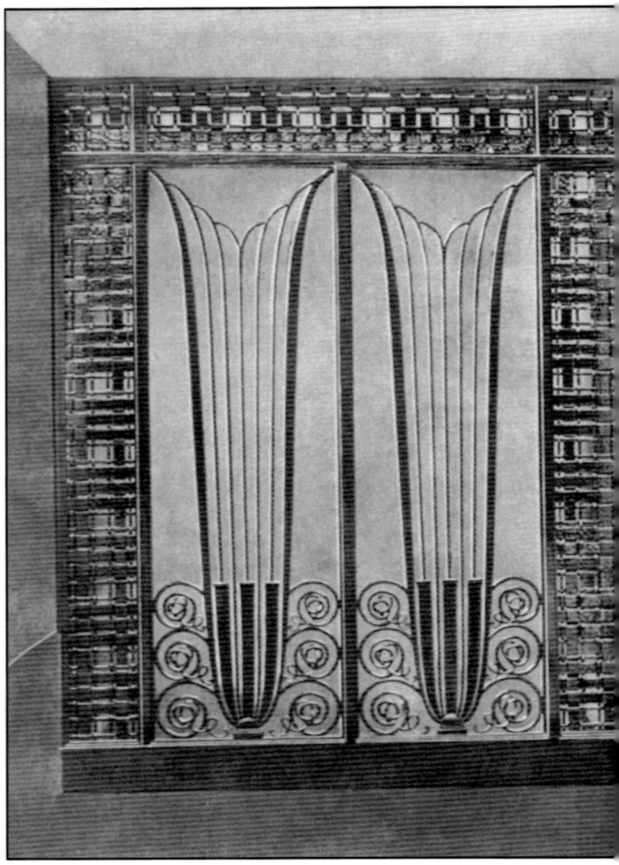

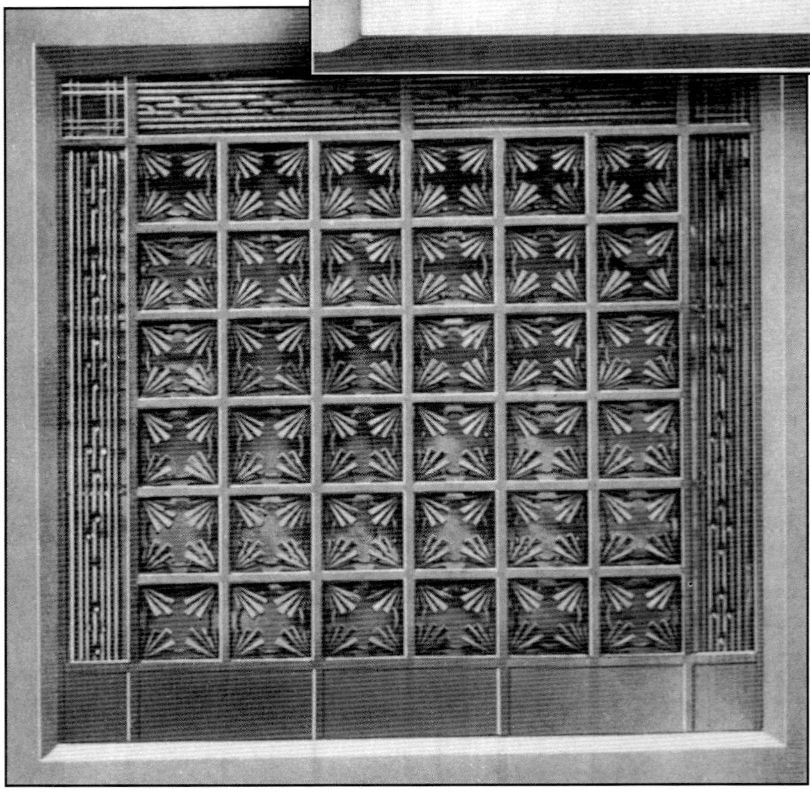

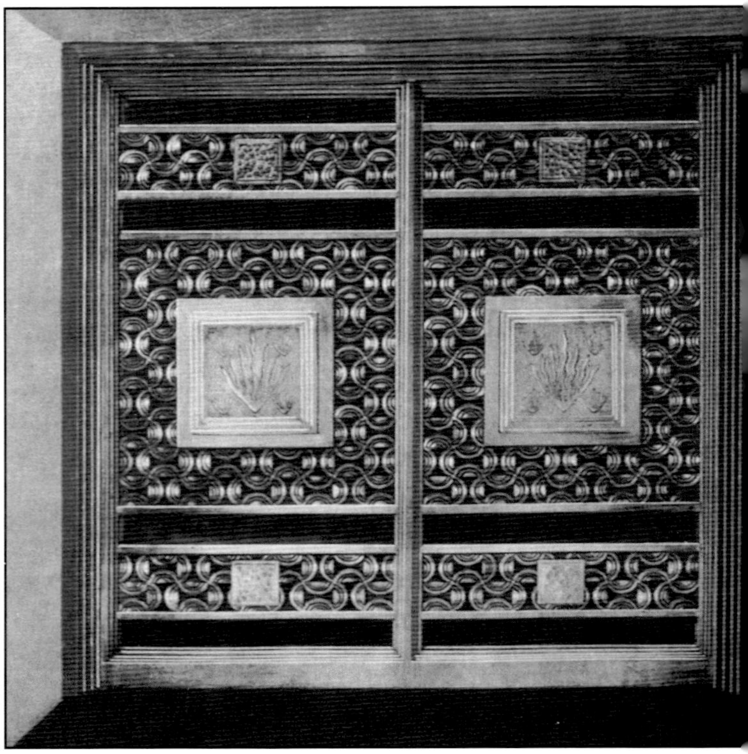

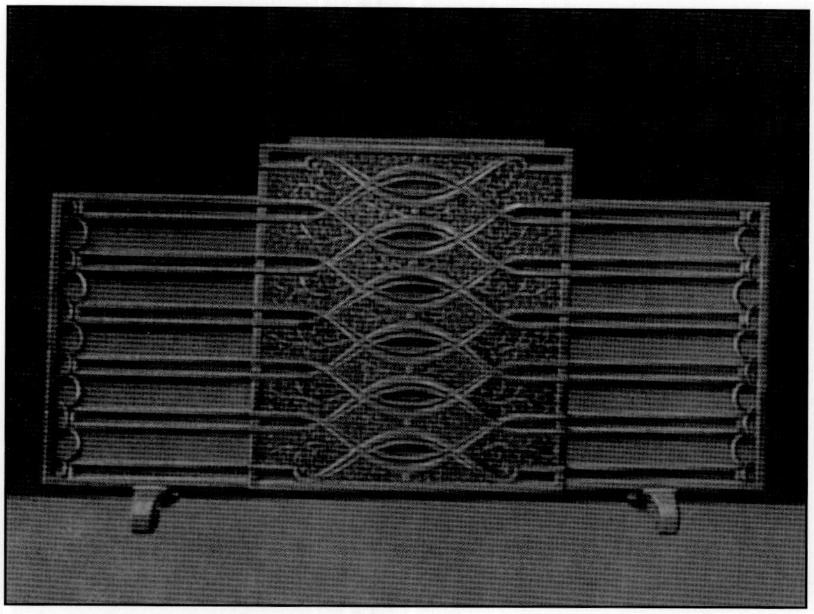

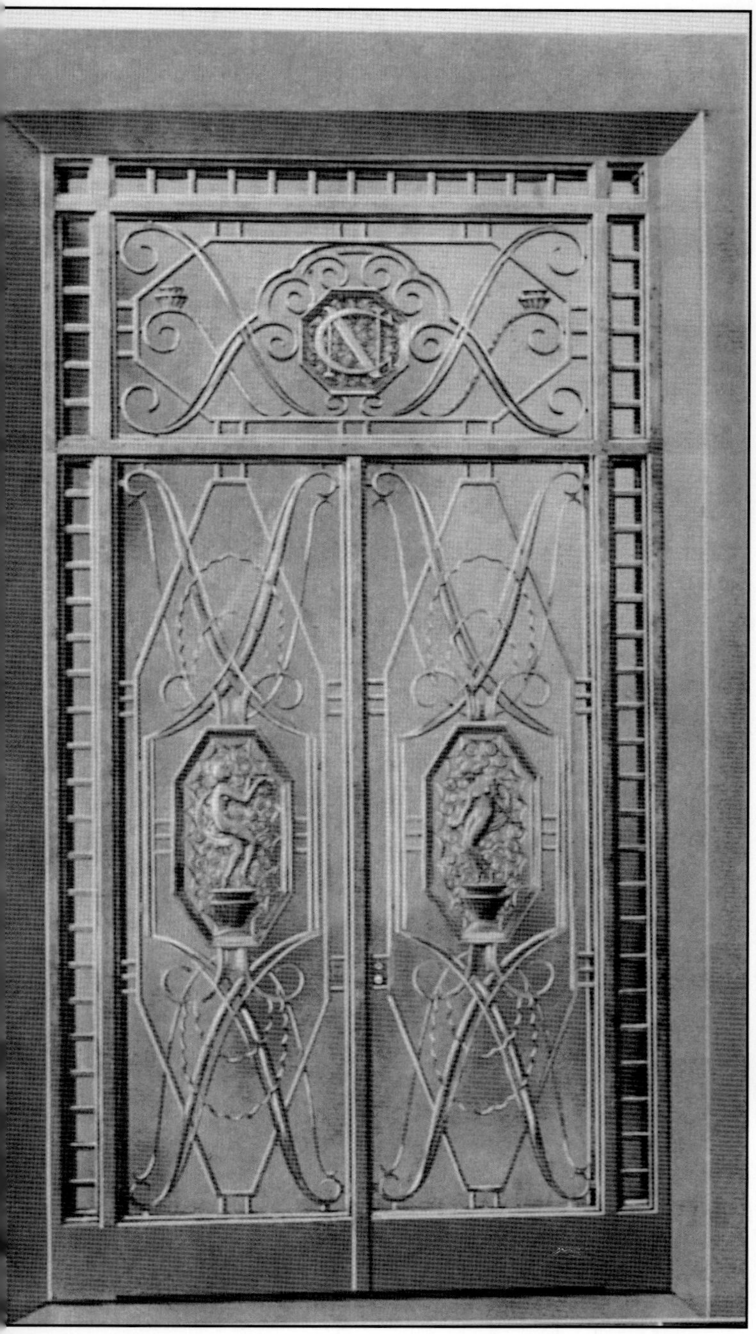

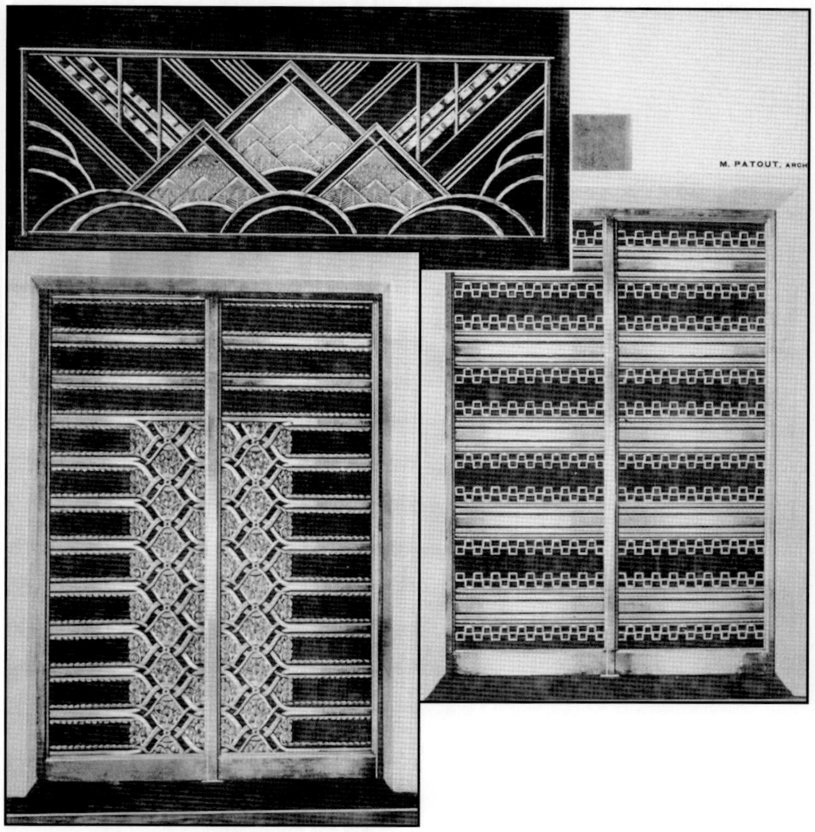
M. PATOUT, ARCH

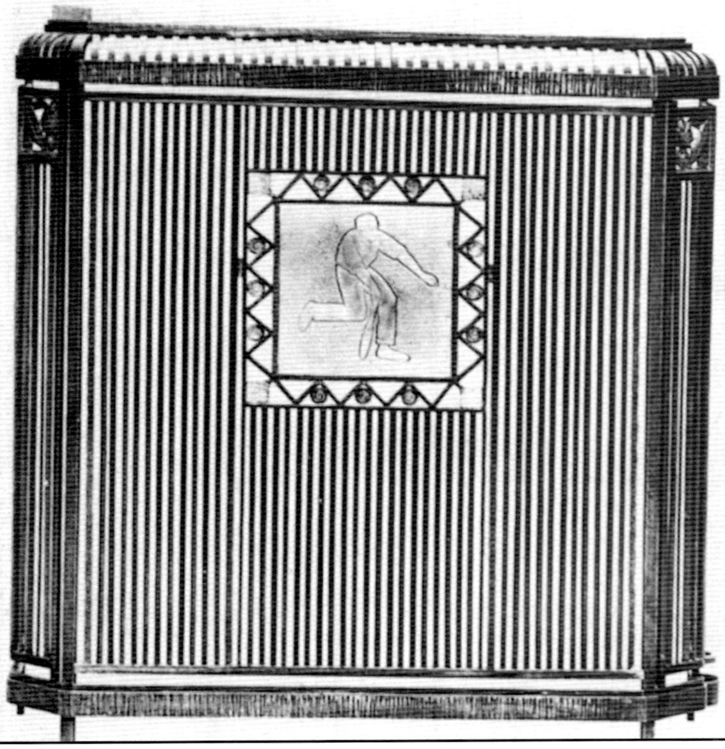

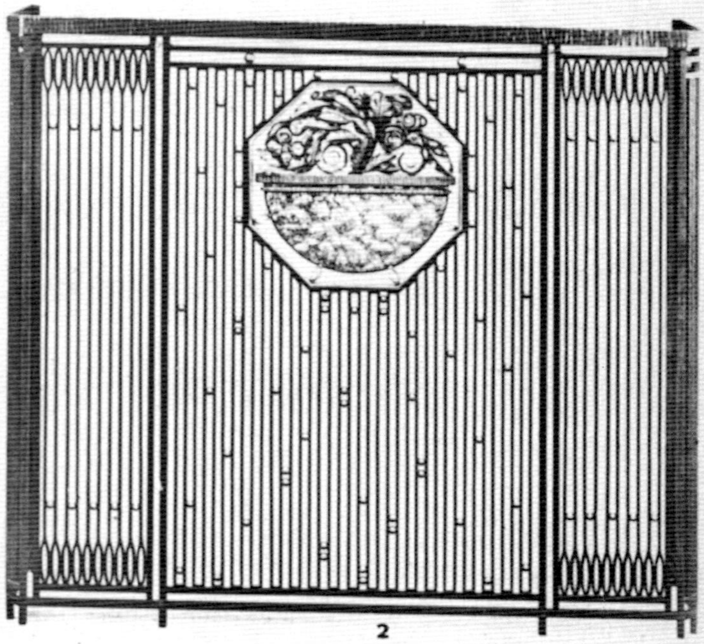

2

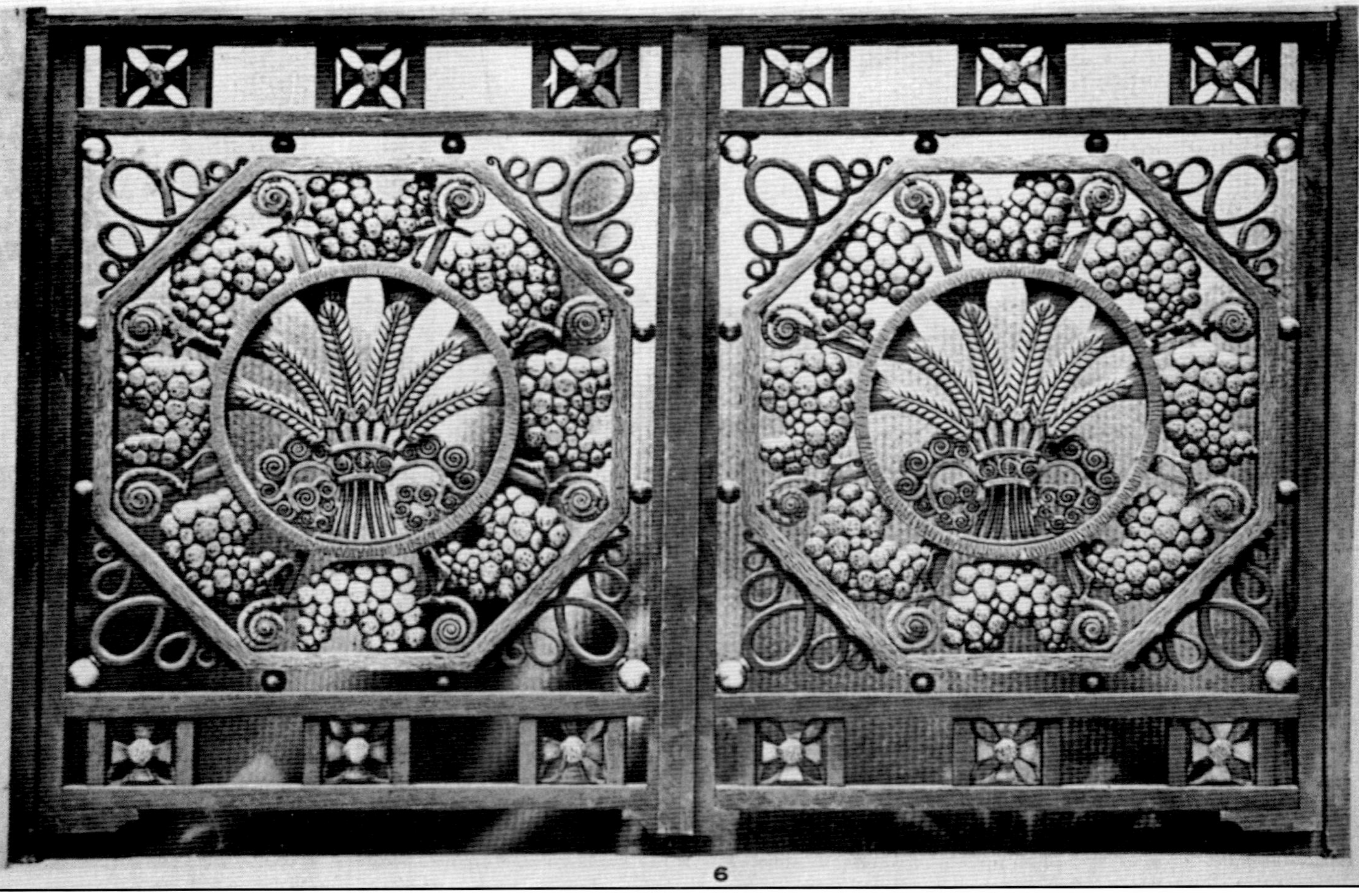

6

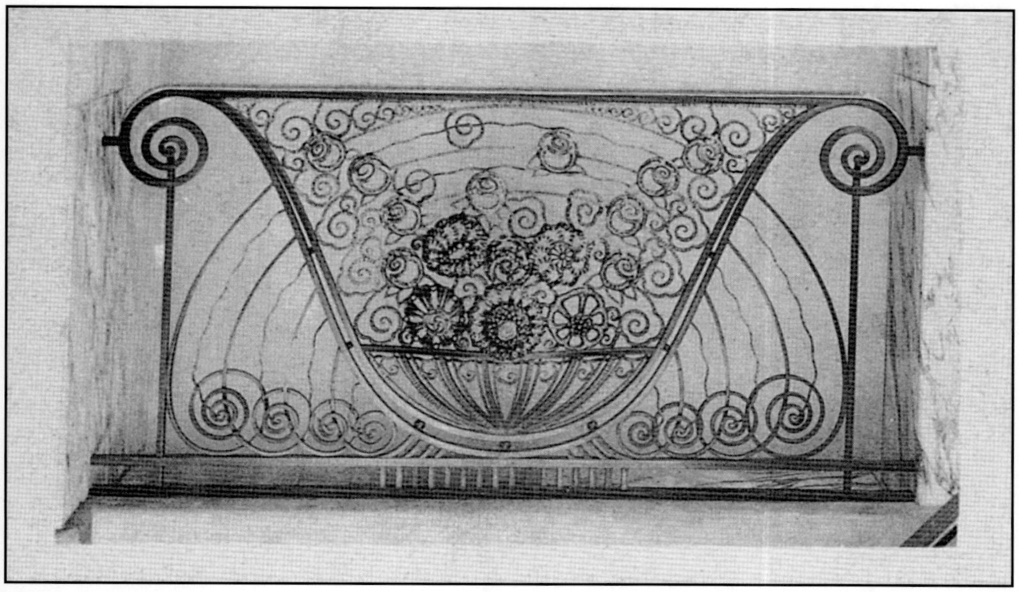

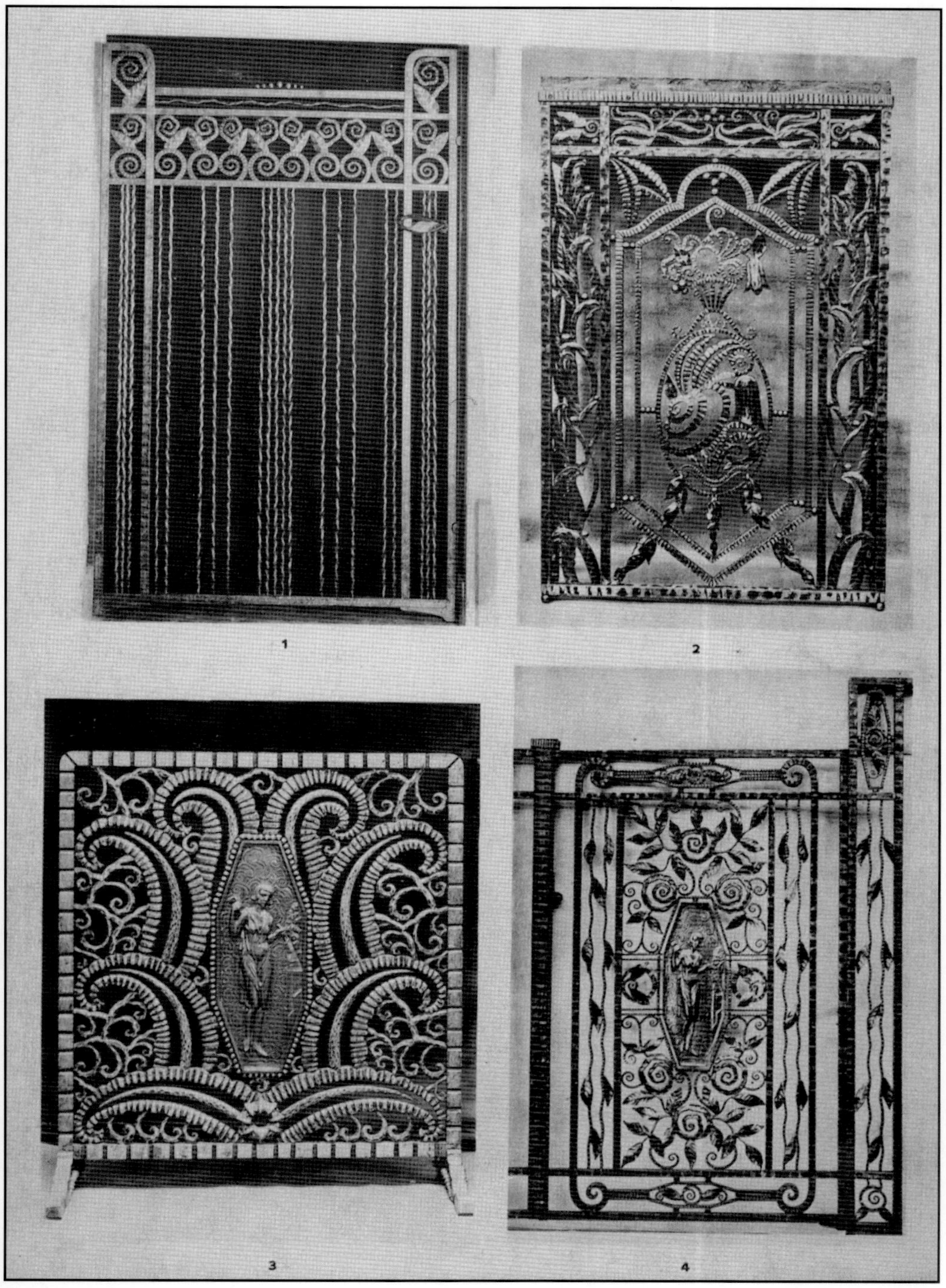
1
2
3
4

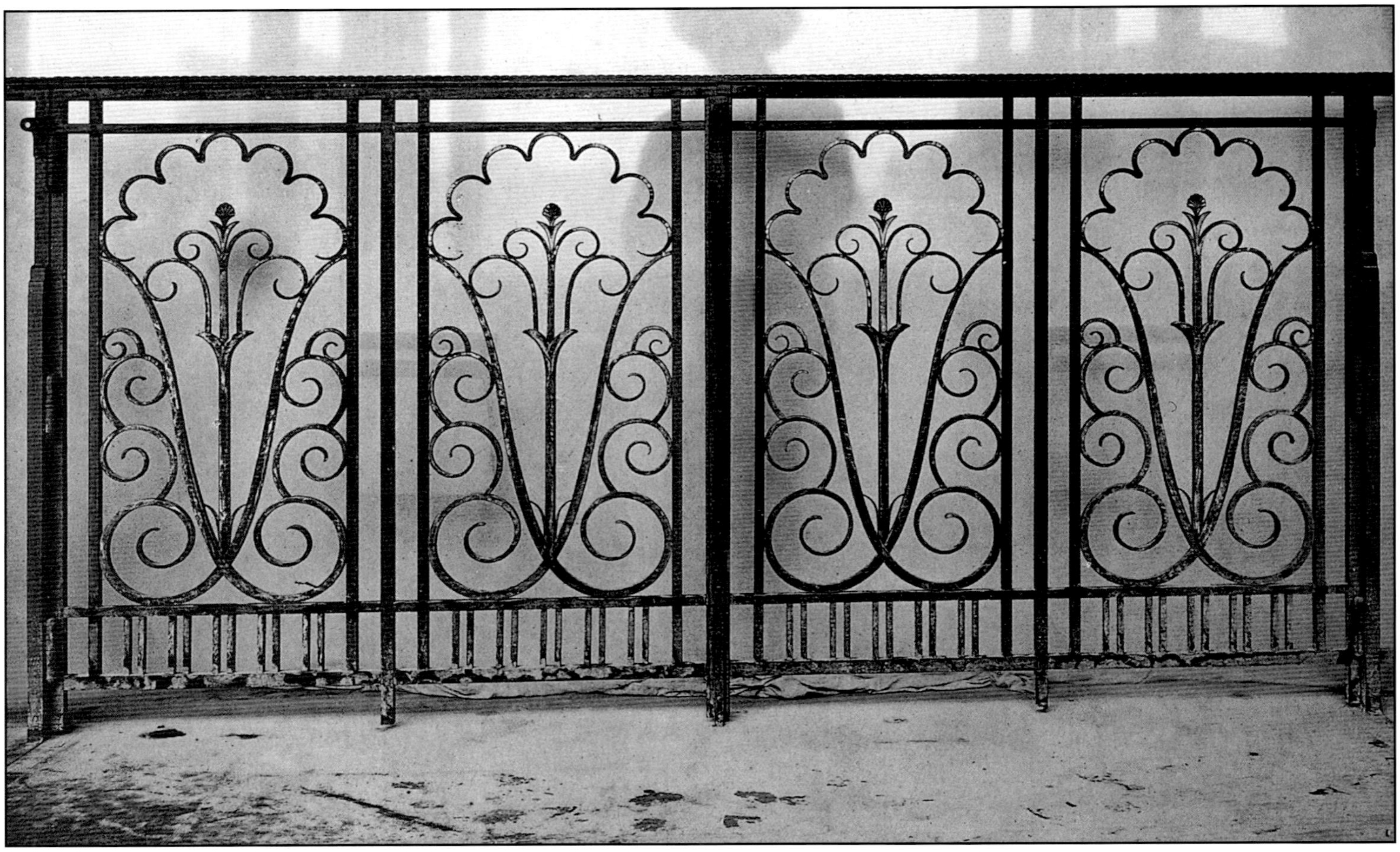

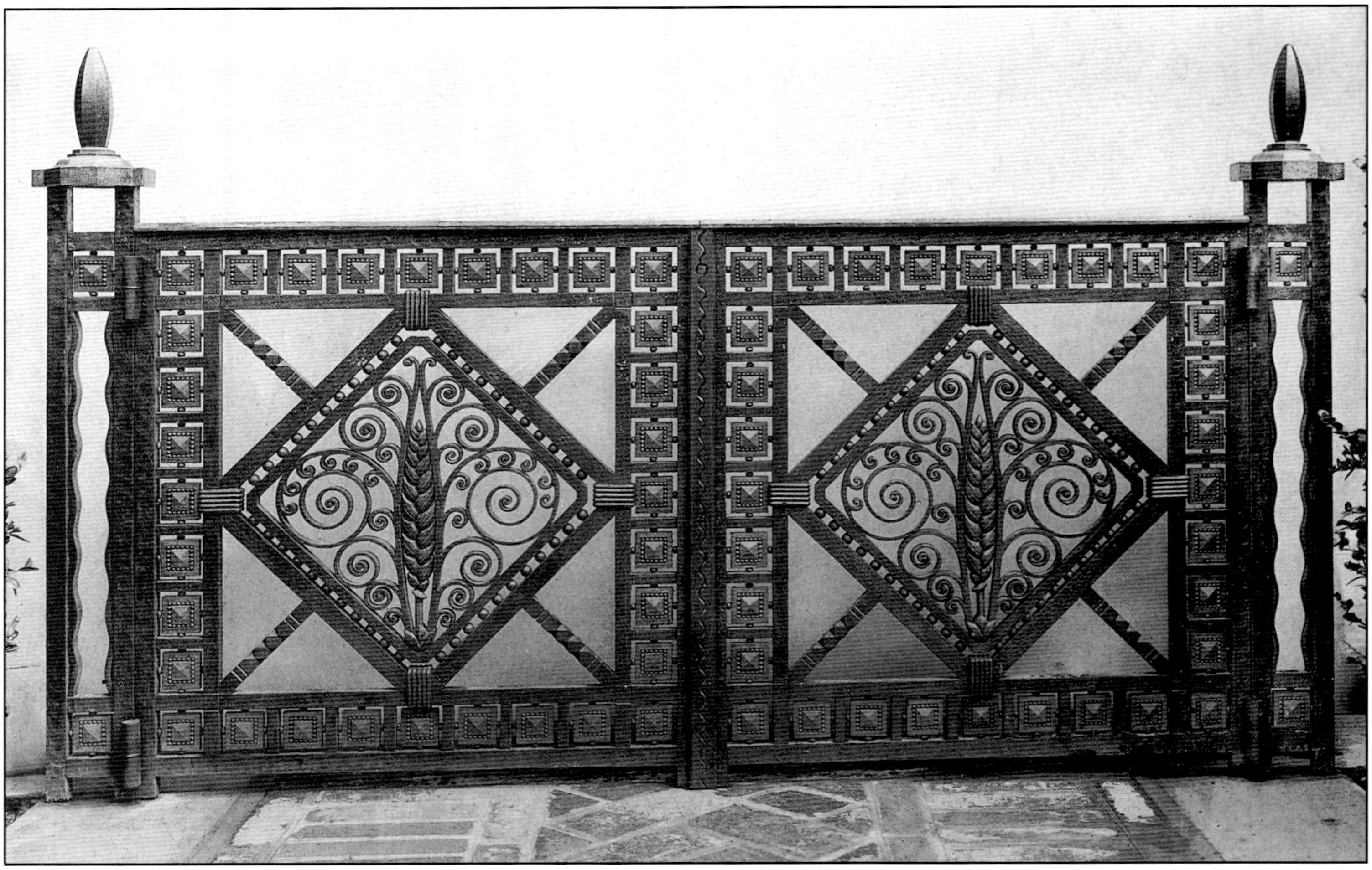

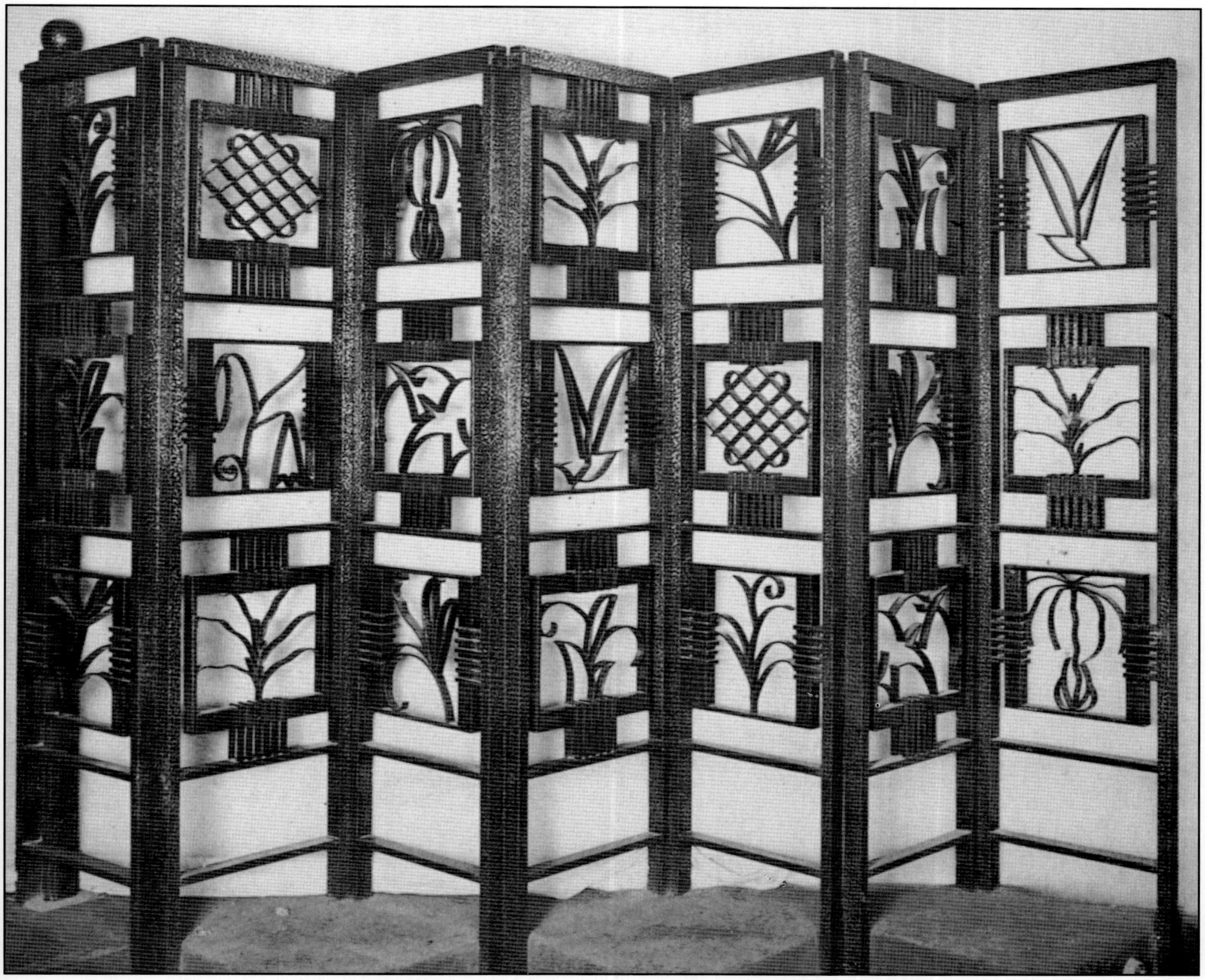

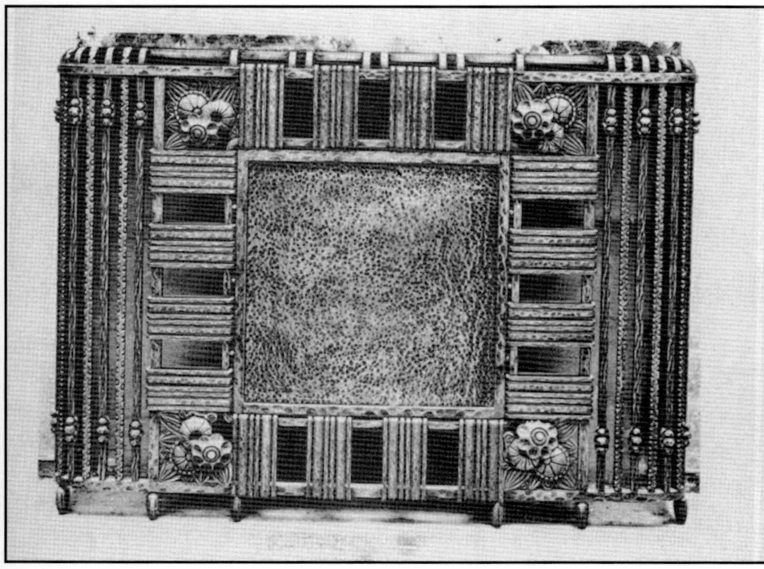

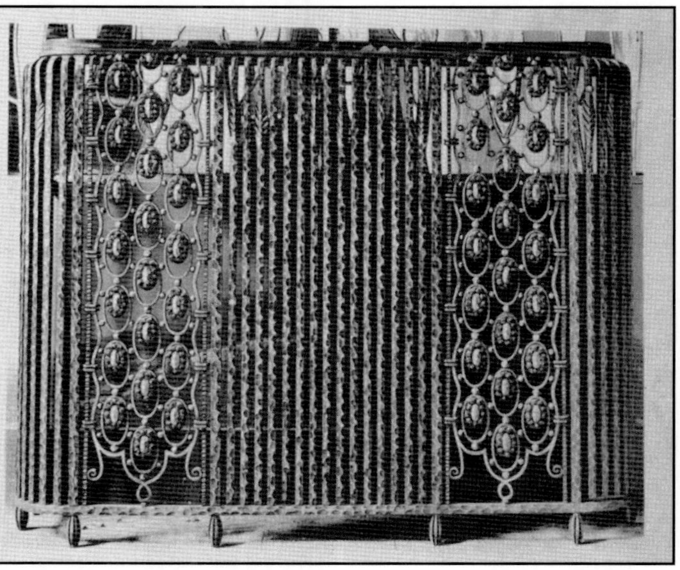

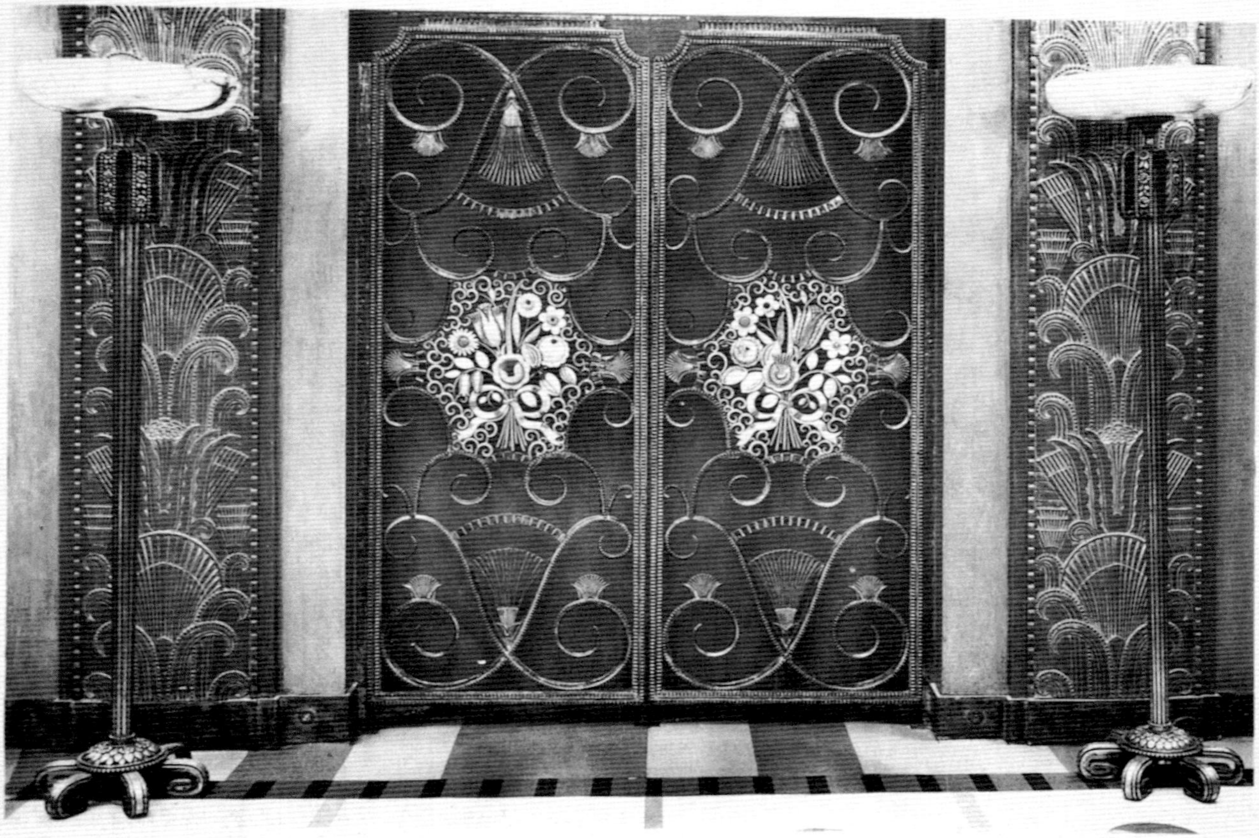

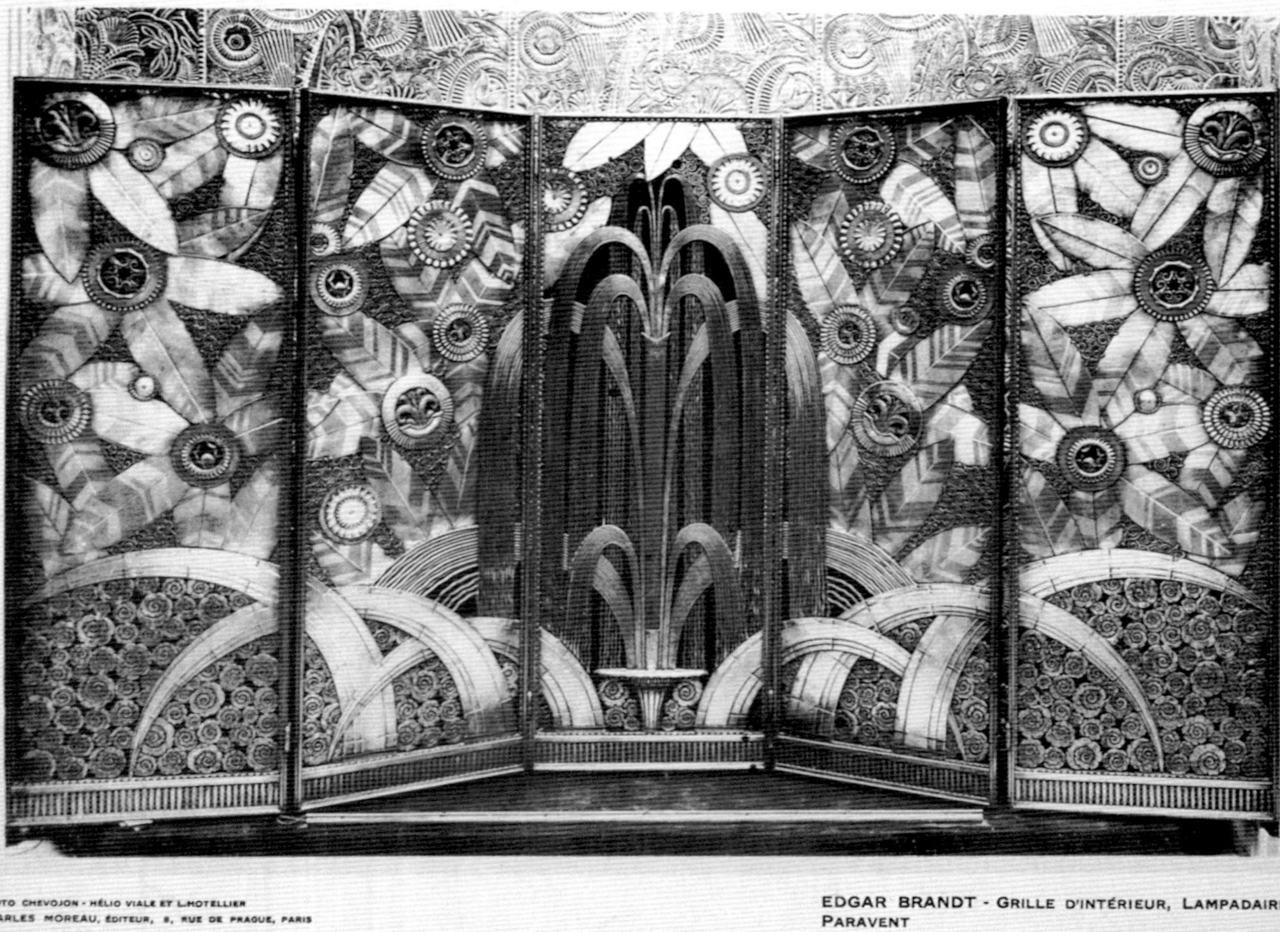

PHOTO CHEVOJON - HÉLIO VIALE ET L.HOTELLIER
CHARLES MOREAU, ÉDITEUR, 8, RUE DE PRAGUE, PARIS

EDGAR BRANDT - GRILLE D'INTÉRIEUR, LAMPADAIRES, PARAVENT

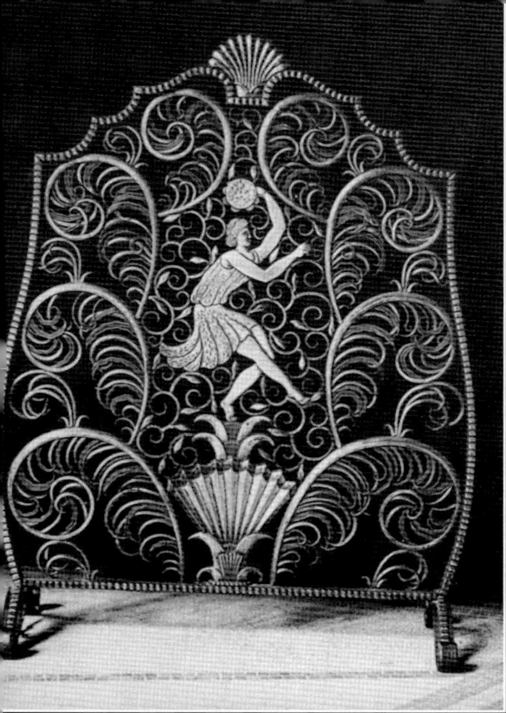
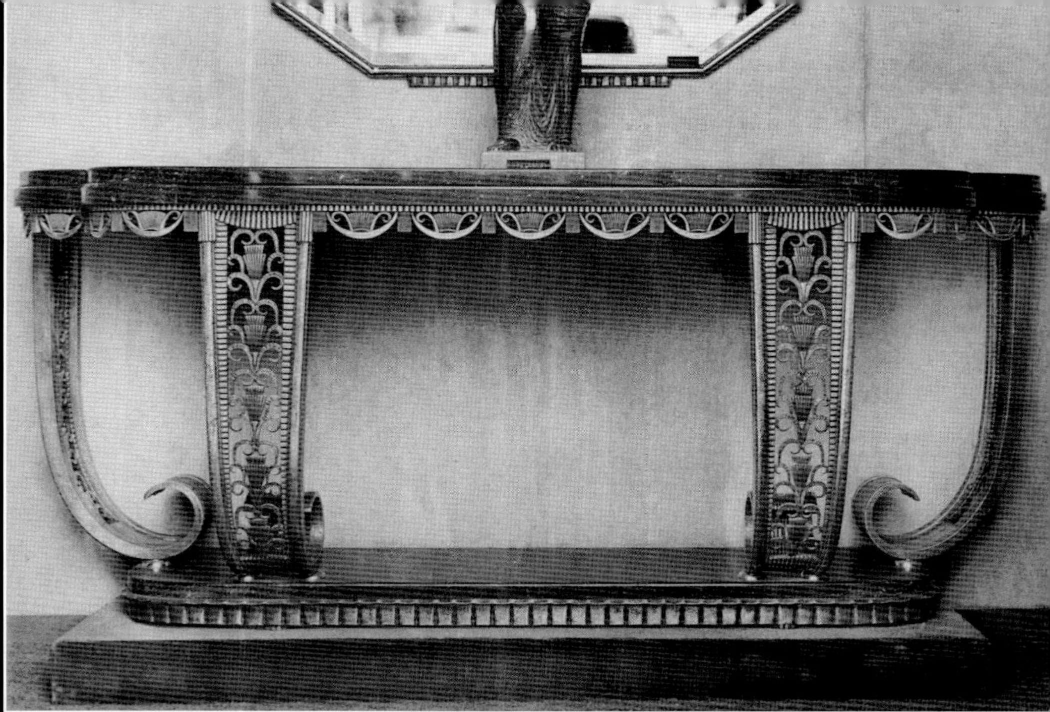
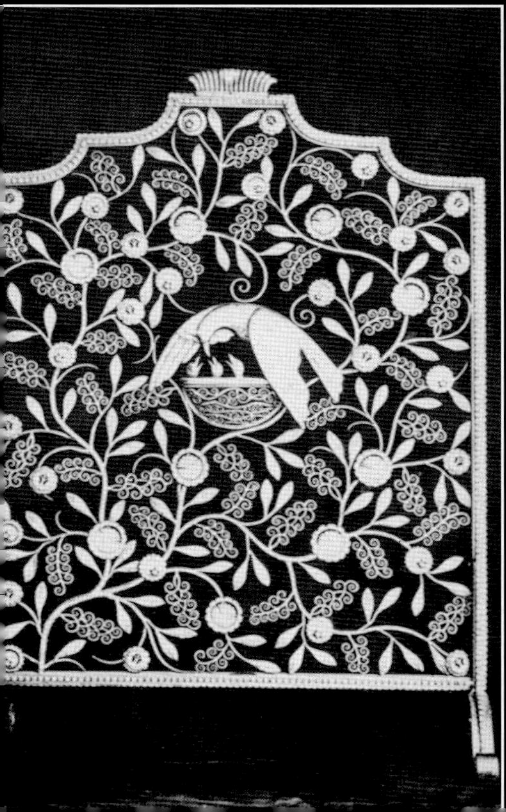
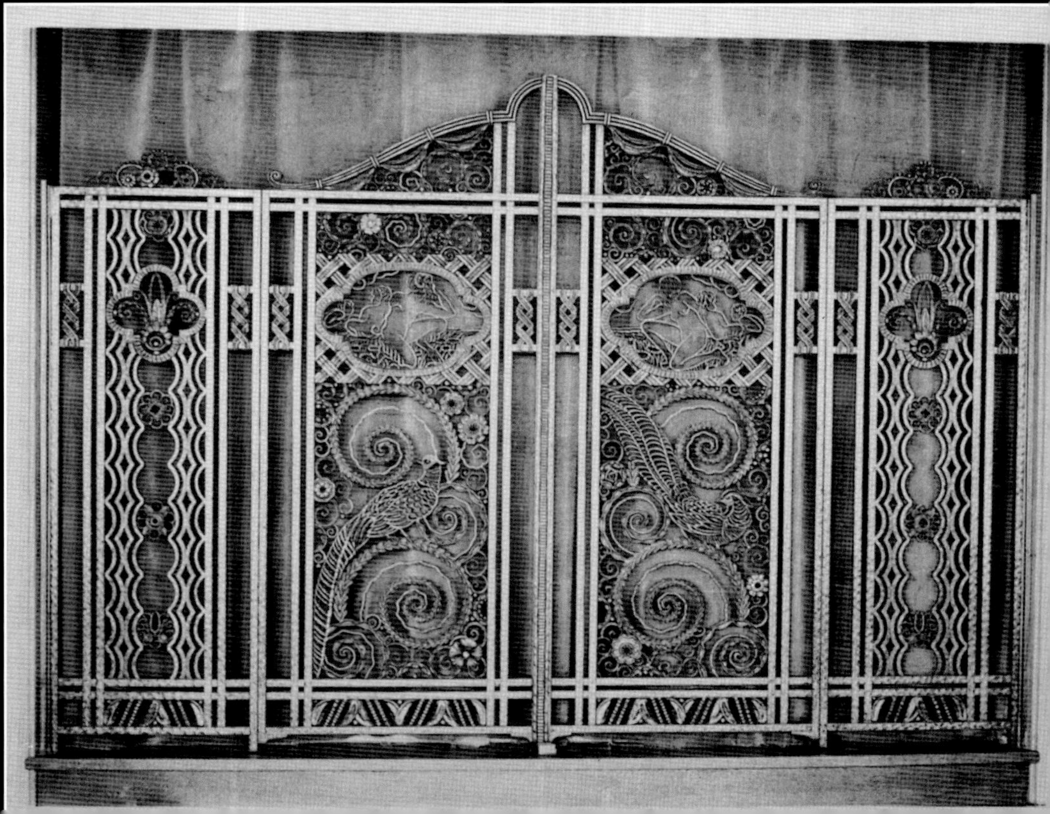

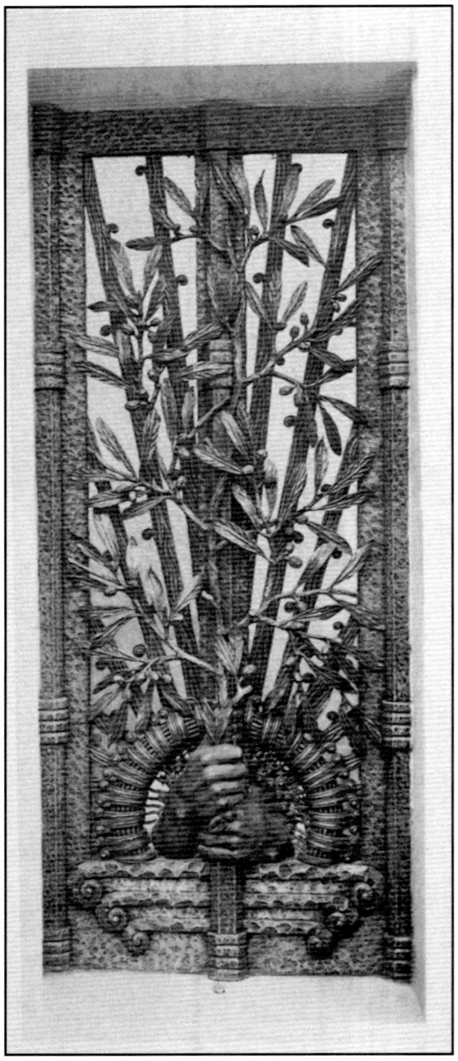

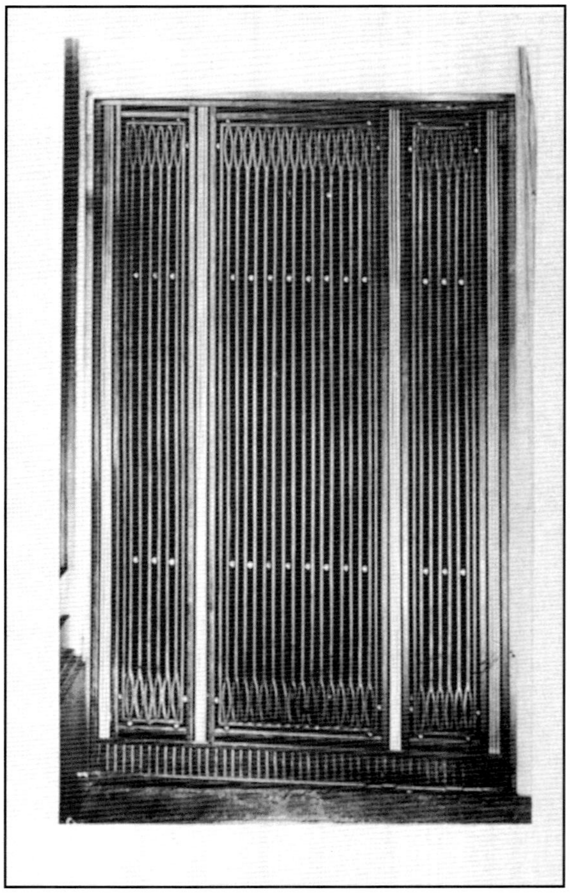

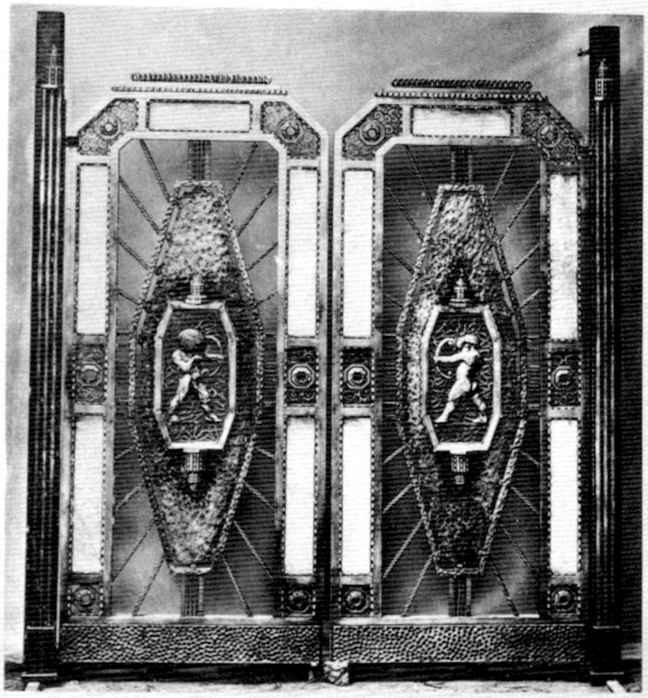

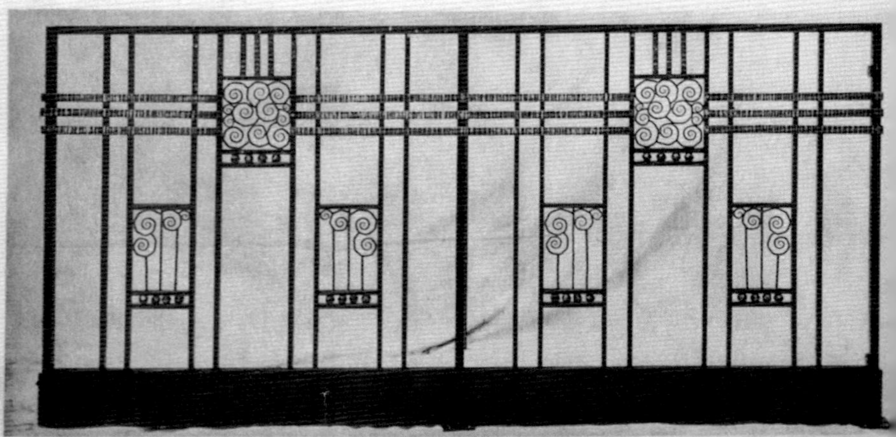

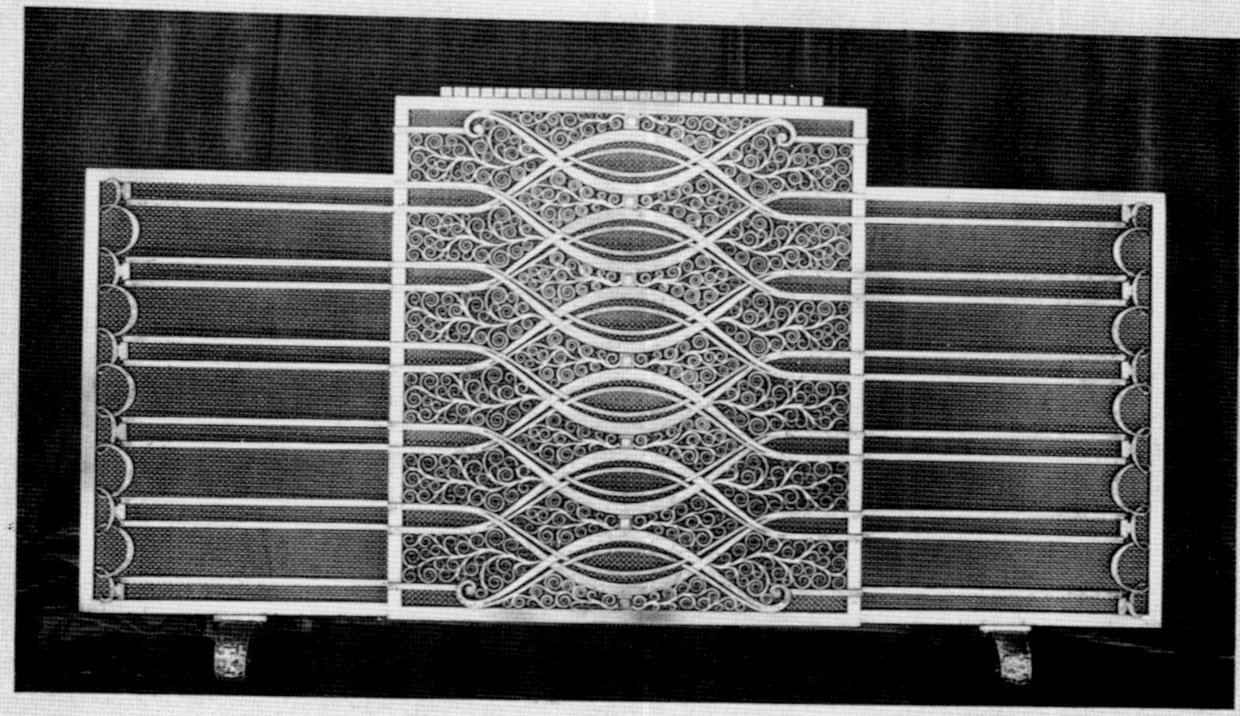

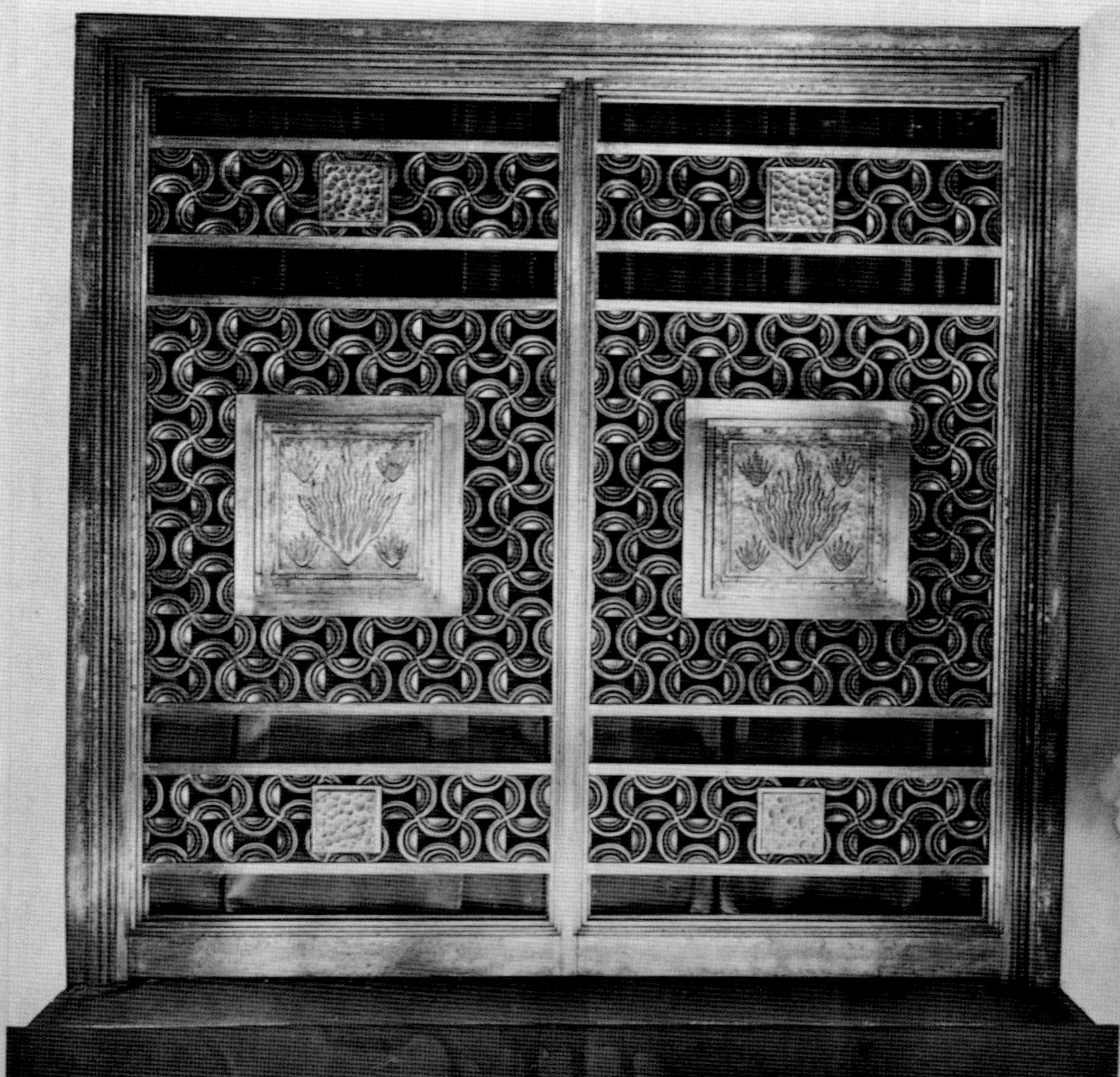

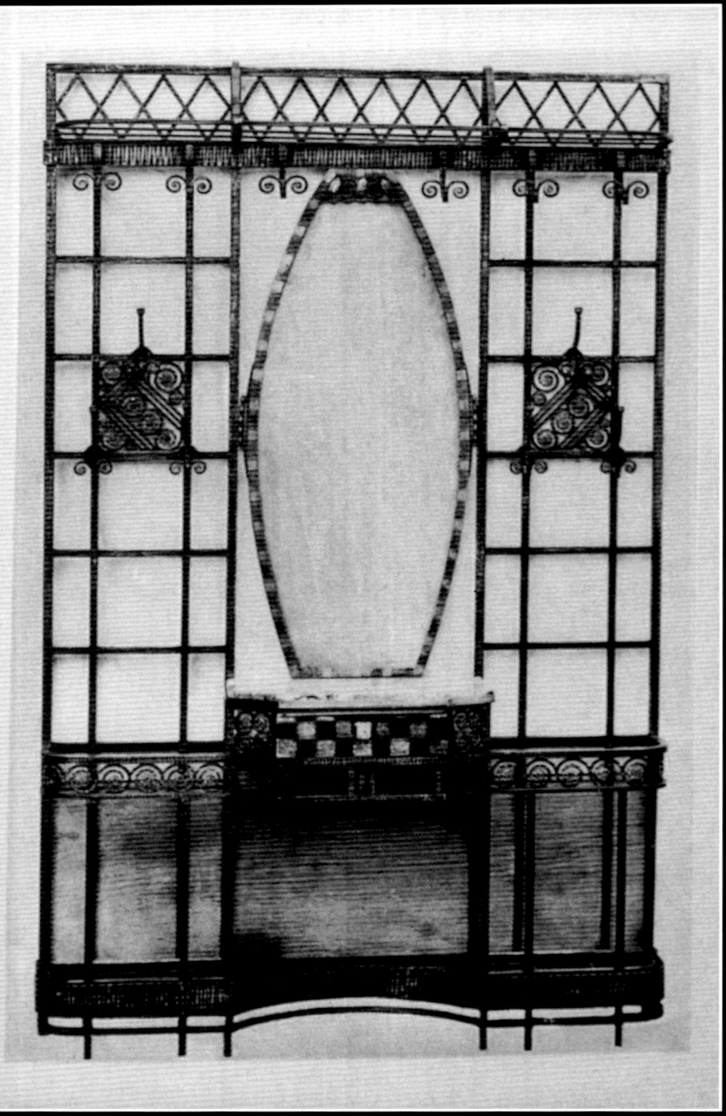

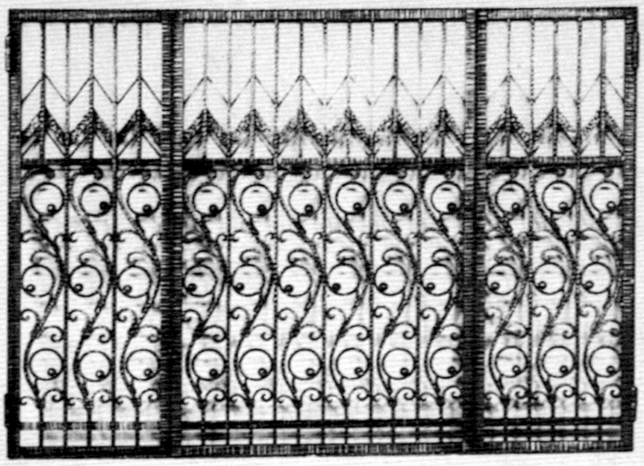

2

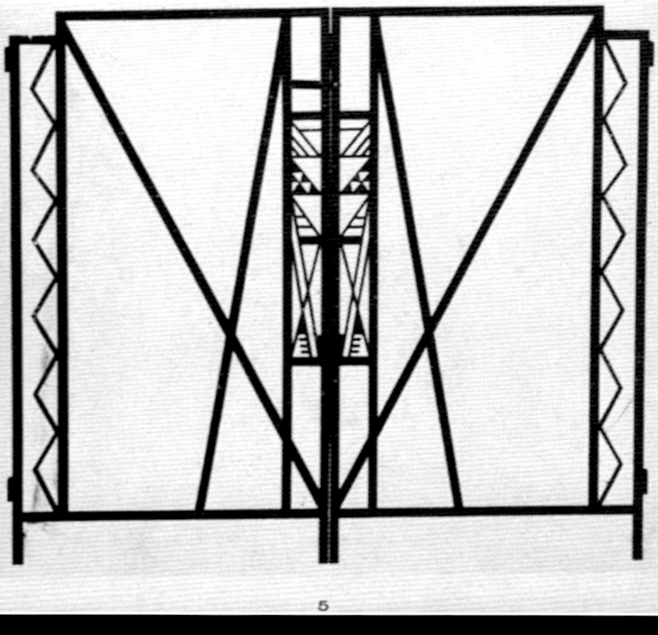

5

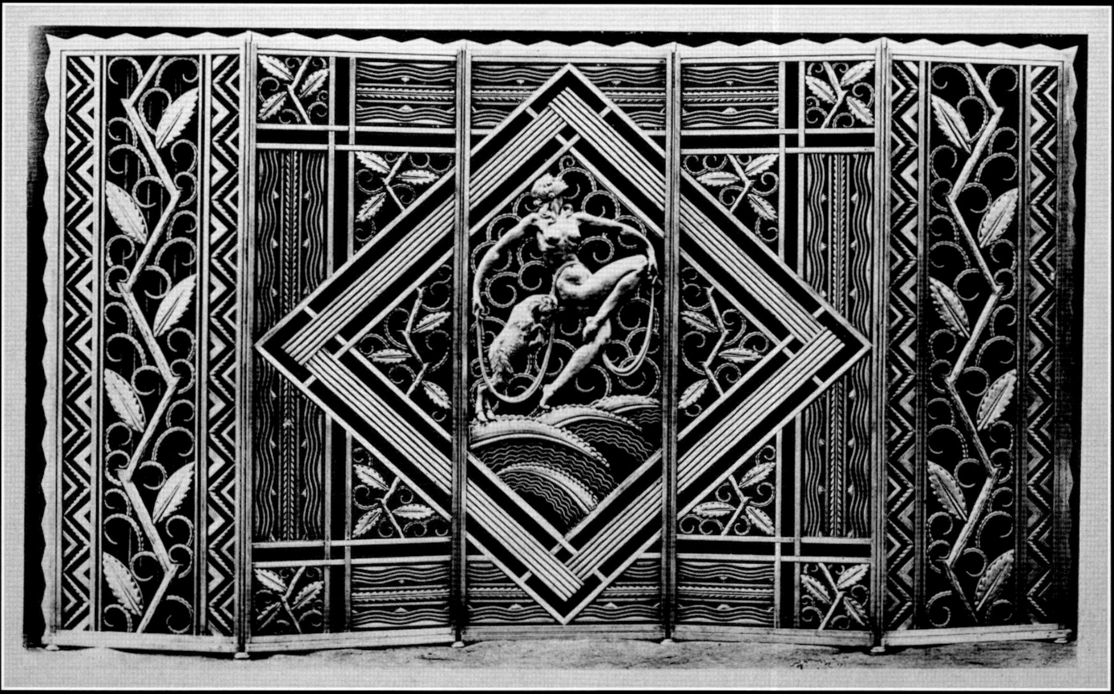

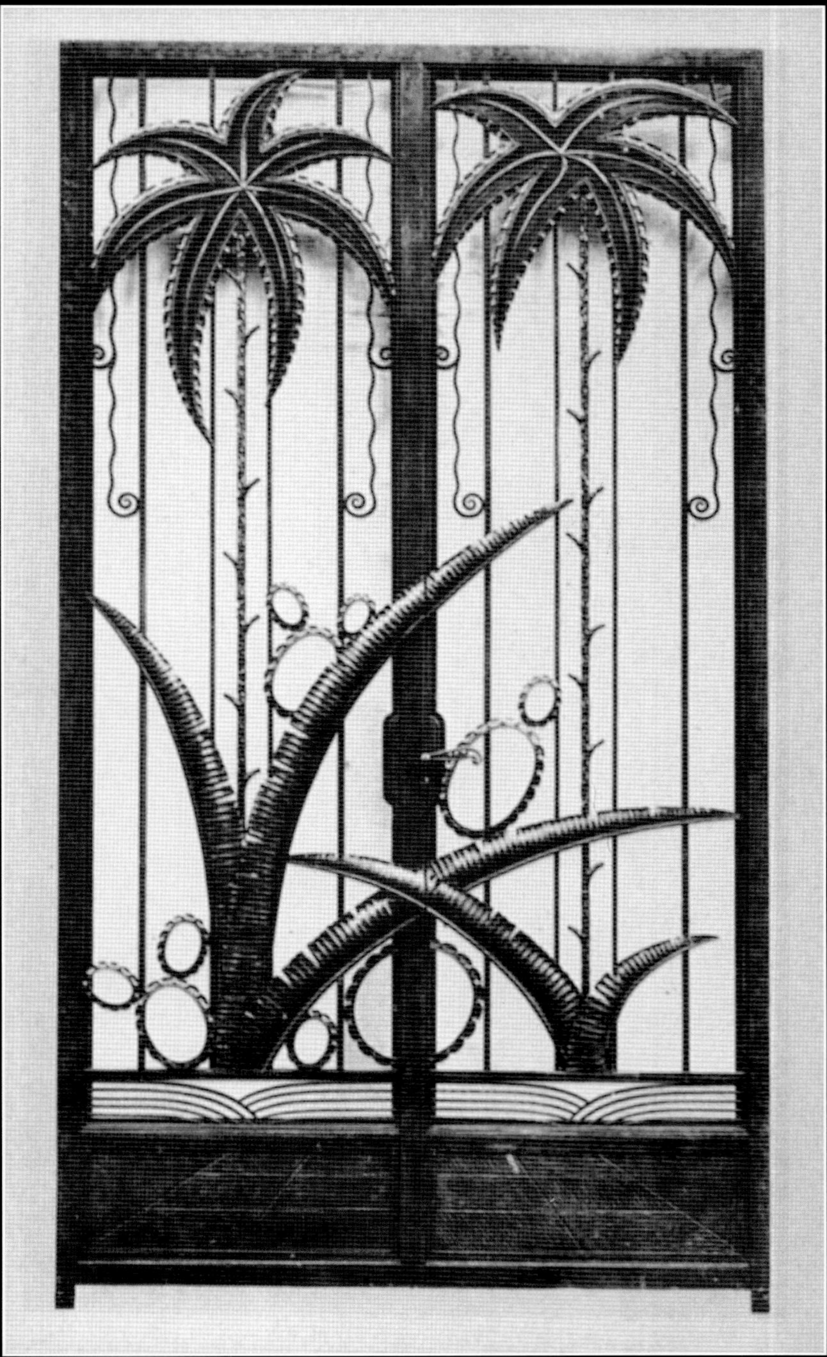

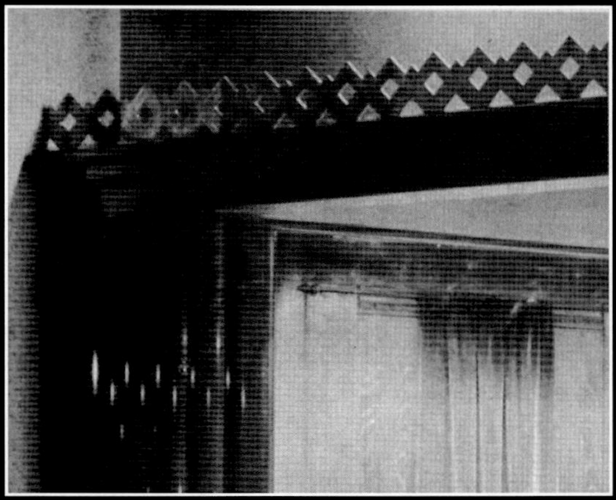

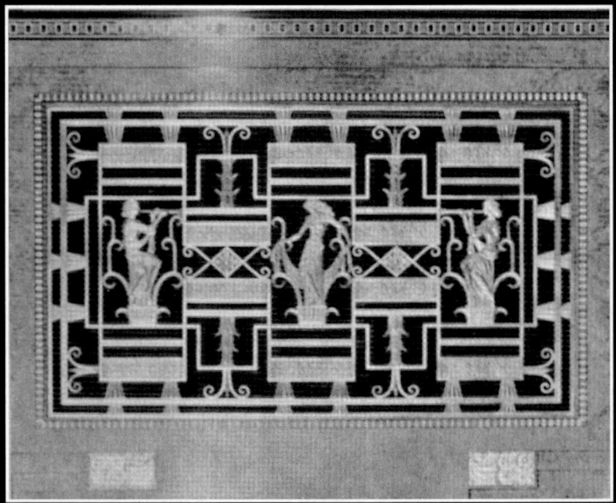

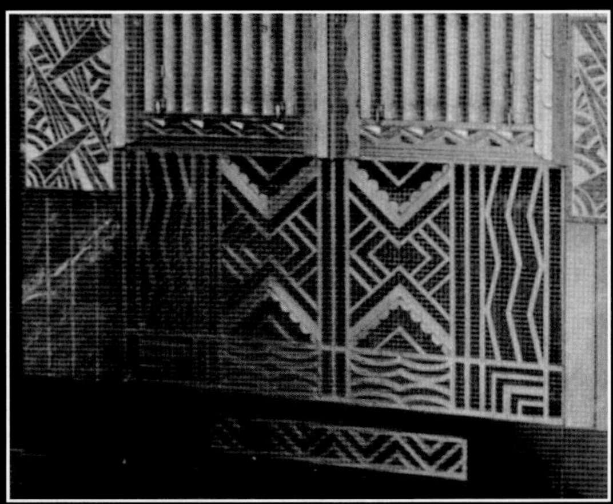

Morgan, Walls & Clements

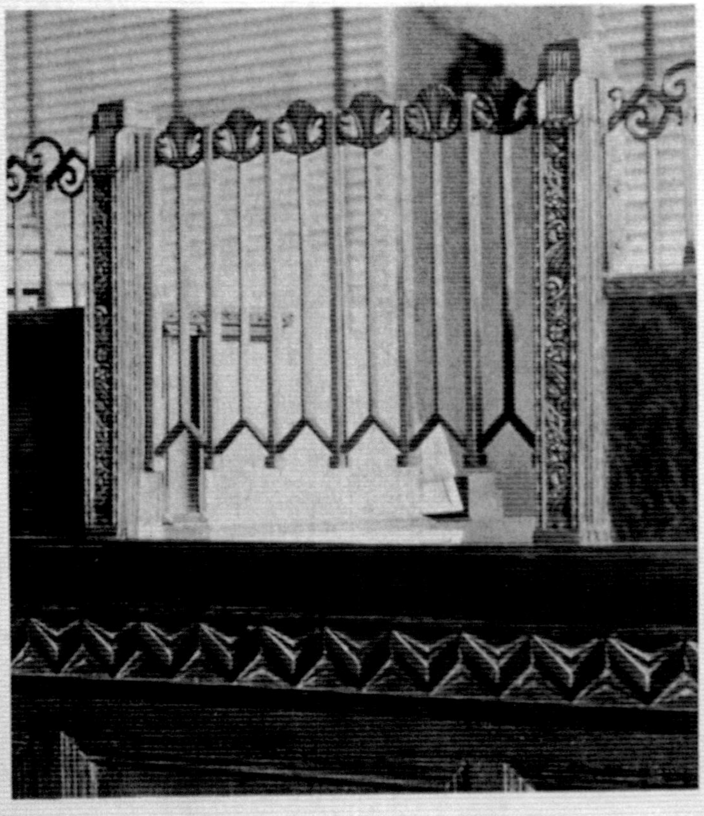

W. H. Harrison

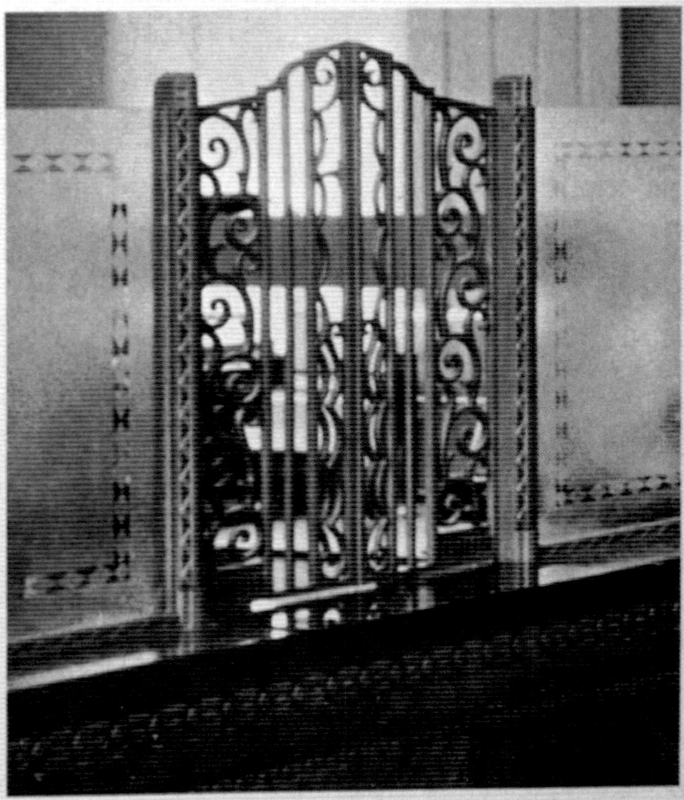

John and Donald B. Parkinson

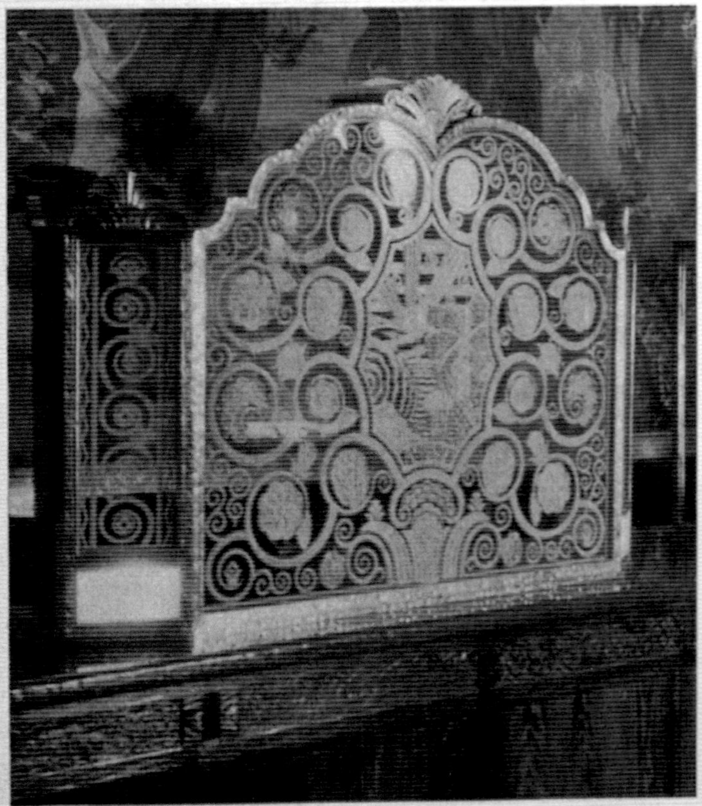

Morgan, Walls & Clements

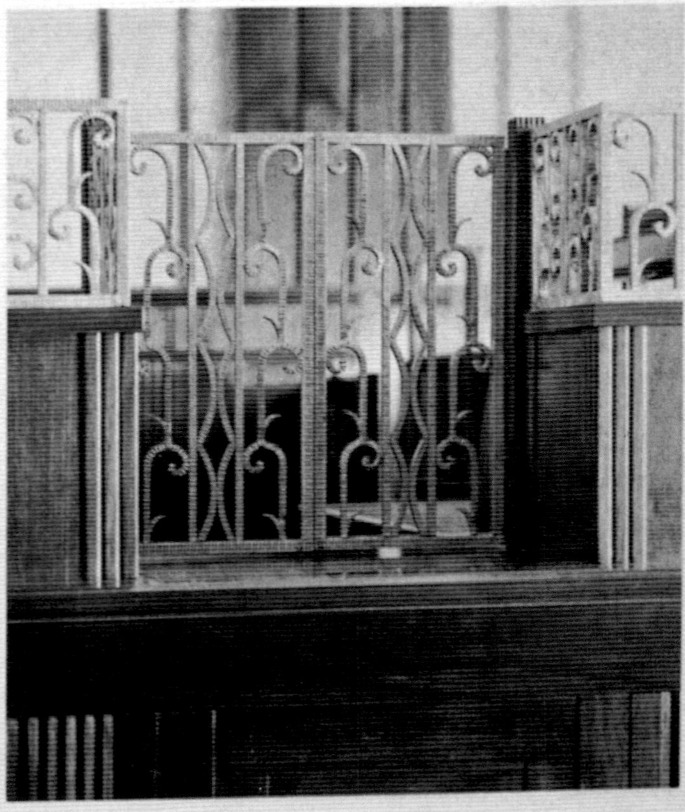

Staircases & Railings

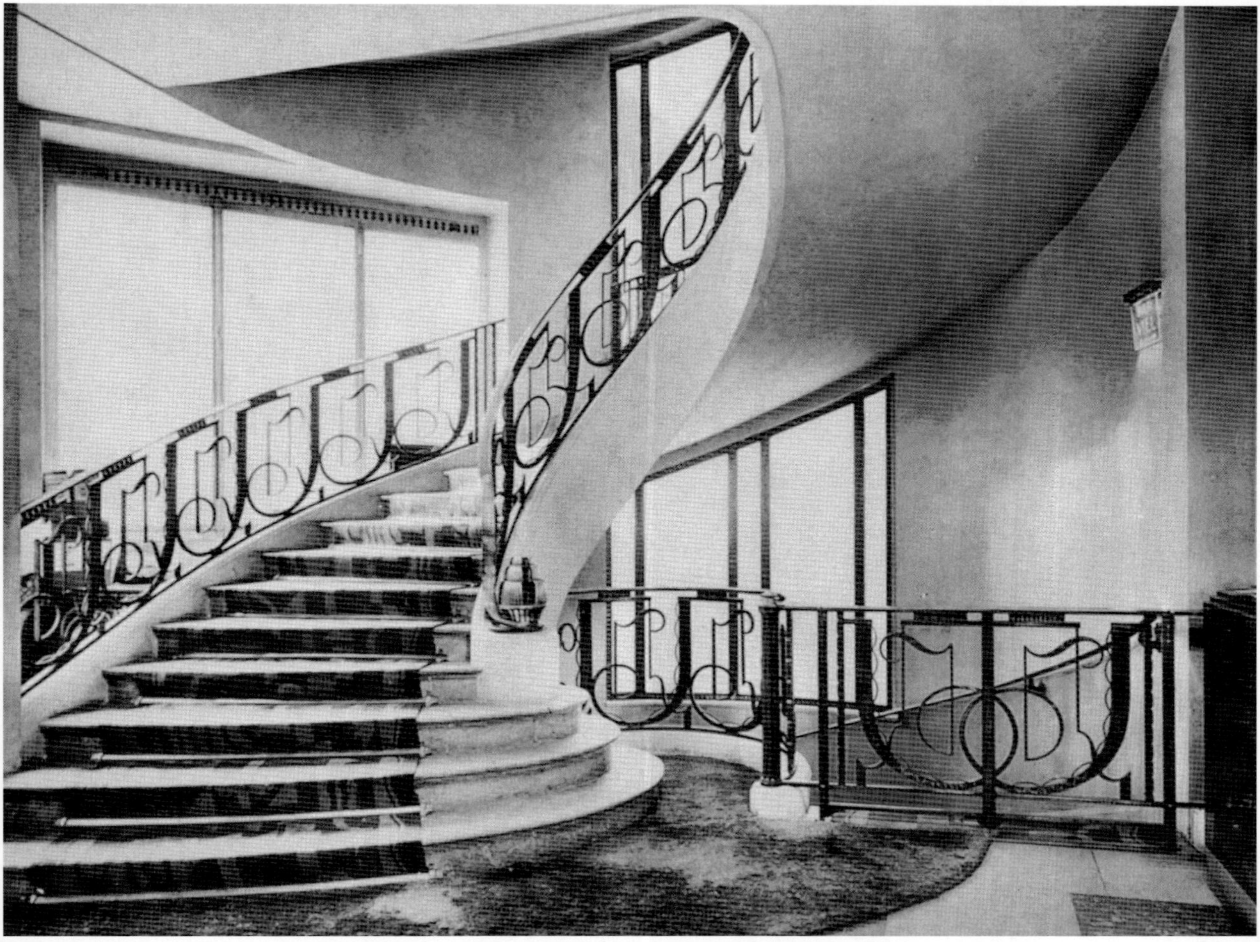

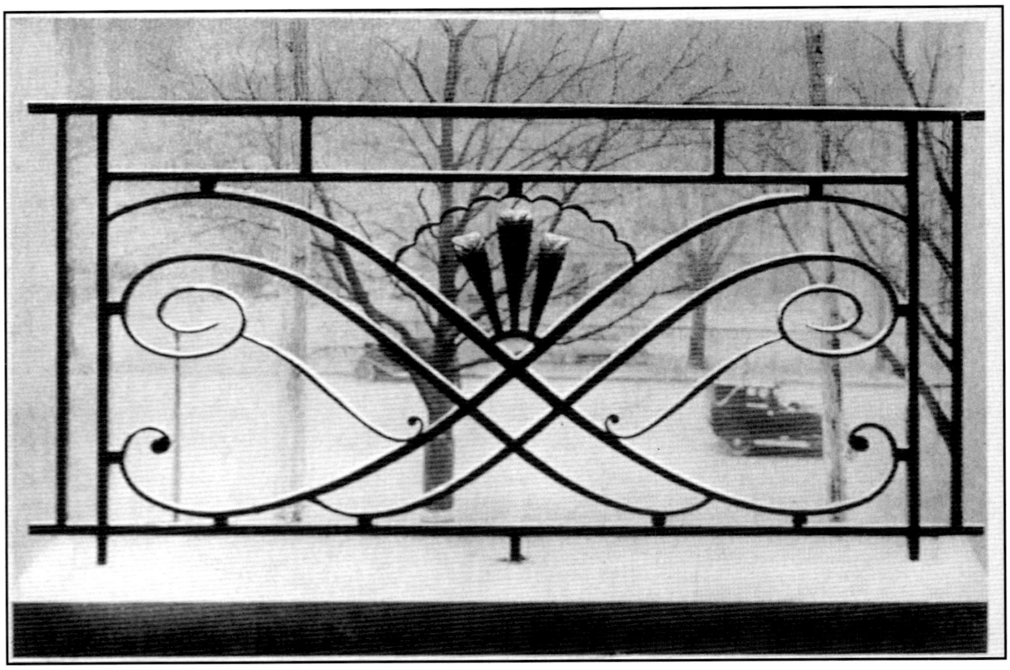

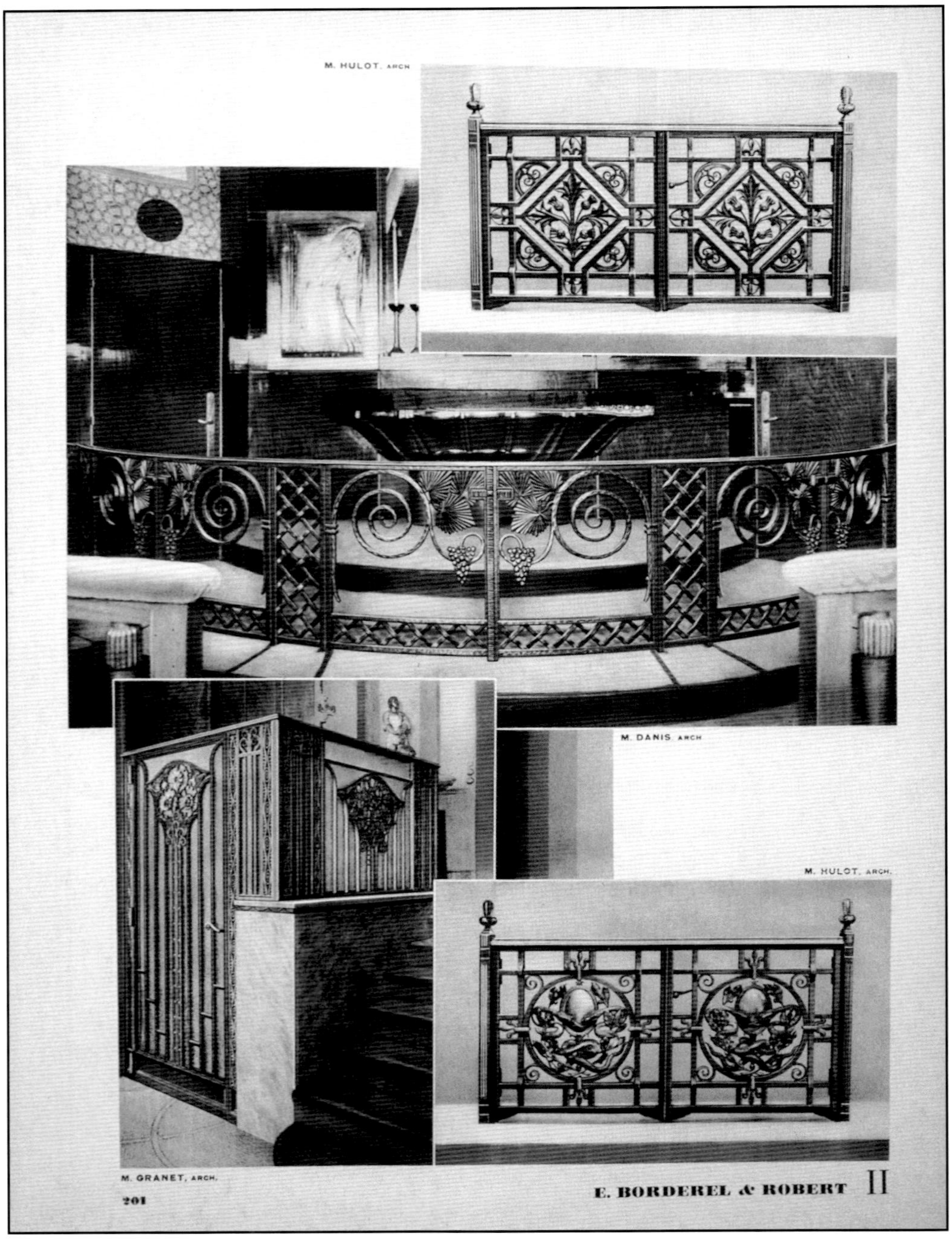
M. HULOT, ARCH
M. DANIS, ARCH
M. HULOT, ARCH.
M. GRANET, ARCH.
201
E. BORDEREL & ROBERT
II

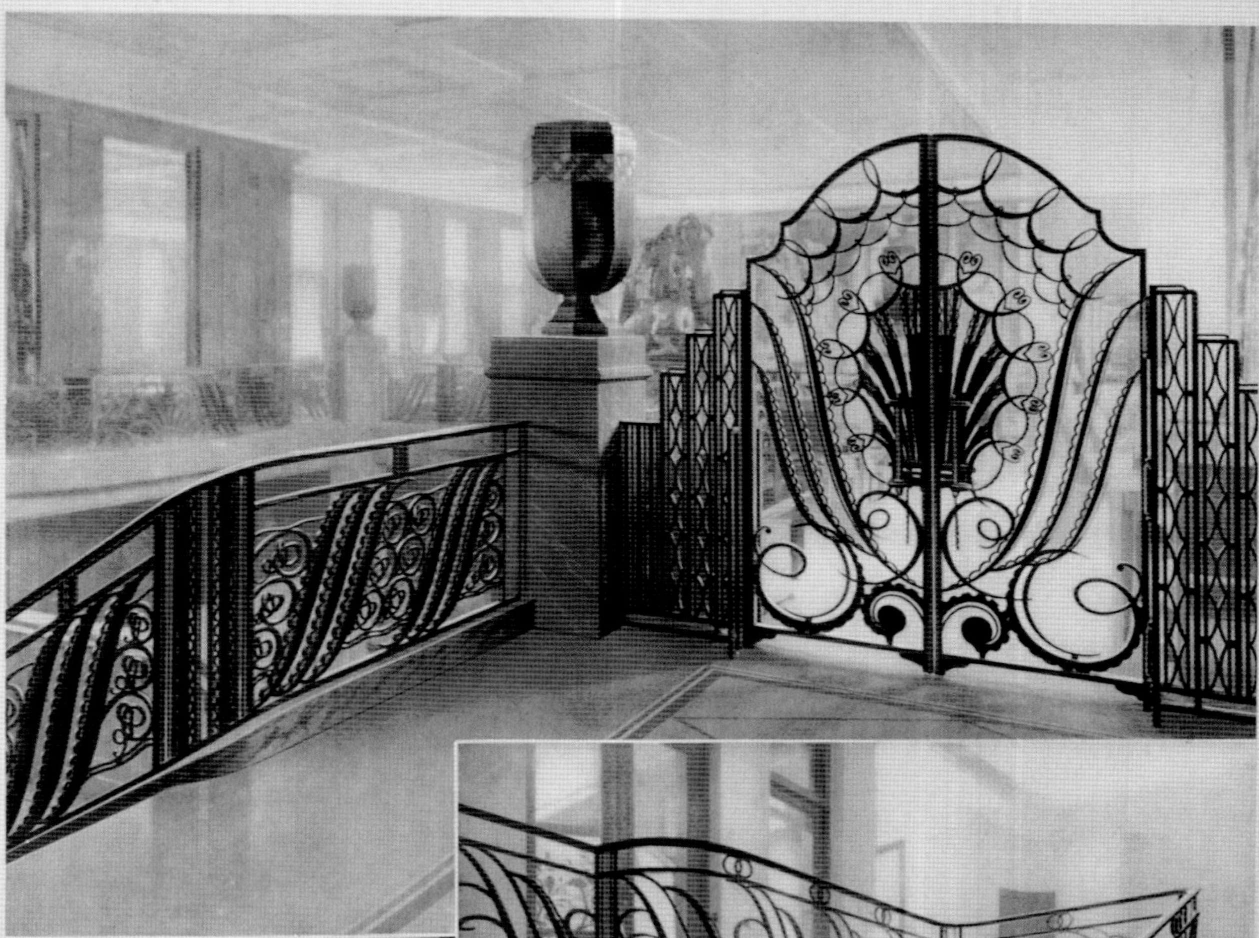

M. BOUWENS DE BOIJEN, ARCH

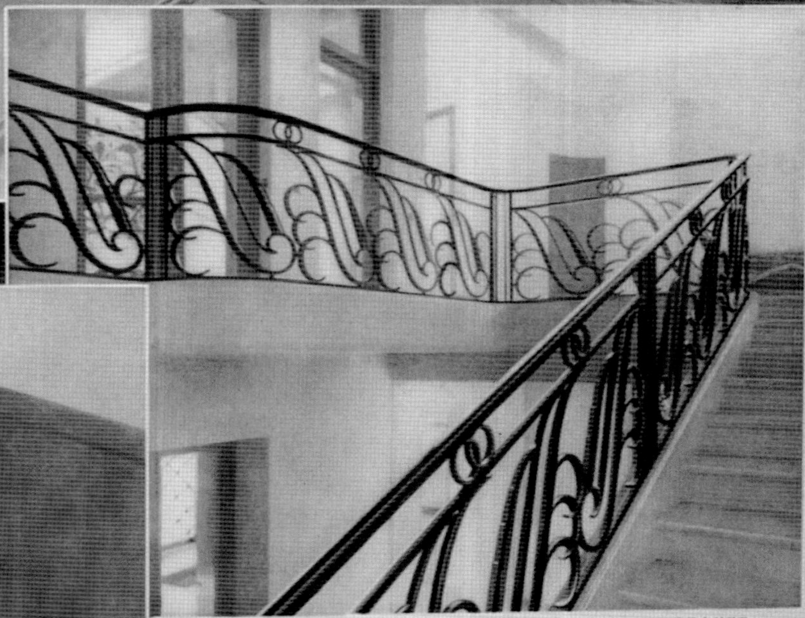

M. GRANET, ARCH.

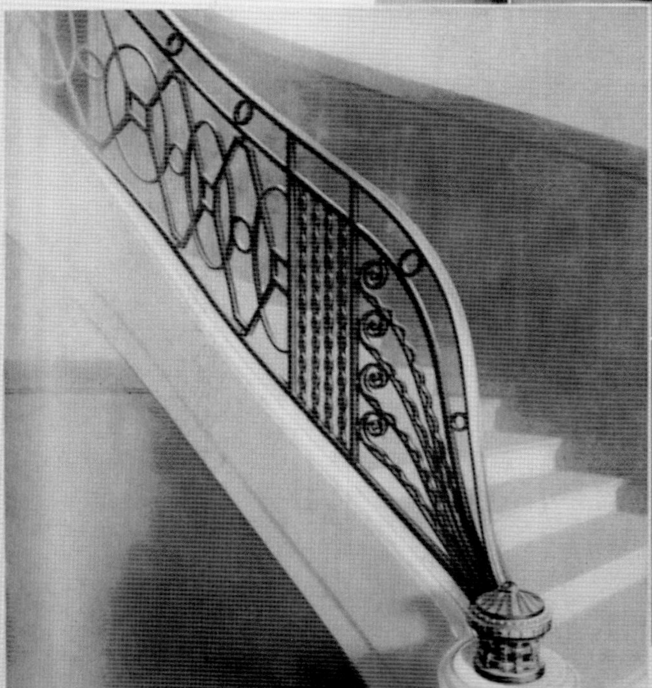

M. PATOUILLARD-DEMORIANE, ARCH.

202

E. BORDEREL & ROBERT II

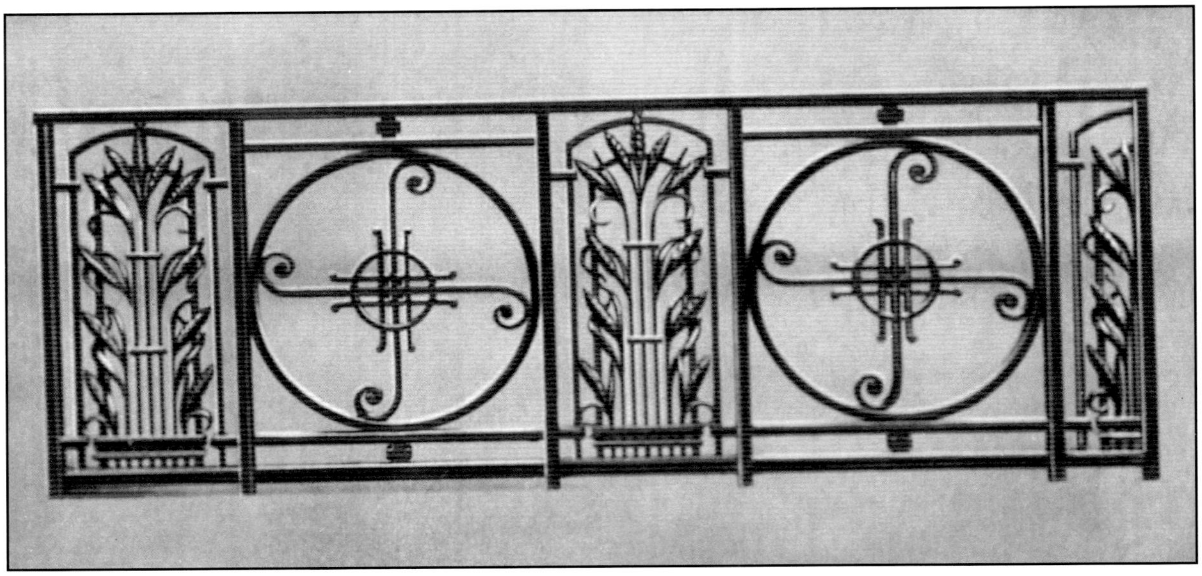

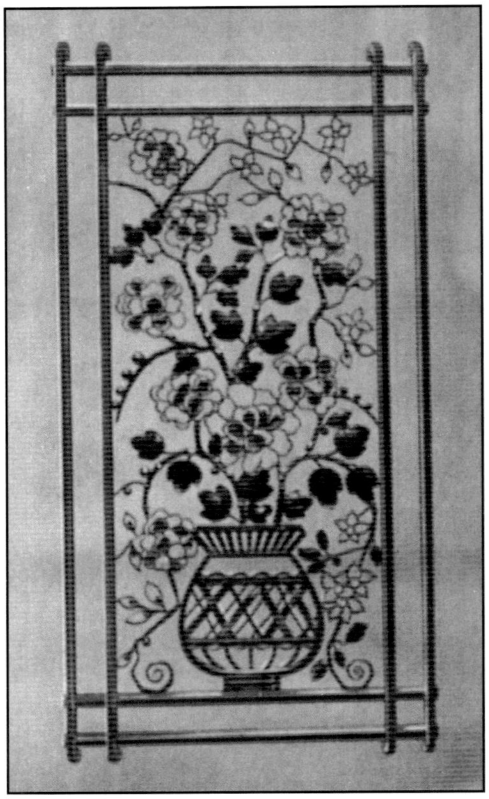

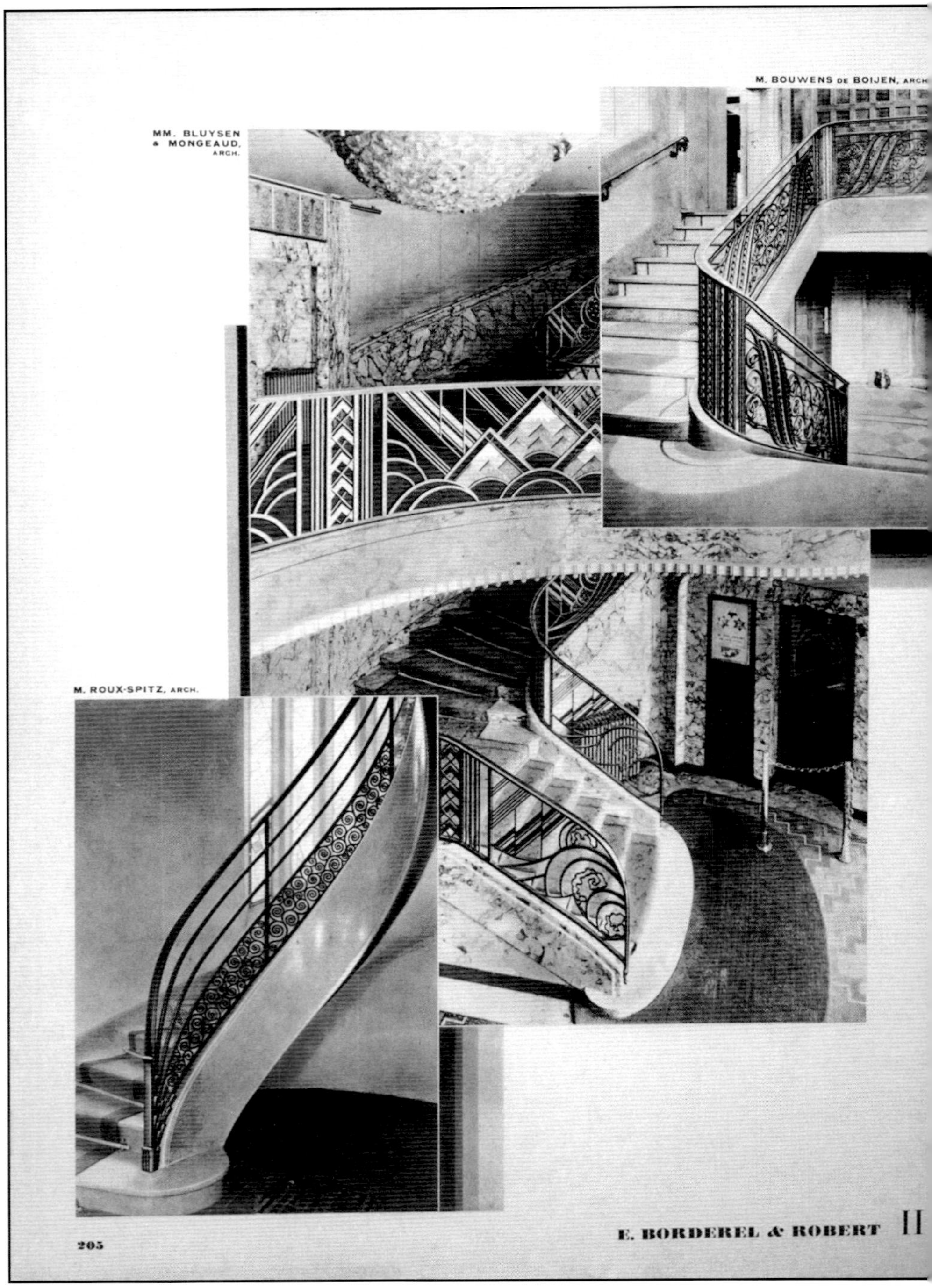
M. BOUWENS DE BOIJEN, ARCH
MM. BLUYSEN & MONGEAUD, ARCH.
M. ROUX-SPITZ, ARCH.
205
E. BORDEREL & ROBERT II

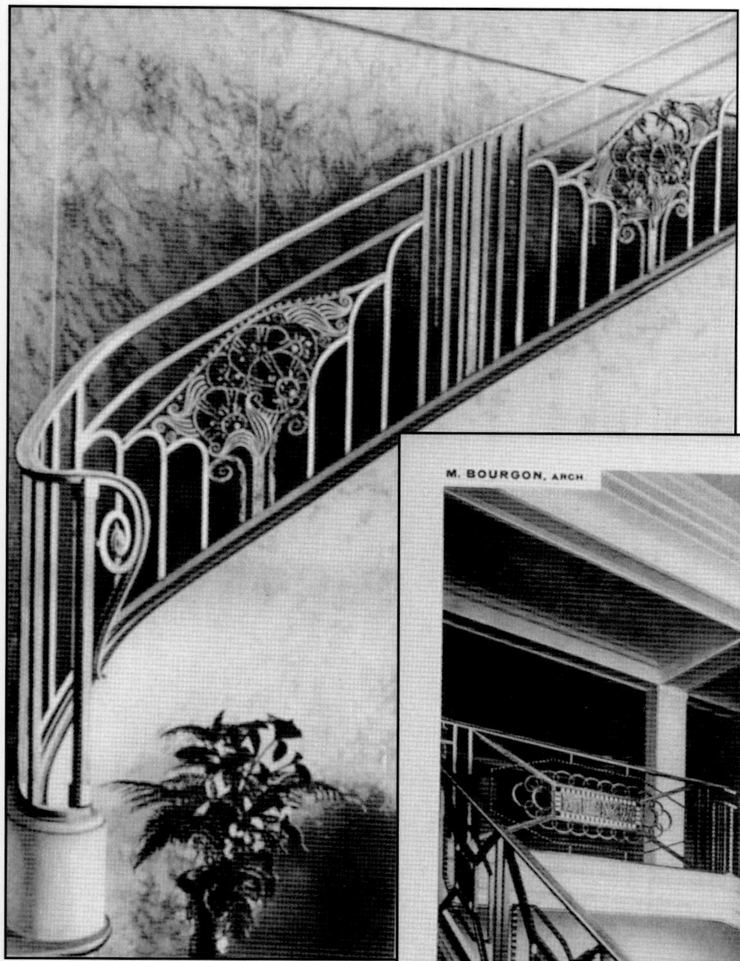

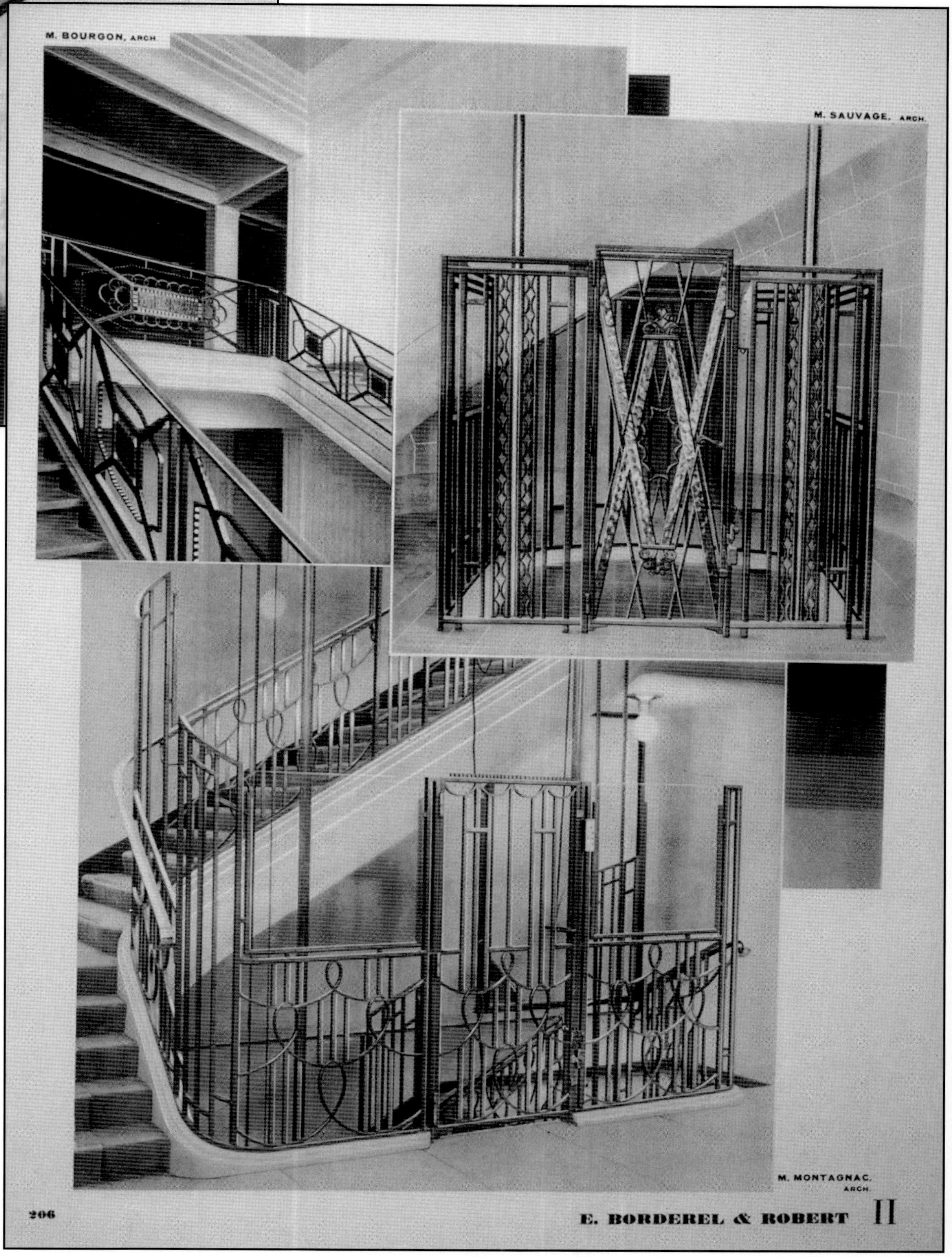
M. BOURGON, ARCH.
M. SAUVAGE, ARCH.
M. MONTAGNAC, ARCH.
206
E. BORDEREL & ROBERT
II

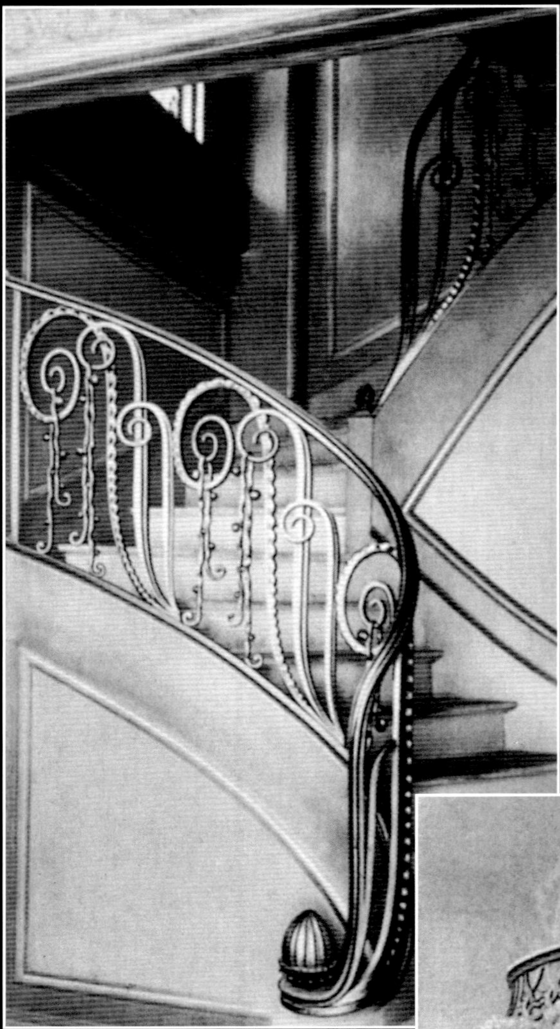

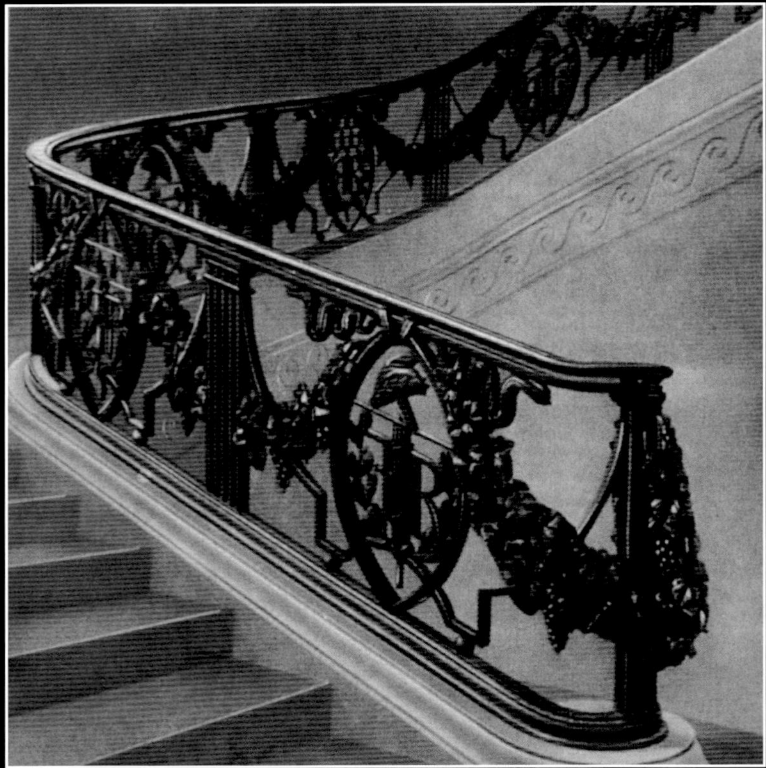

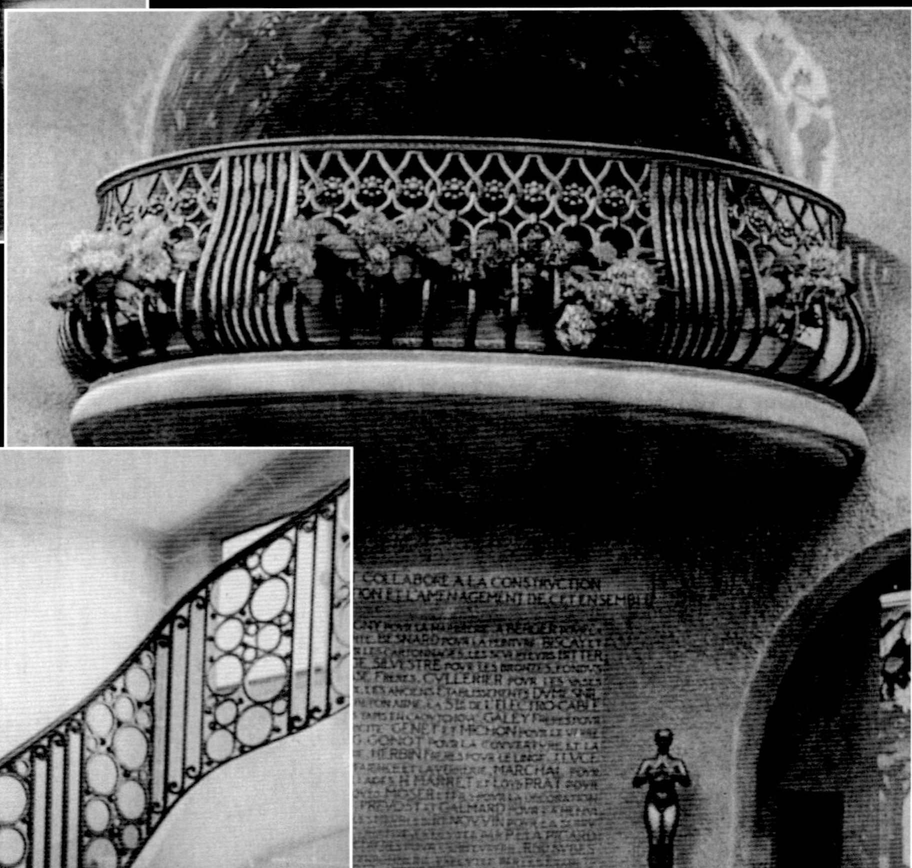
COLLABORE A LA CONSTRVCTION

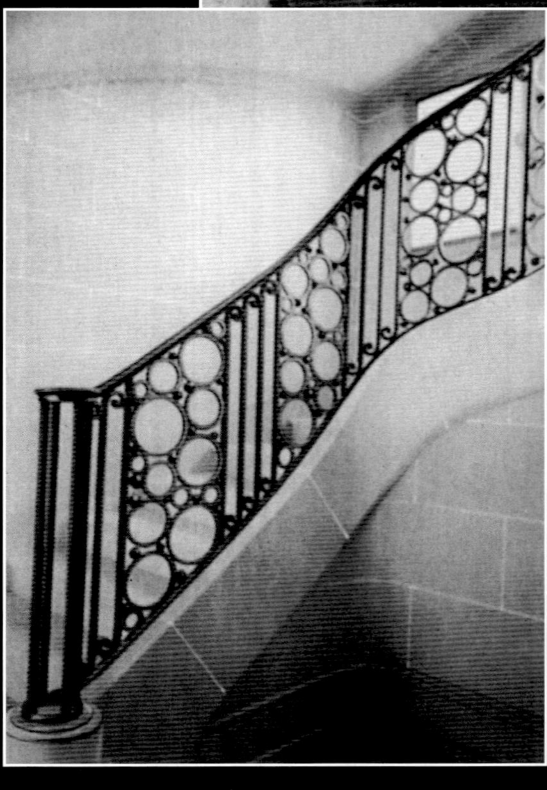

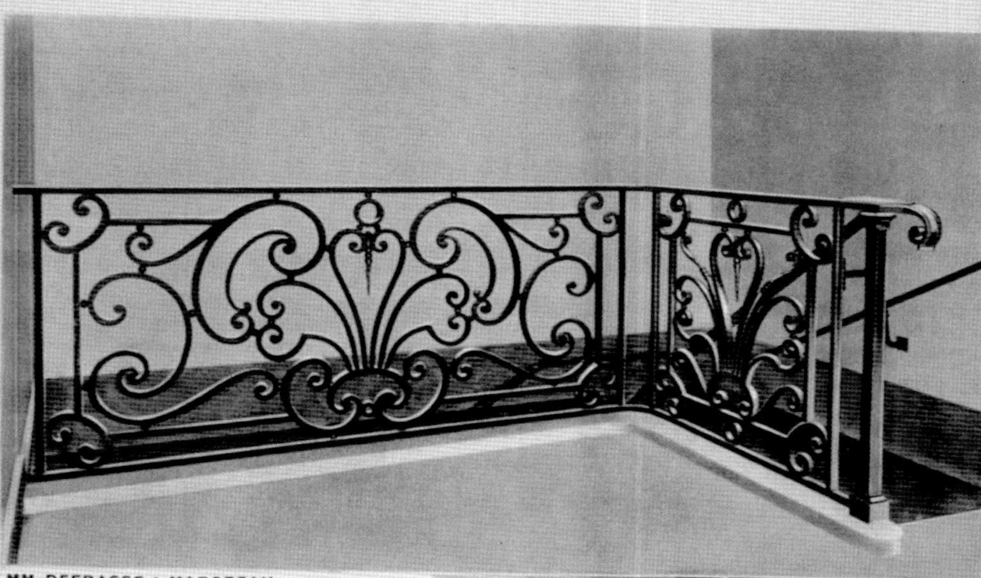

MM. DEFRASSE & MAROZEAU, ARCH

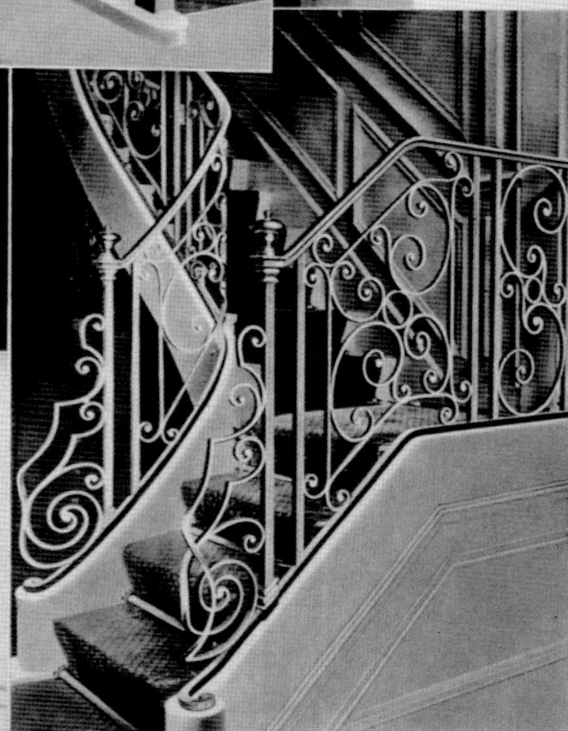

M. MAROZEAU, ARCH.

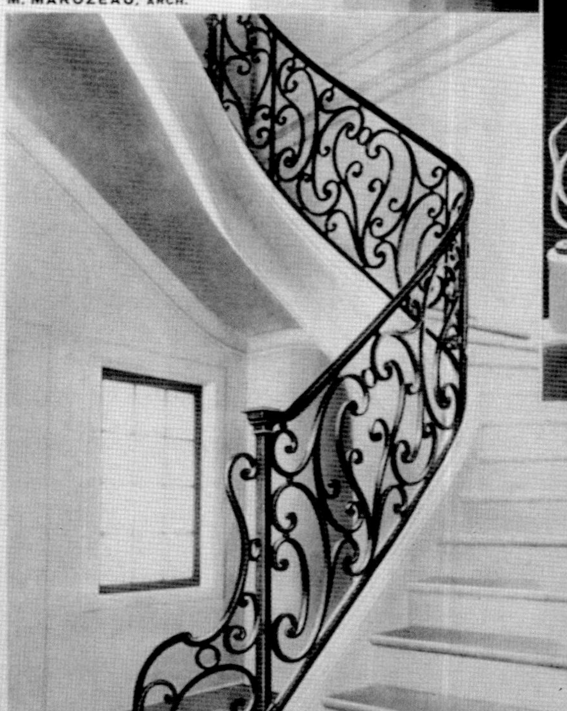

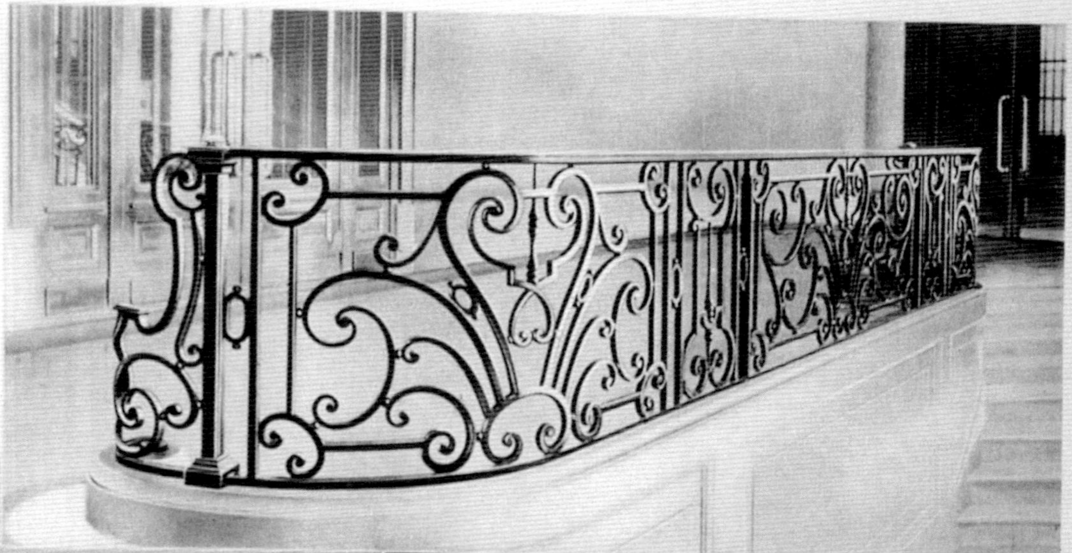

MM. DEFRASSE ET GUILLEMIN TARAYRE, ARCH.

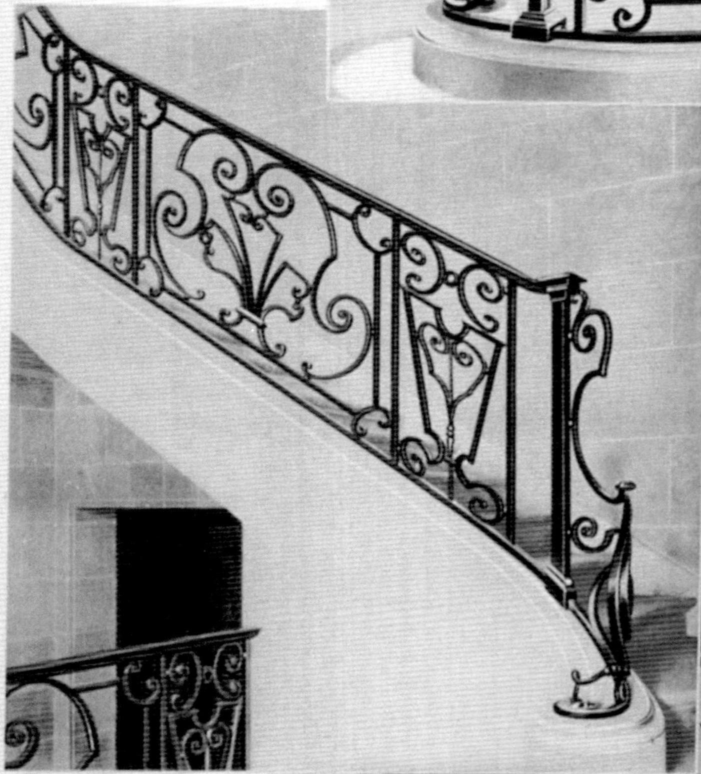

M. GREBER, ARCH.

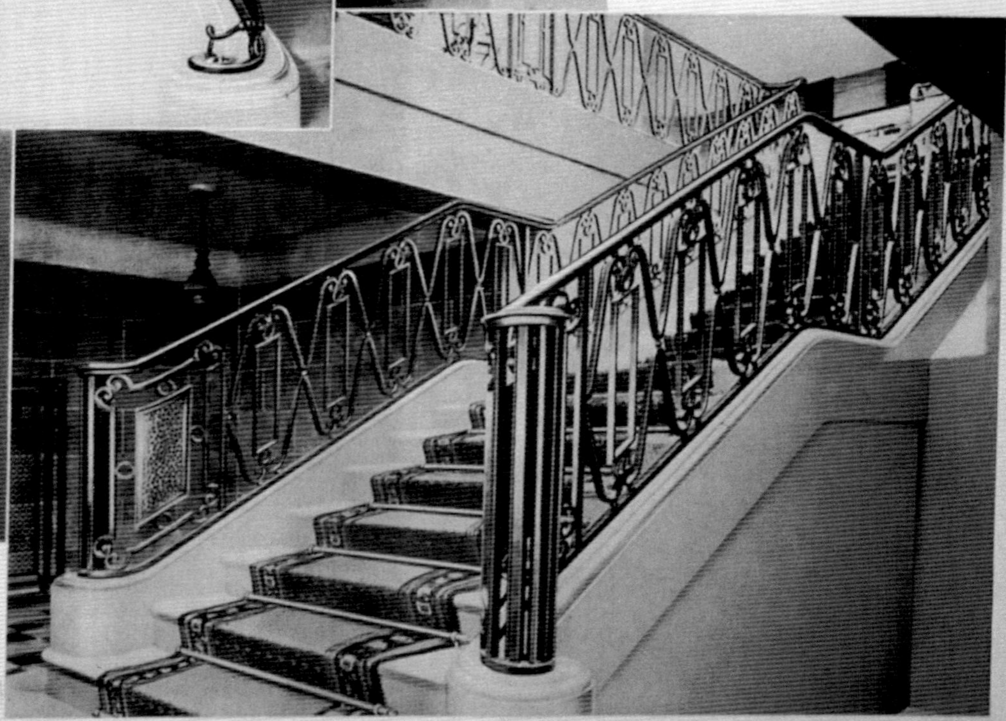

MM. DEFRASSE & HAUG, ARCH.

406 E. BORDEREL & ROBERT IV

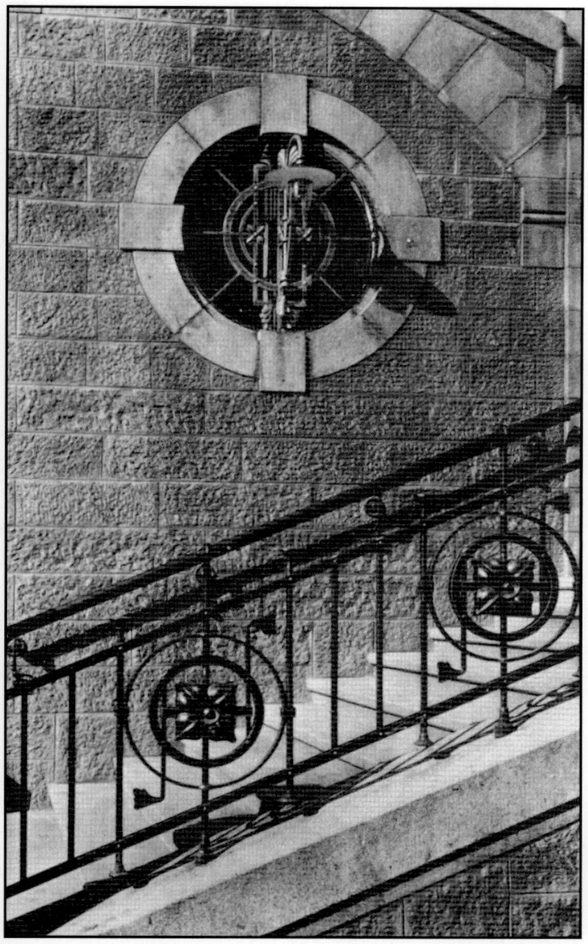

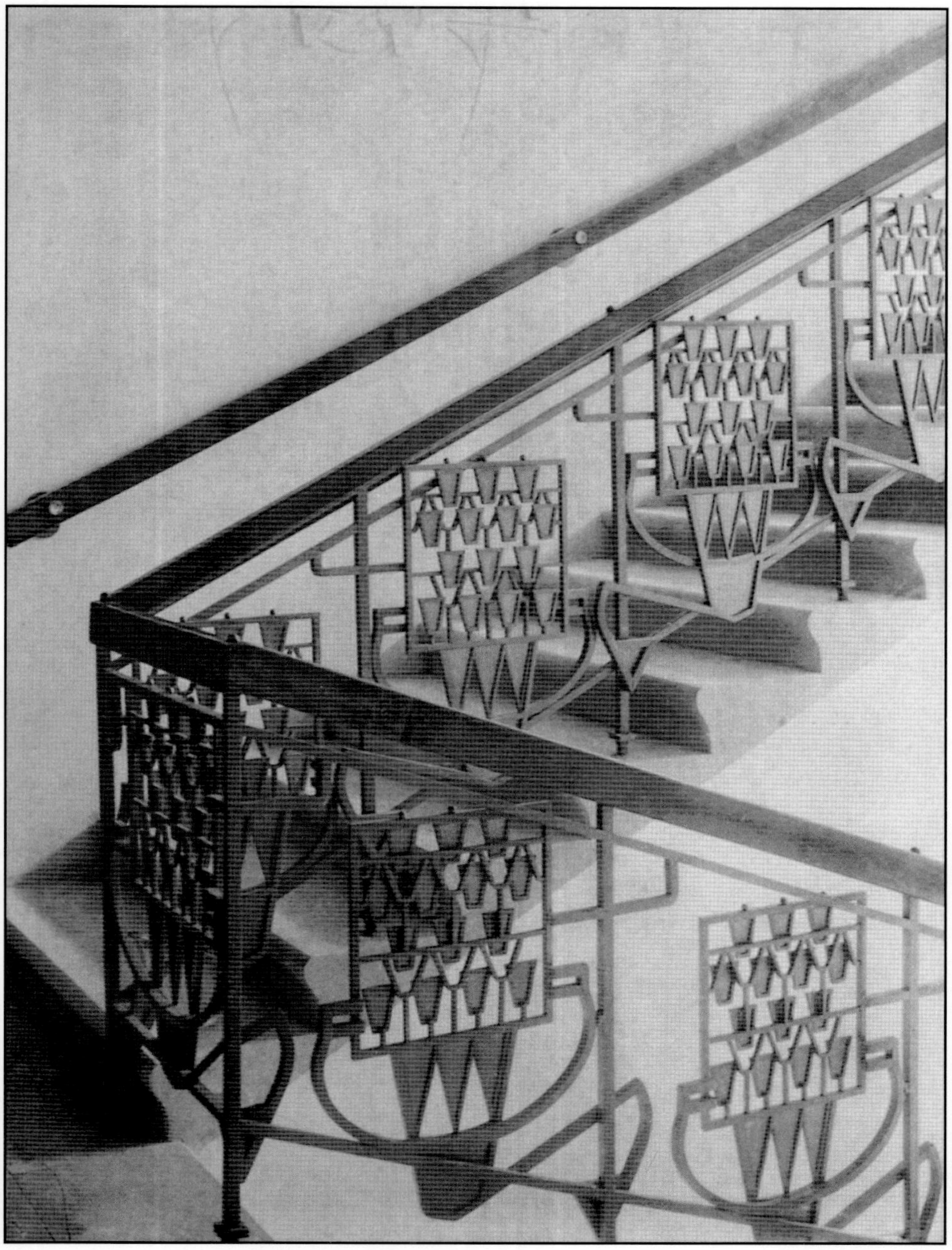

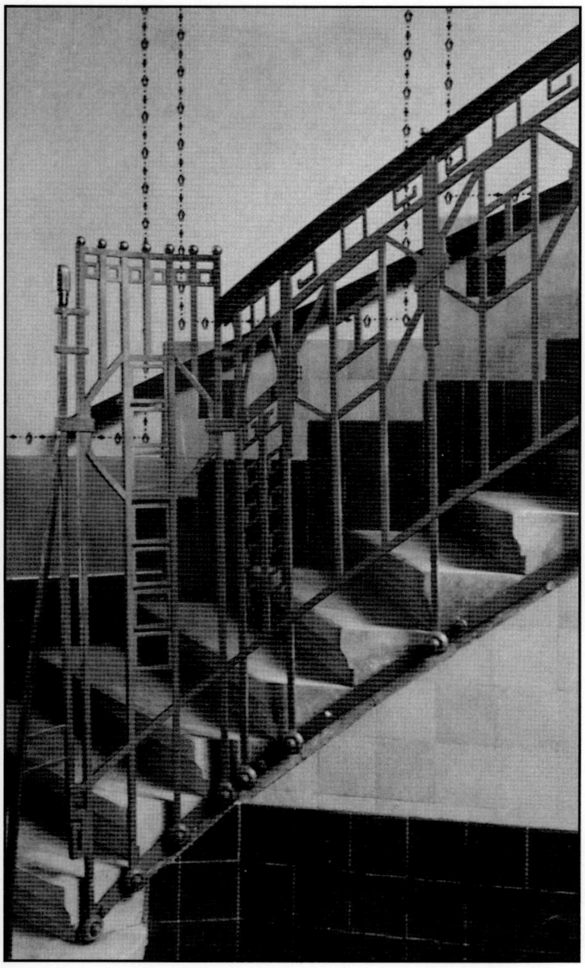

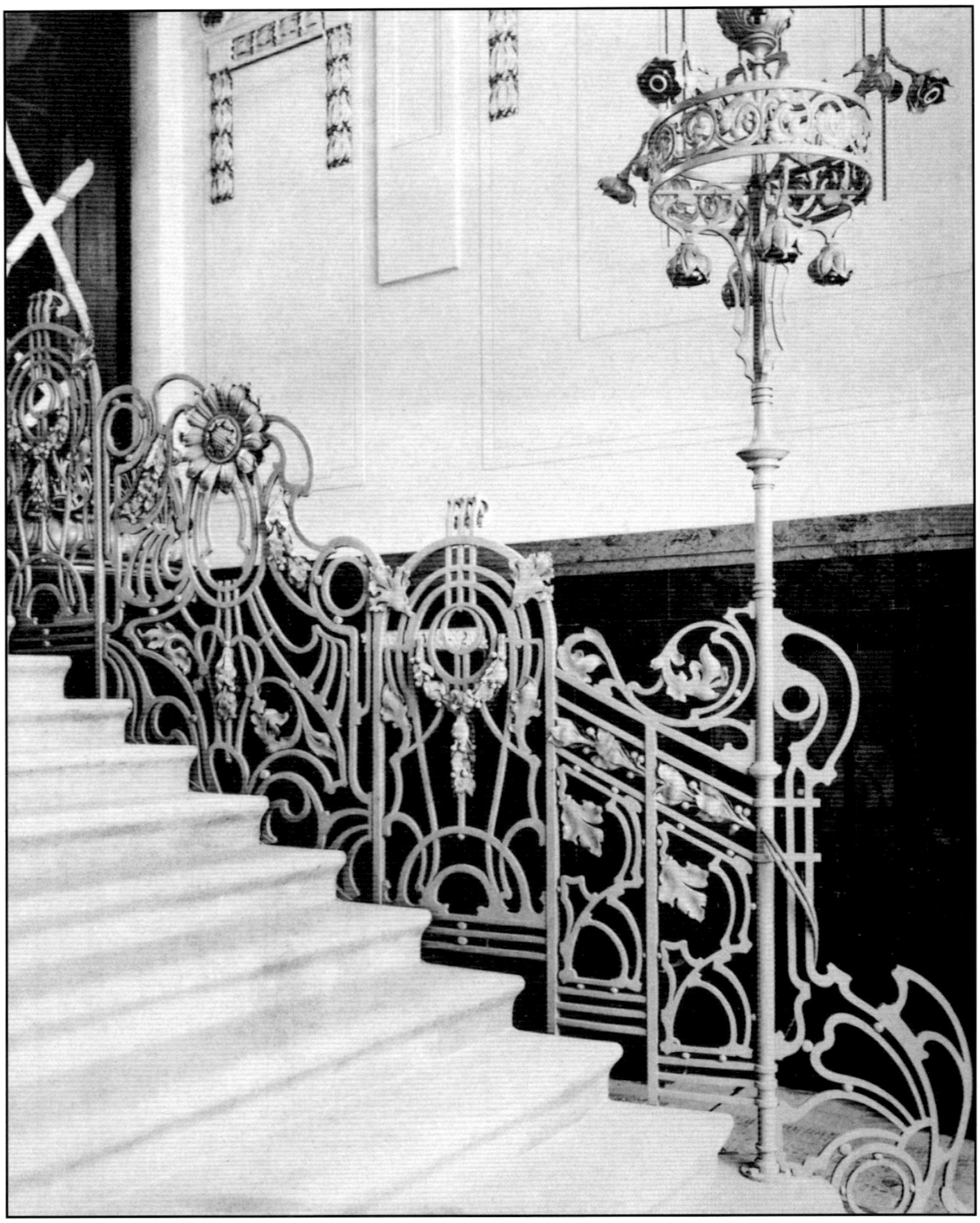

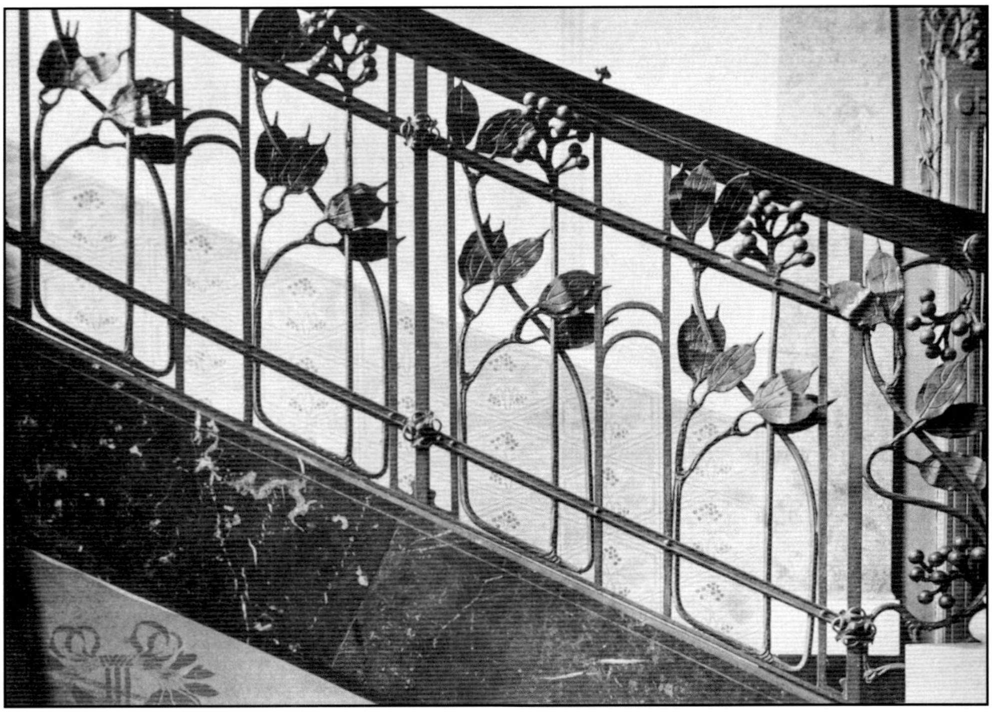

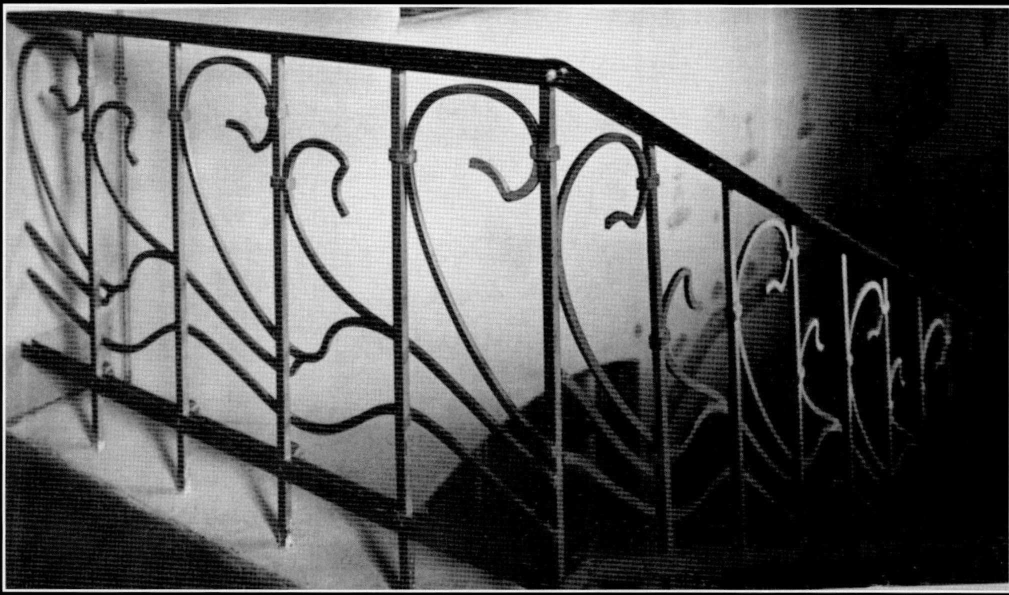

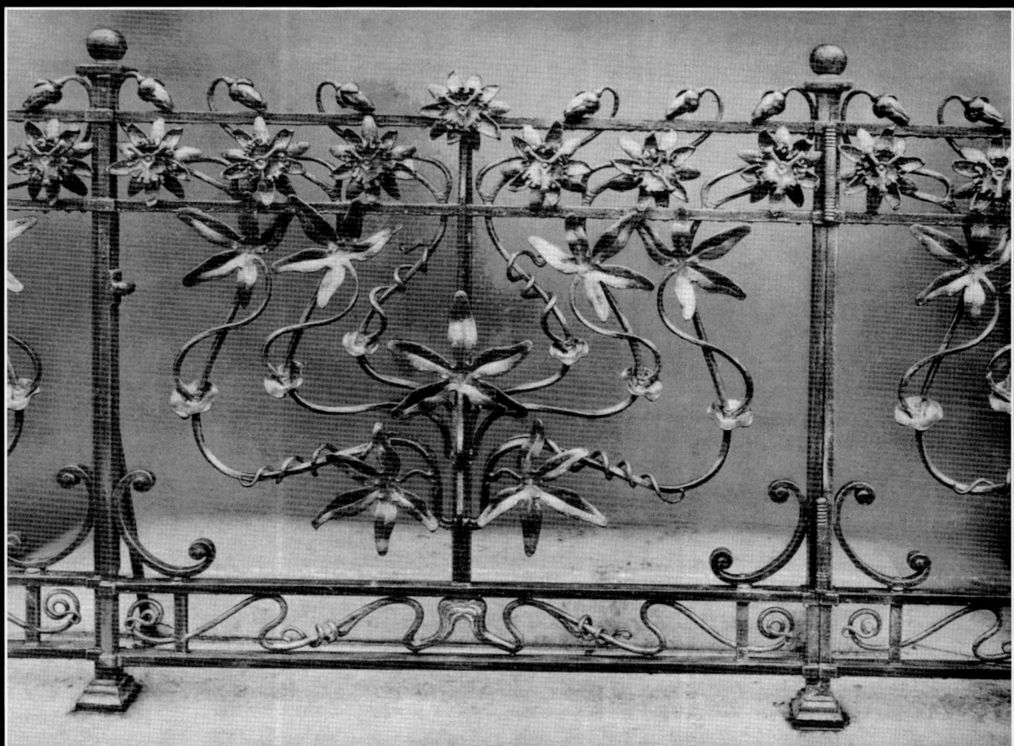

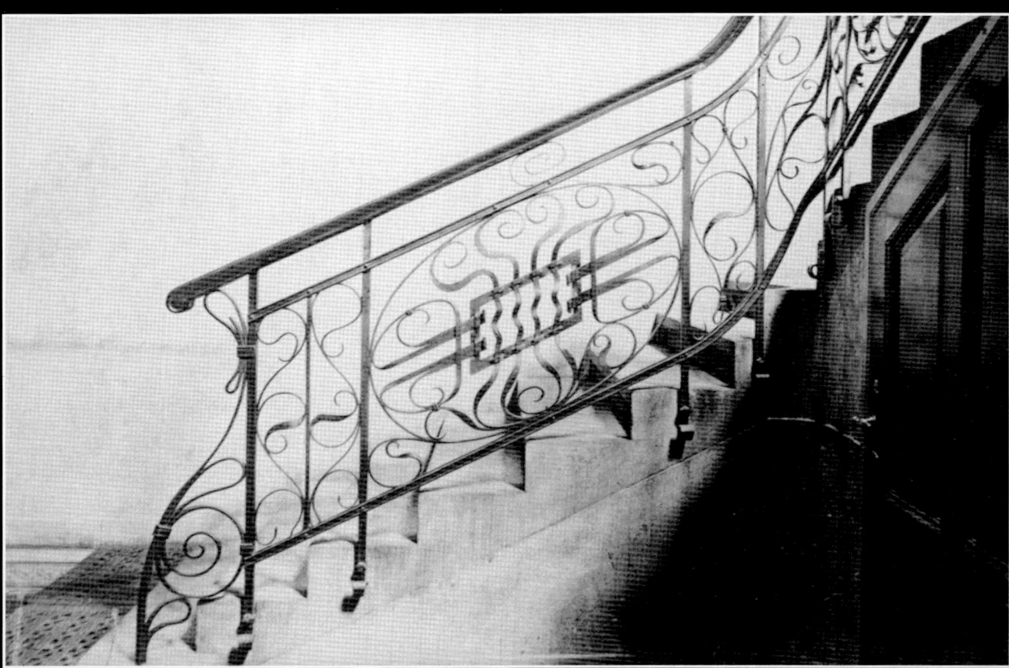

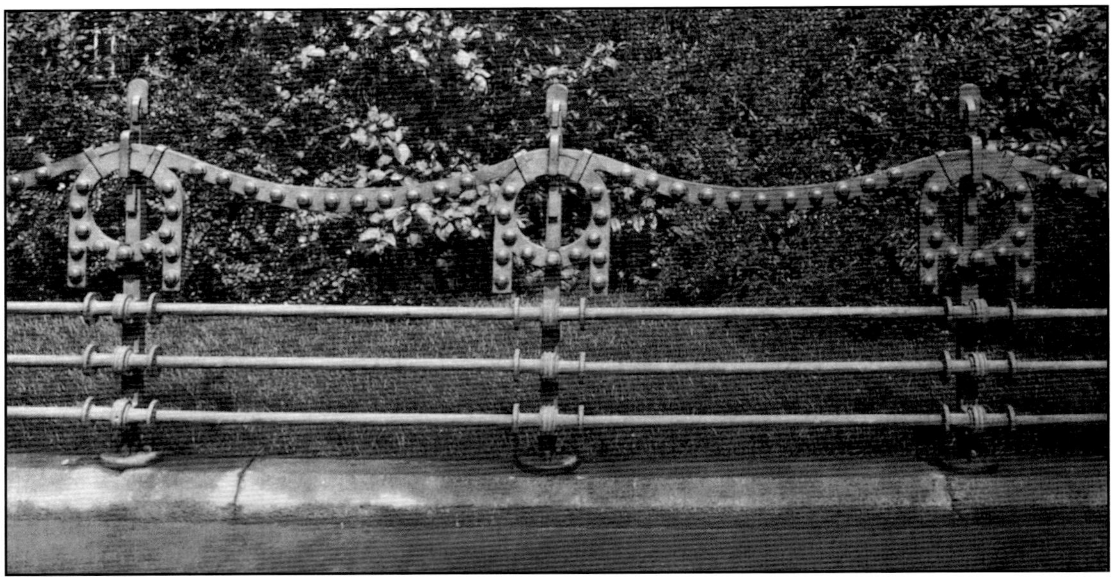

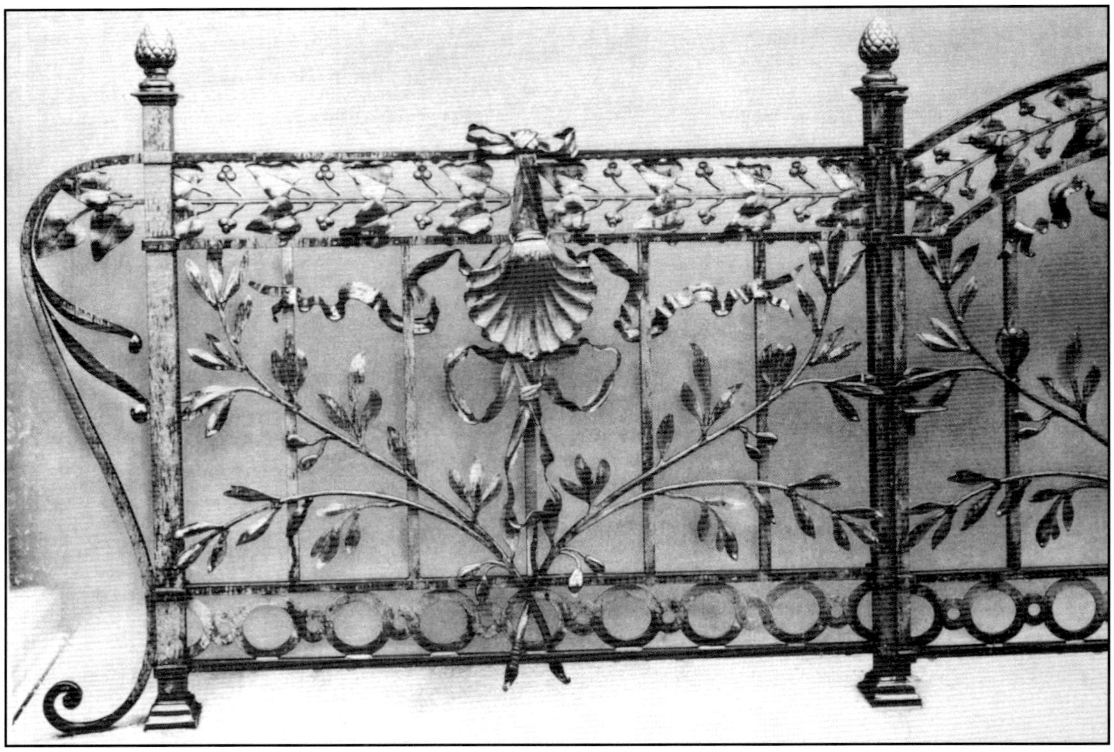

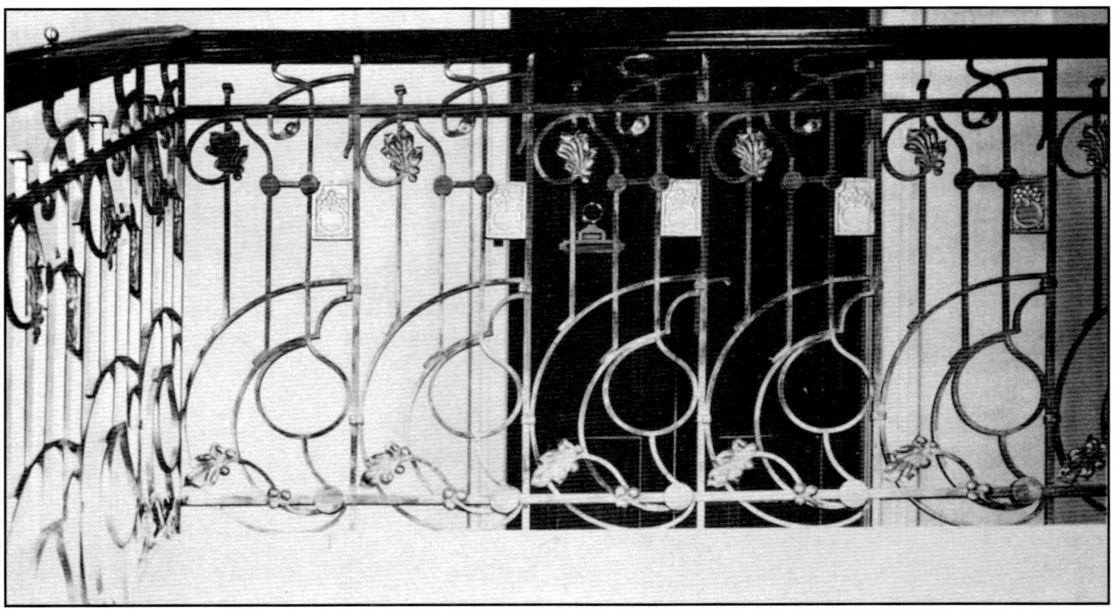

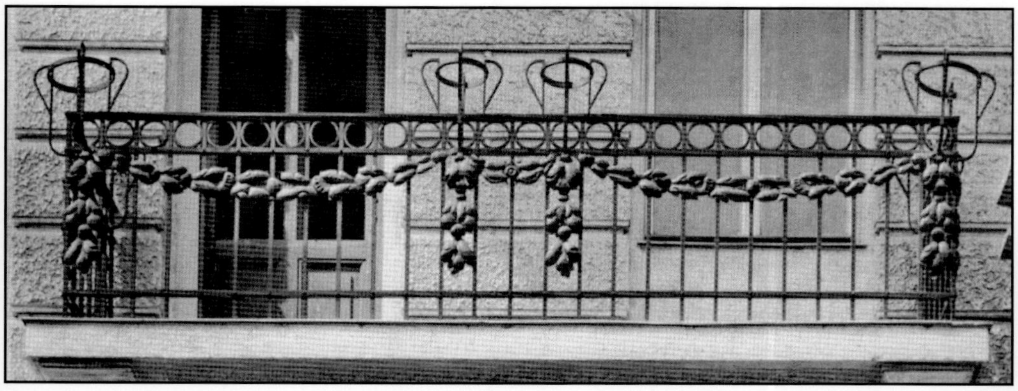

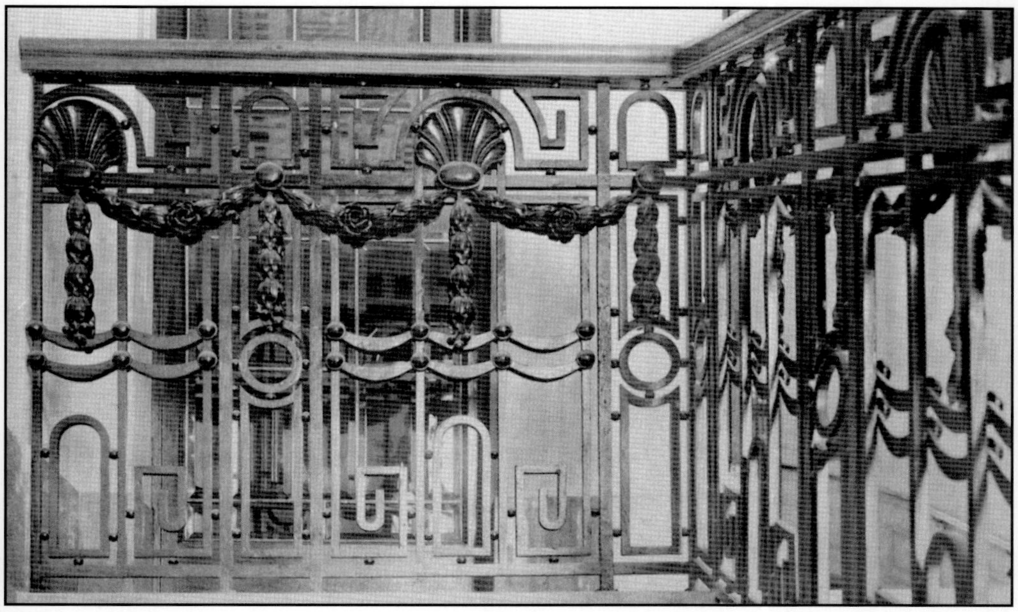

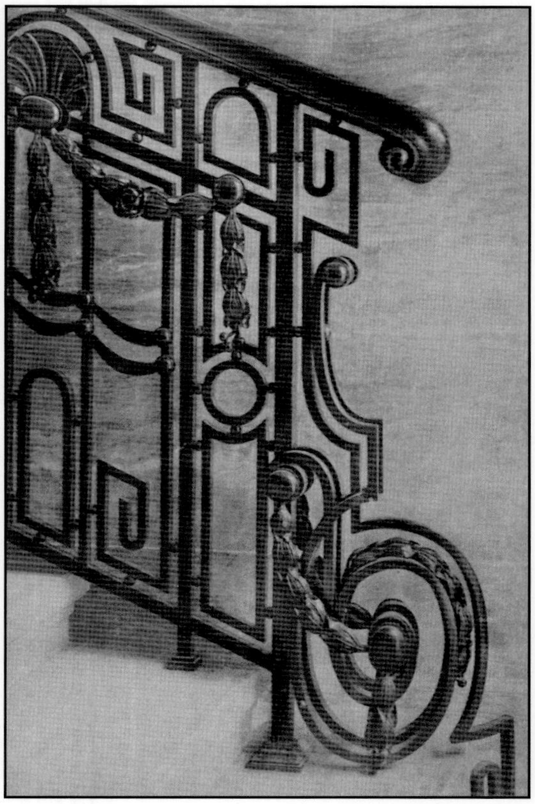

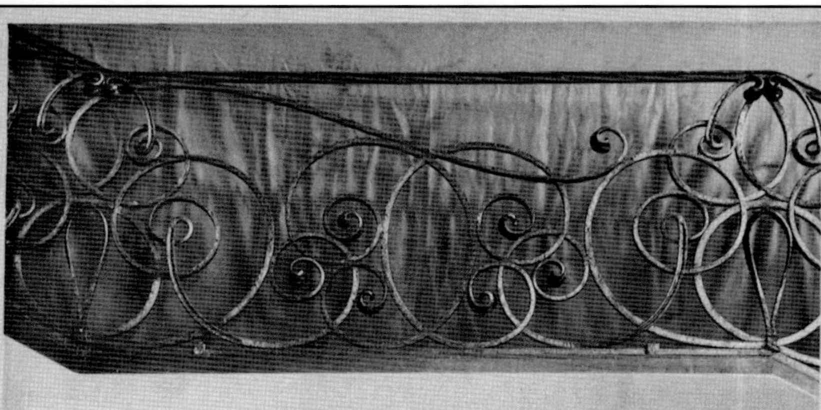

1

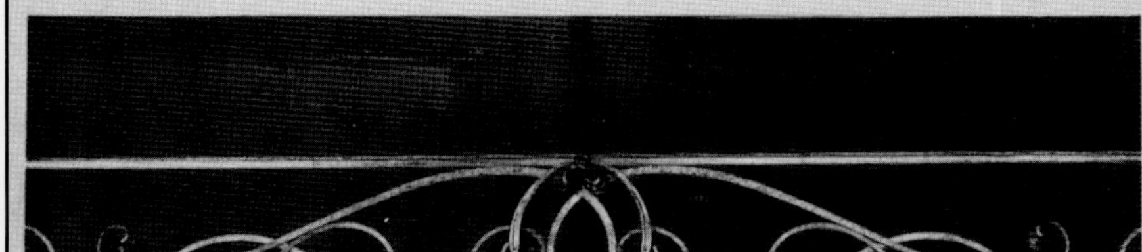

2

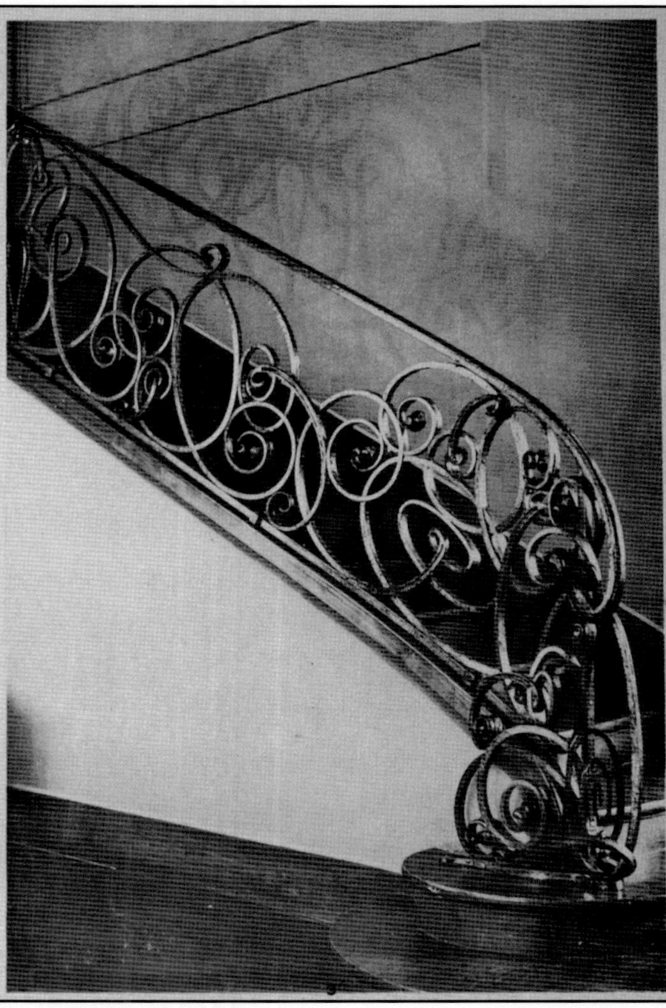

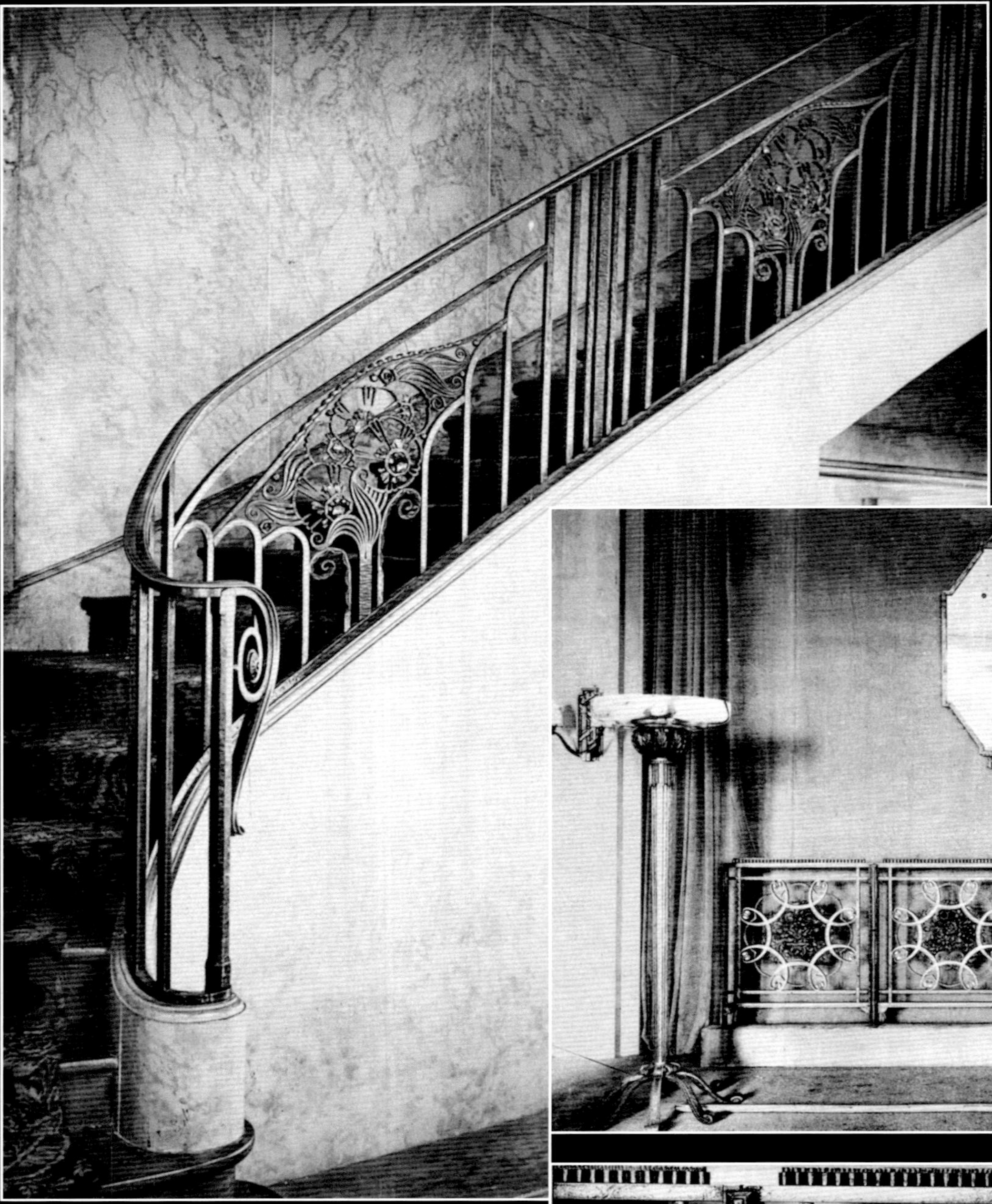
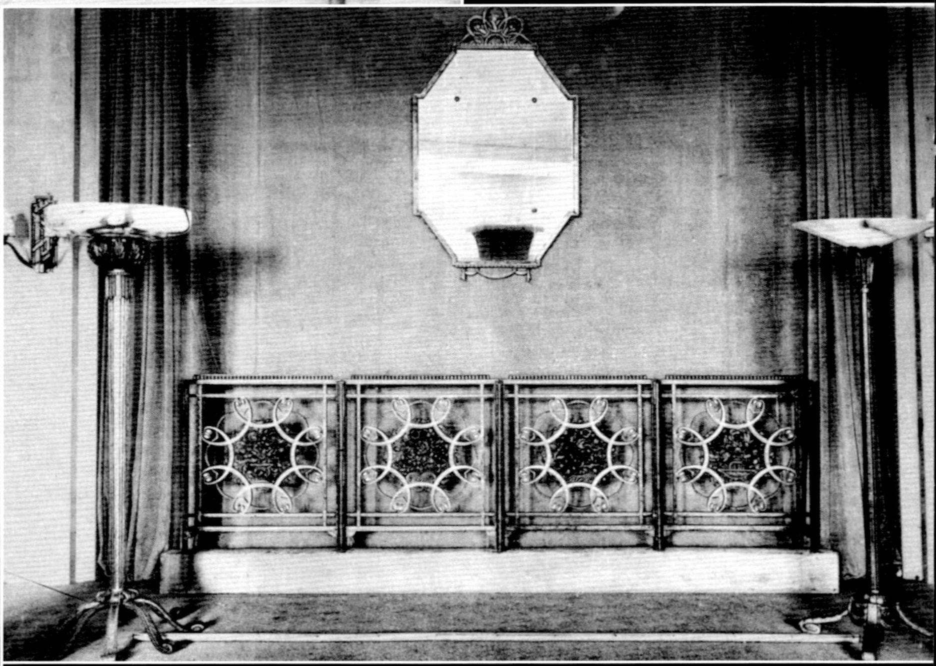
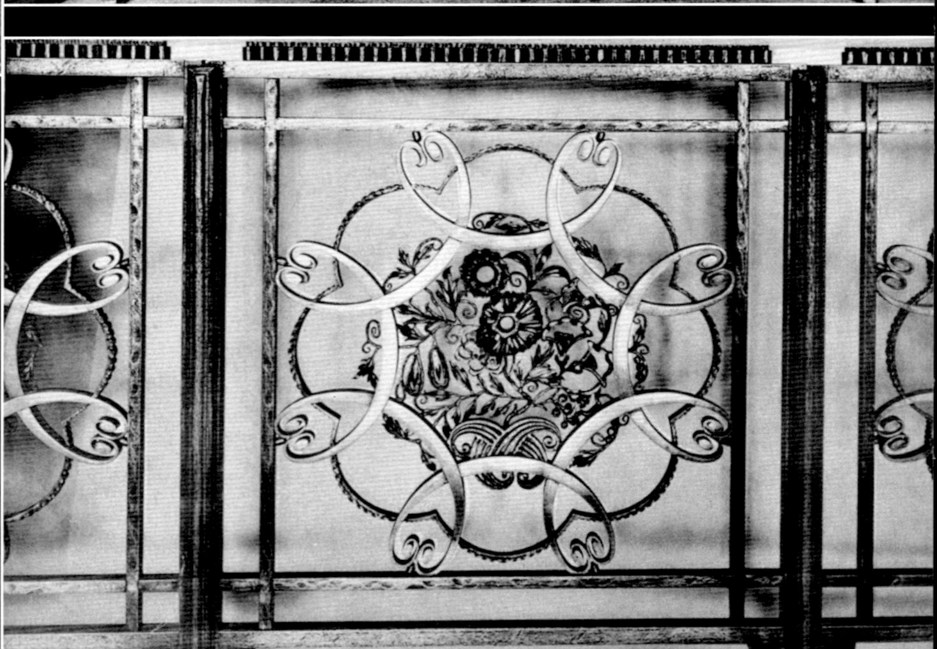

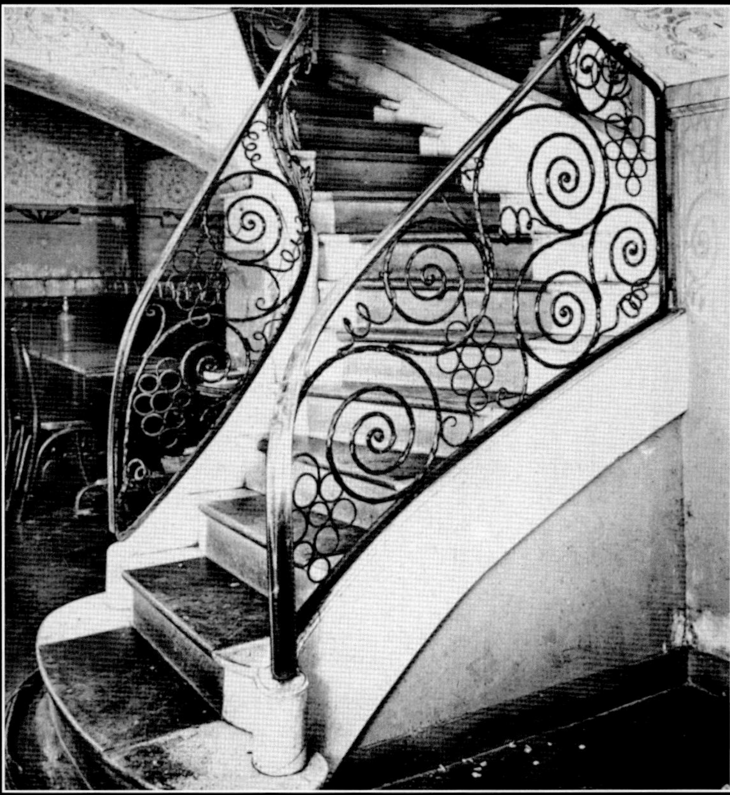

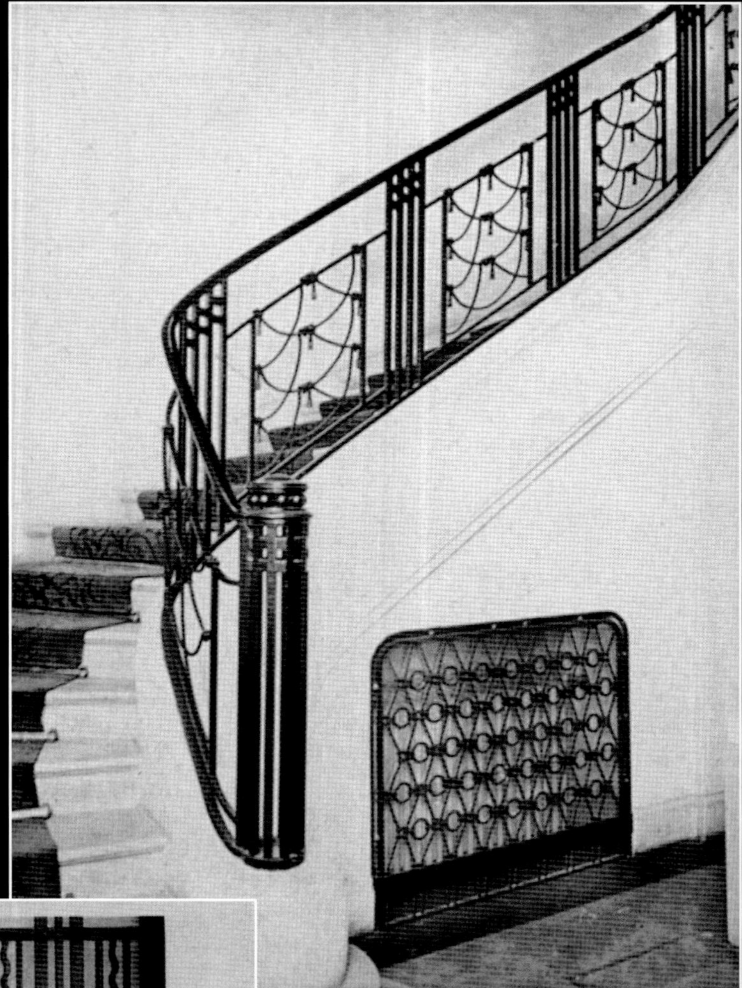

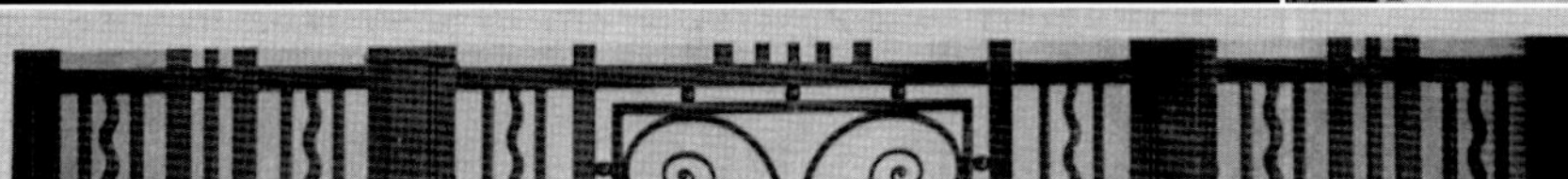

1

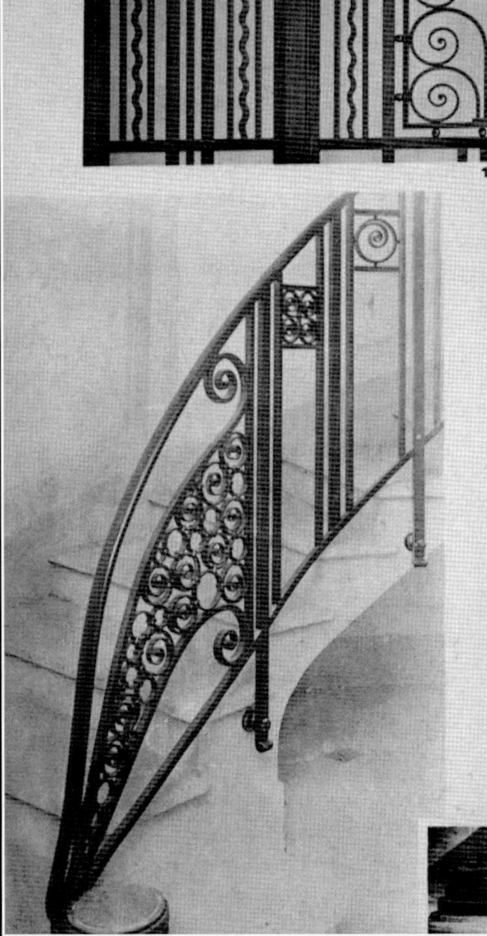

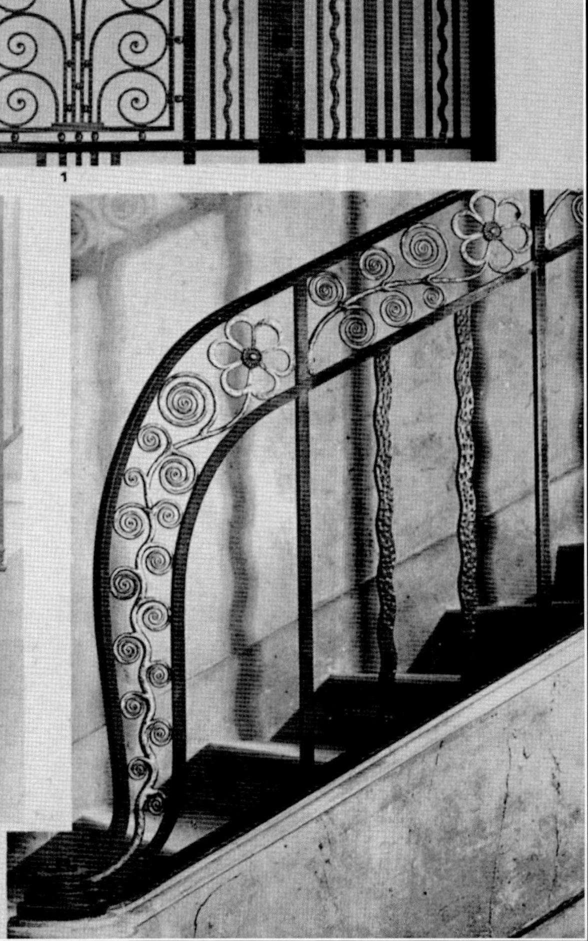

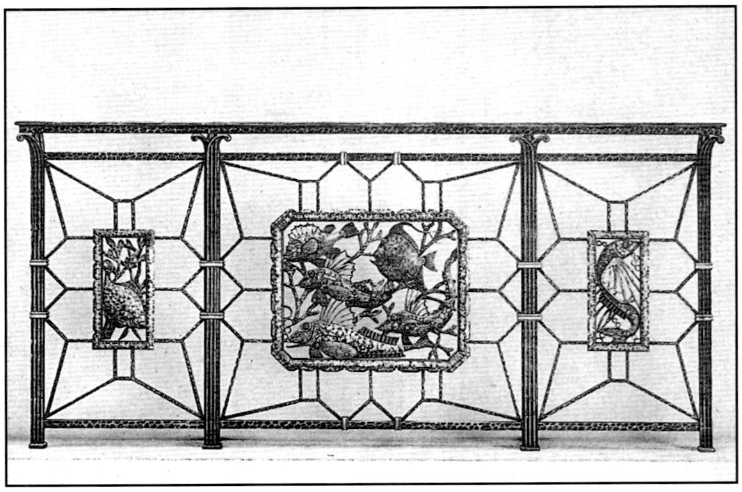

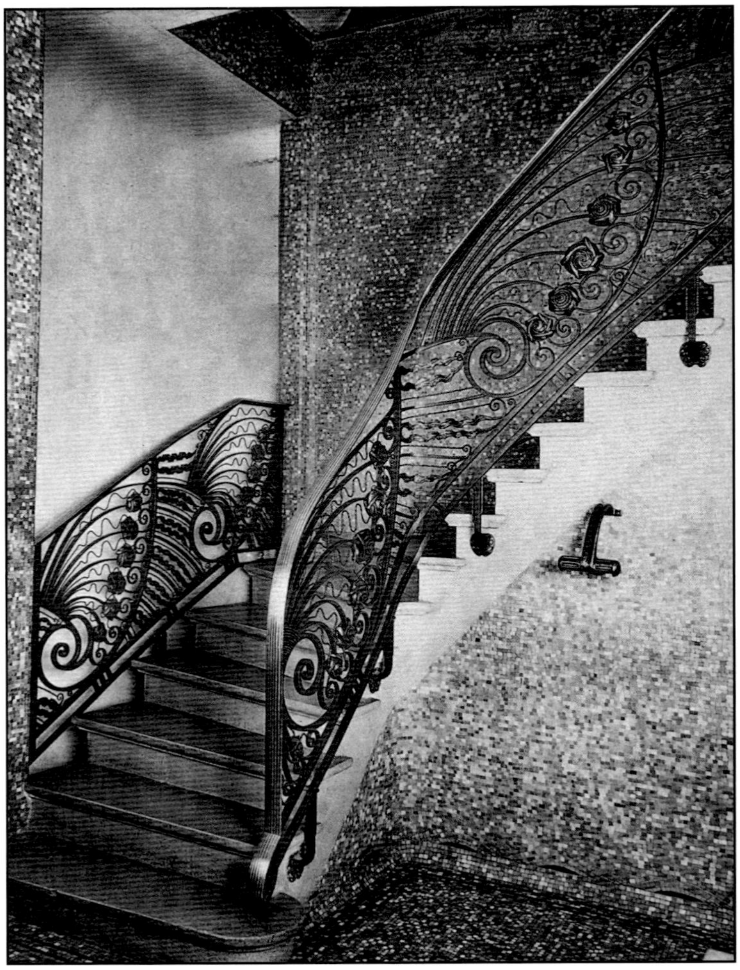

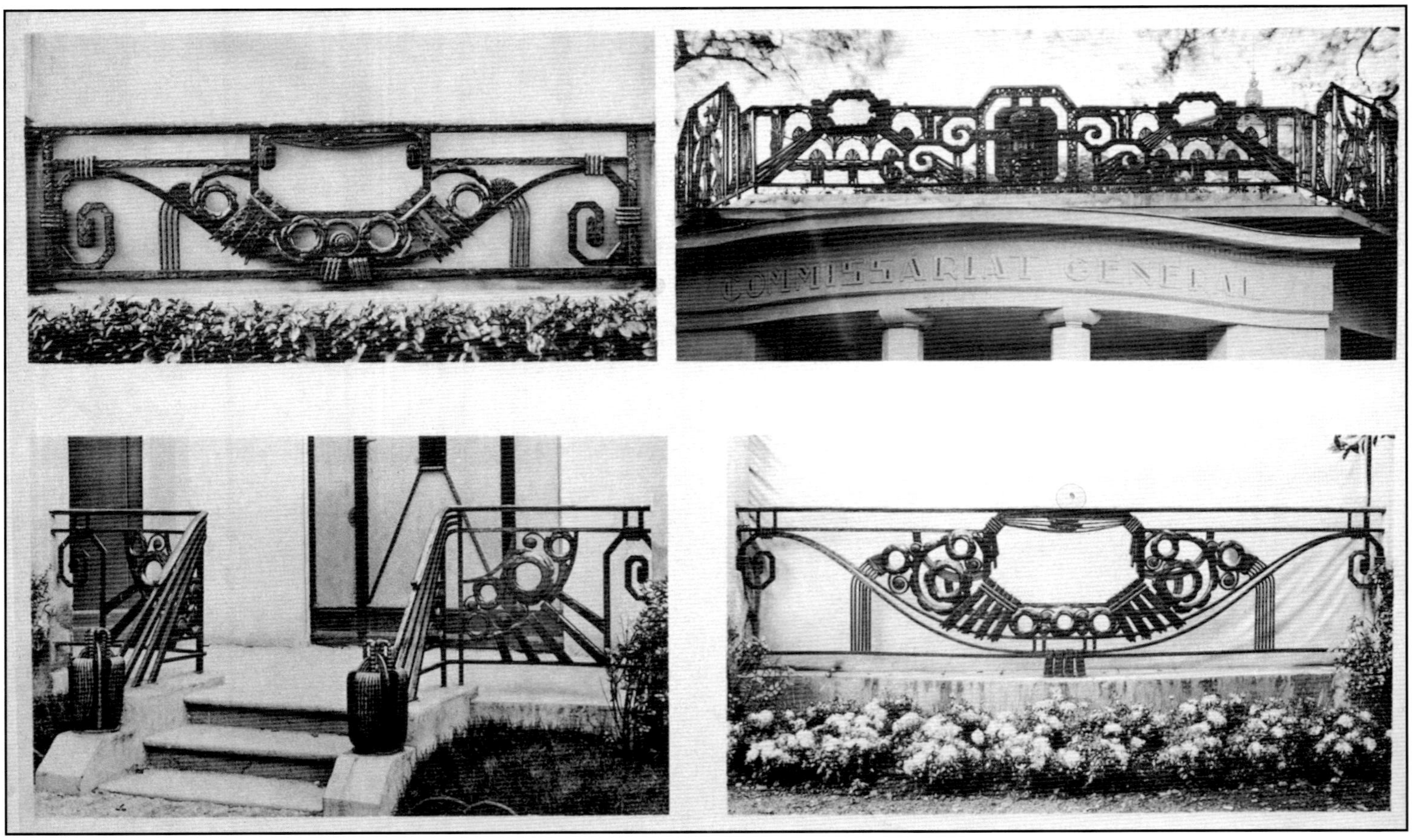

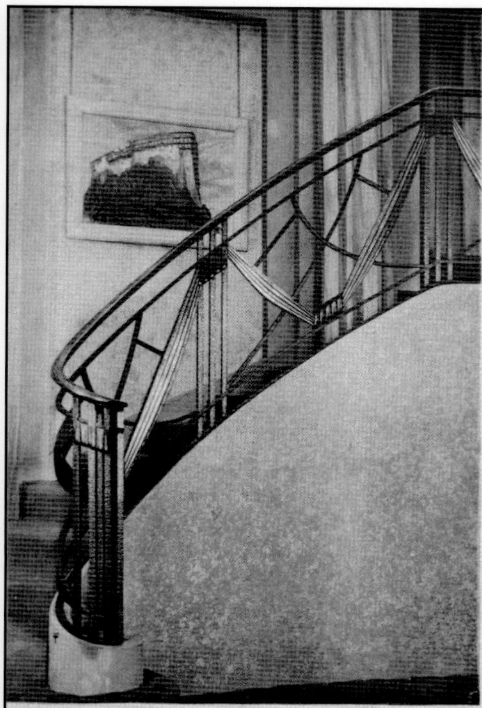

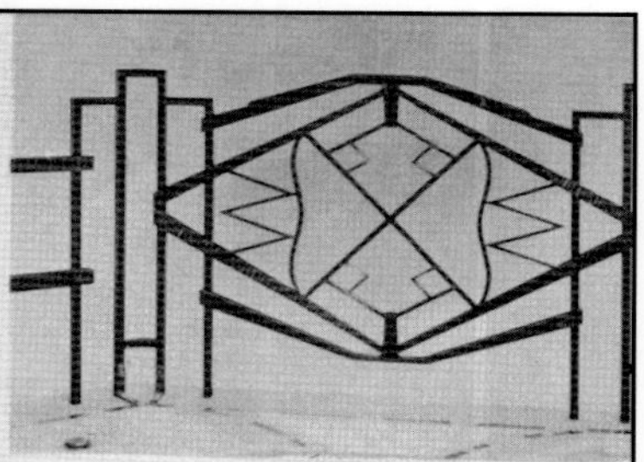

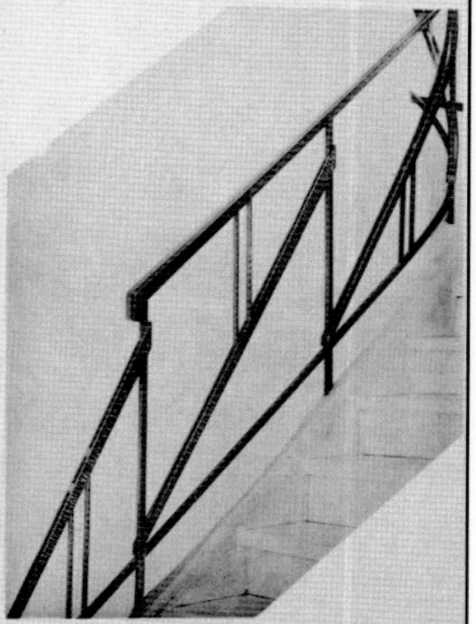

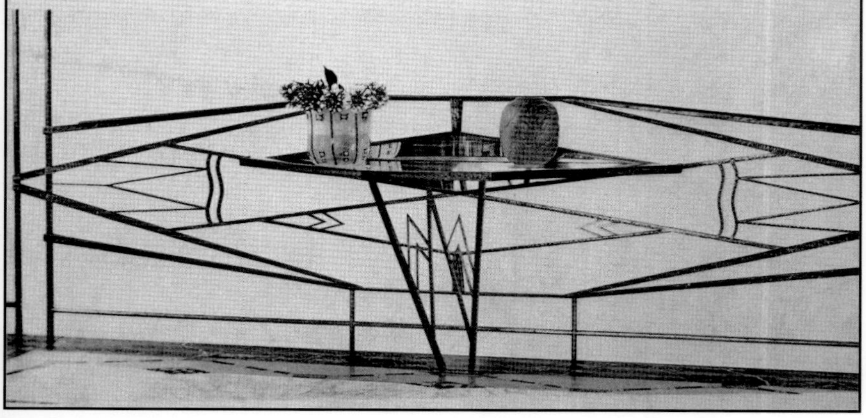

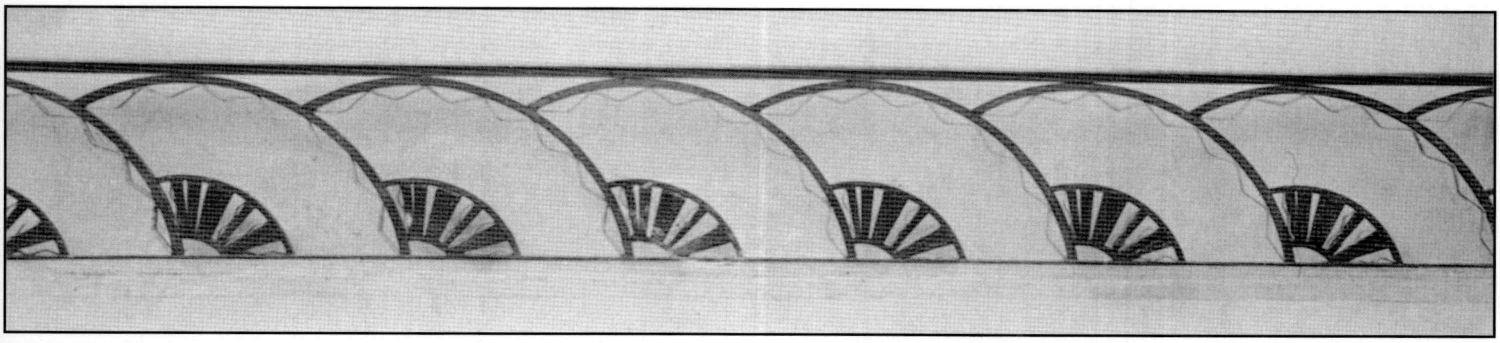

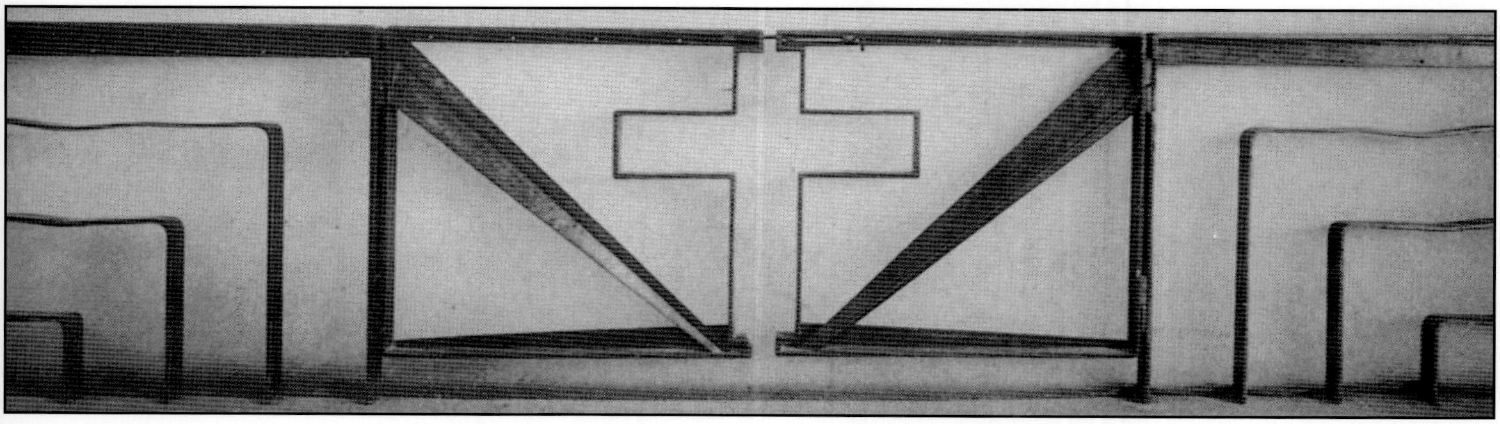

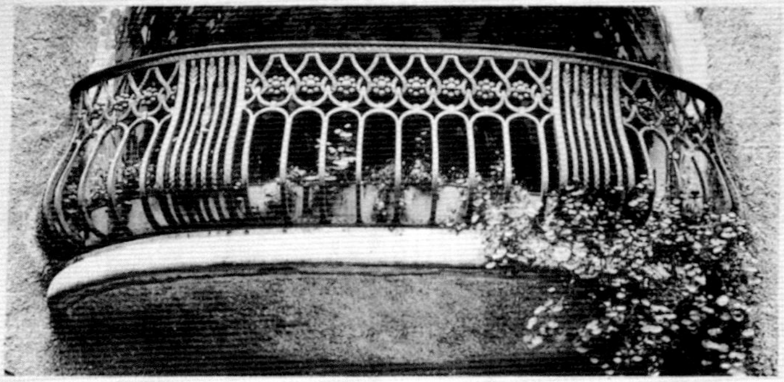
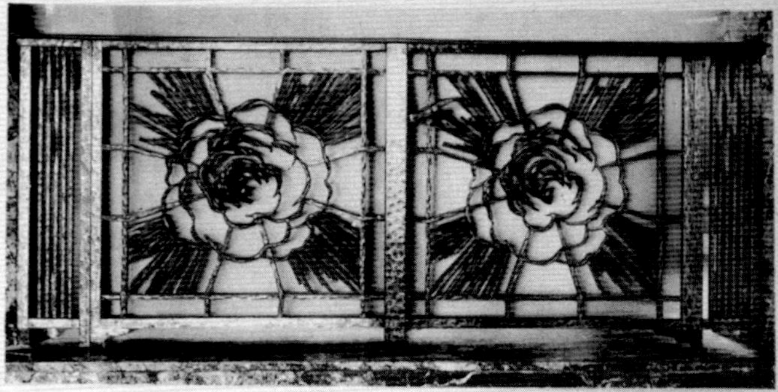
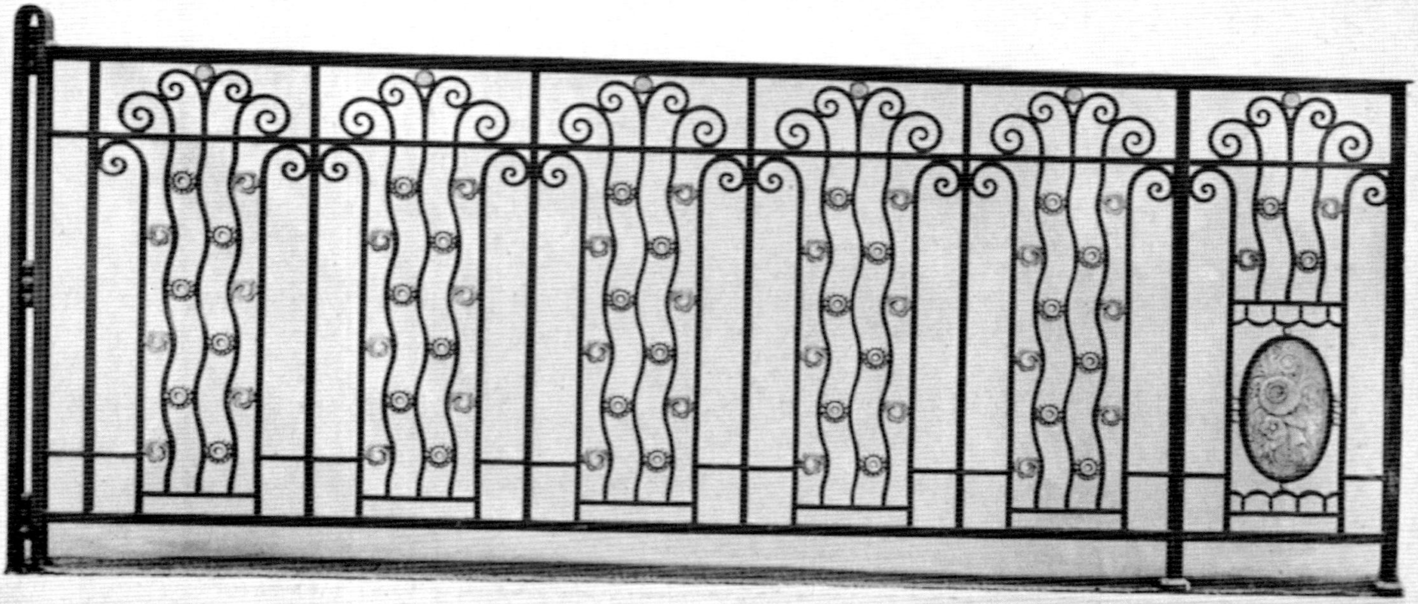
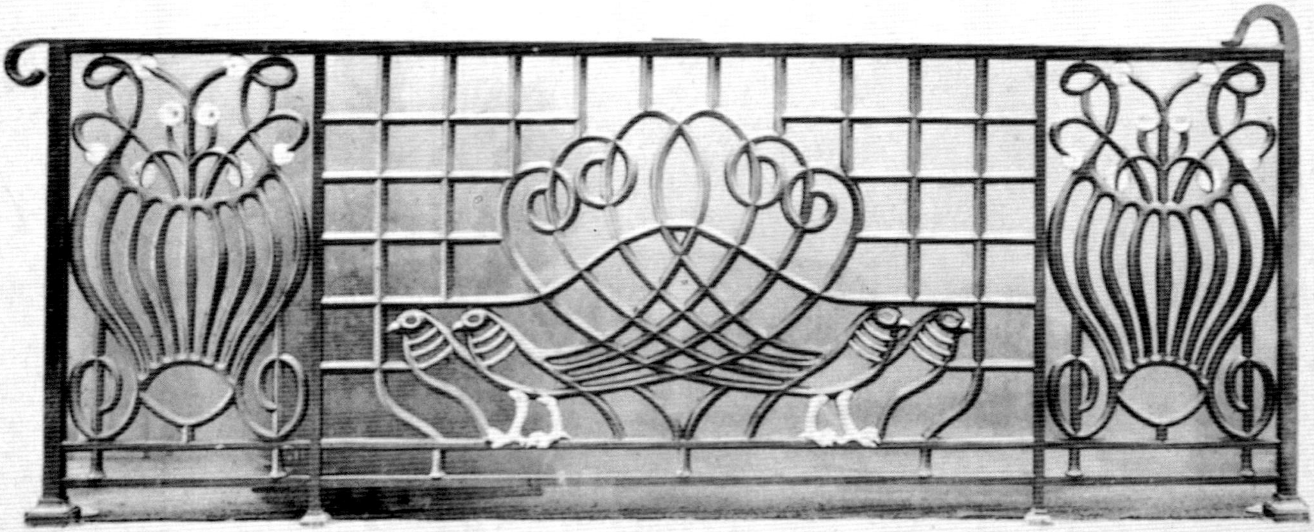

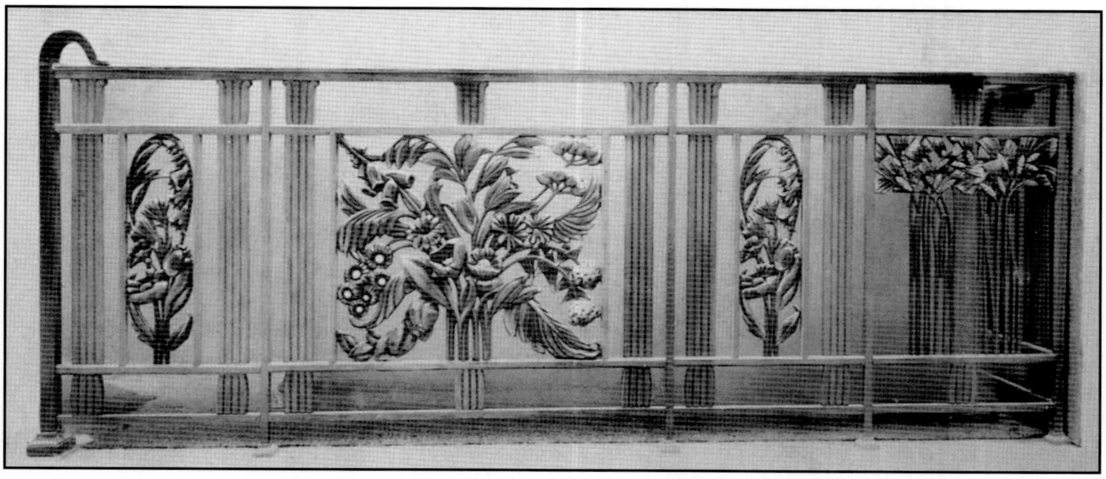

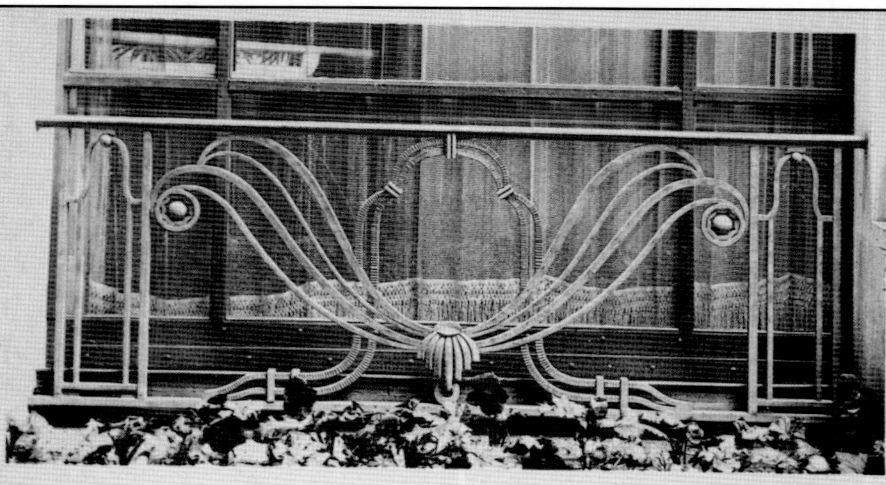

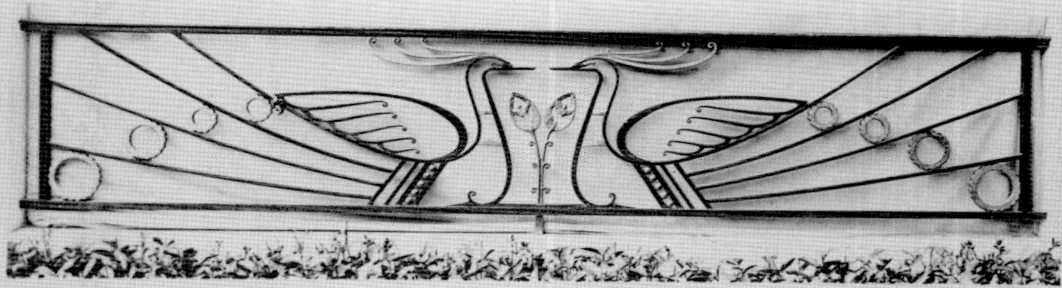

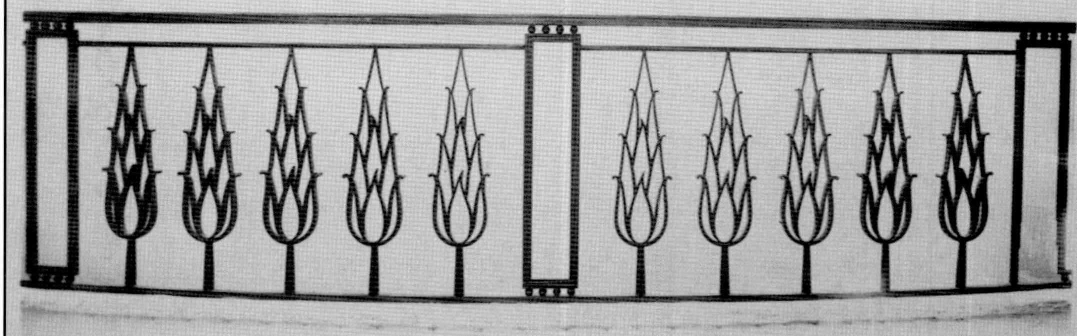

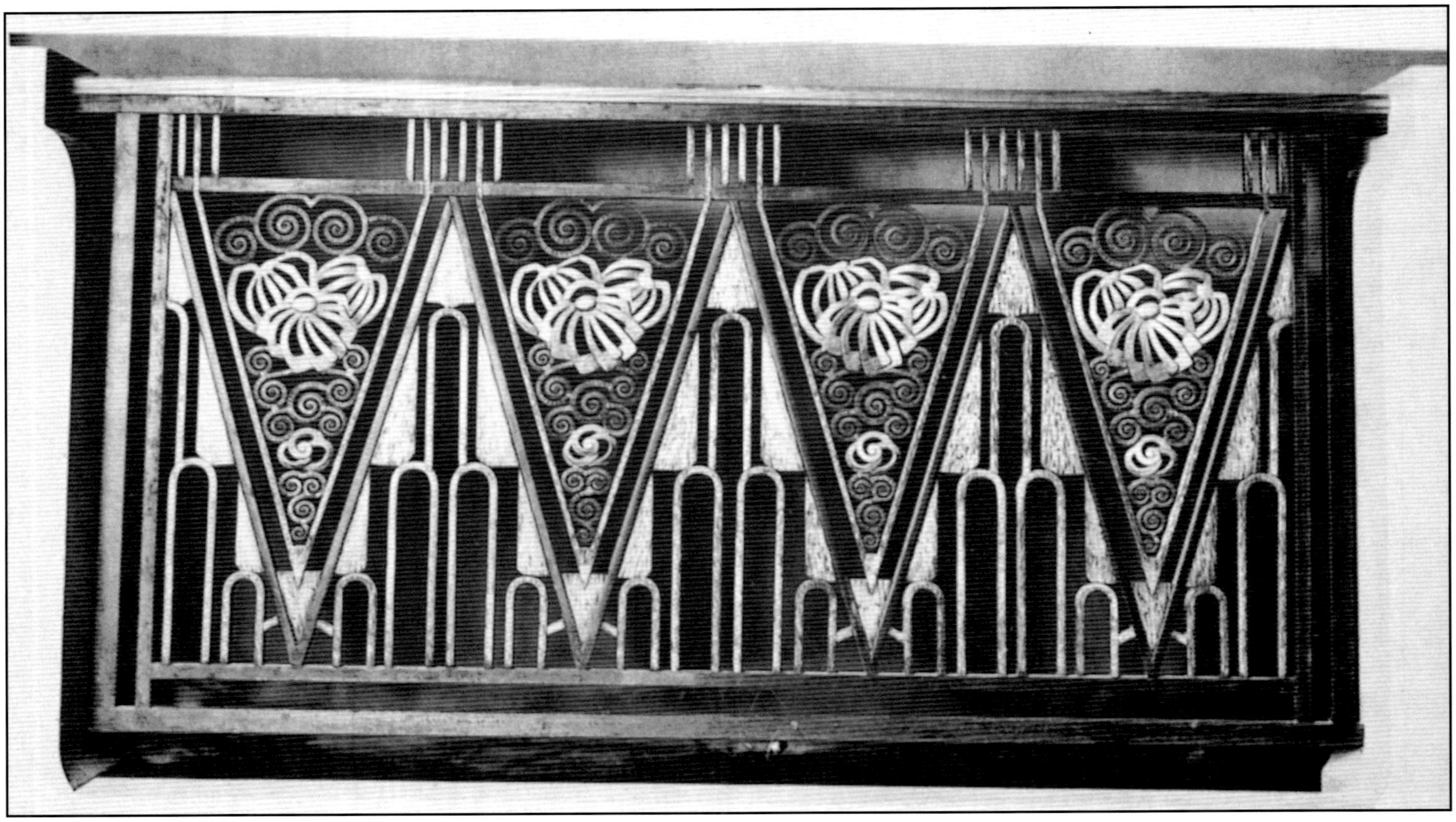

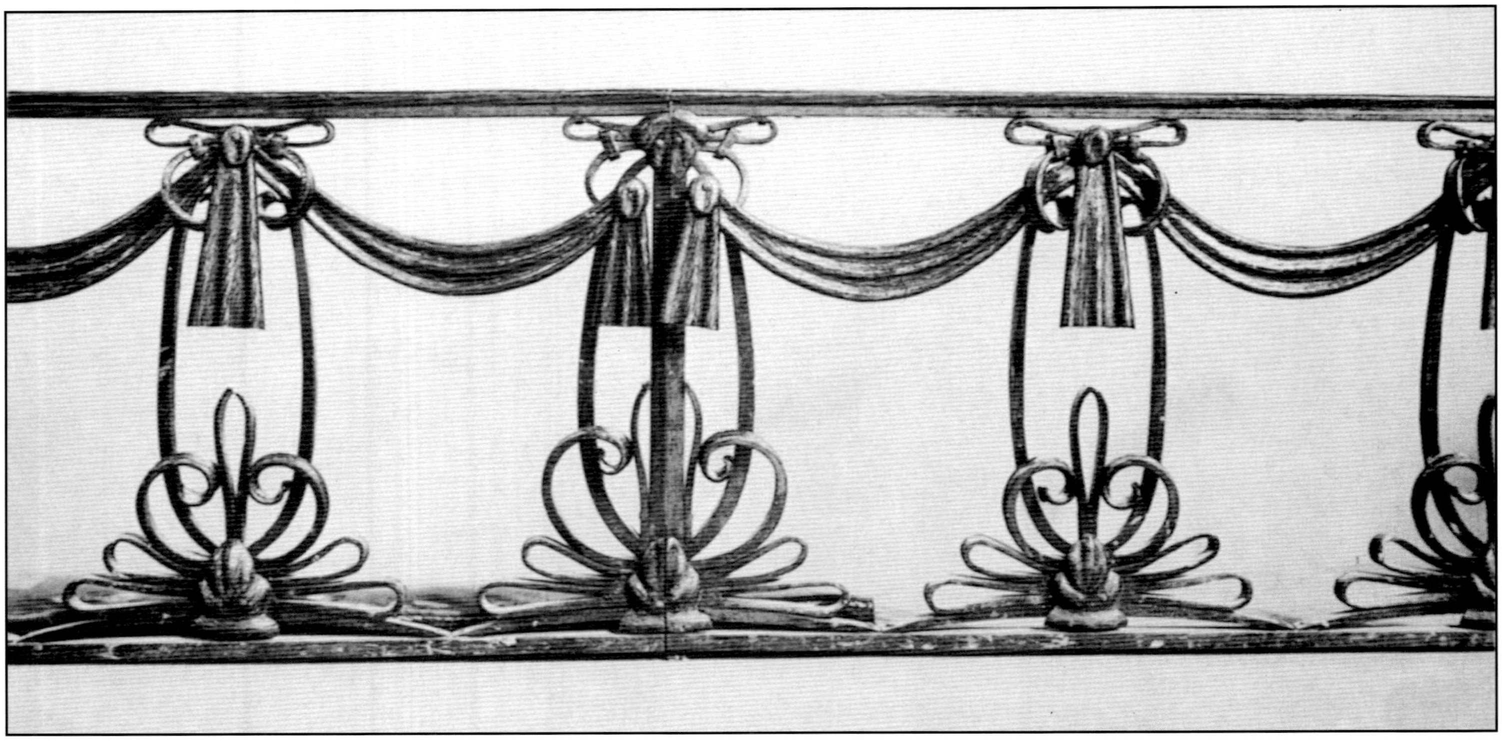

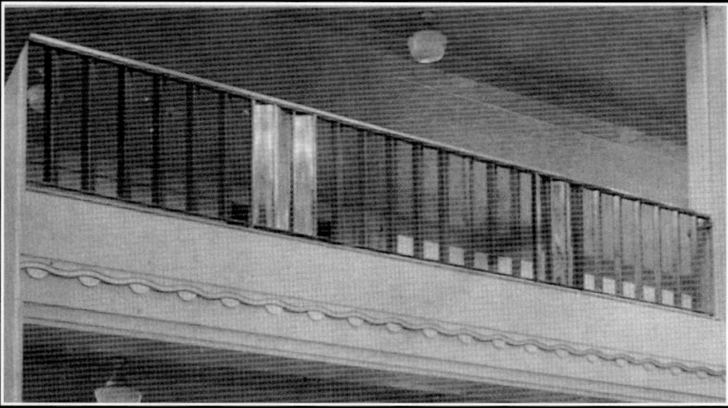

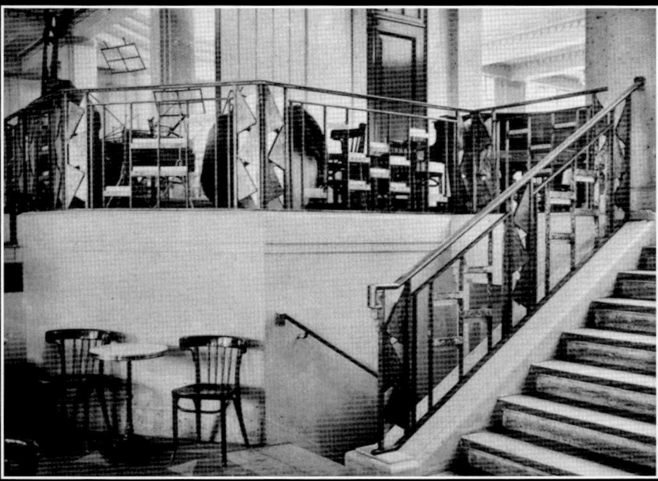

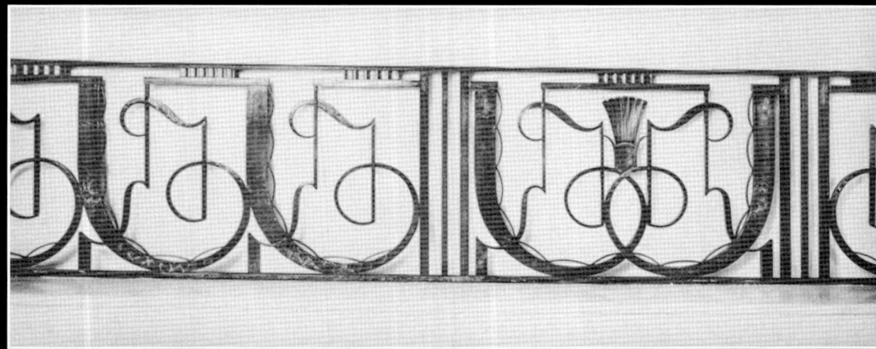

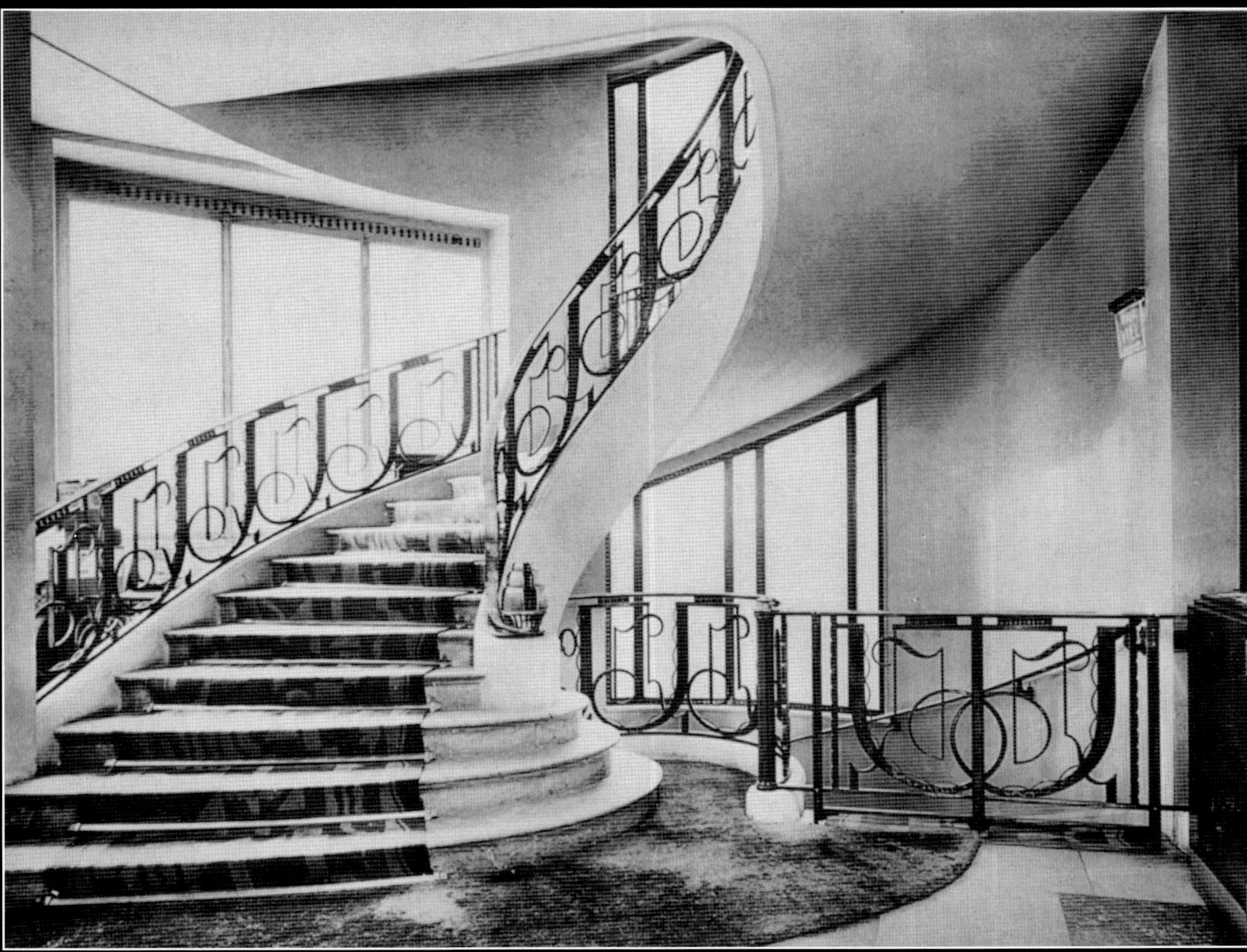

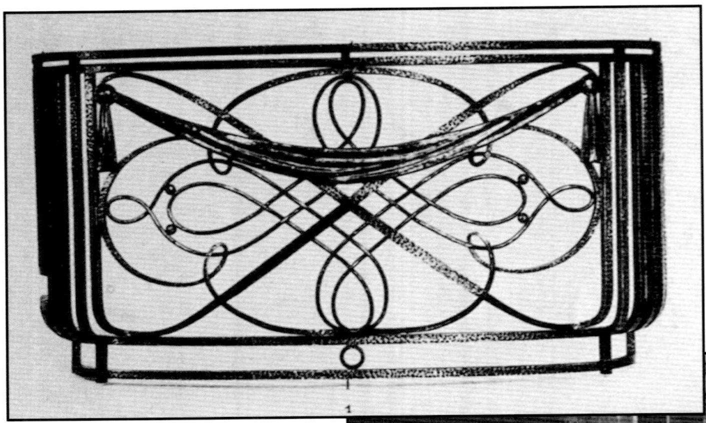

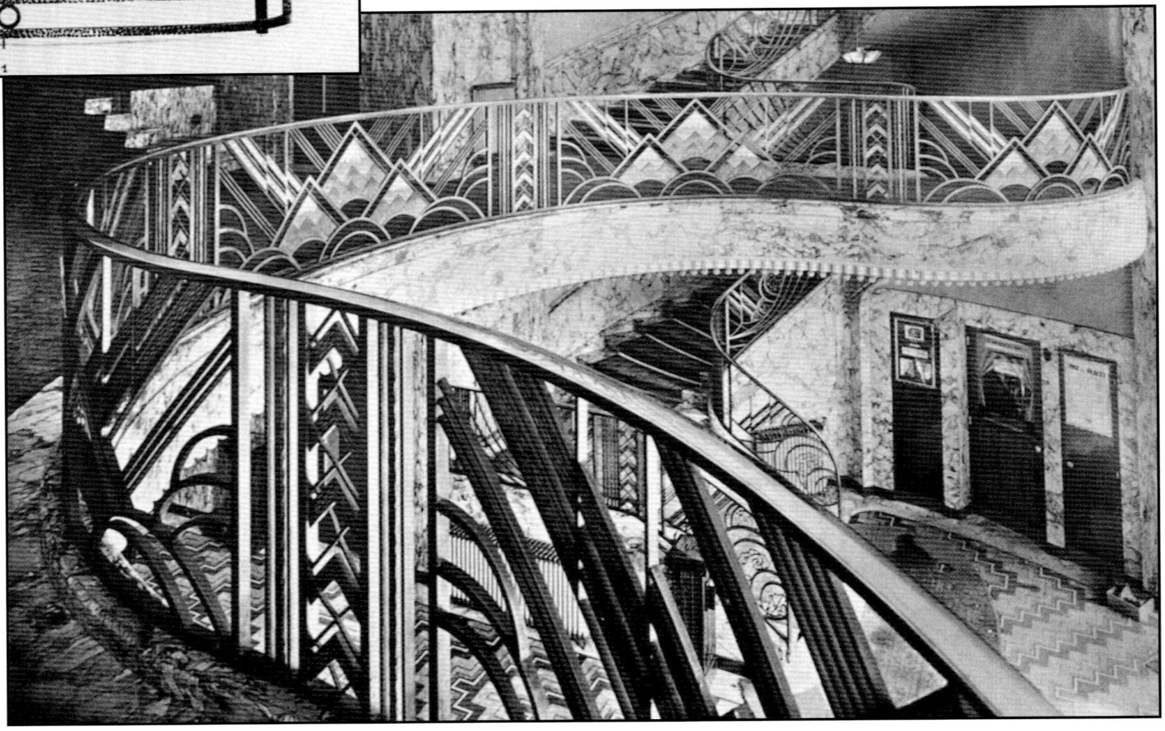

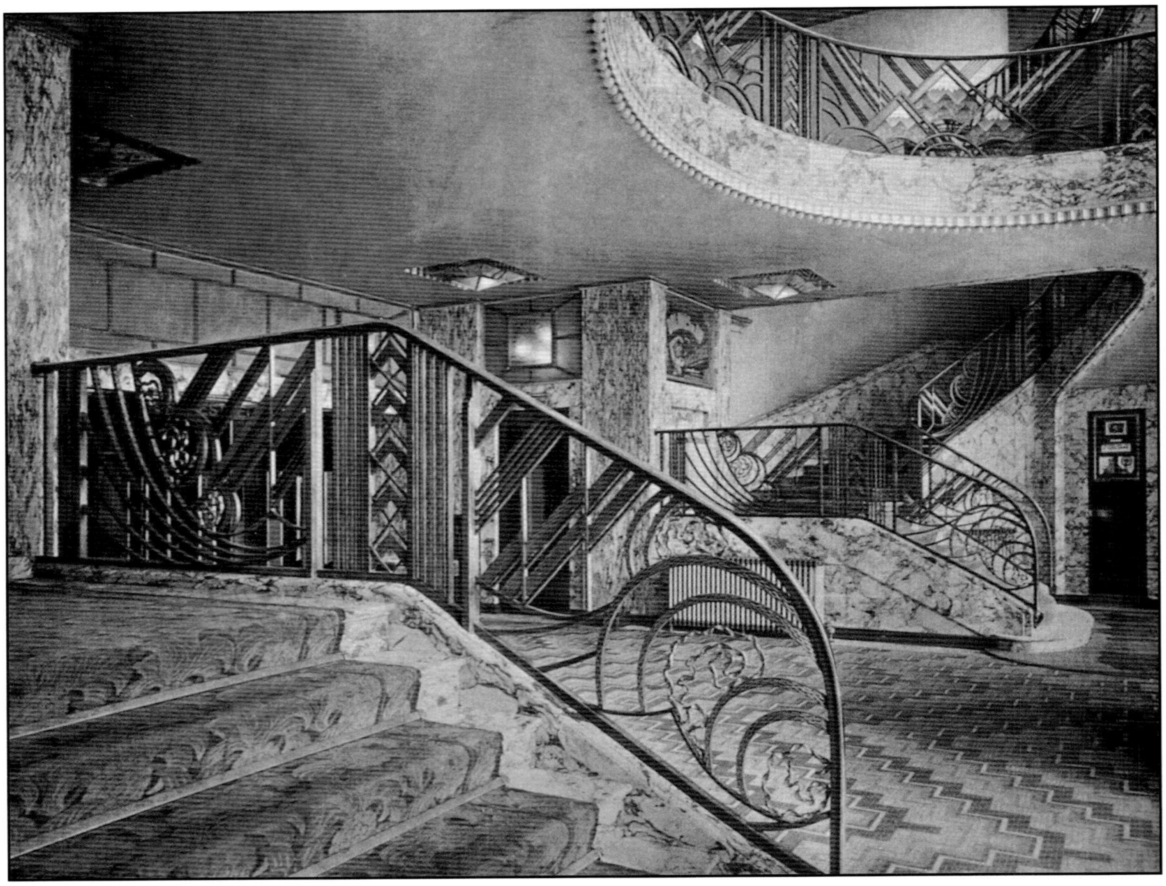

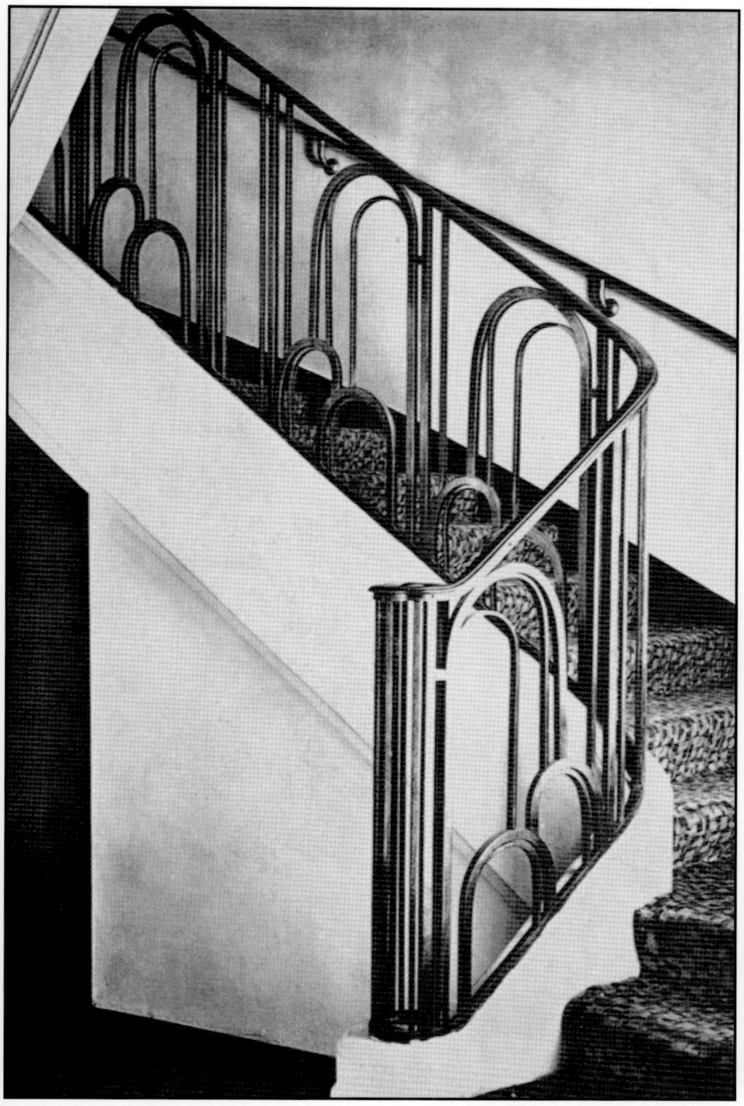

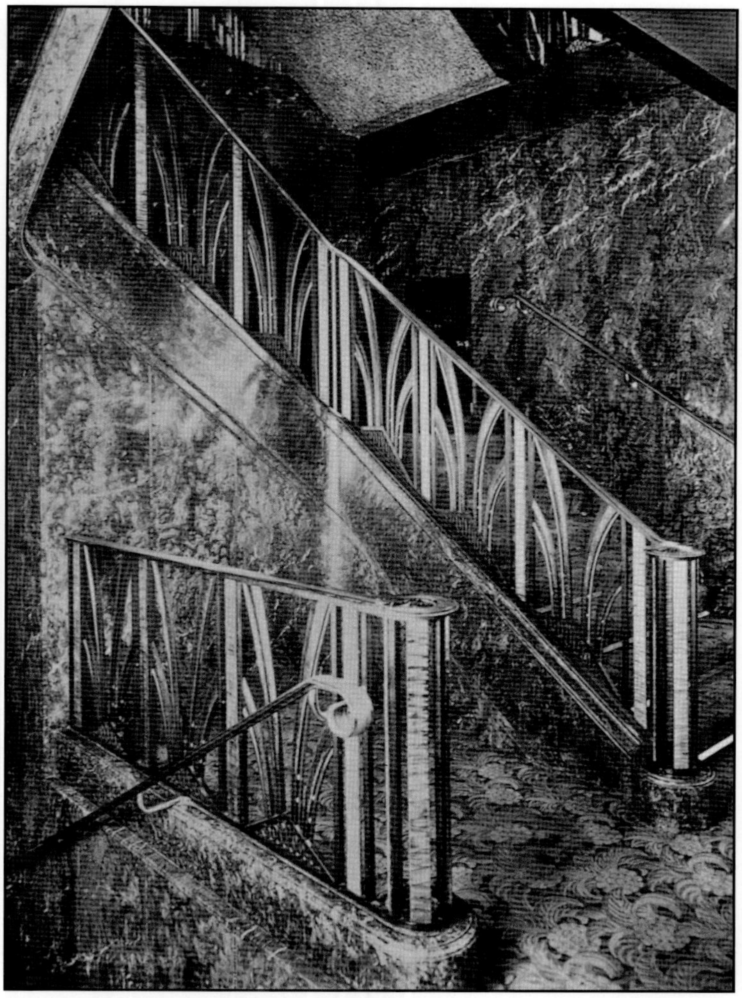

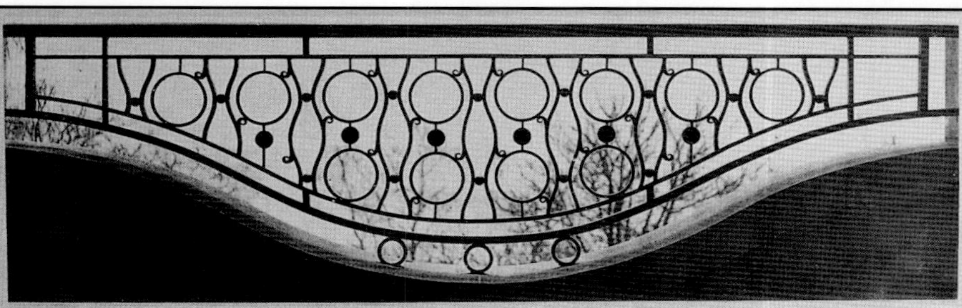

1

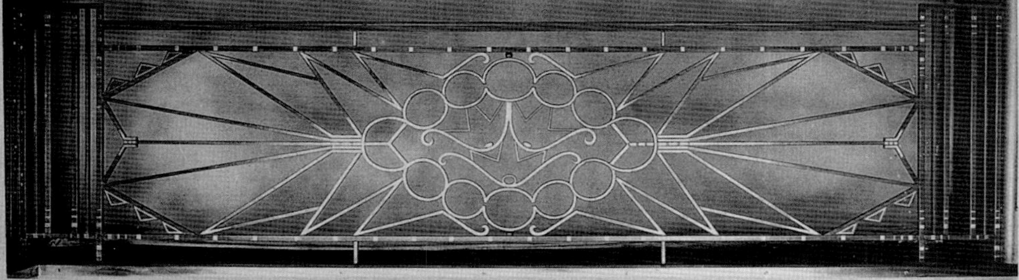

2

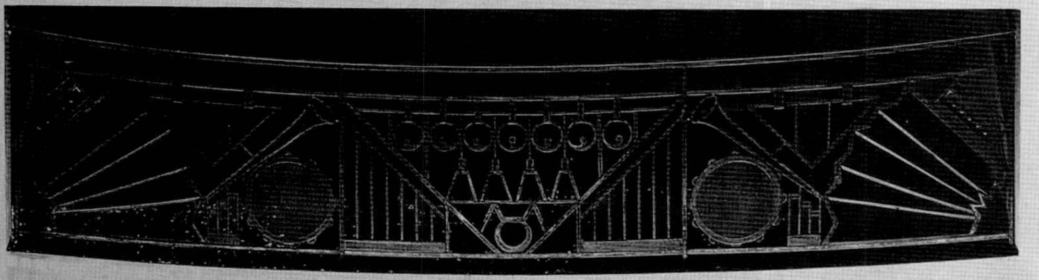

3

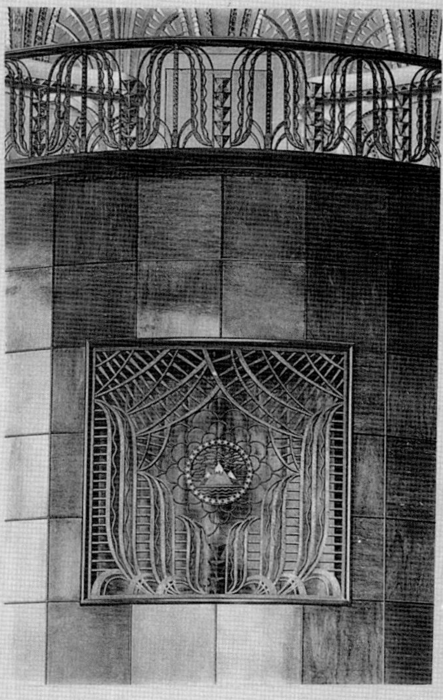

4

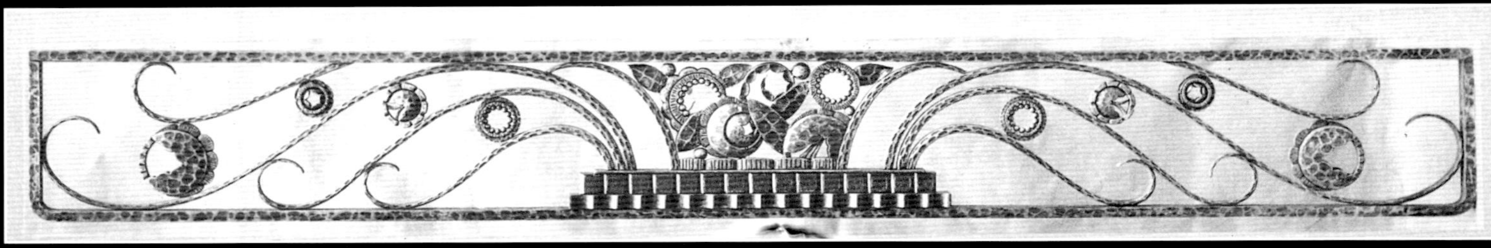

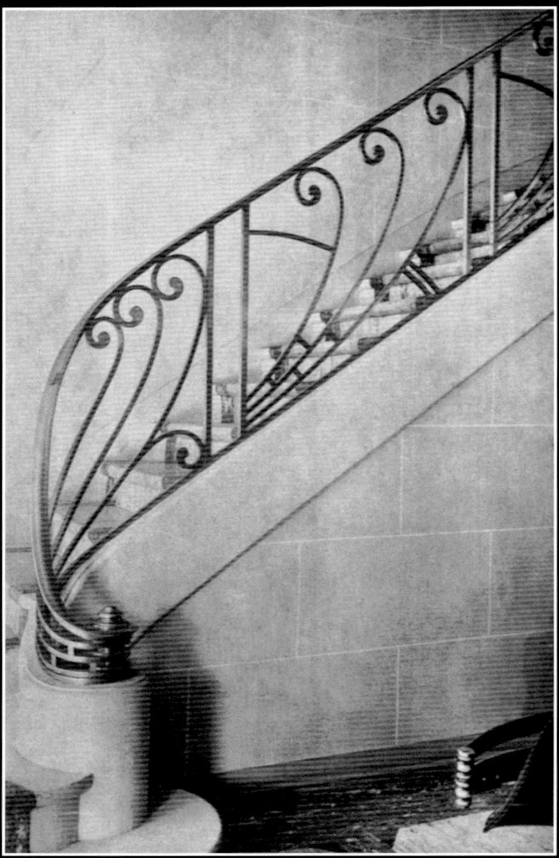

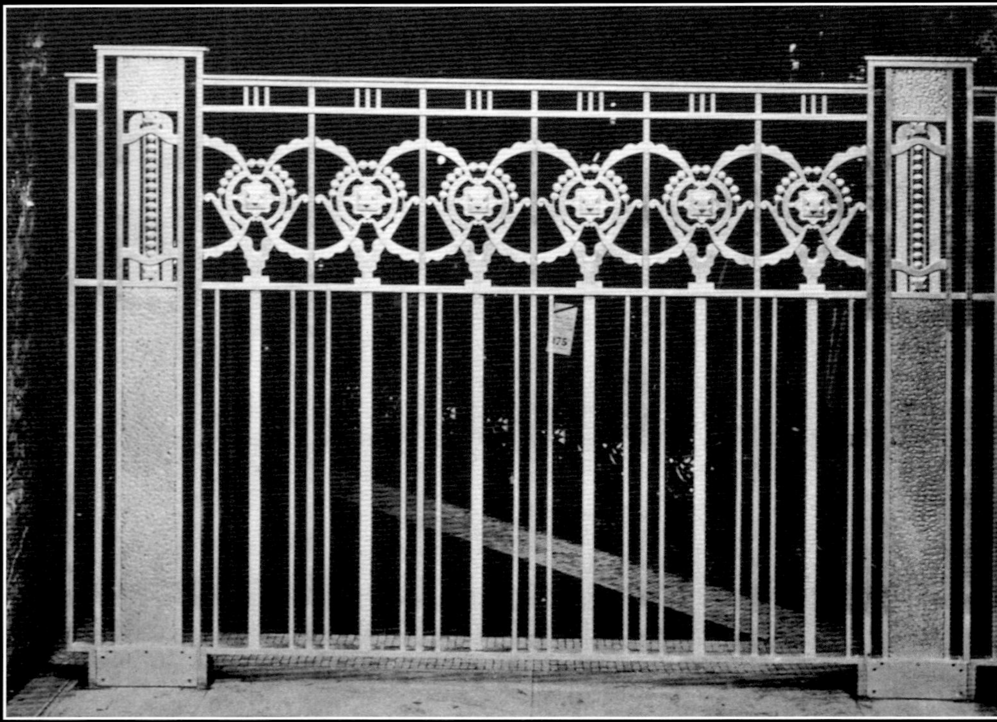

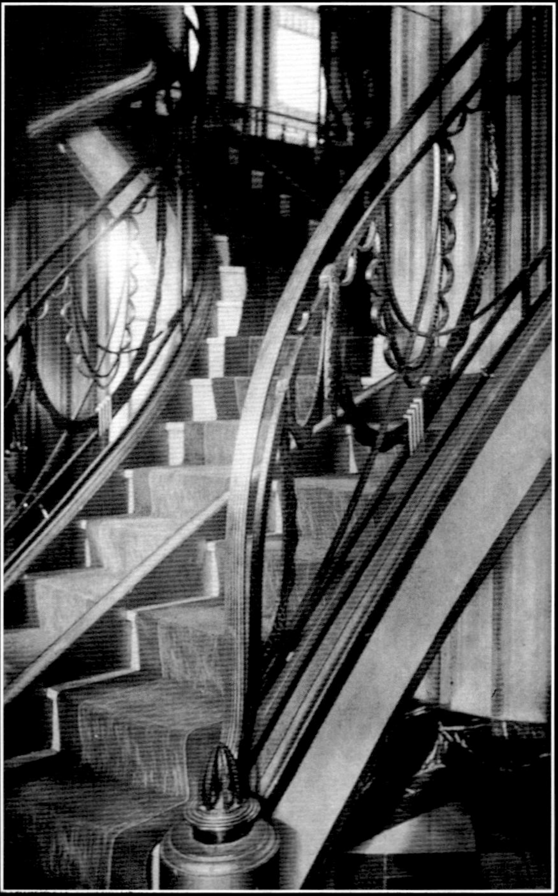

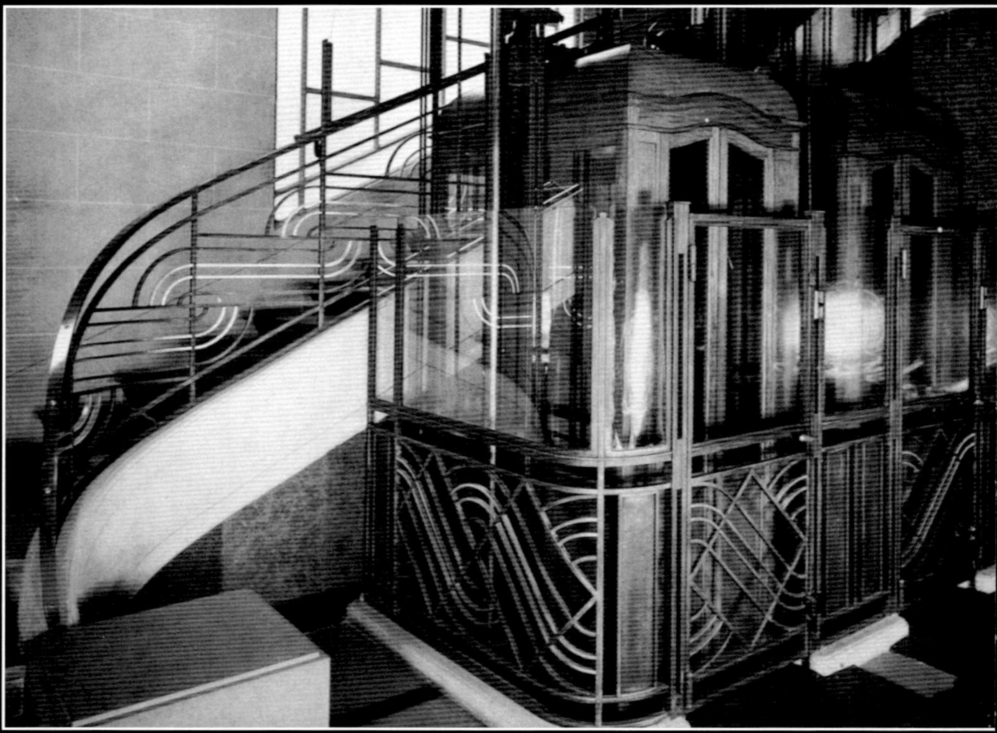

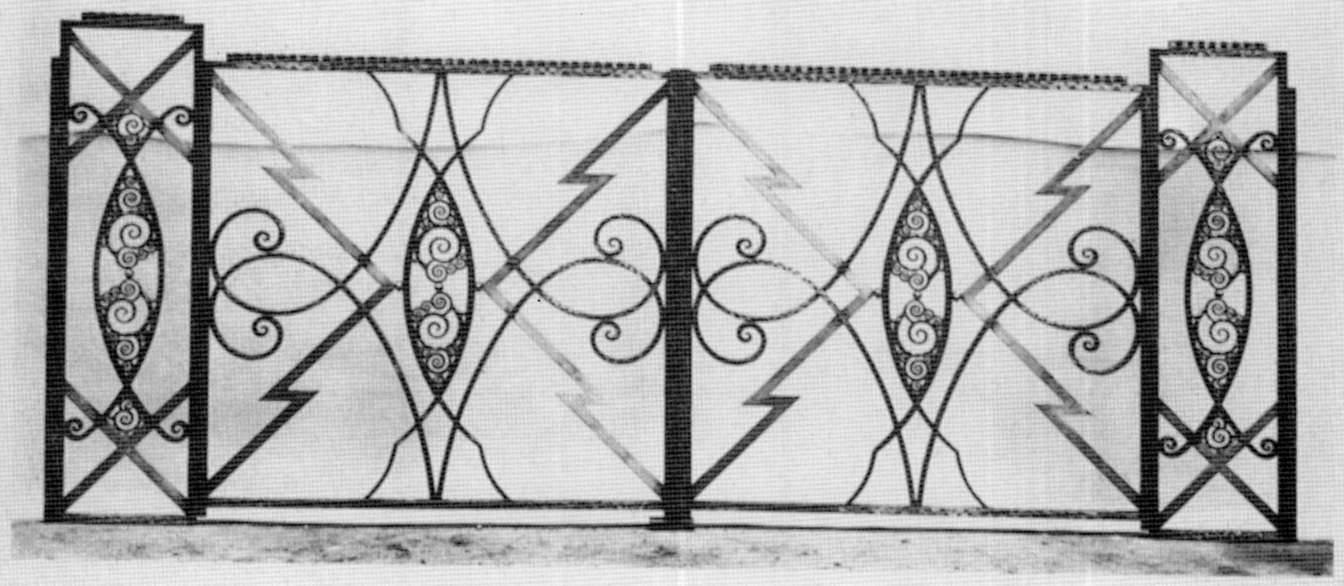

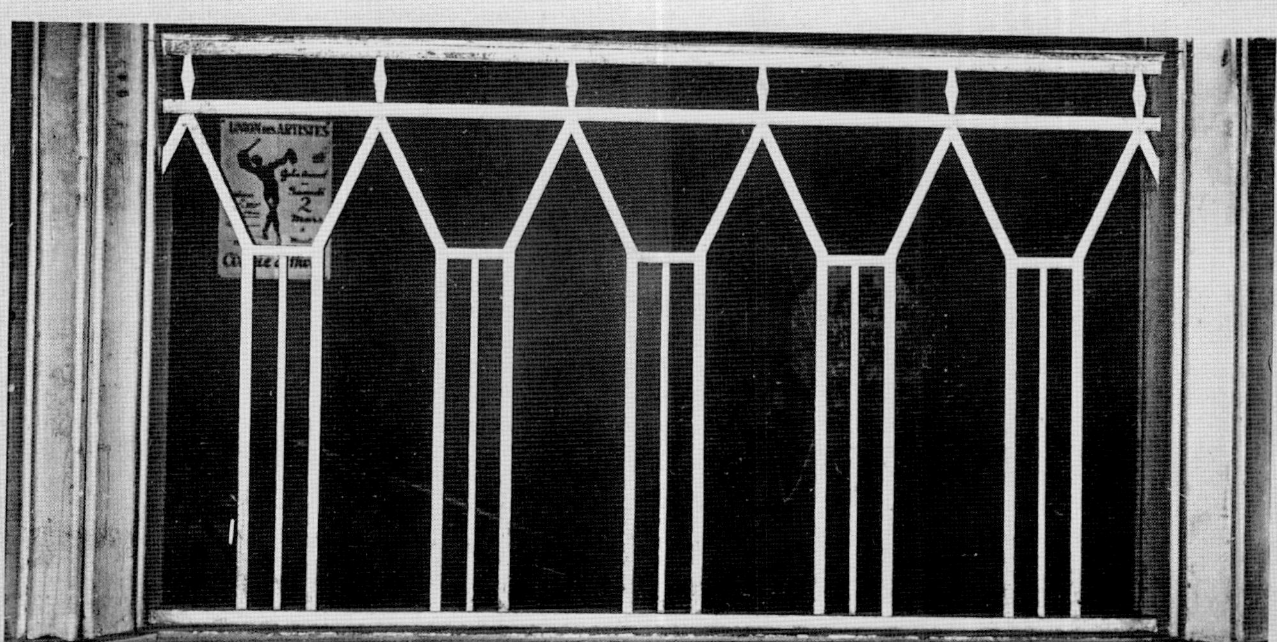
UNION des ARTISTES
2

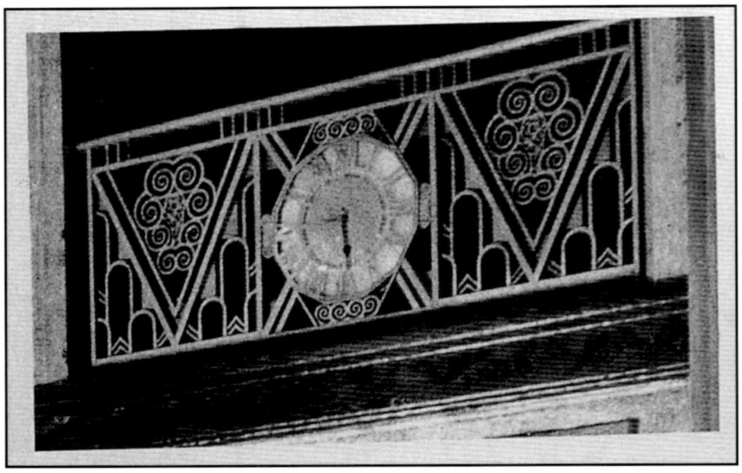

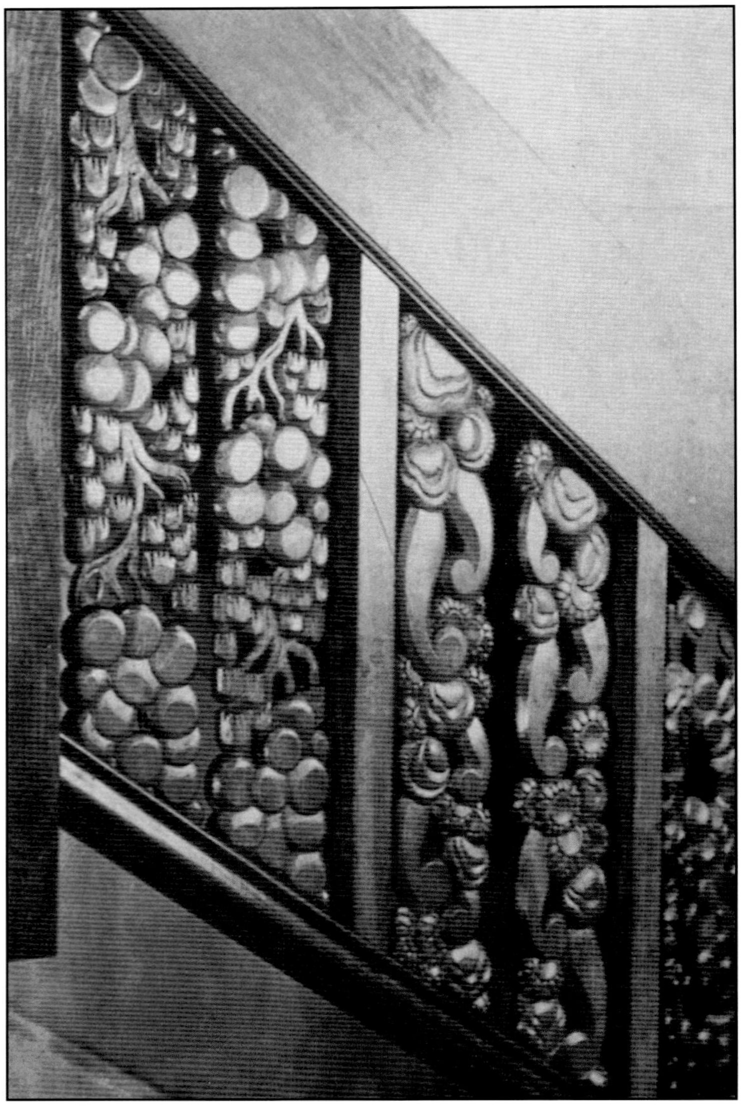

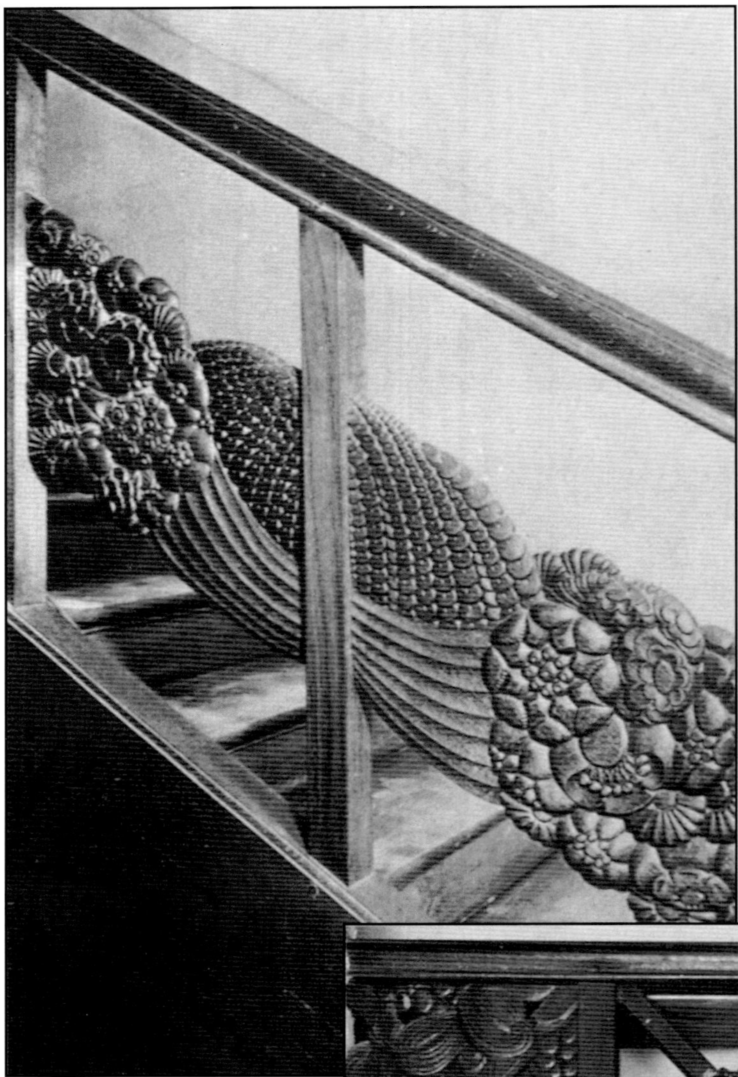

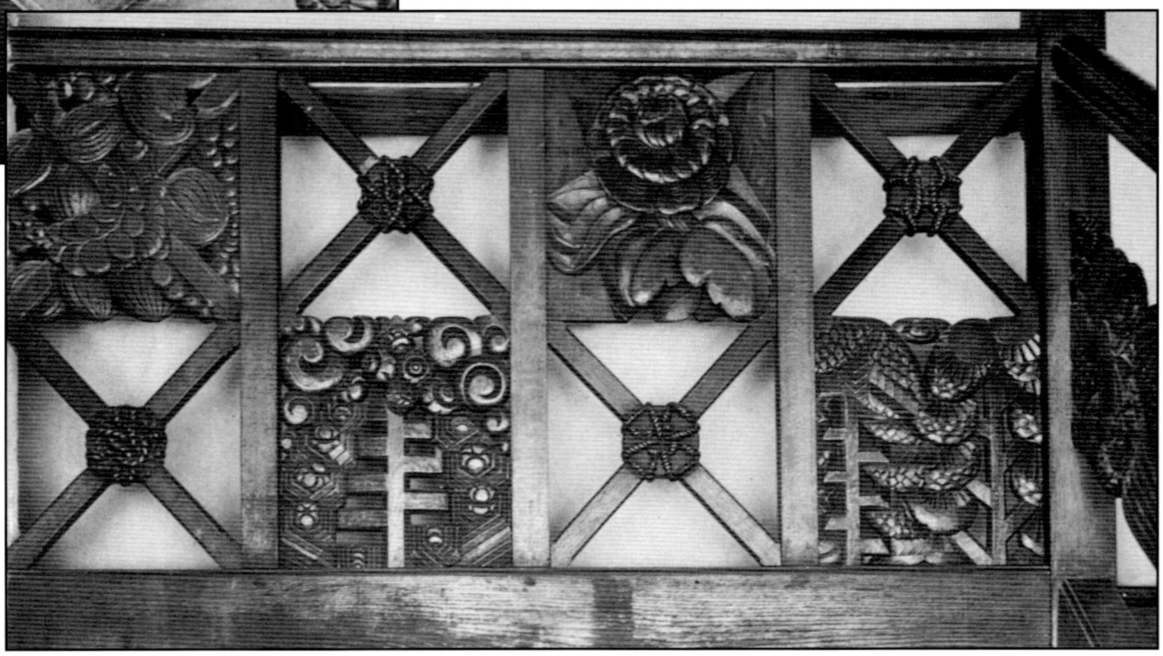

Light Fixtures

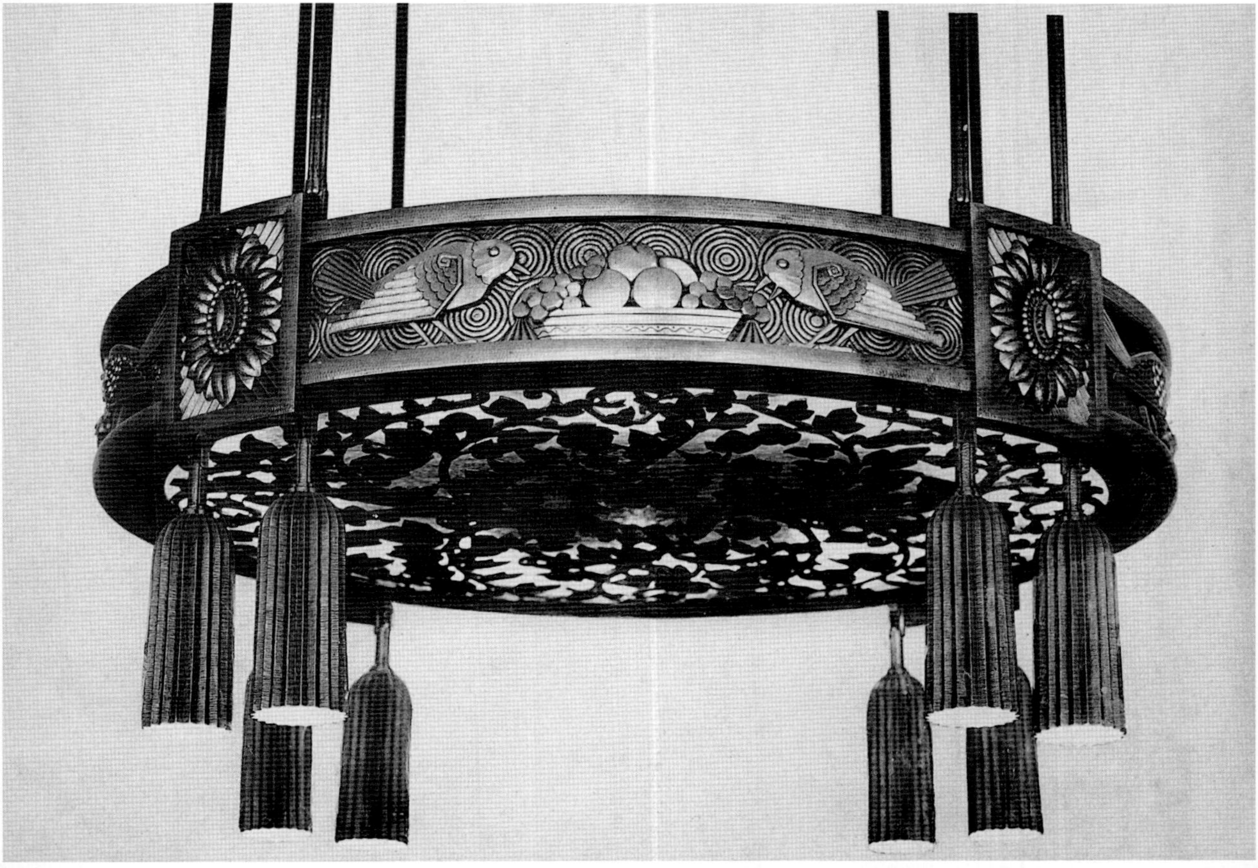

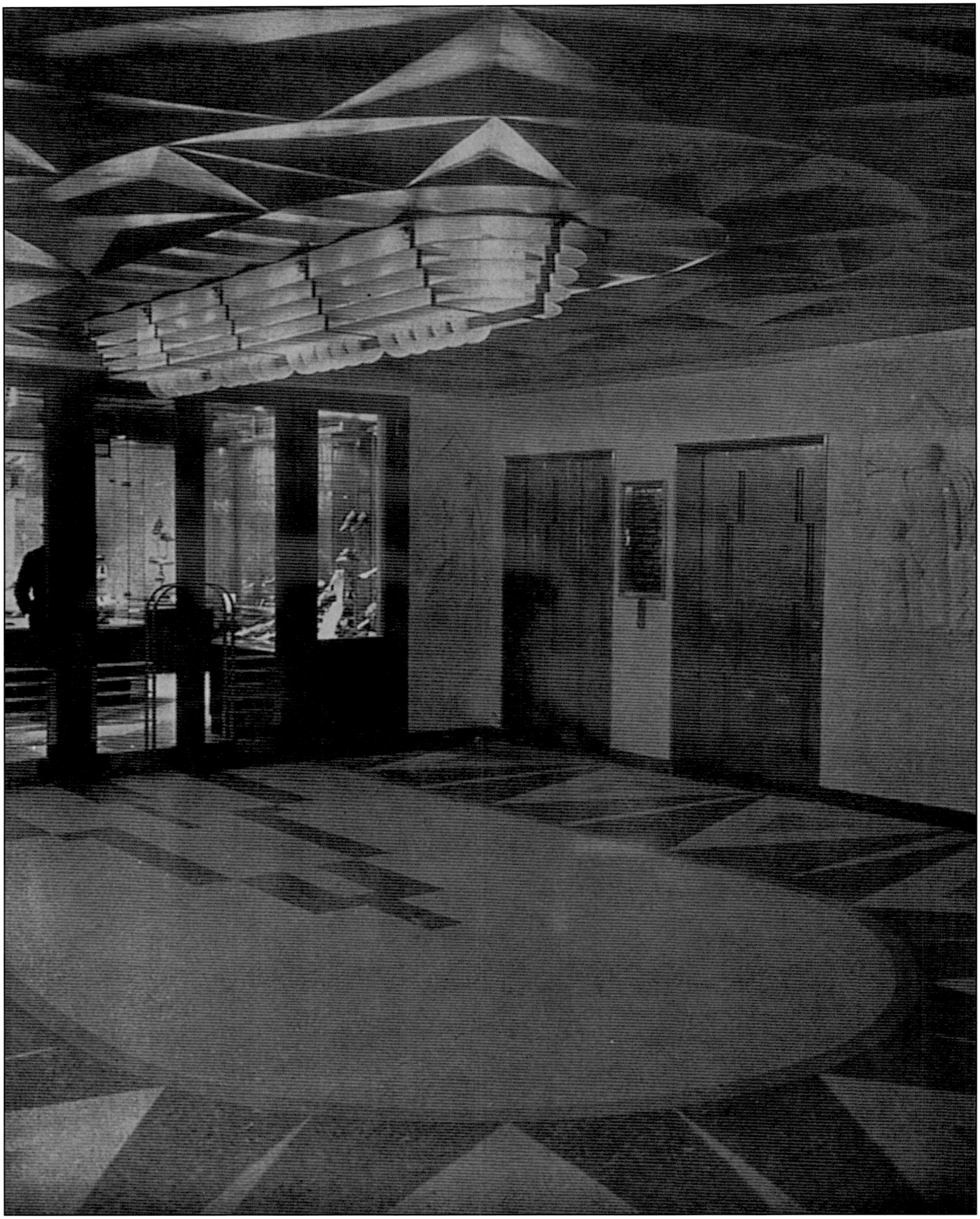

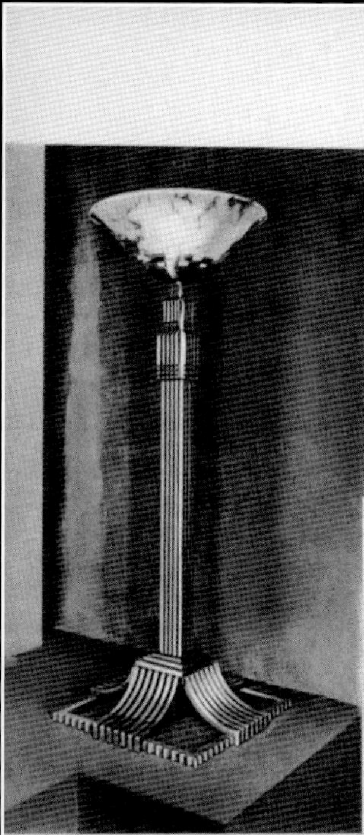

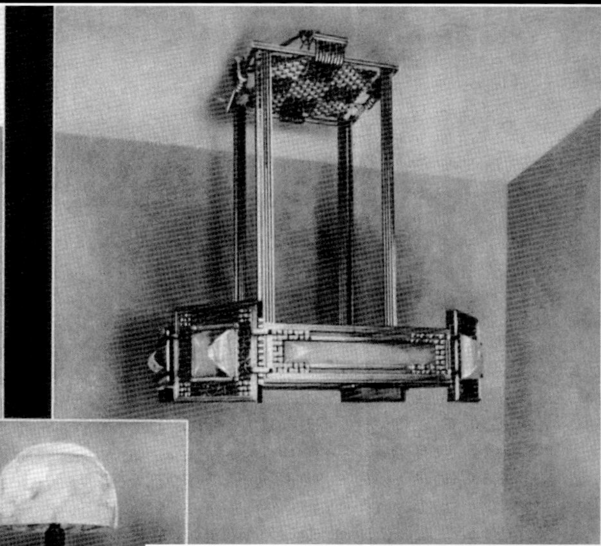

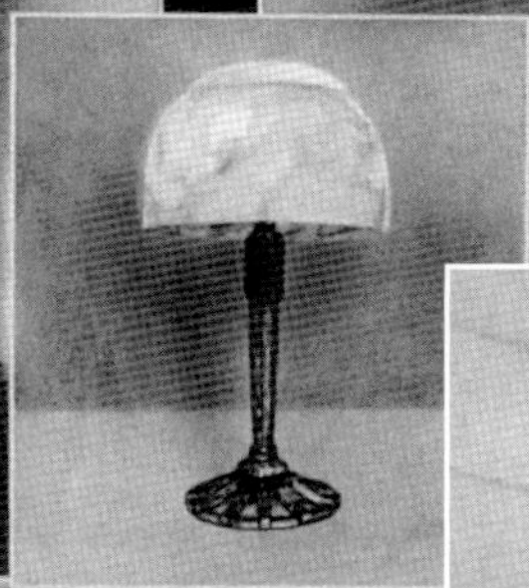

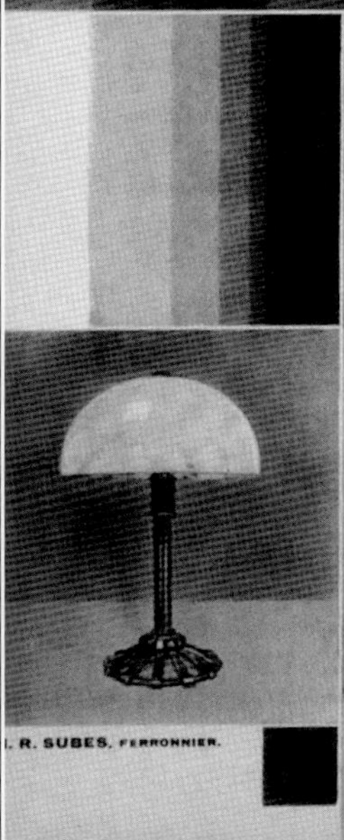
R. SUBES, FERRONNIER.

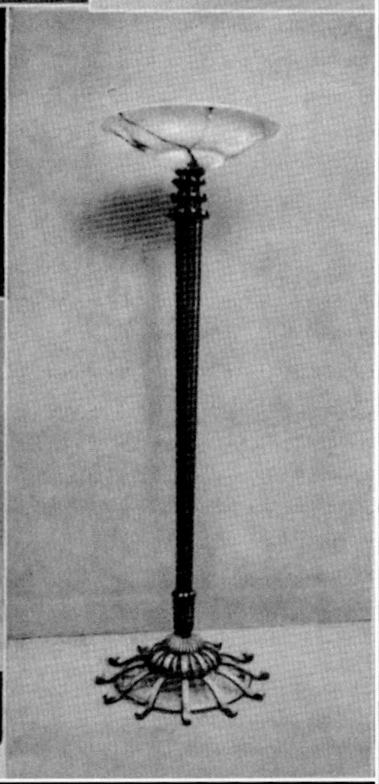

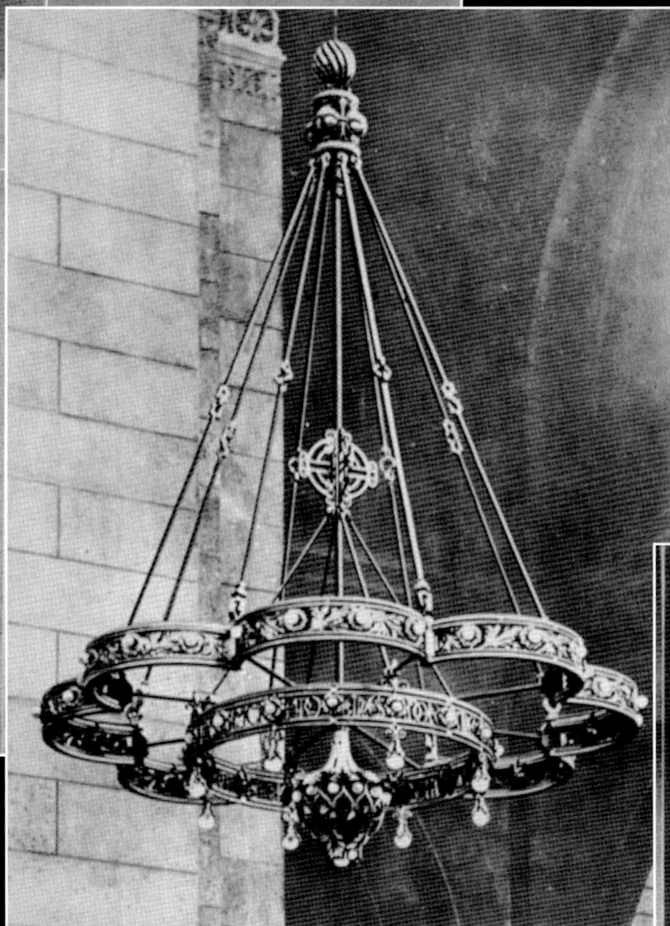

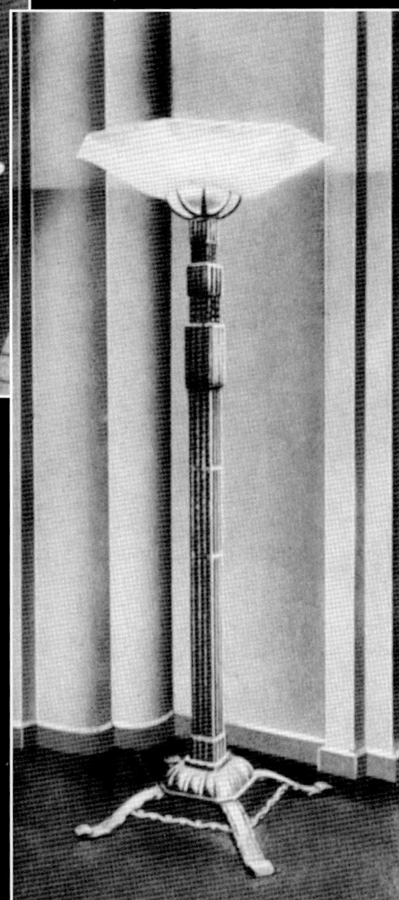

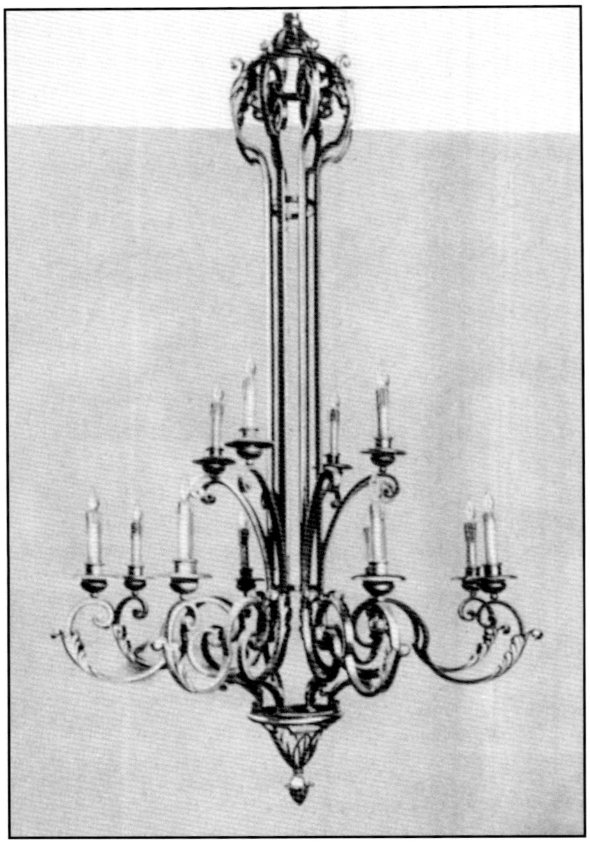

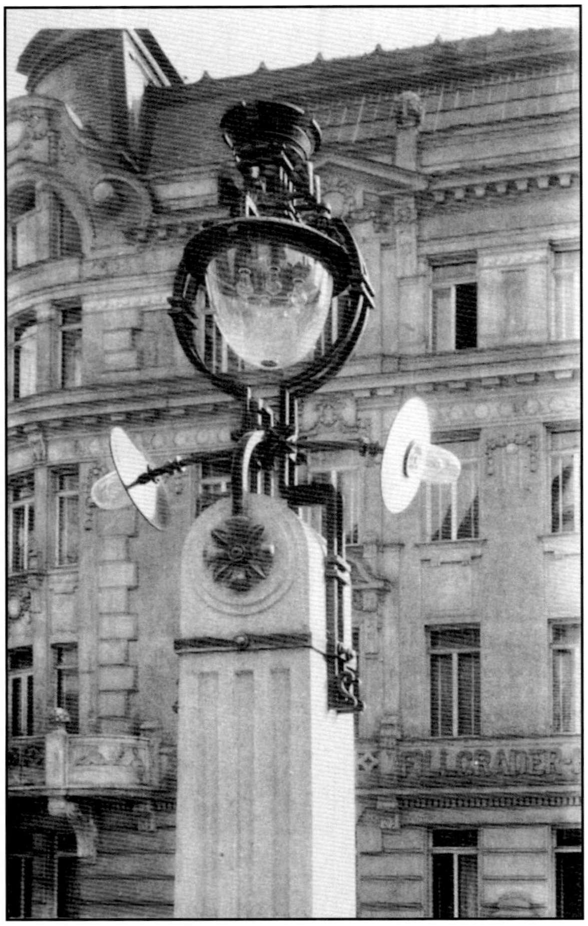
FILLGRADER

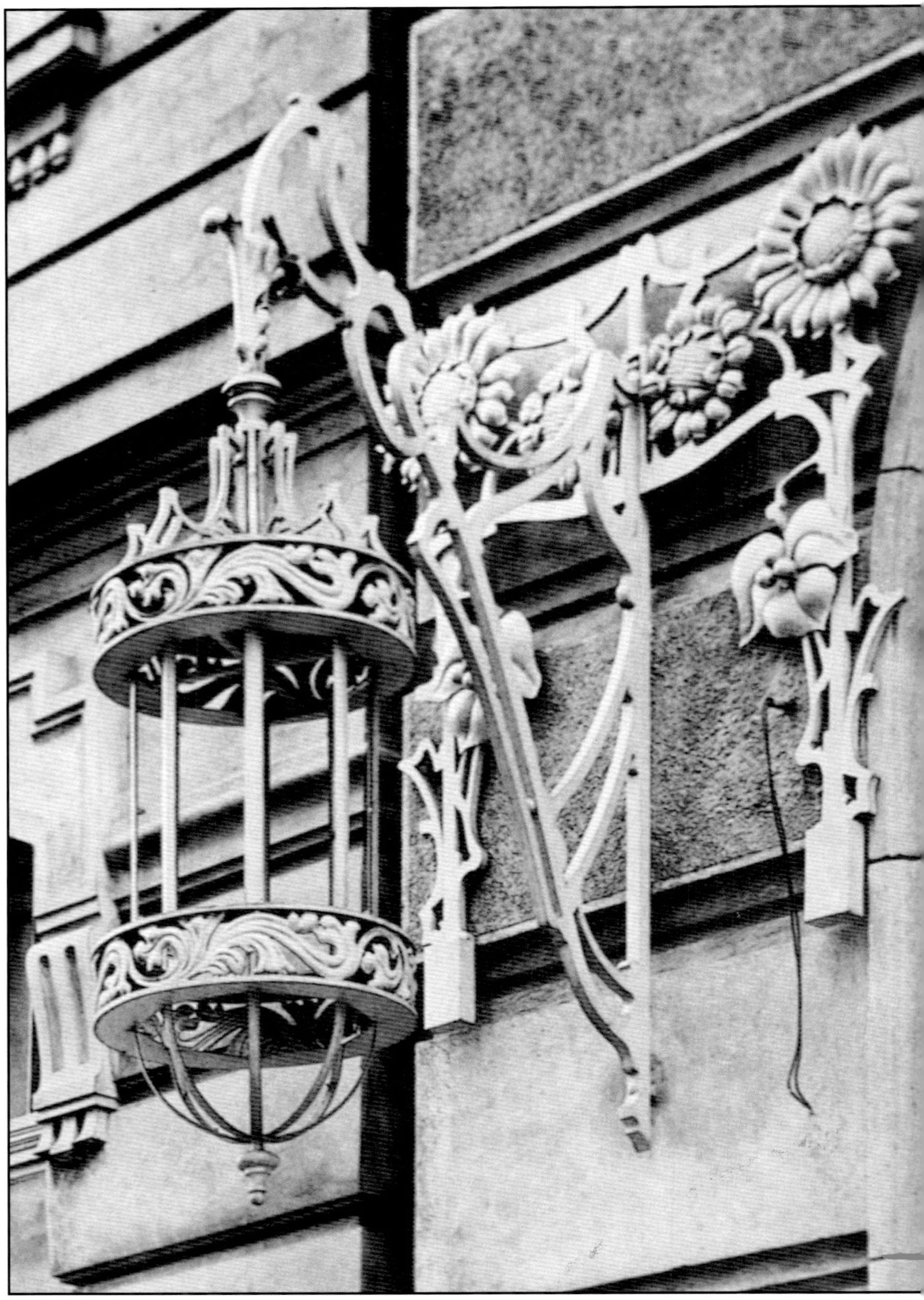

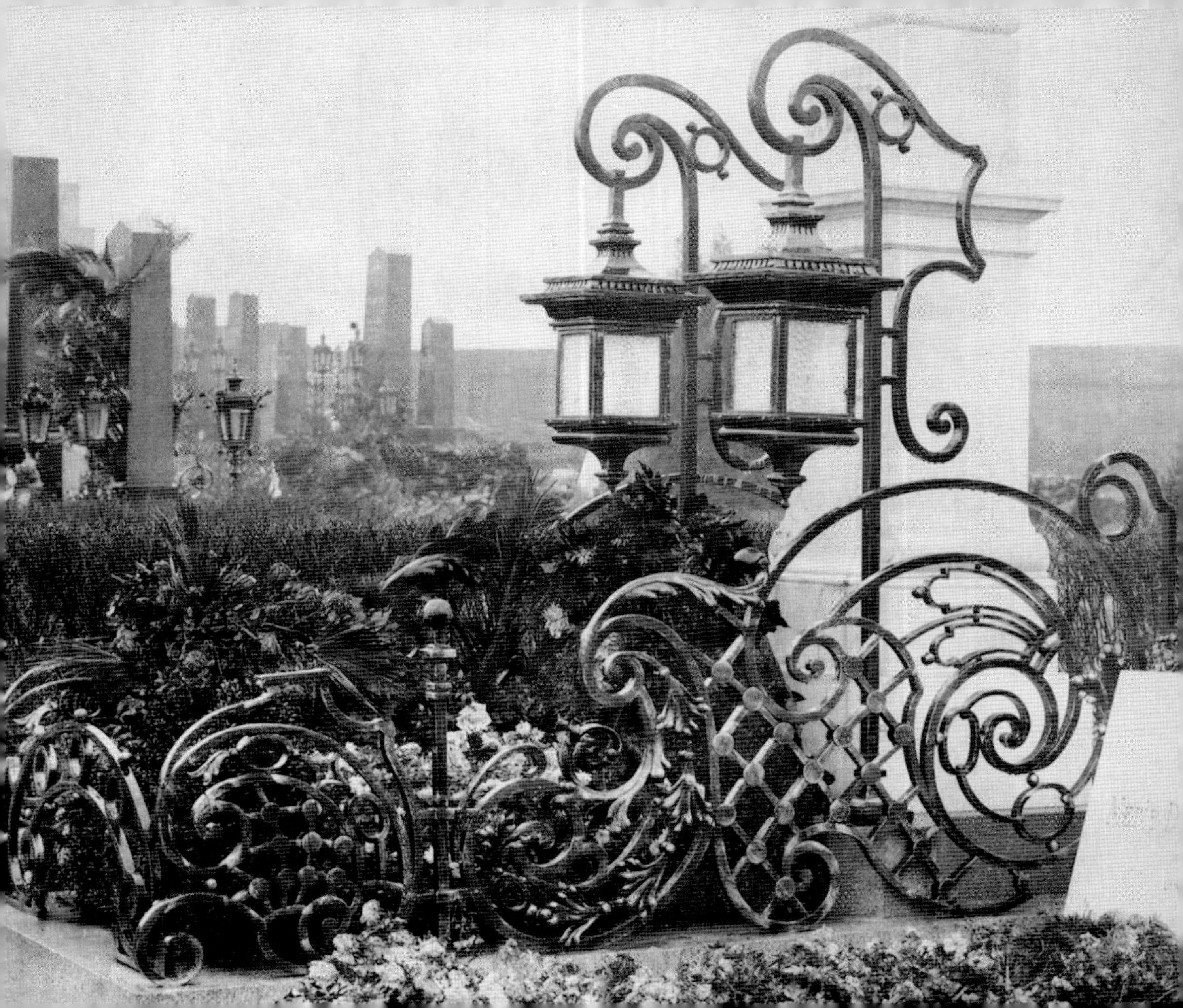

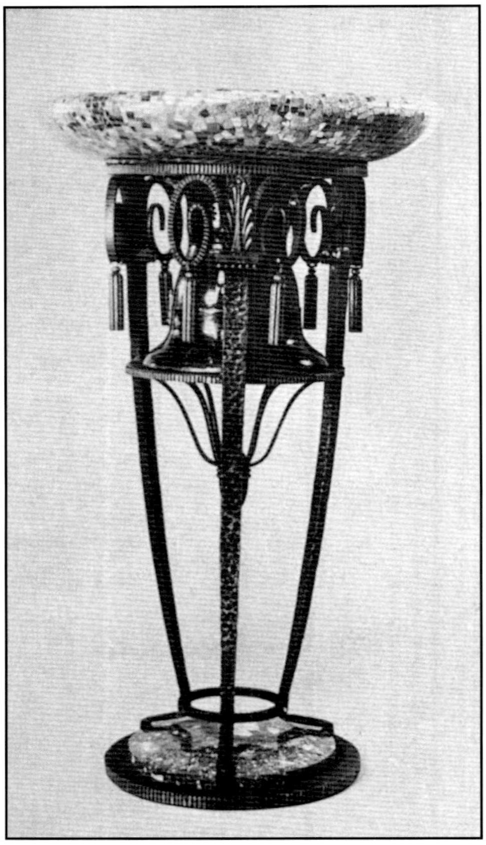

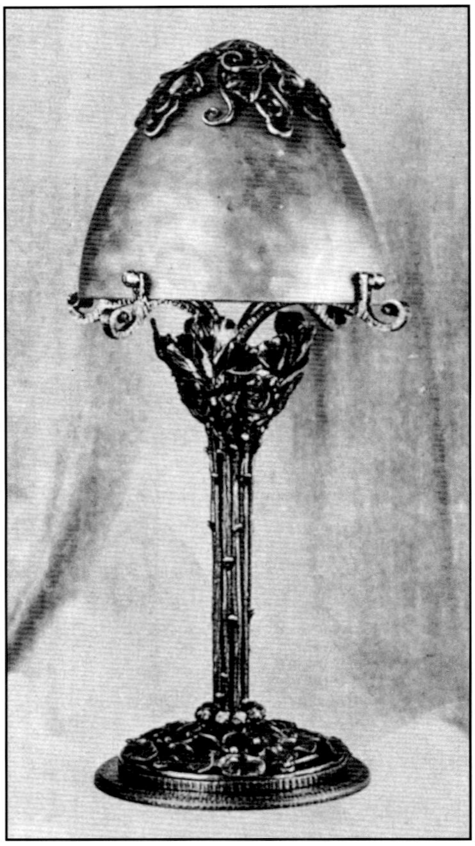

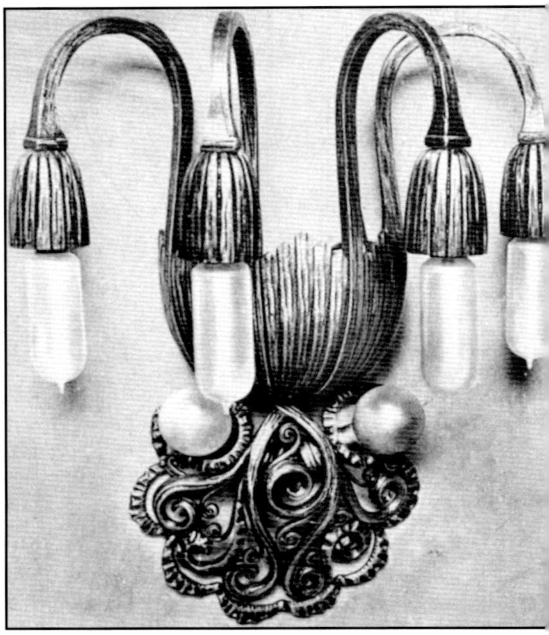

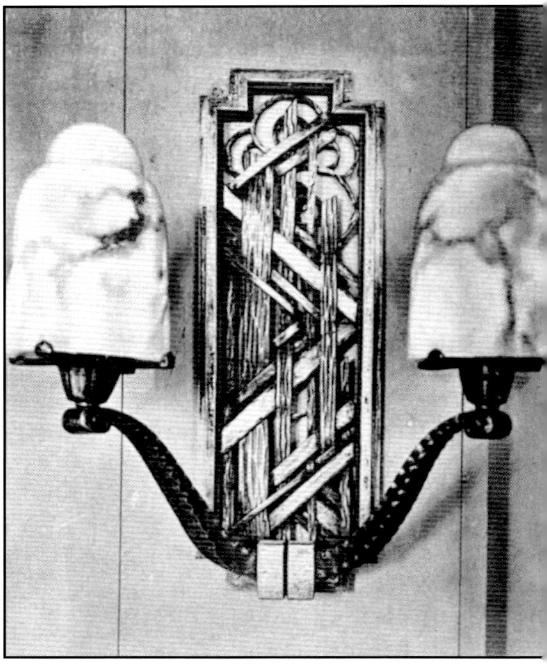

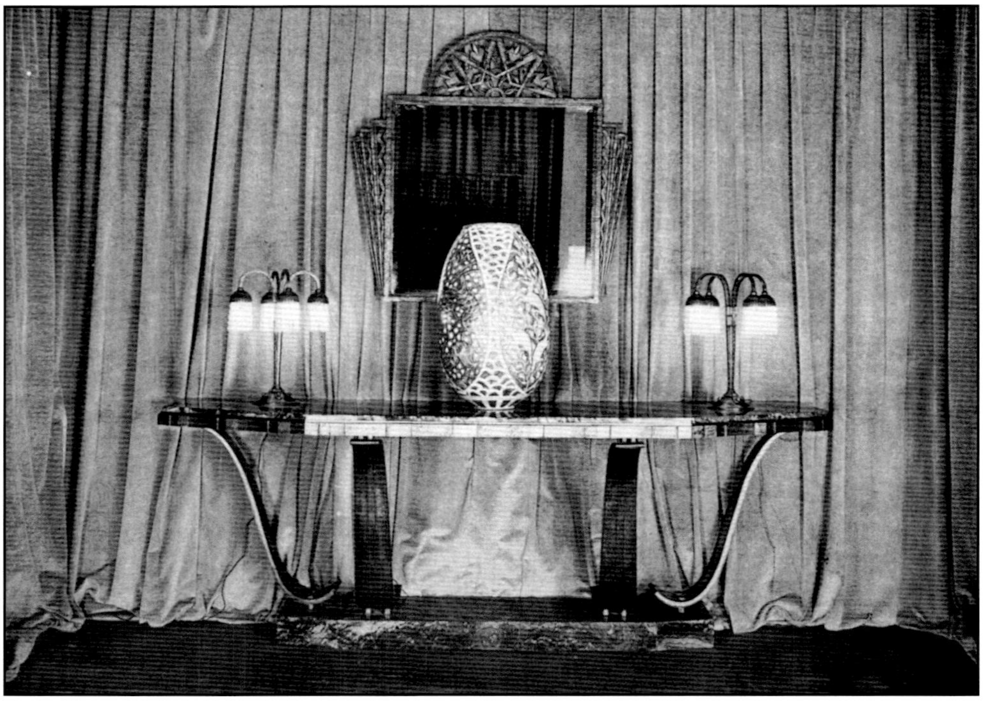

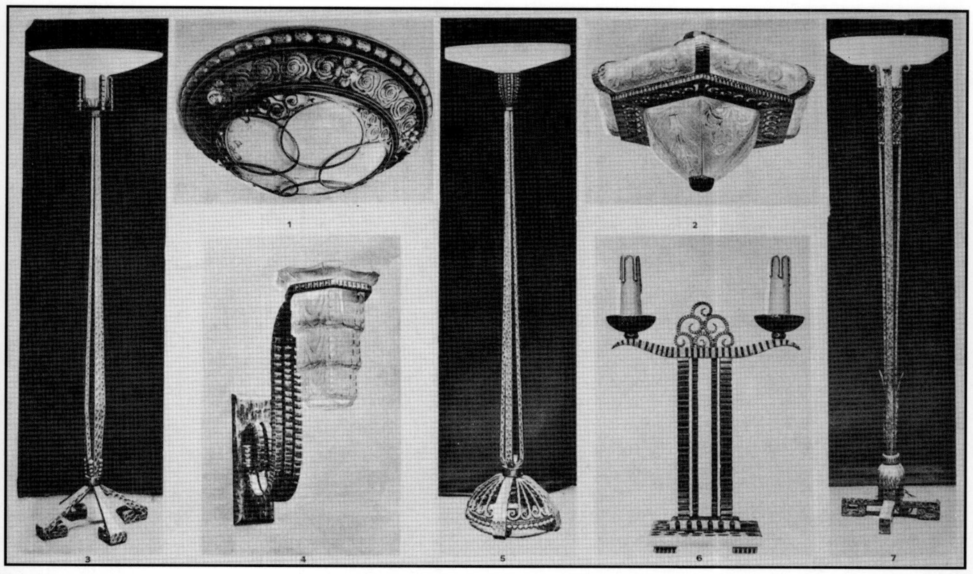

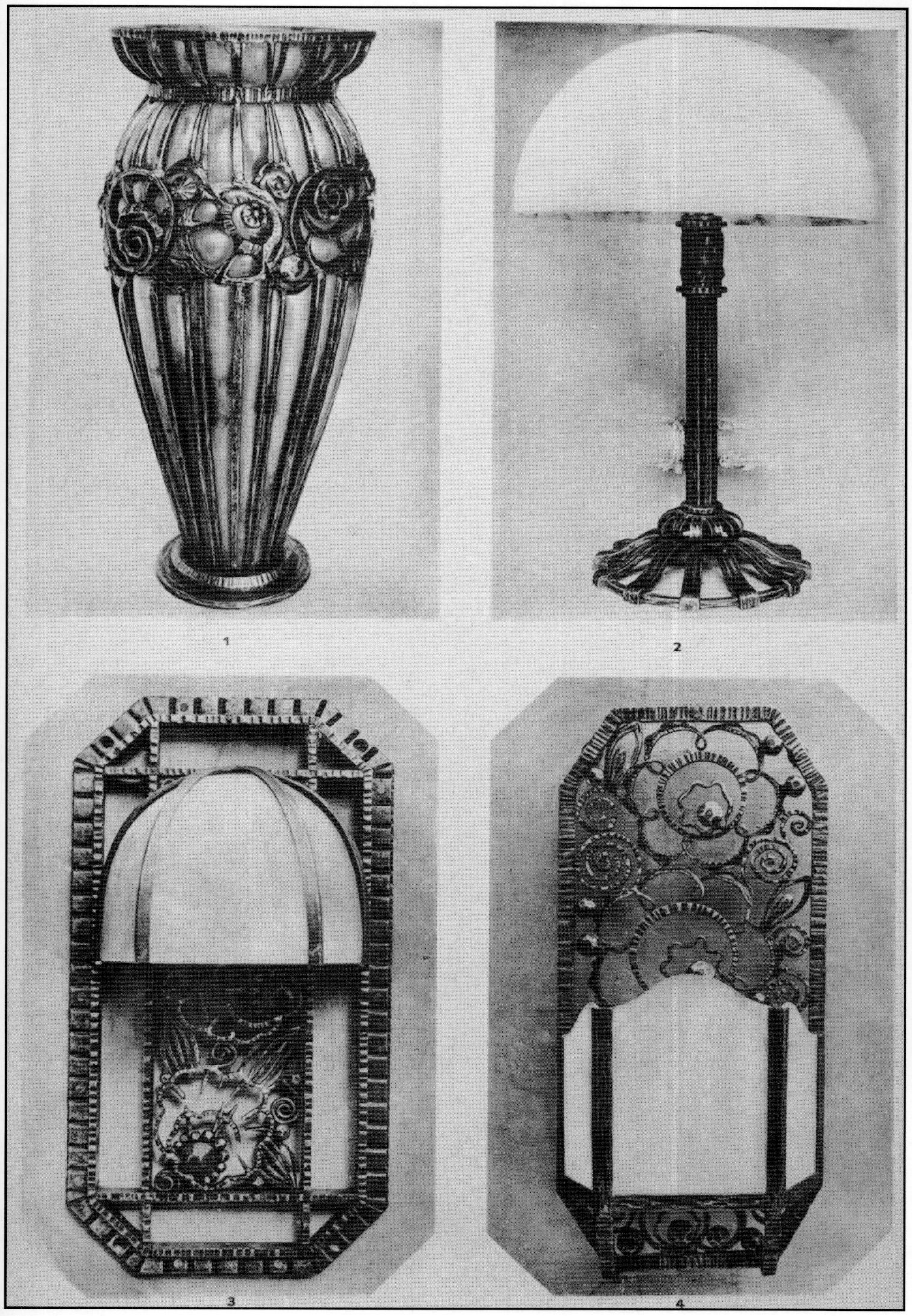

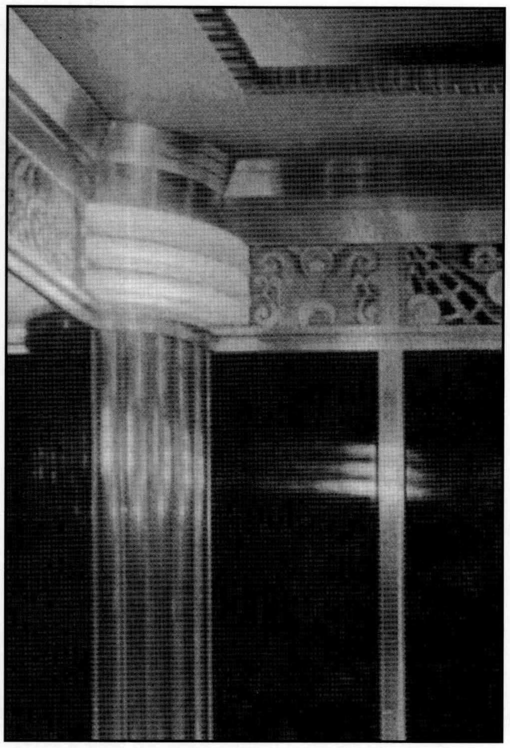

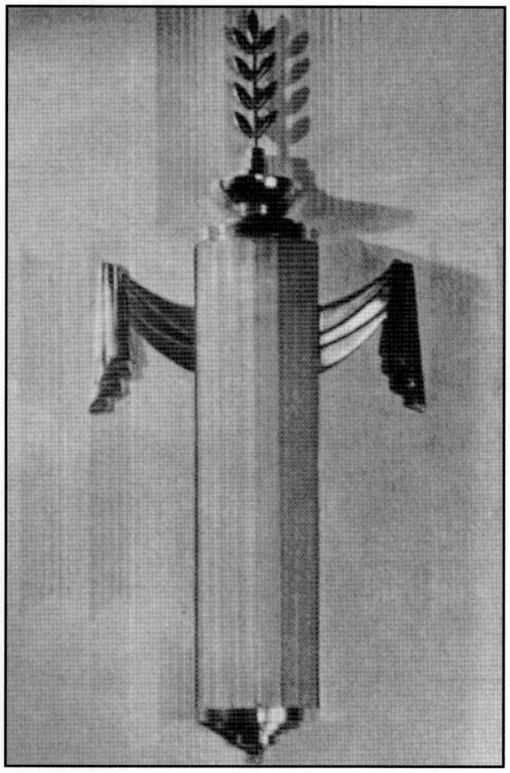

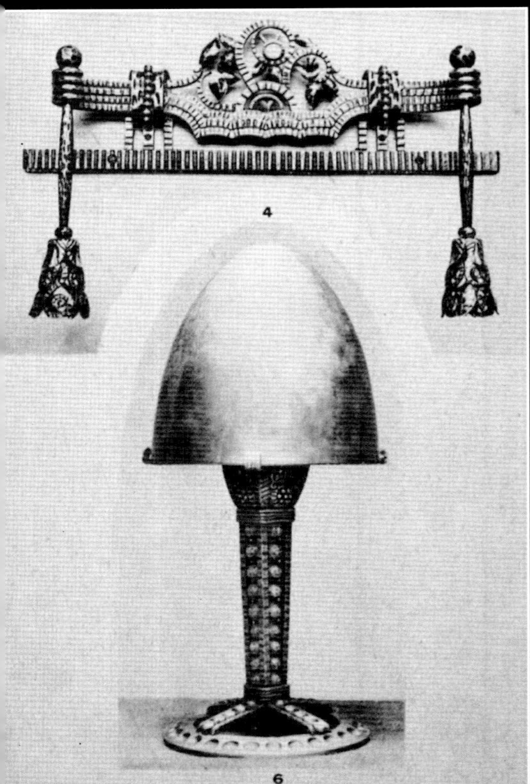
4
6

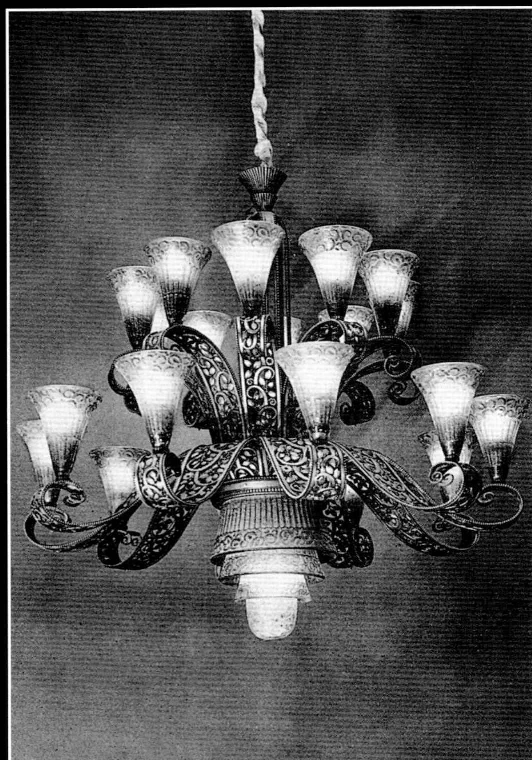

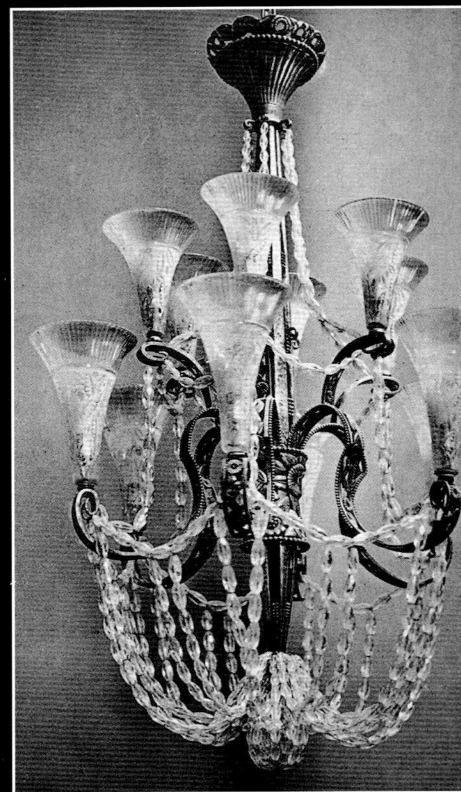

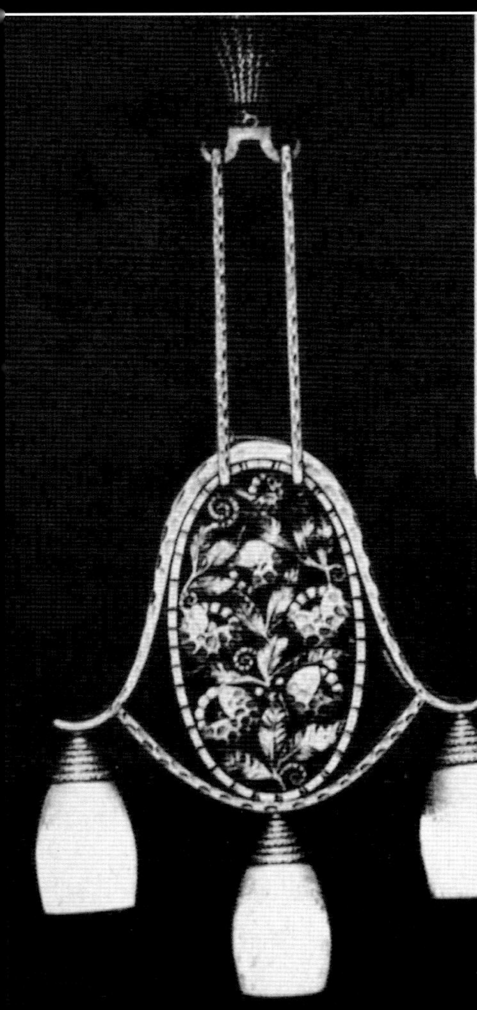

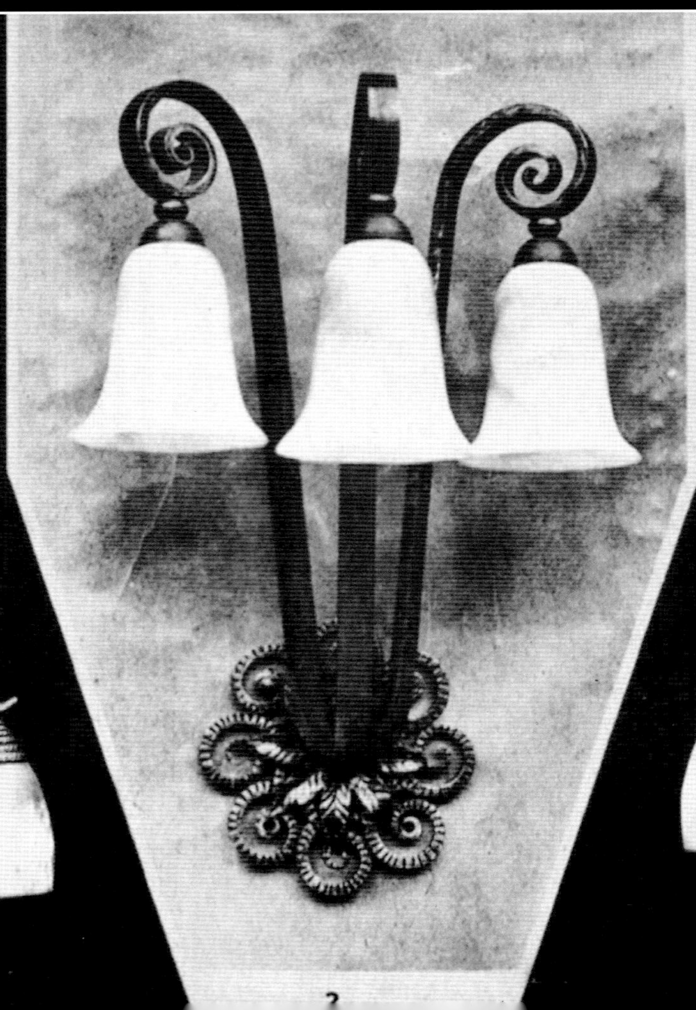

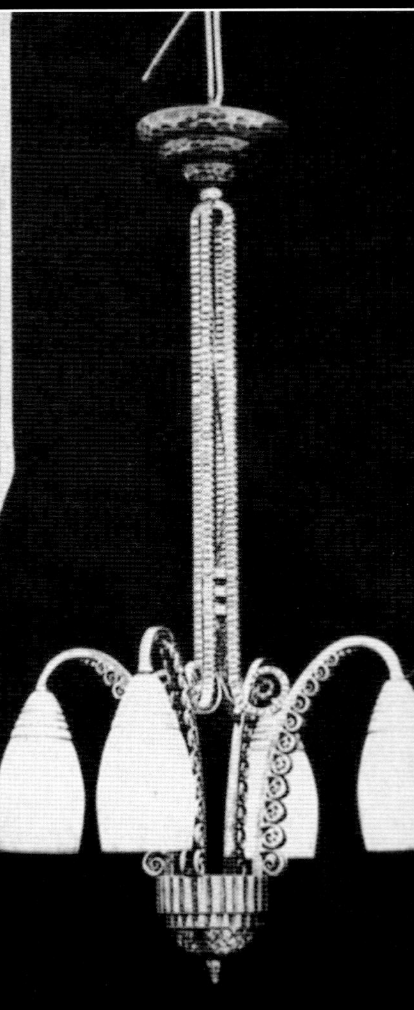

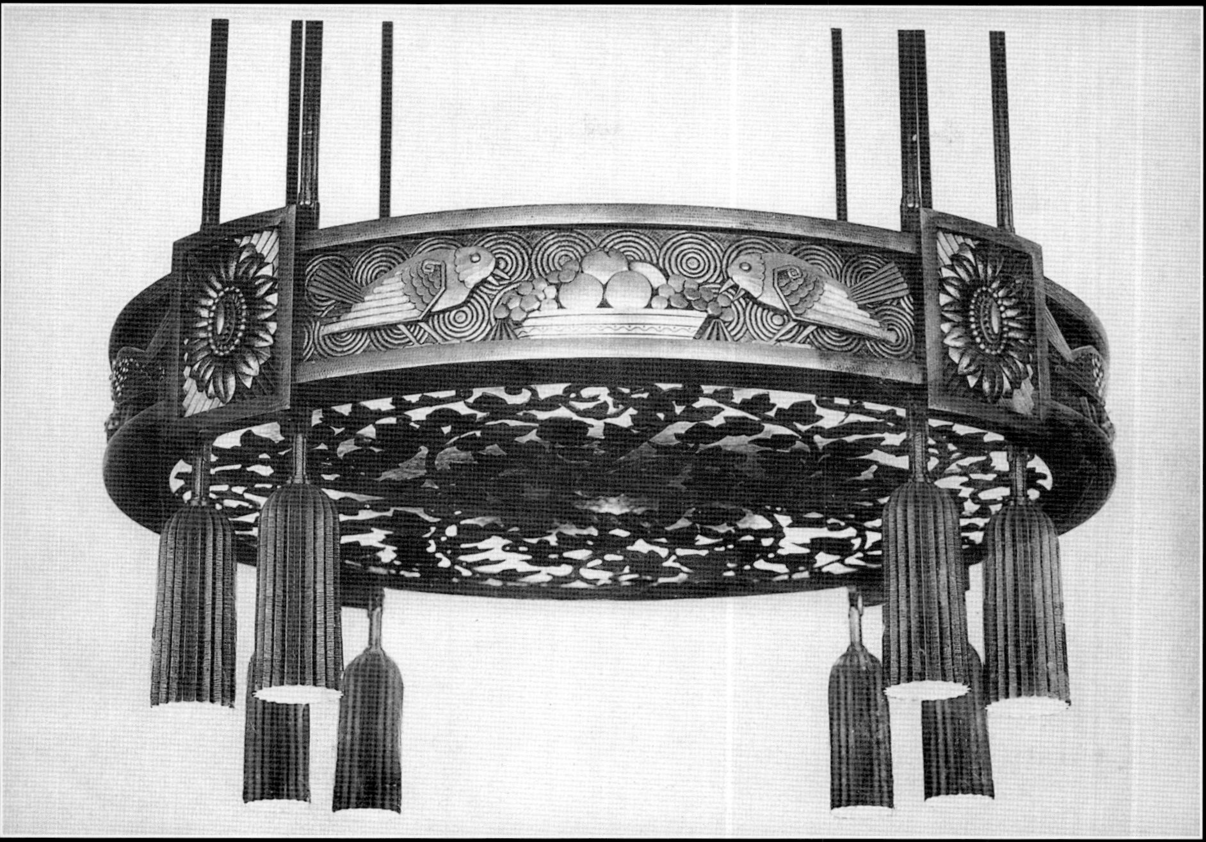

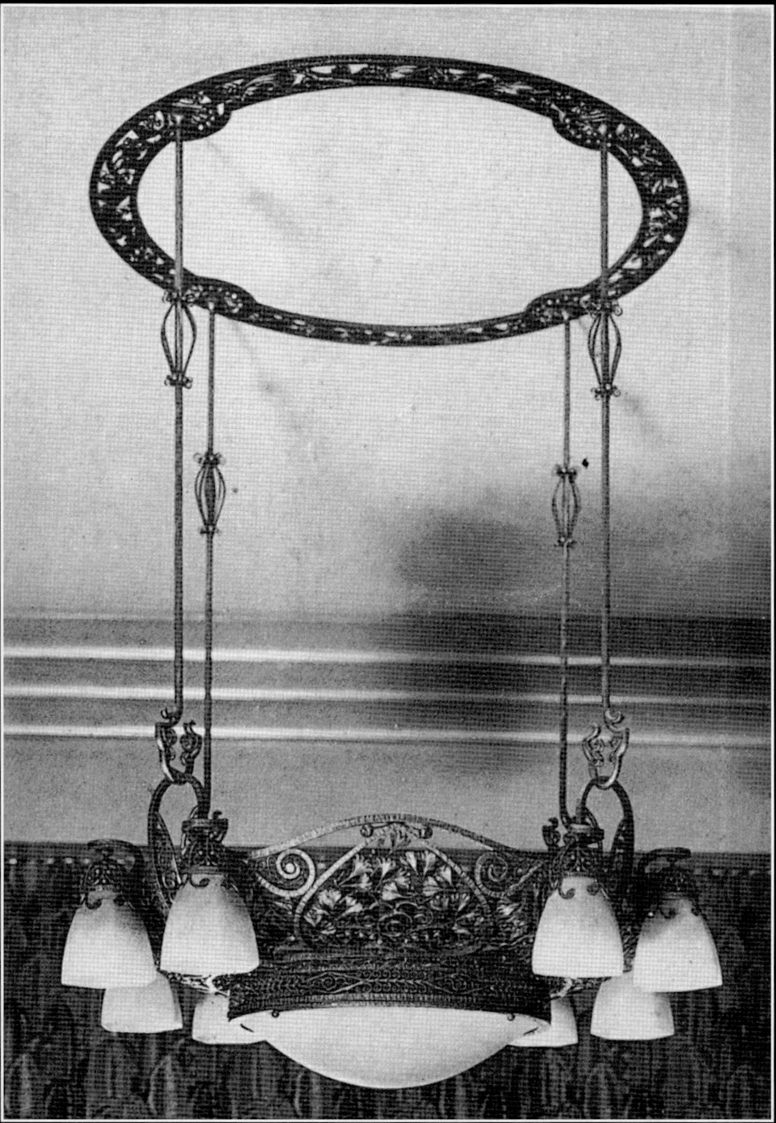

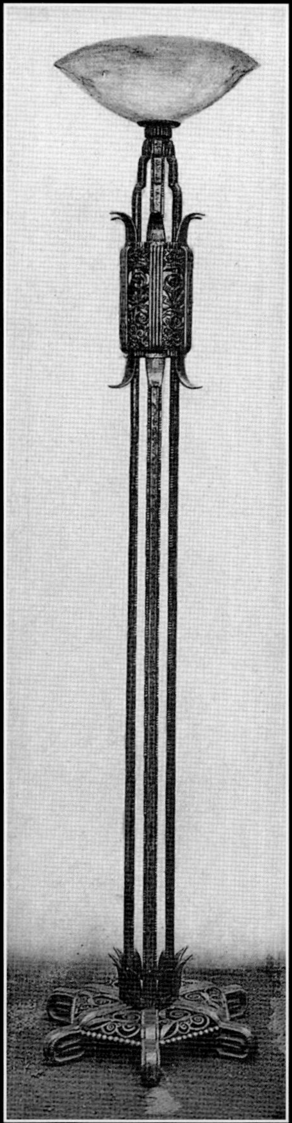

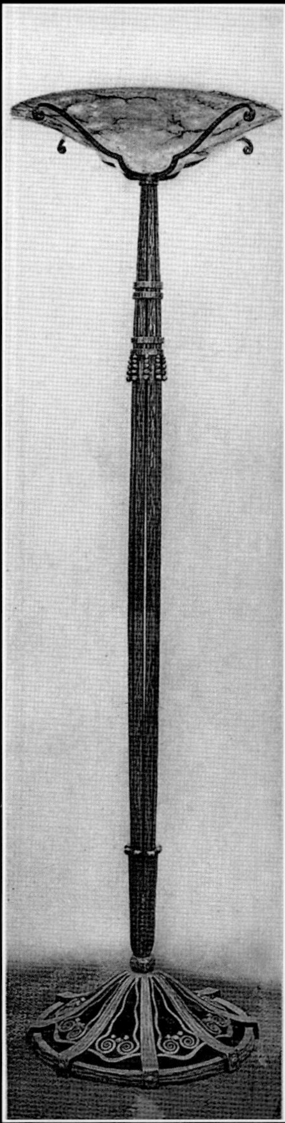

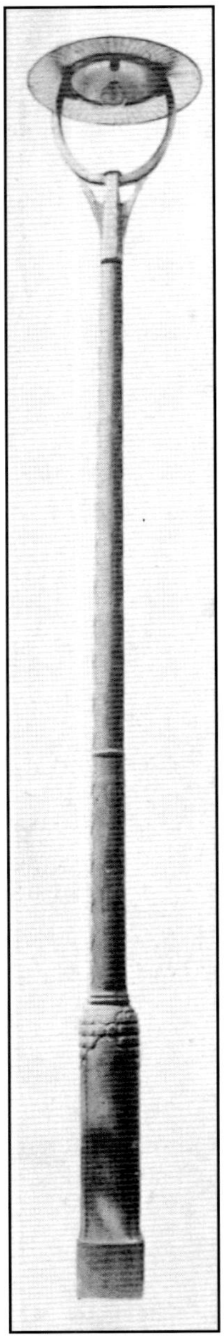

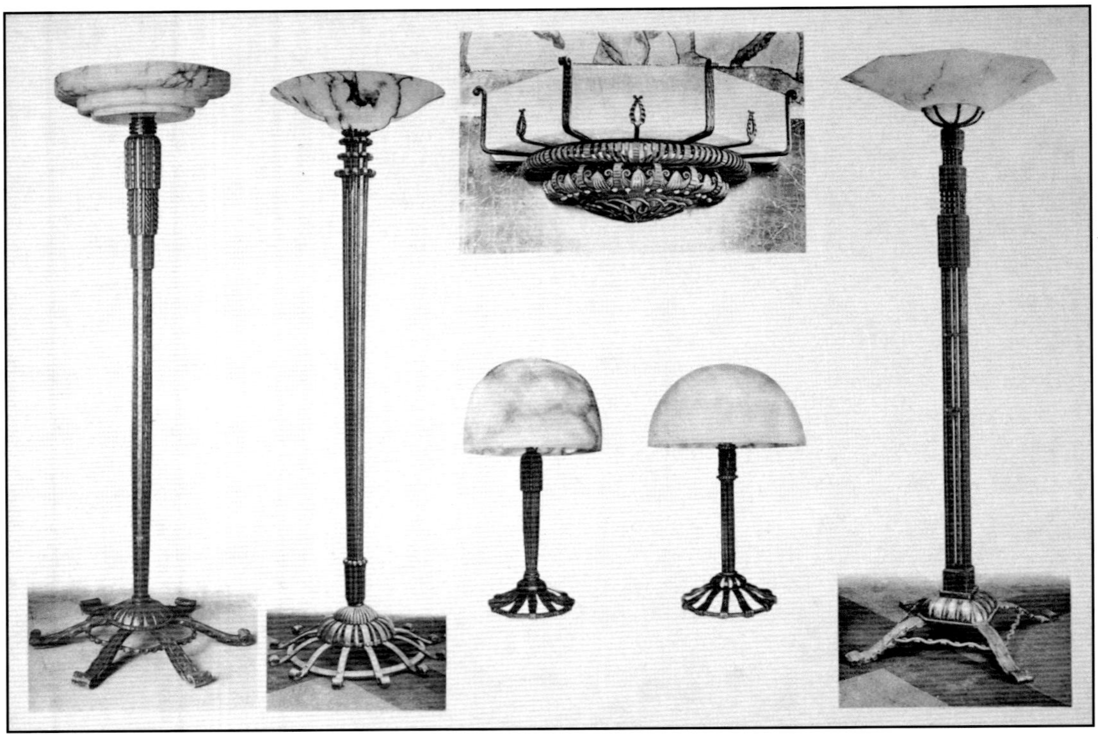

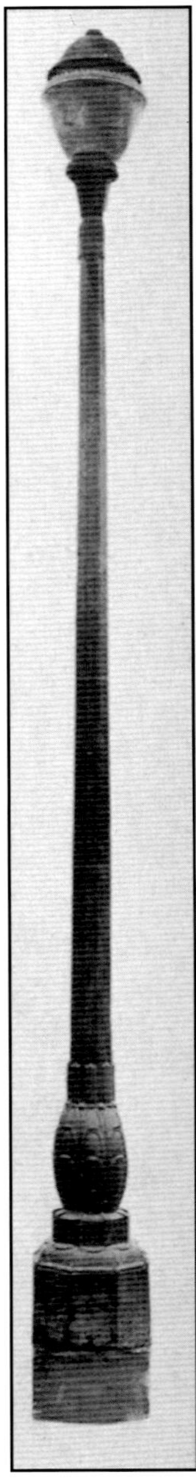

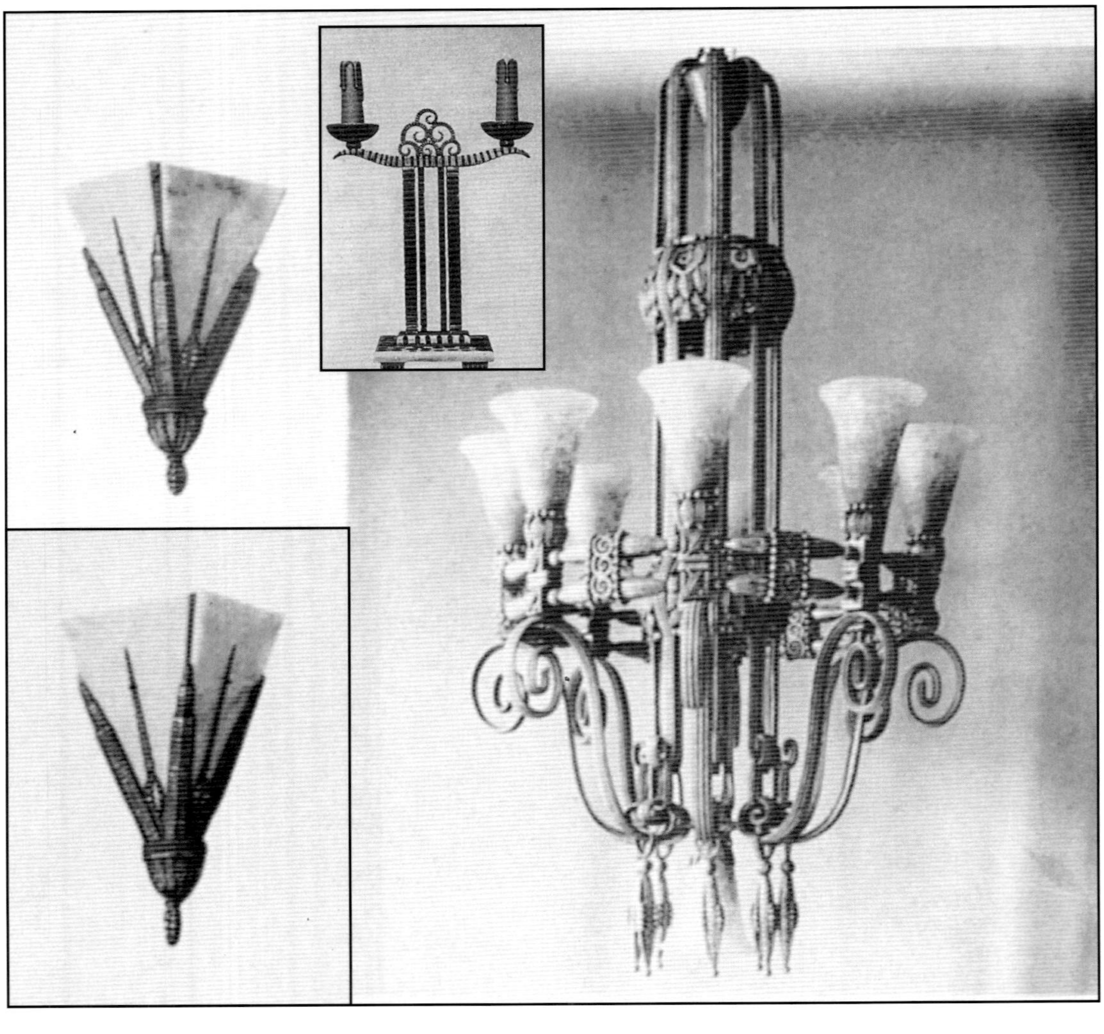

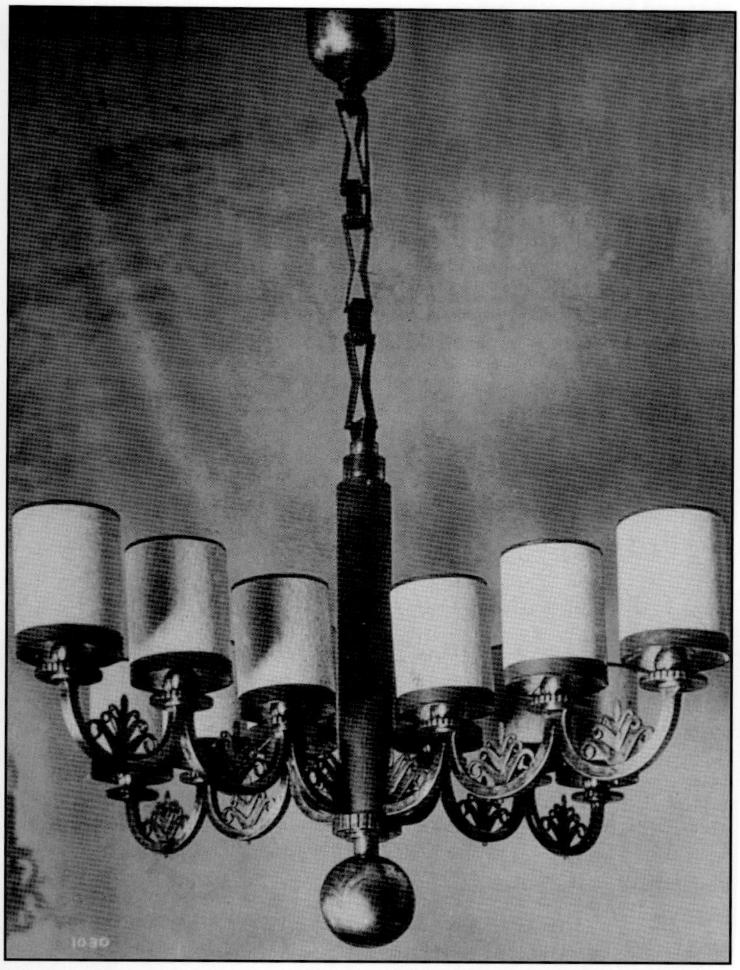

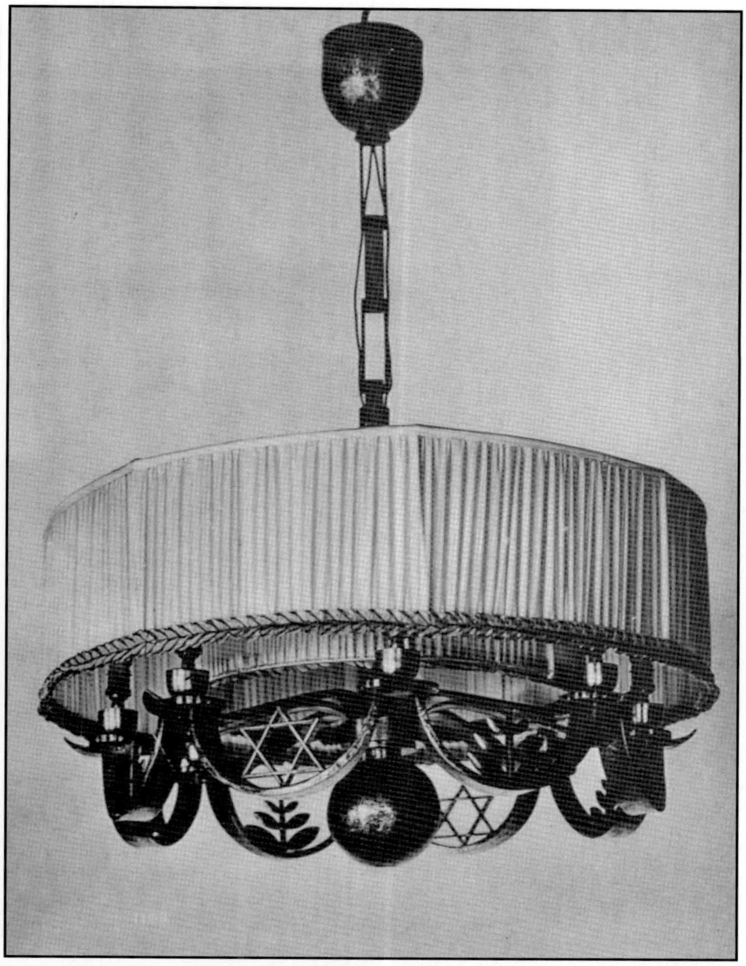

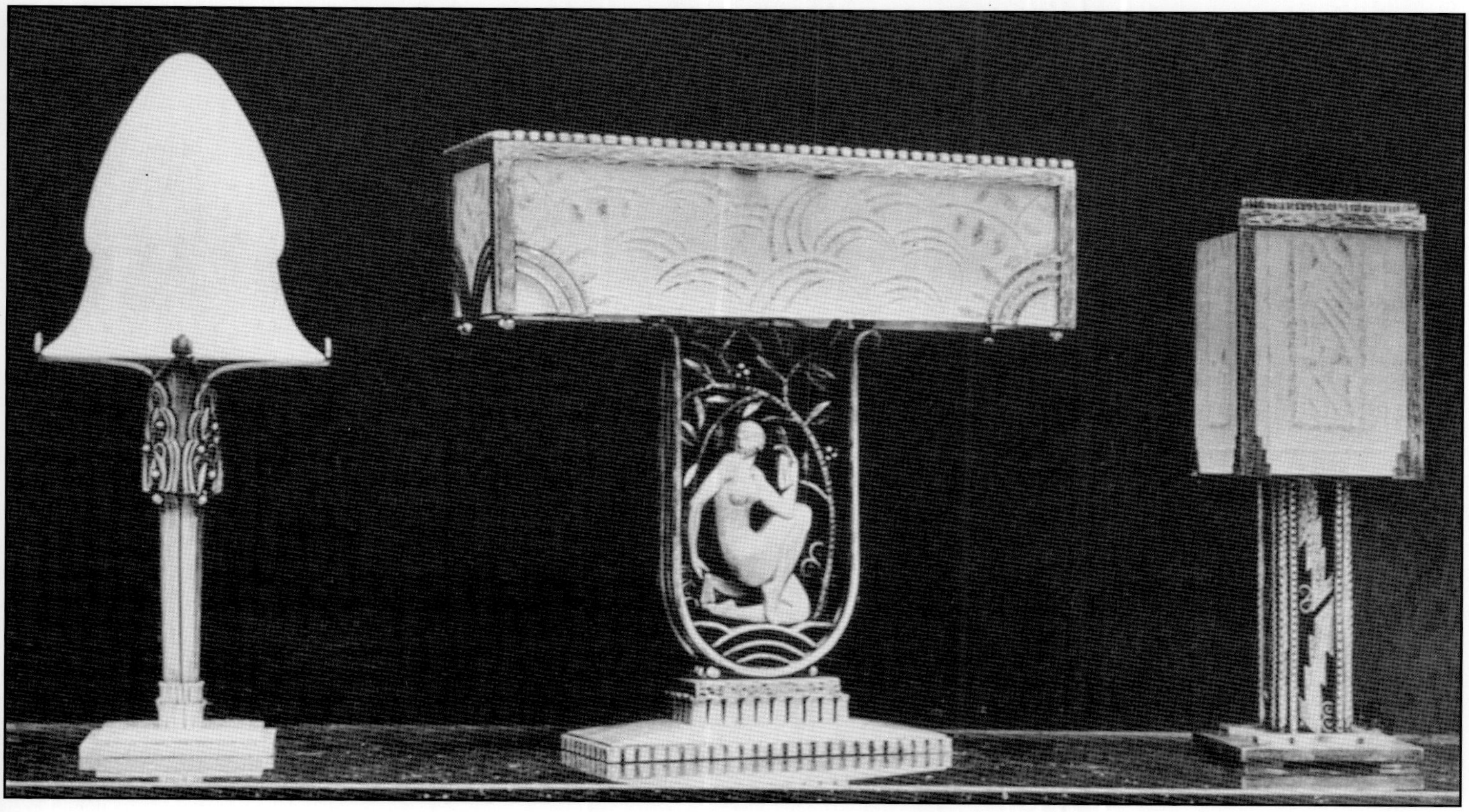

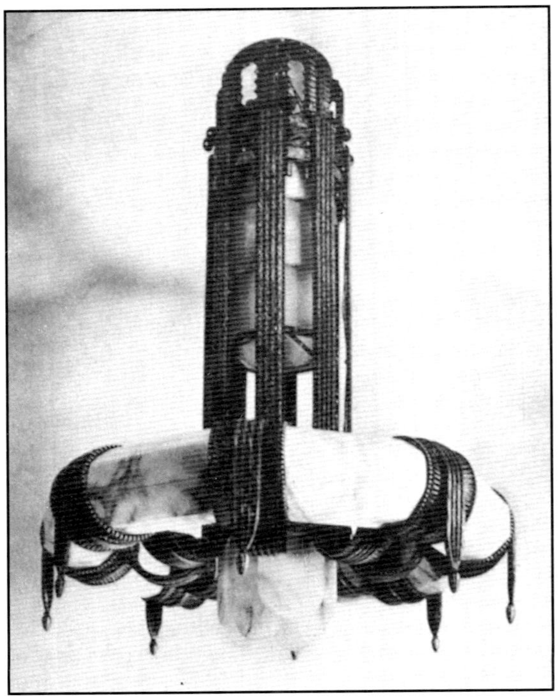

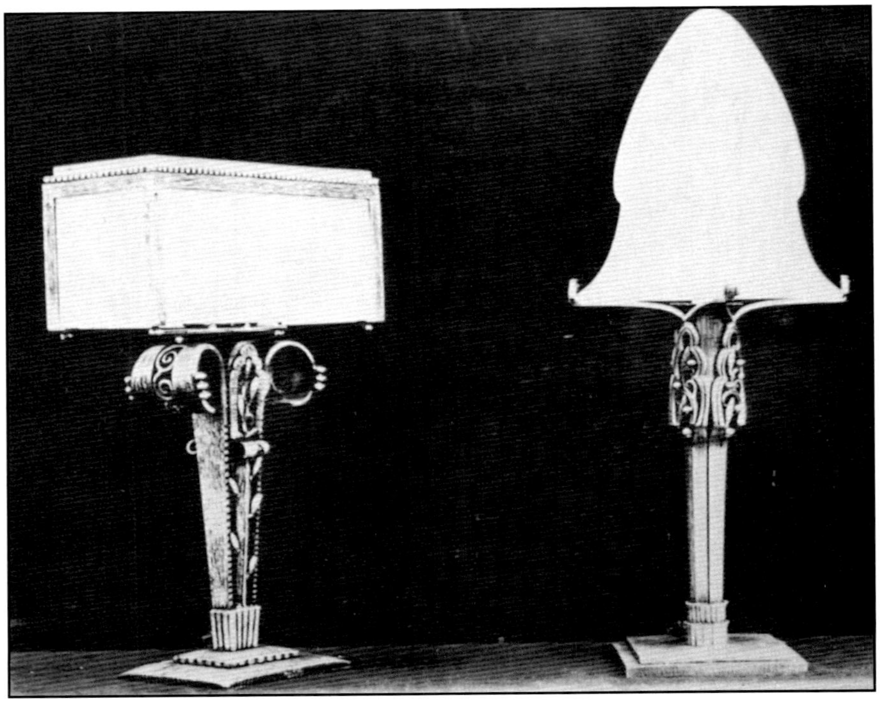

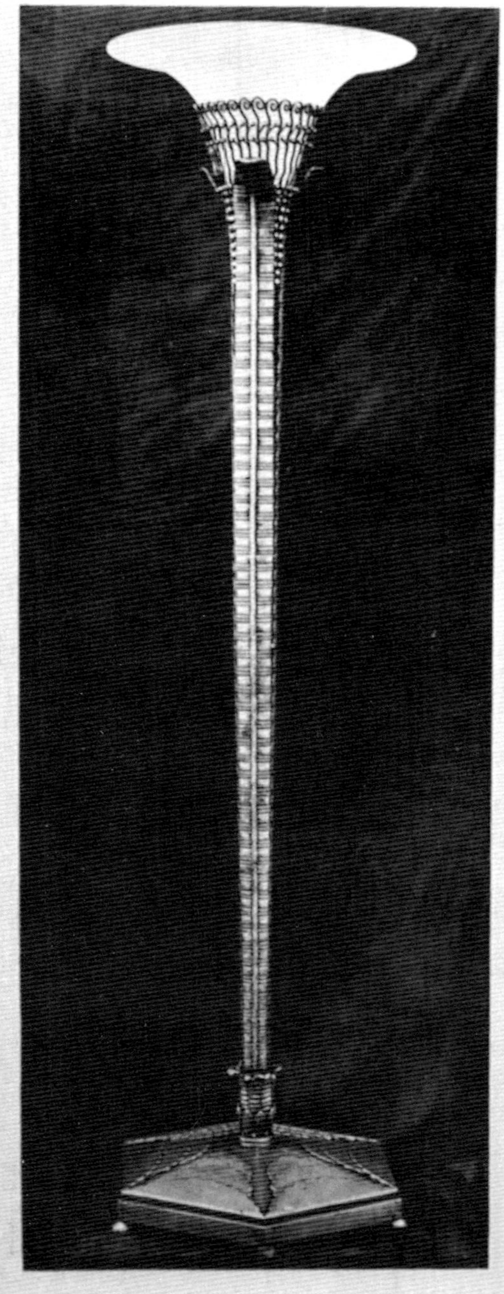

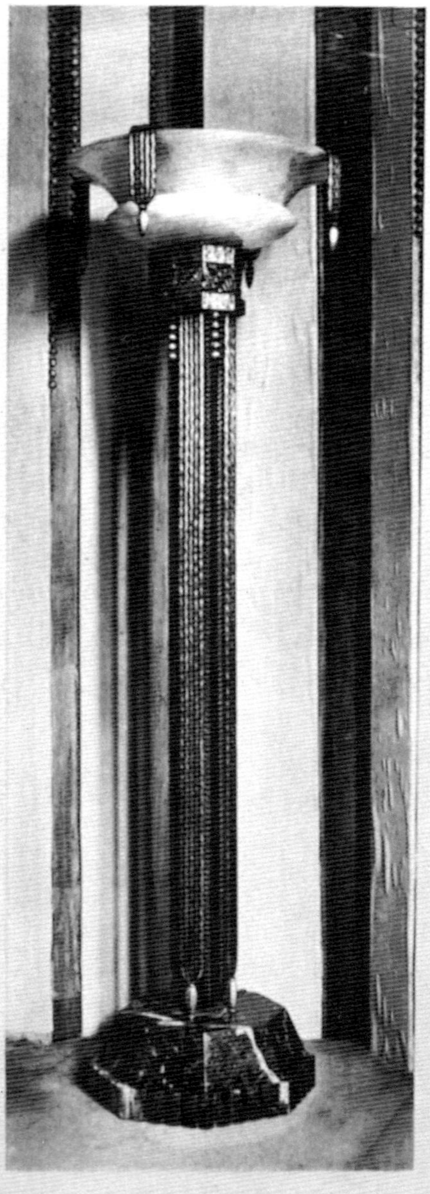

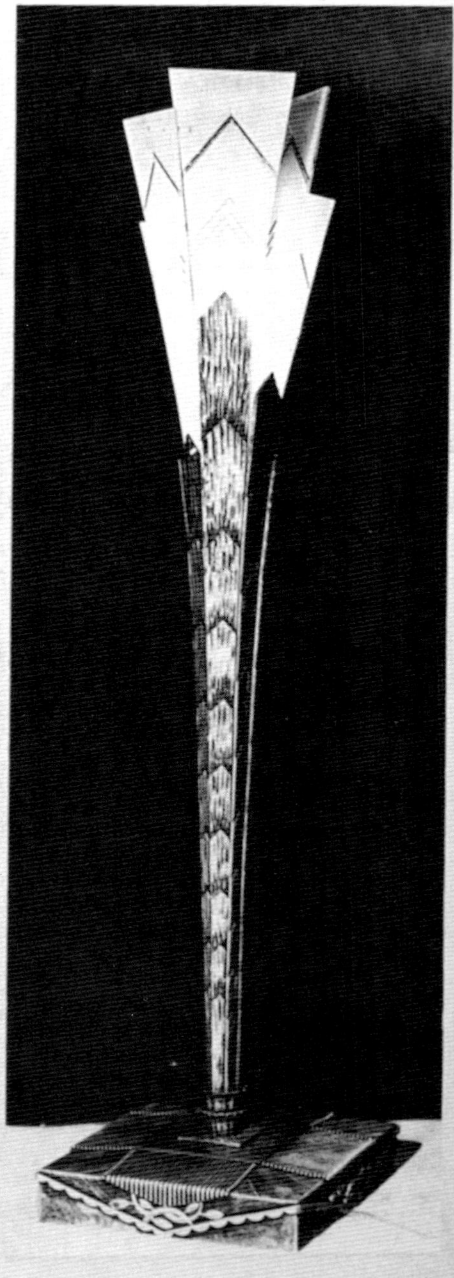

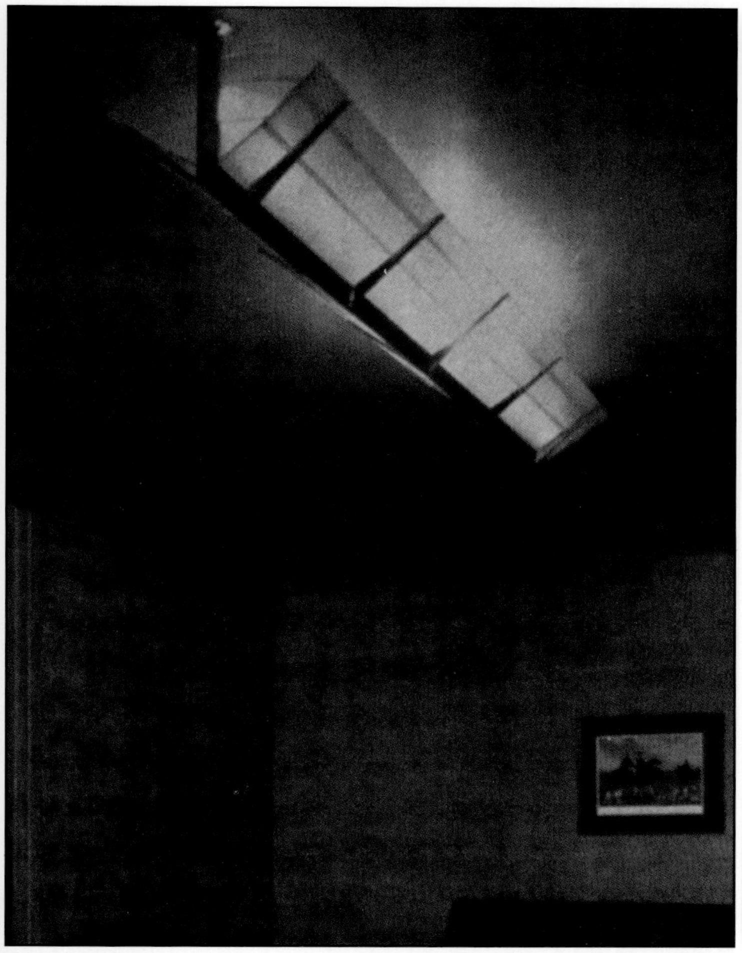

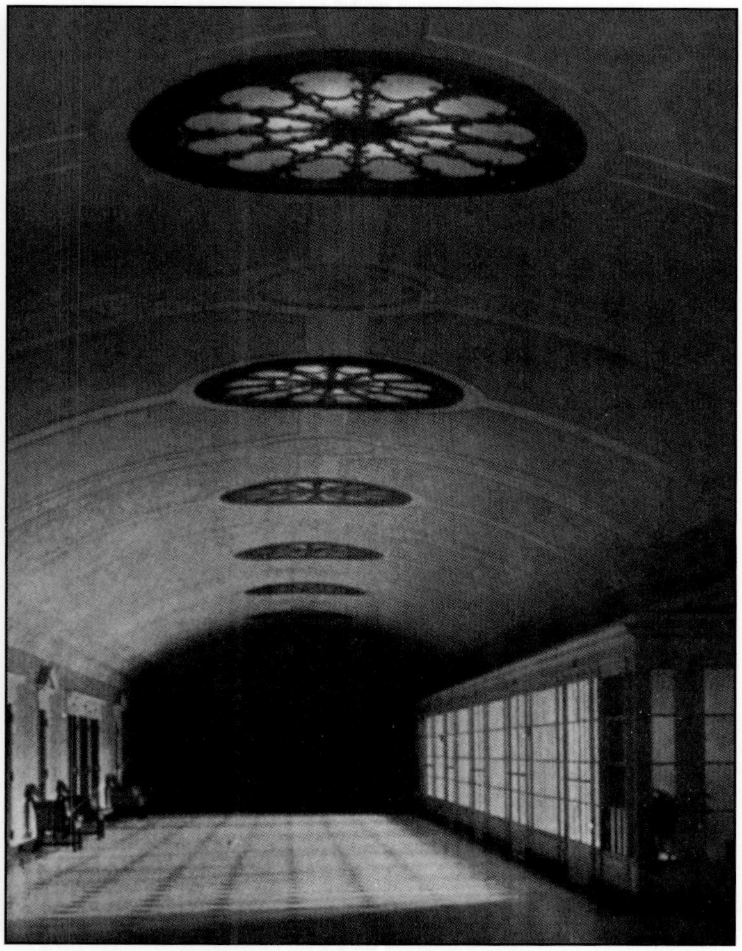

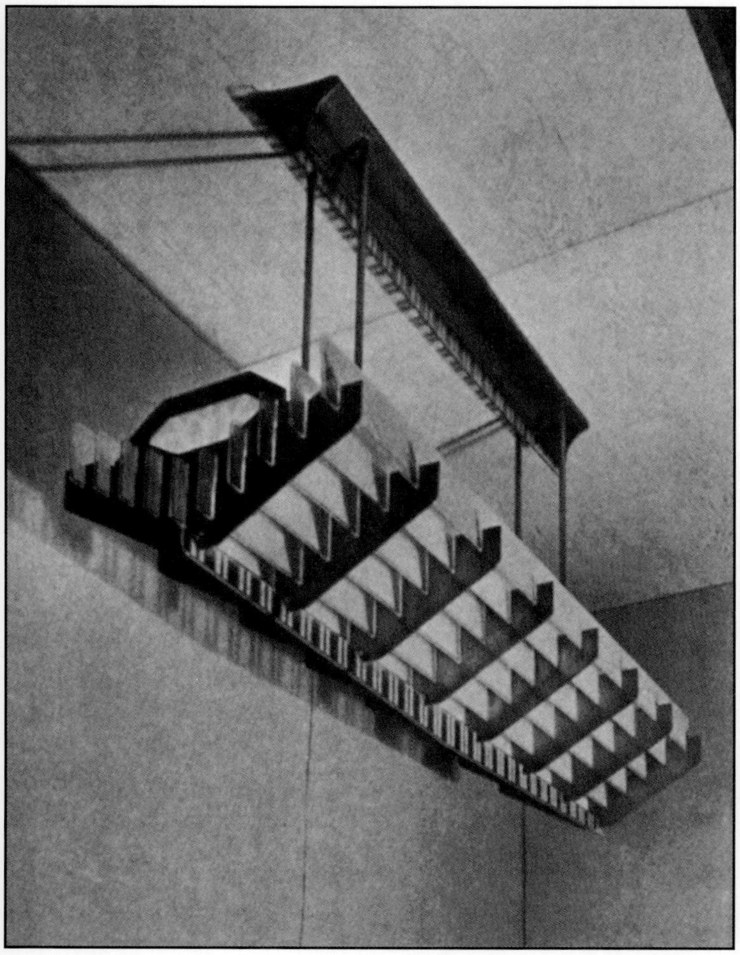

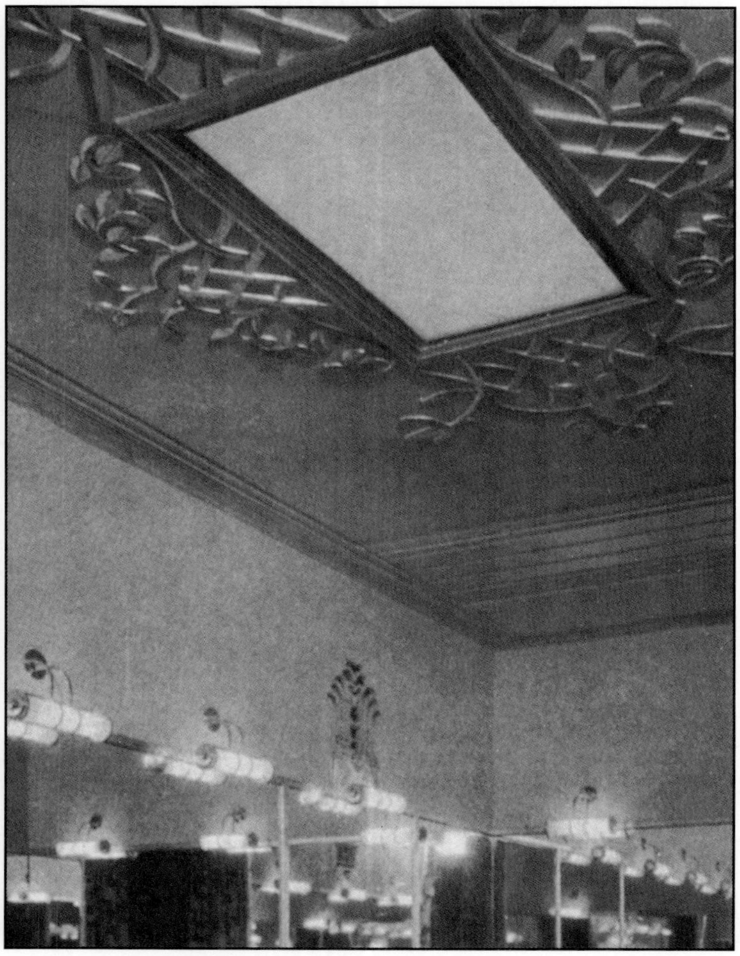

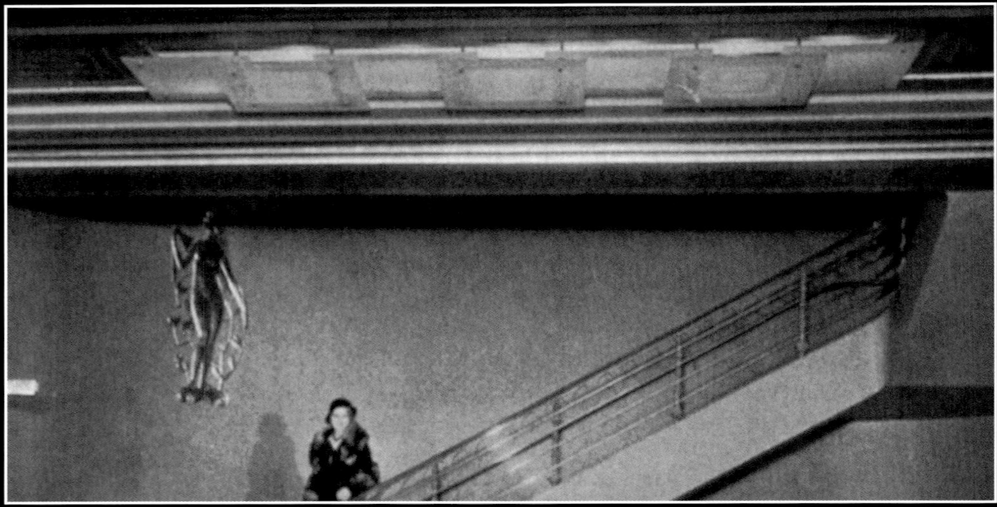

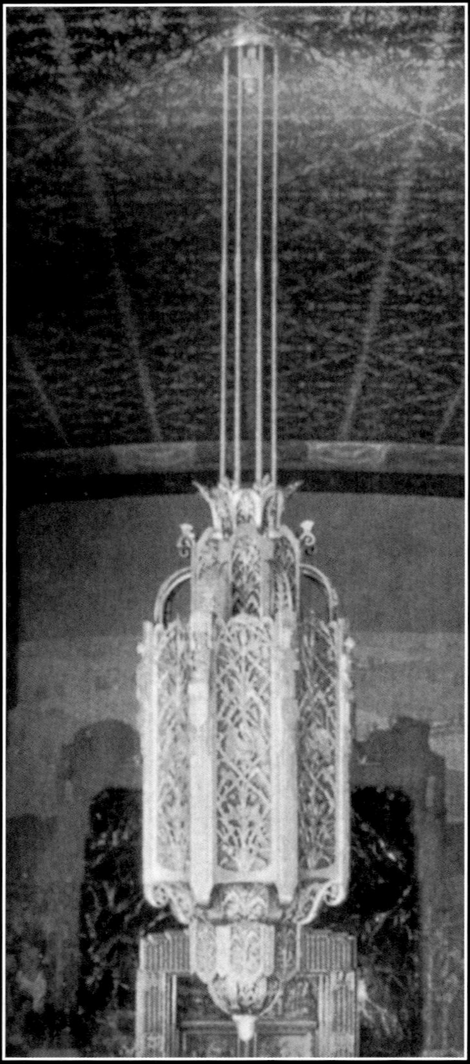

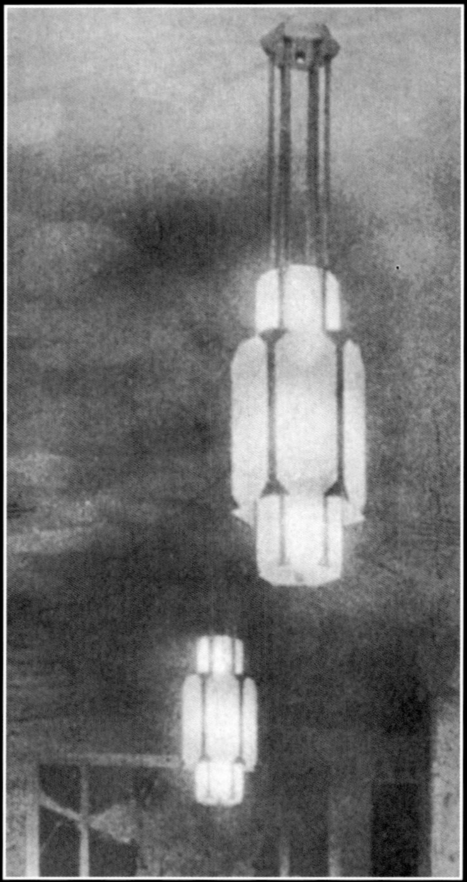

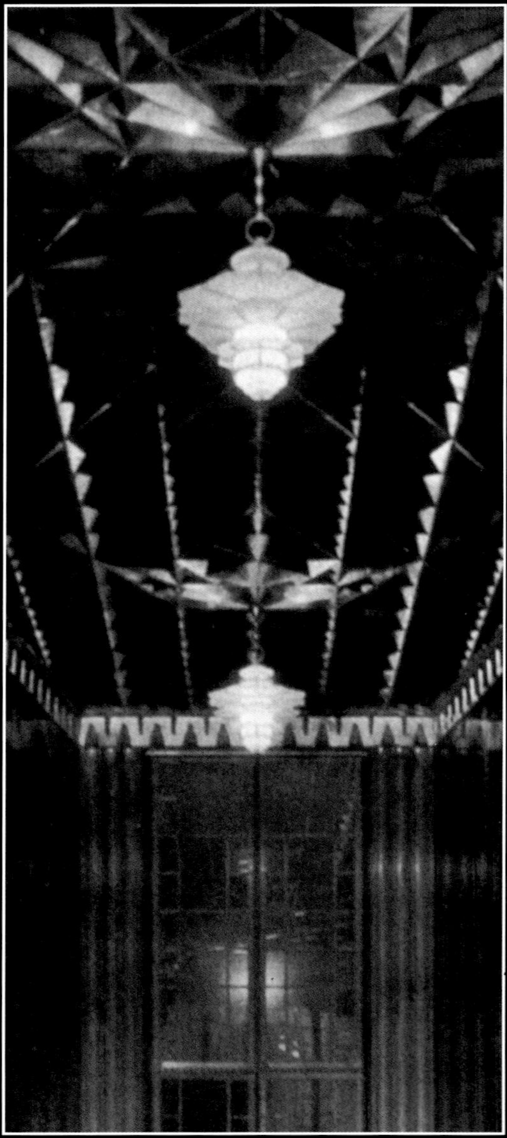

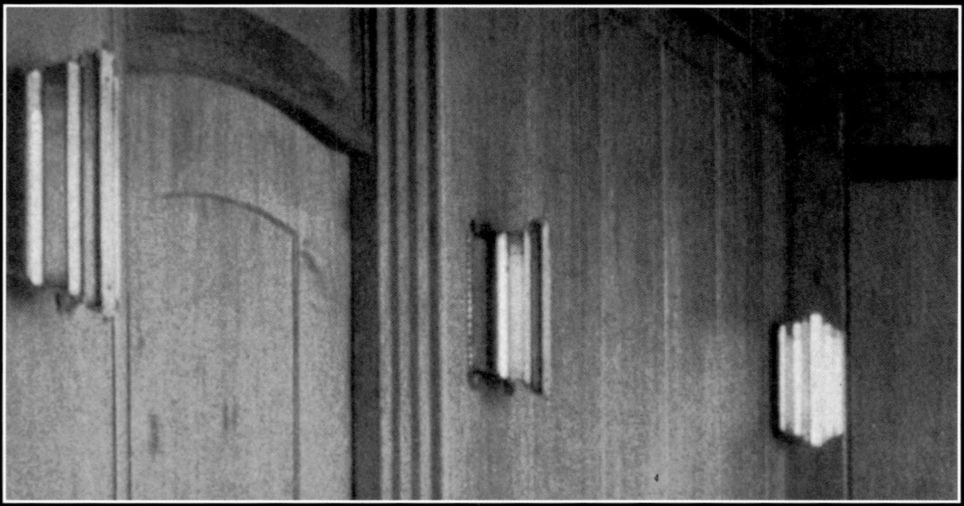

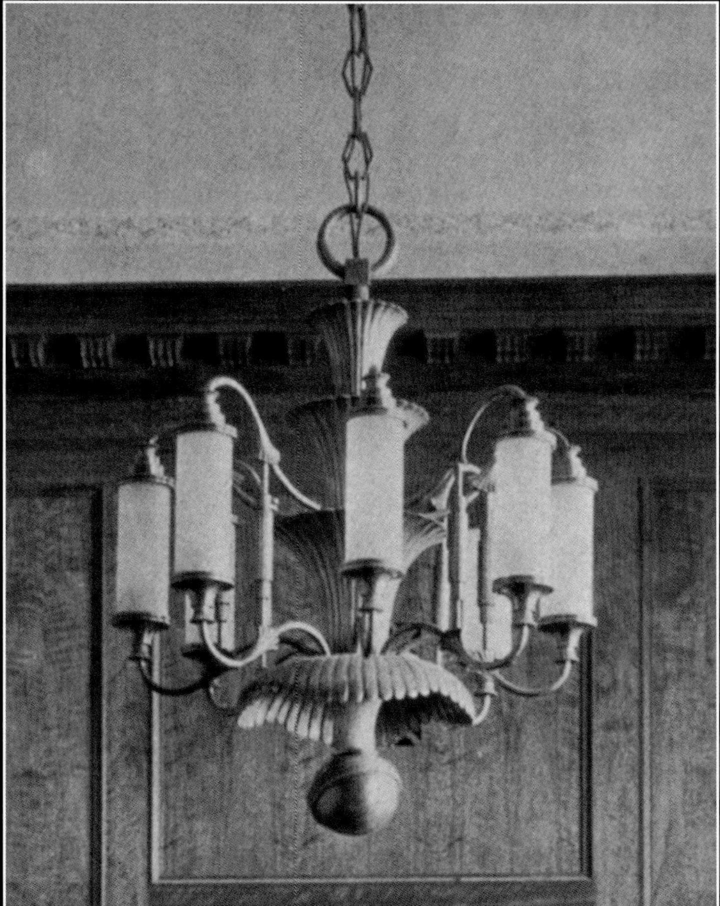
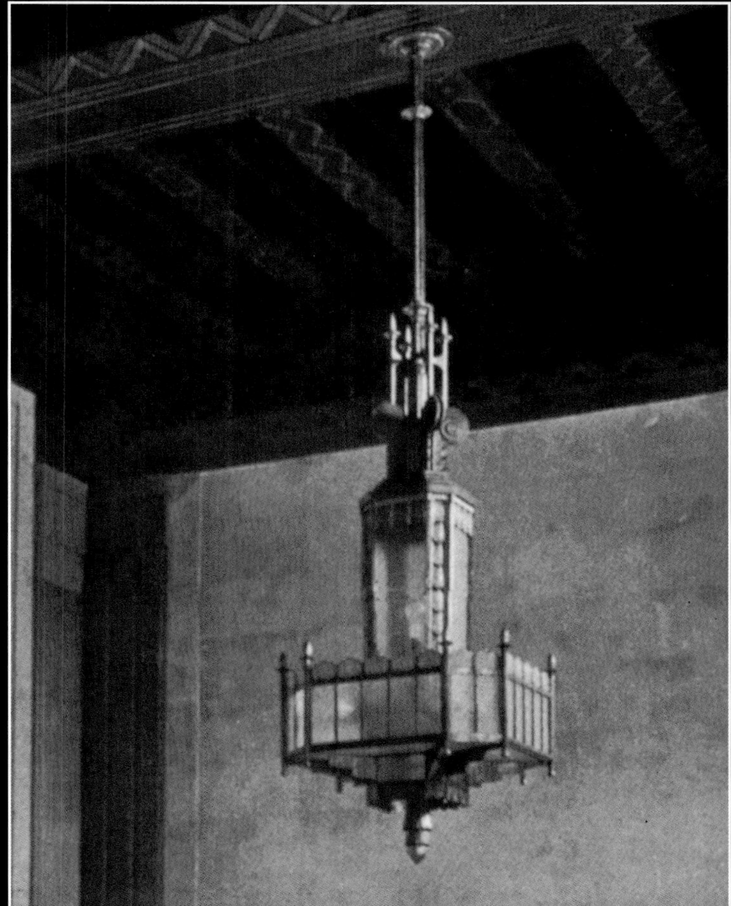
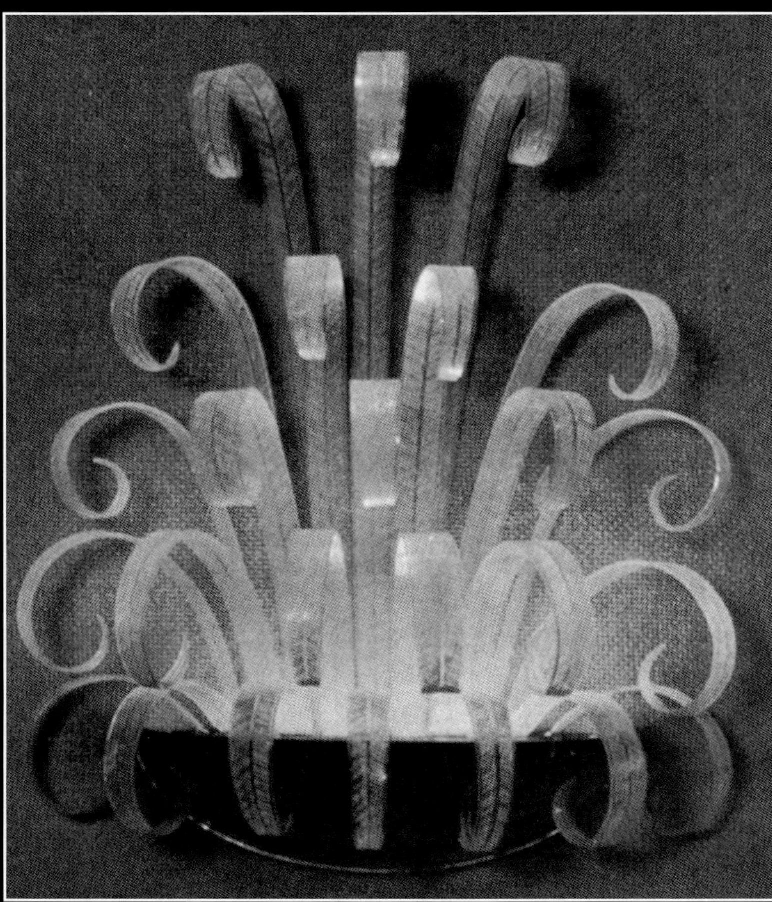
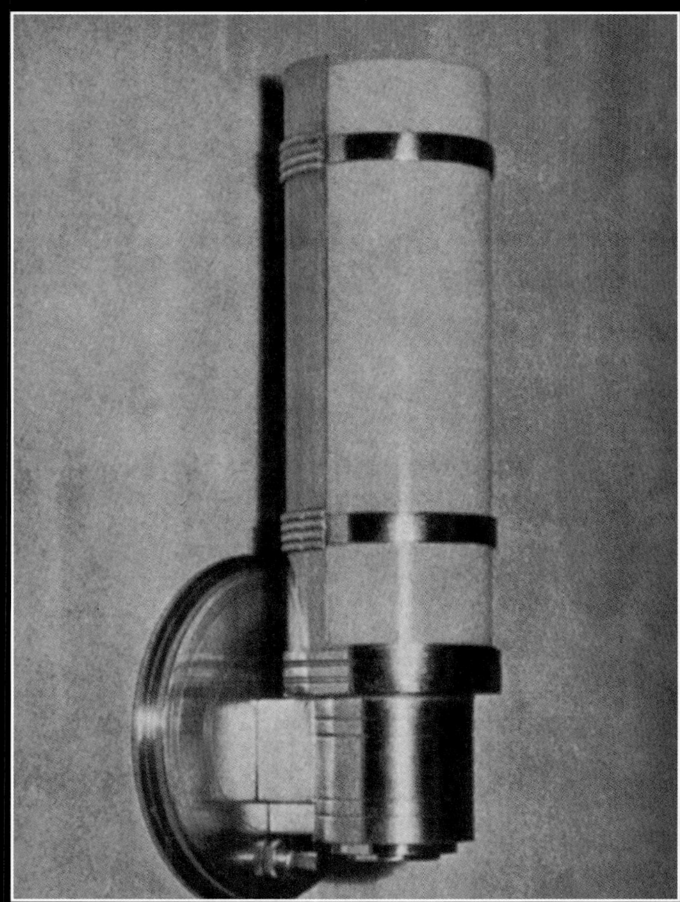

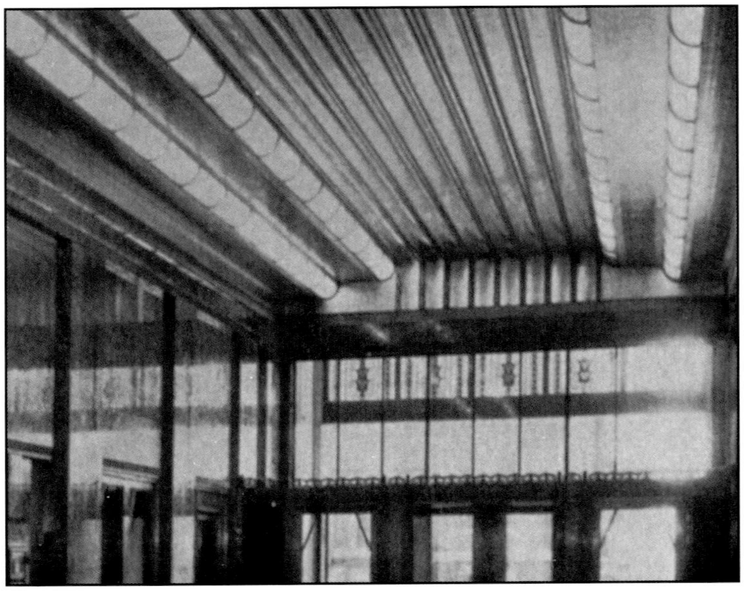

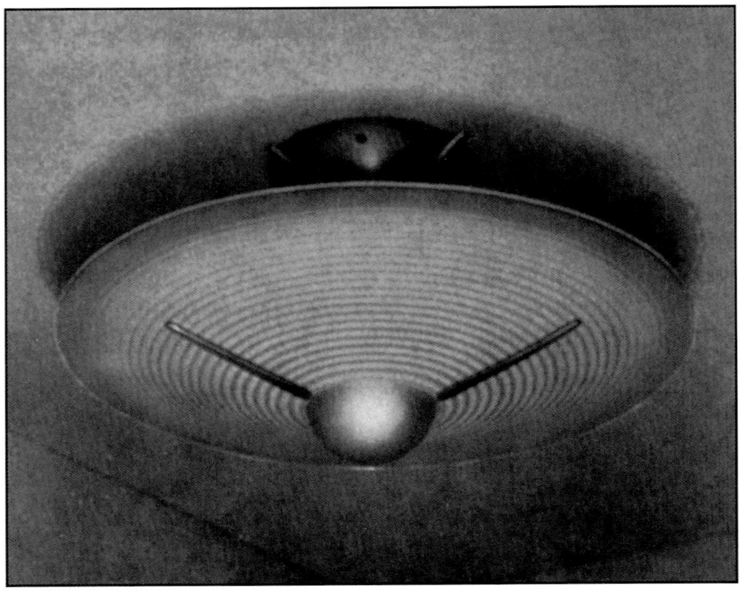

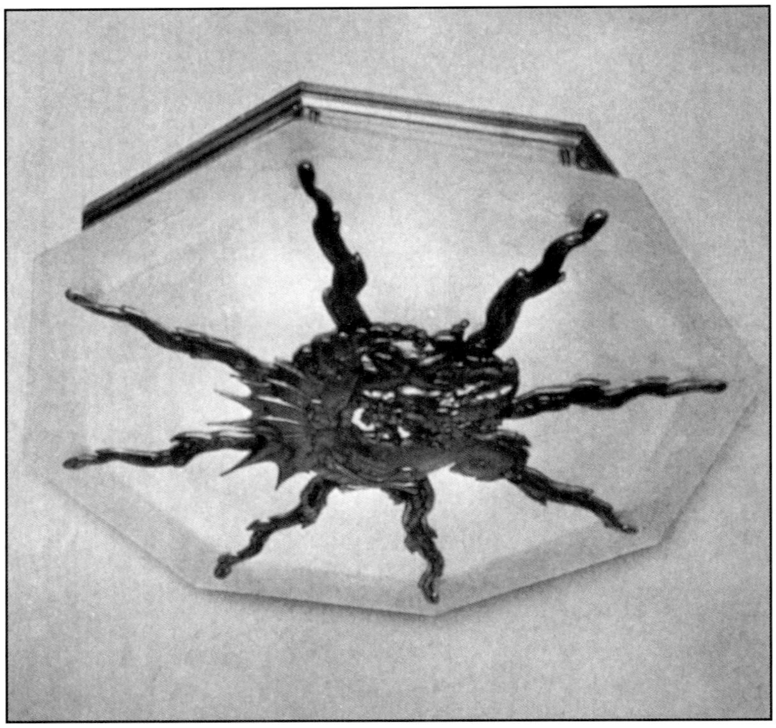

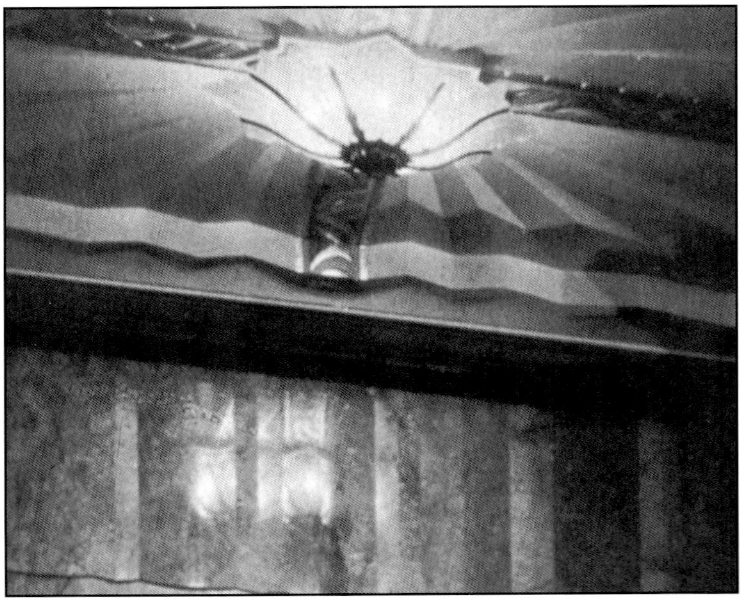

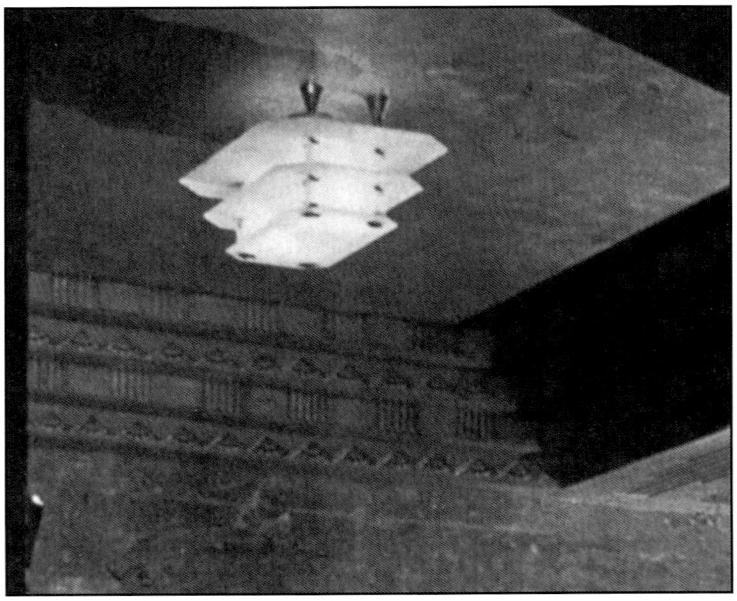

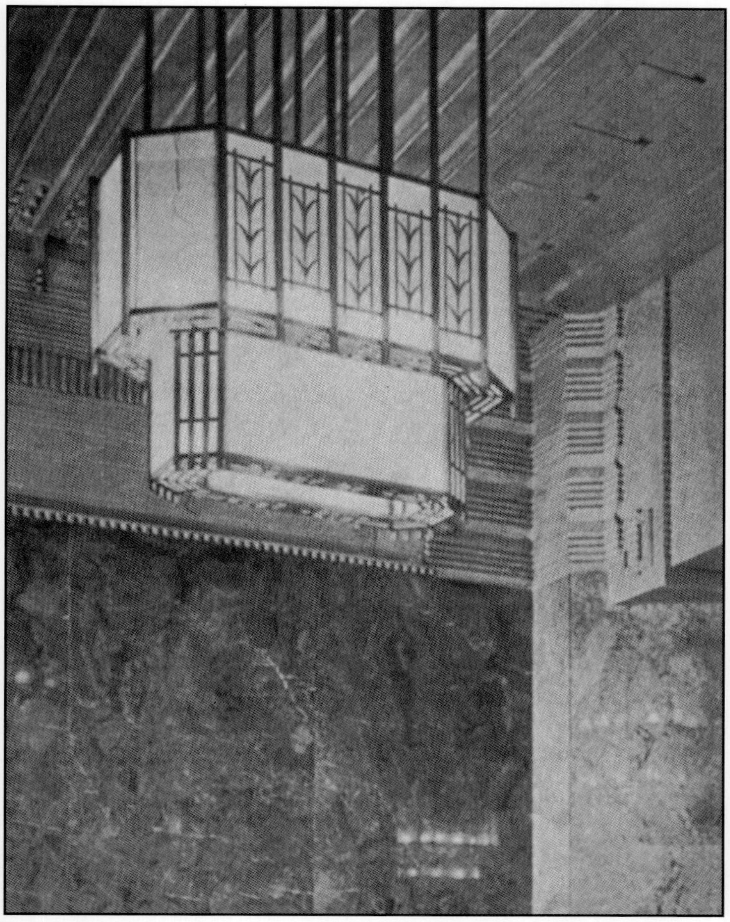

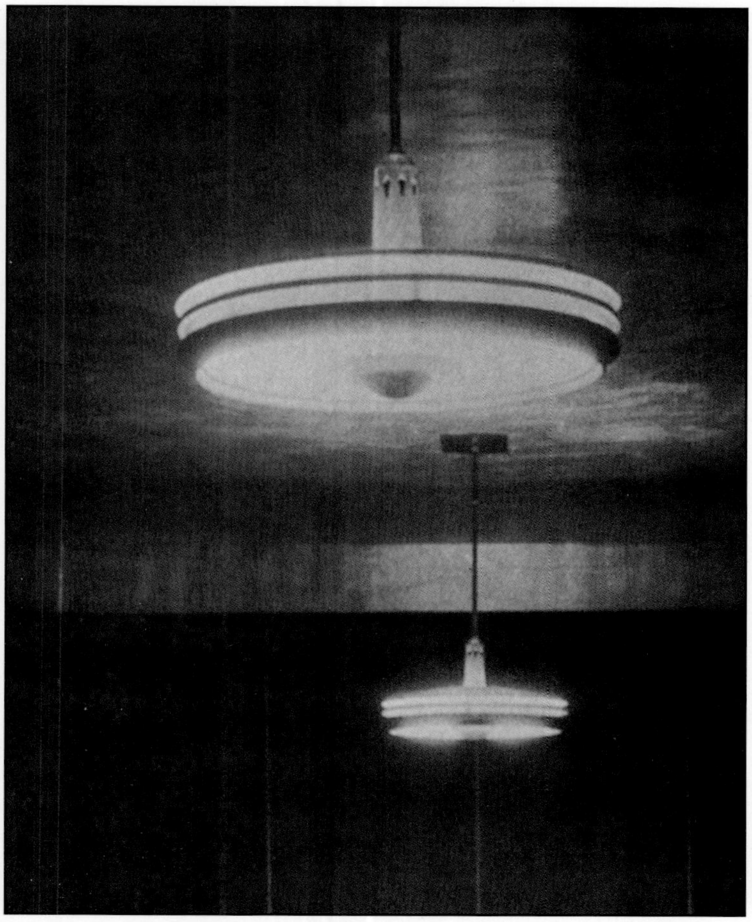

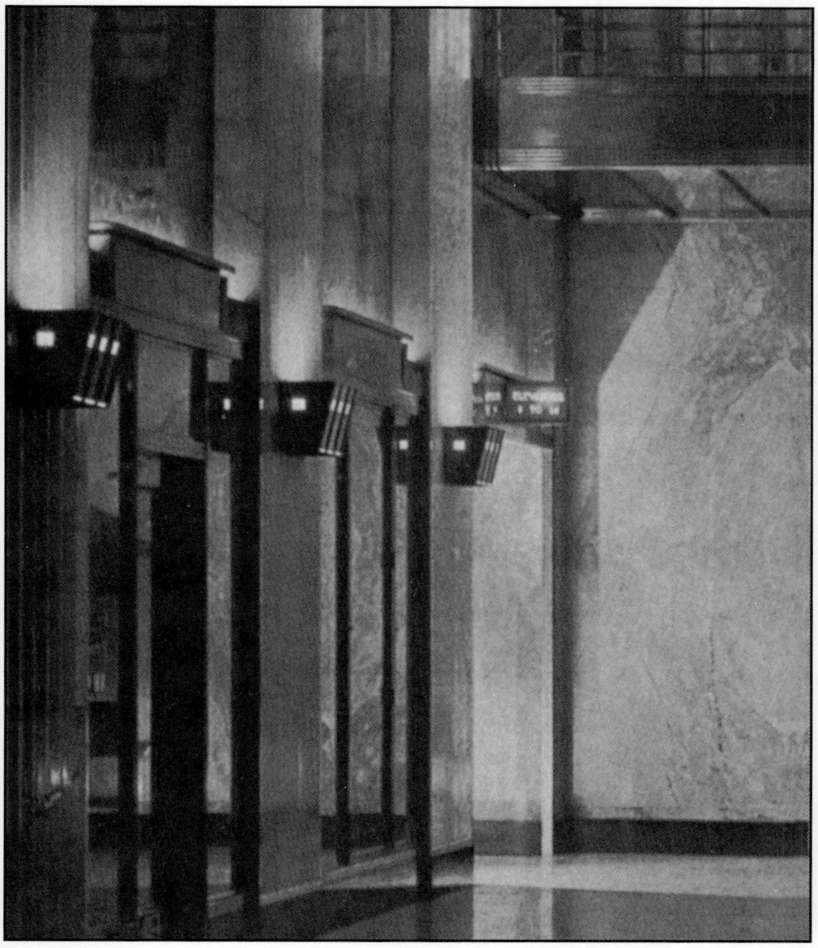

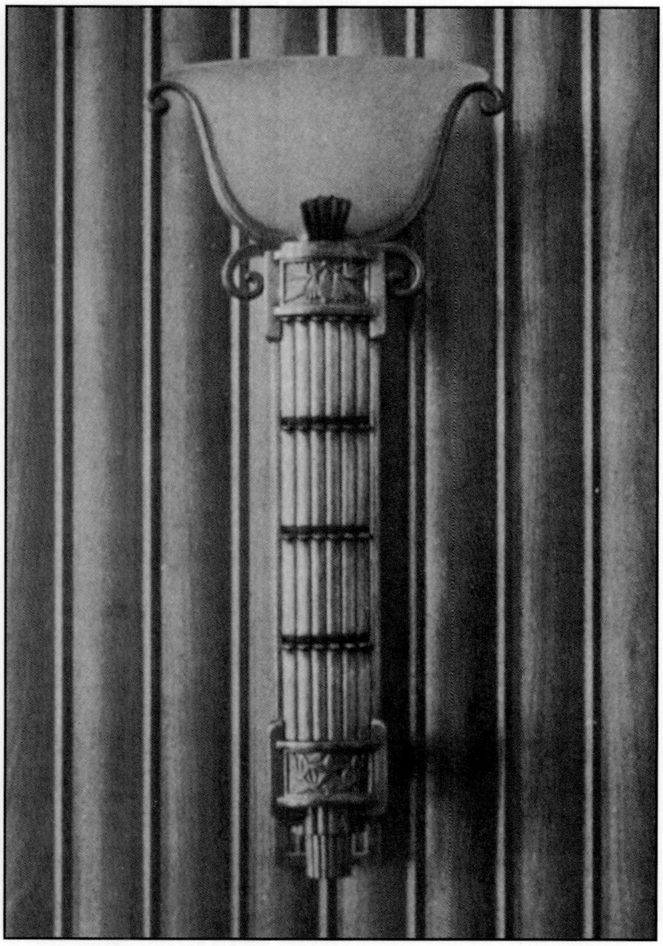

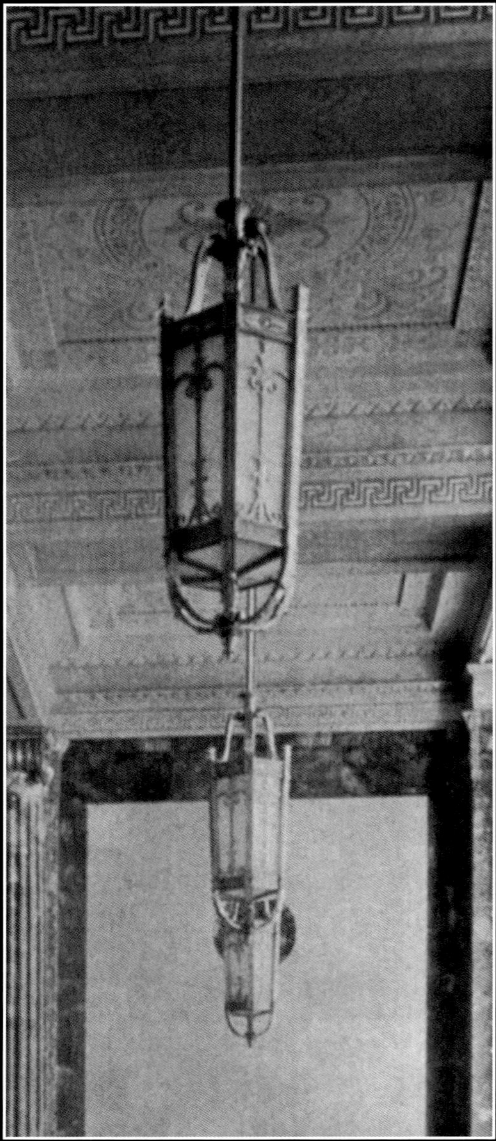

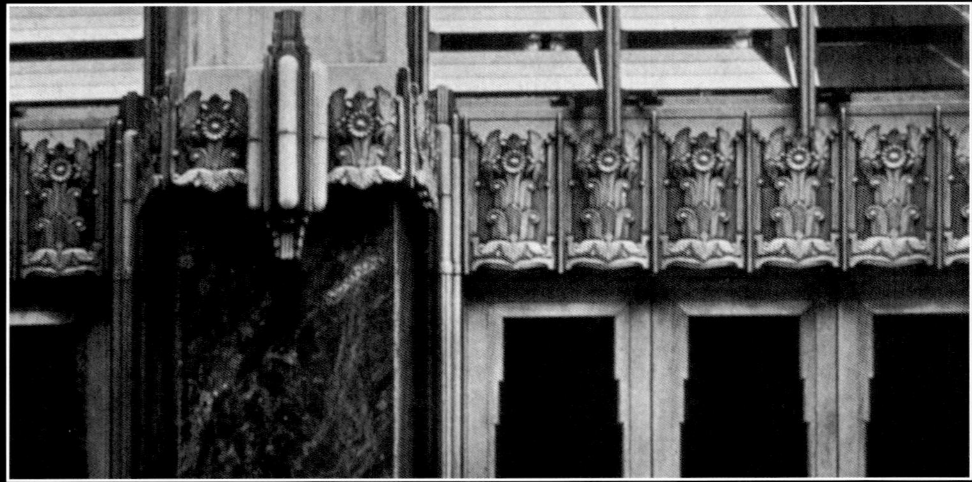

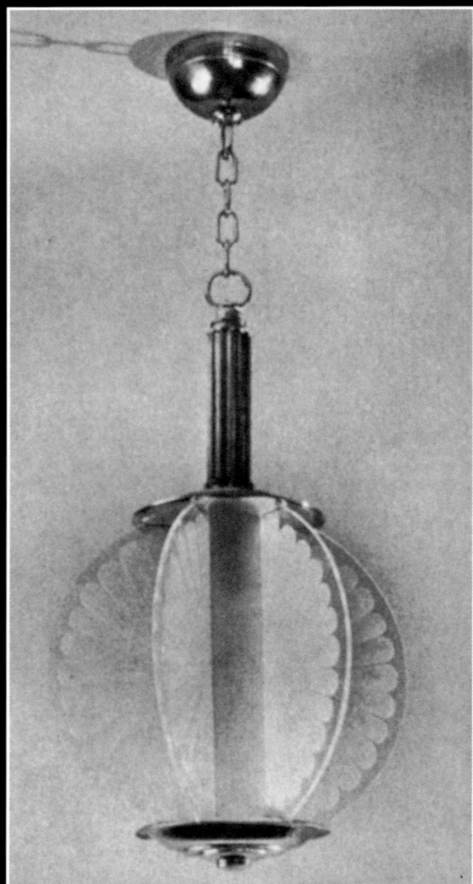

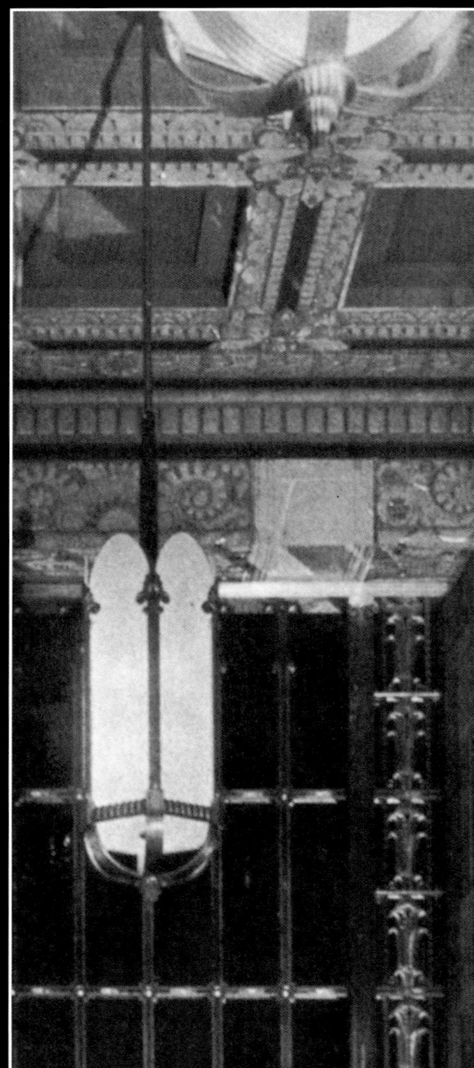

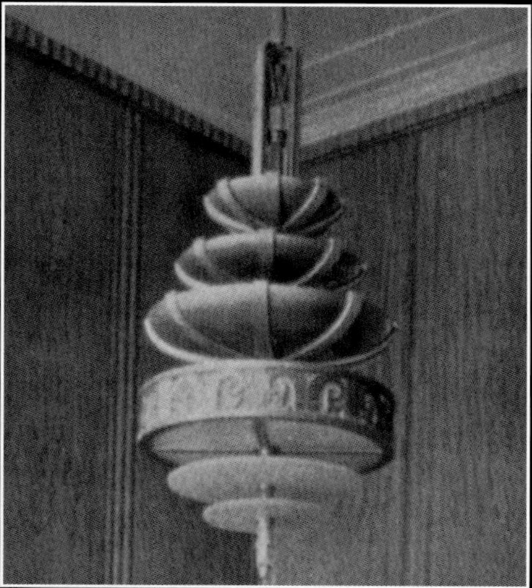

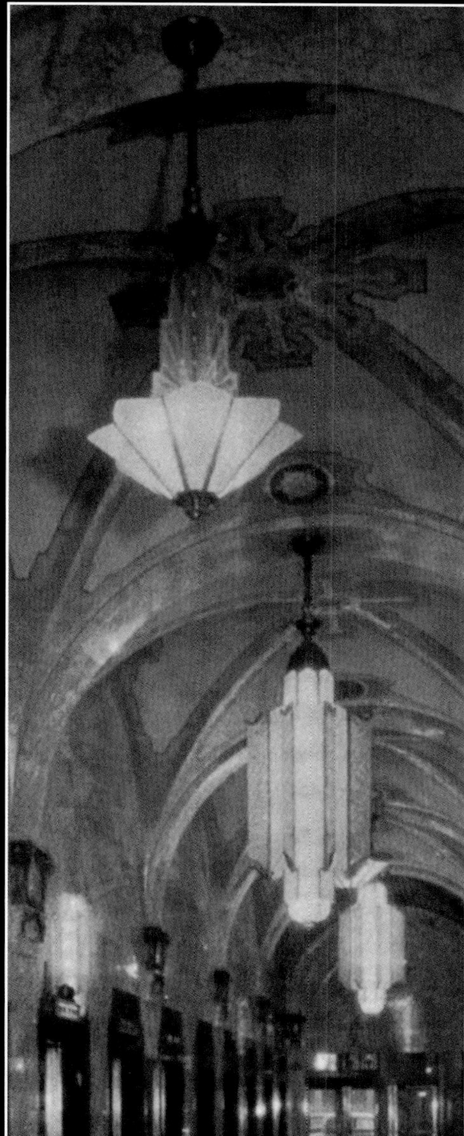

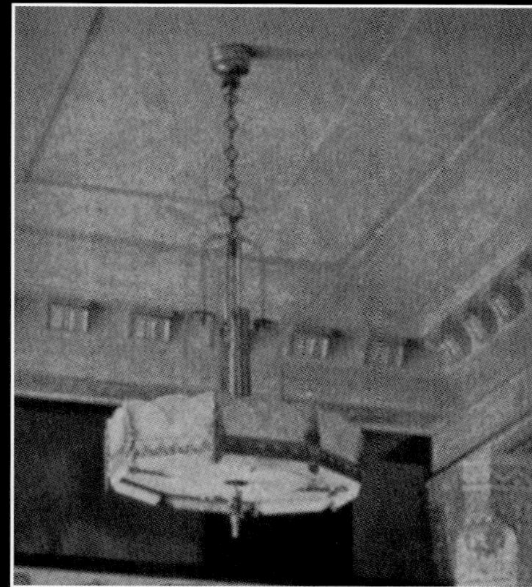

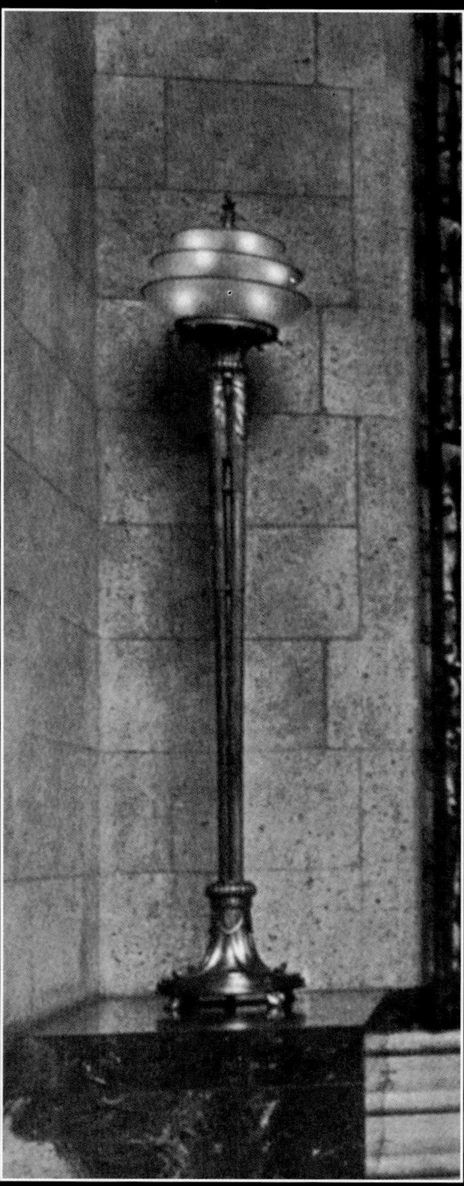

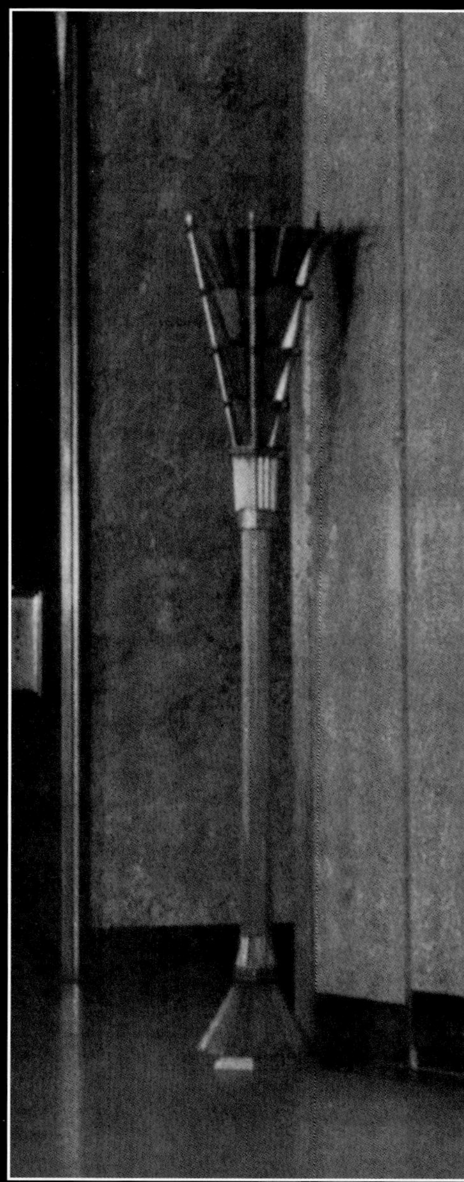

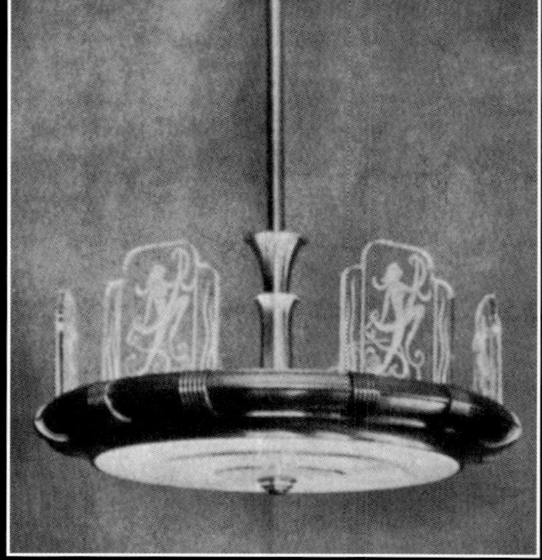

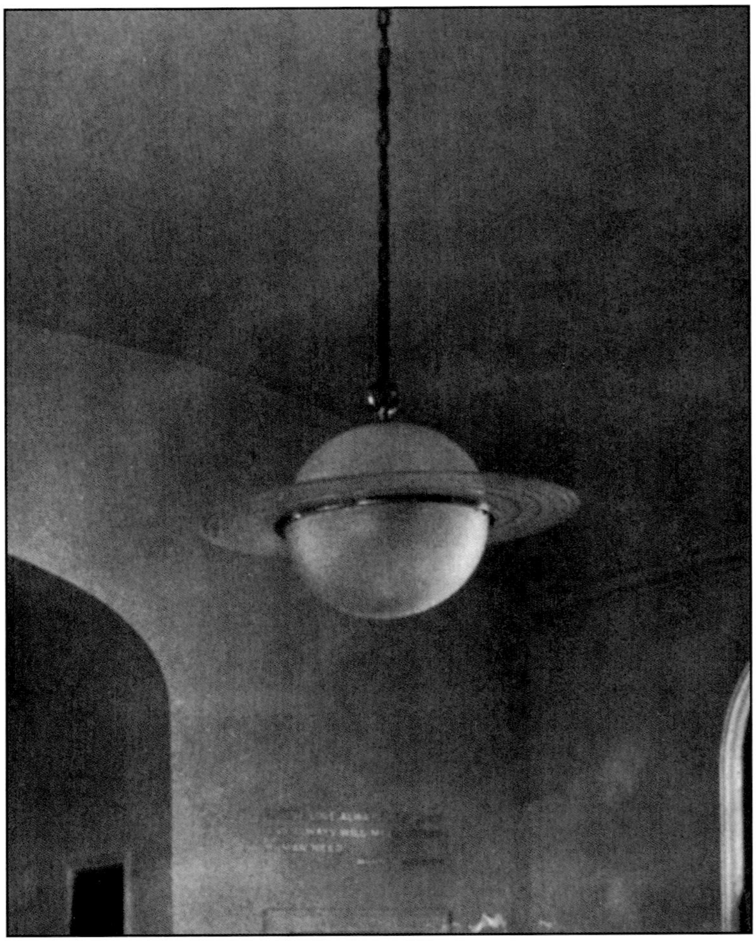

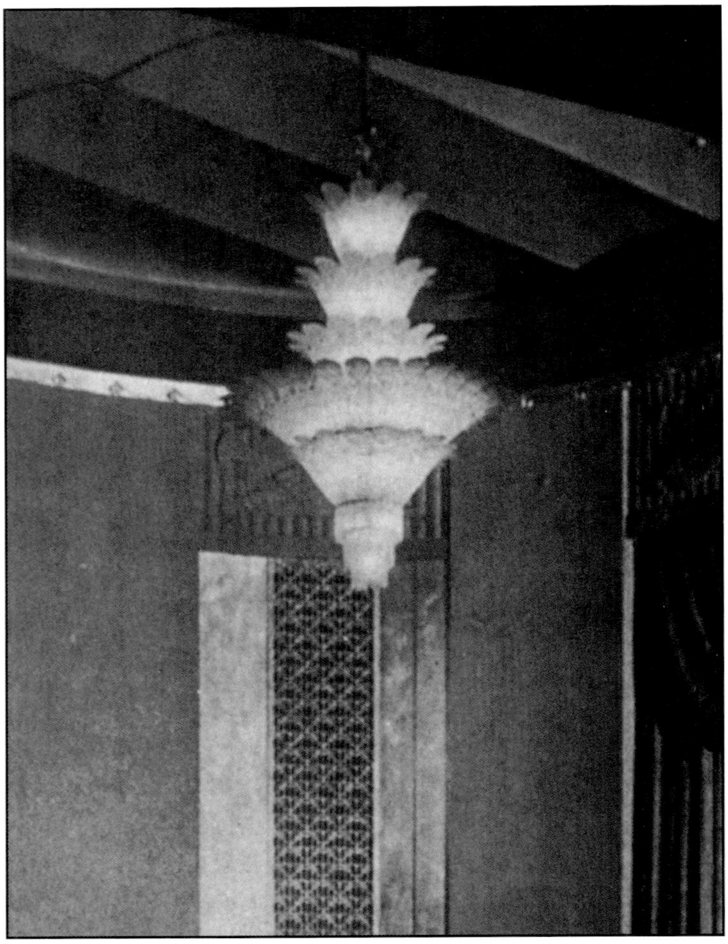

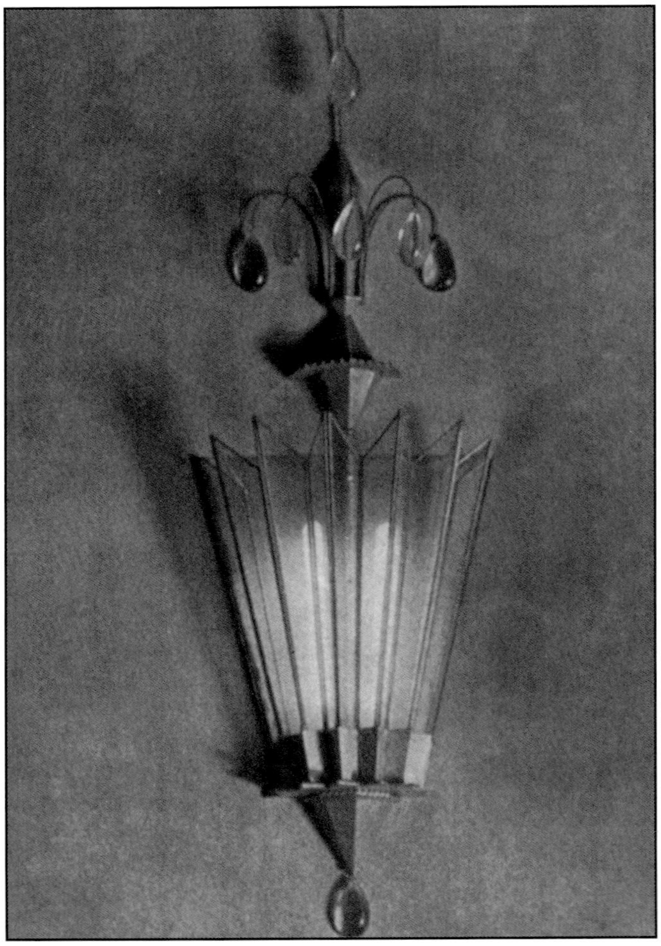

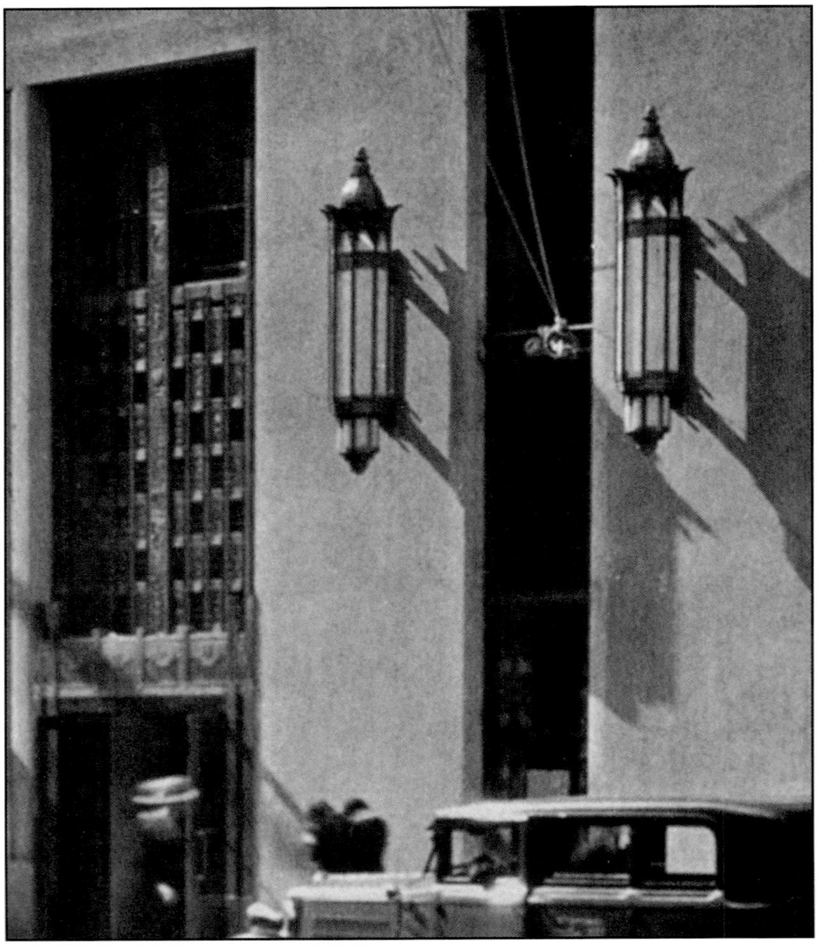

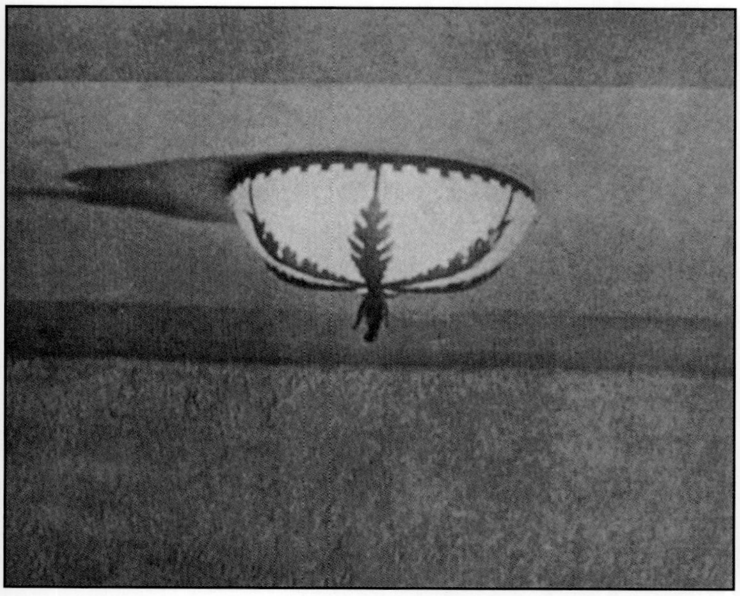

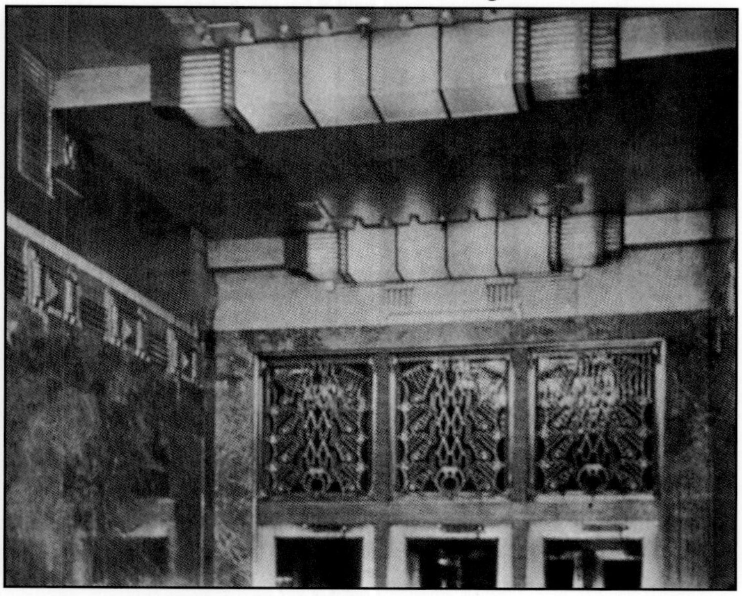

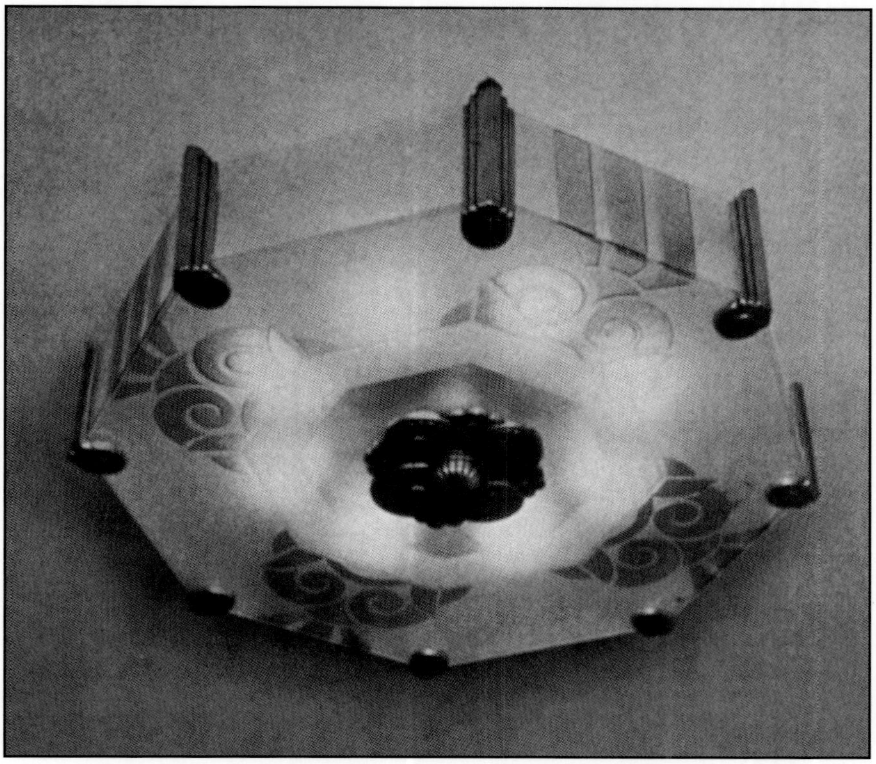

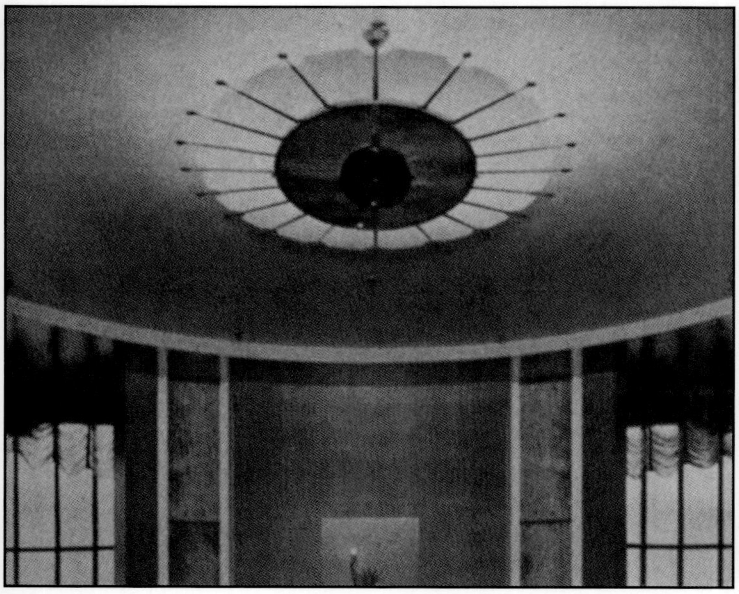

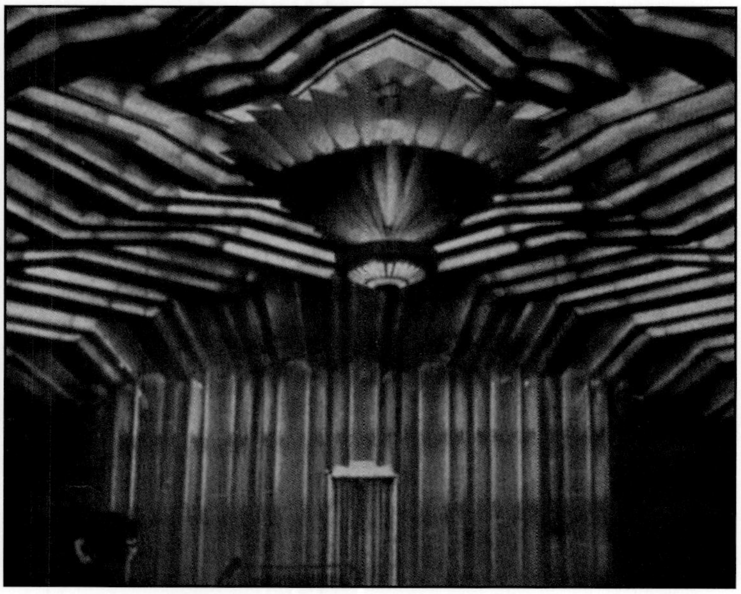

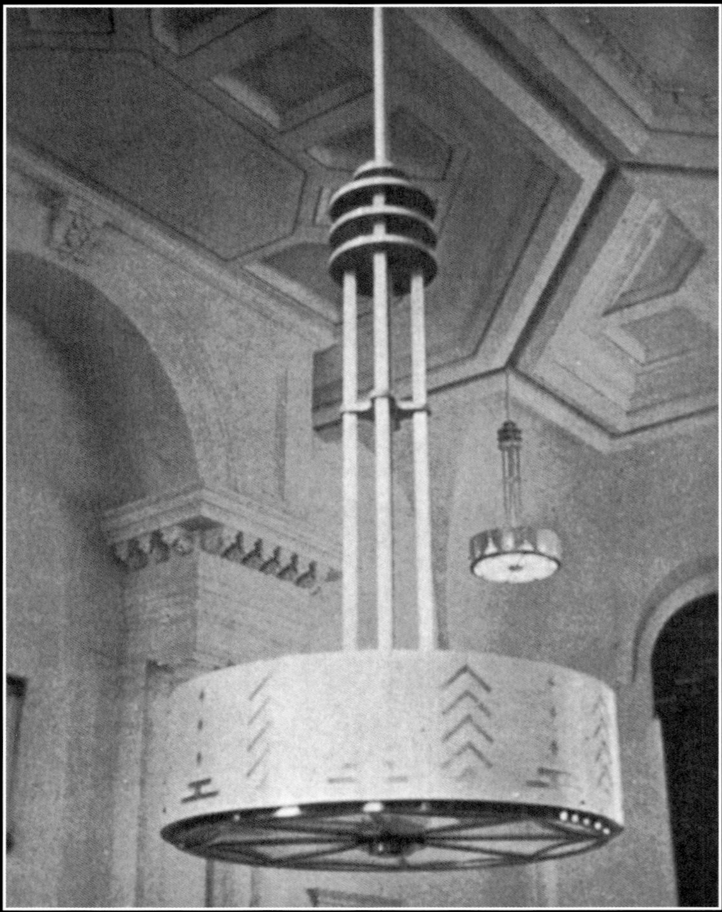

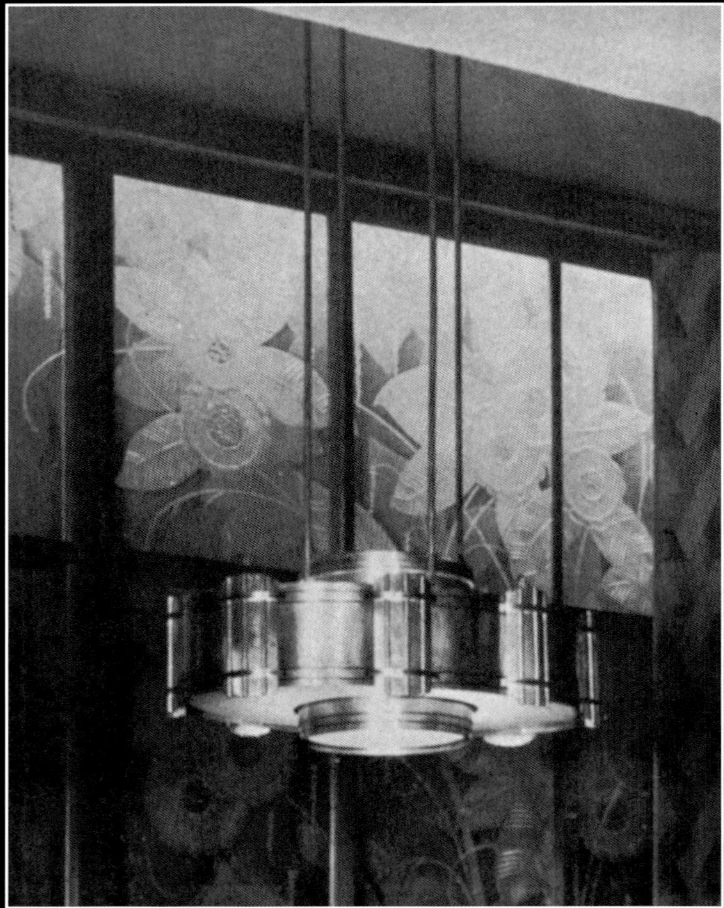

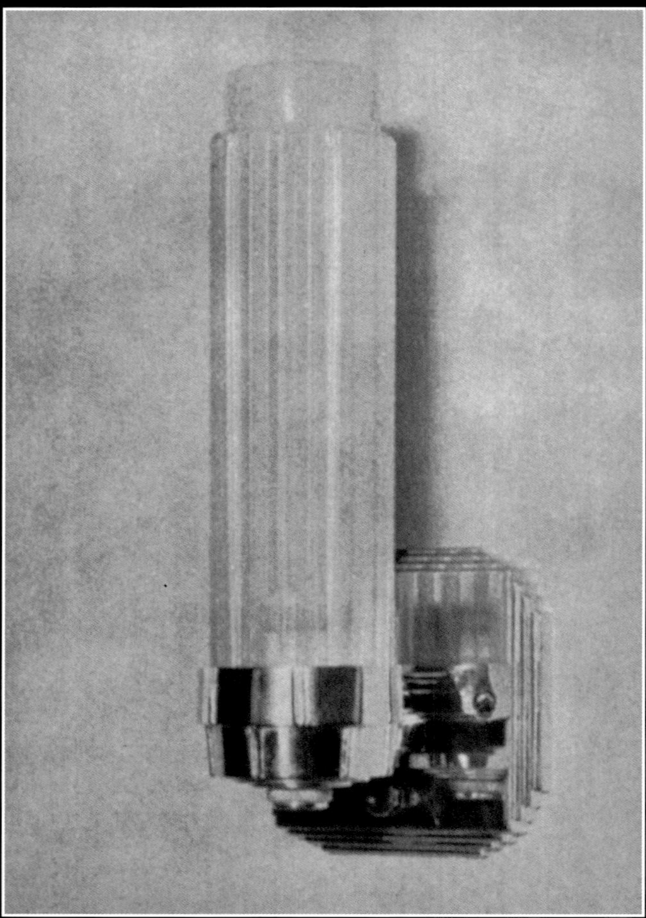

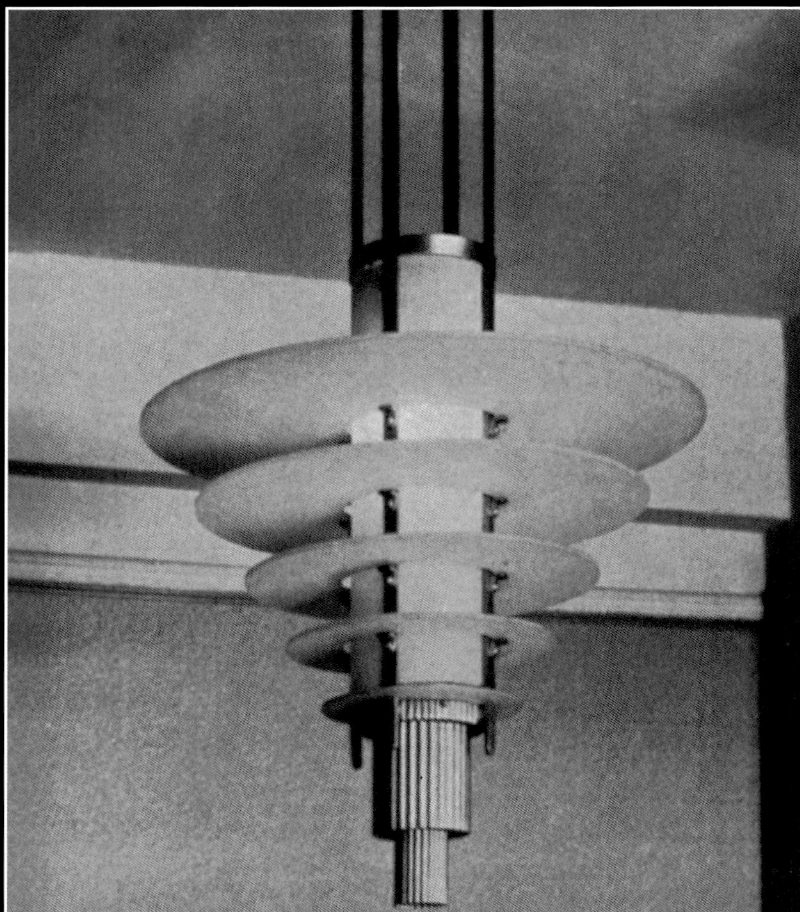

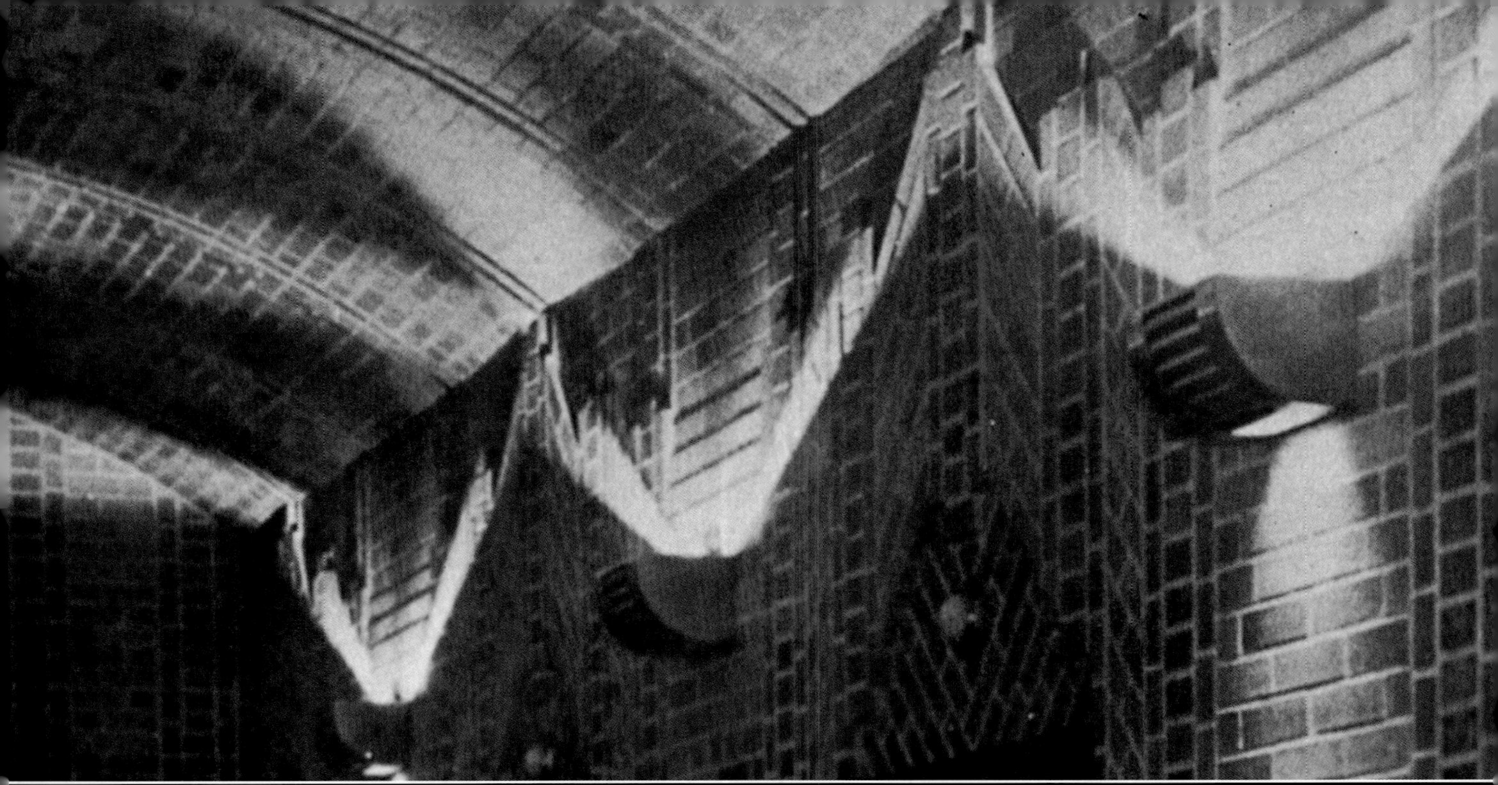
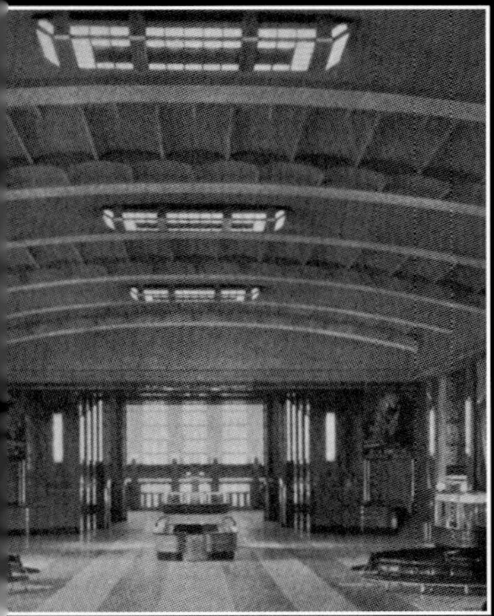
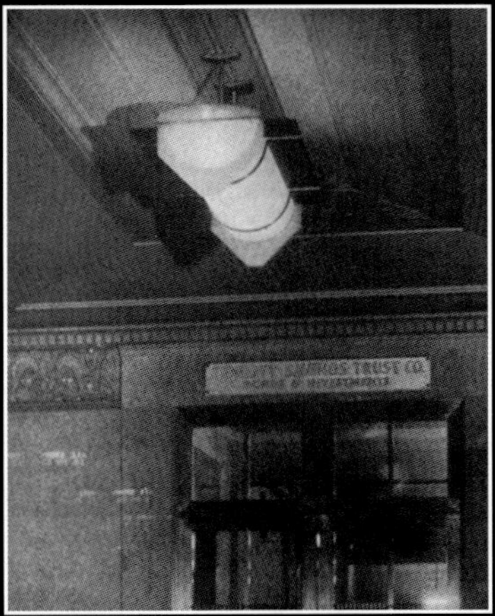
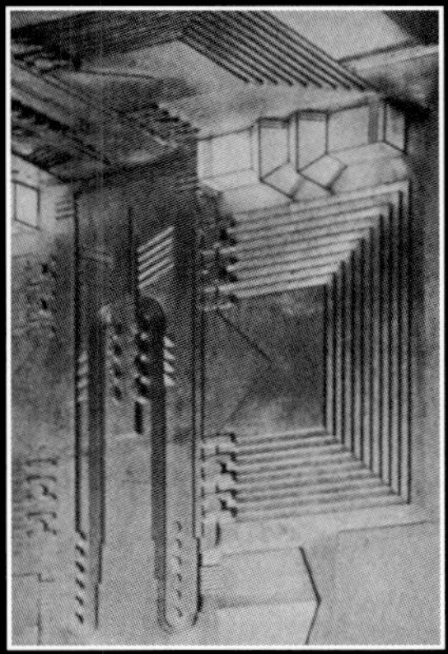
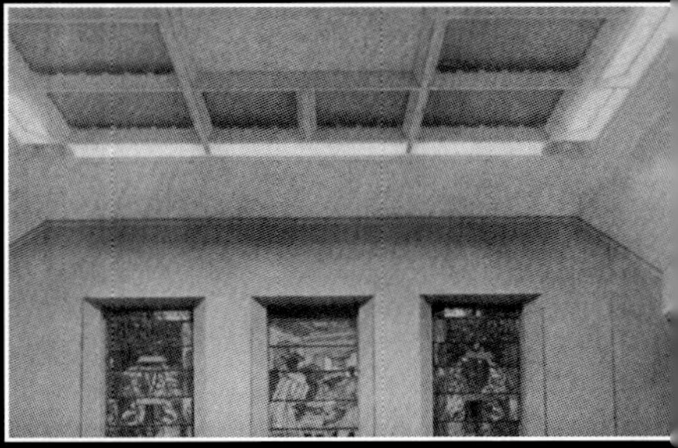
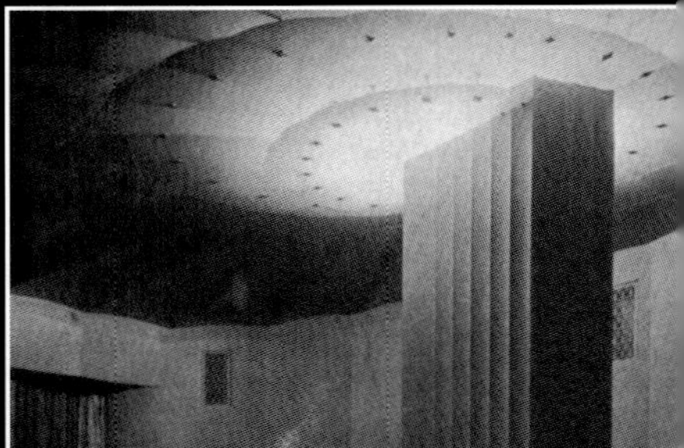
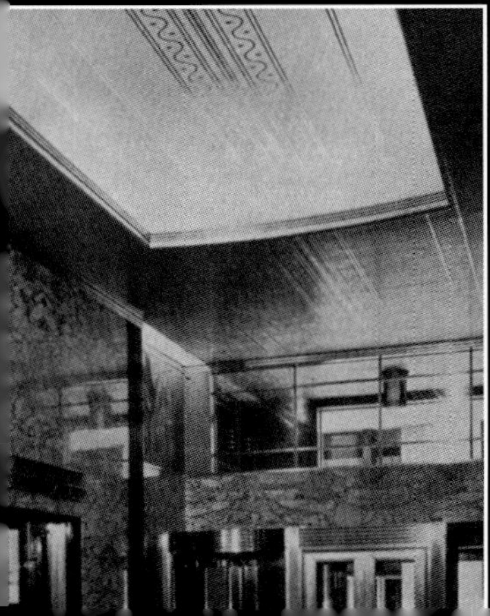
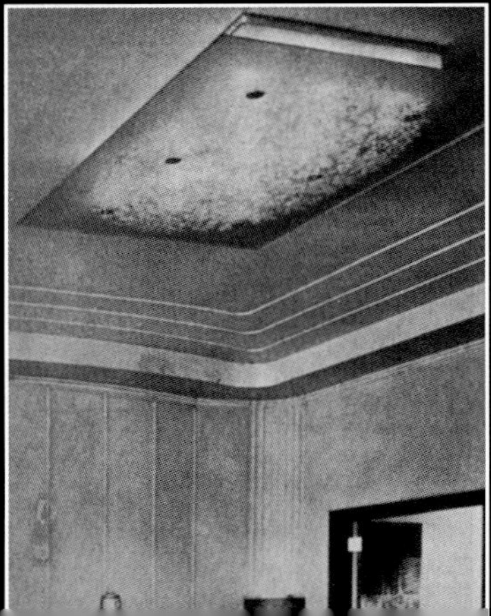
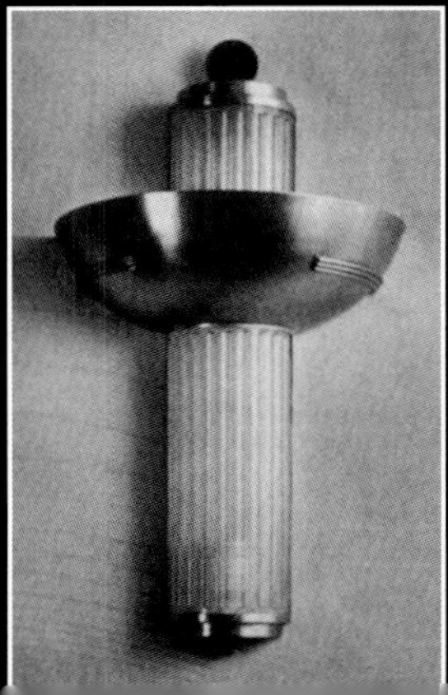
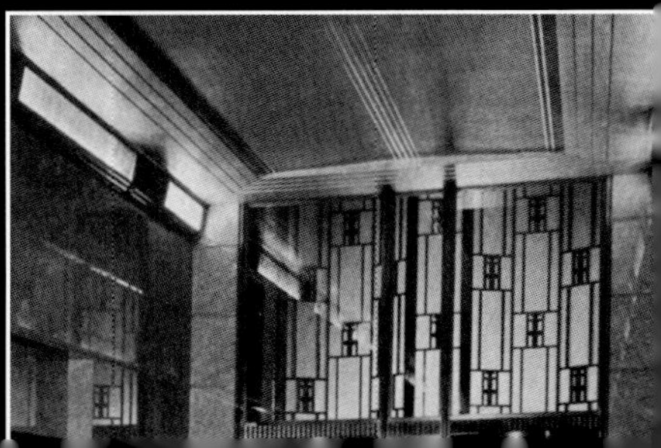

1

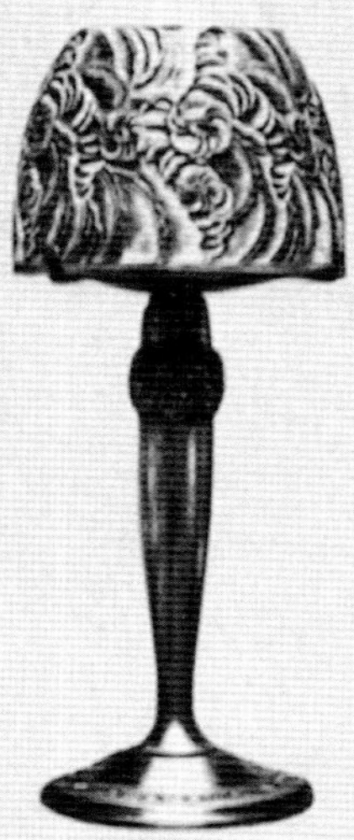

3

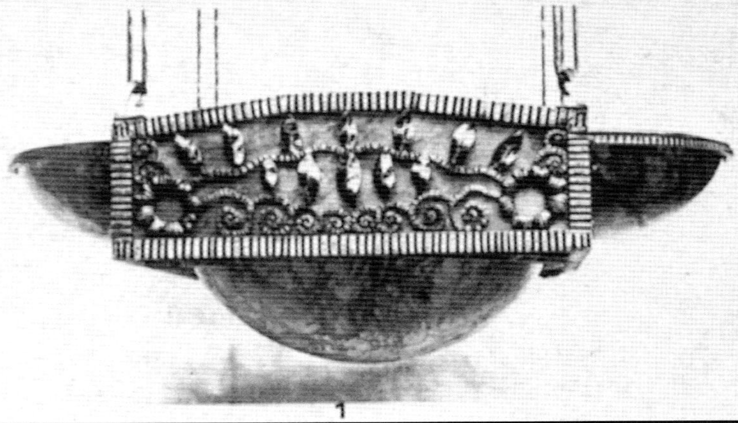

1

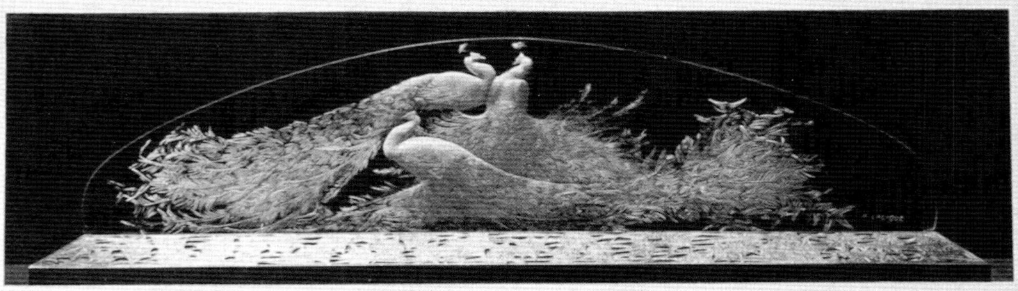

1

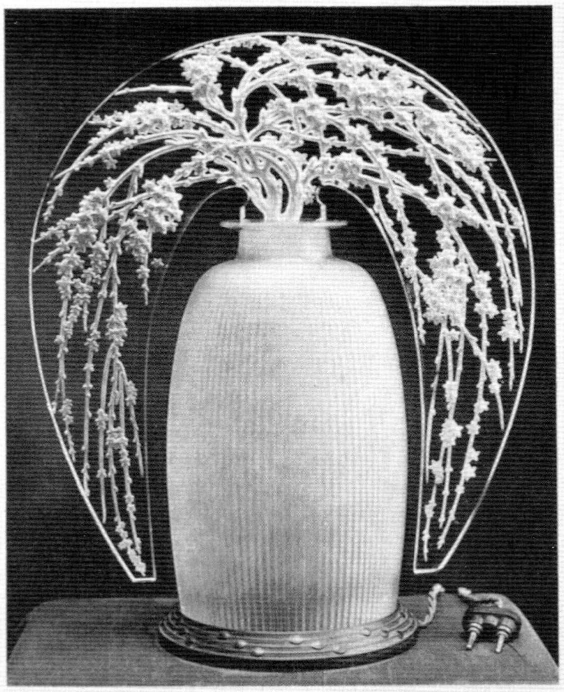

2

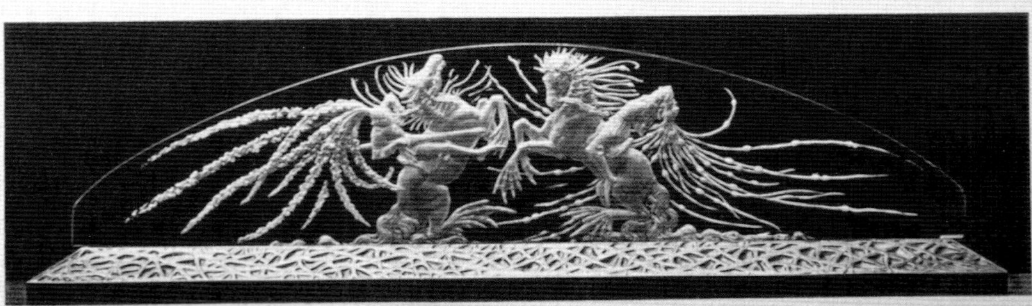

3

Façades, Awnings, & Outdoor Windows

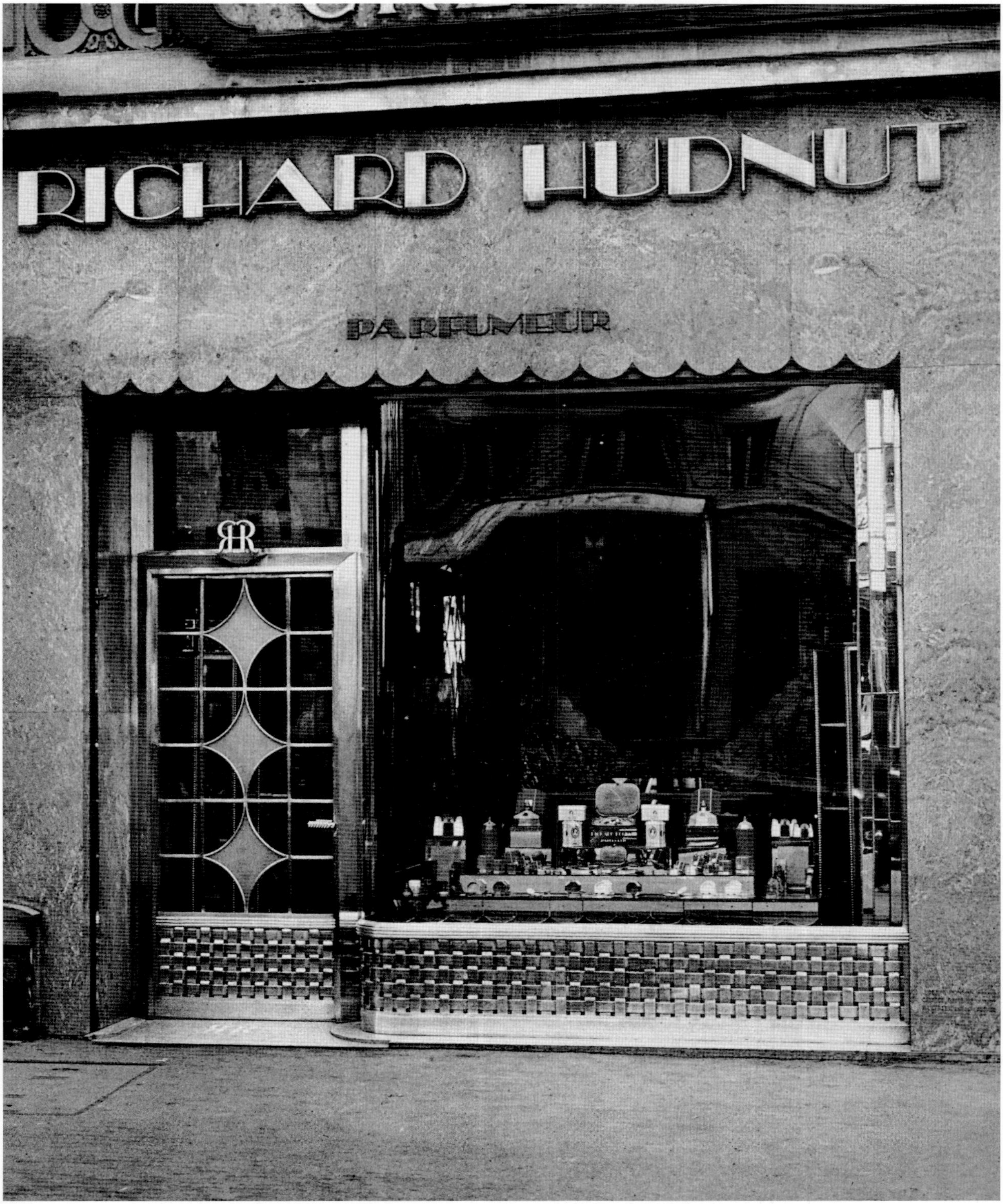

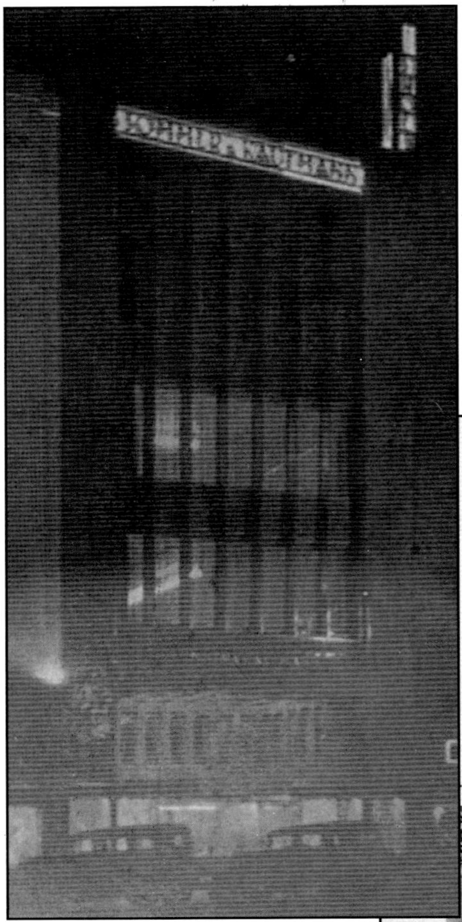

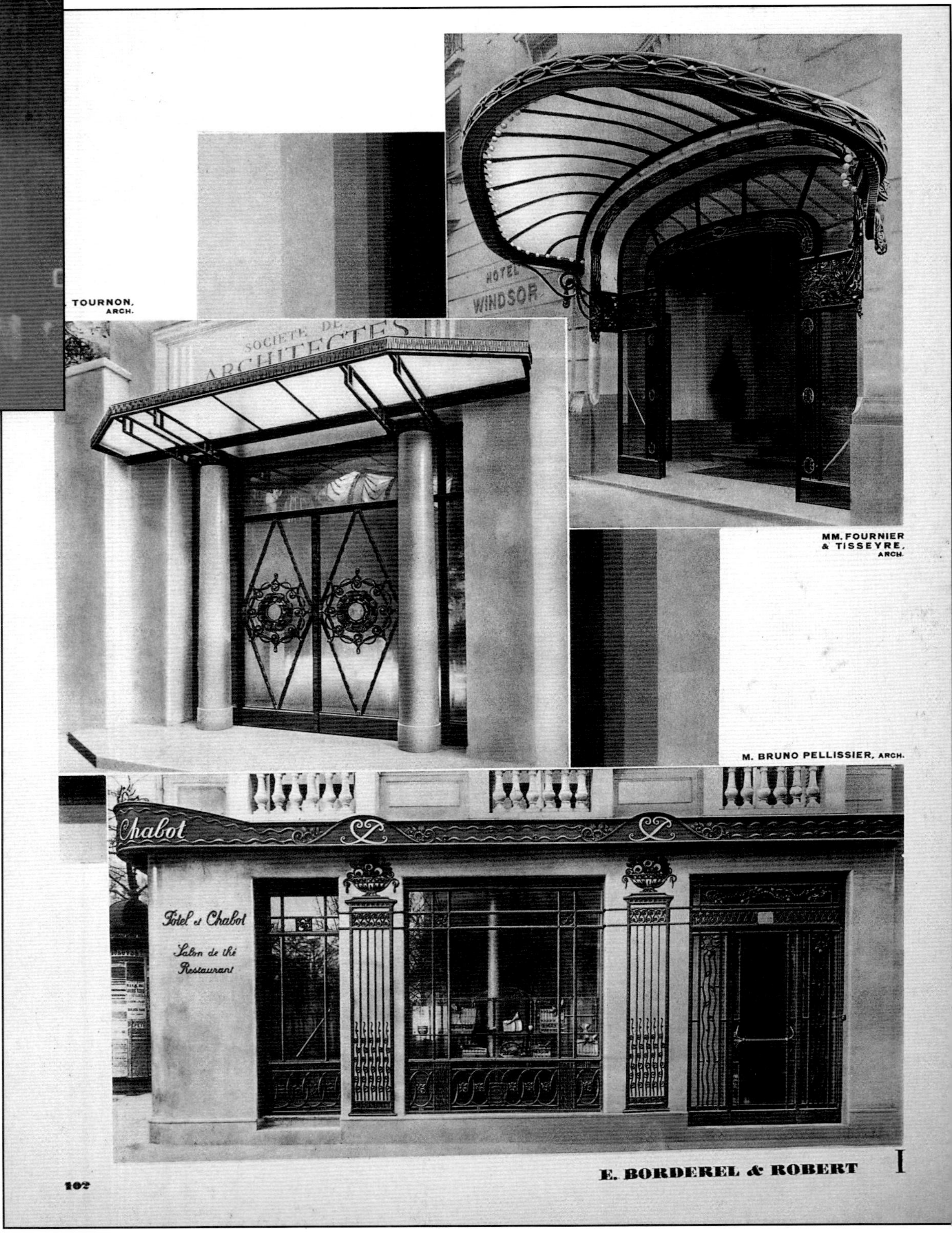
TOURNON, ARCH.
HÔTEL WINDSOR
SOCIETE DE ARCHITECTES
MM. FOURNIER & TISSEYRE, ARCH.
M. BRUNO PELLISSIER, ARCH.
Chabot
Hôtel Chabot
Salon de thé
Restaurant
102
E. BORDEREL & ROBERT
I

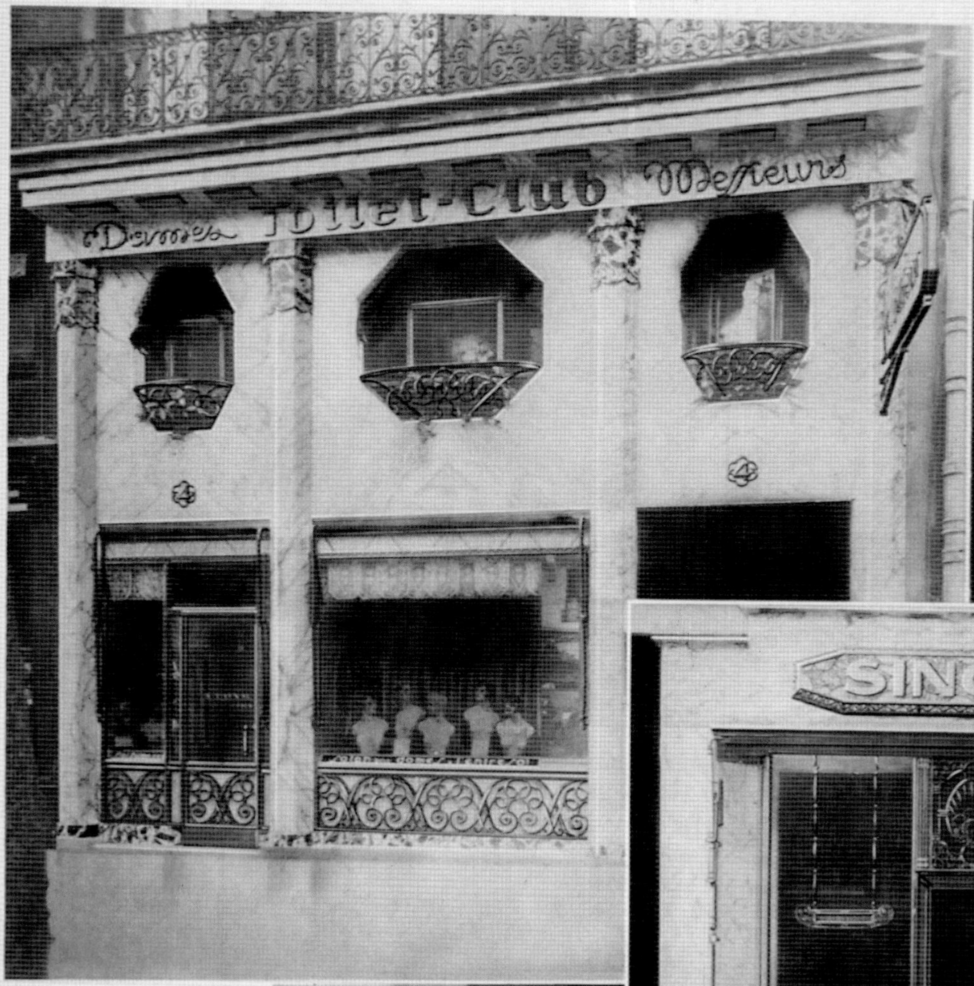

M. A. VOIS, ARCH.

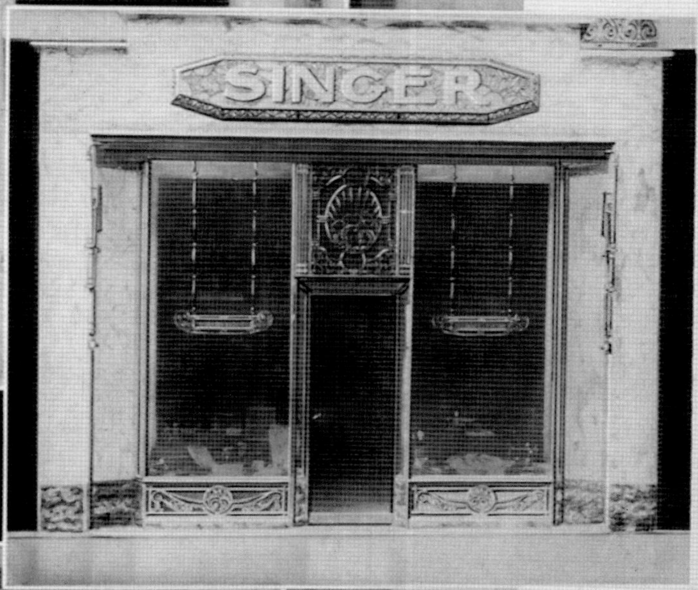

MM. BAHRMANN & ARNOULD, ARCH.

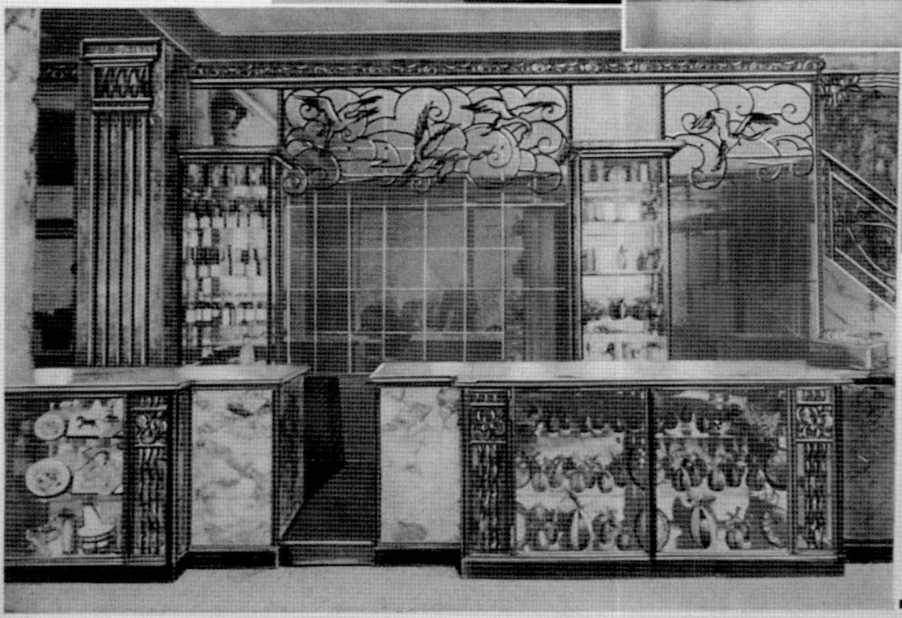

M. BRUNO PELLISSIER, ARCH.

MM. PATOUILLARD & PELLECHET, ARCH

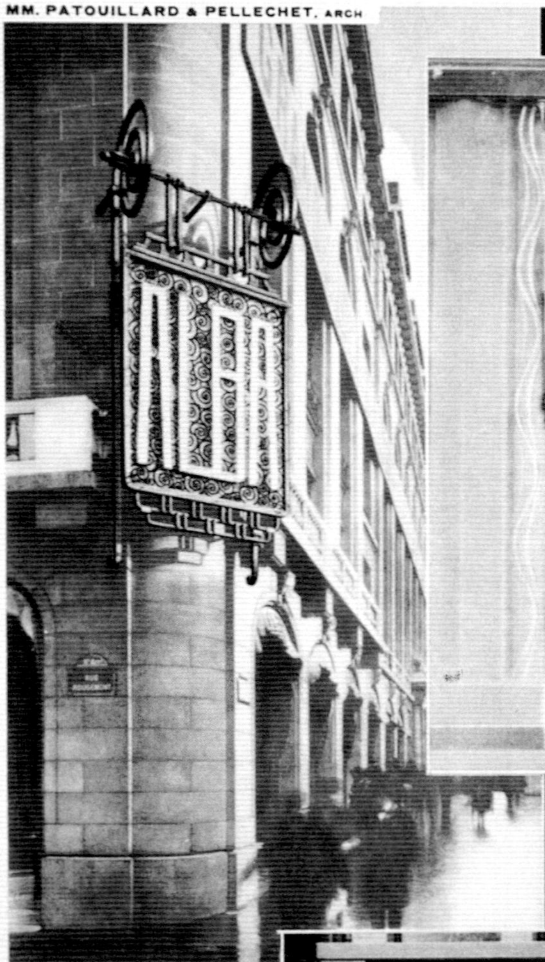

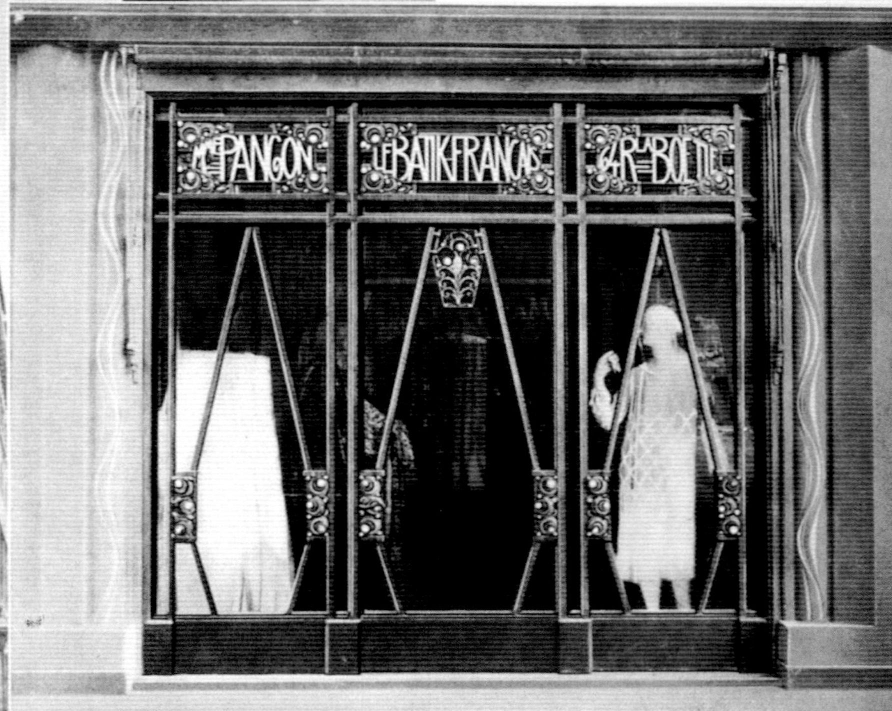

M. HAUBOLD, ARCH.

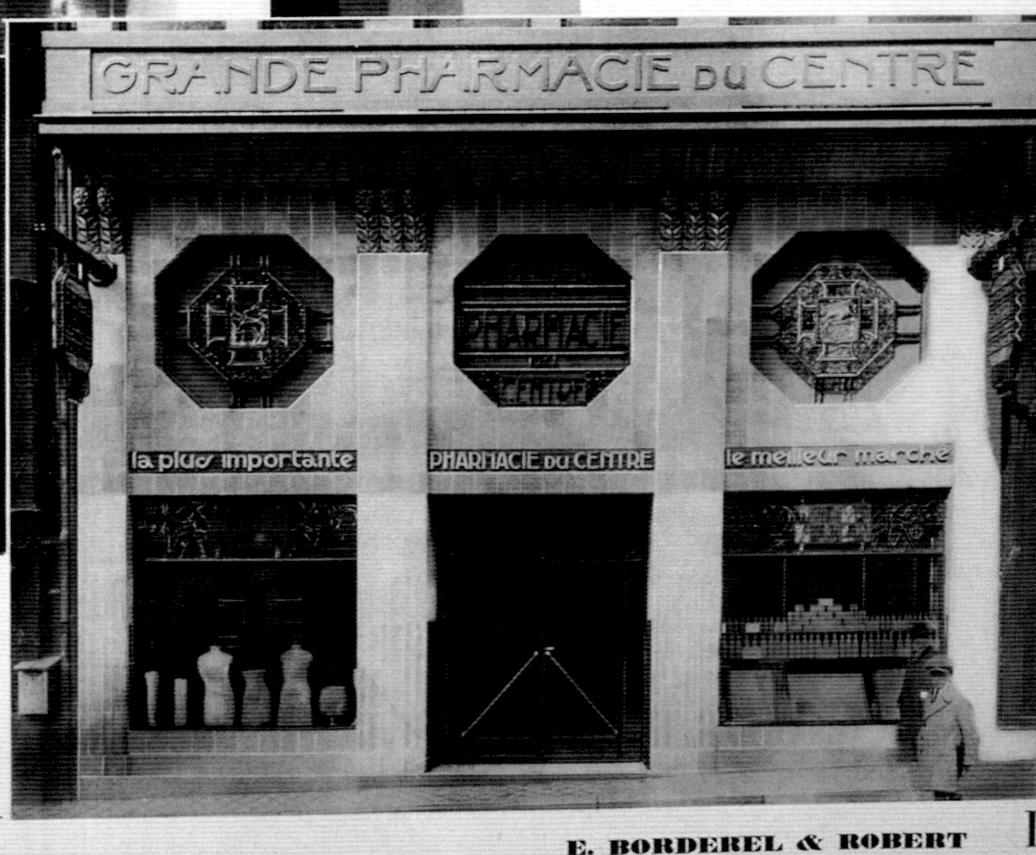

M. HAMELET, ARCH.

E. BORDEREL & ROBERT I

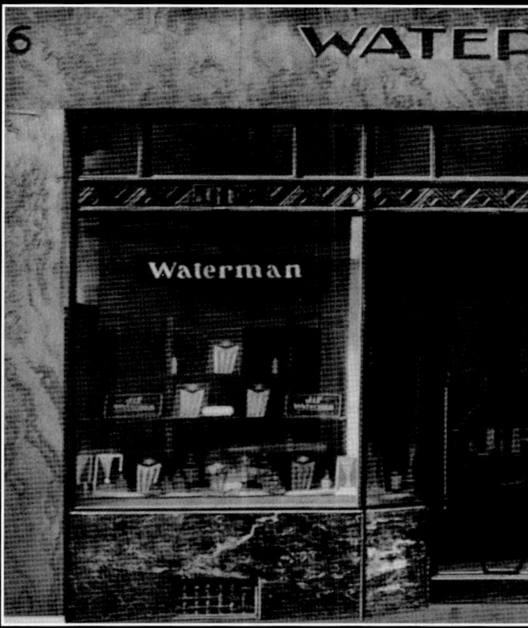
Waterman

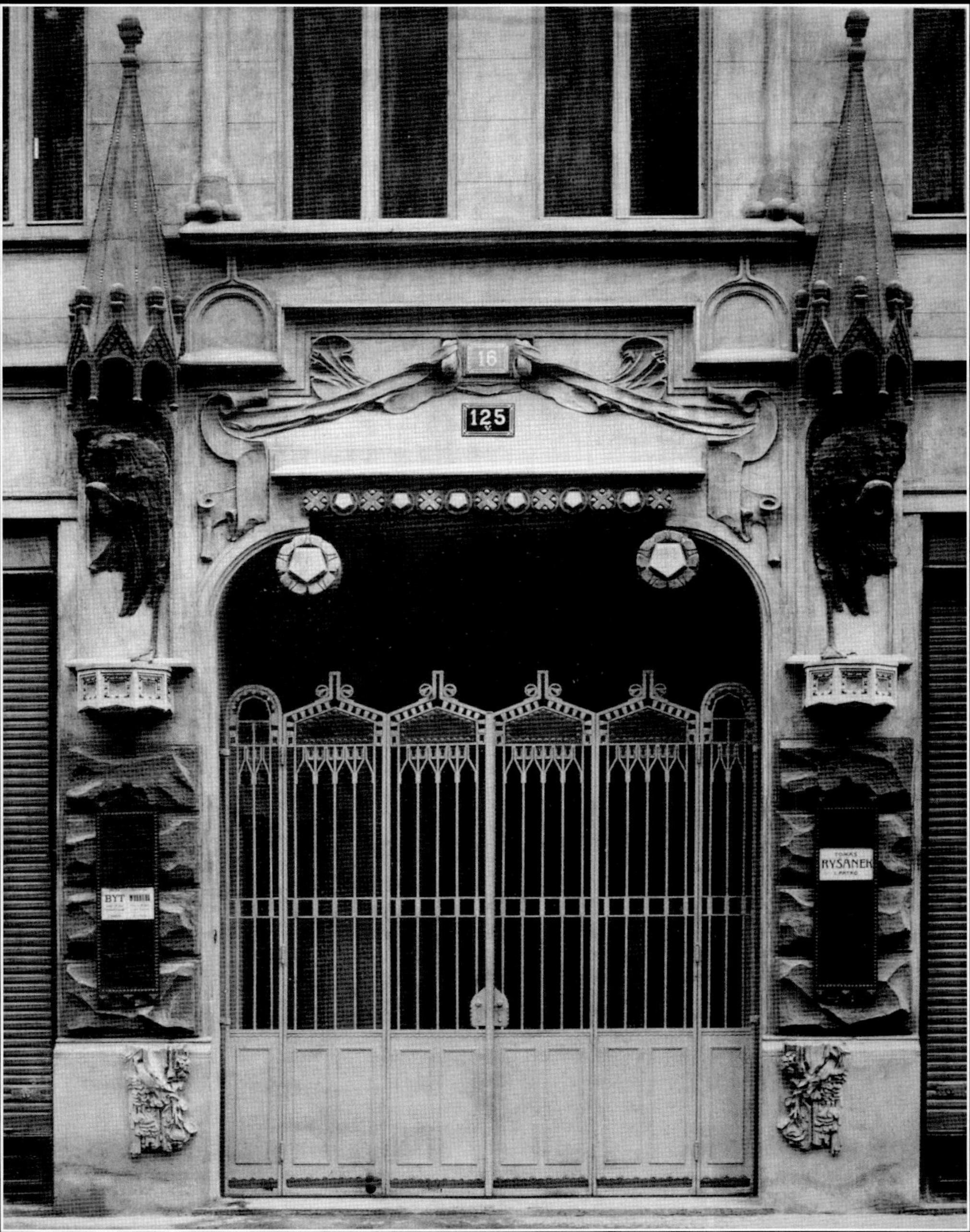
16
125
BYT

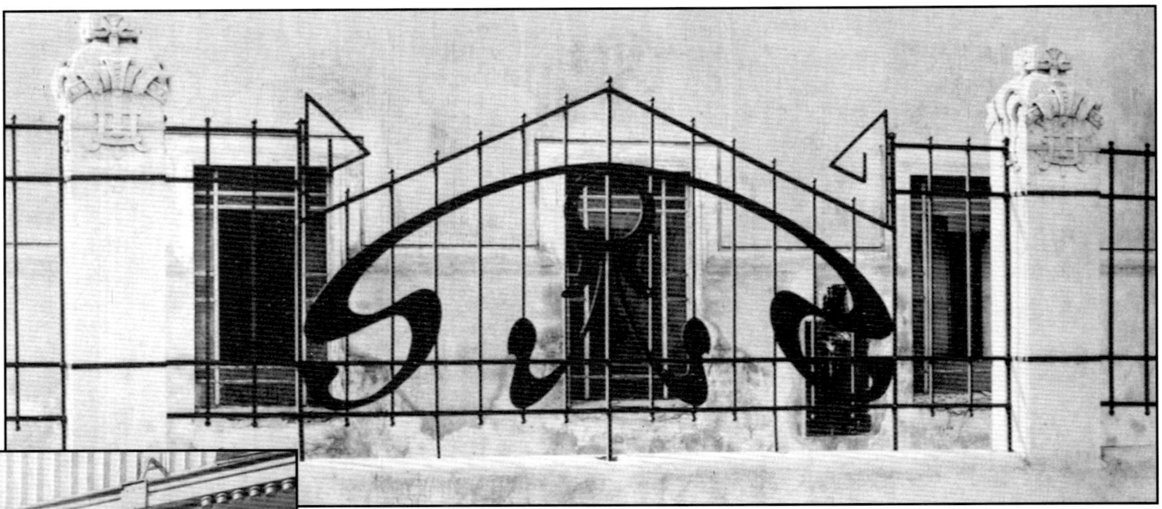

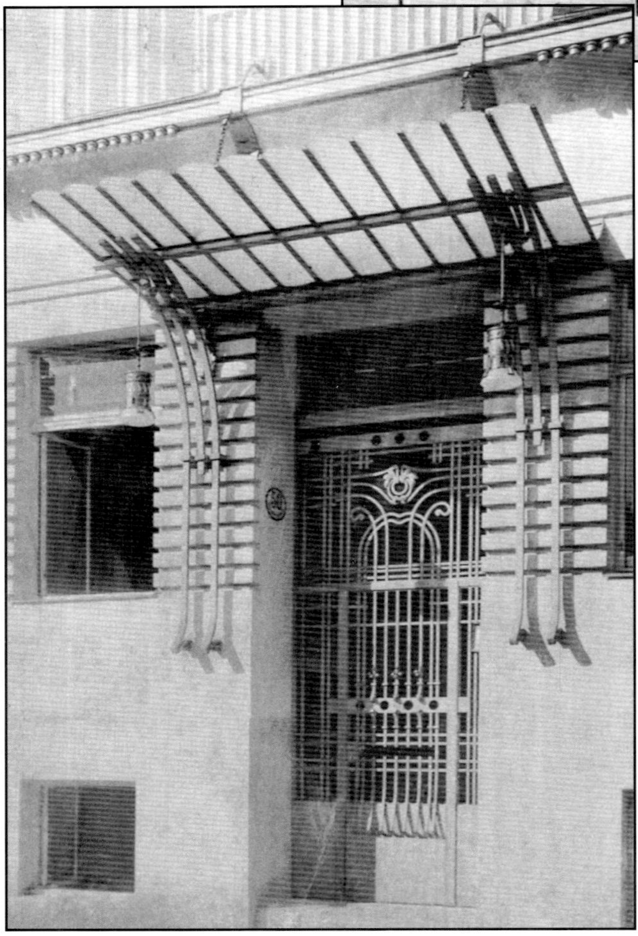

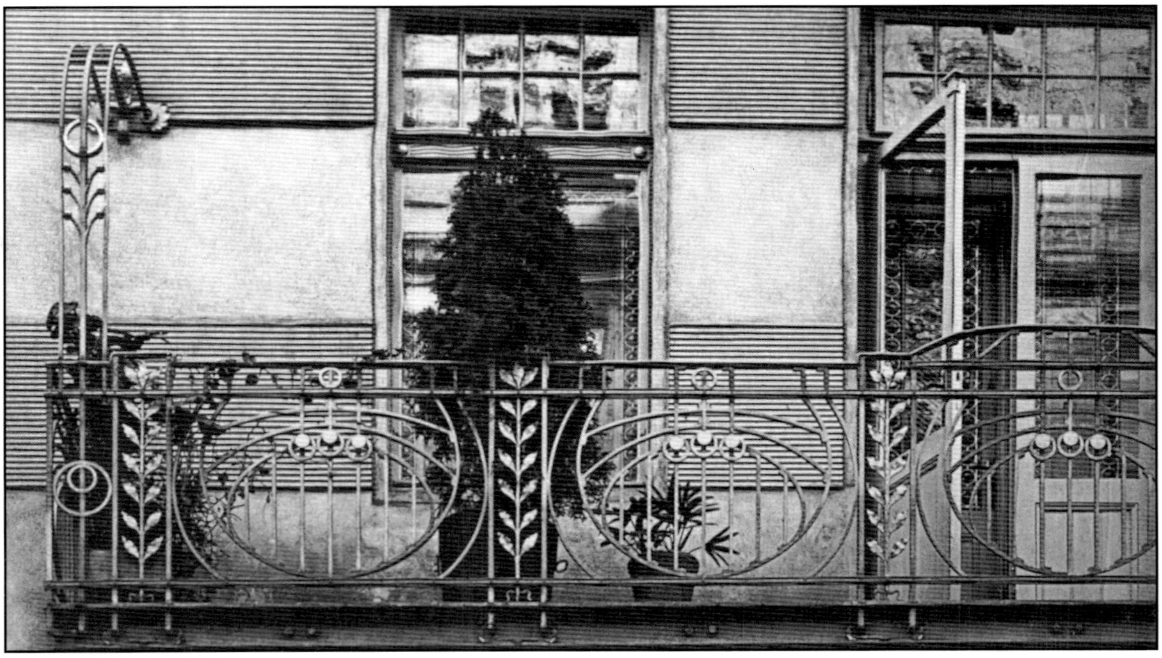

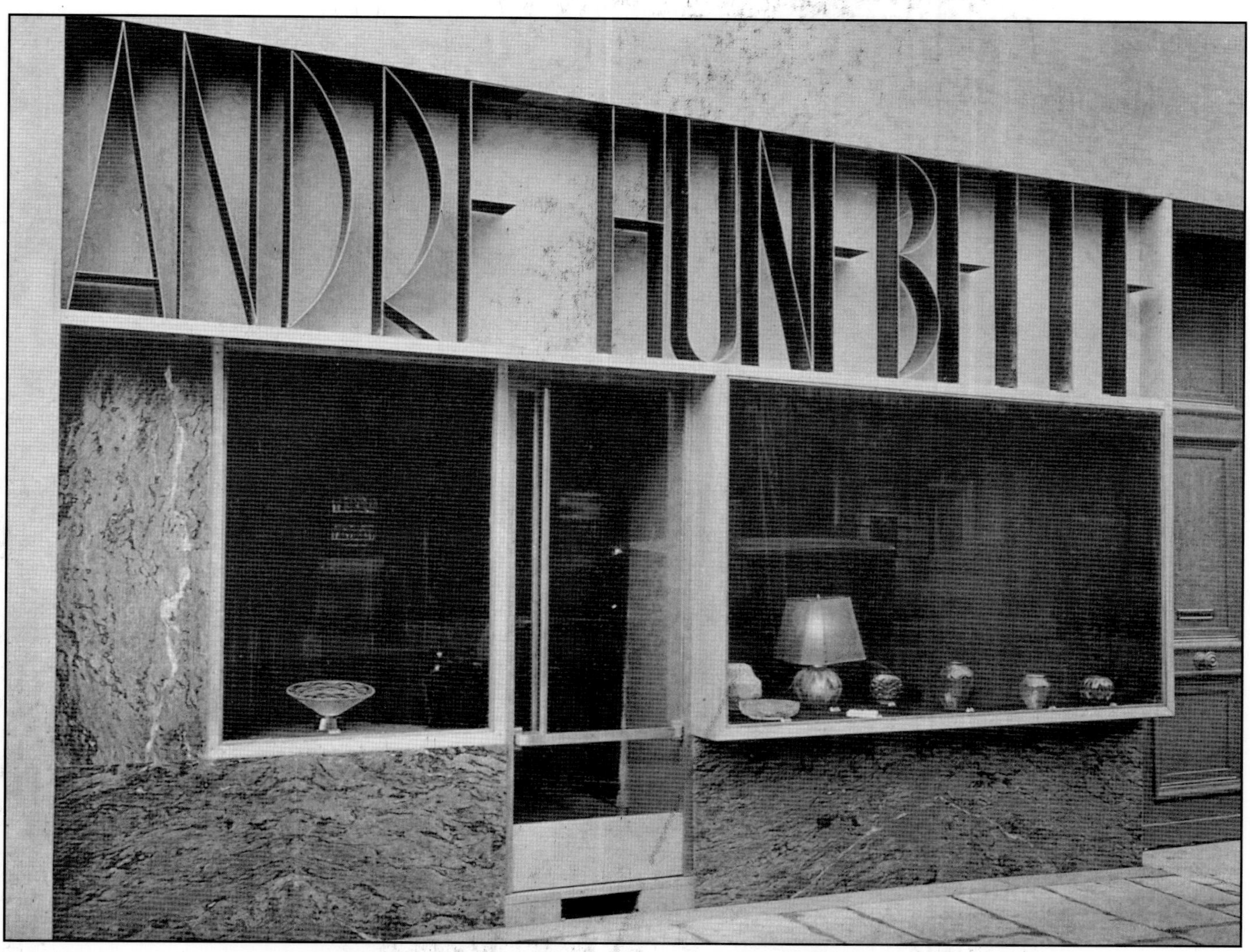

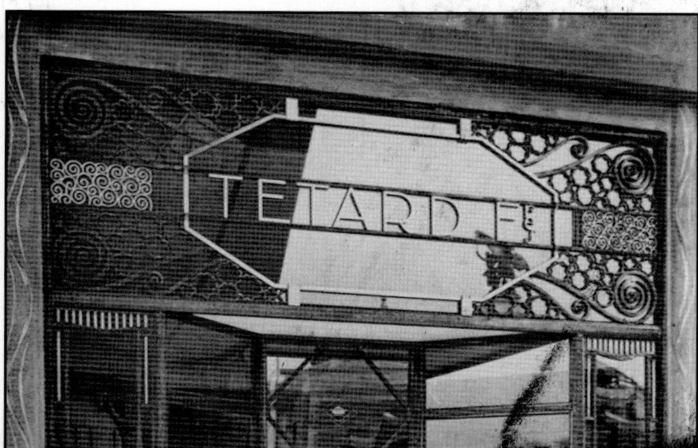
TETARD

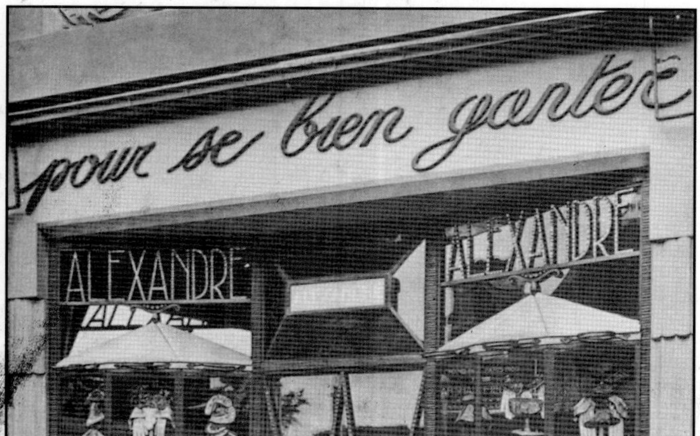
pour se bien ganter
ALEXANDRE
ALEXANDRE

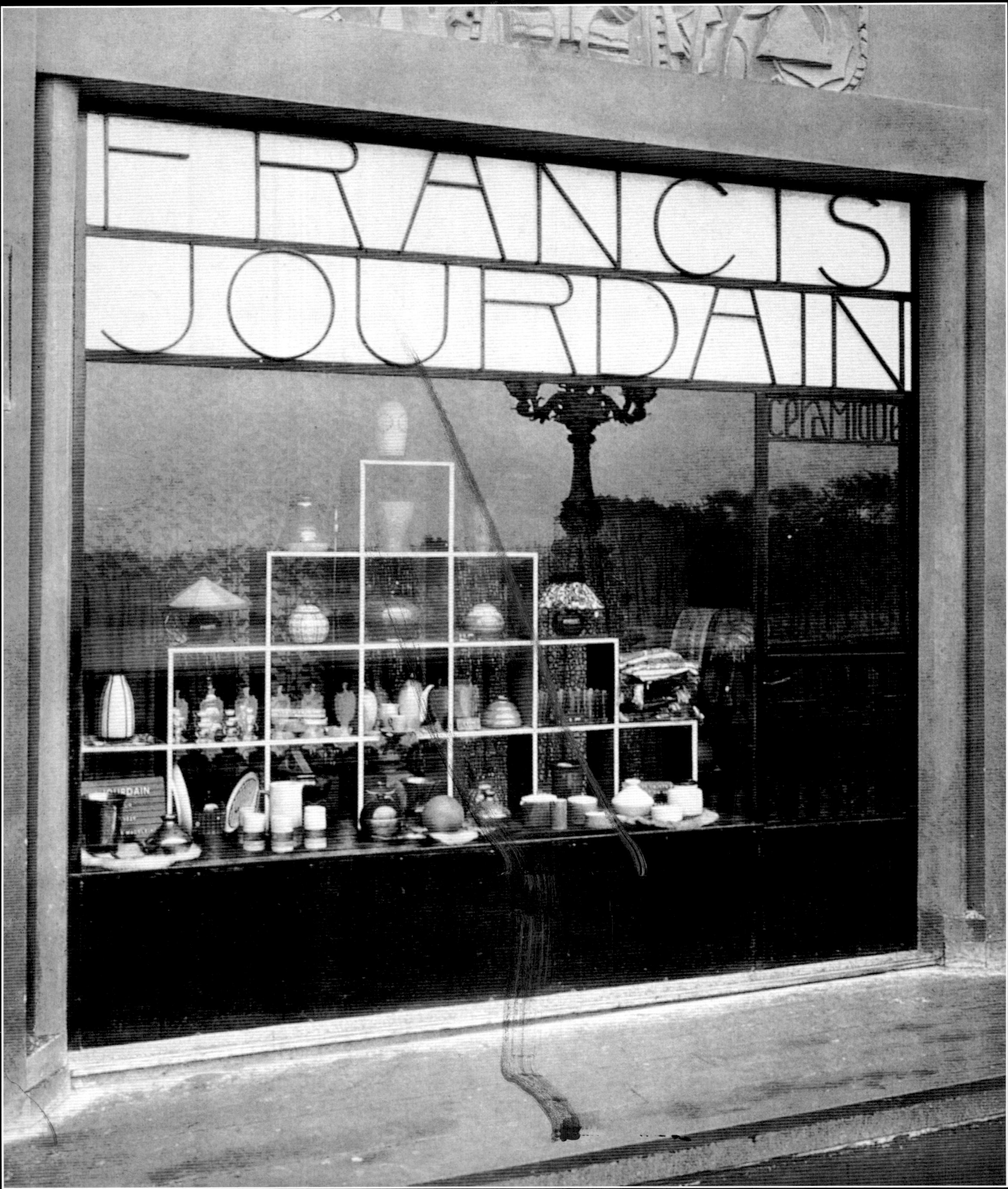
FRANCIS
JOURDAIN
CERAMIQUE

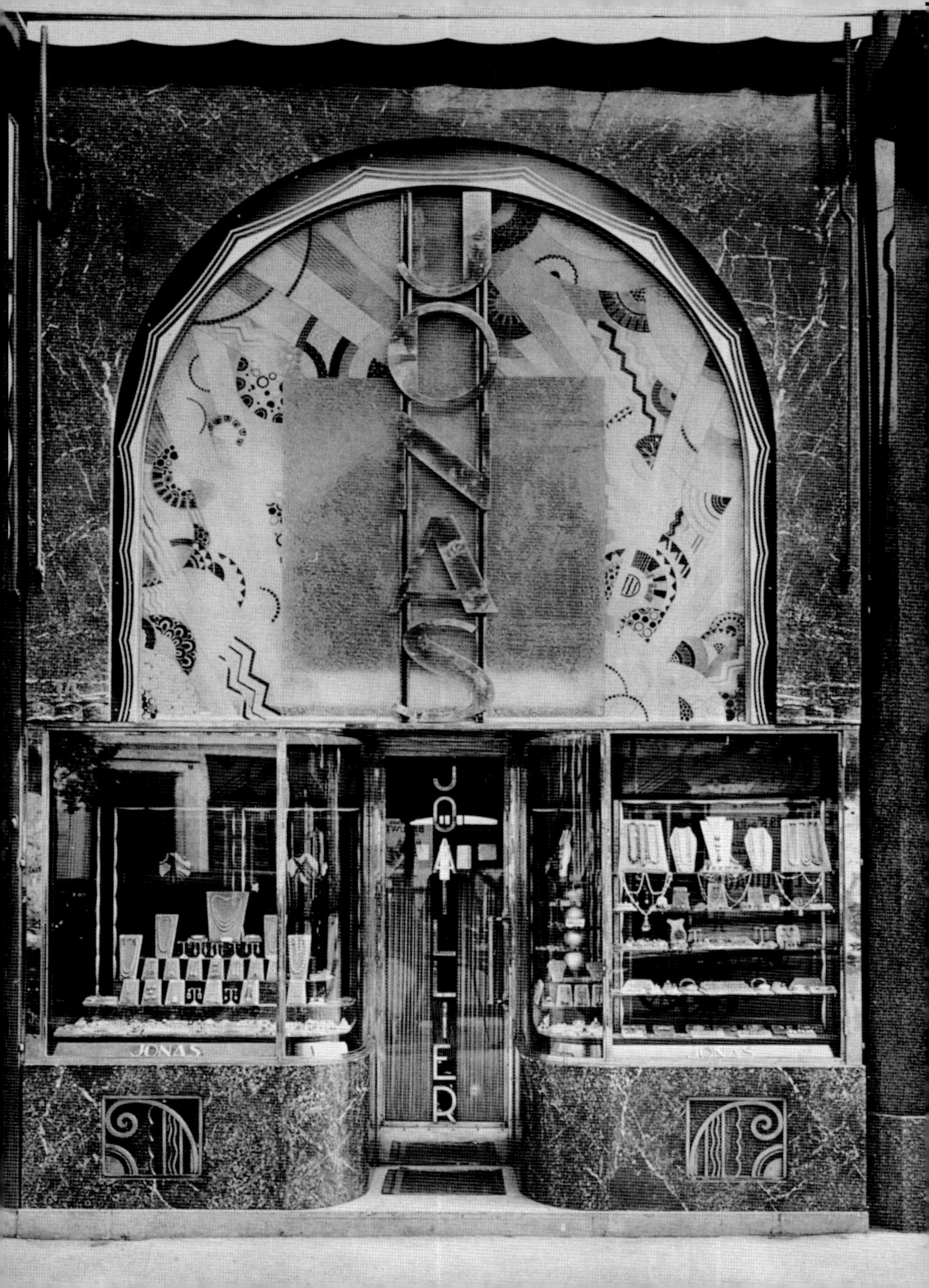
JONAS
JOAILLIER
JONAS

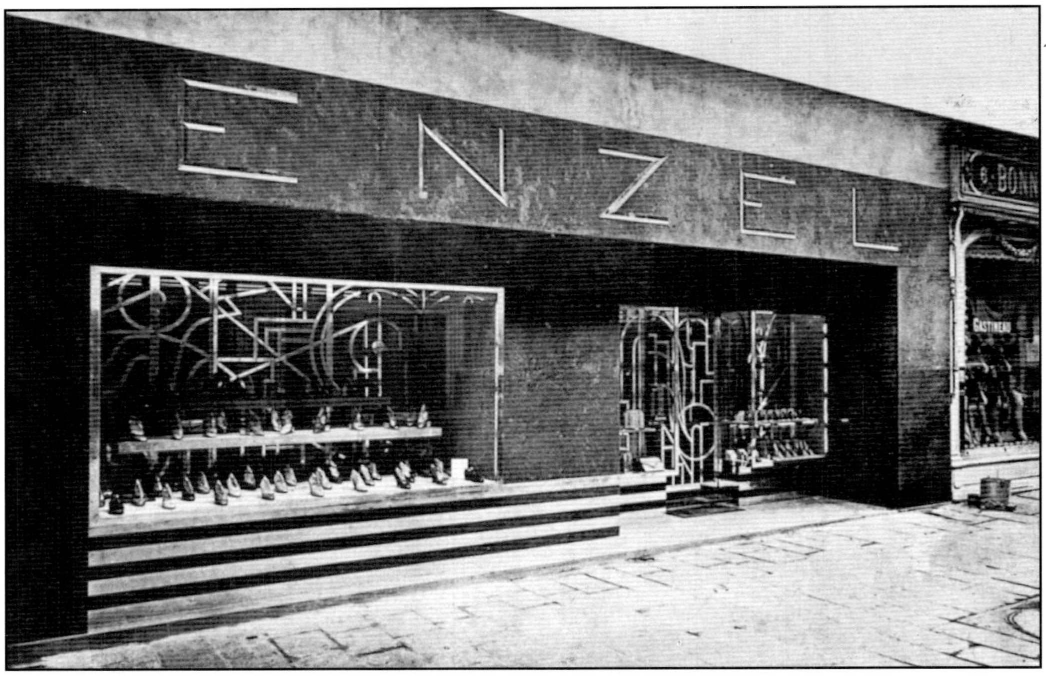
ENZEL

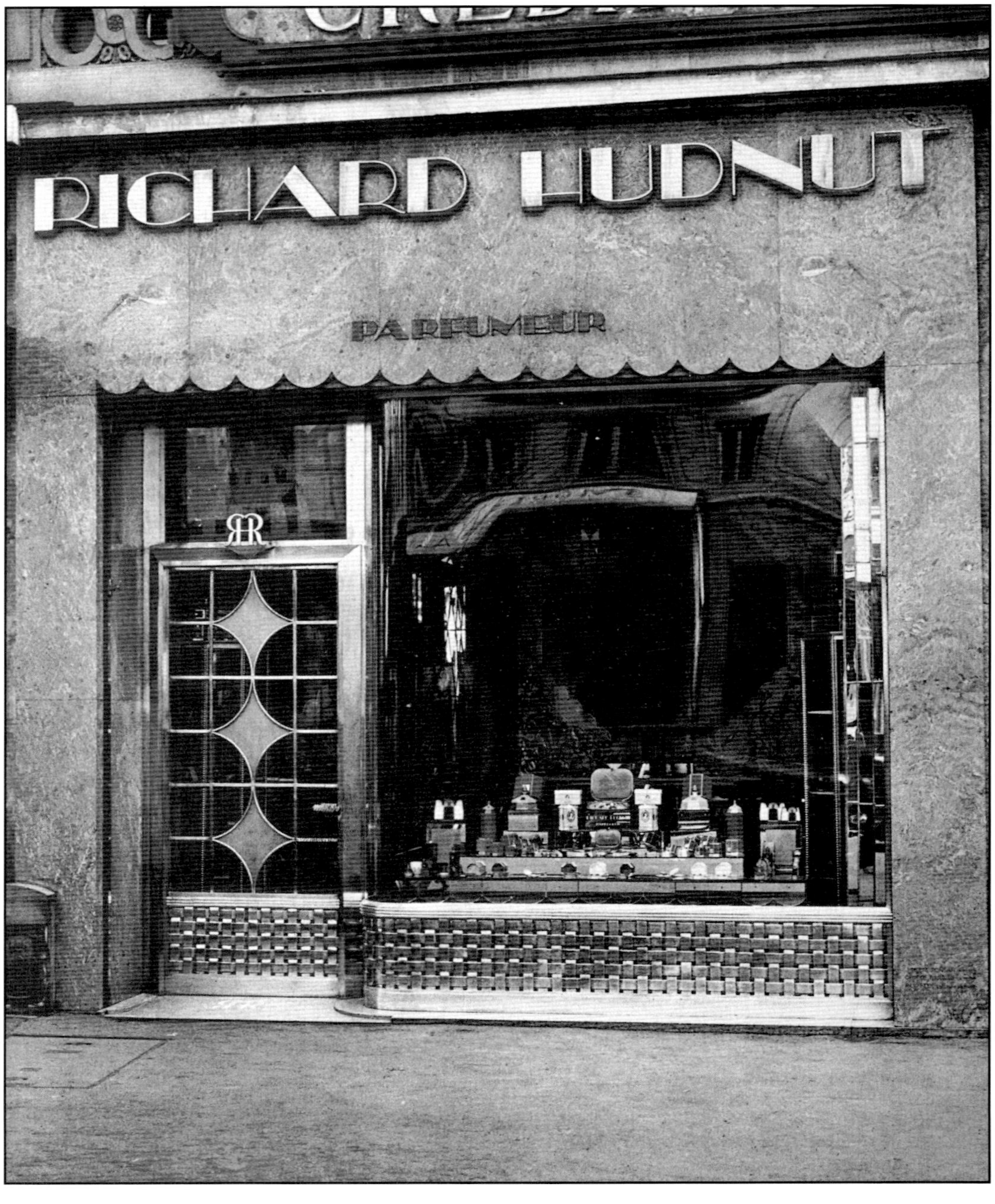
RICHARD HUDNUT
PARFUMEUR

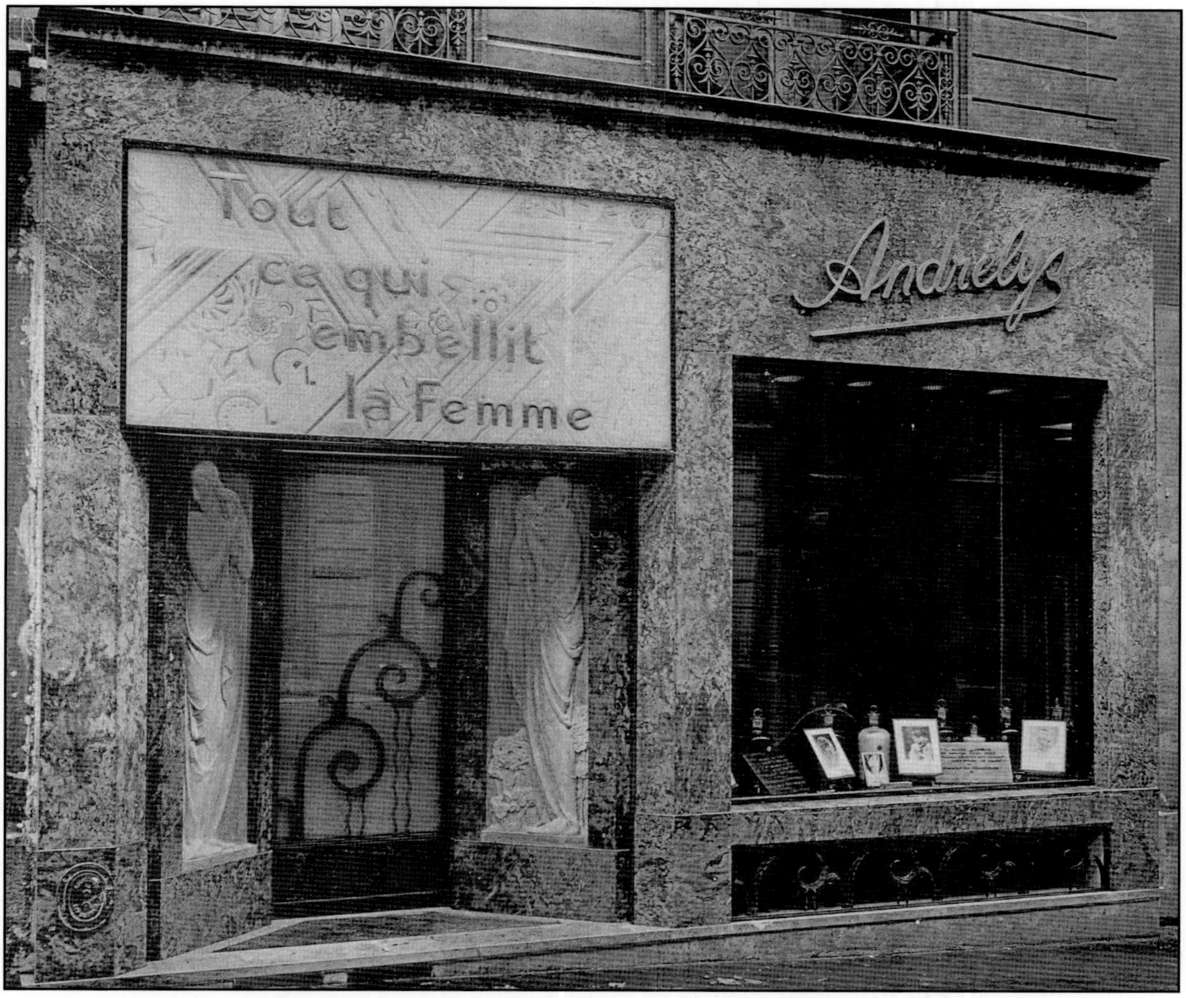
Tout ce qui embellit la Femme
Andrelys

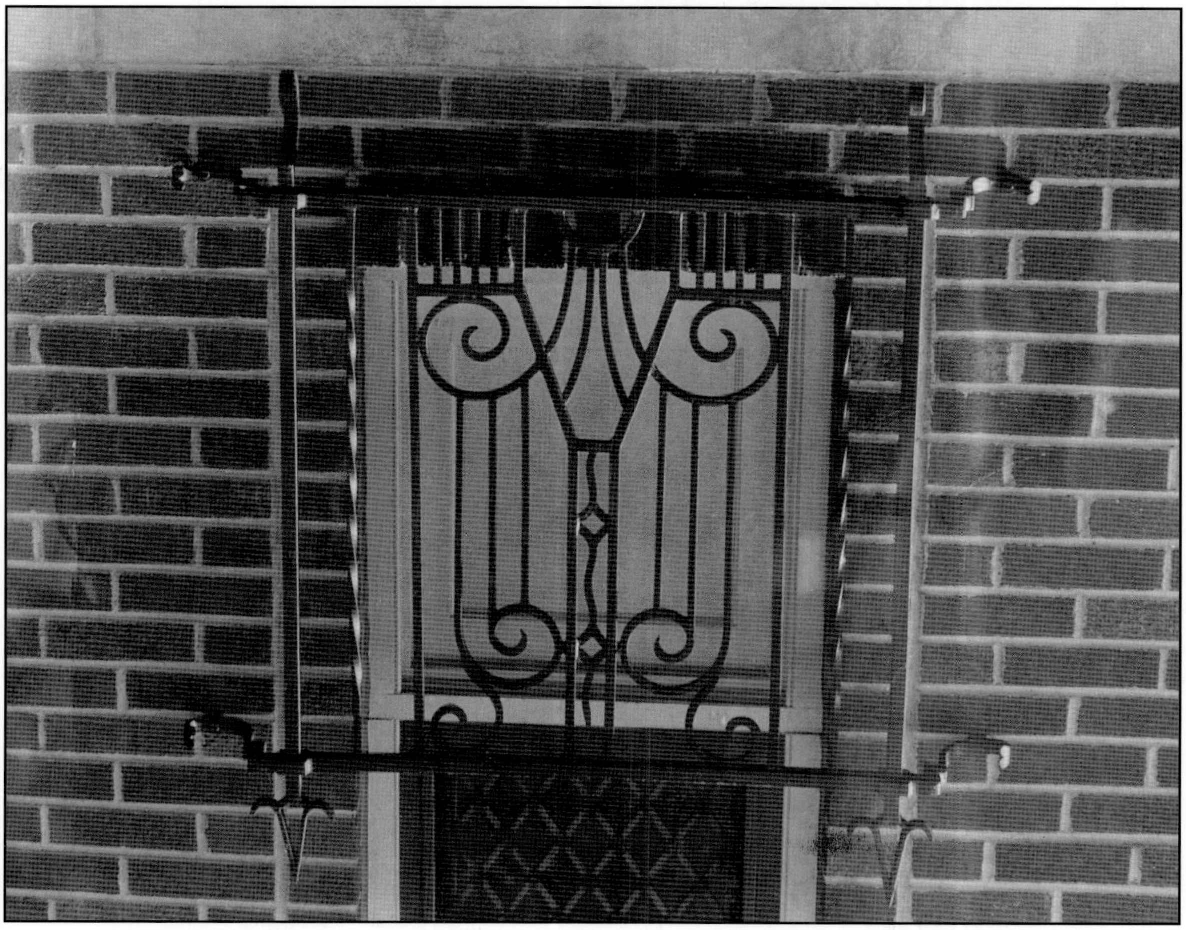

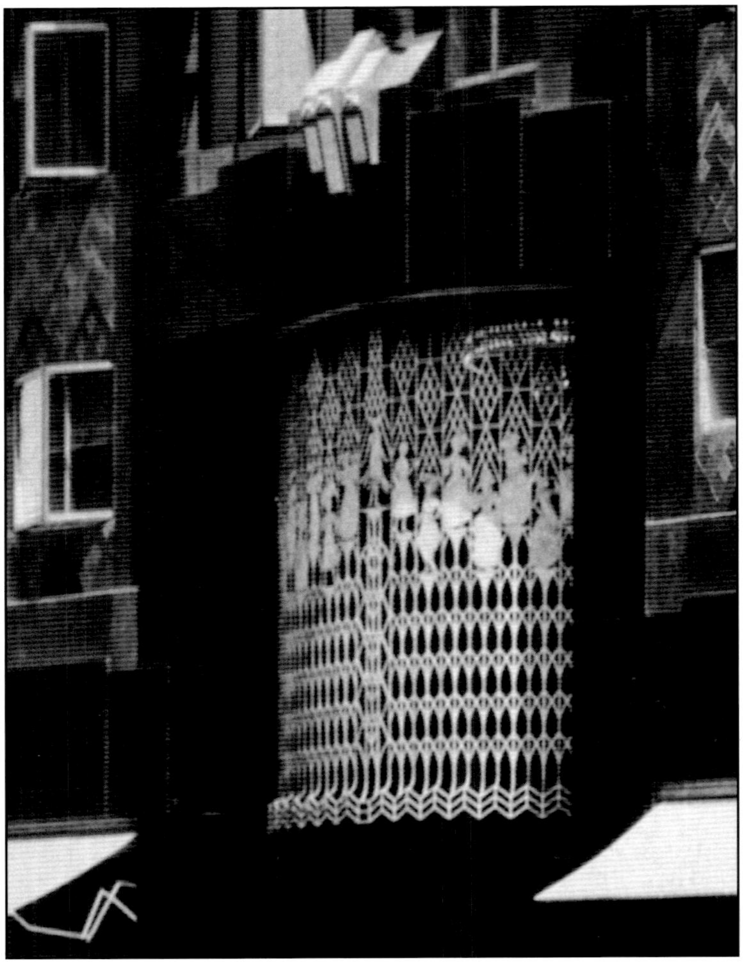

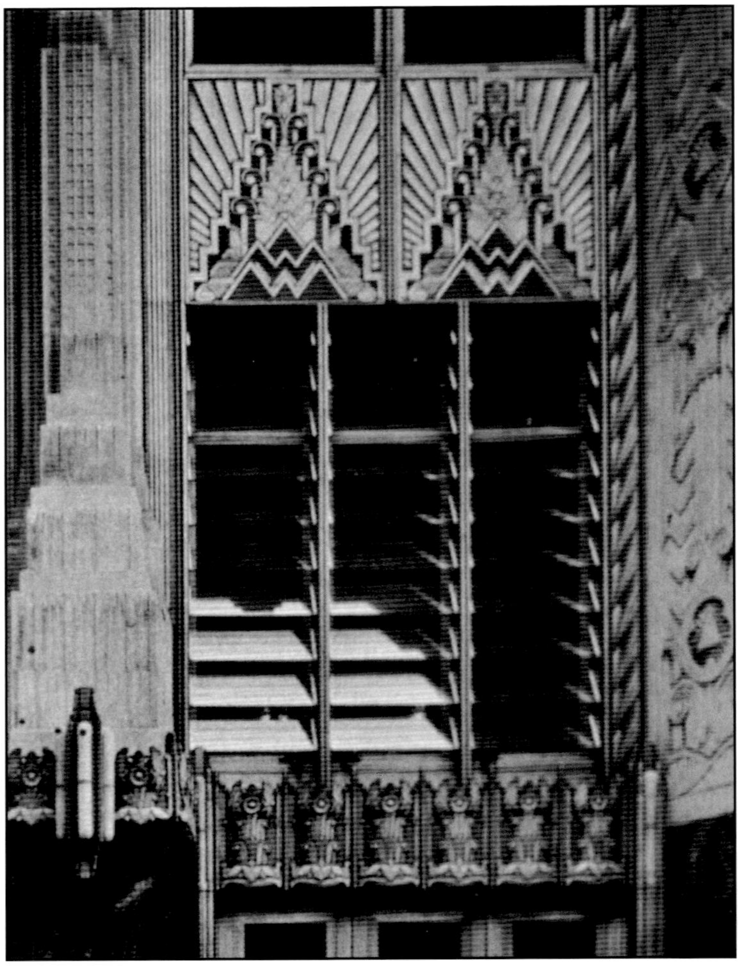

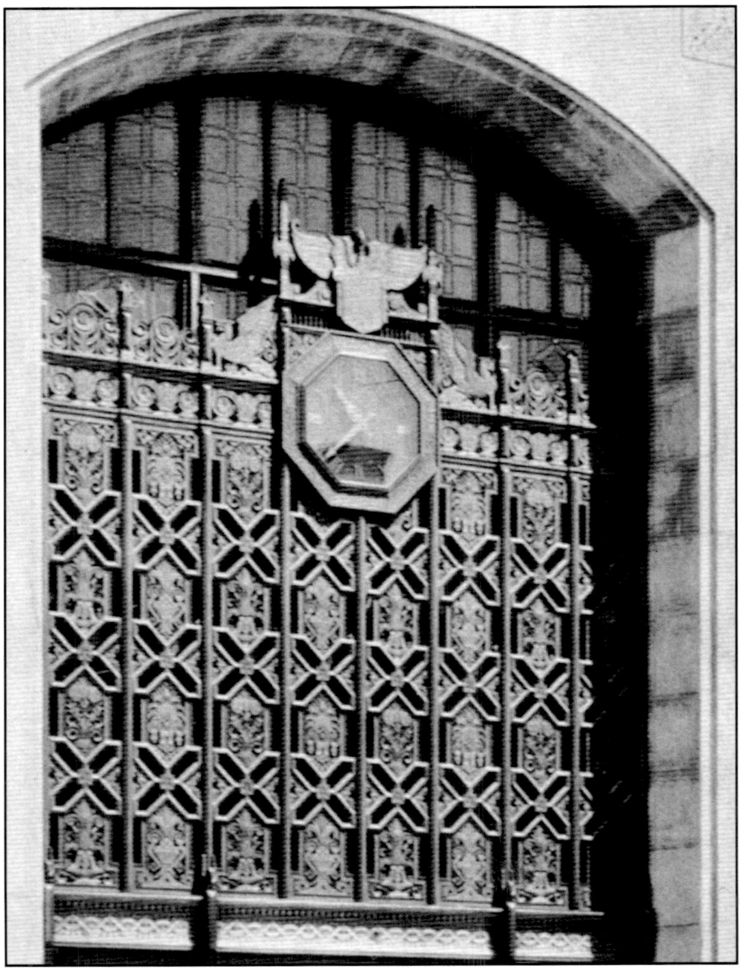

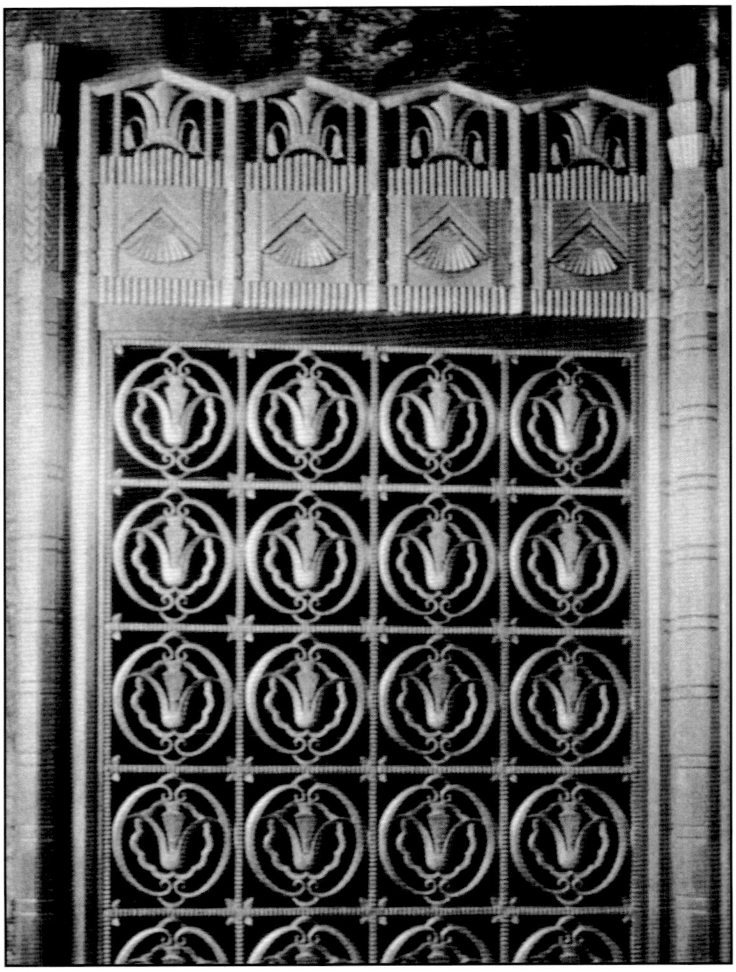

Furniture, Fireplaces, Vases, & Mirrors

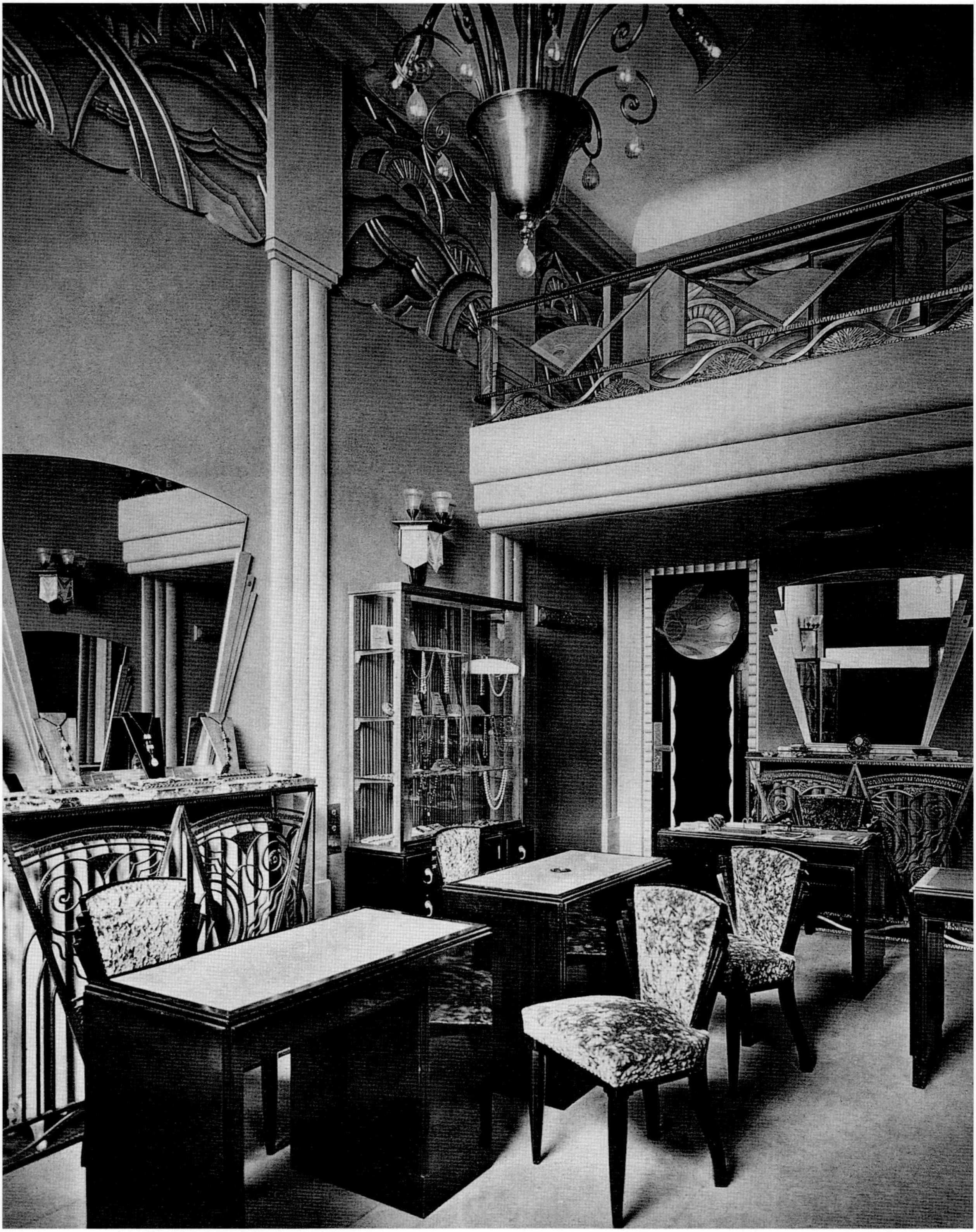

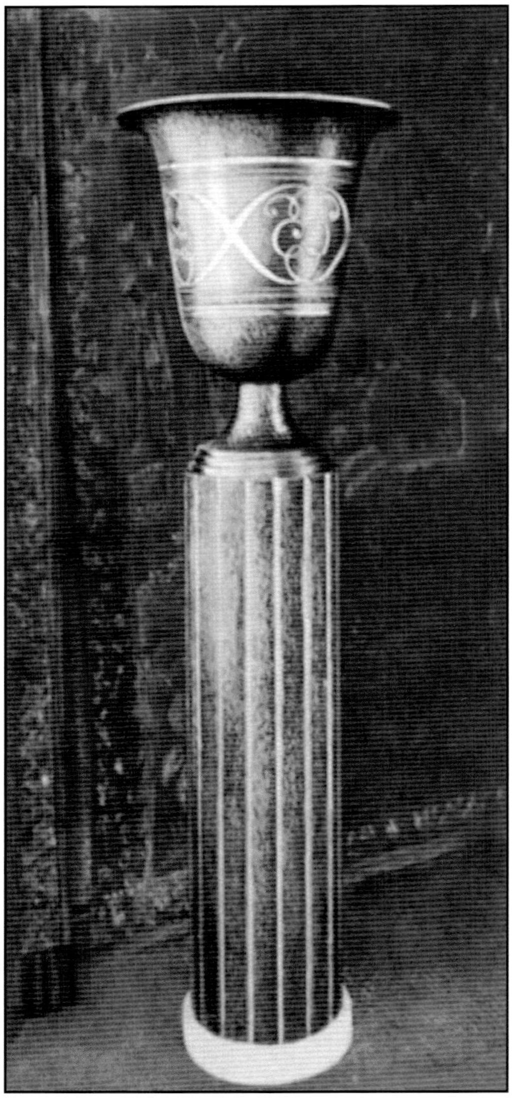

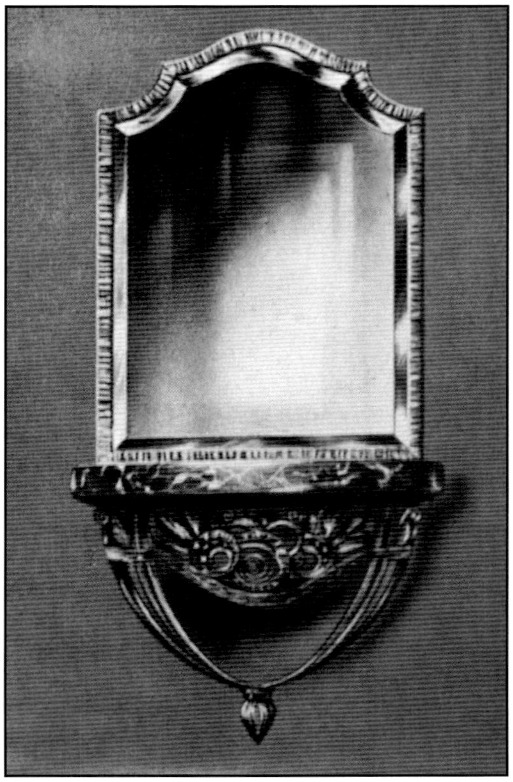

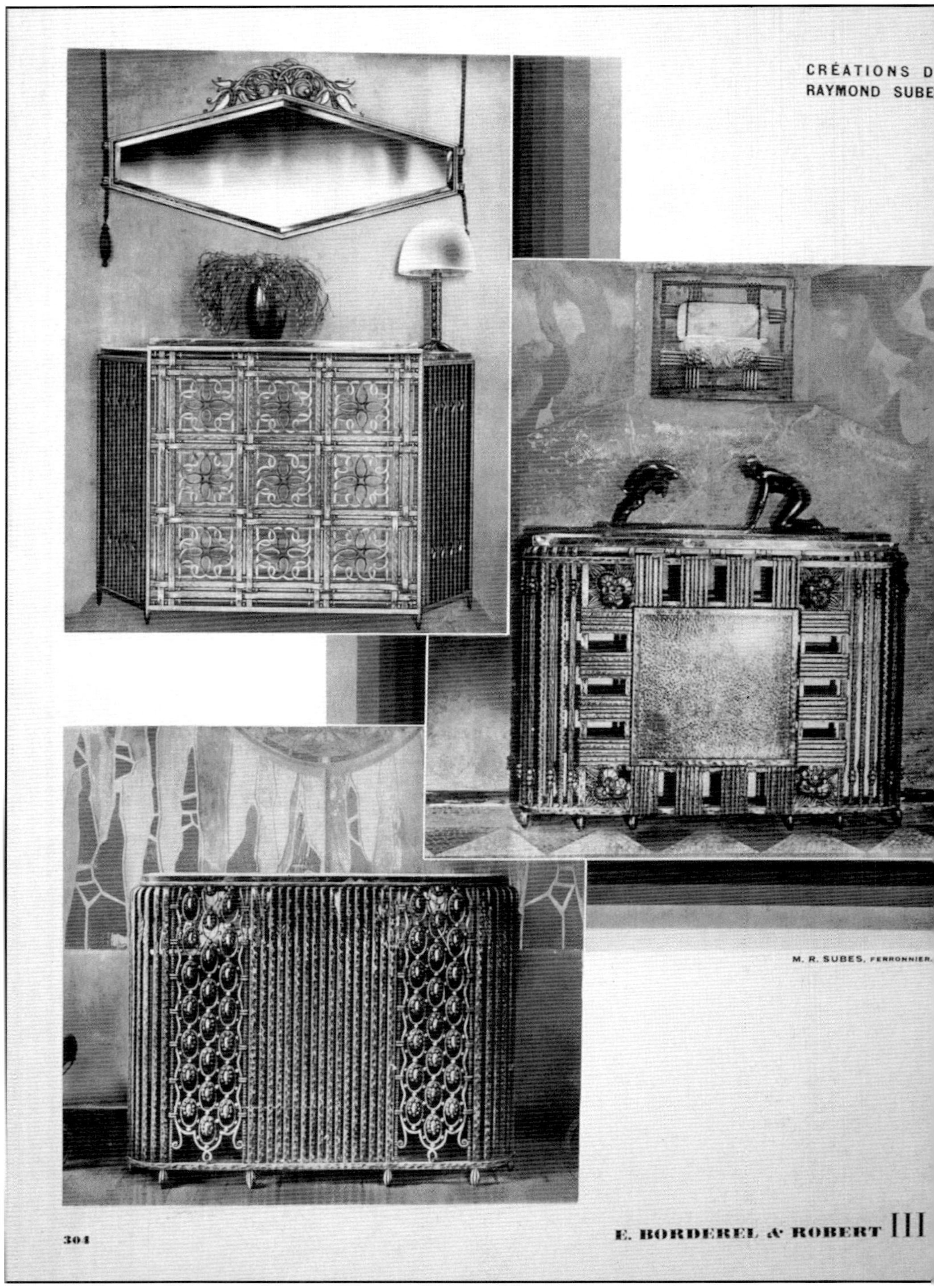

CRÉATIONS D
RAYMOND SUBE

M. R. SUBES, FERRONNIER.

304

E. BORDEREL & ROBERT III

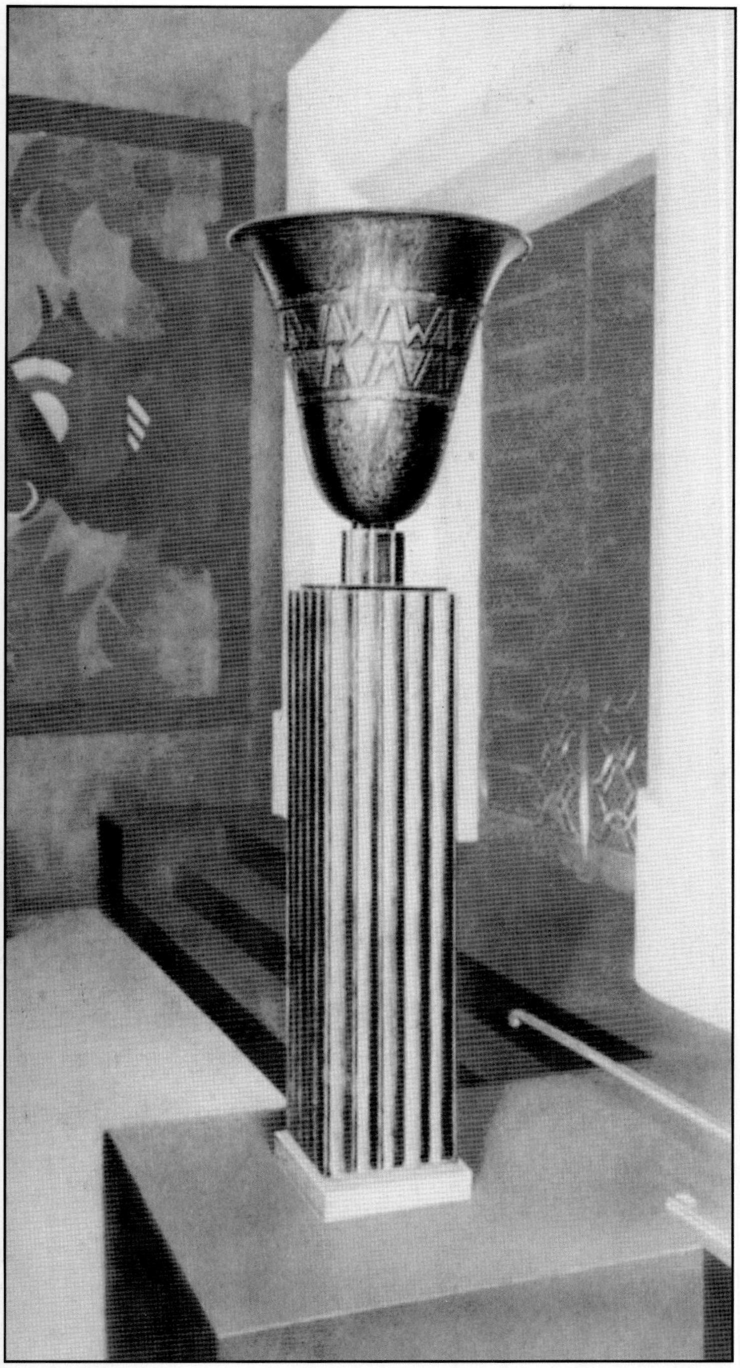

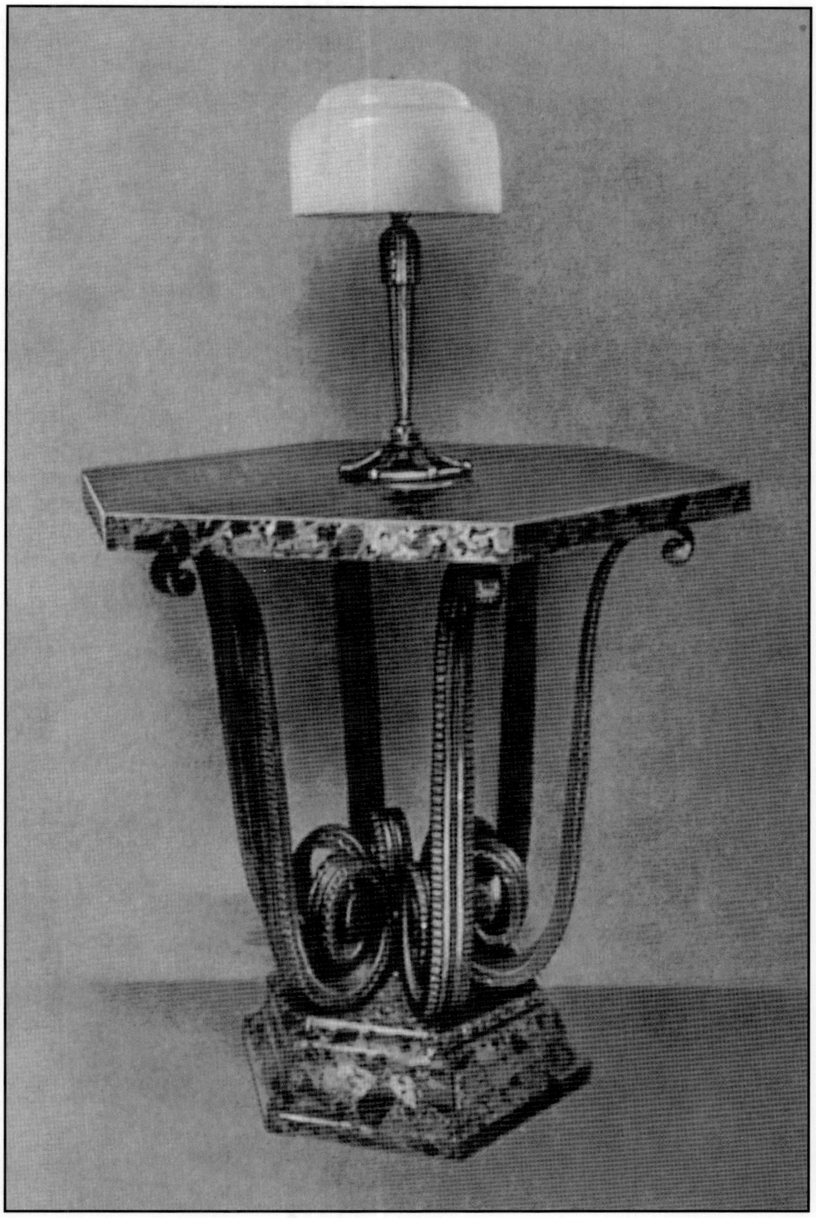

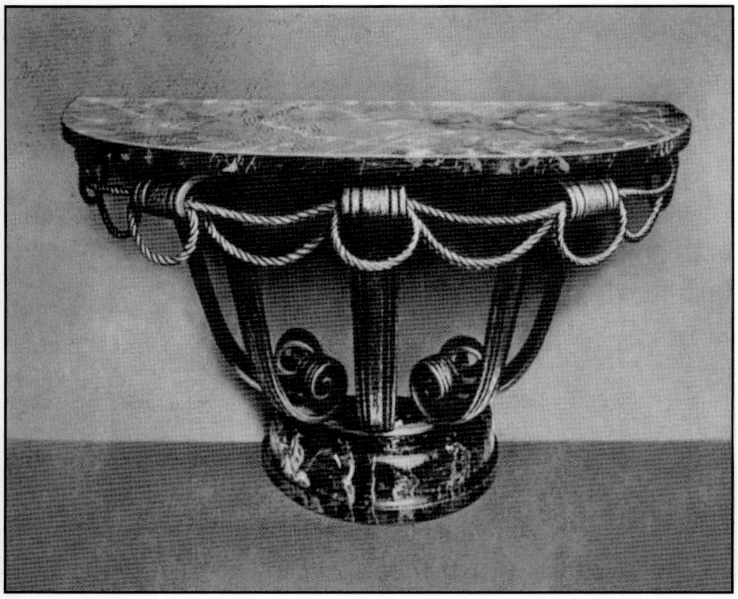

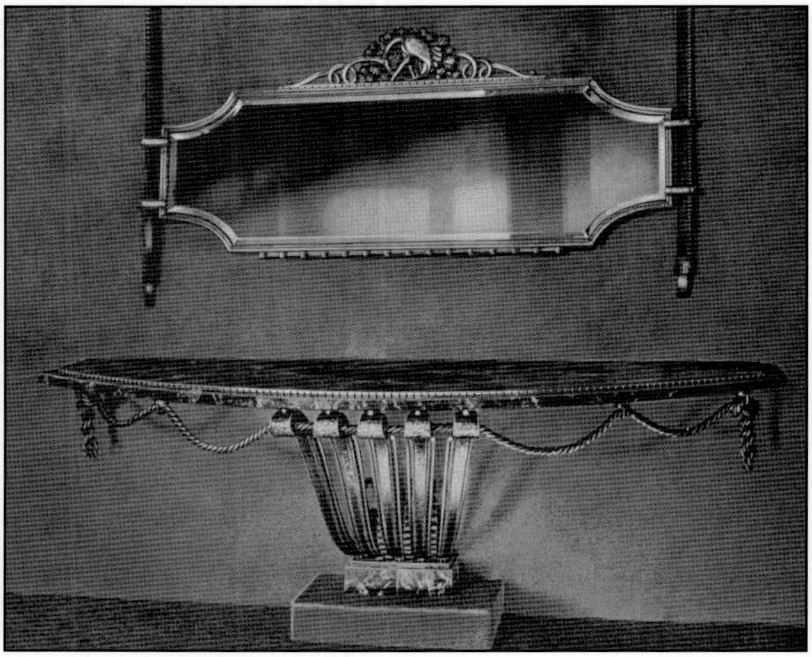

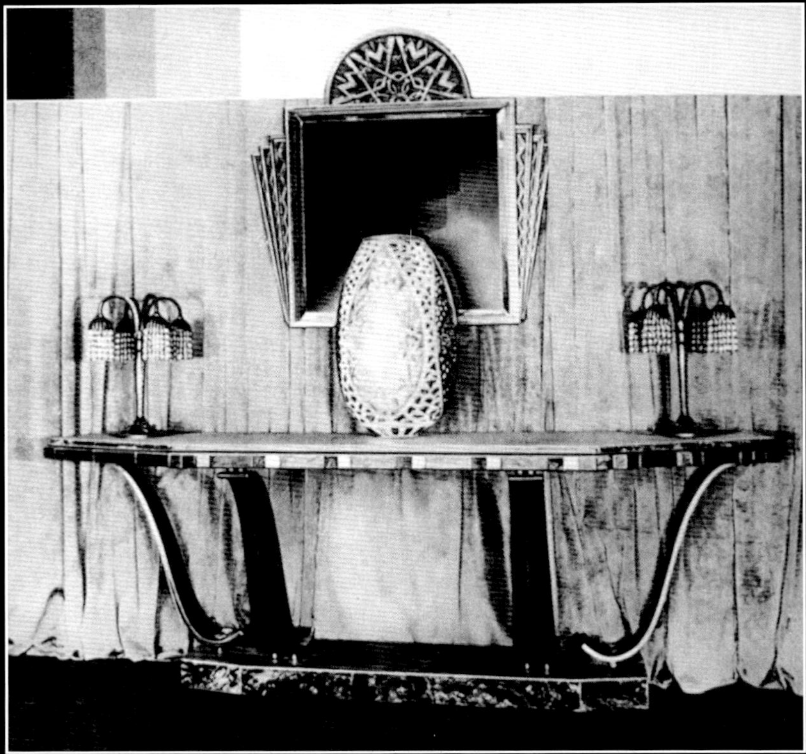

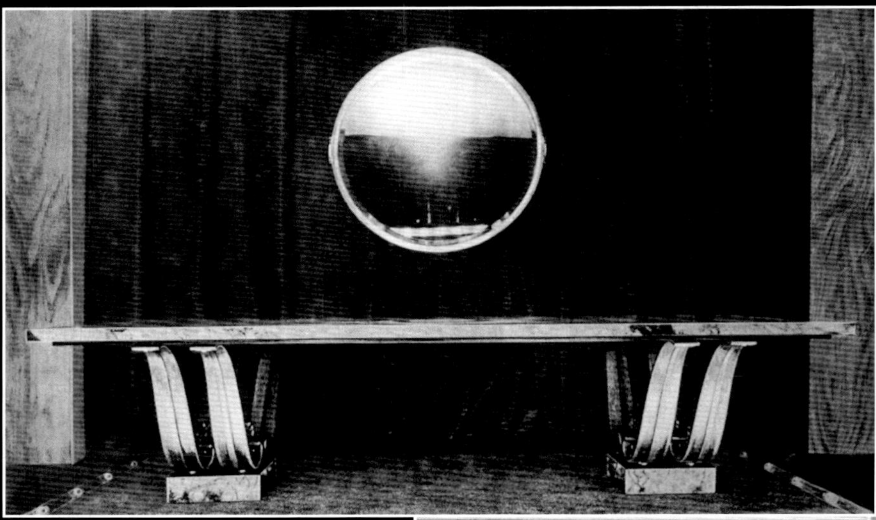

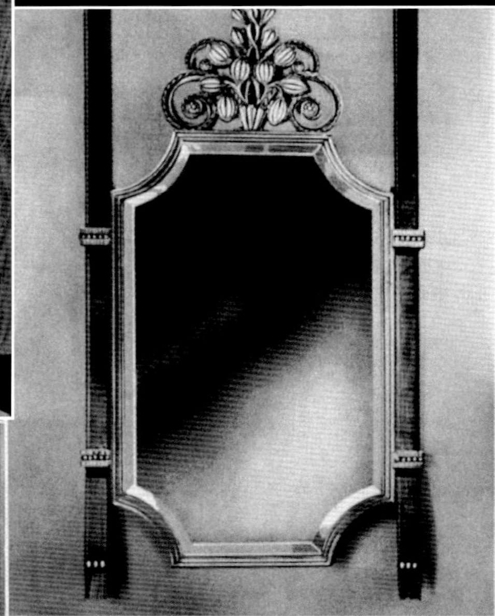

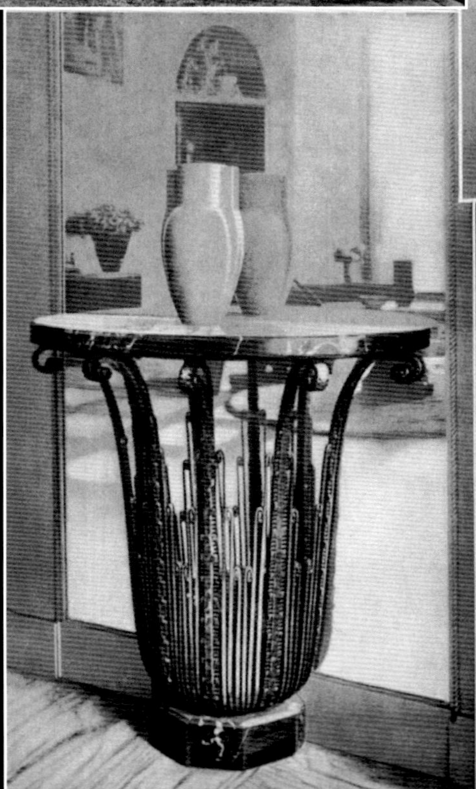

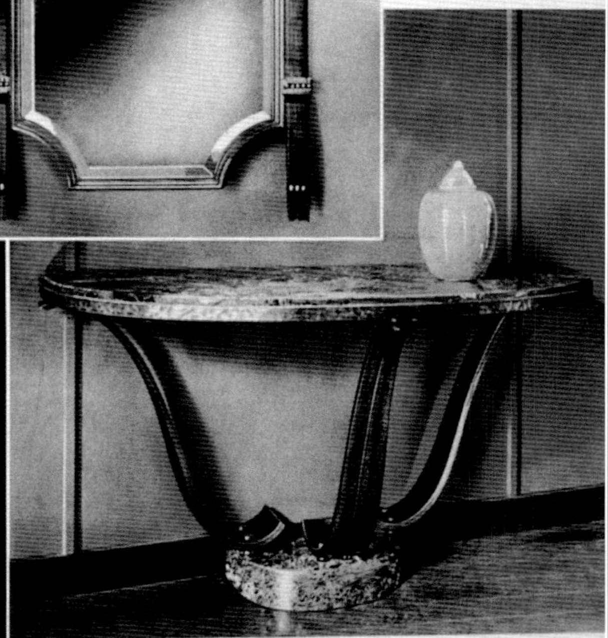

M. R. SUBES, FERRONNIER

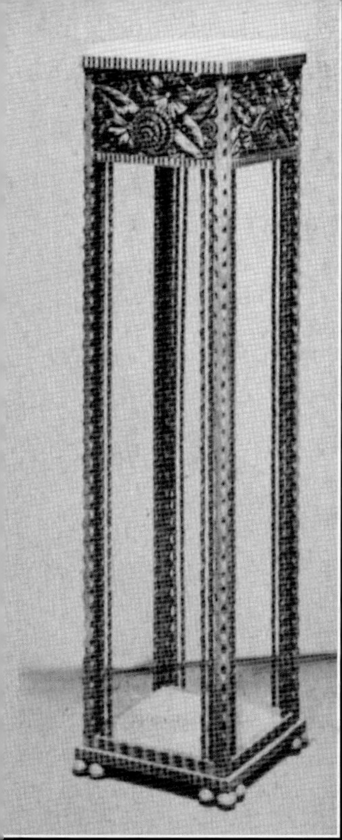

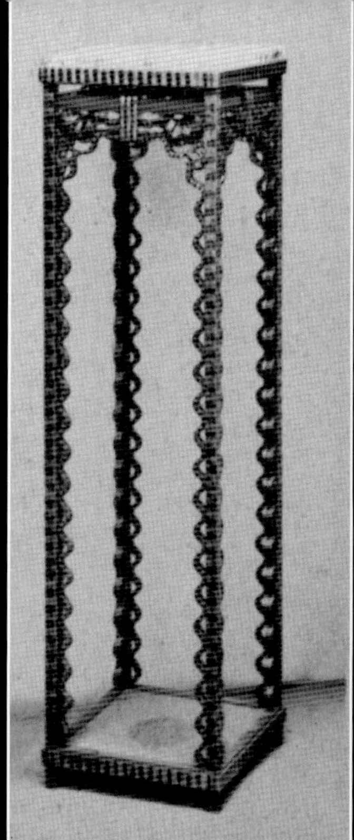

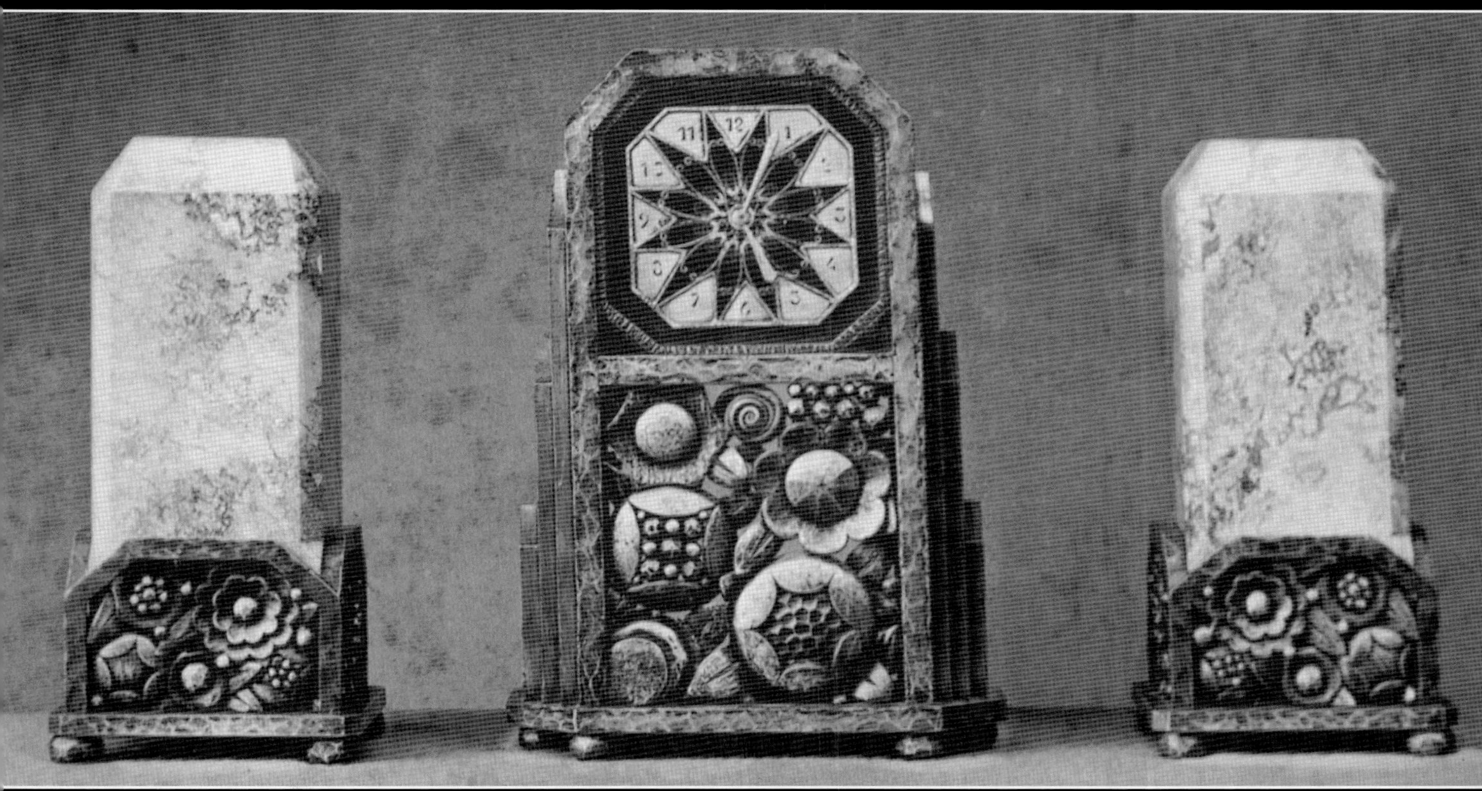

1

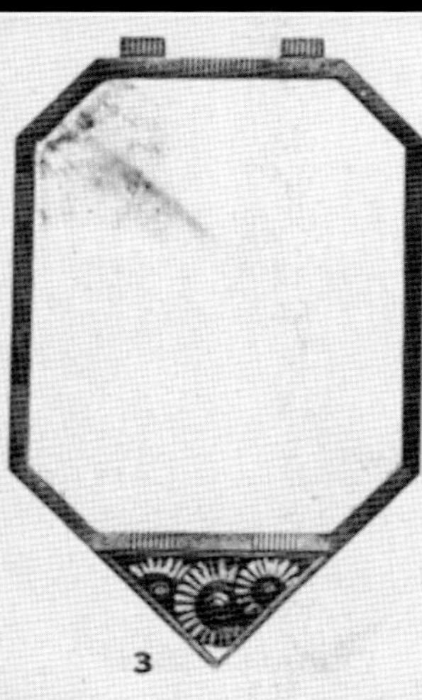

3

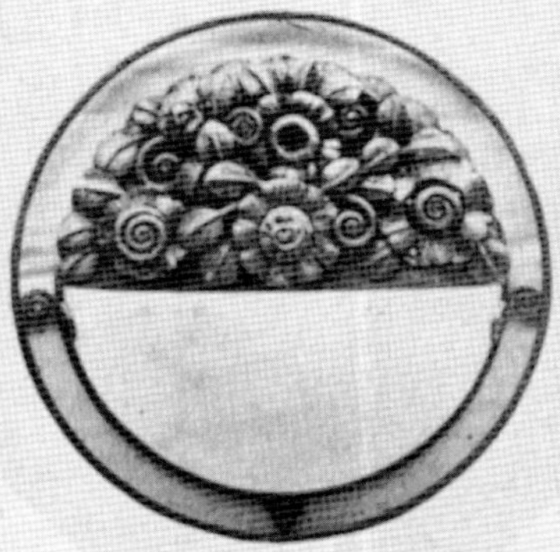

4

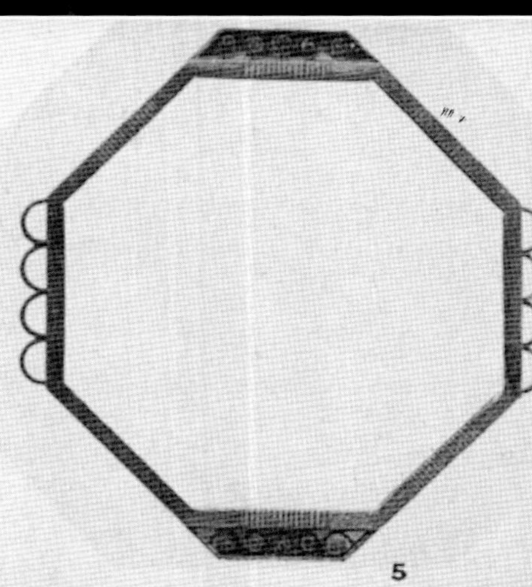

5

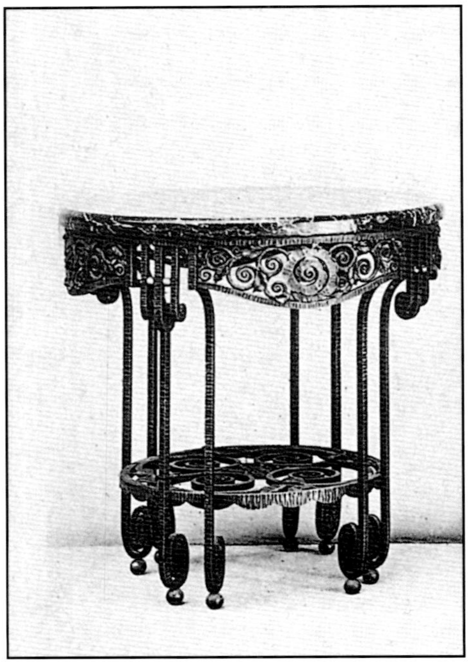

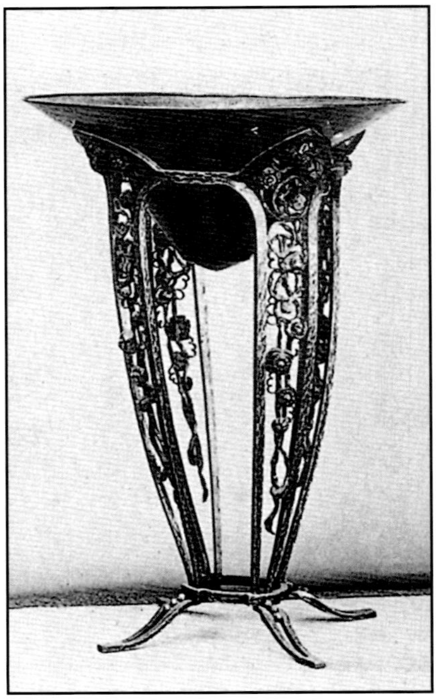

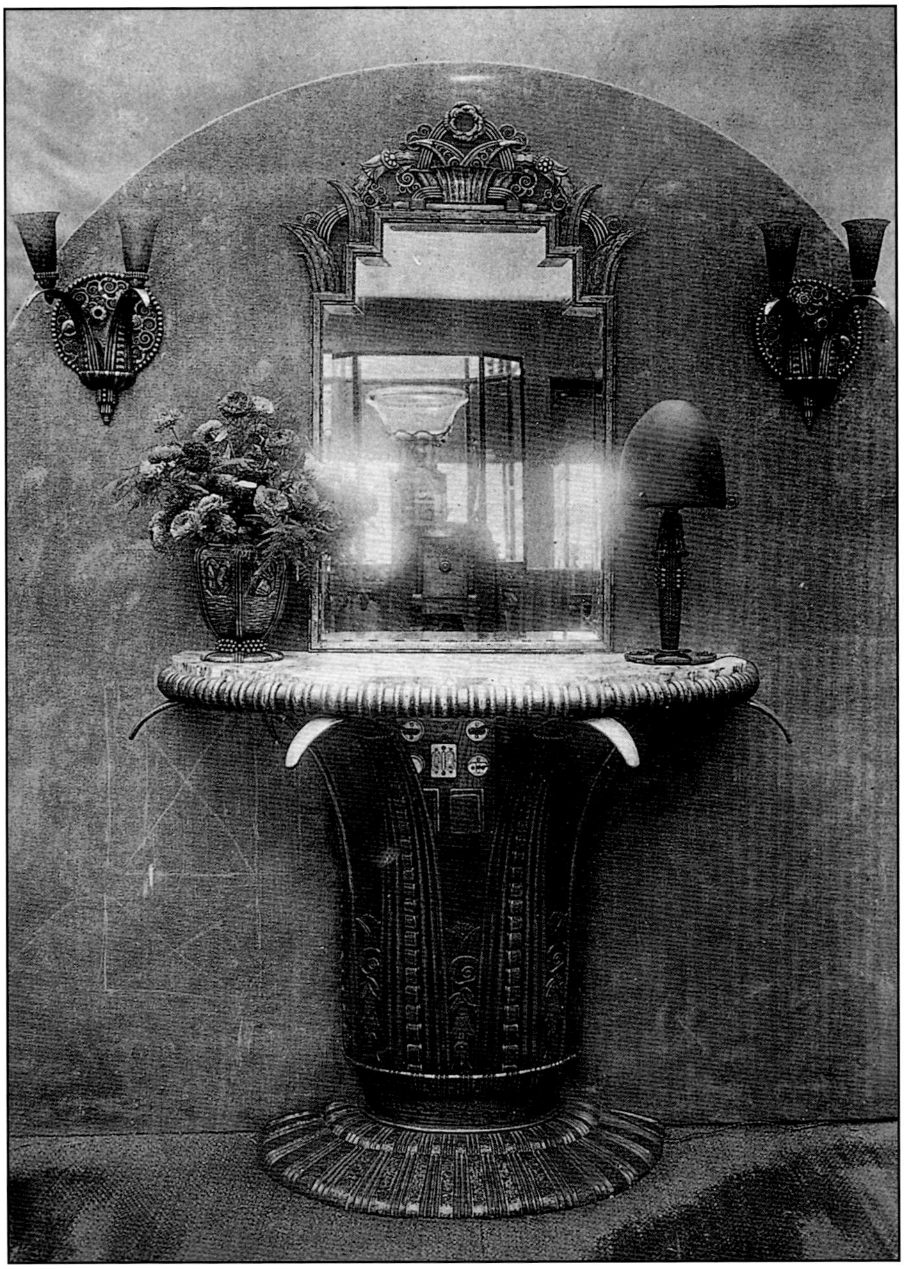

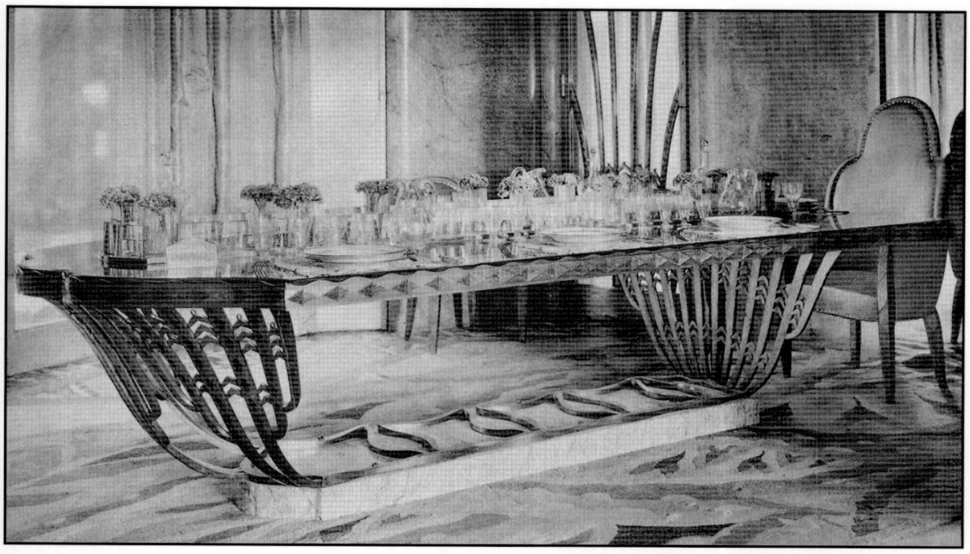

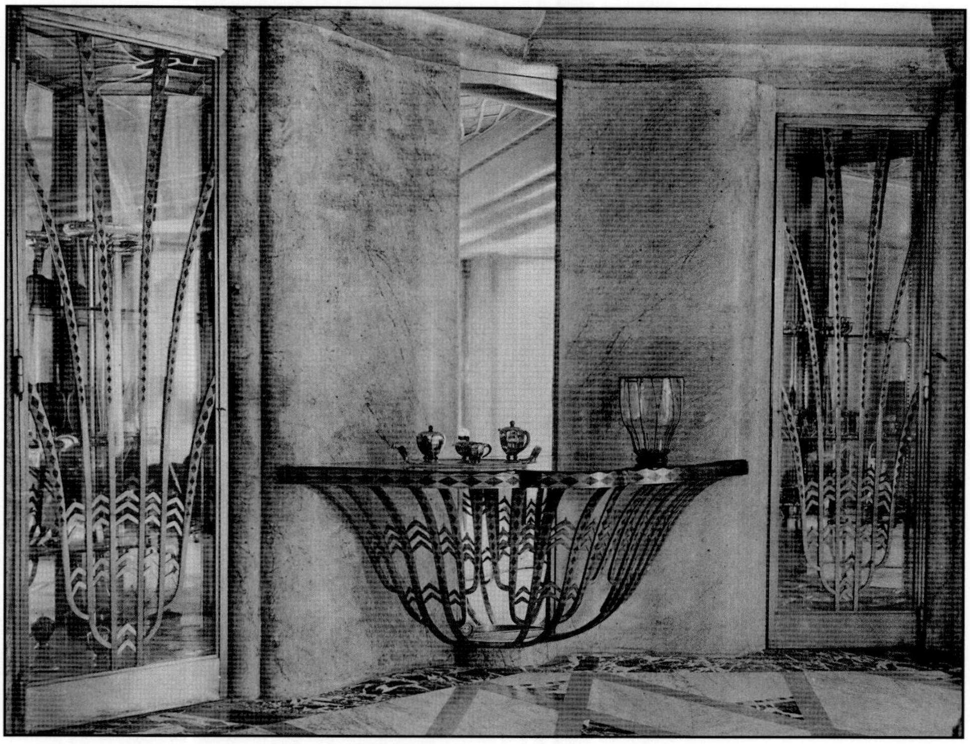

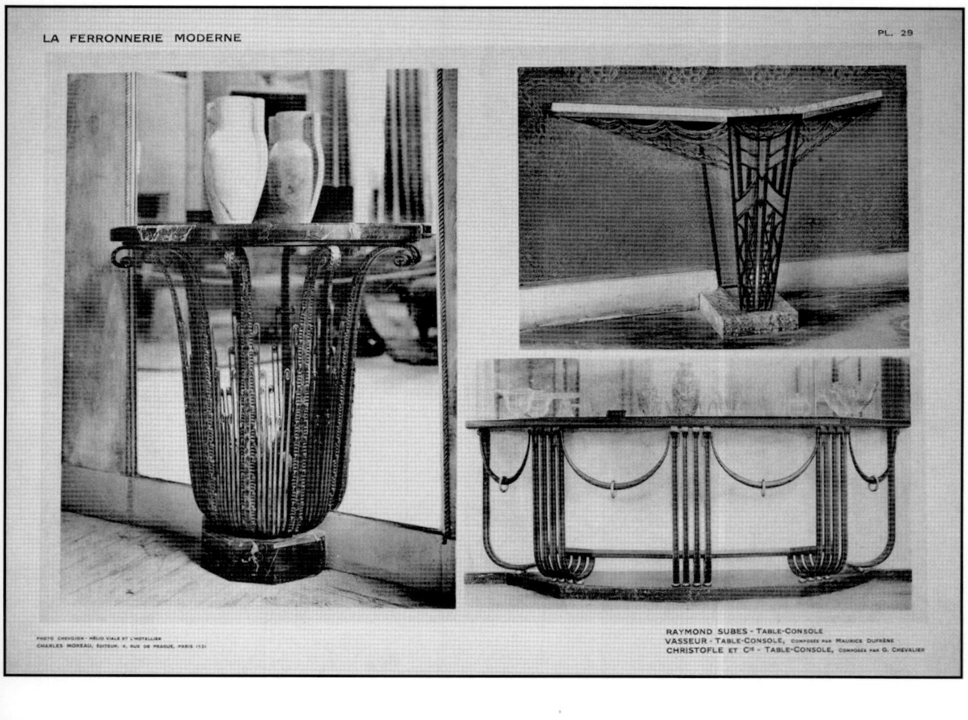
LA FERRONNERIE MODERNE
PL. 29
PHOTO CHEVOJON - HÉLIO VIALE ET L'HOTELLIER
CHARLES MOREAU, ÉDITEUR, 7, RUE DE PRAGUE, PARIS (12)
RAYMOND SUBES - TABLE-CONSOLE
VASSEUR - TABLE-CONSOLE, COMPOSÉE PAR MAURICE DUFRÊNE
CHRISTOFLE ET CIE - TABLE-CONSOLE, COMPOSÉE PAR G. CHEVALIER

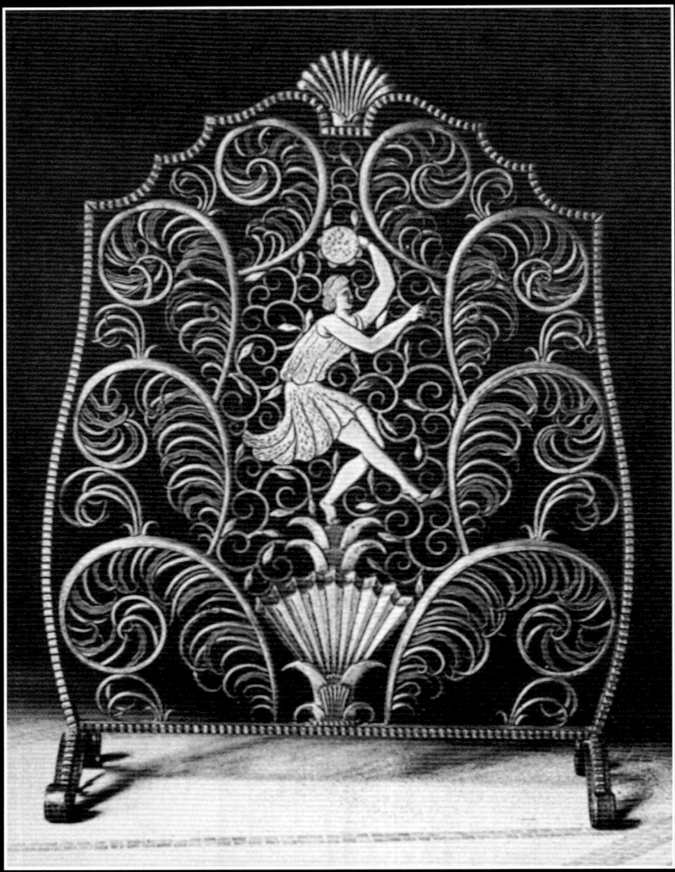

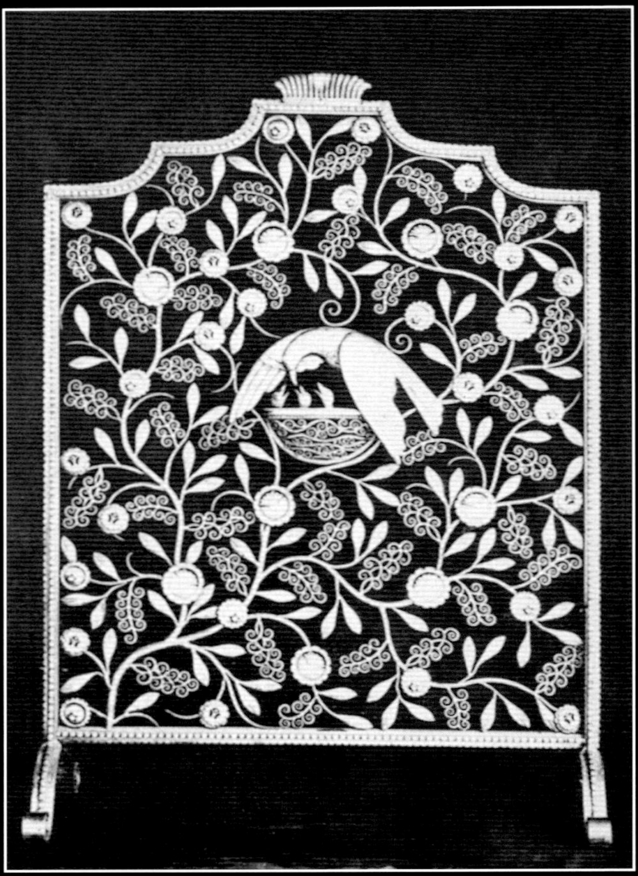

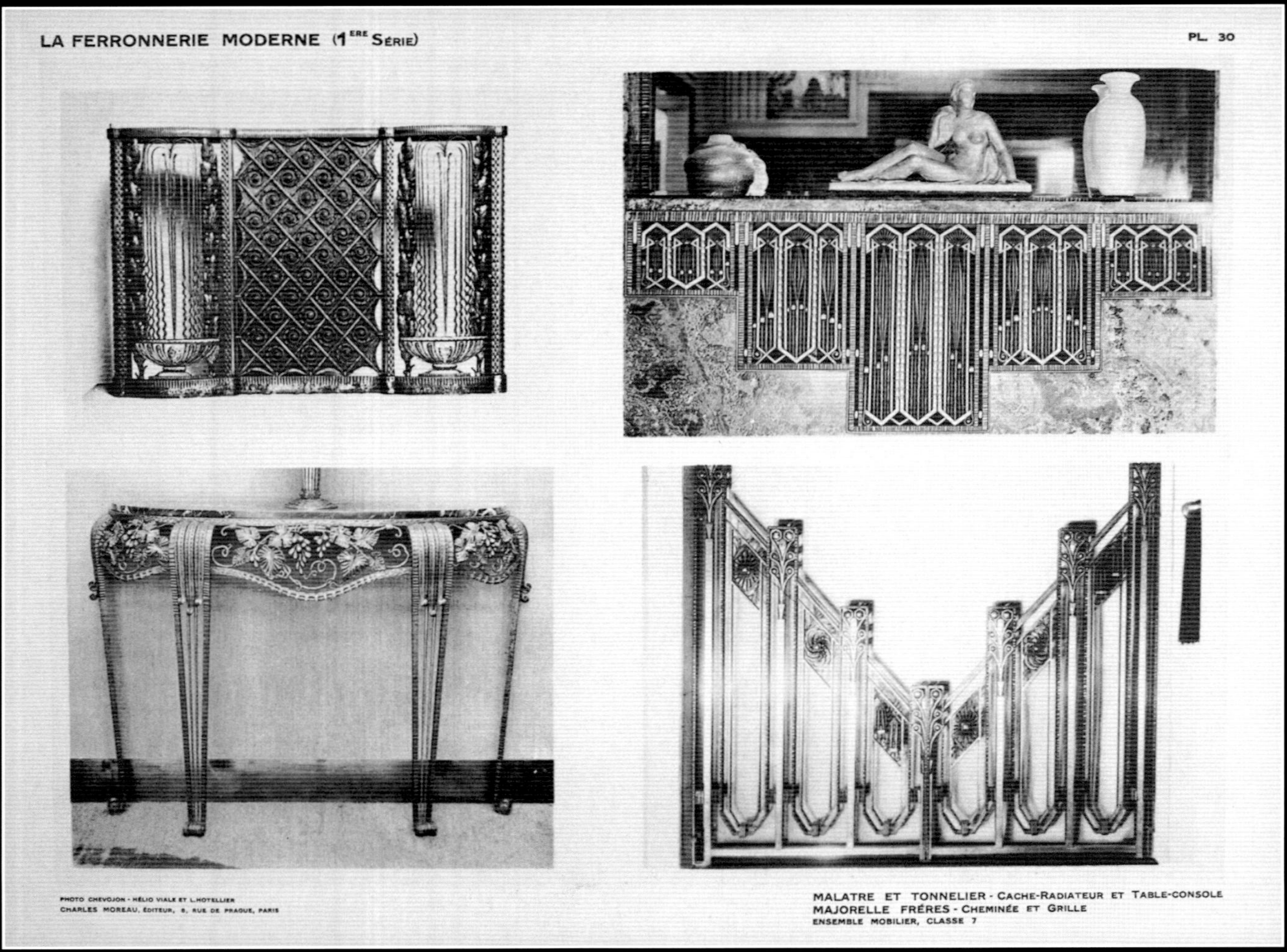

LA FERRONNERIE MODERNE (1ERE SÉRIE)

PL. 30

PHOTO CHEVOJON - HÉLIO VIALE ET L.HOTELLIER
CHARLES MOREAU, ÉDITEUR, 8, RUE DE PRAGUE, PARIS

MALATRE ET TONNELIER - CACHE-RADIATEUR ET TABLE-CONSOLE
MAJORELLE FRÉRES - CHEMINÉE ET GRILLE
ENSEMBLE MOBILIER, CLASSE 7

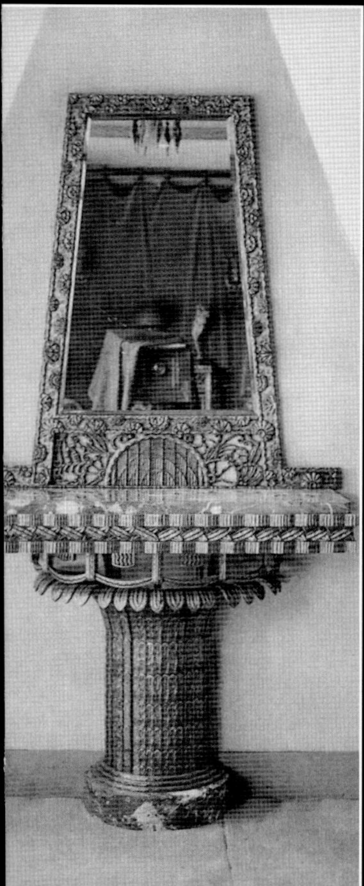

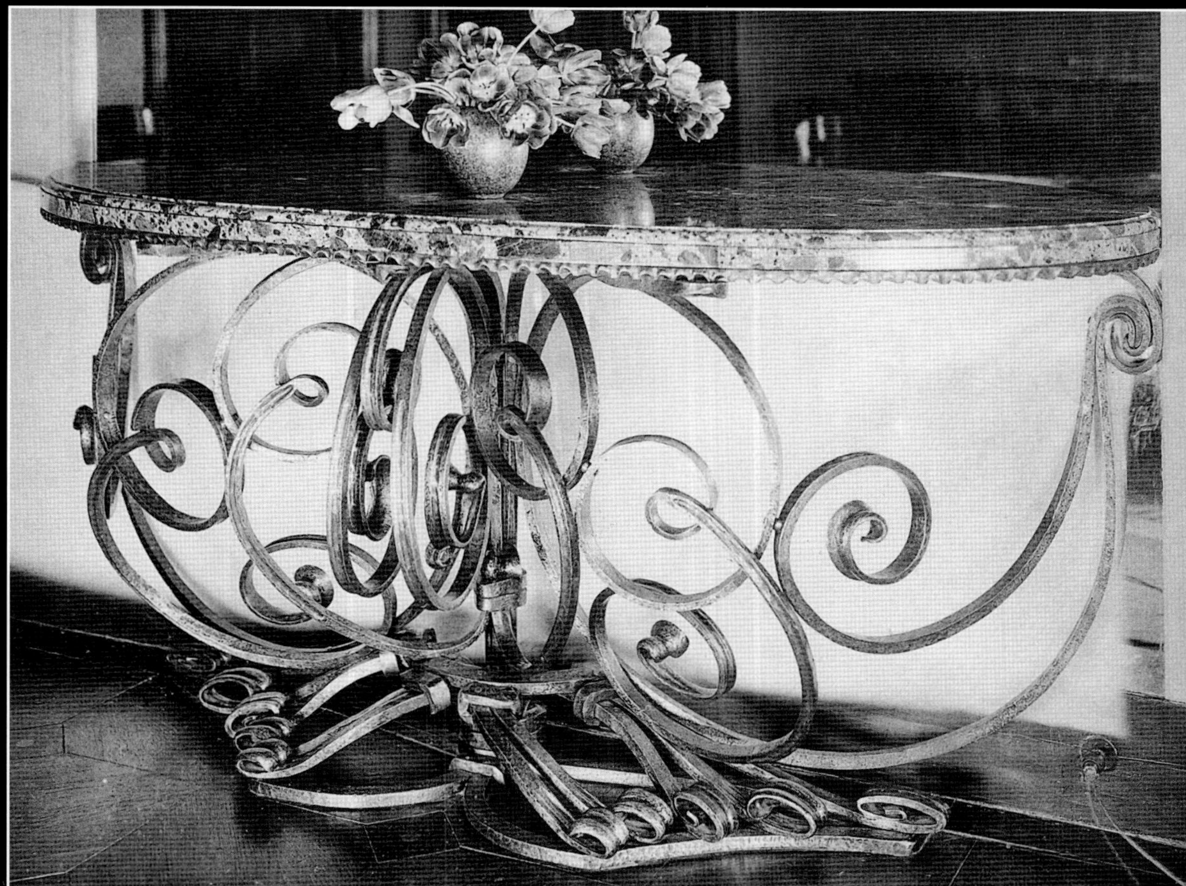

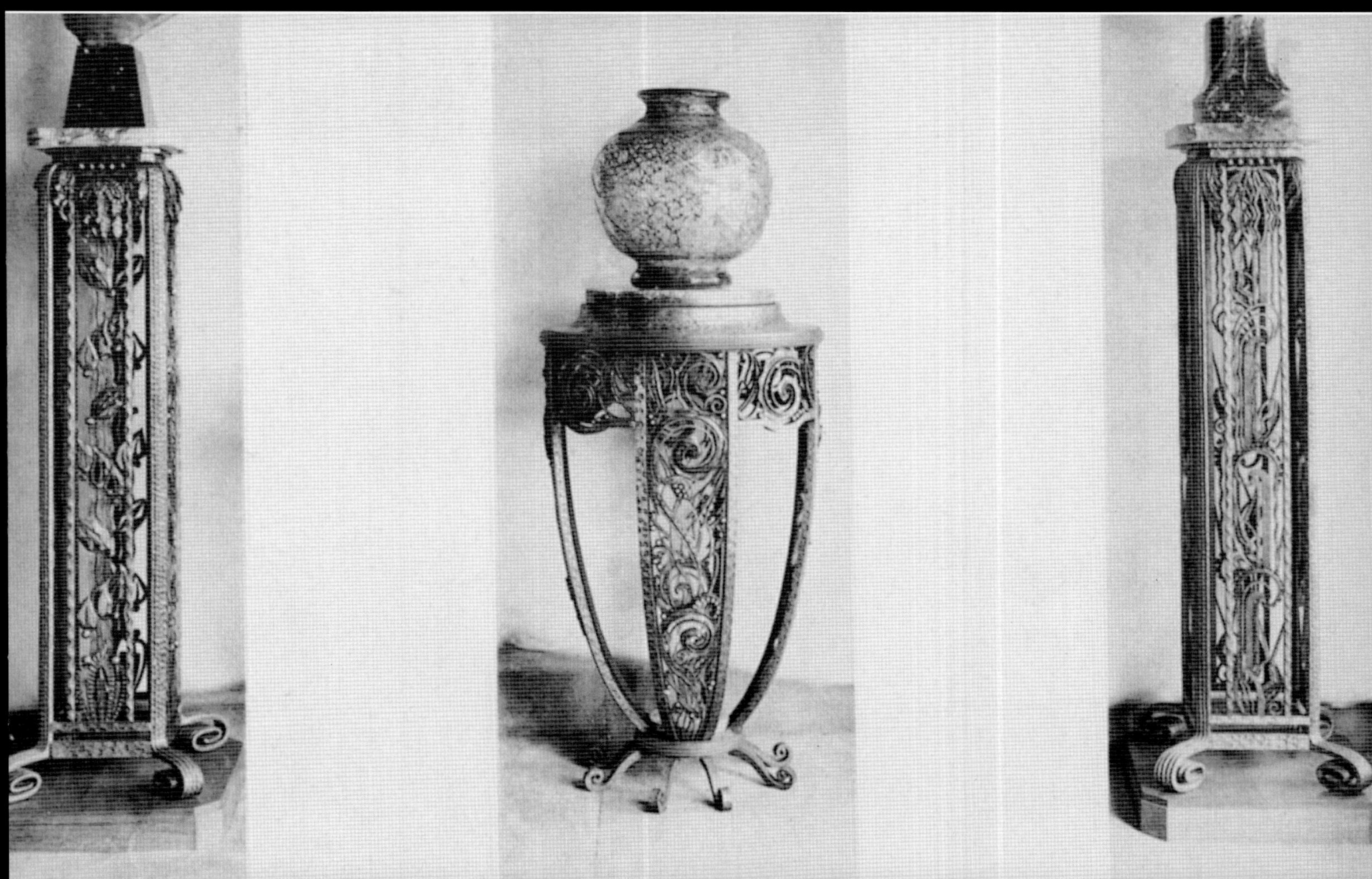

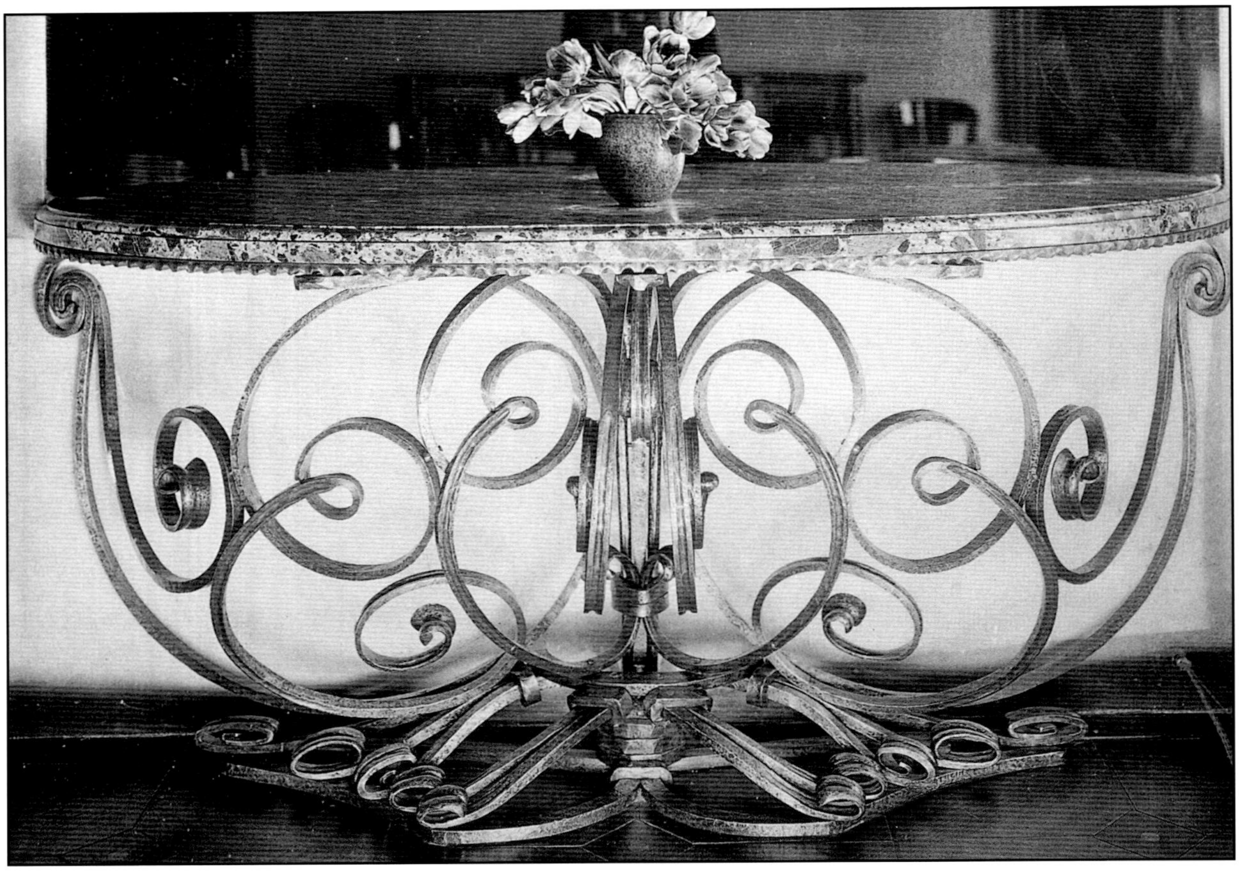

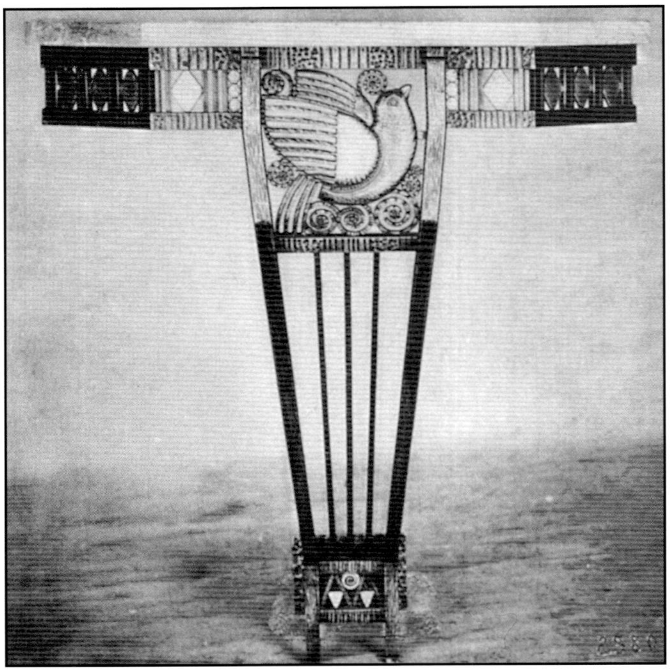

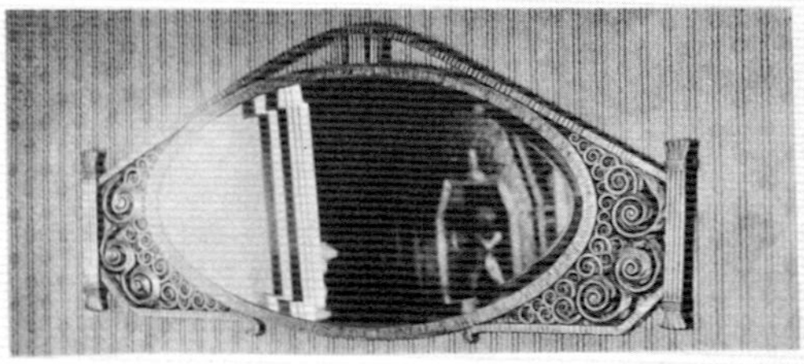

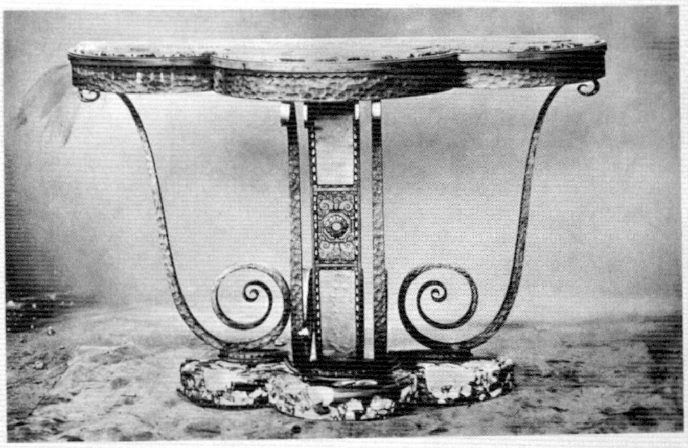

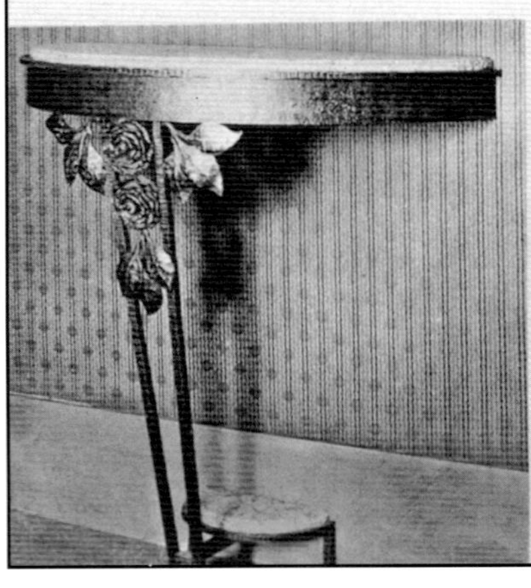

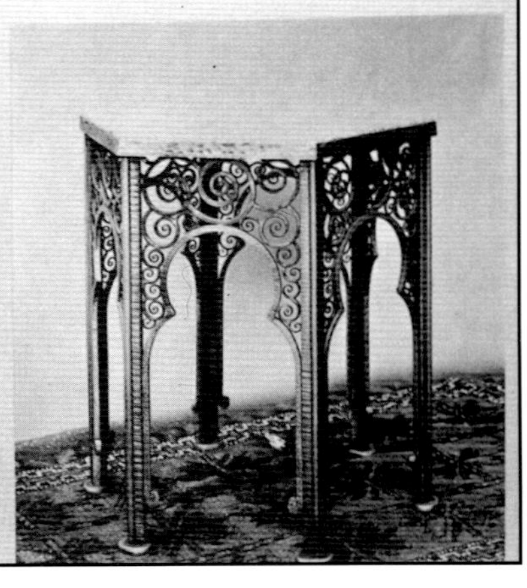

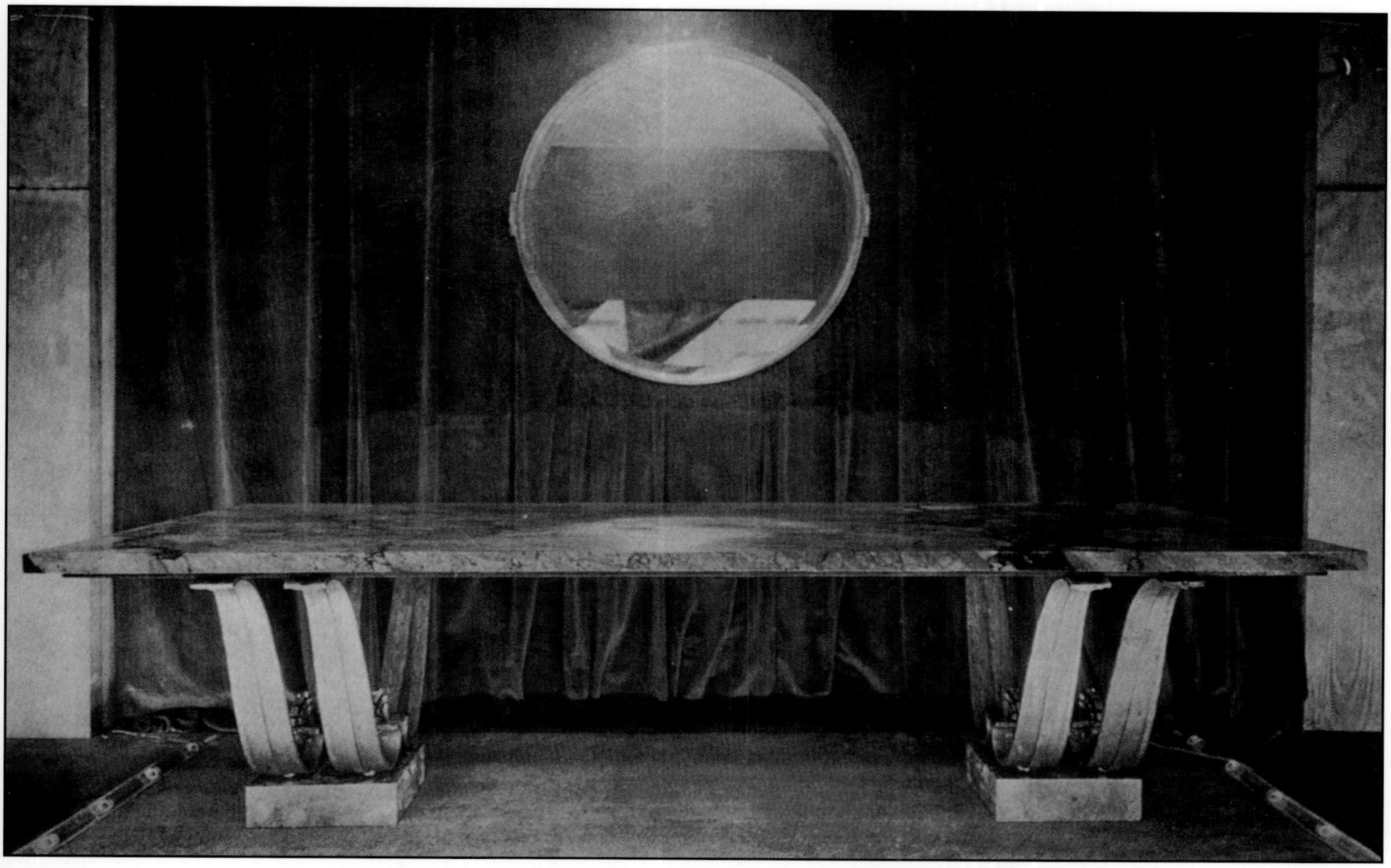

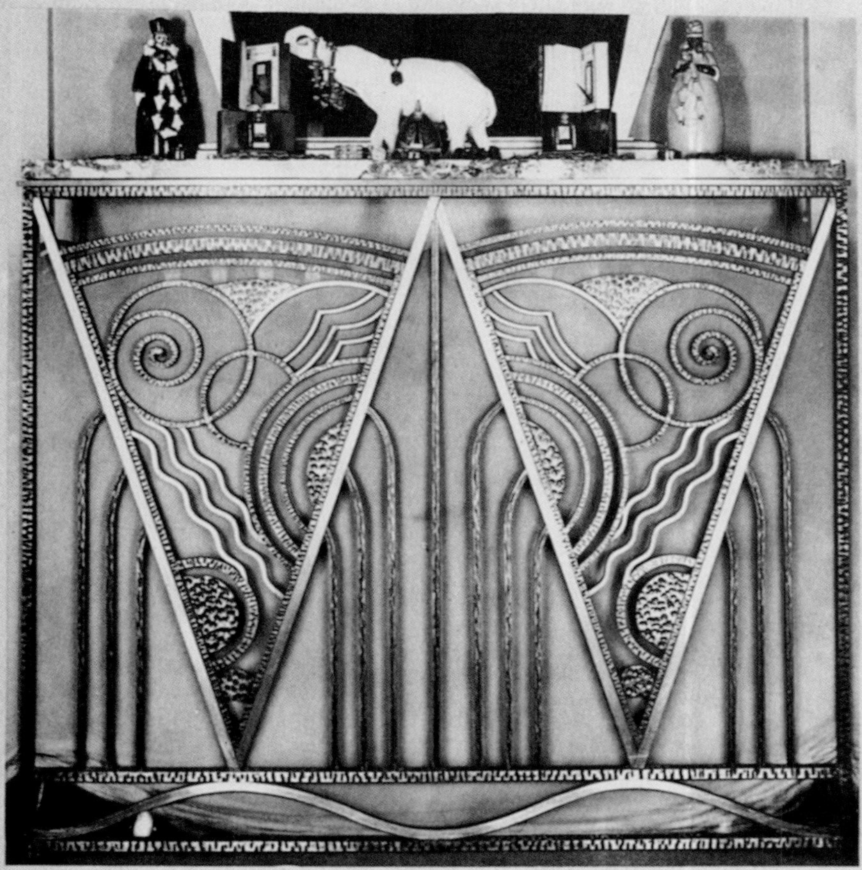

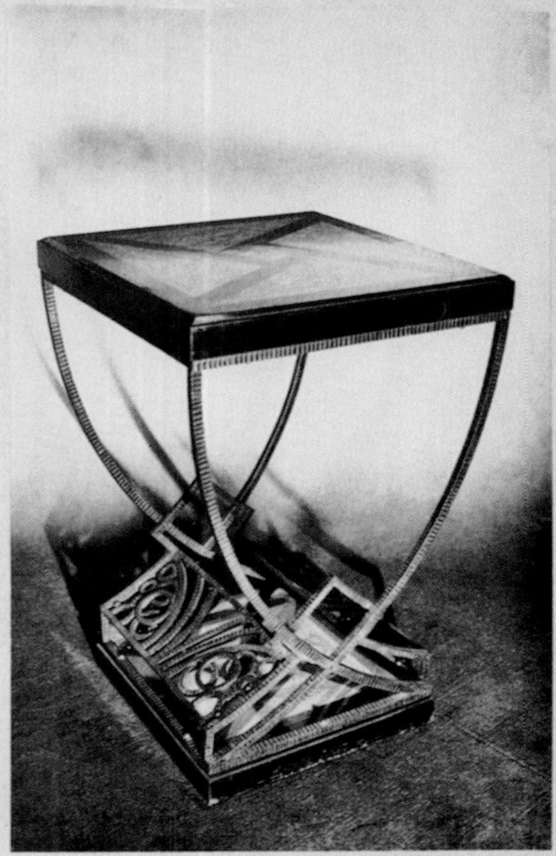

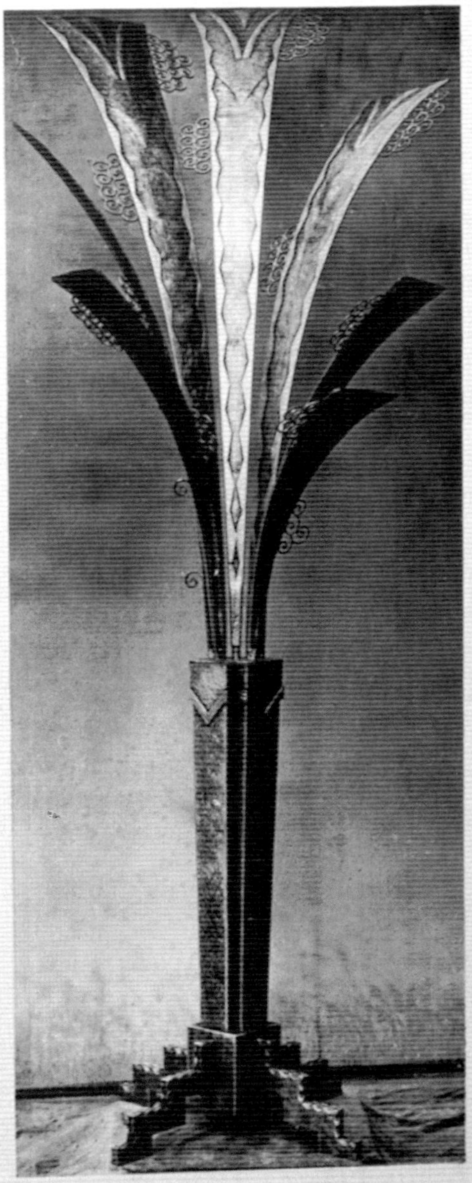

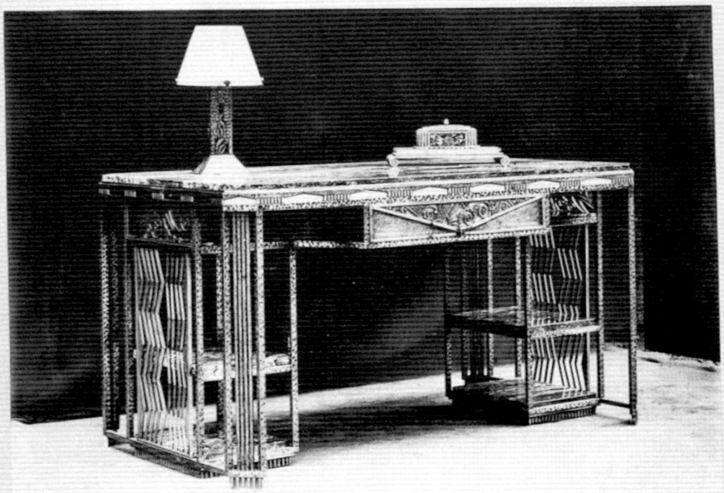

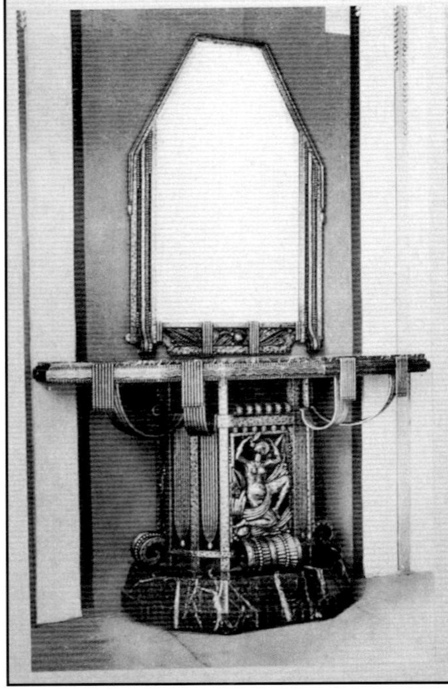

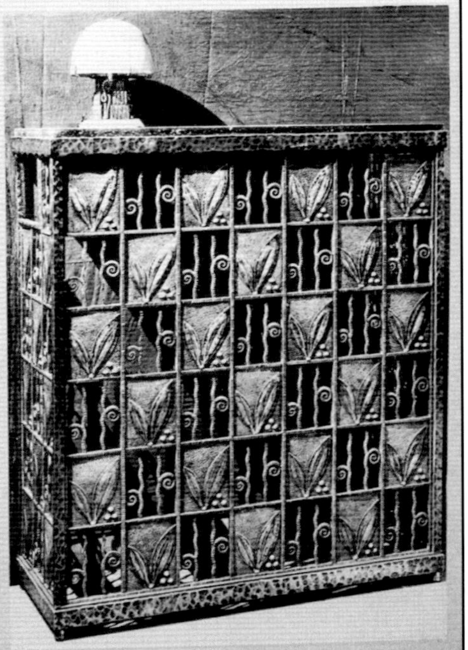

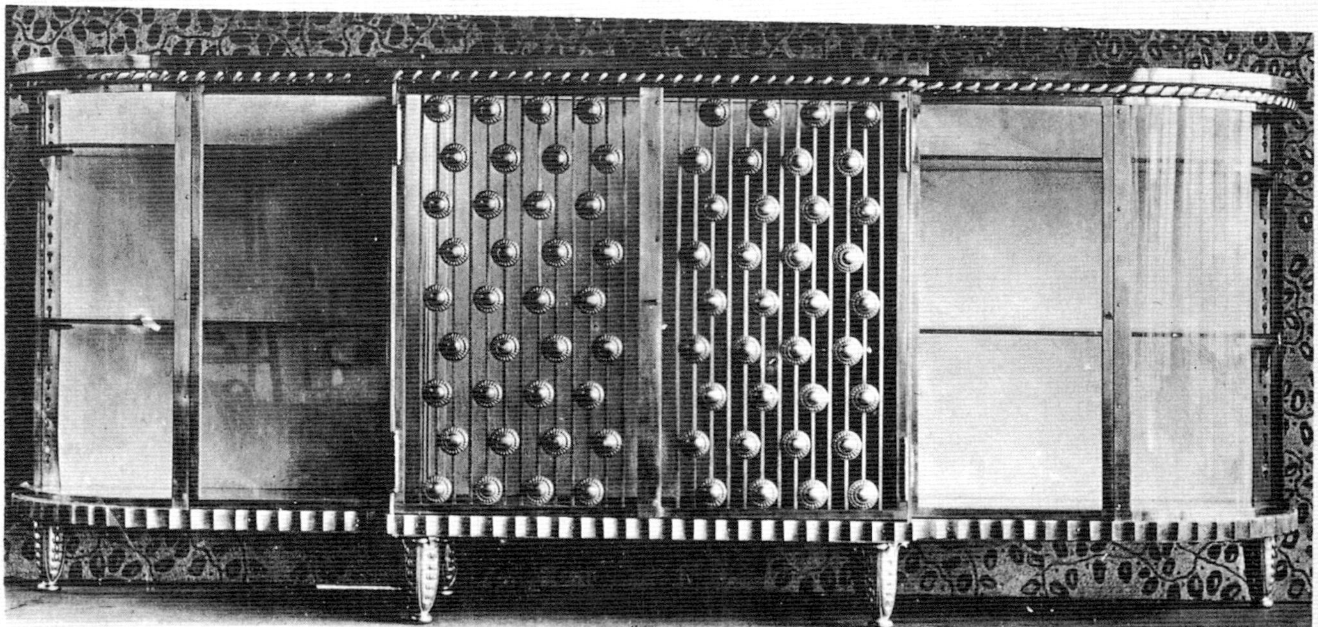

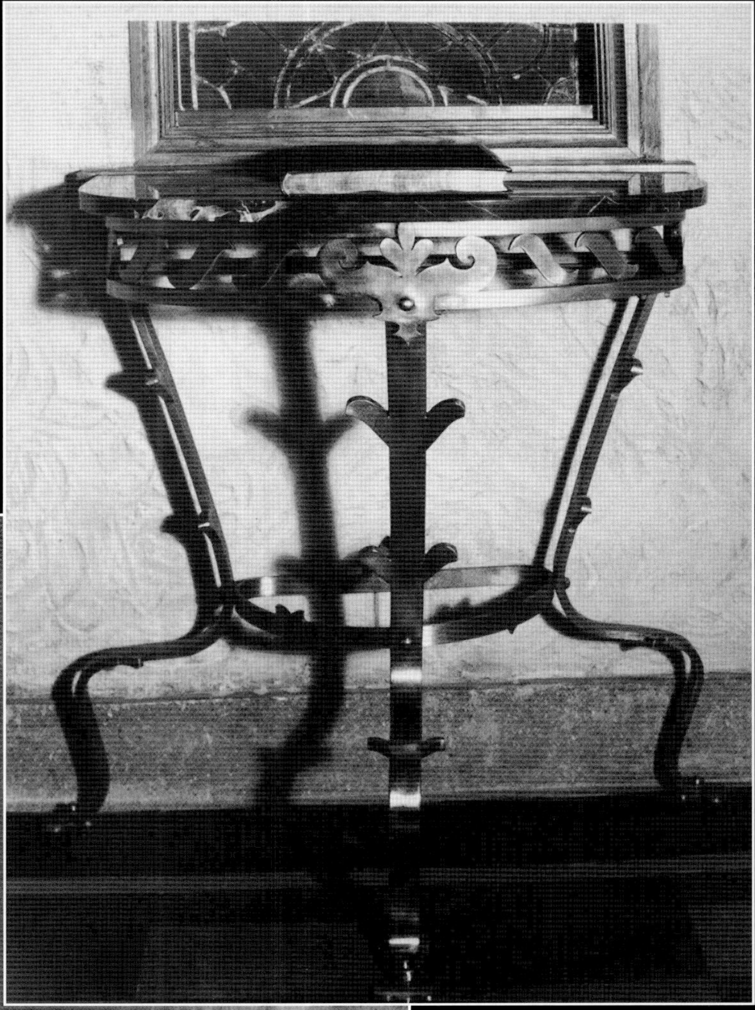

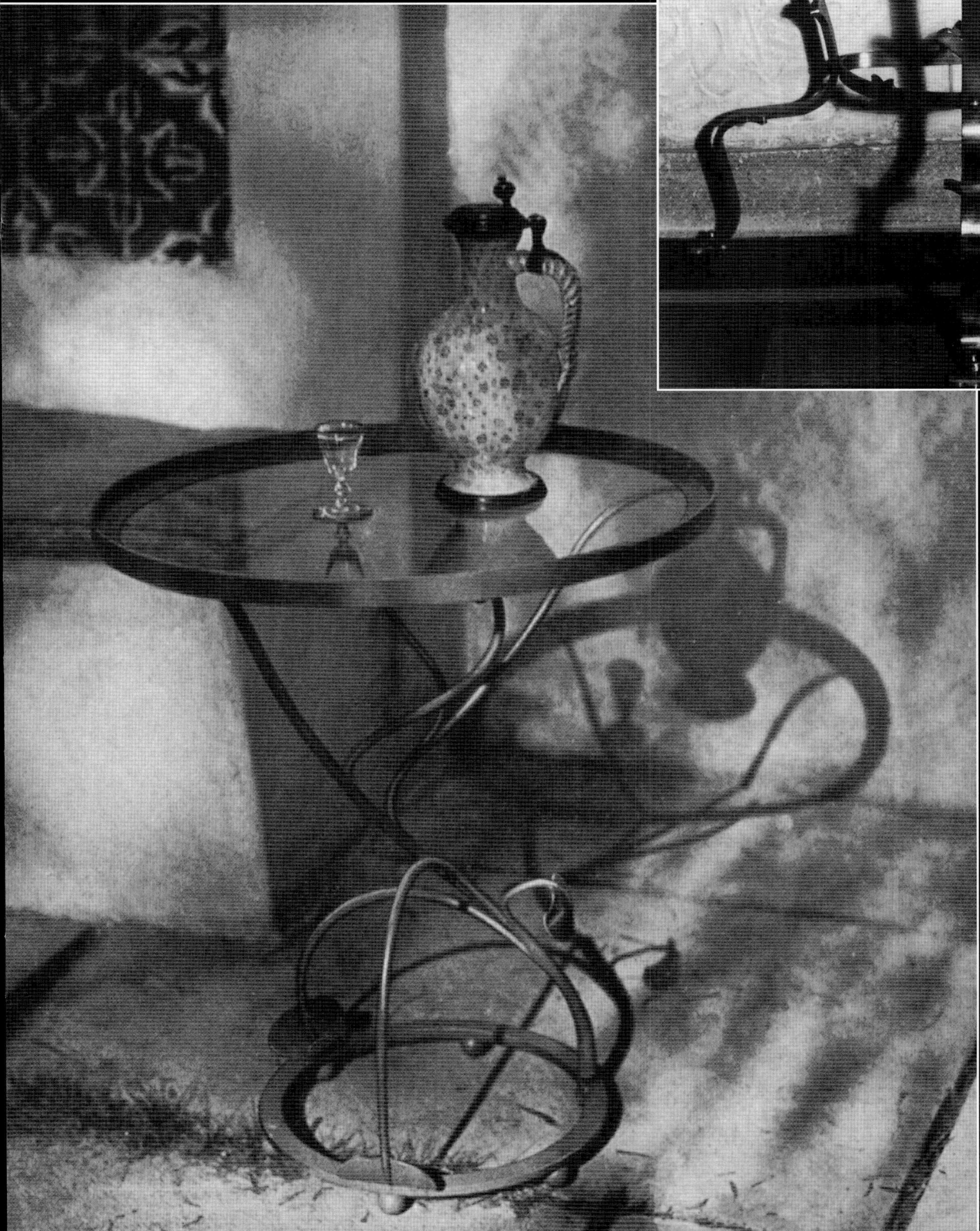

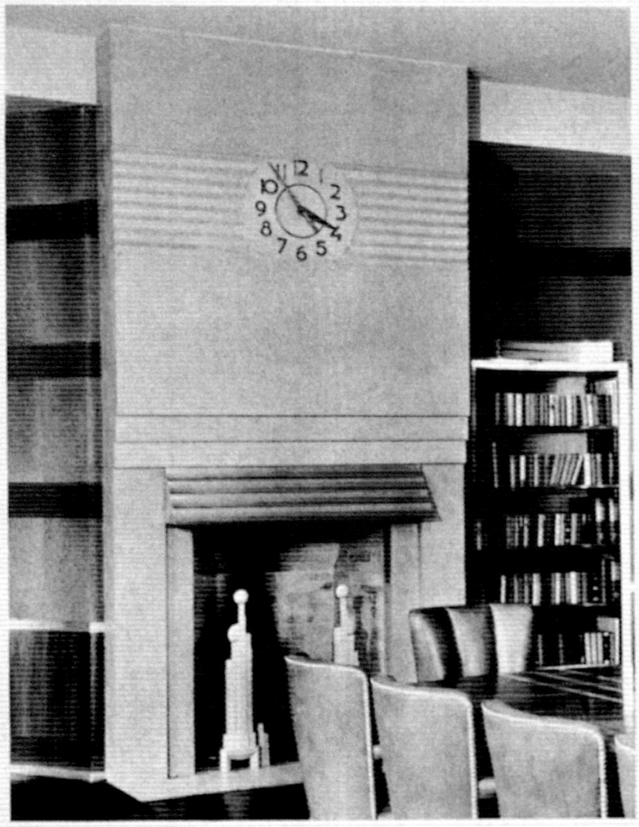

Fellheimer & Wagner

Shreve, Lamb & Harmon

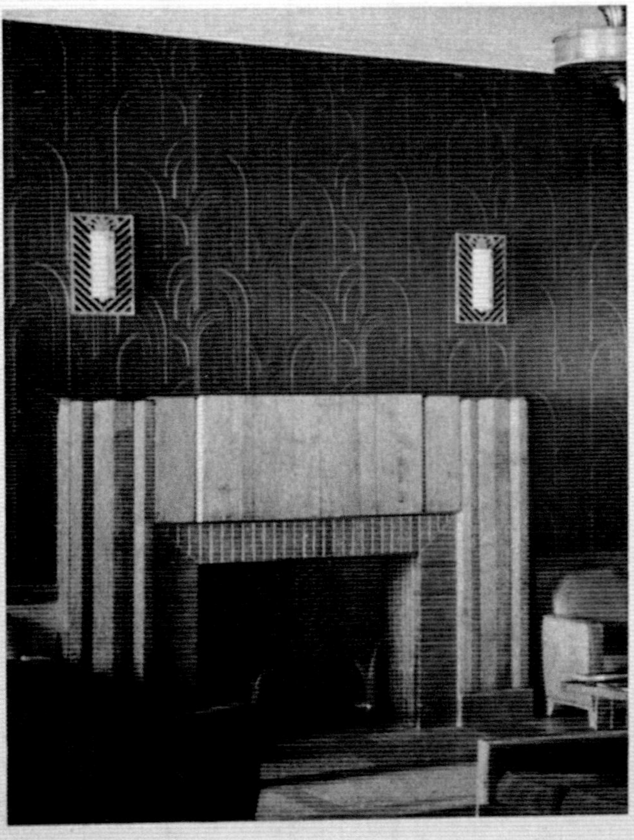

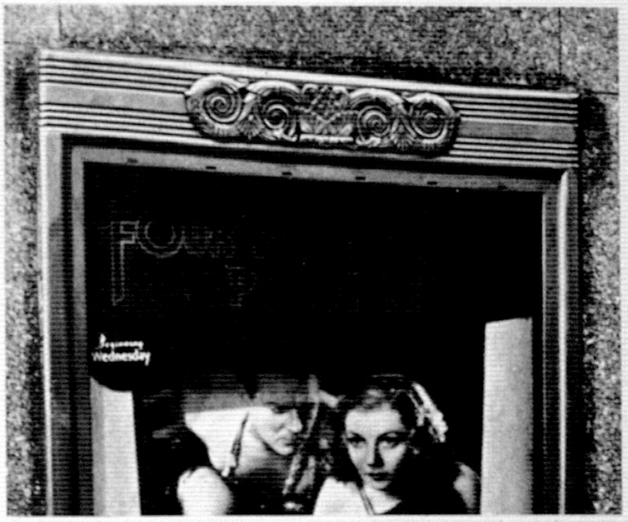

Reinhard & Hofmeister; Corbett, Harrison & MacMurray; Hood & Fouilhoux

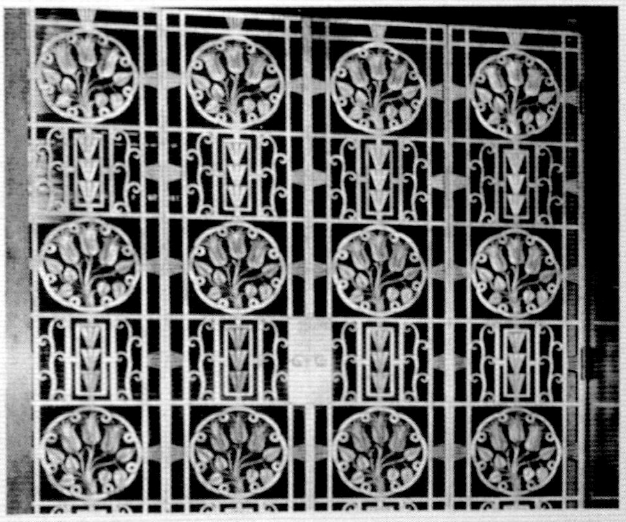

Schultze & Weaver

Vahan Hagopian

© *Amemya*

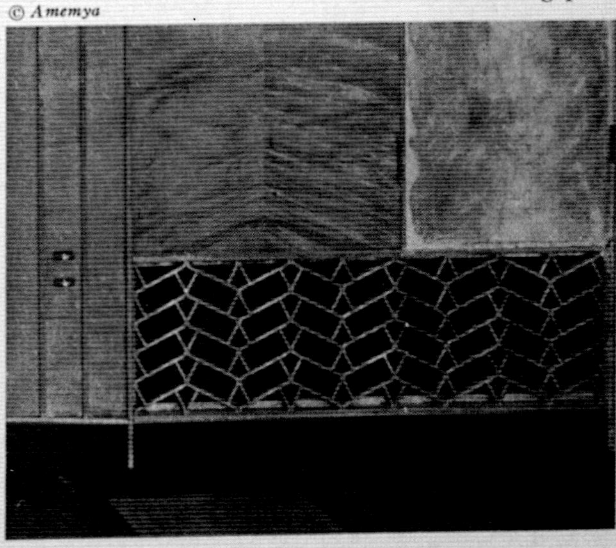

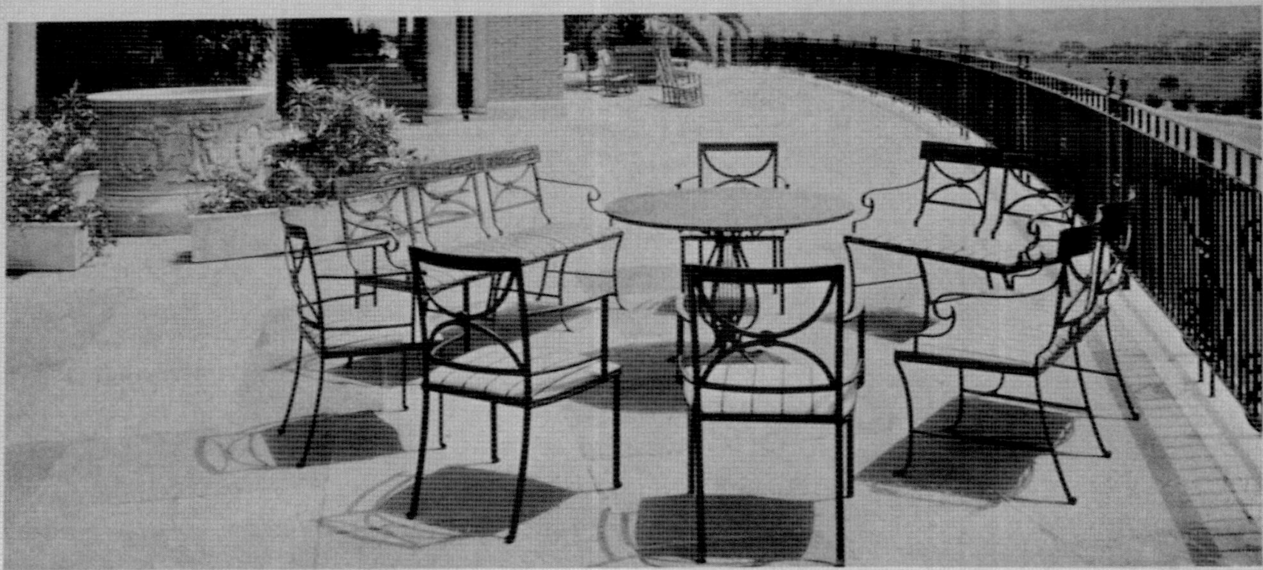

Robert Van Esdorf

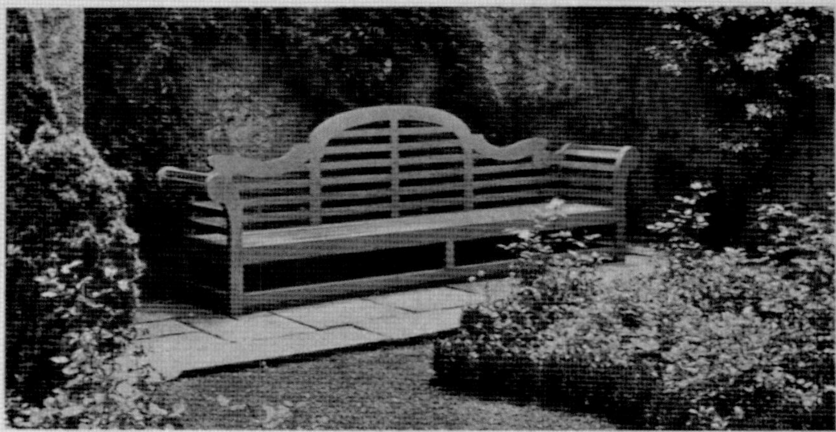

Ellen Shipman

Clarence Fowler

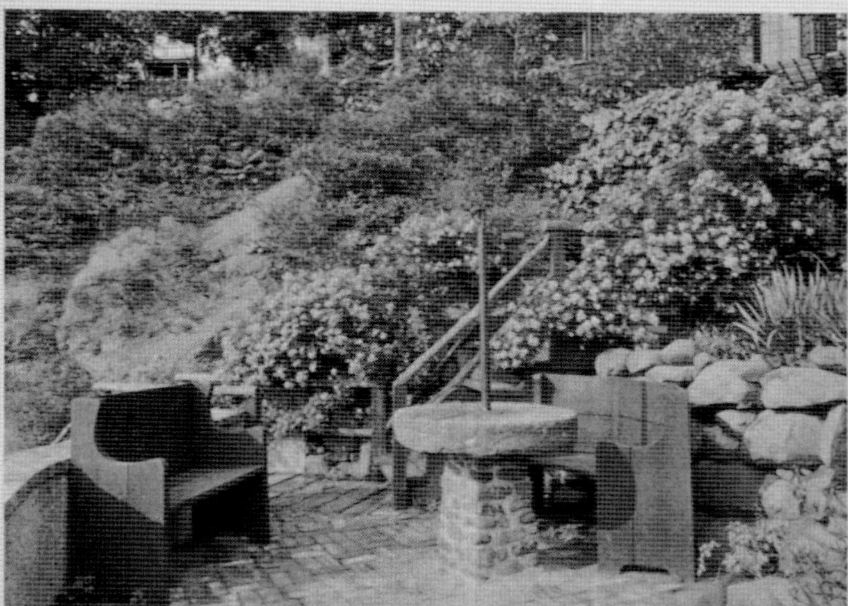

Robert Ludlow Fowler, Jr.; Arden Studios, Inc.

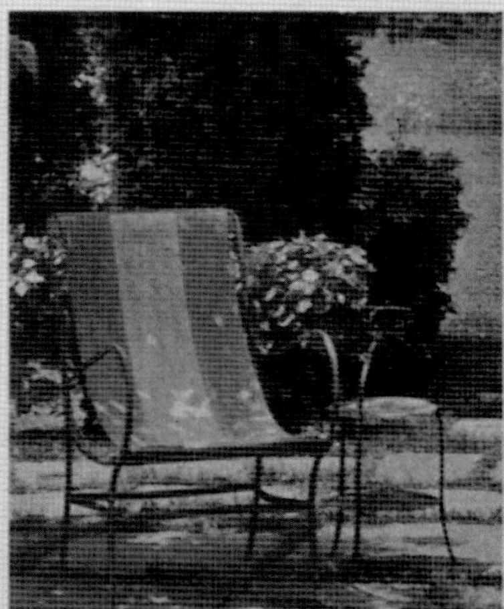

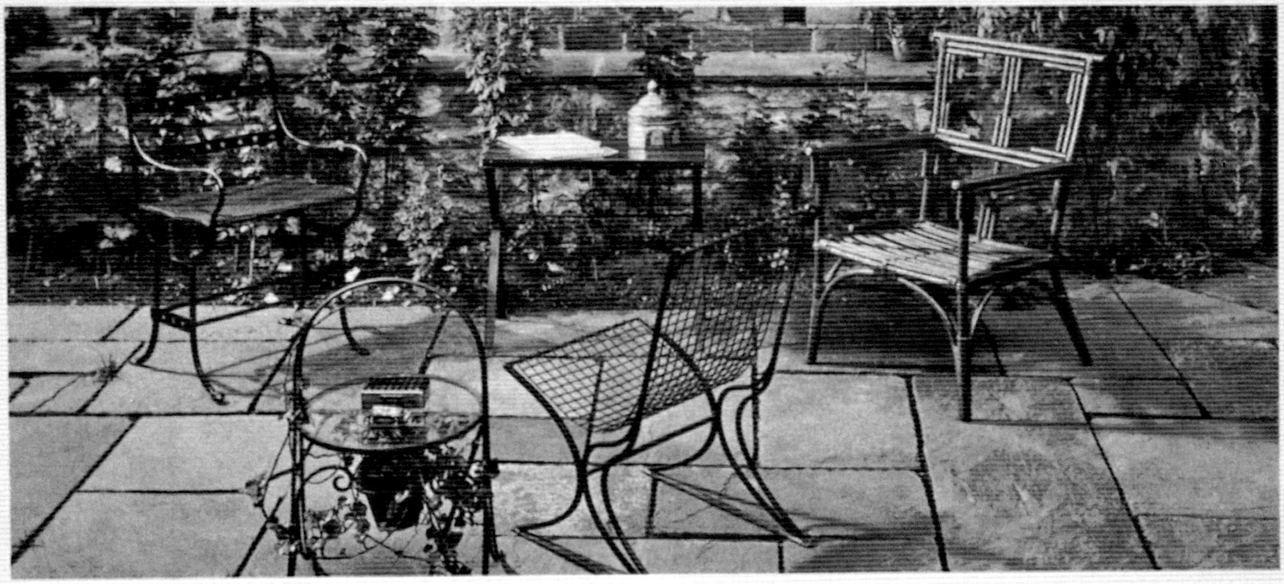

Arden Studios, Inc.

Bradley Delehanty; Isabel Pendleton

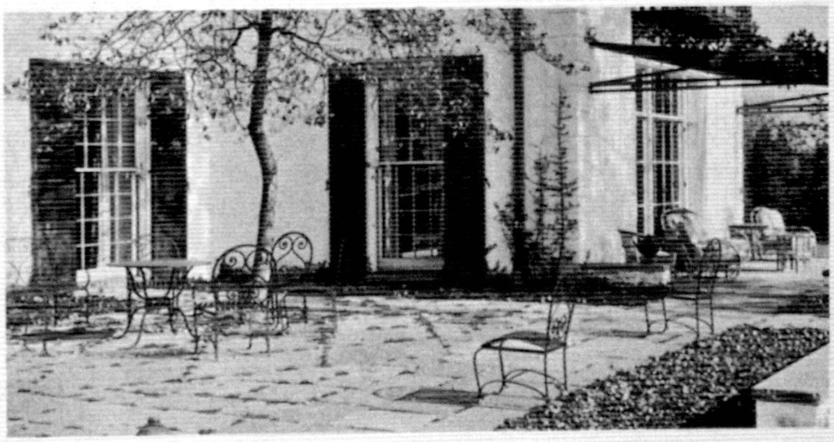

Arden Studios, Inc.

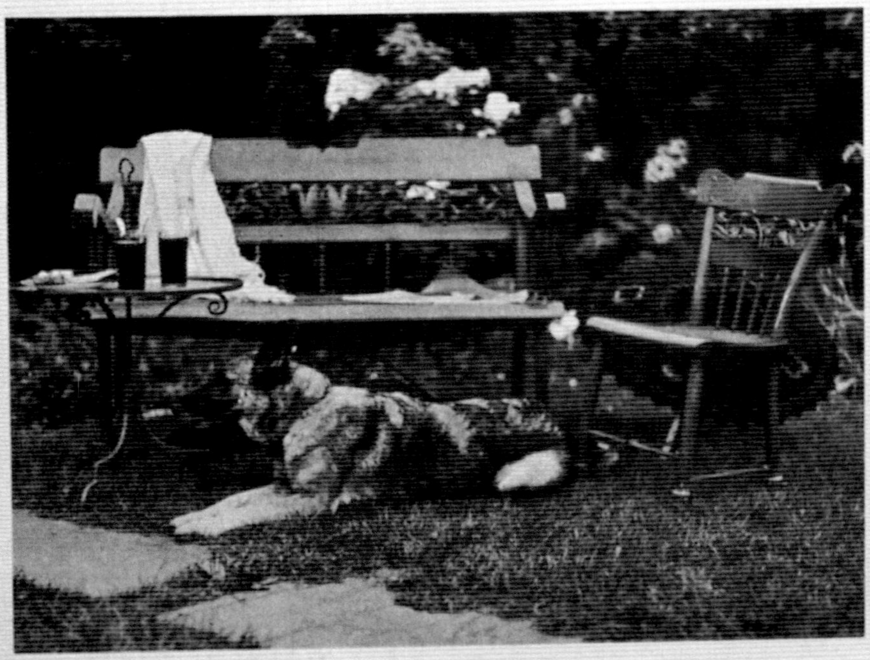

Imported marble seat in a garden by Olmsted Brothers

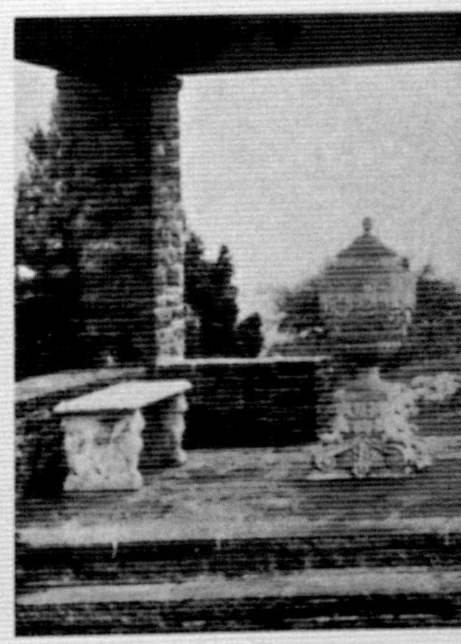

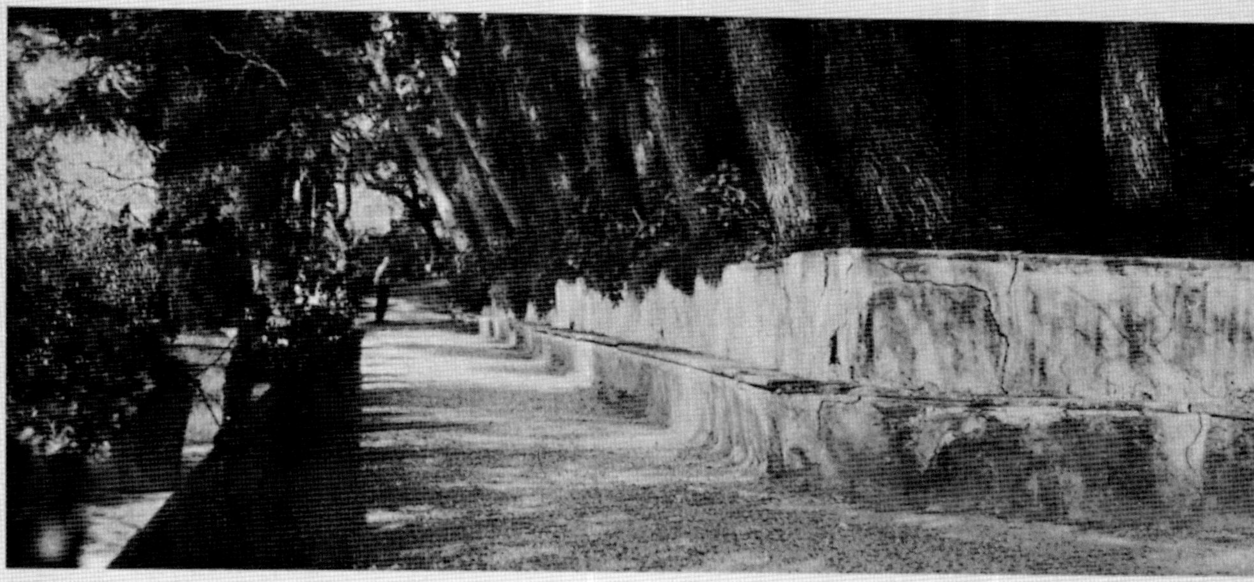

"Raixa," Spain, from the collection of Eleanor Roche

Richard H. Moen

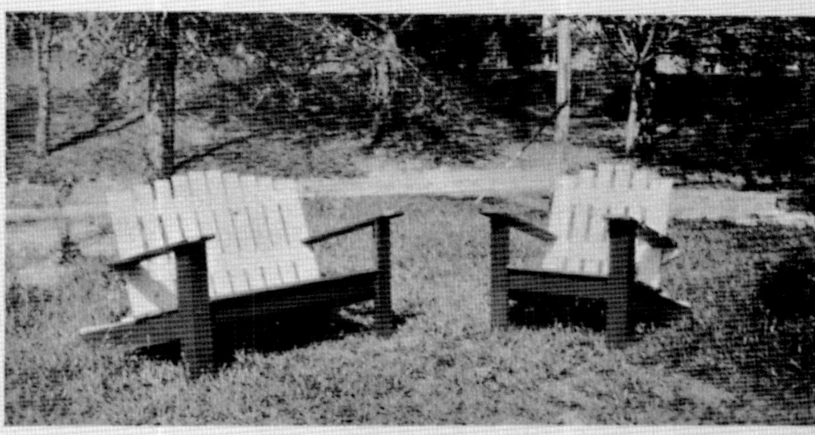

In the Walter C. Teagle estate, Portchester, N. Y.

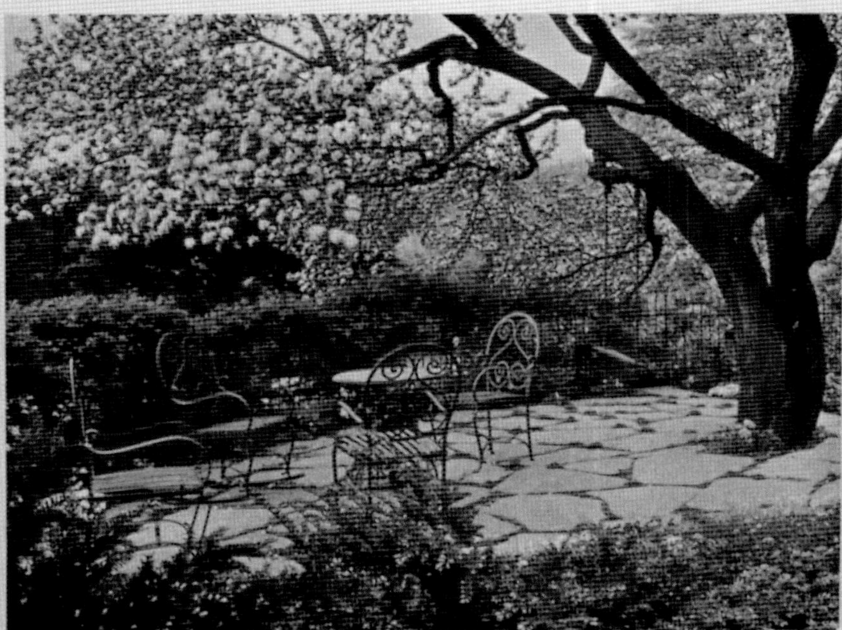

Kenneth MacDonald, Jr.

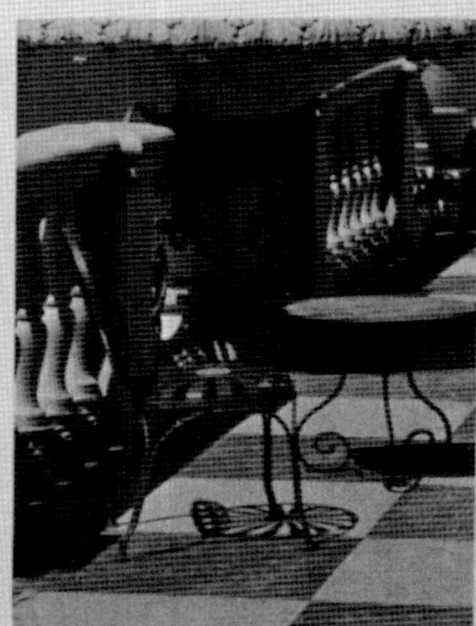

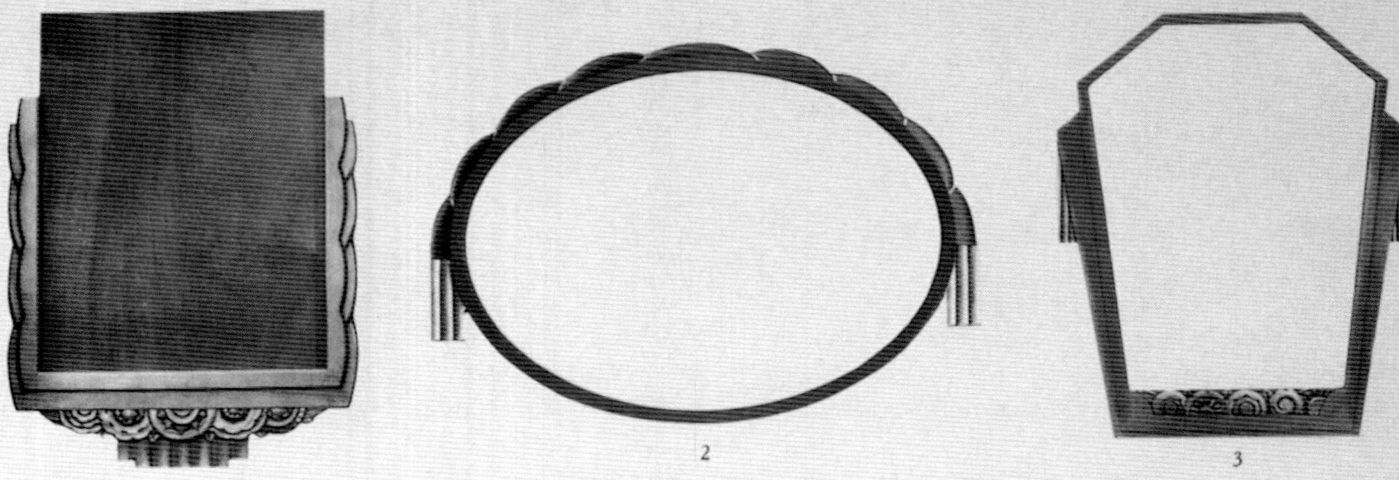

1 2 3

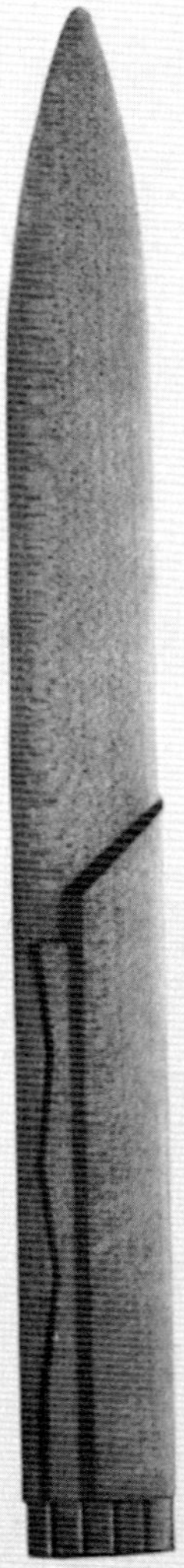

5

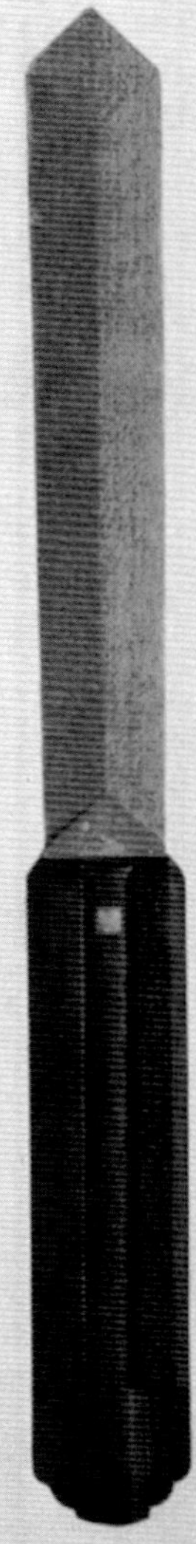

7

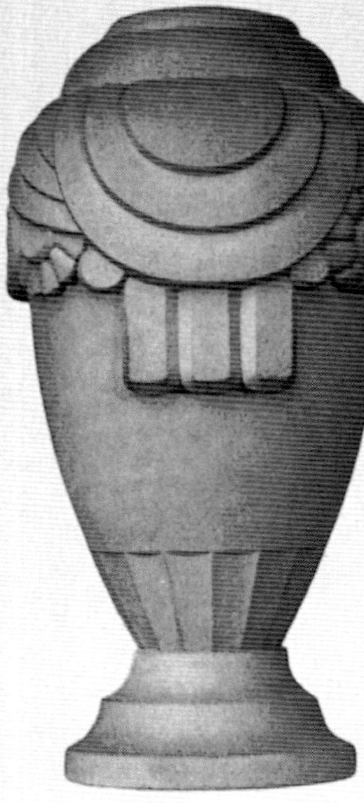

1

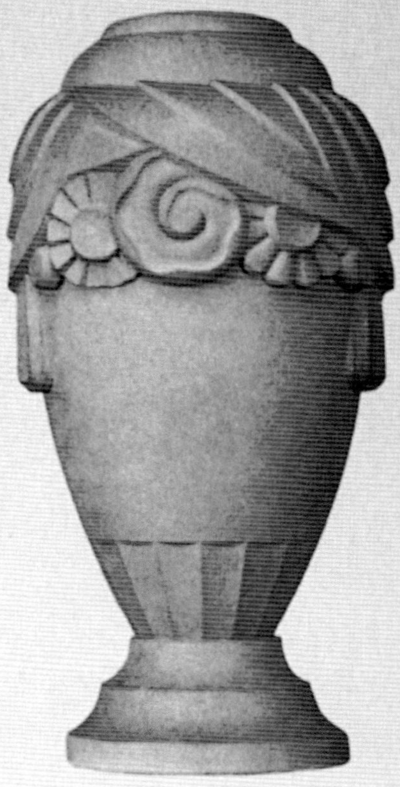

3

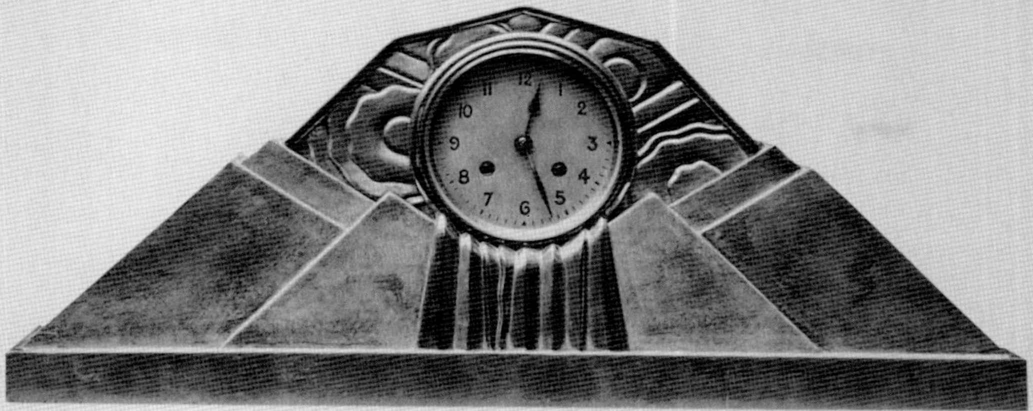

4

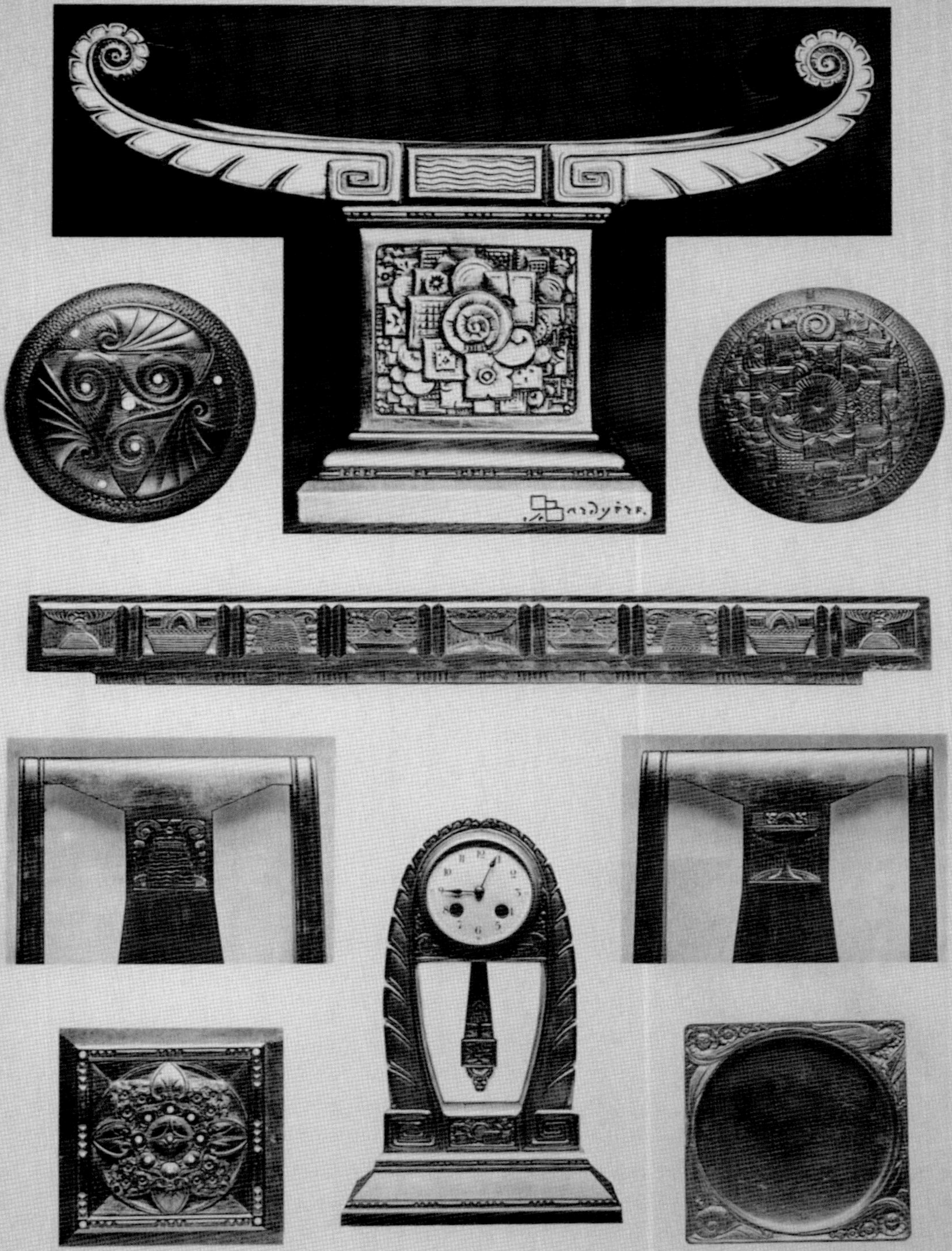

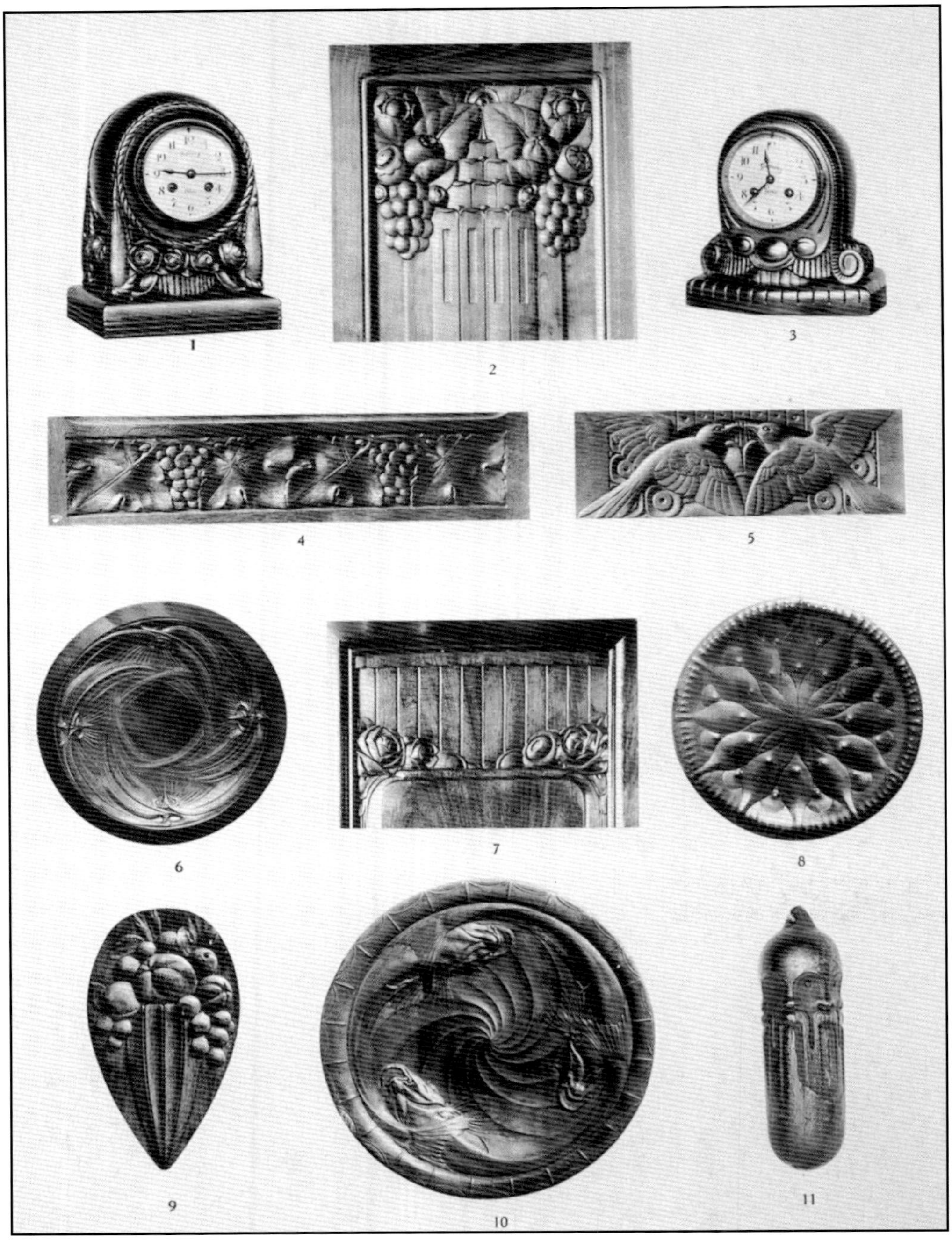

1 2 3 4 5 6 7 8 9 10 11

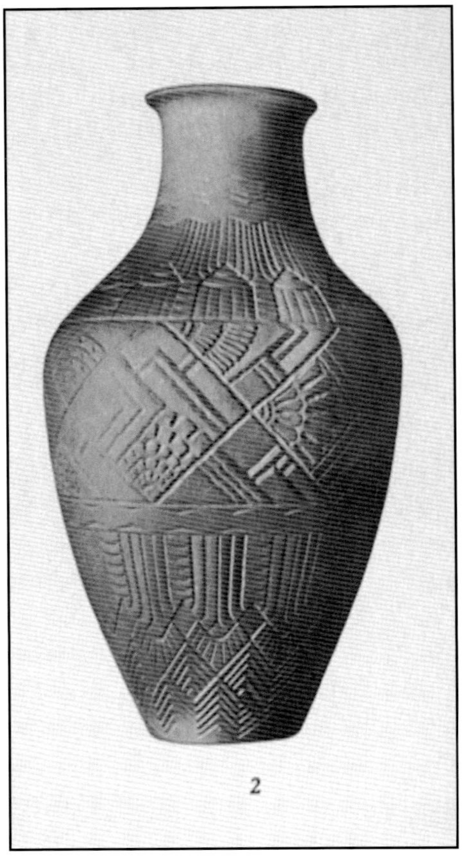

2

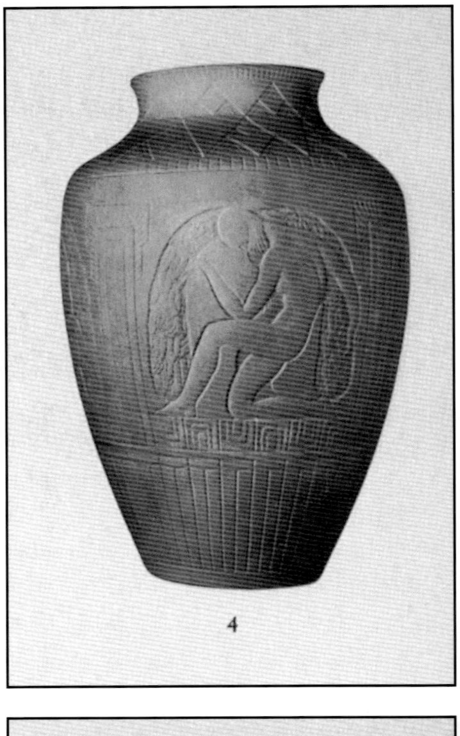

4

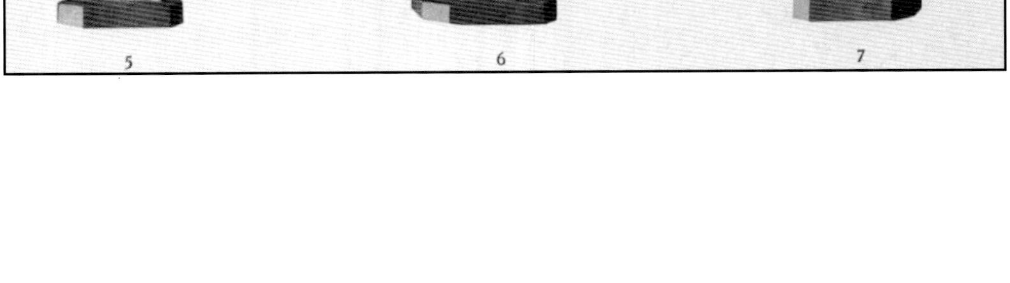

5 6 7

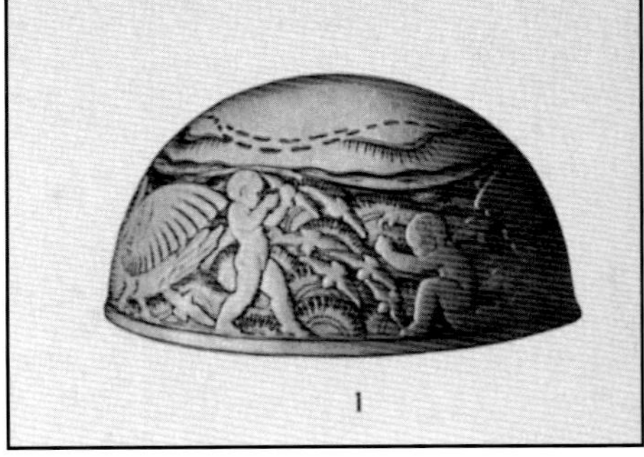

1

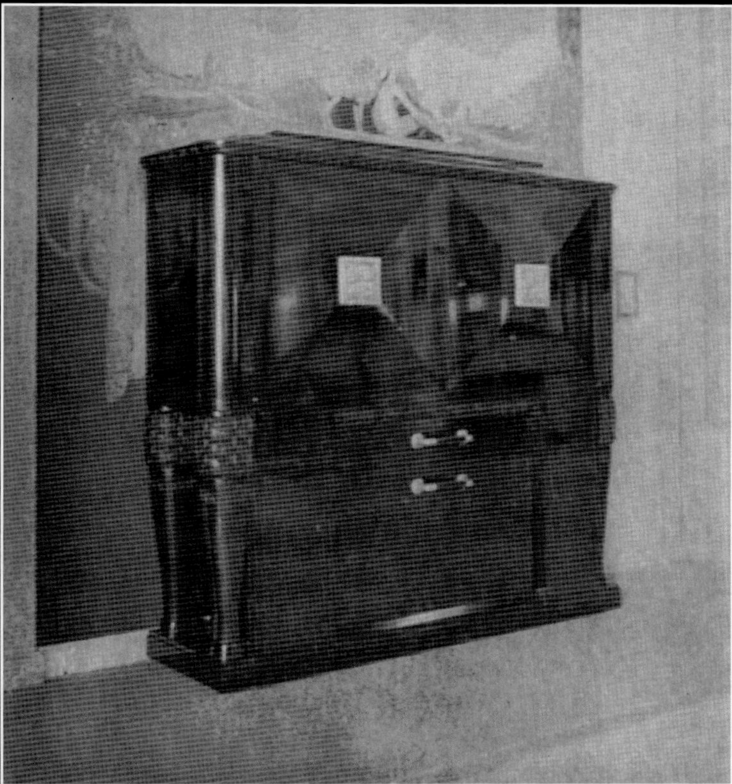

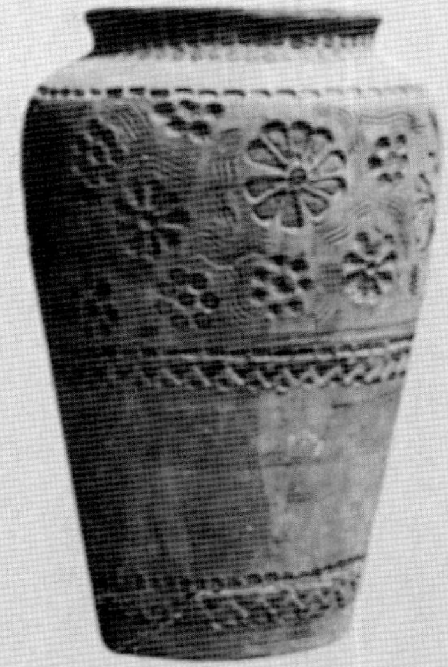

10

3

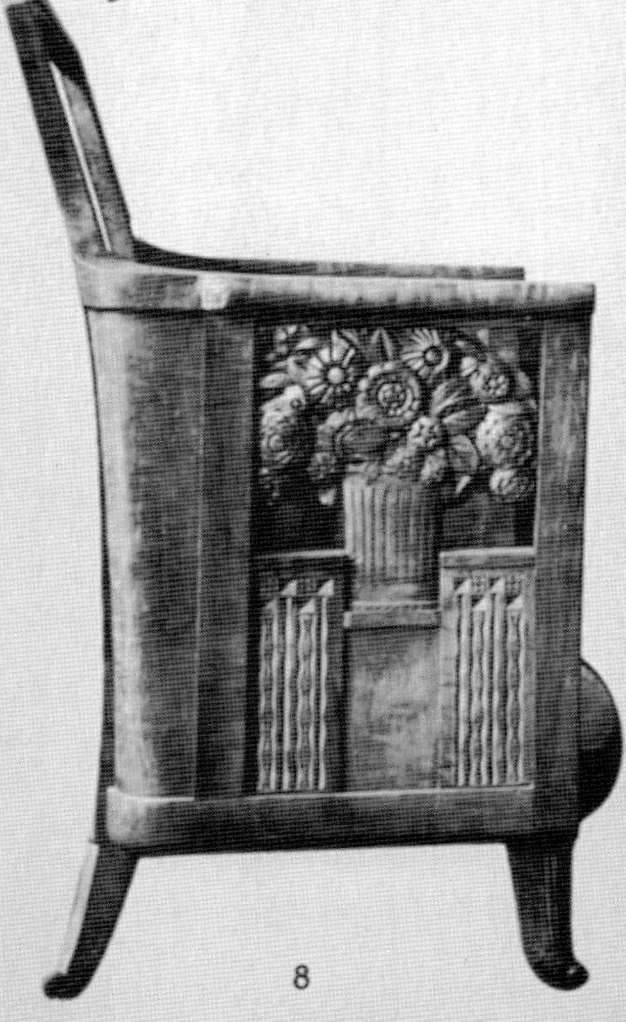

8

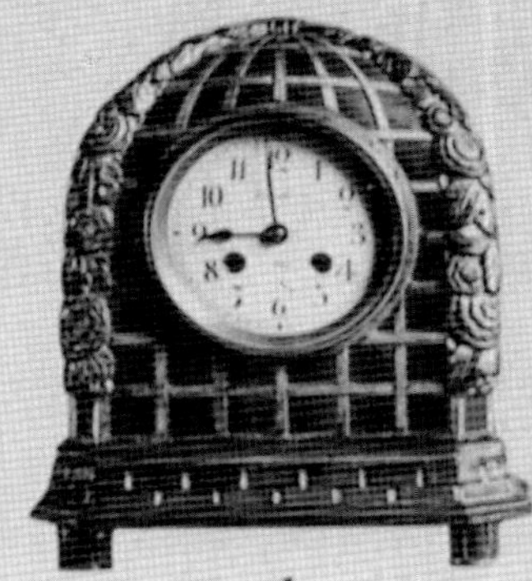

1

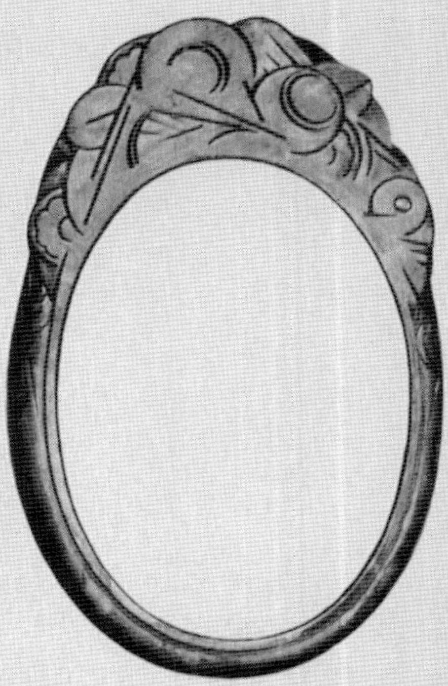

5

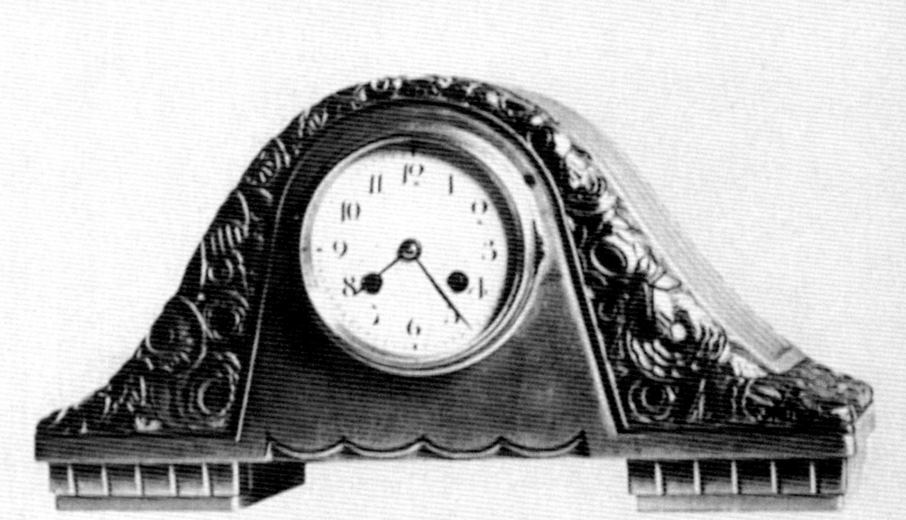

4

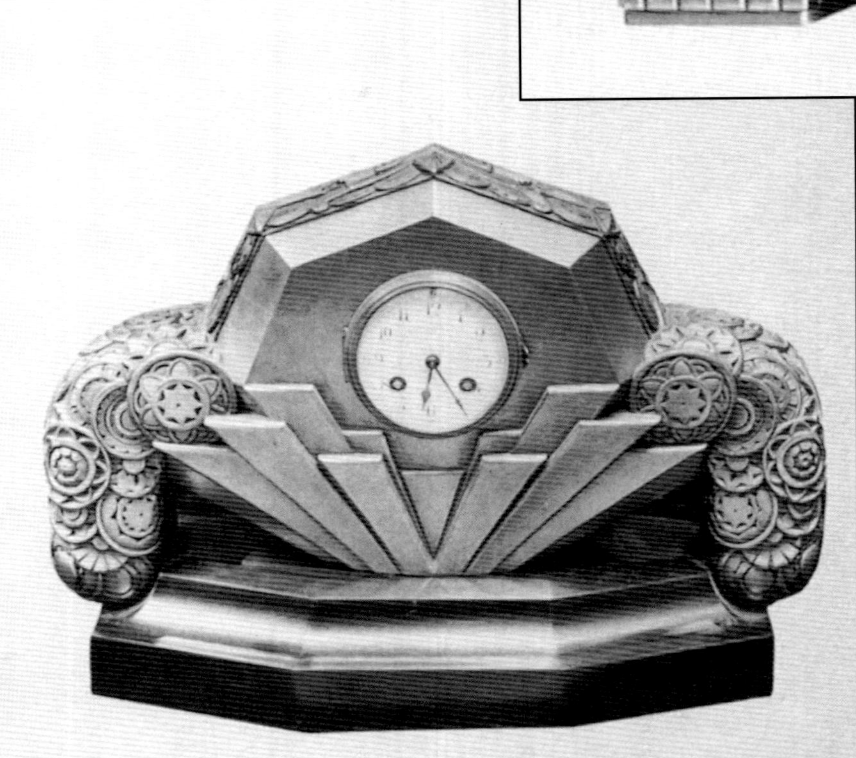

6

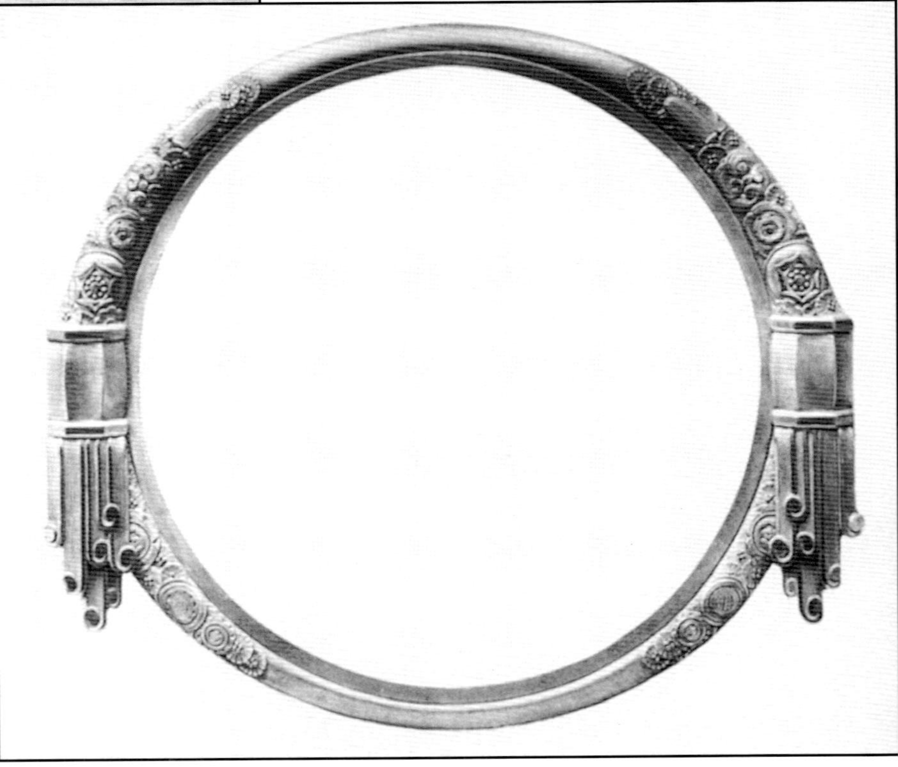

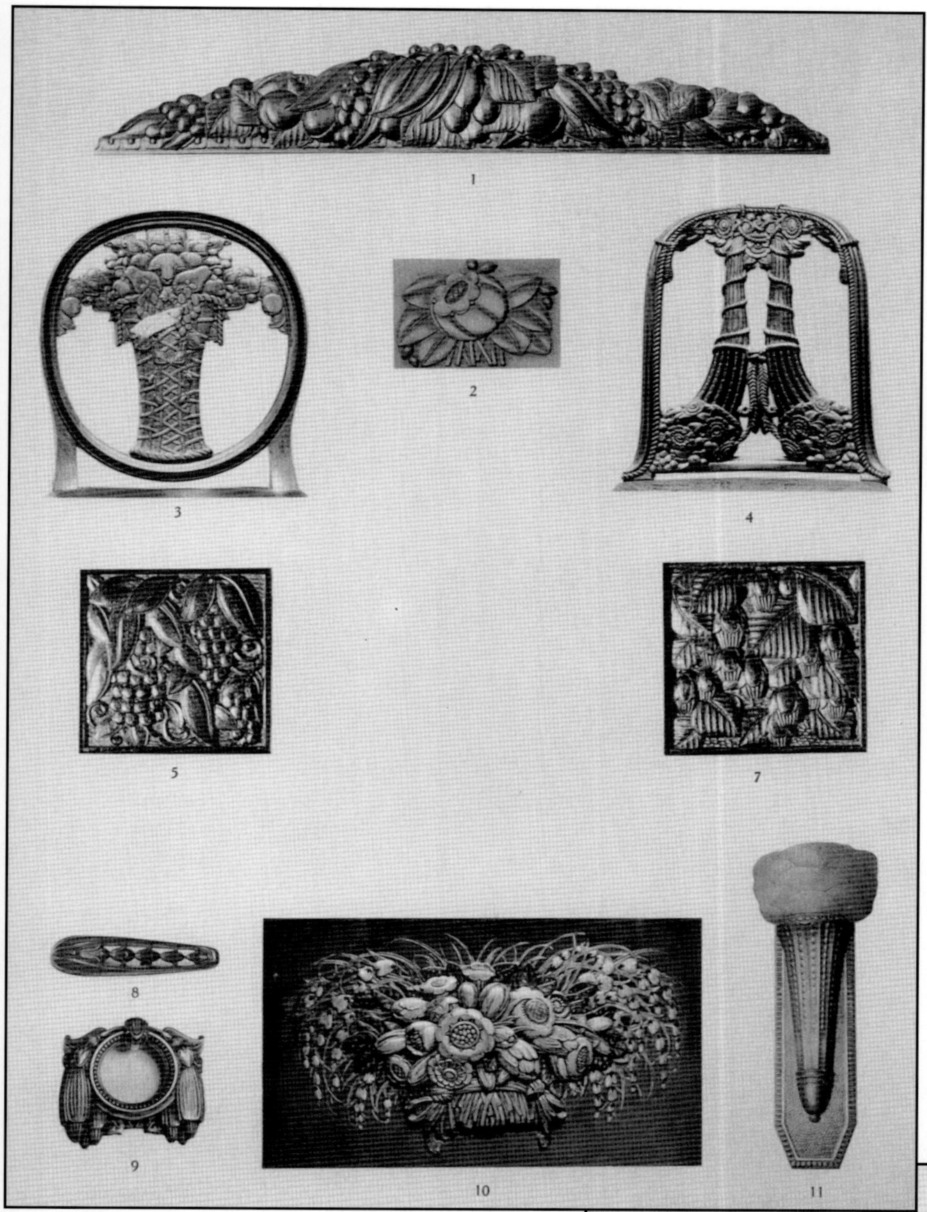
1
2
3
4
5
7
8
9
10
11

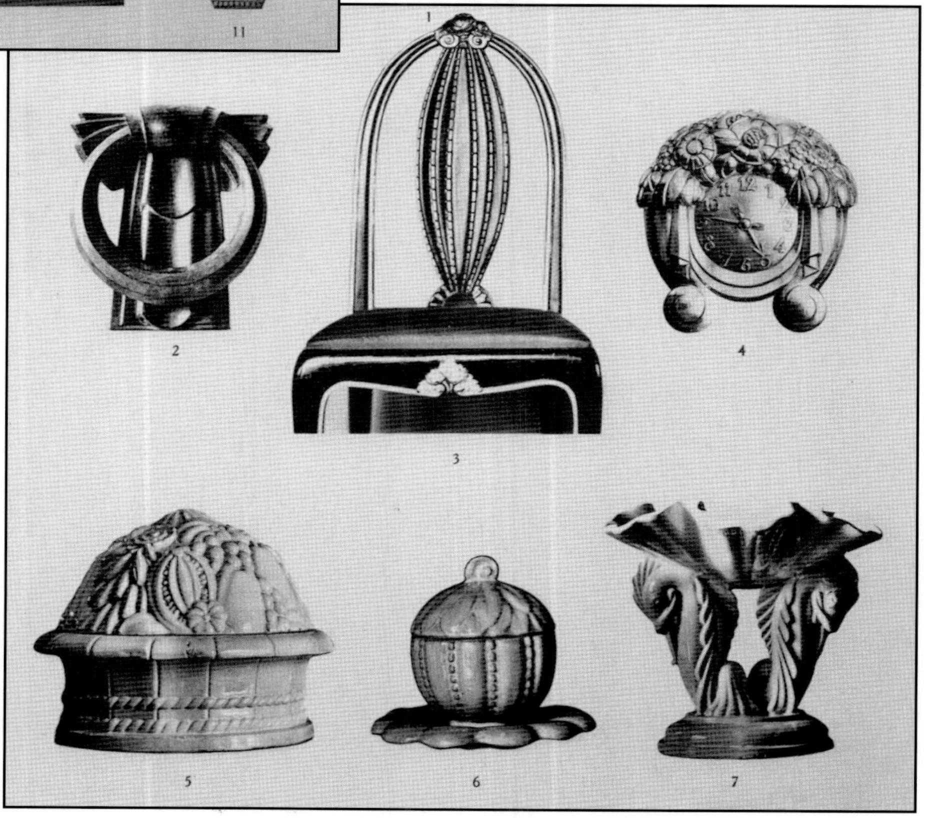
1
2
3
4
5
6
7

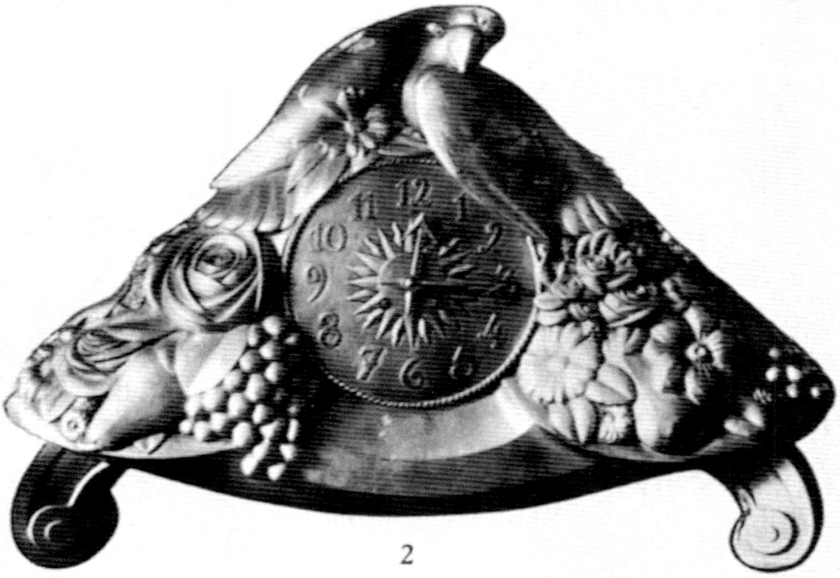

2

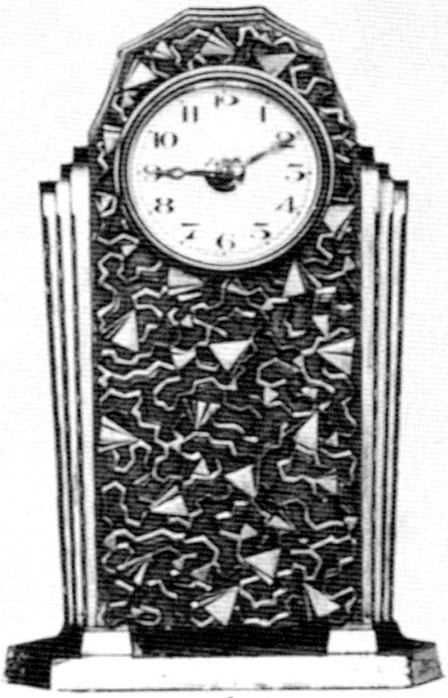

1

4

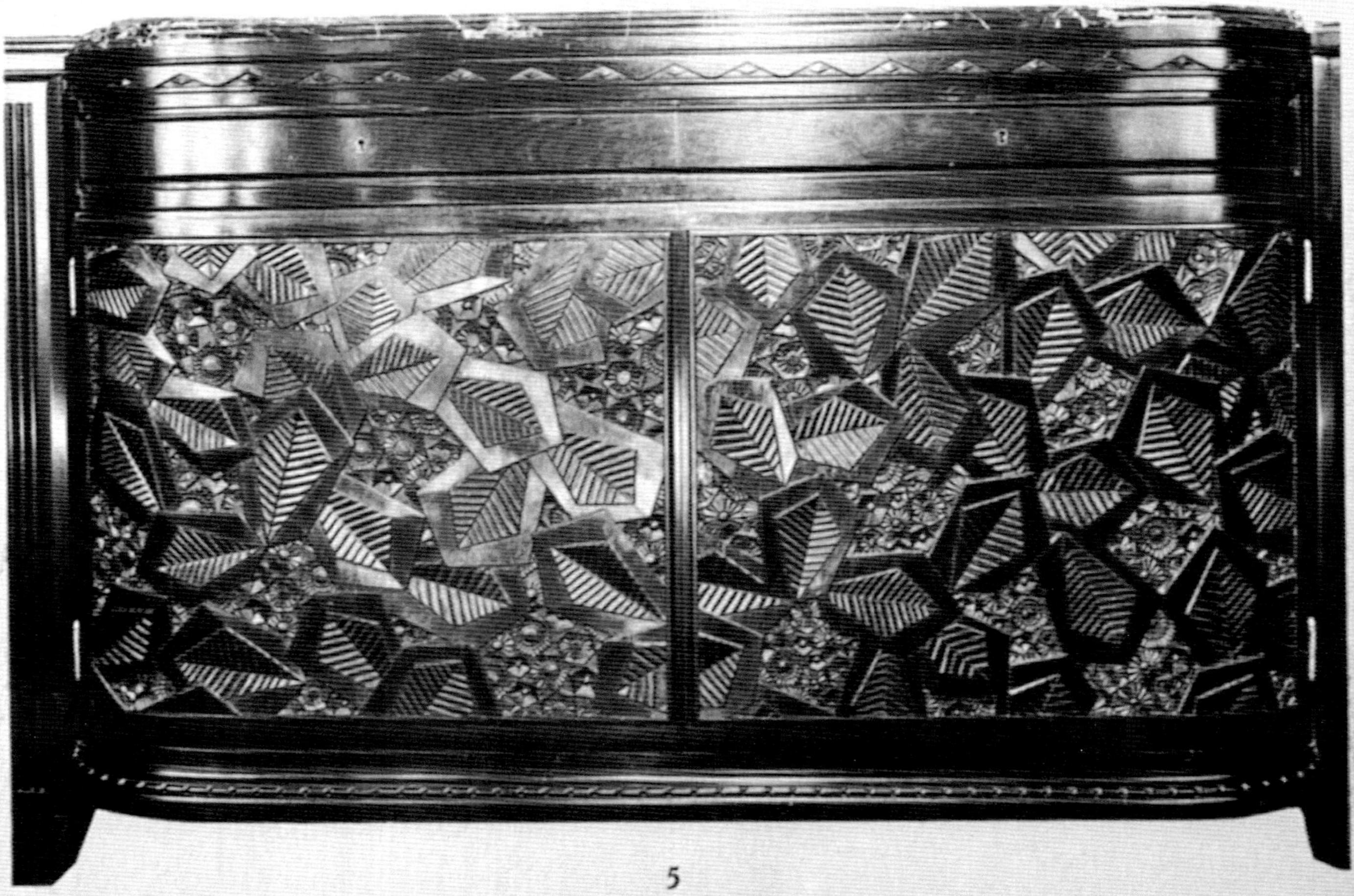

5

Pl. 17

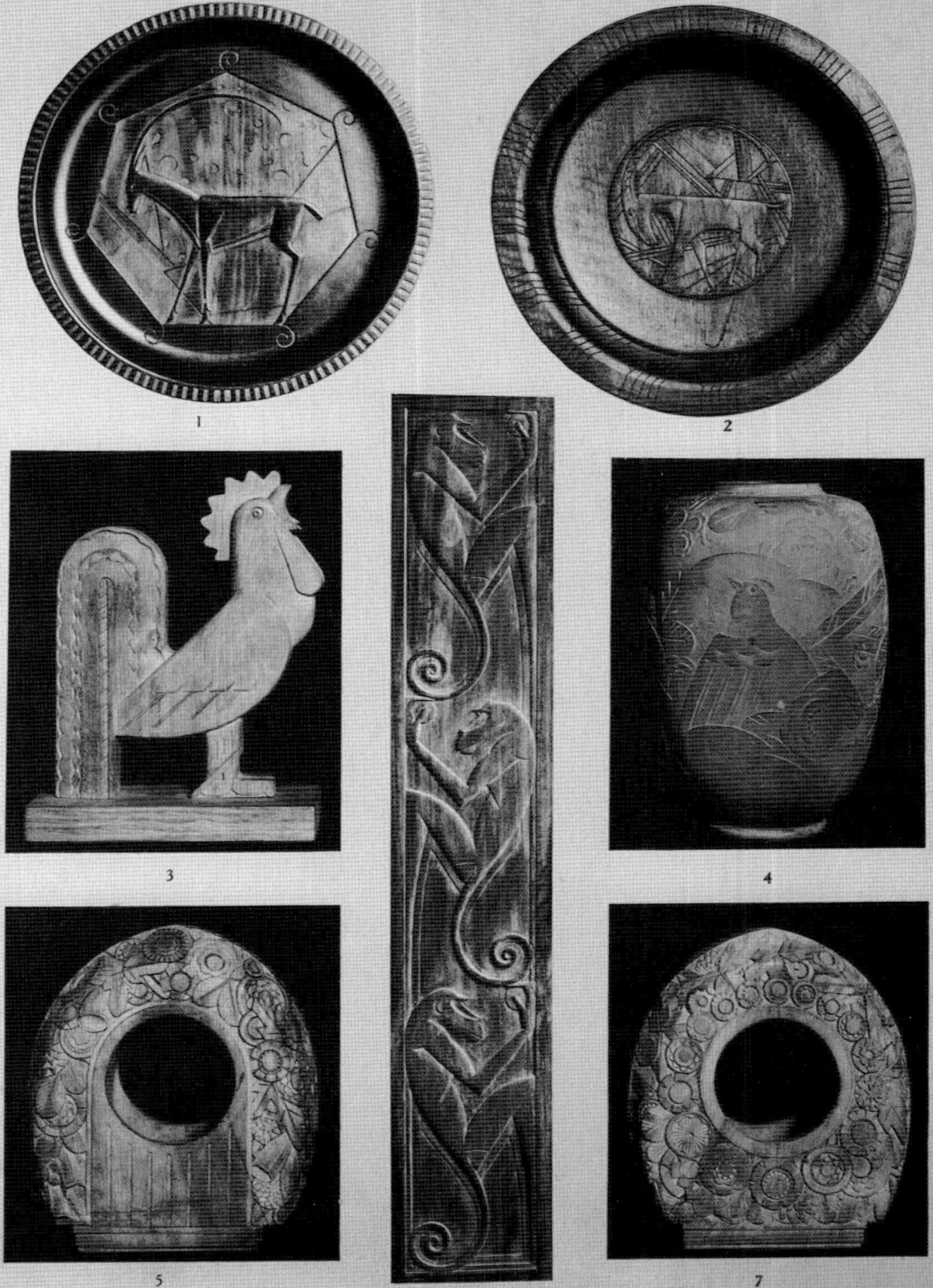

1 2 3 4 5 6 7

Charles Moreau, éditeur, 8, Rue de Prague, Paris (XIIe)

Hélio Léon Marotte, Paris

JALLOT

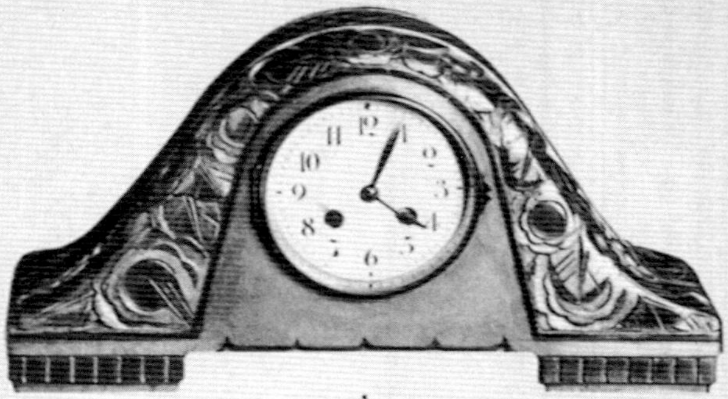

1

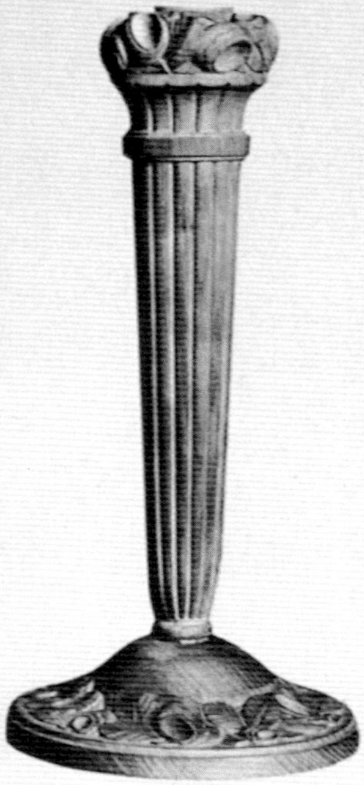

2

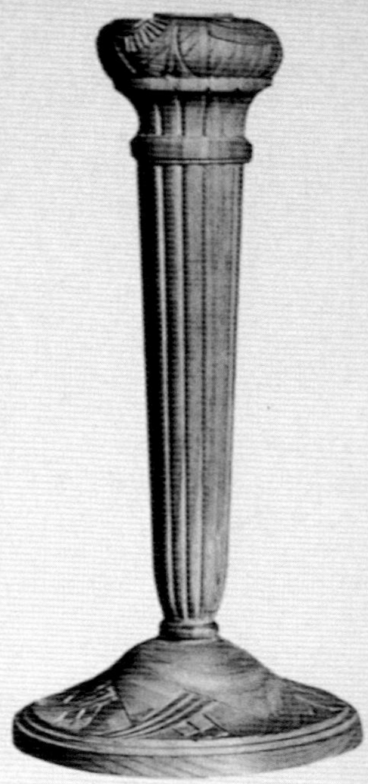

3

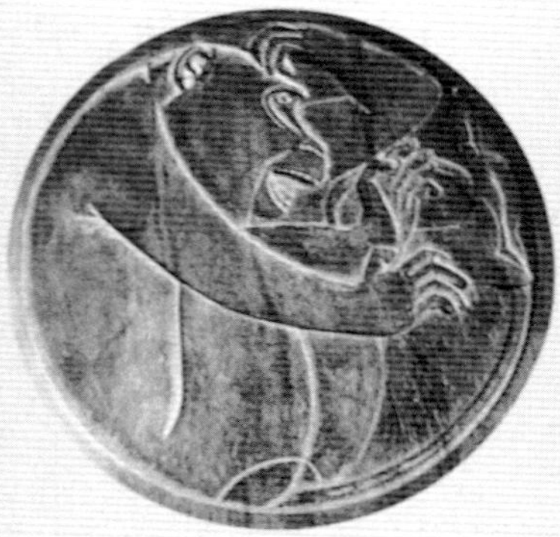

5

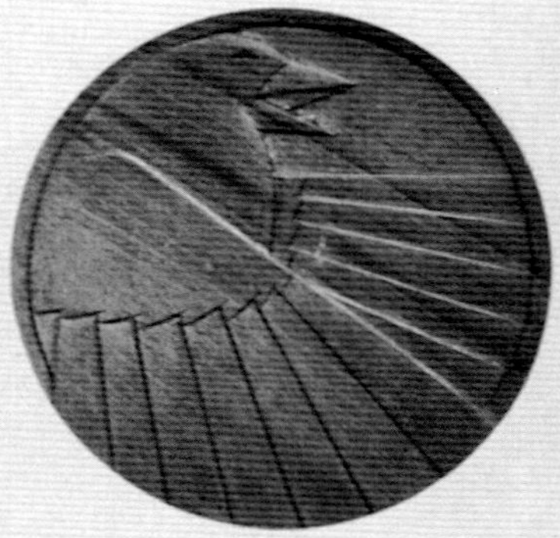

6

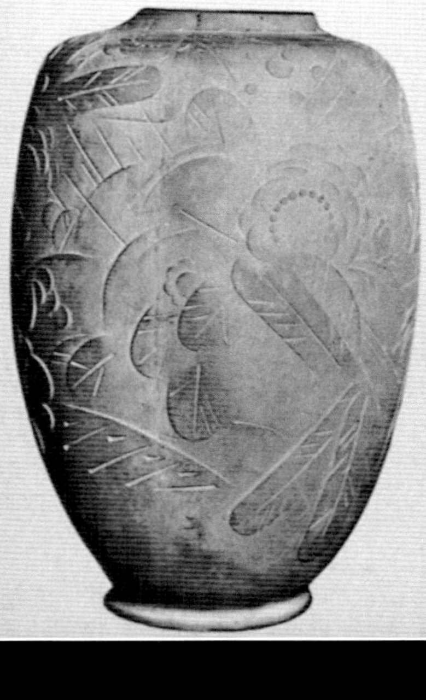

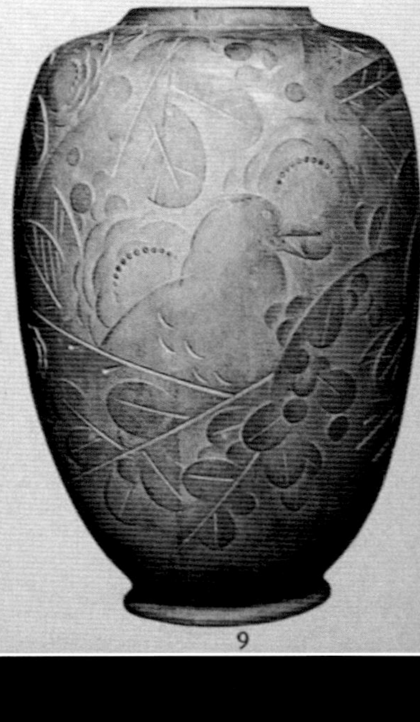

9

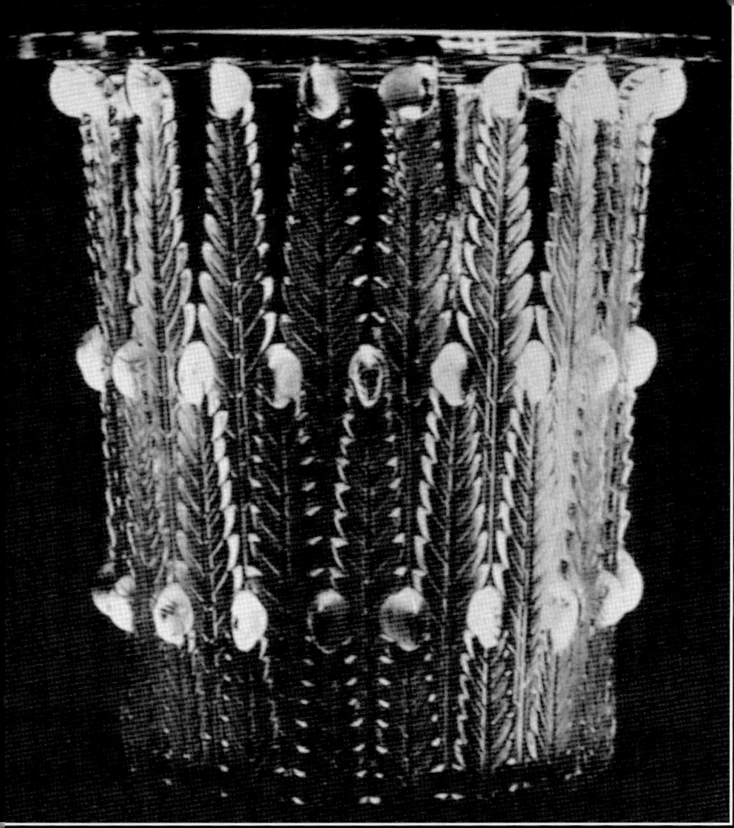

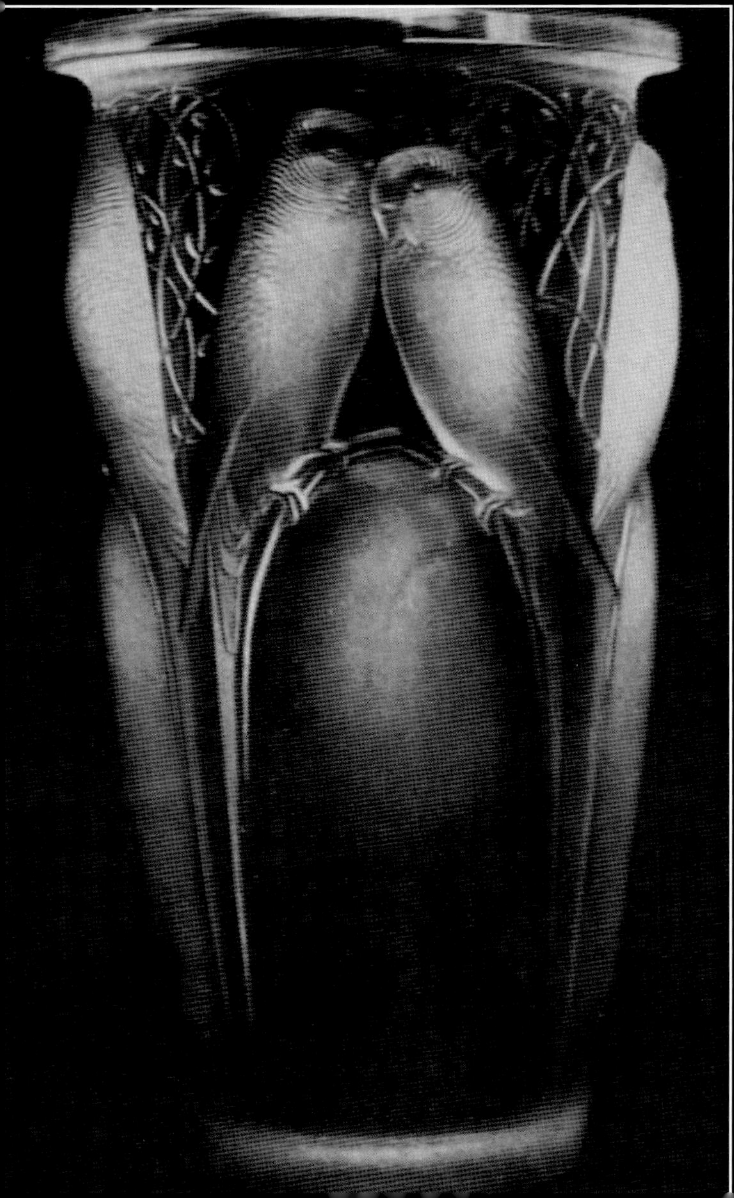

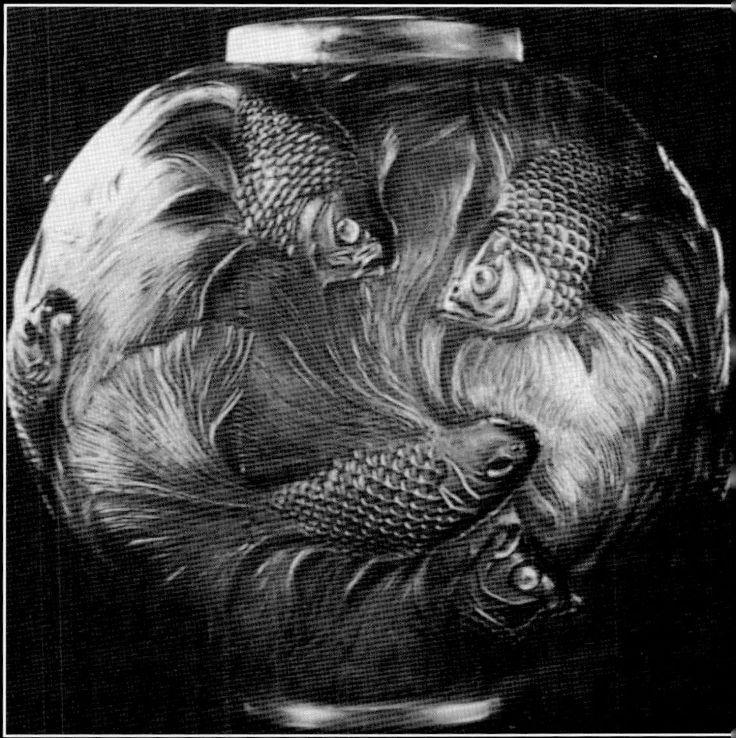

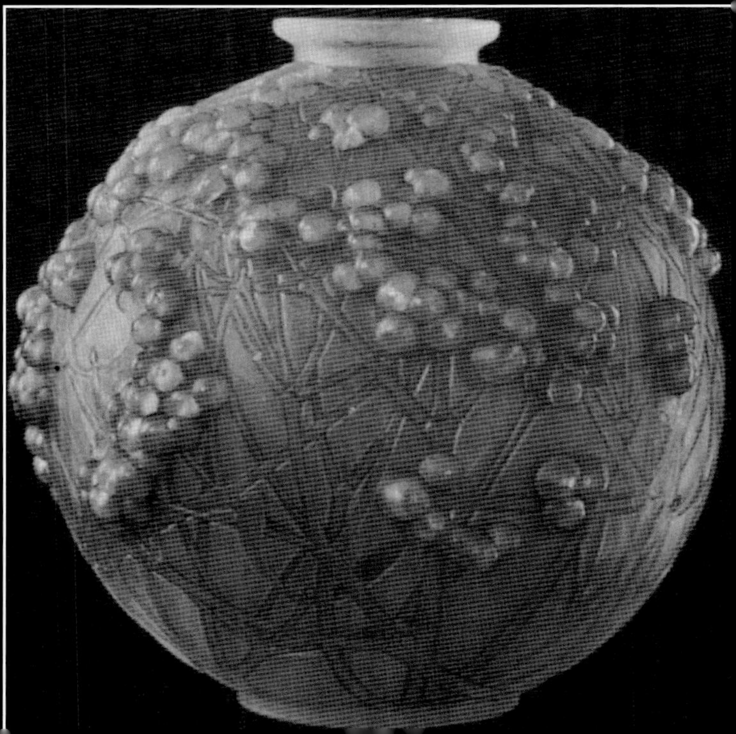

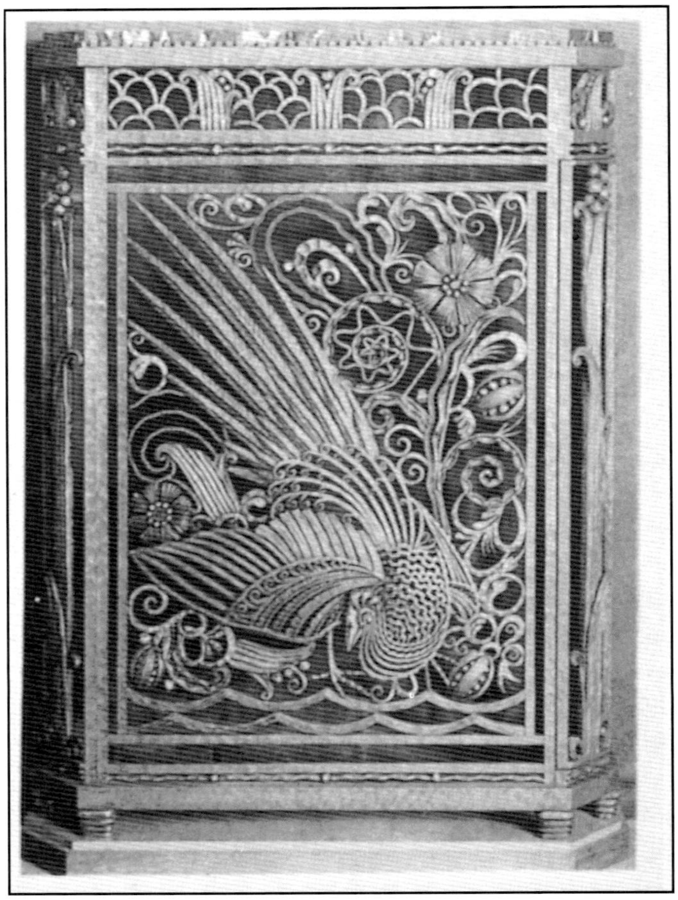

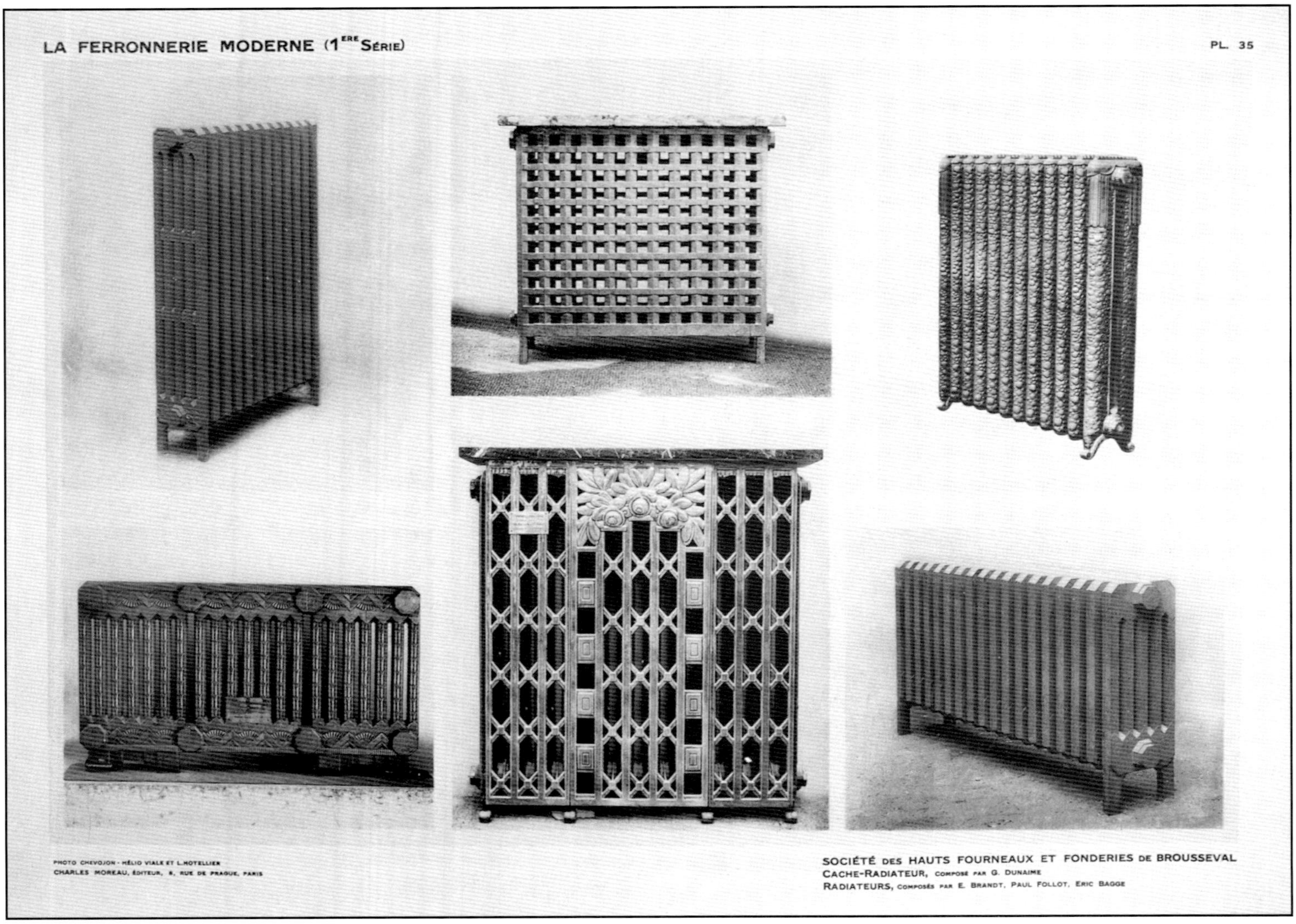
LA FERRONNERIE MODERNE (1ERE SÉRIE)
PL. 35
PHOTO CHEVOJON - HÉLIO VIALE ET L.HOTELLIER
CHARLES MOREAU, ÉDITEUR, 8, RUE DE PRAGUE, PARIS
SOCIÉTÉ DES HAUTS FOURNEAUX ET FONDERIES DE BROUSSEVAL
CACHE-RADIATEUR, COMPOSÉ PAR G. DUNAIME
RADIATEURS, COMPOSÉS PAR E. BRANDT, PAUL FOLLOT, ERIC BAGGE

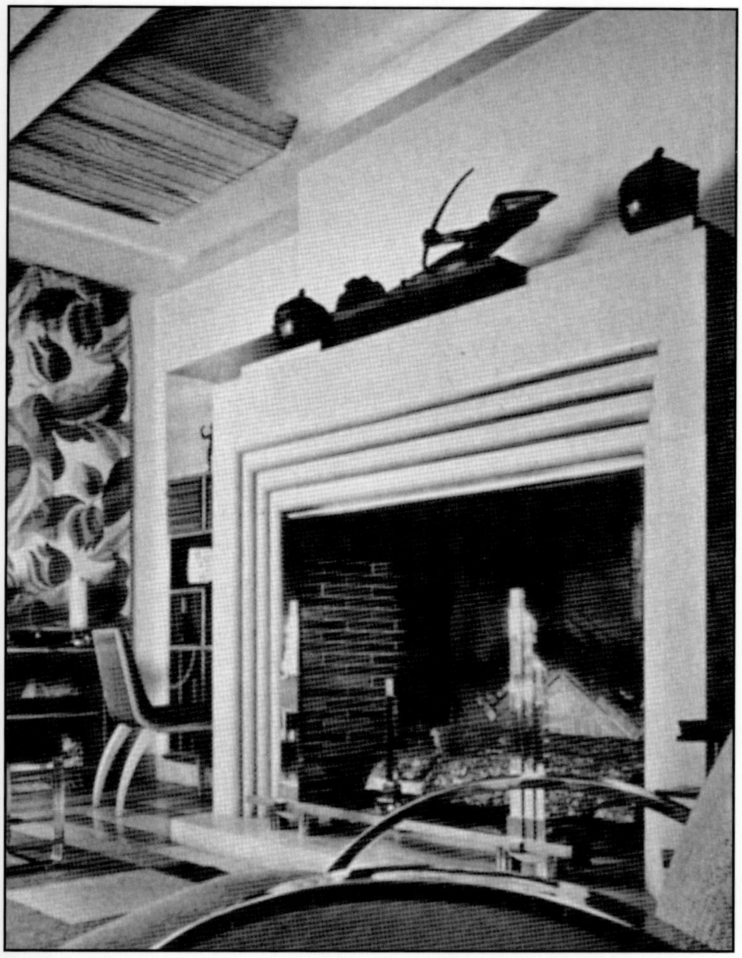

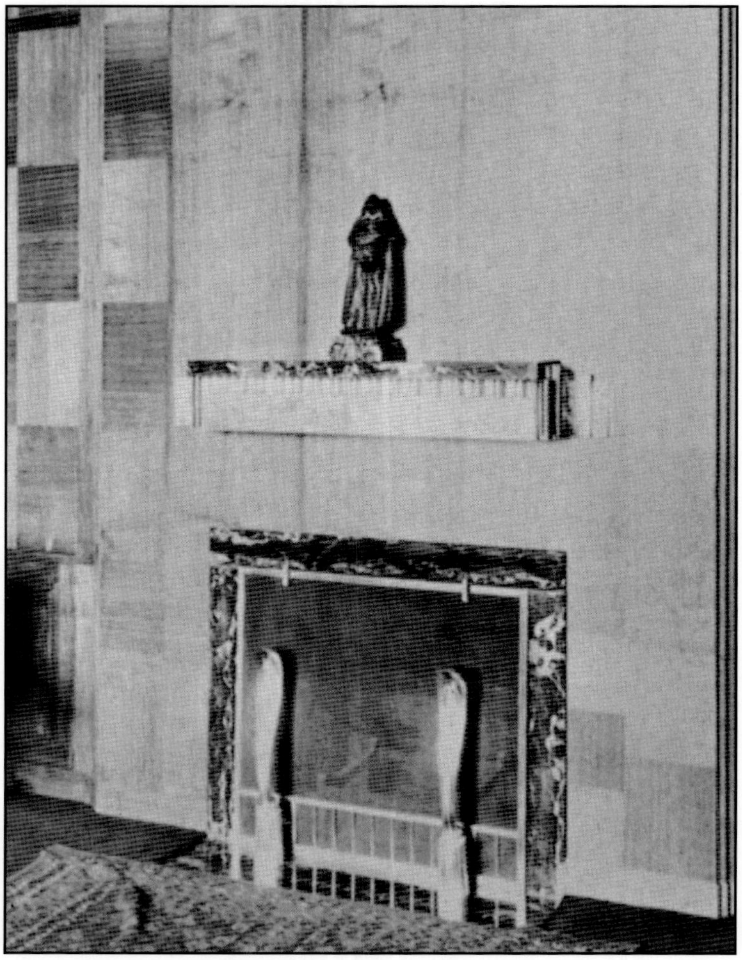

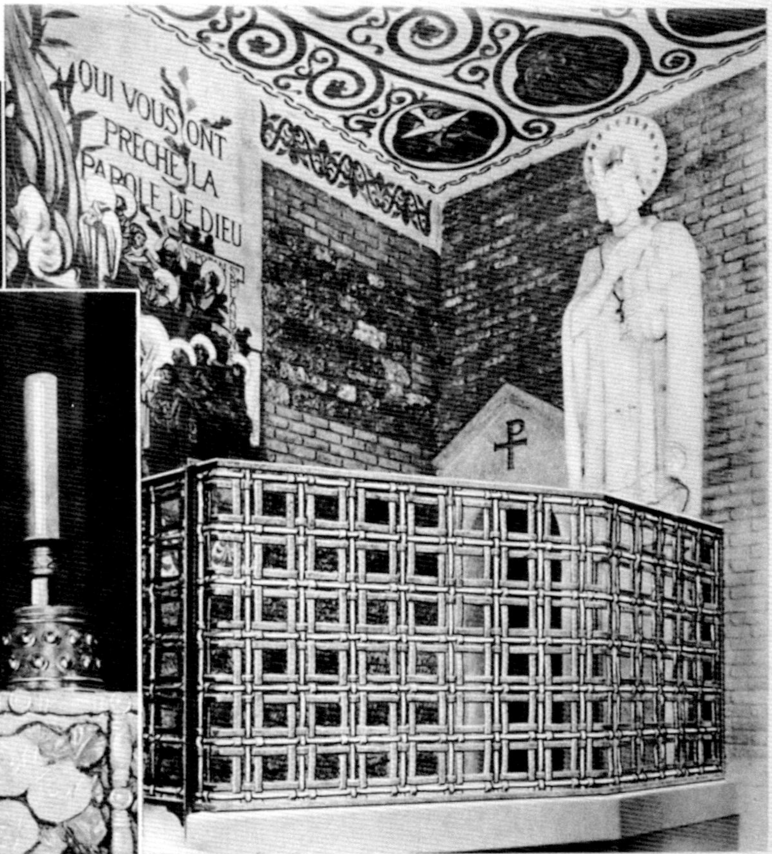

M. MARRAST, ARCH.

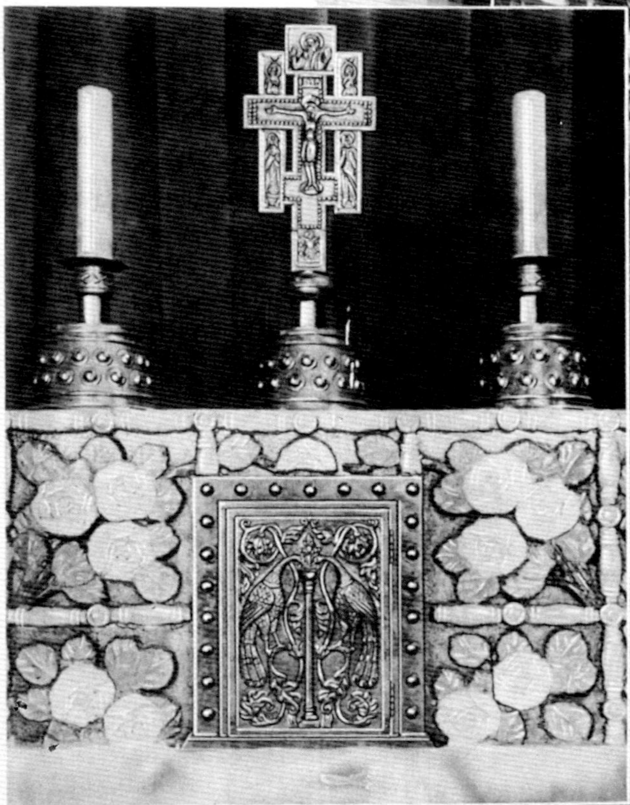

M. MARRAST, ARCH.

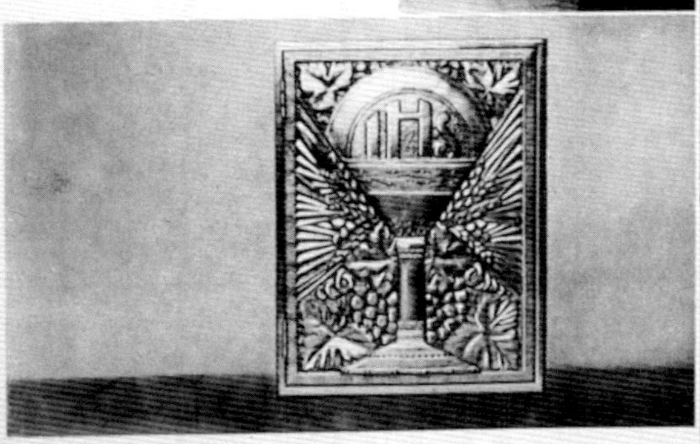

M. BRUNET, ARCH.

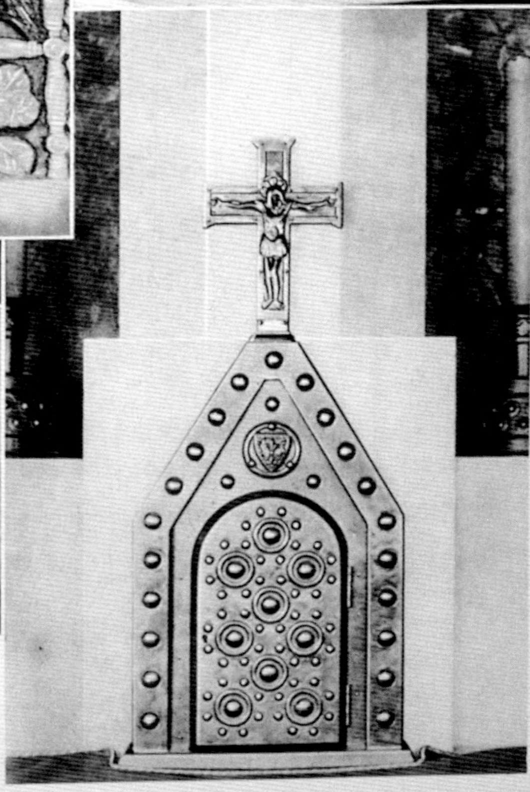

M. MARRAST, ARCH.

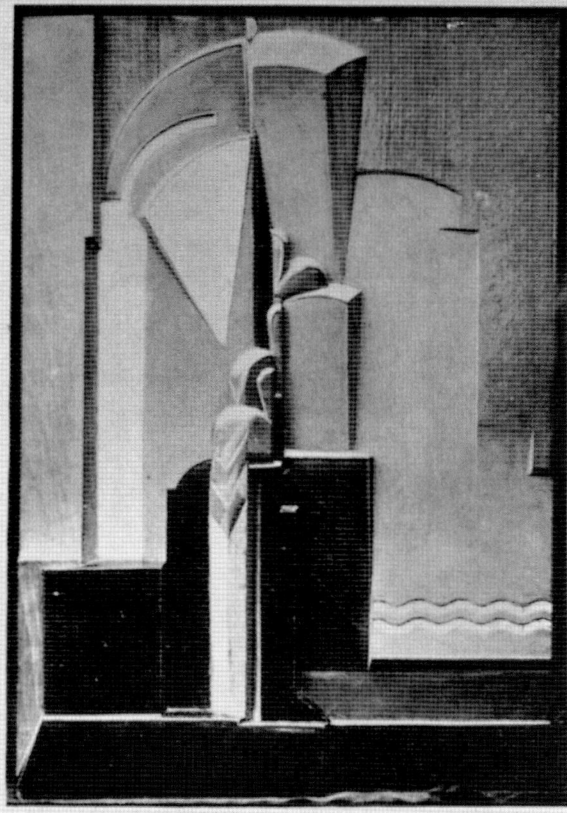

1

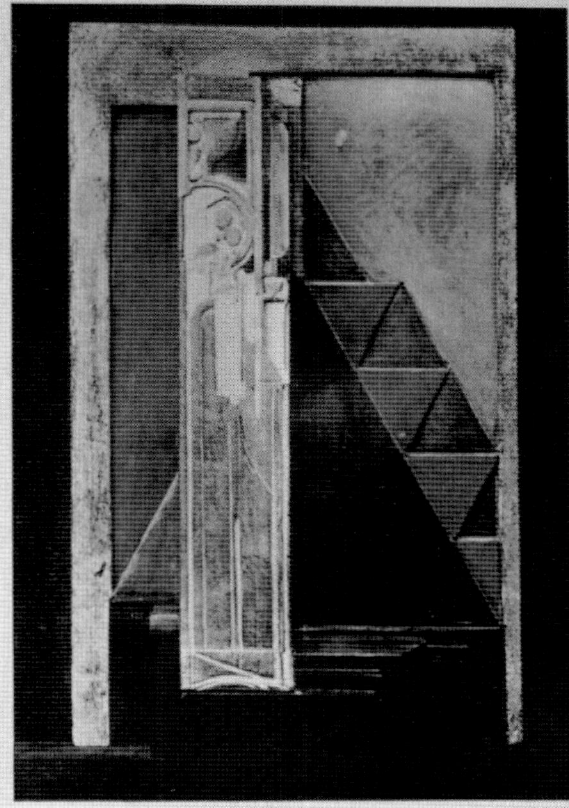

2

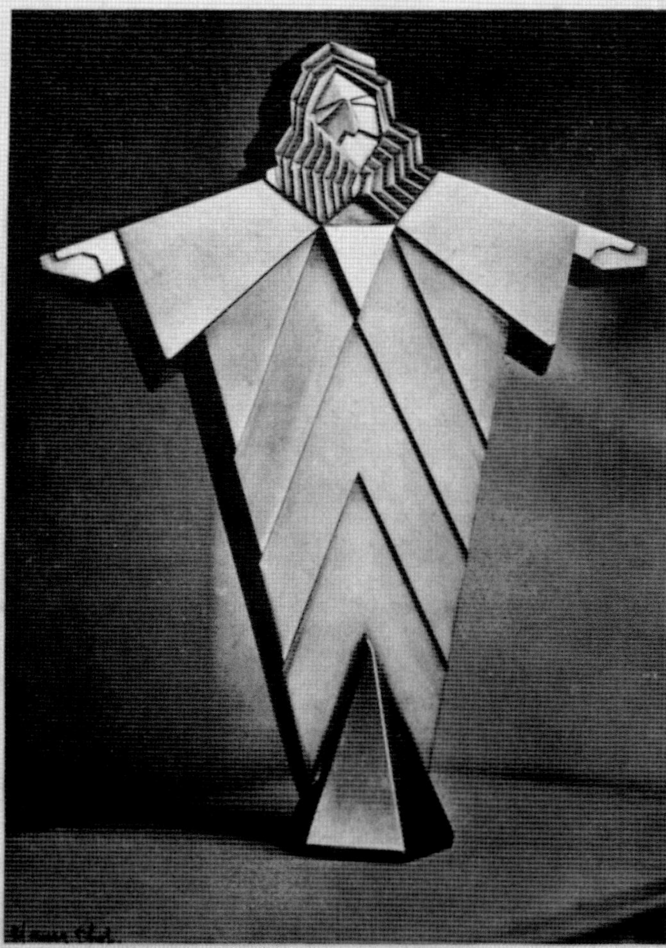

3

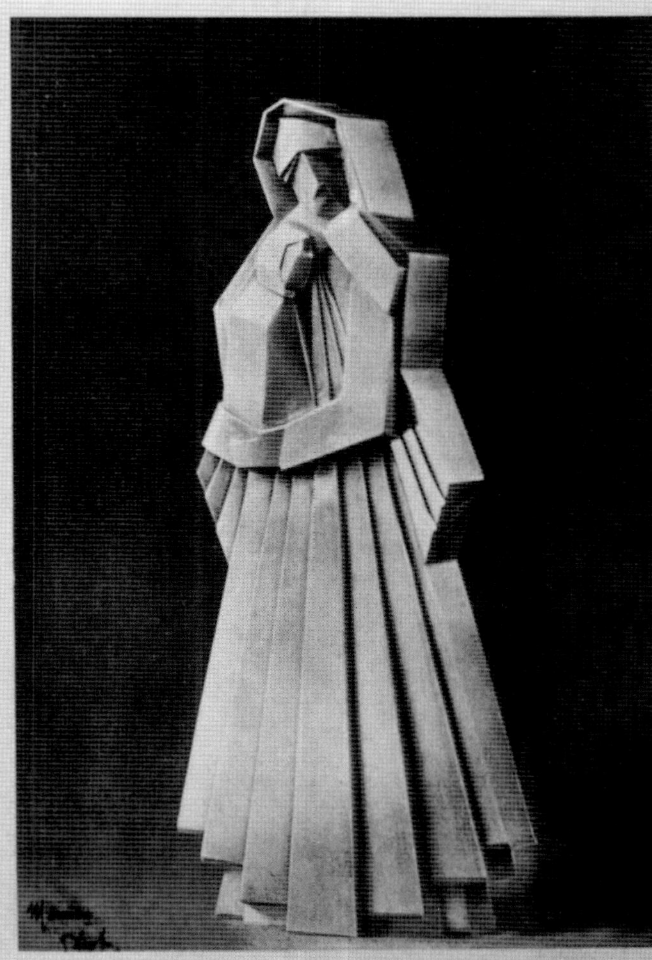

4

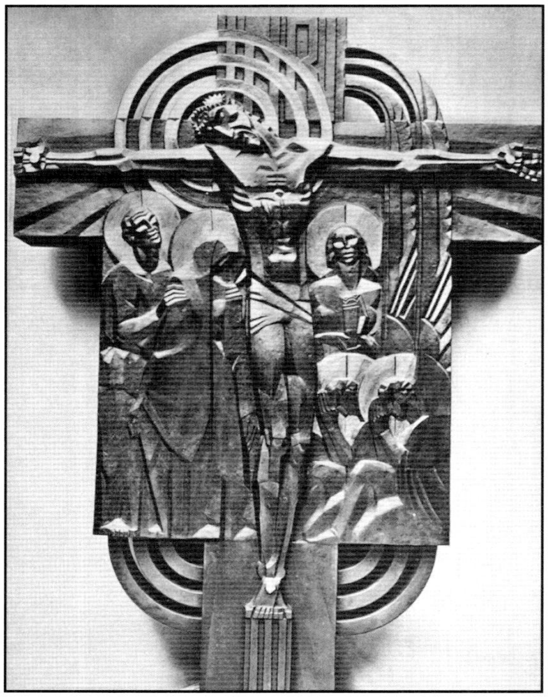

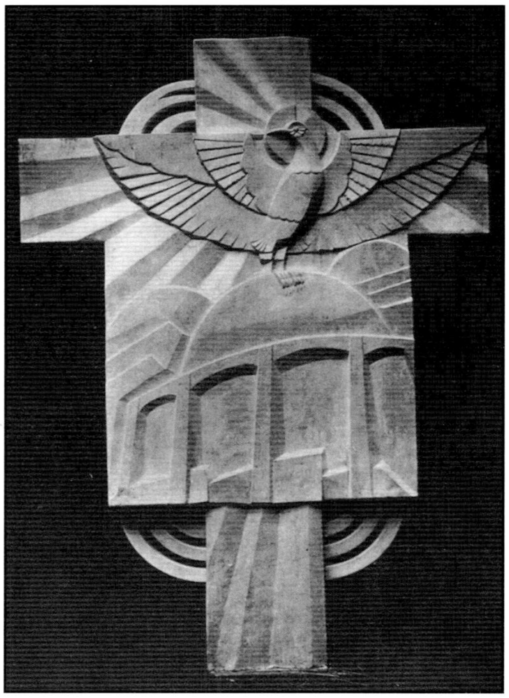

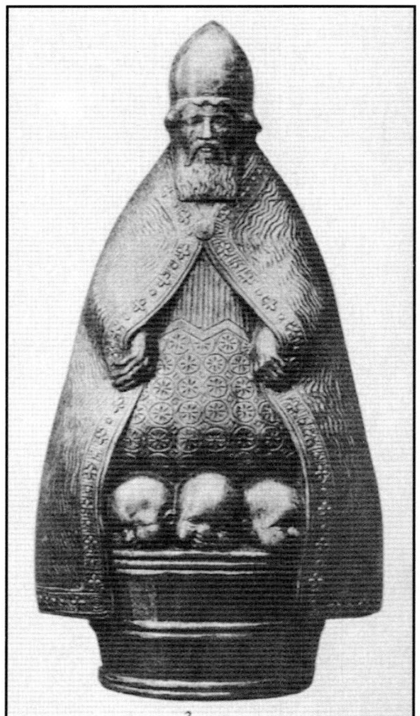

3

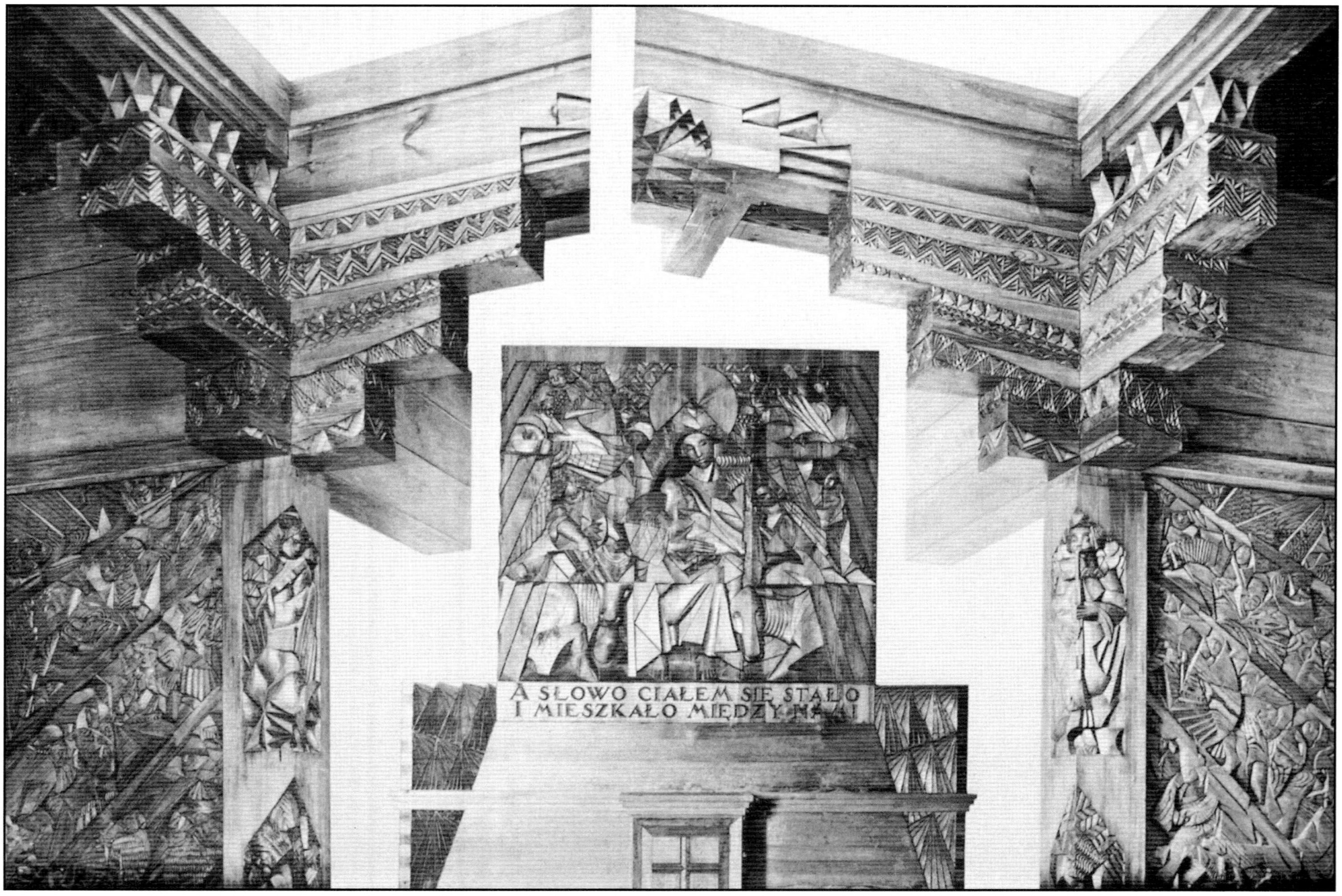

Stonework & Woodwork Relief on Interior Walls and Columns

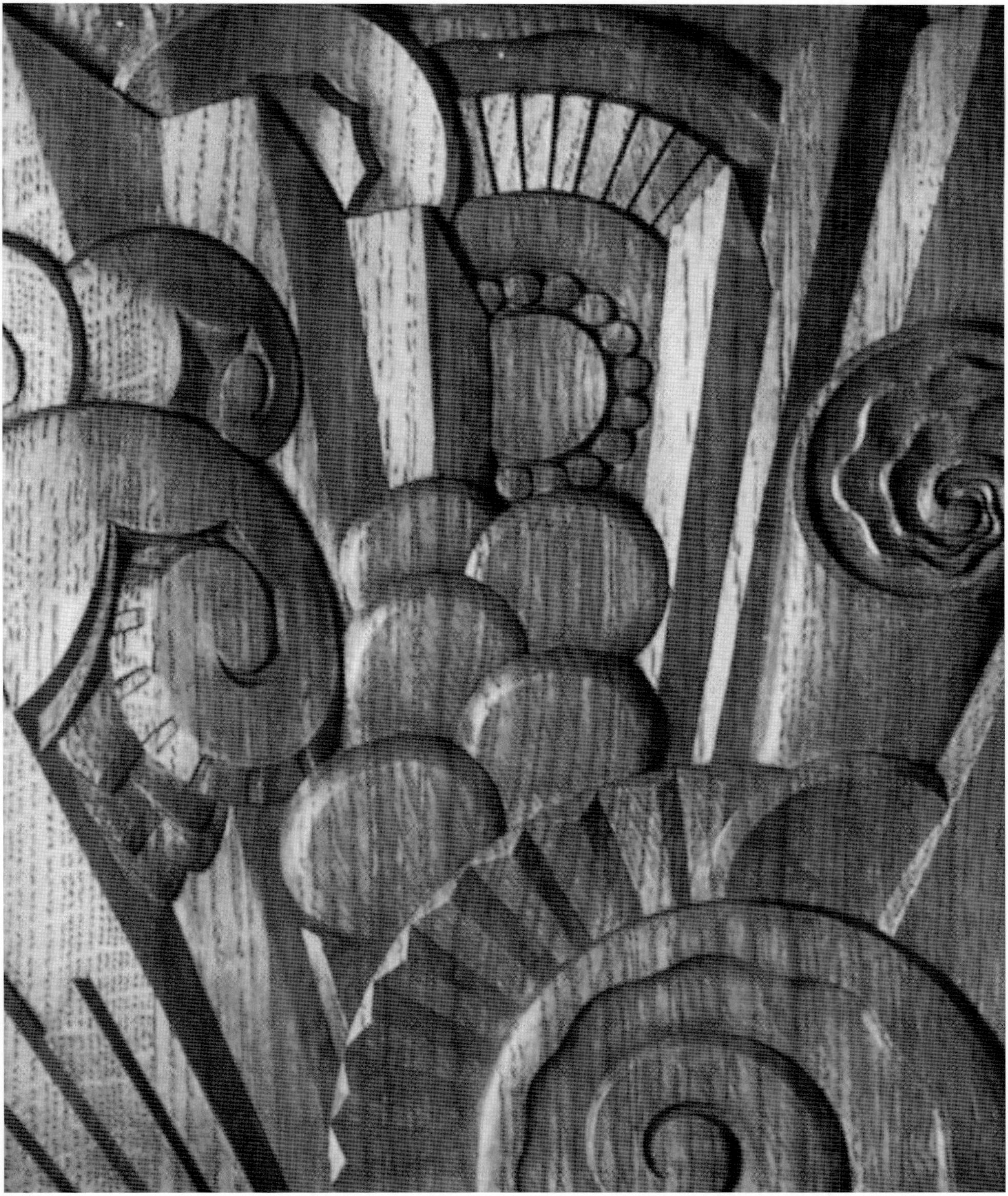

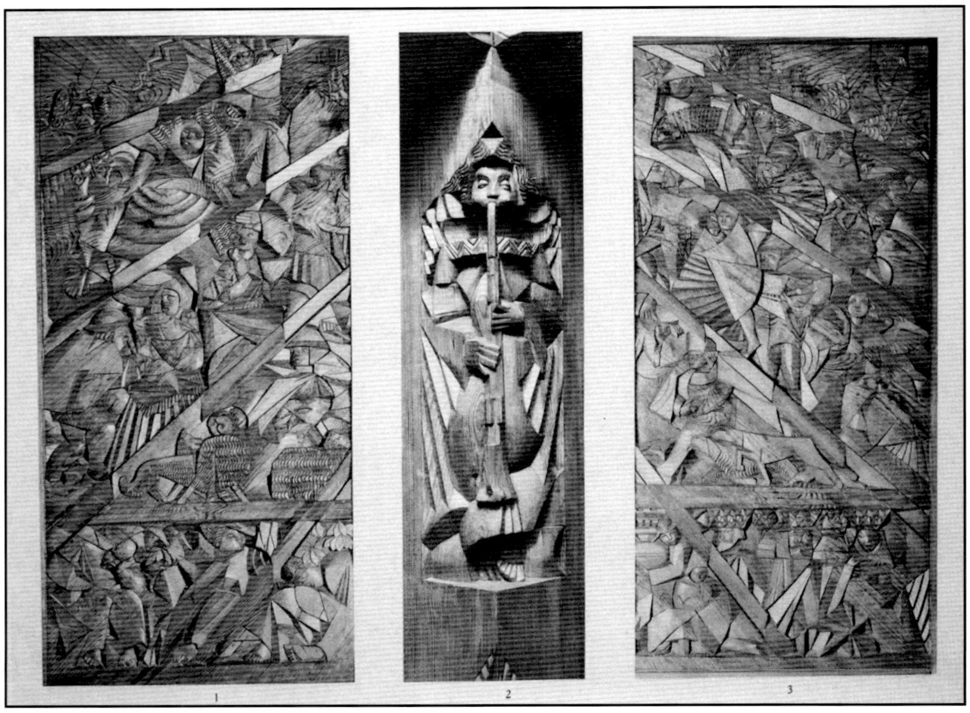
1
2
3

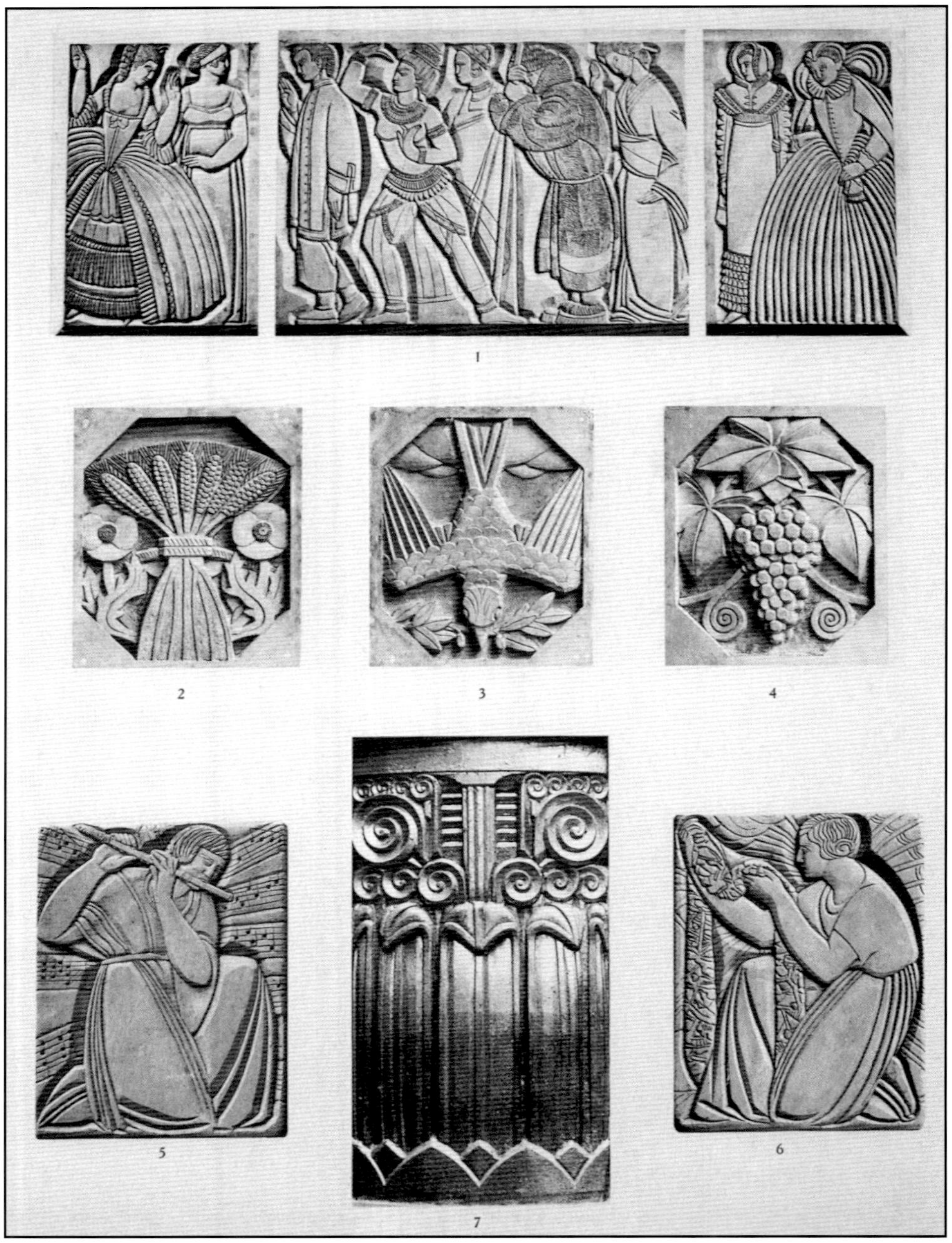
1
2
3
4
5
6
7

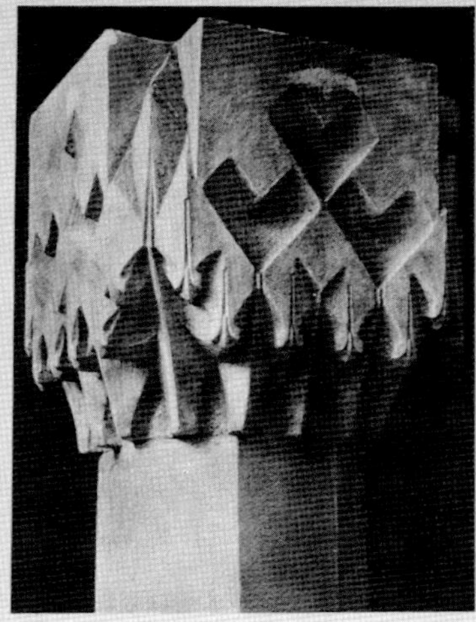
1

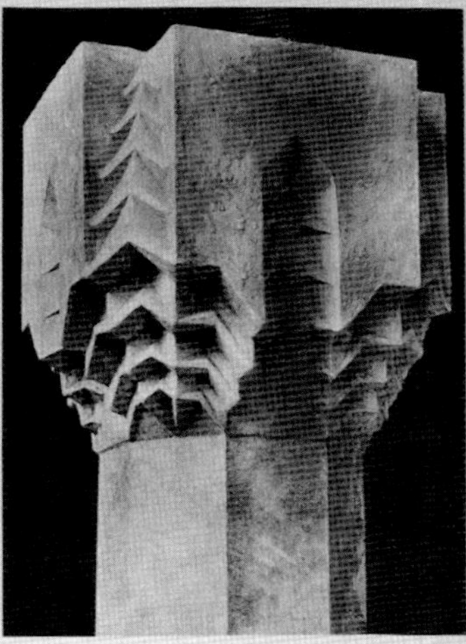
2

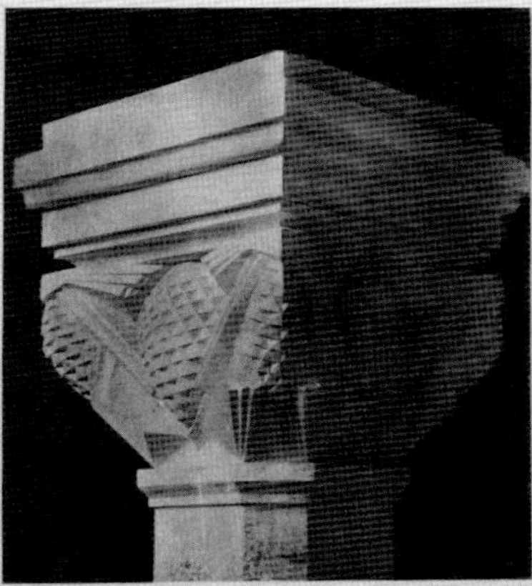
3

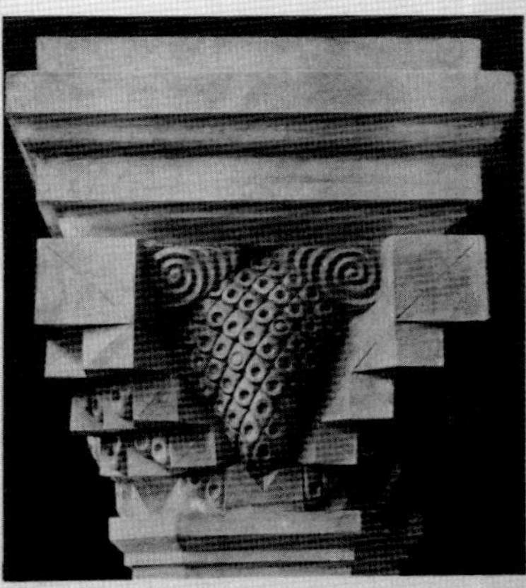
4

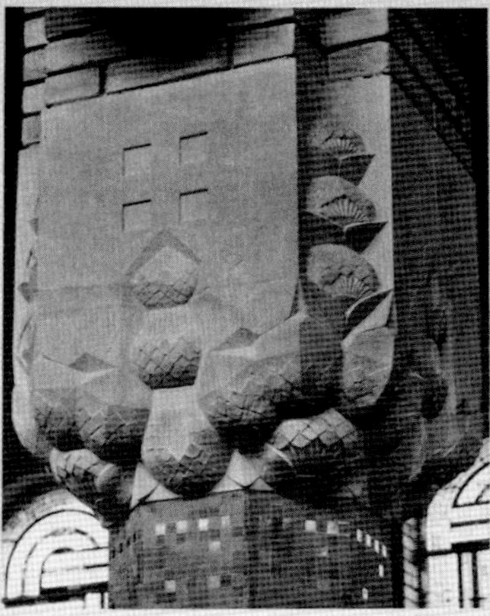
1

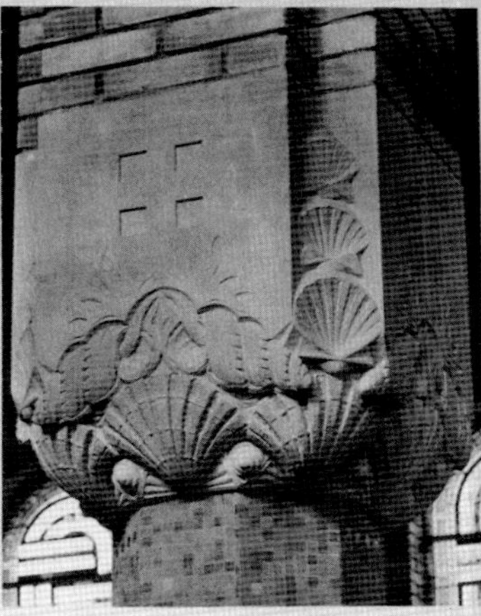
2

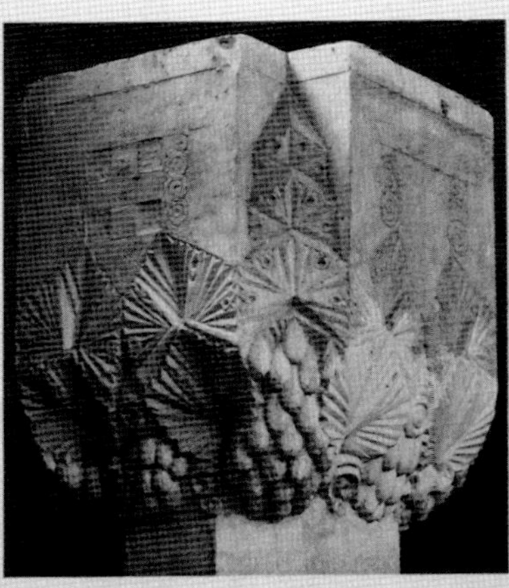
3

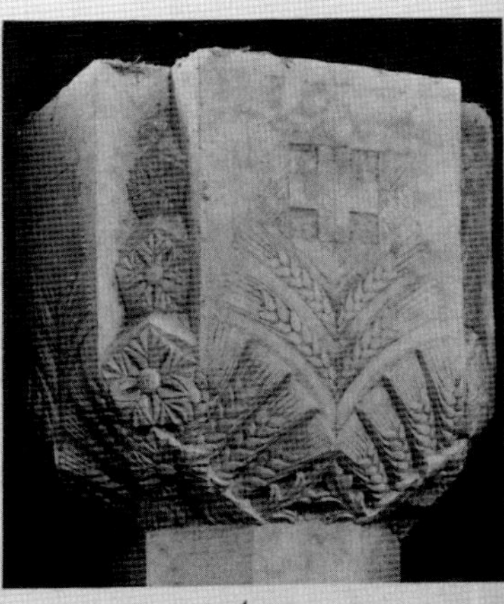
4

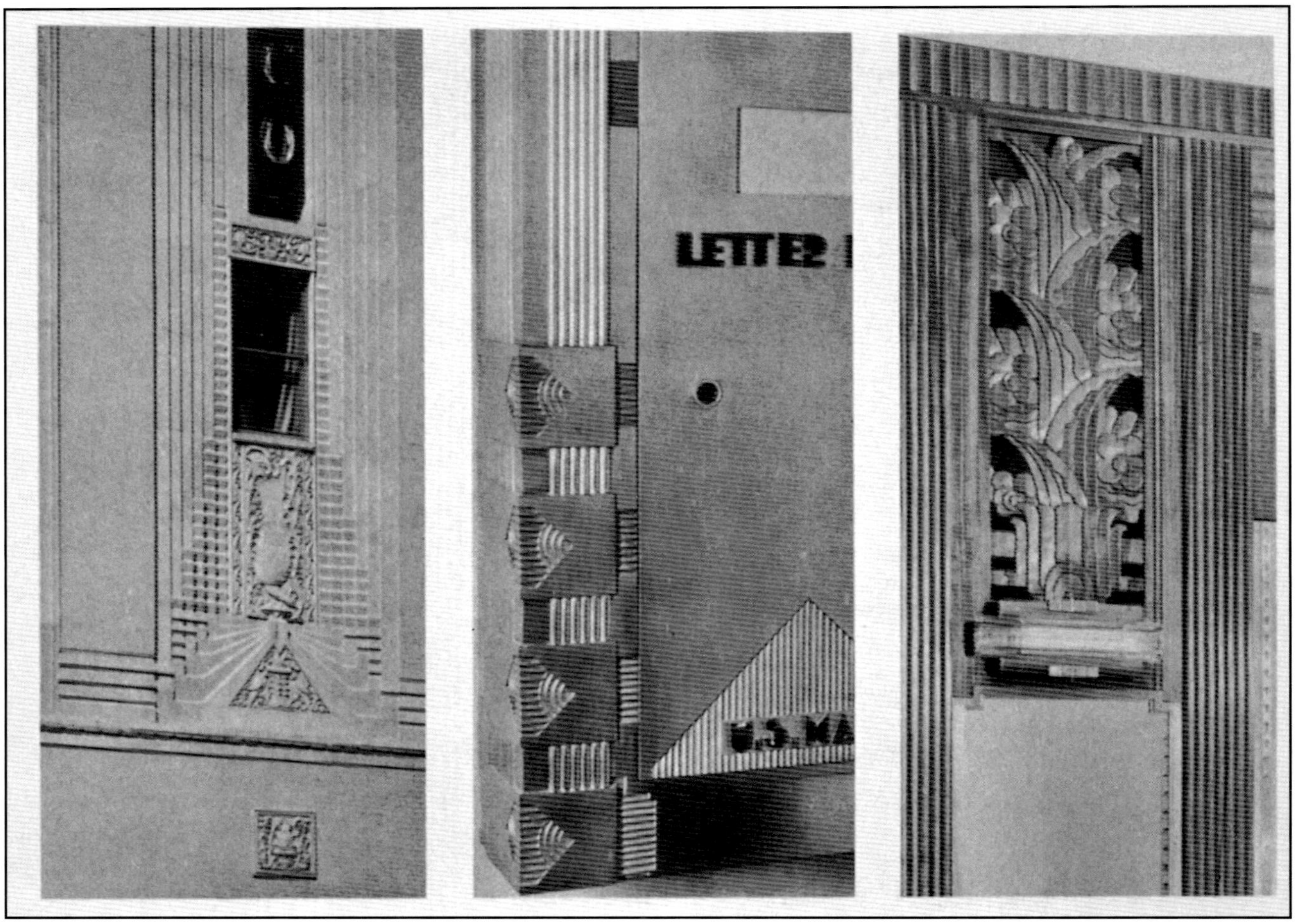

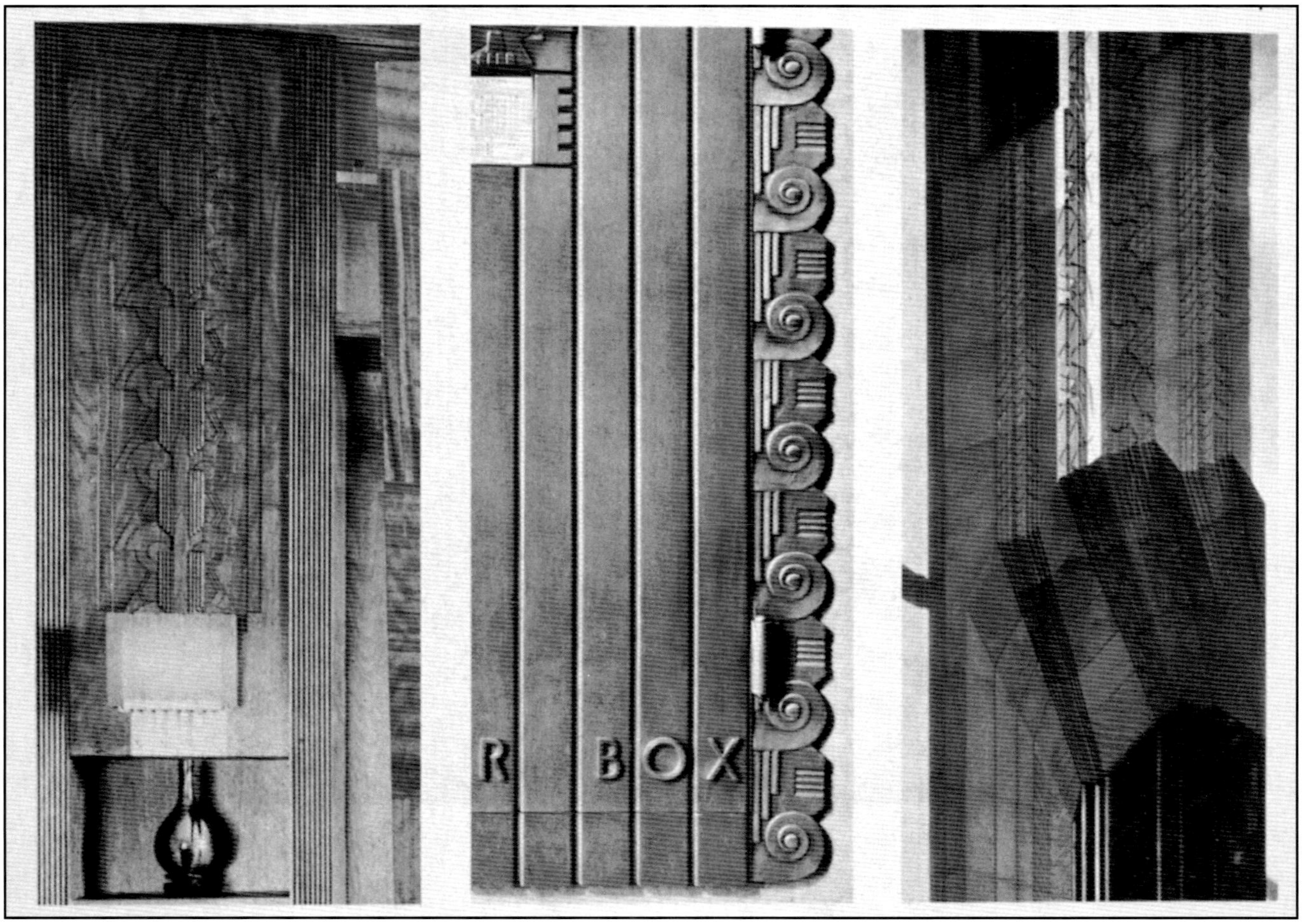
R BOX

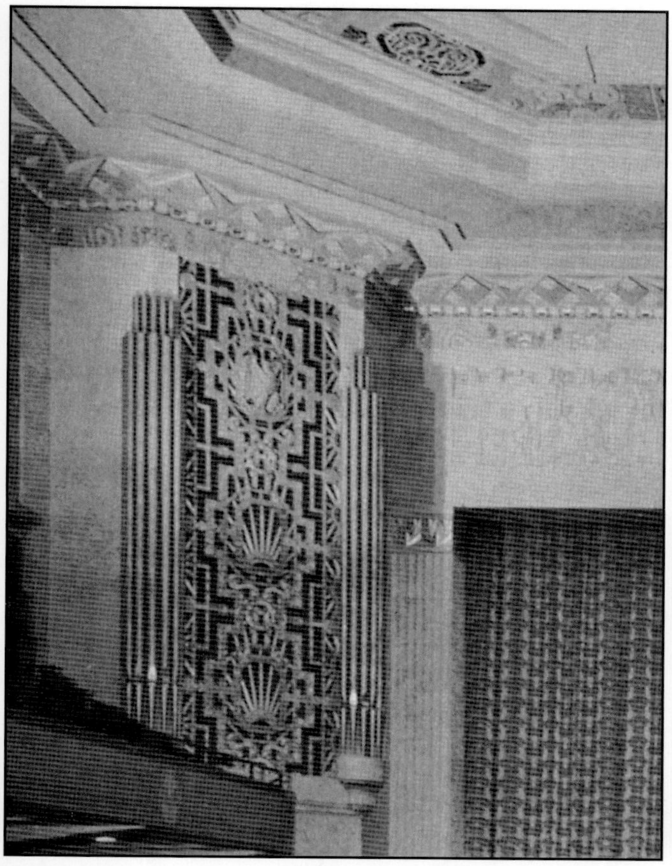

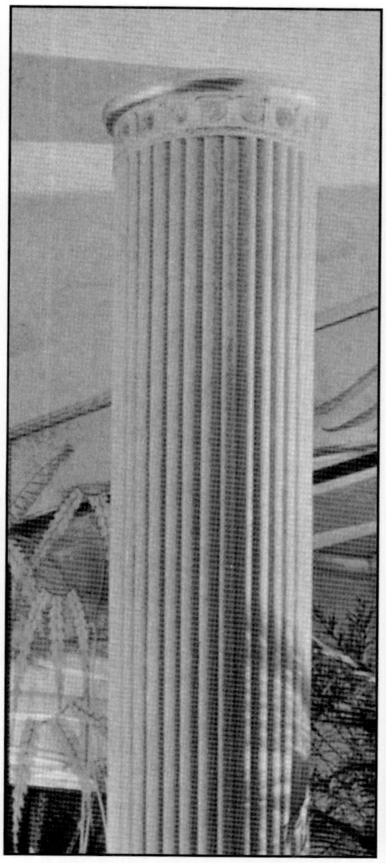

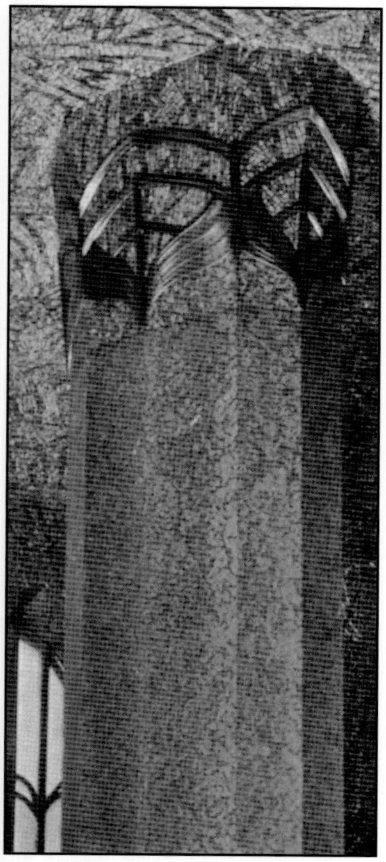

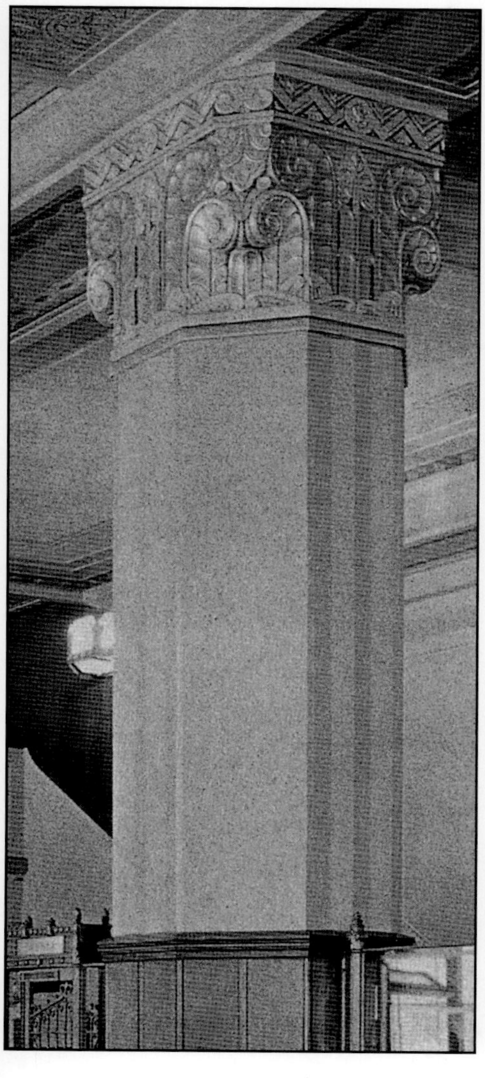

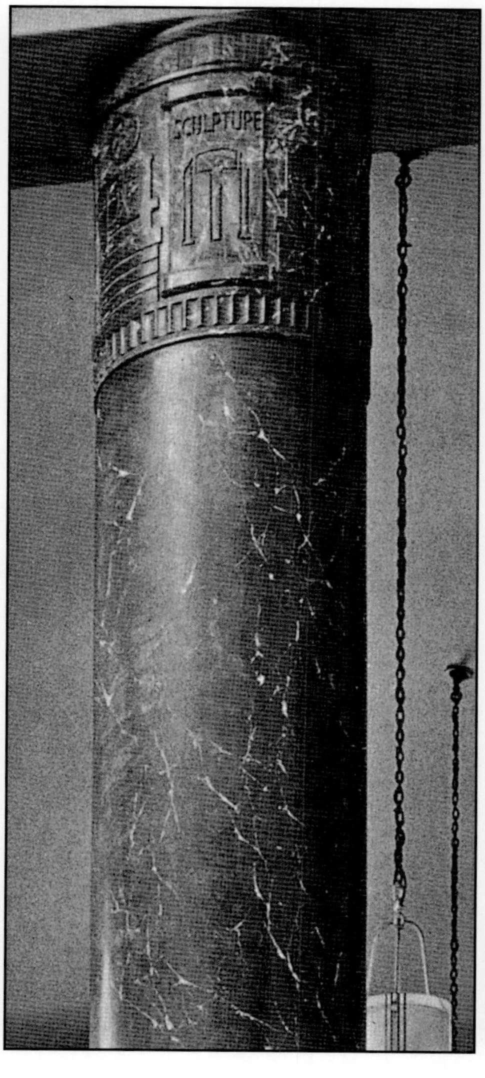
SCULPTURE

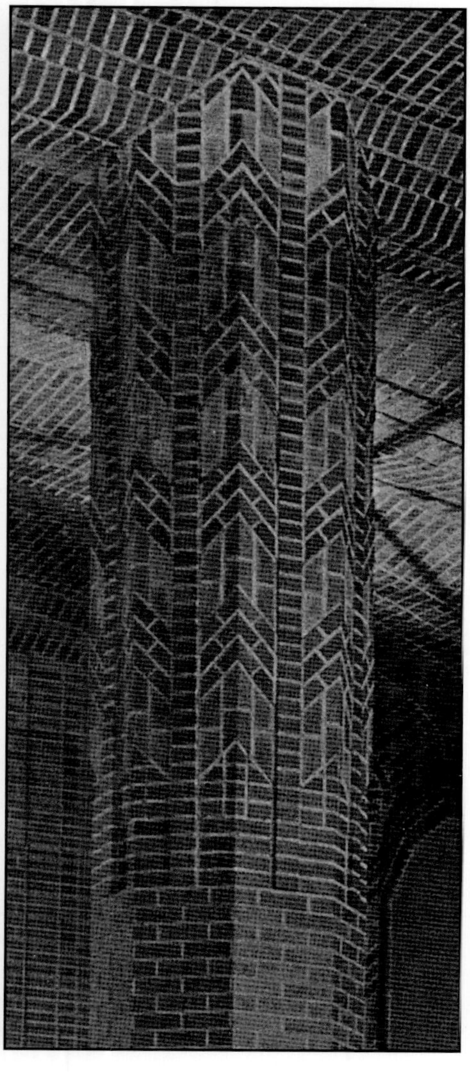

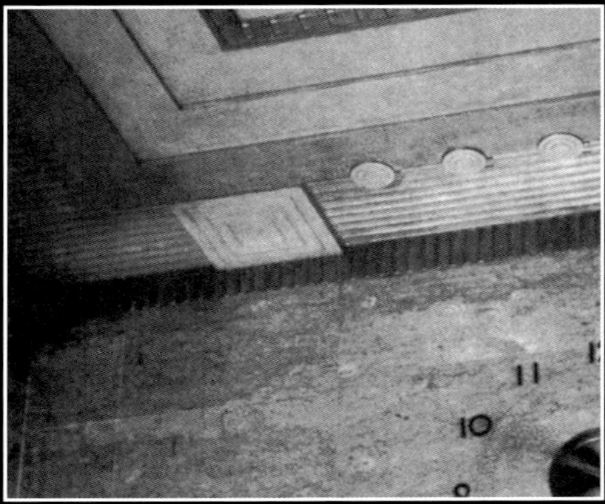
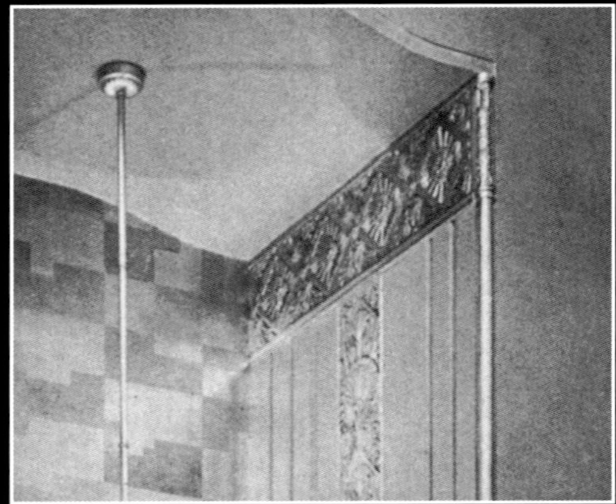
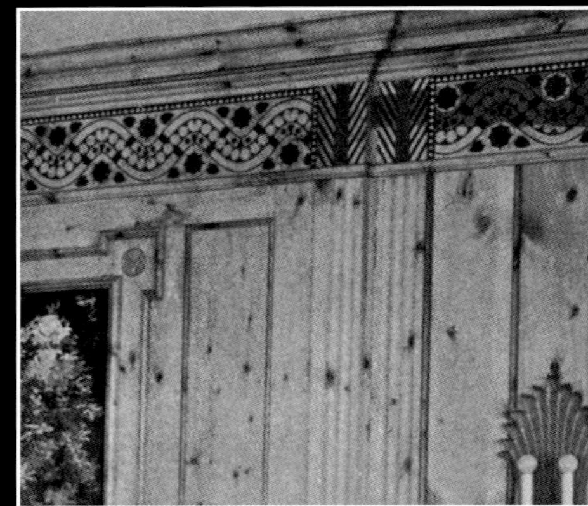
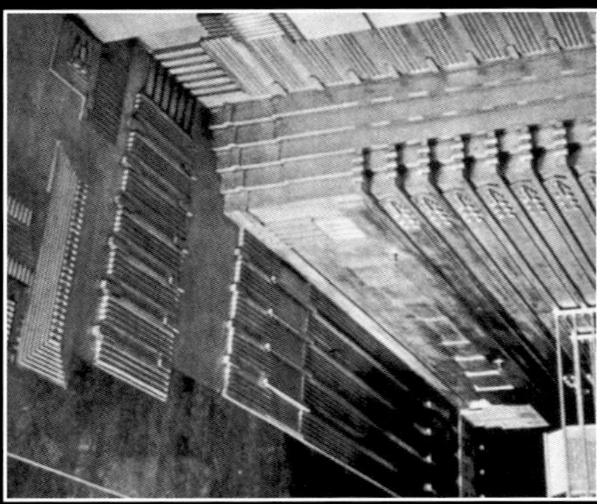
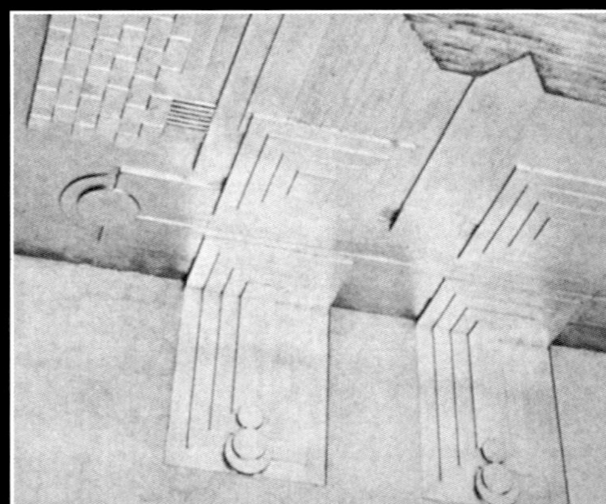
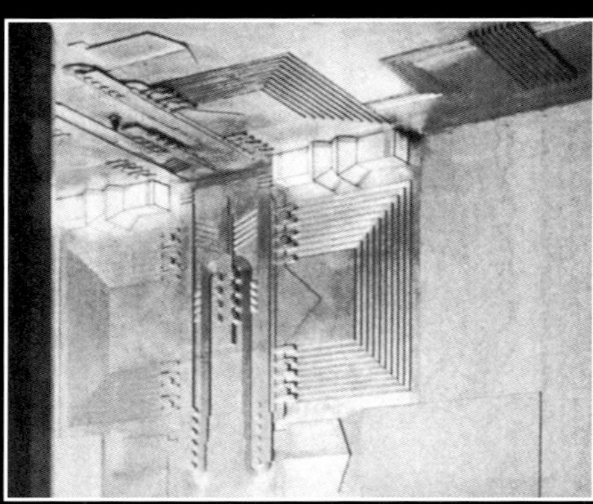
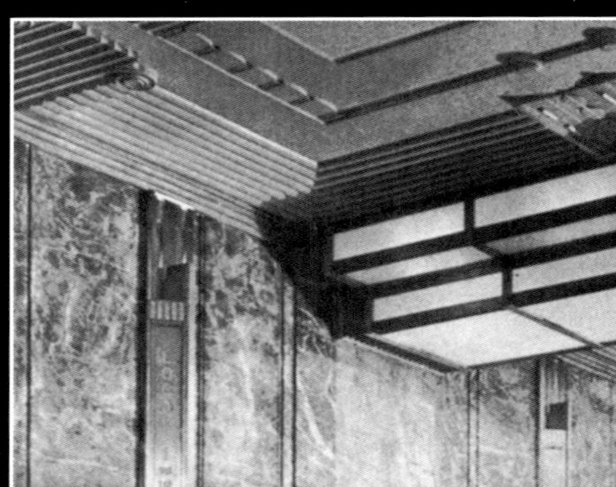
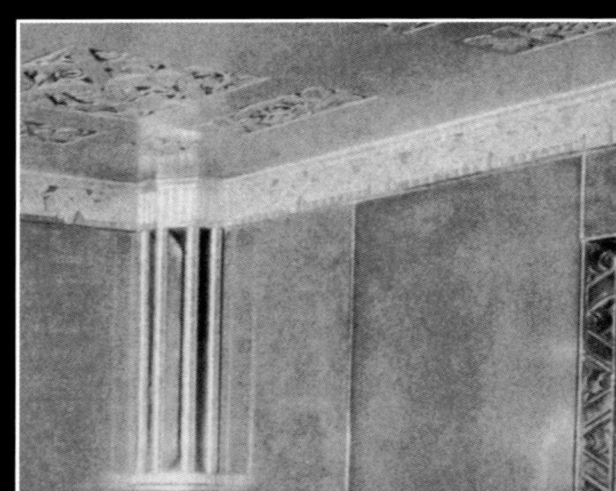
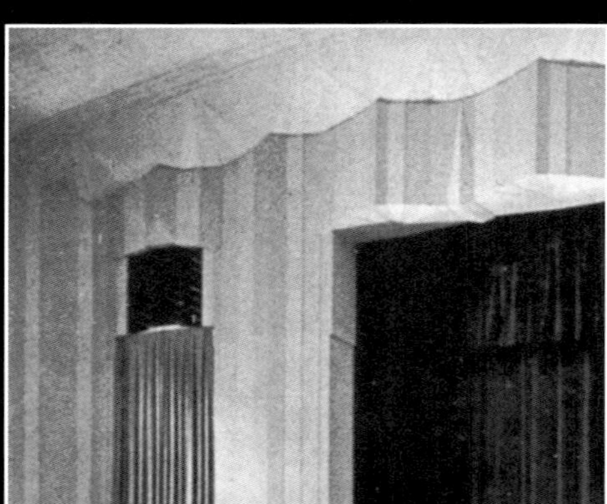
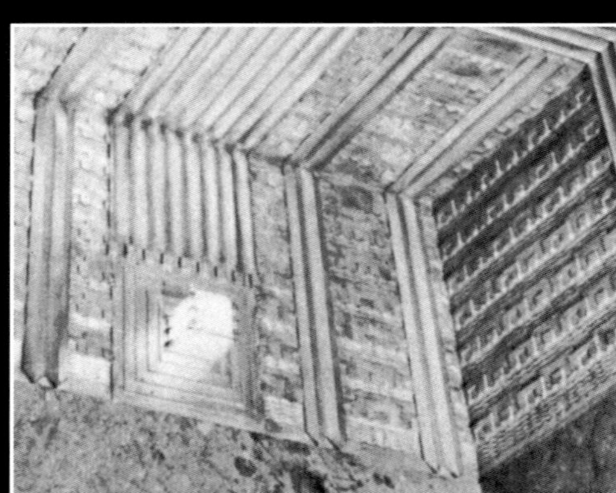
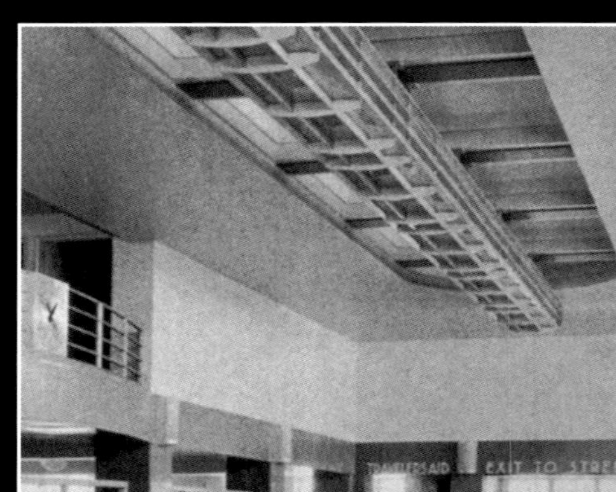

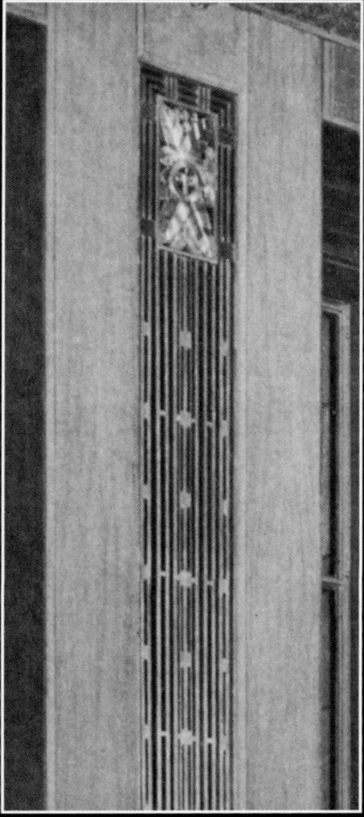
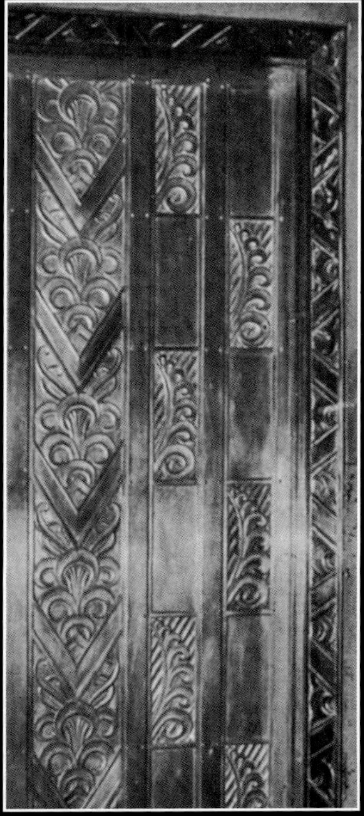
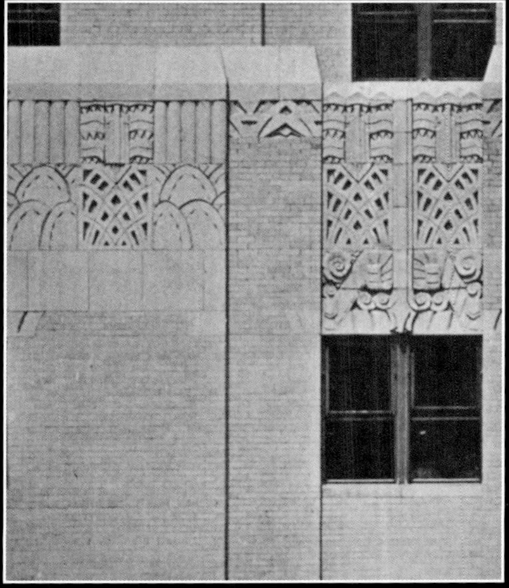
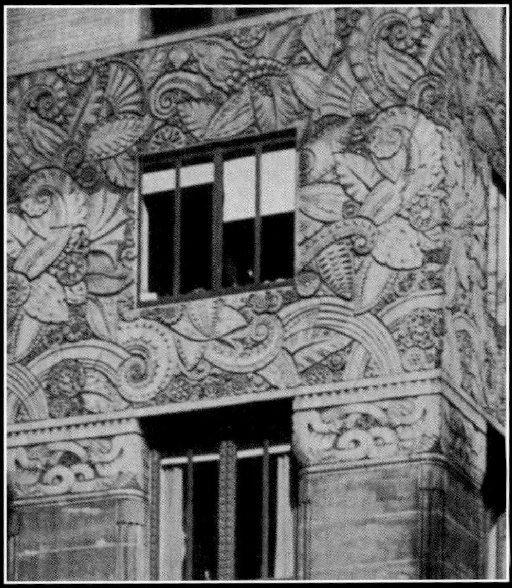
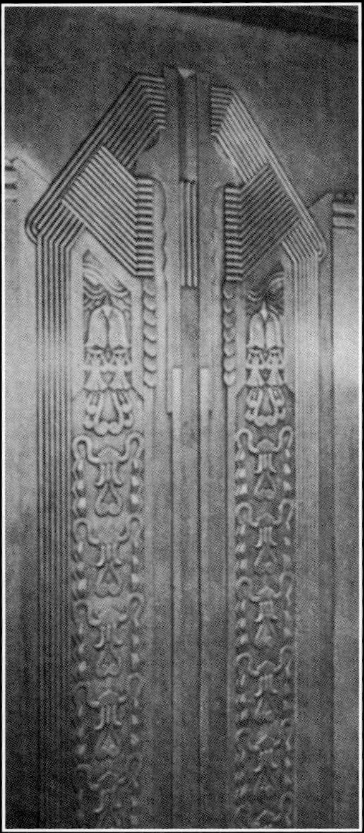
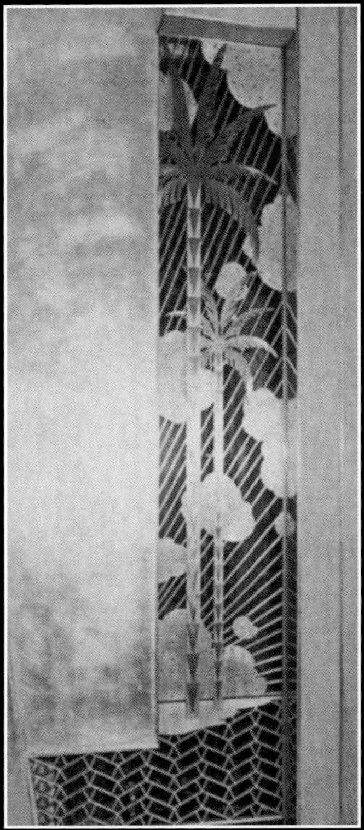
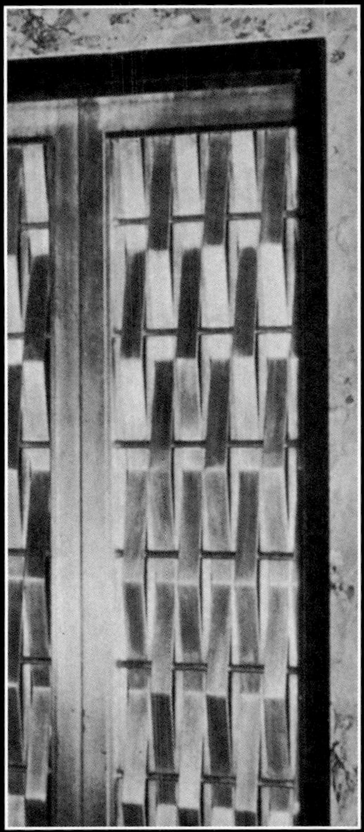

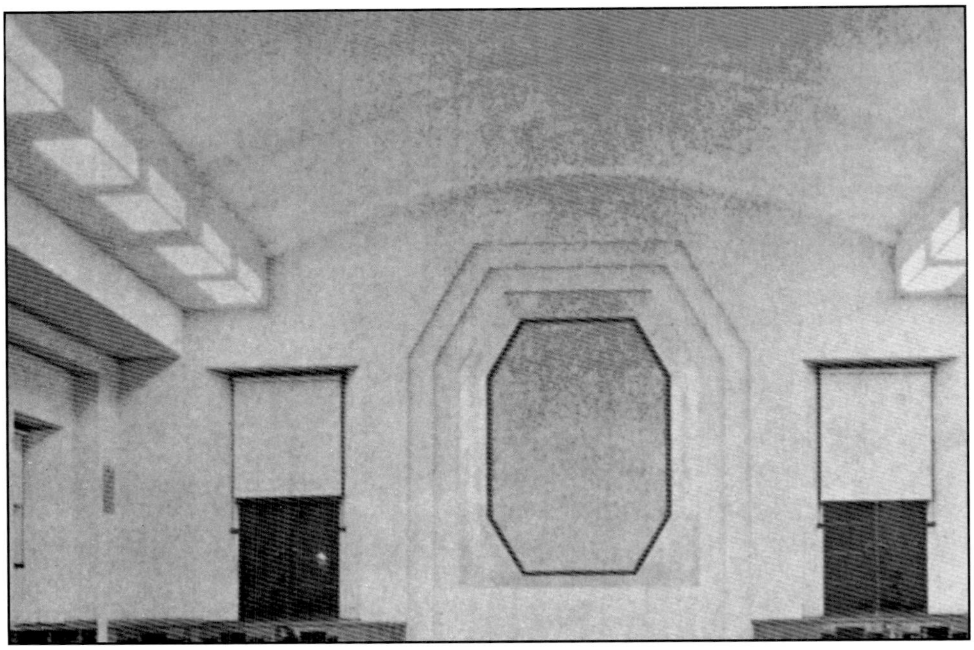

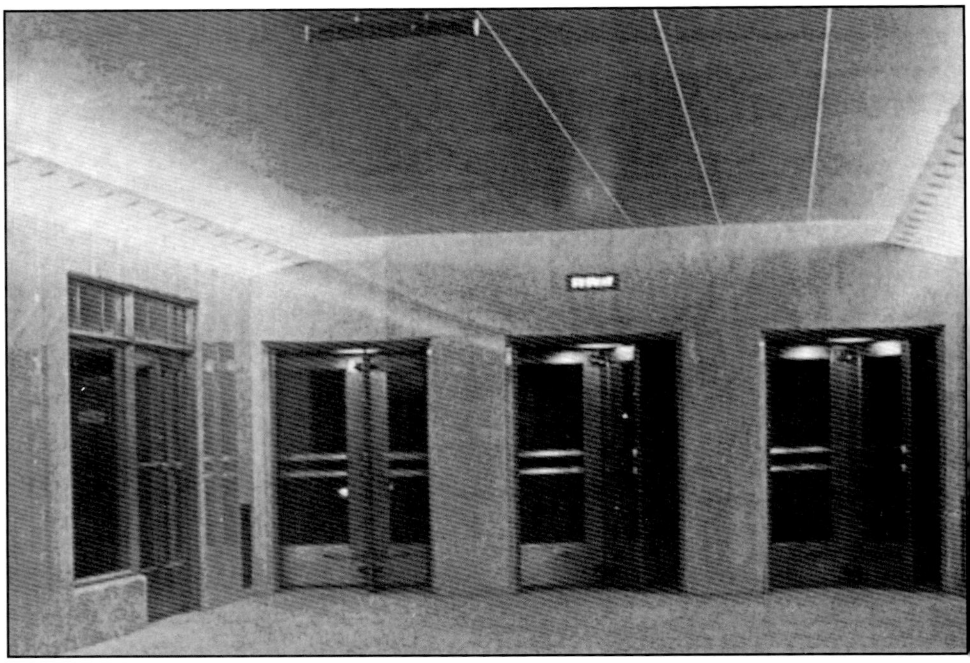

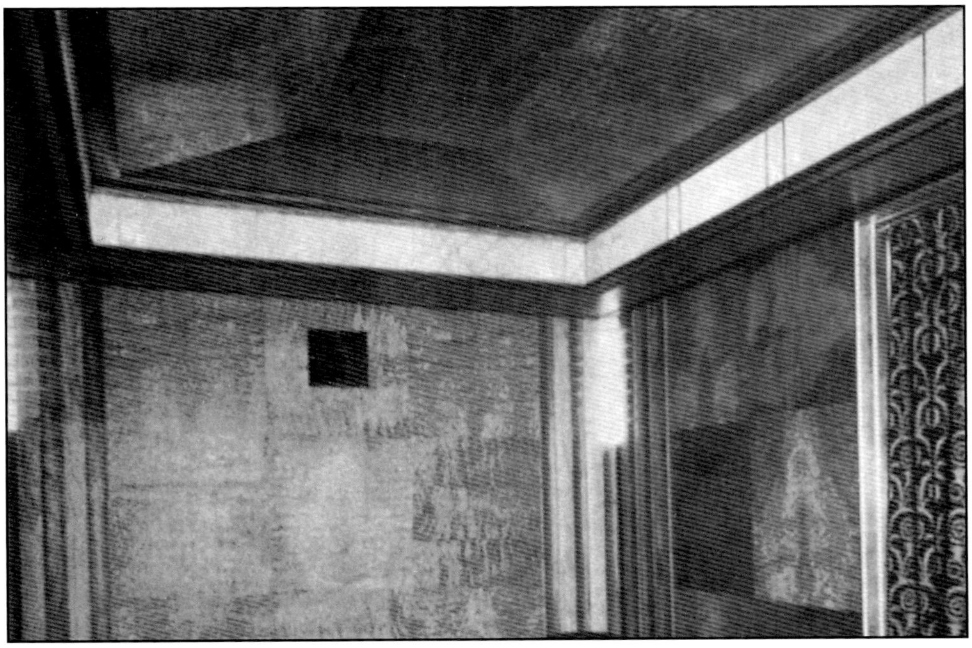

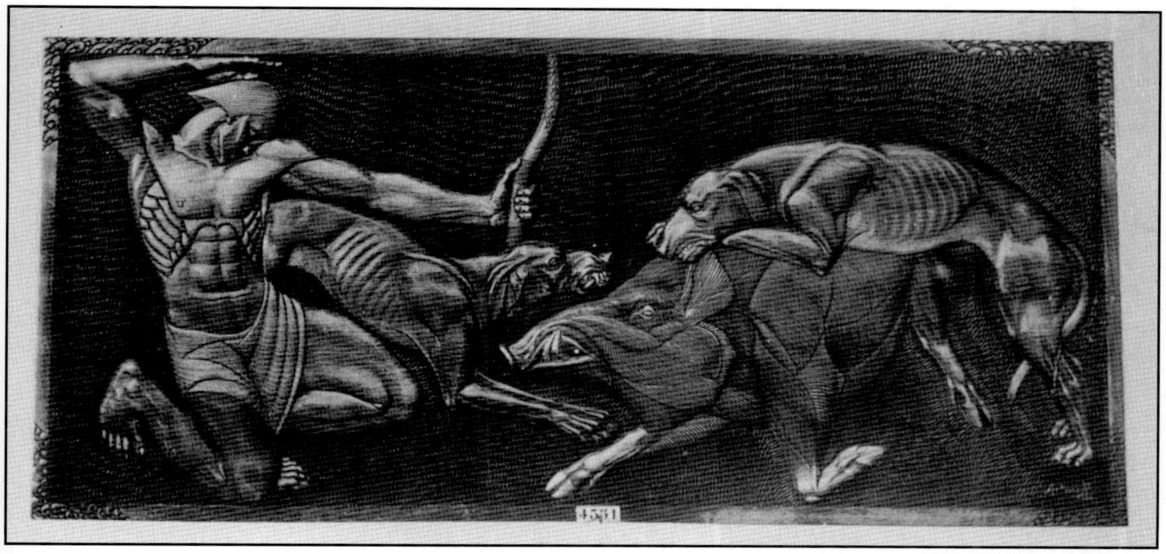
4531

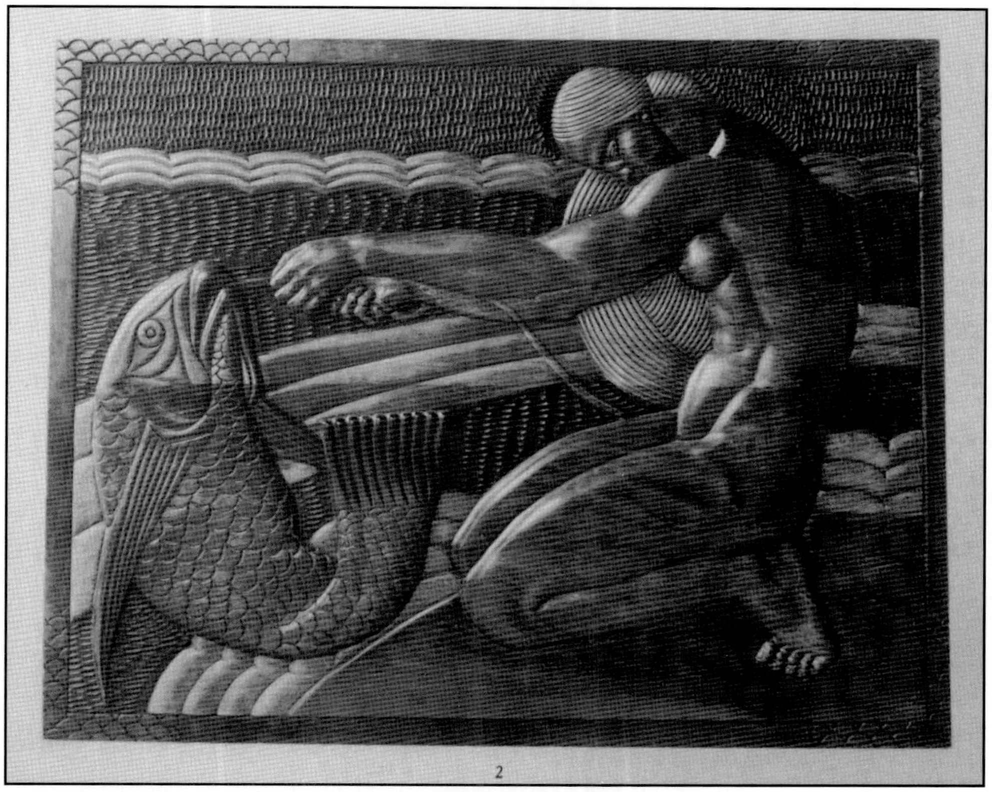
2

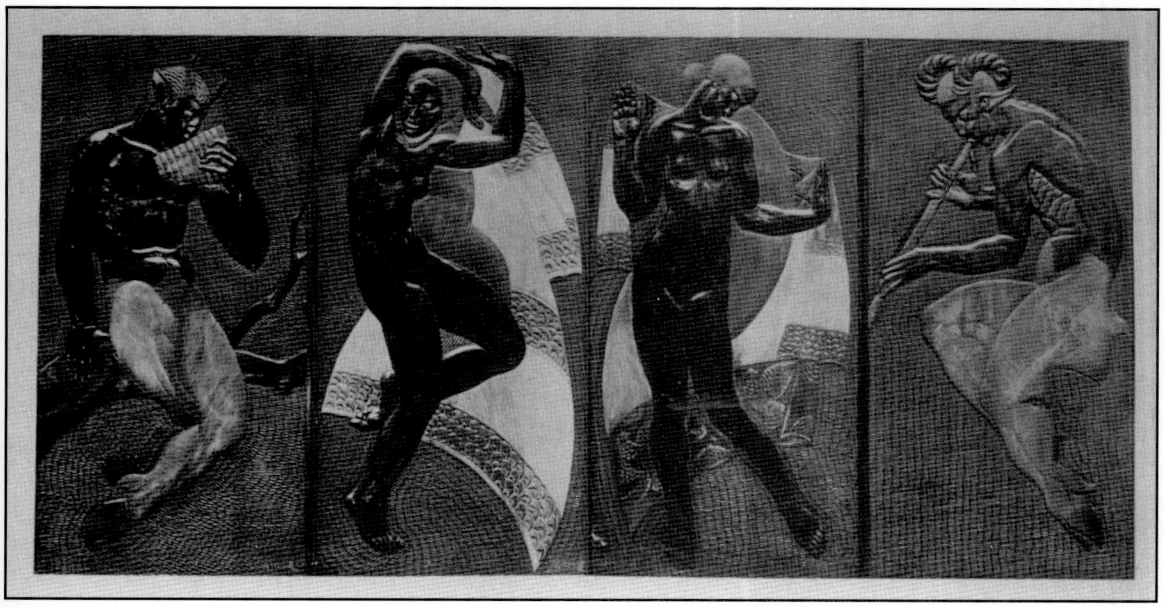

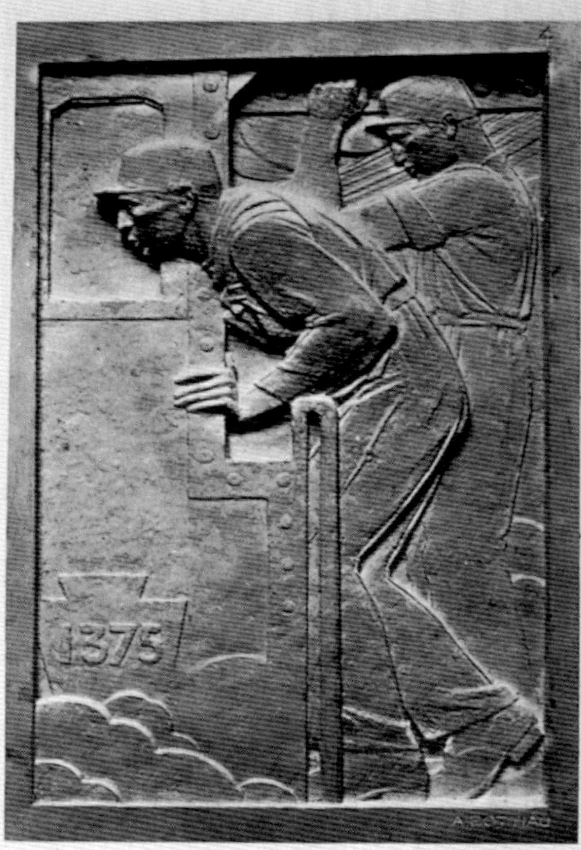

1

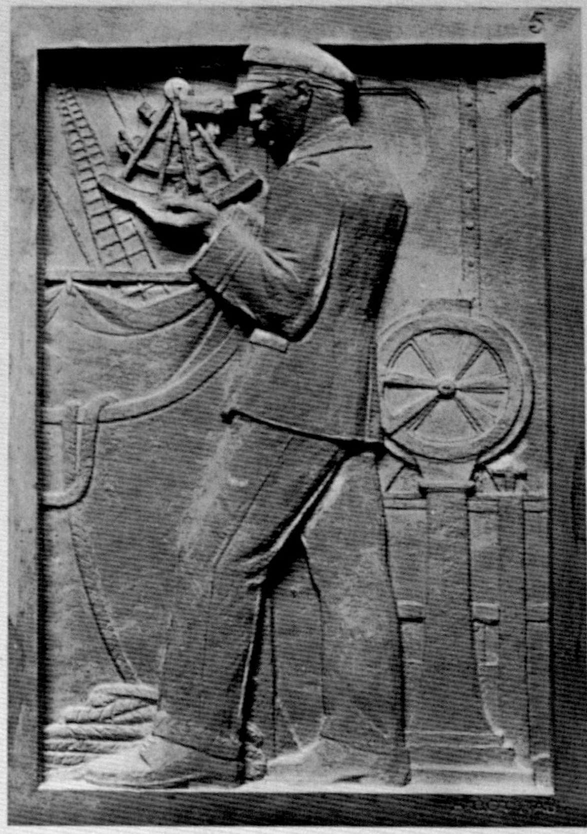

2

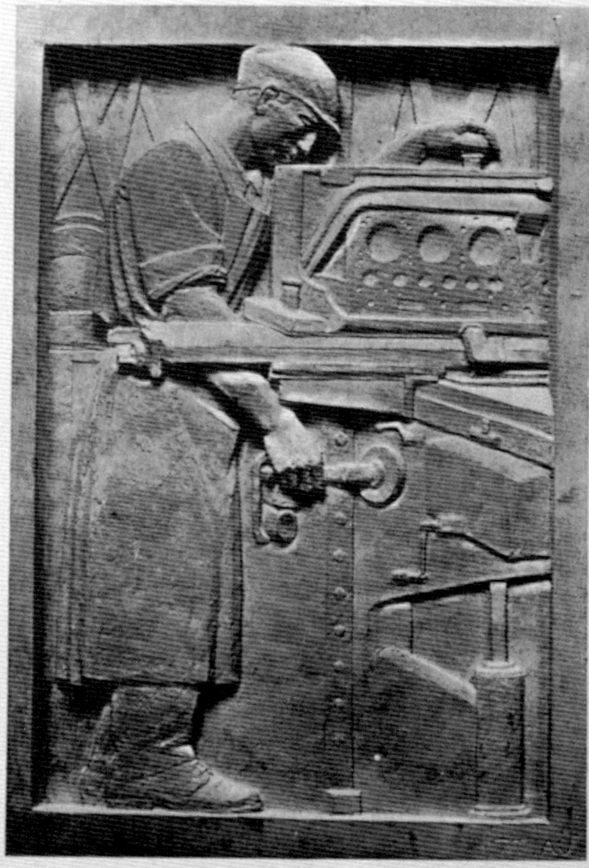

3

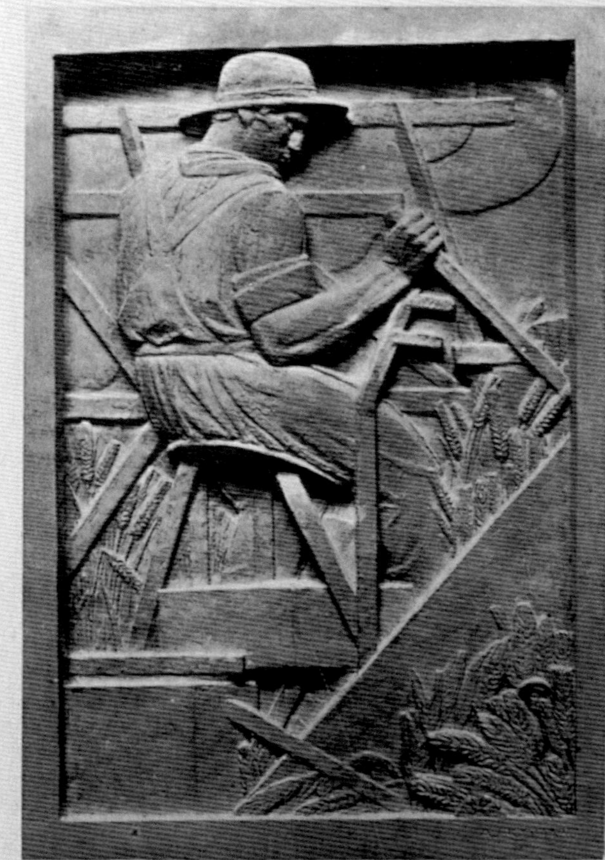

4

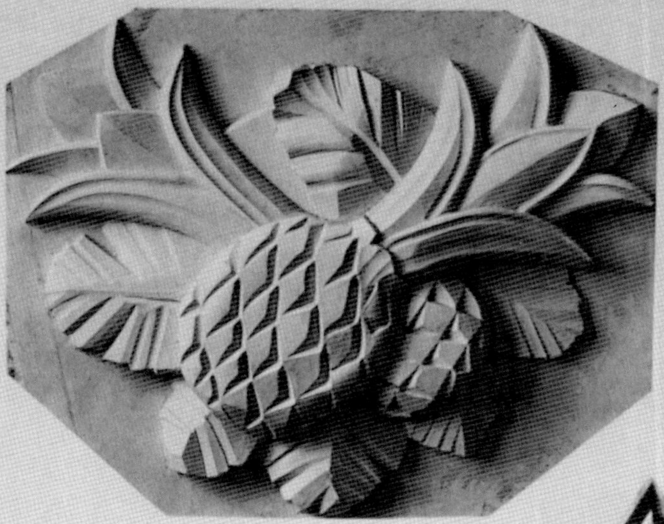

1

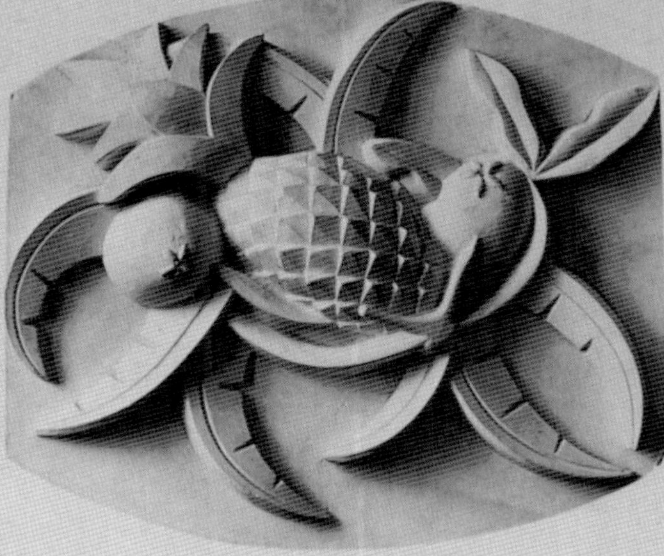

2

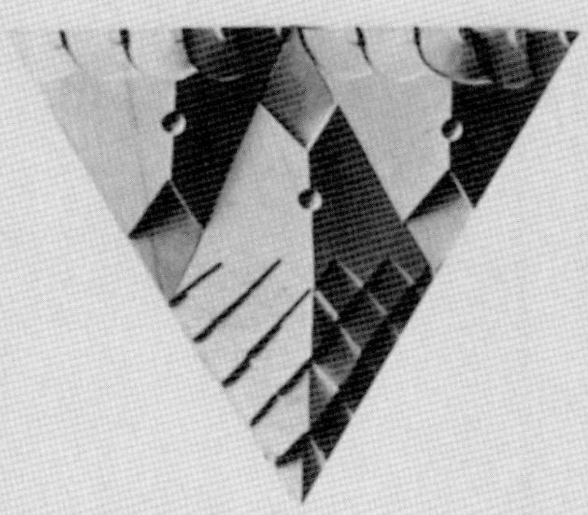

3

4

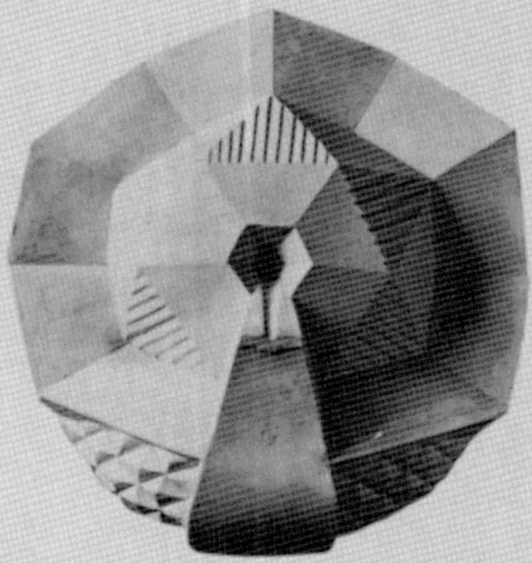

5

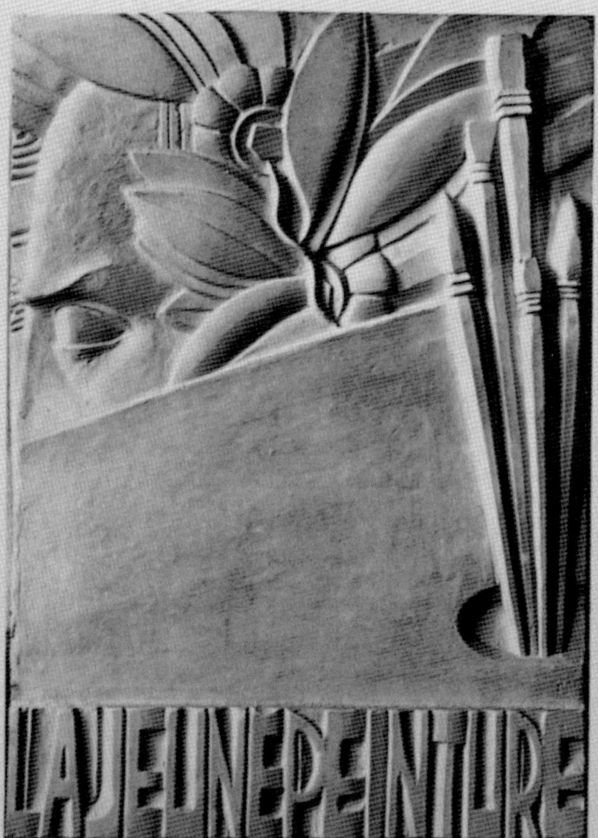

6

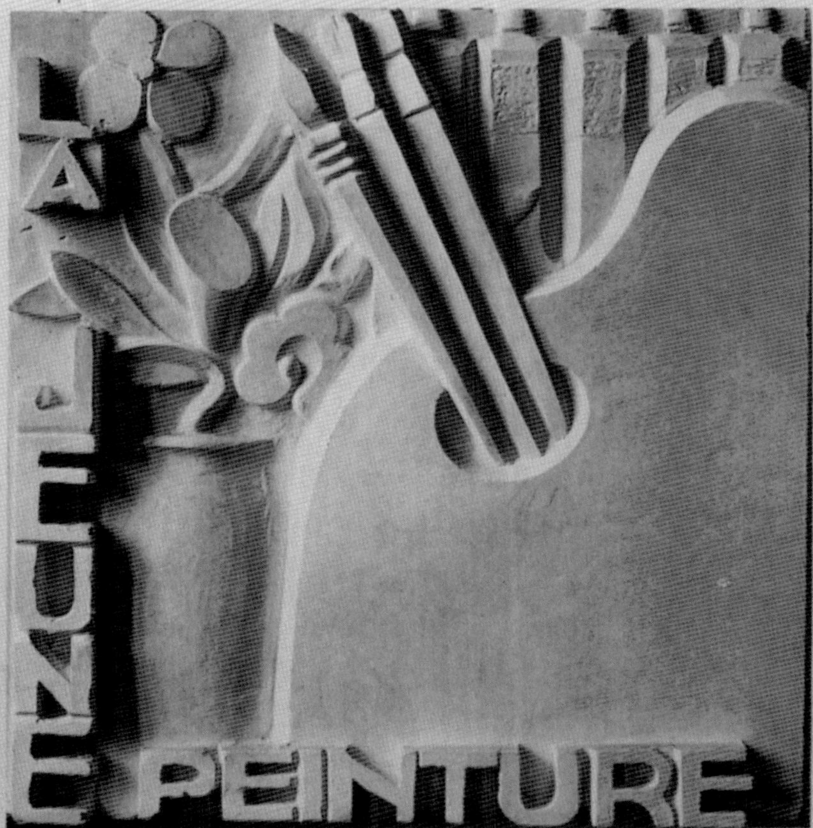

7

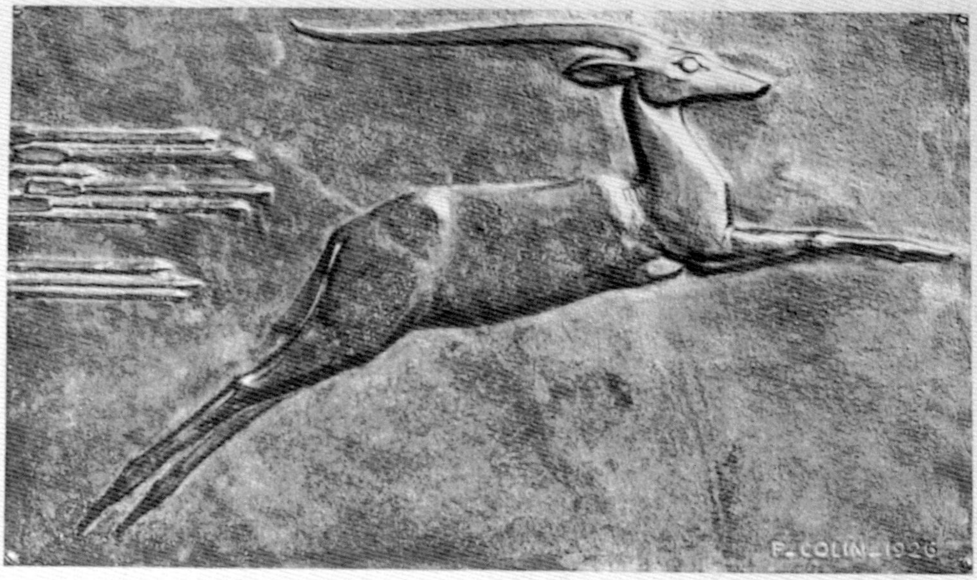

1

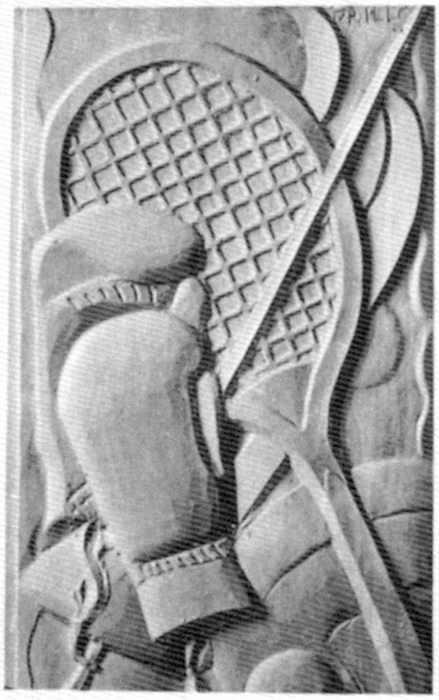

2

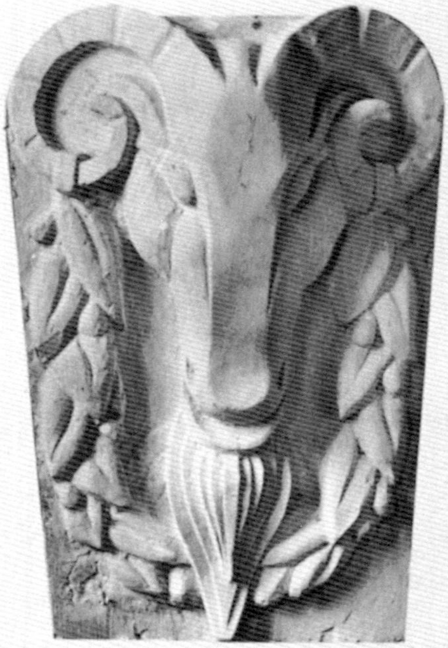

3

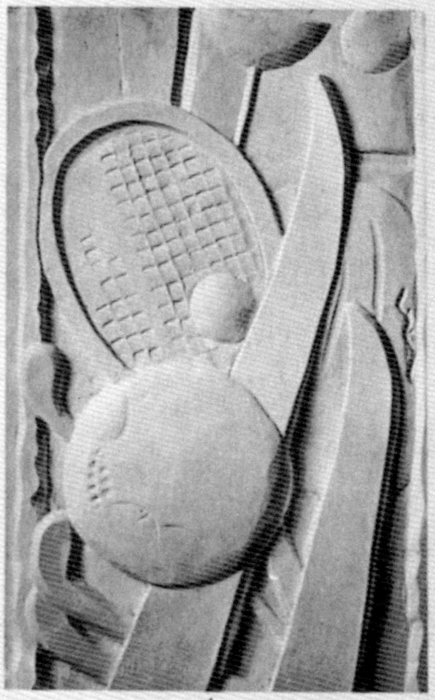

4

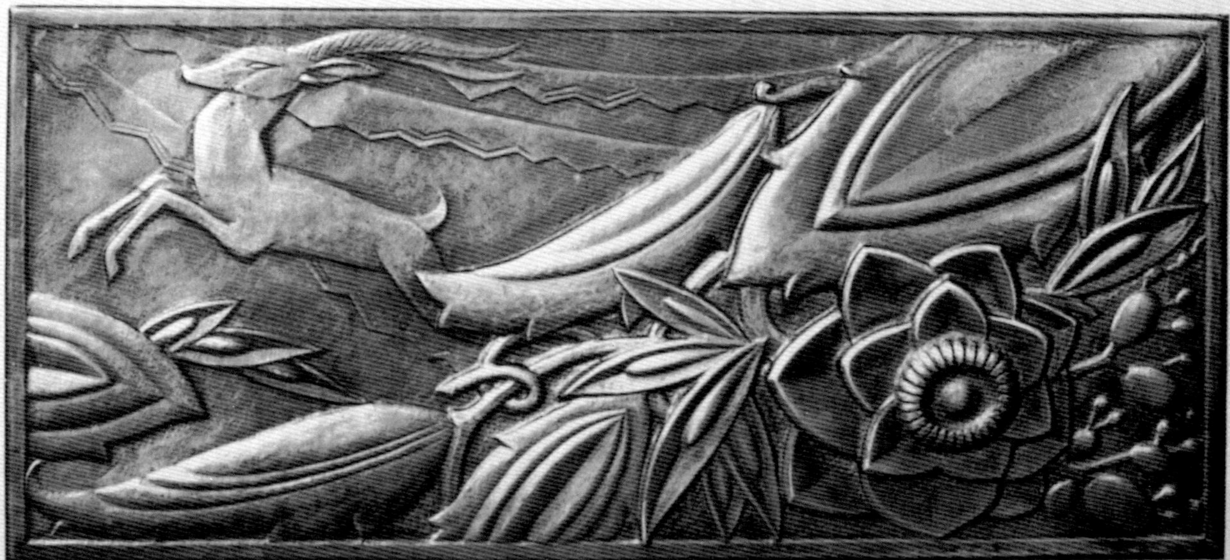

5

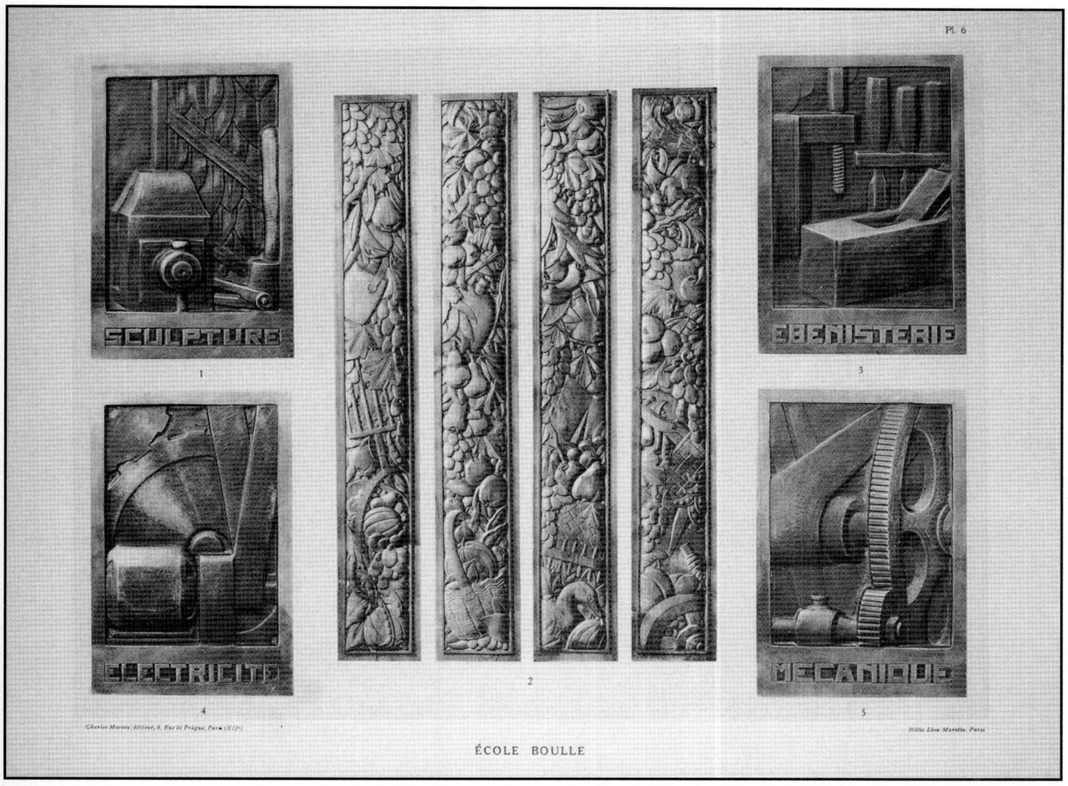
Pl. 6
SCULPTURE
1
EBENISTERIE
3
ELECTRICITE
4
2
MECANIQUE
5
ÉCOLE BOULLE

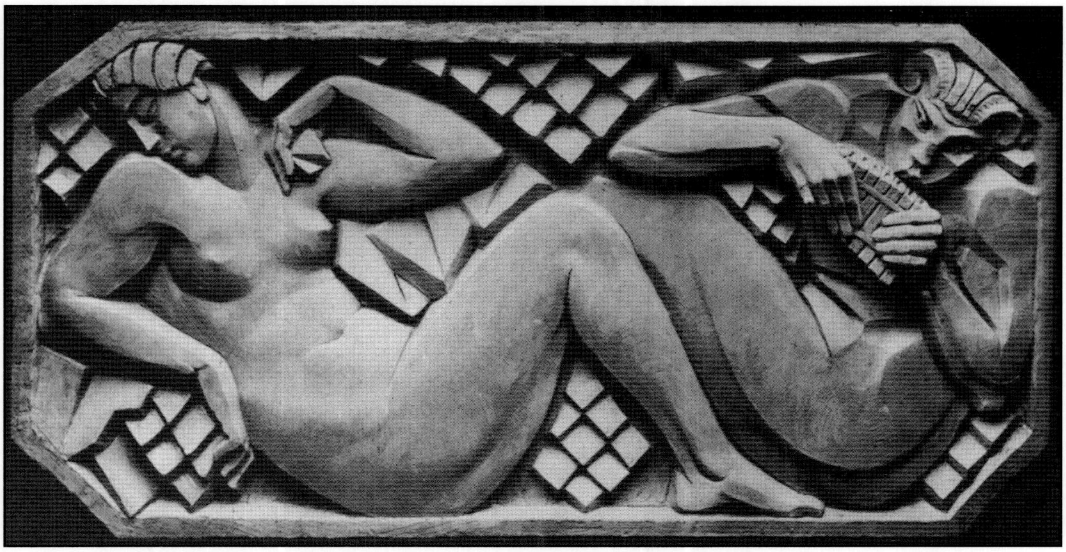

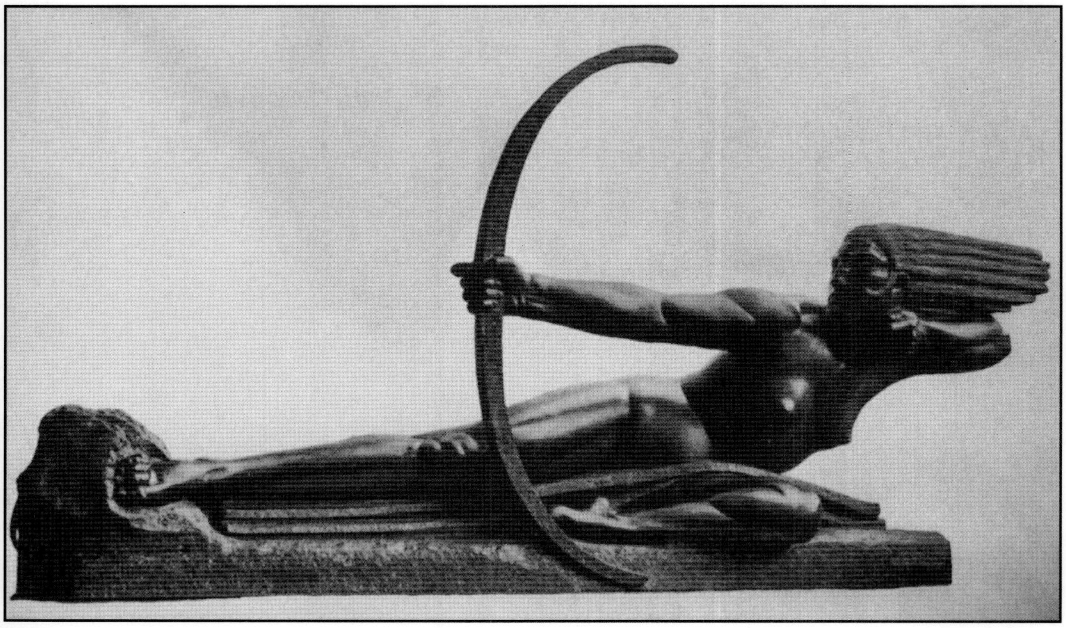

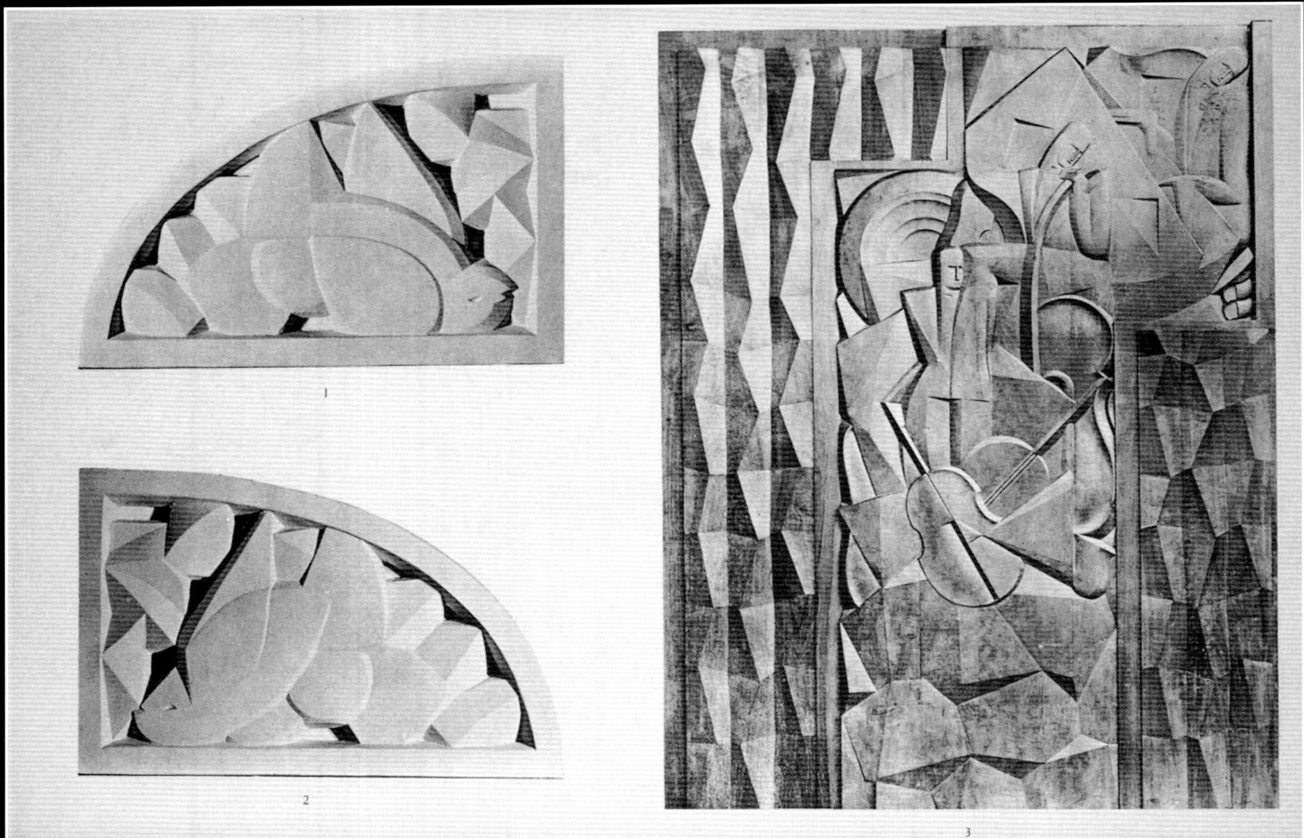

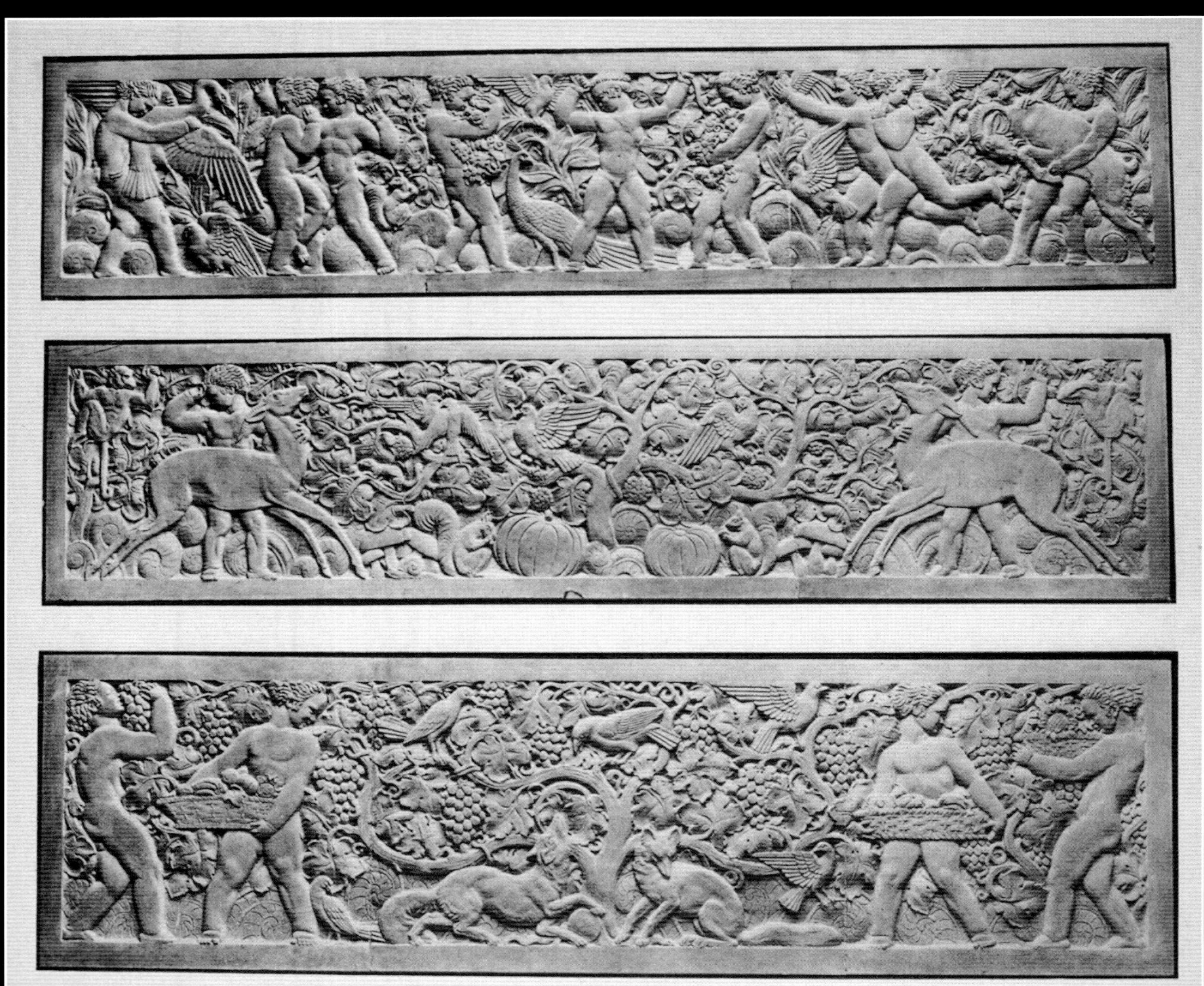

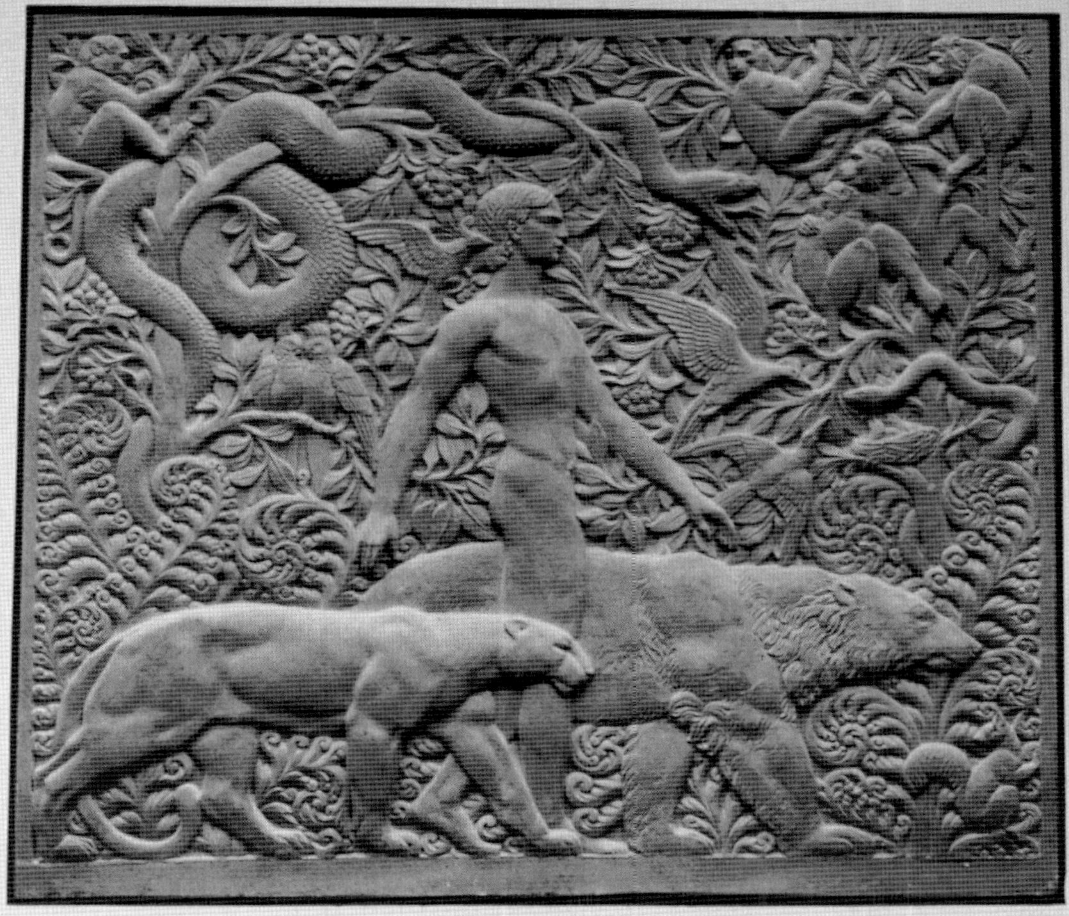

1

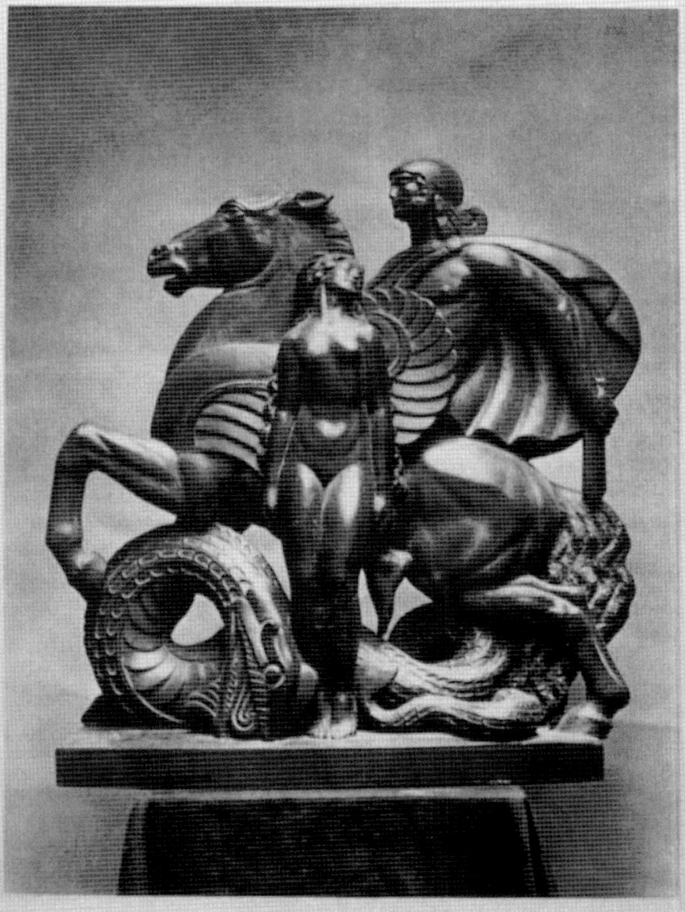

2

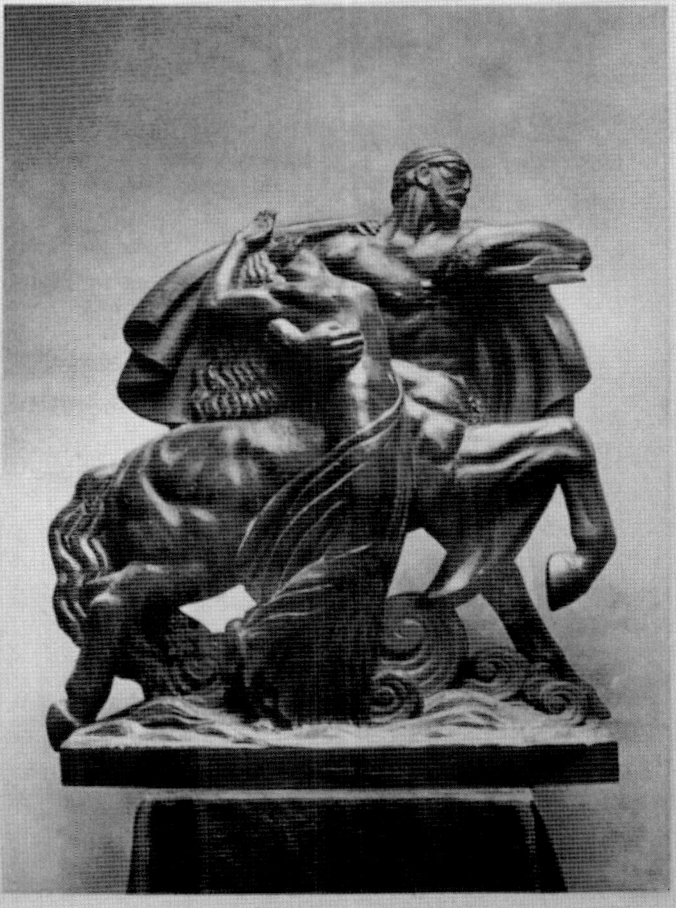

3

2

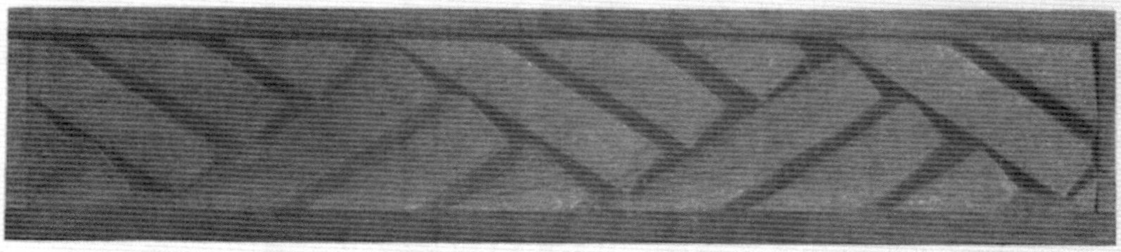

4

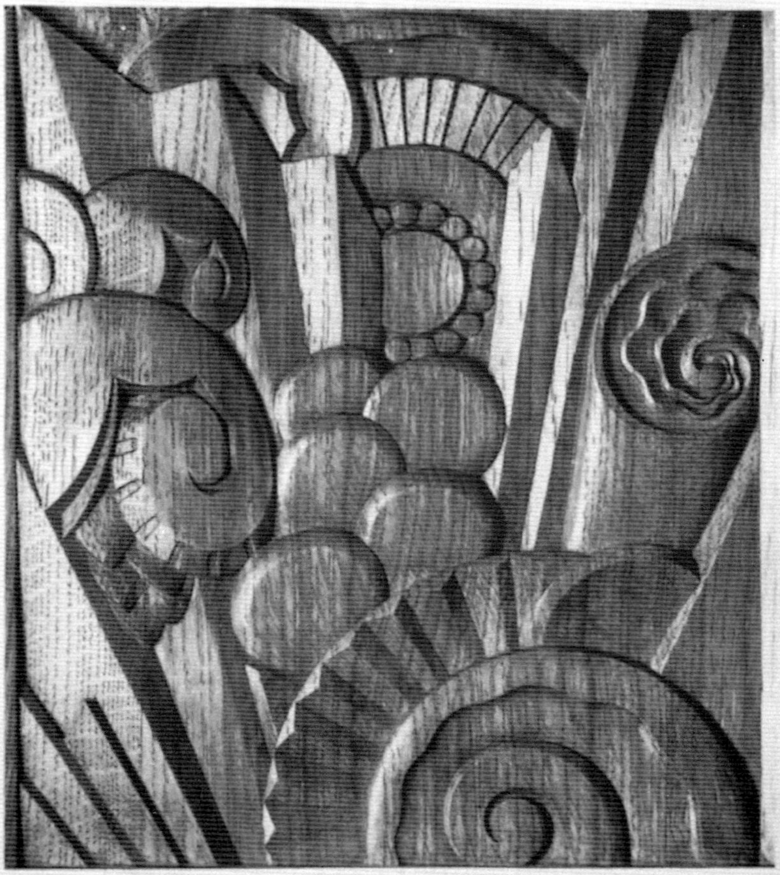

6

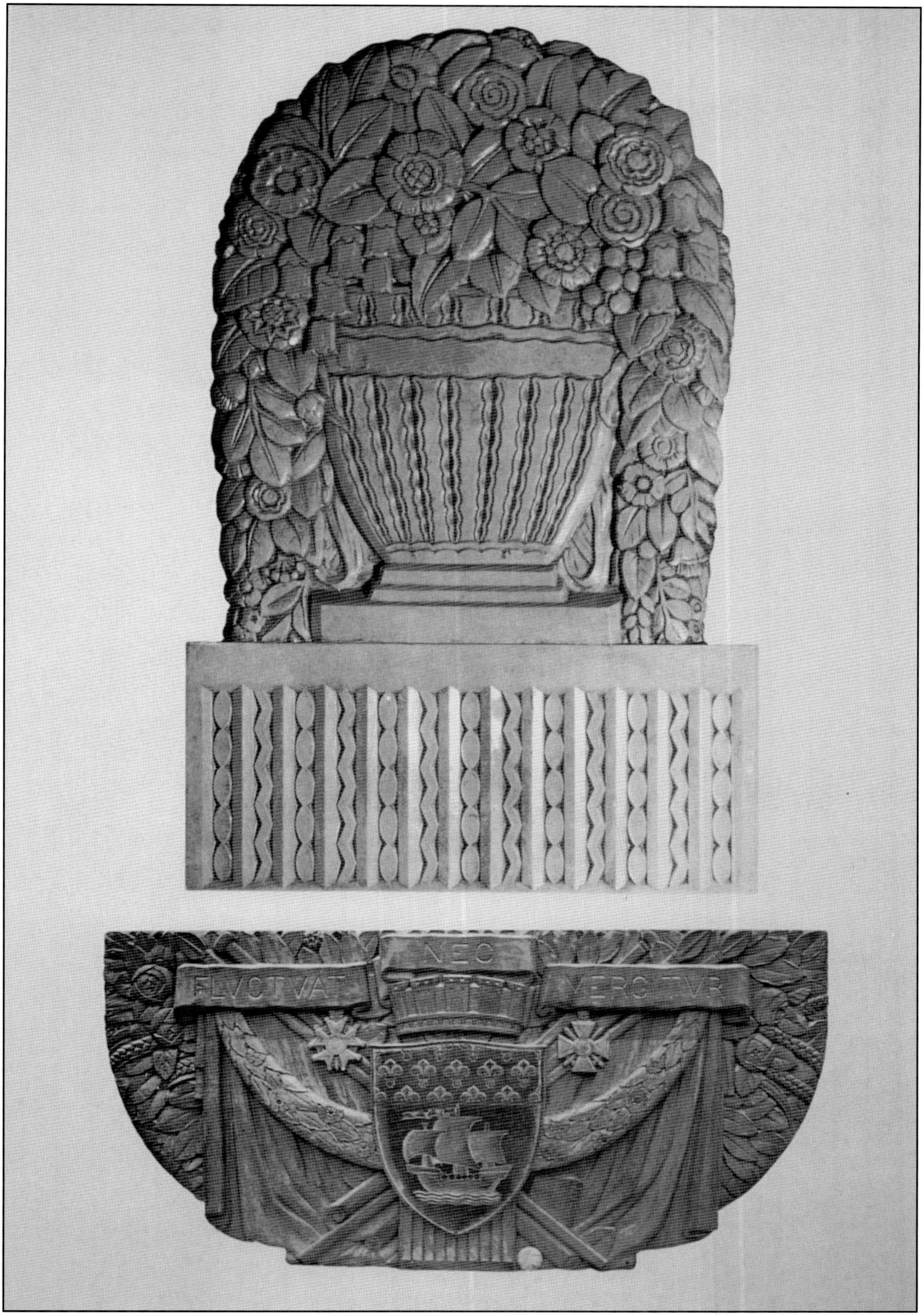
NEC
FLVCTVAT
MERGITVR

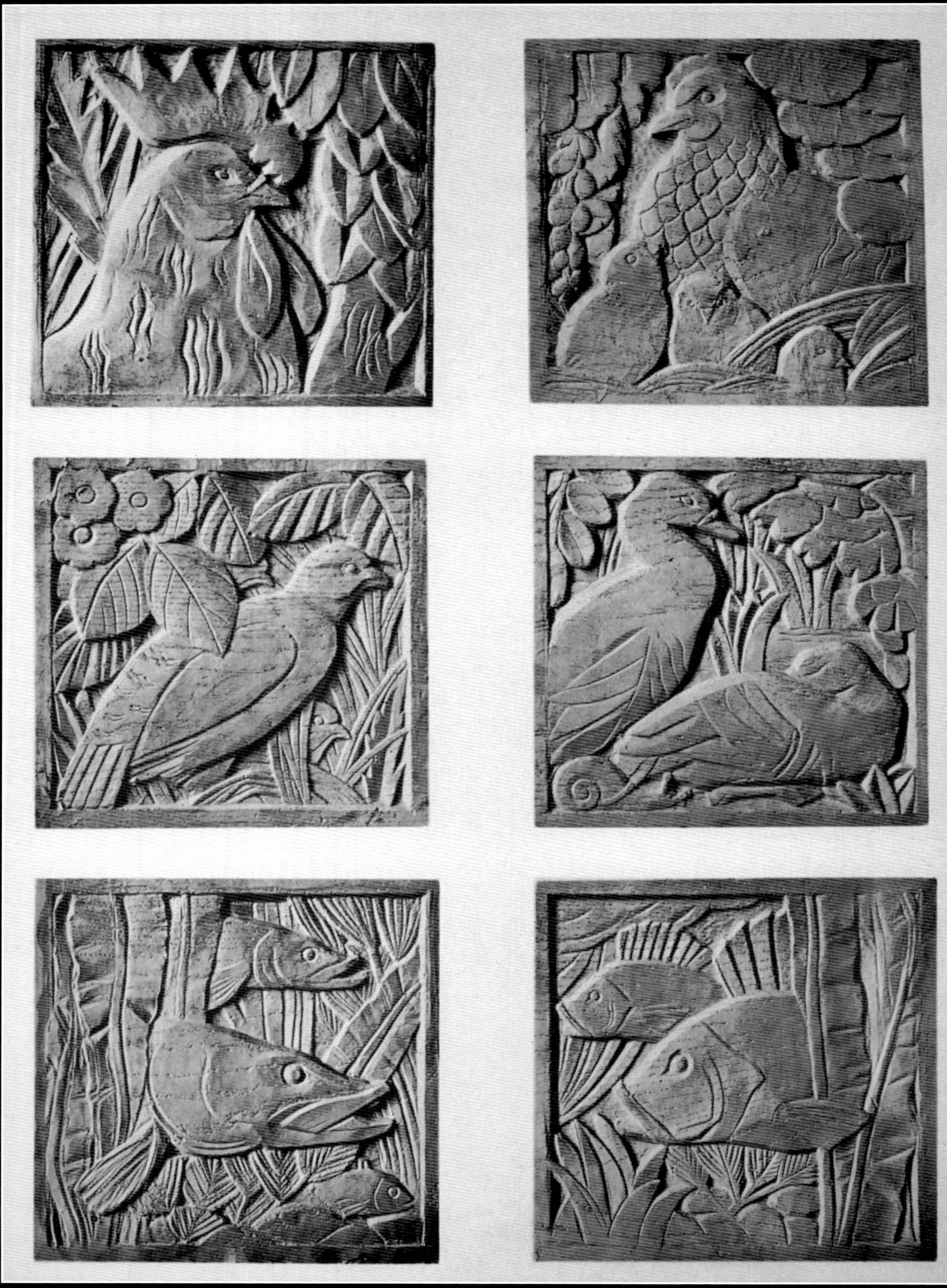

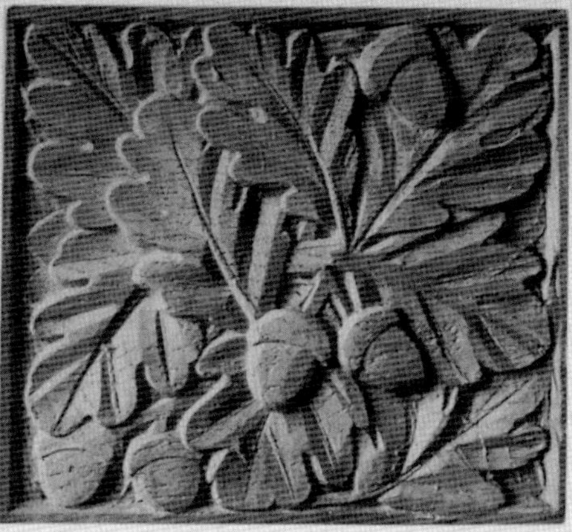

1

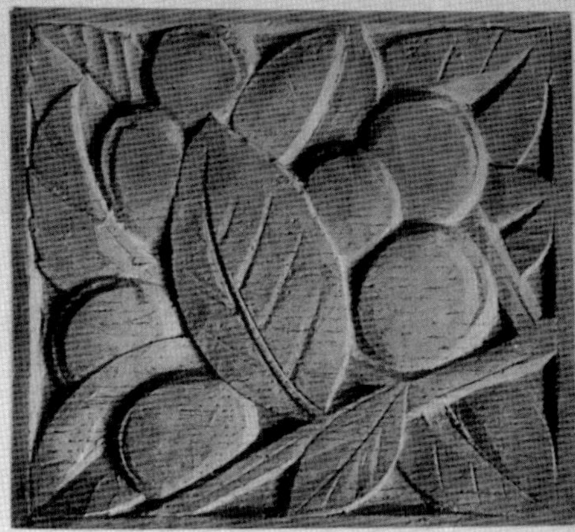

2

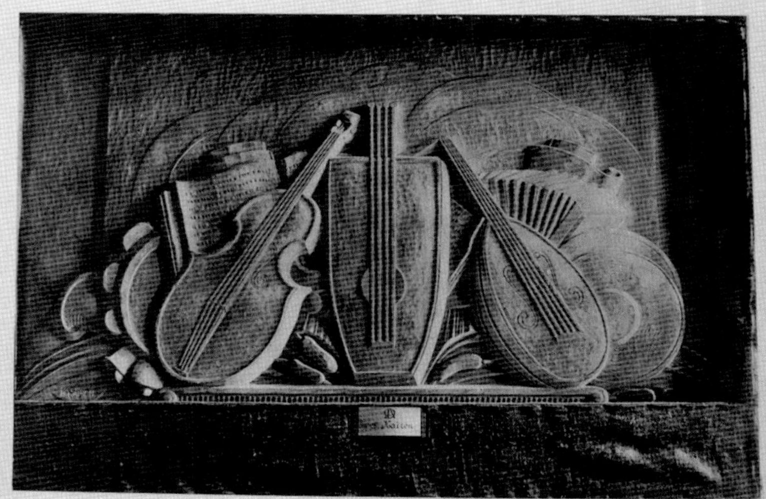

3

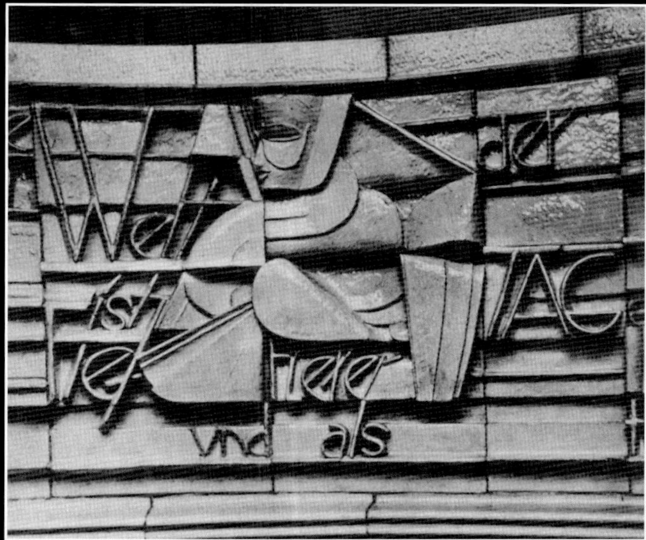

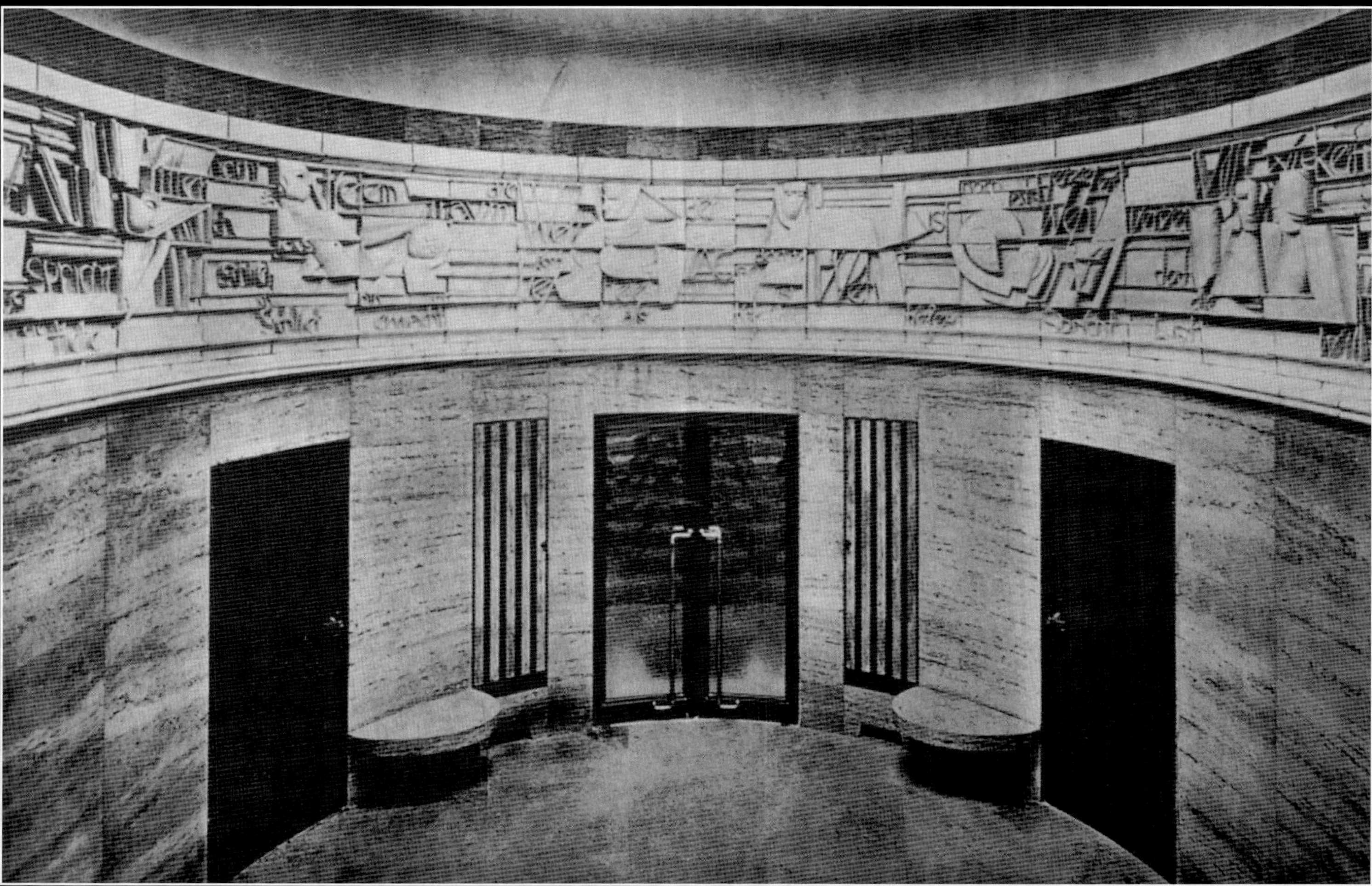

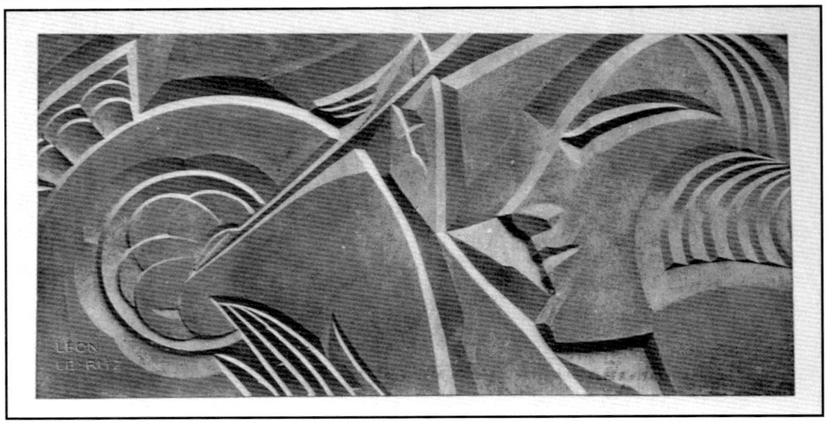

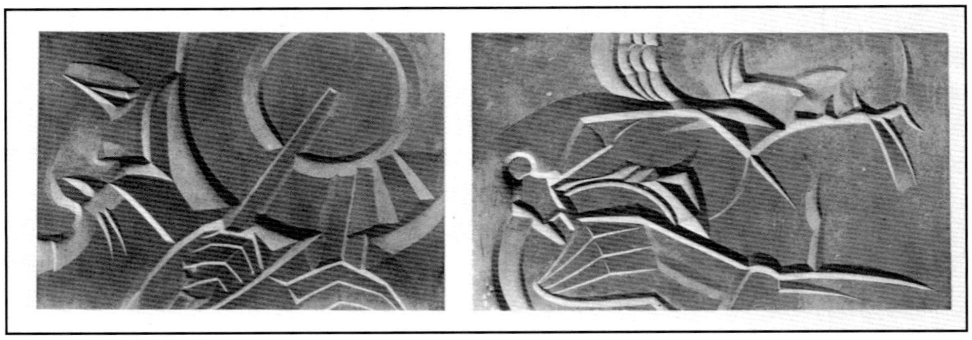

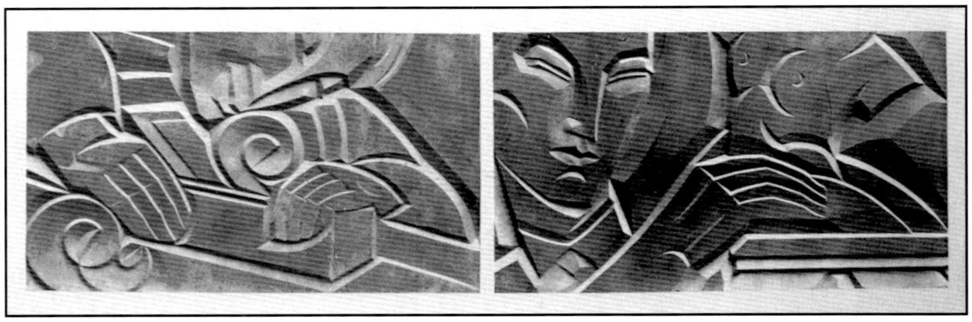

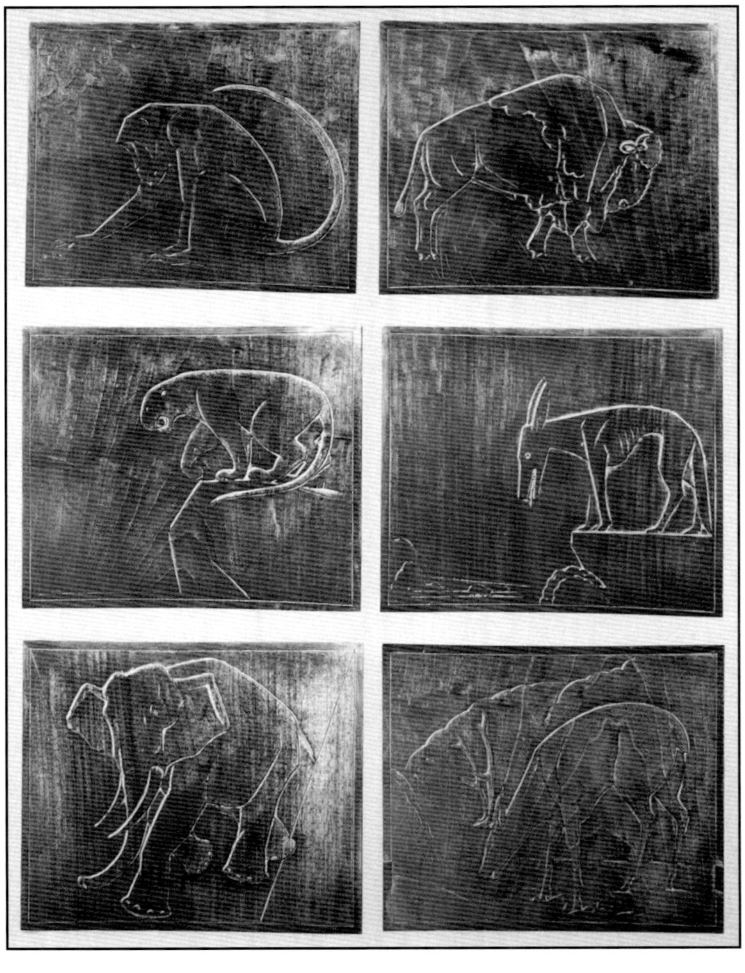

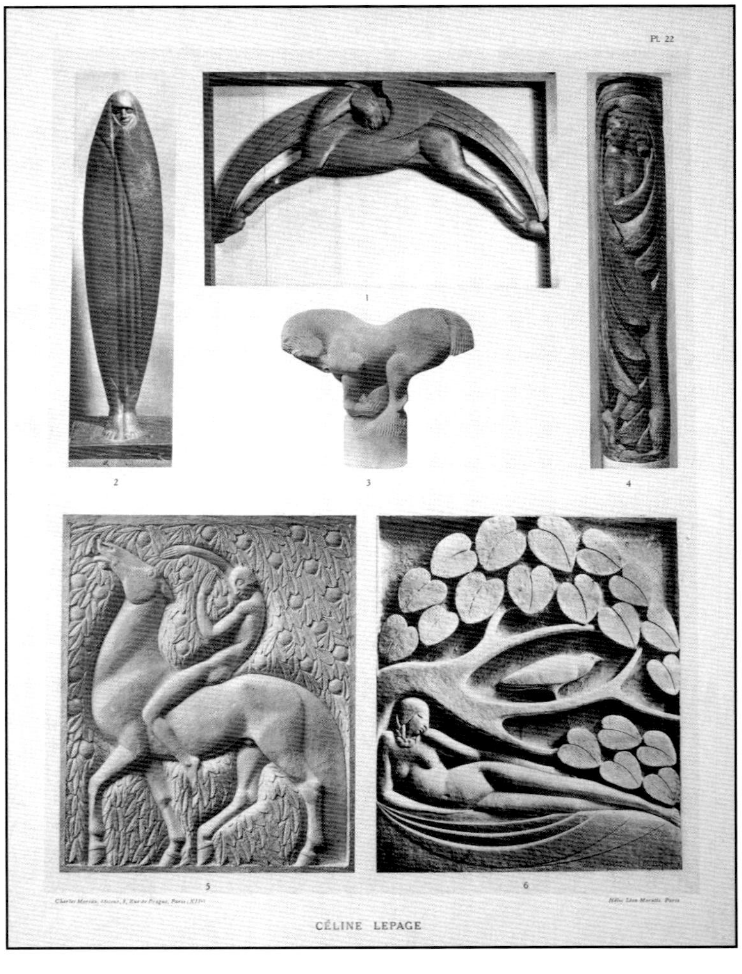
Pl. 22
1
2
3
4
5
6
CÉLINE LEPAGE

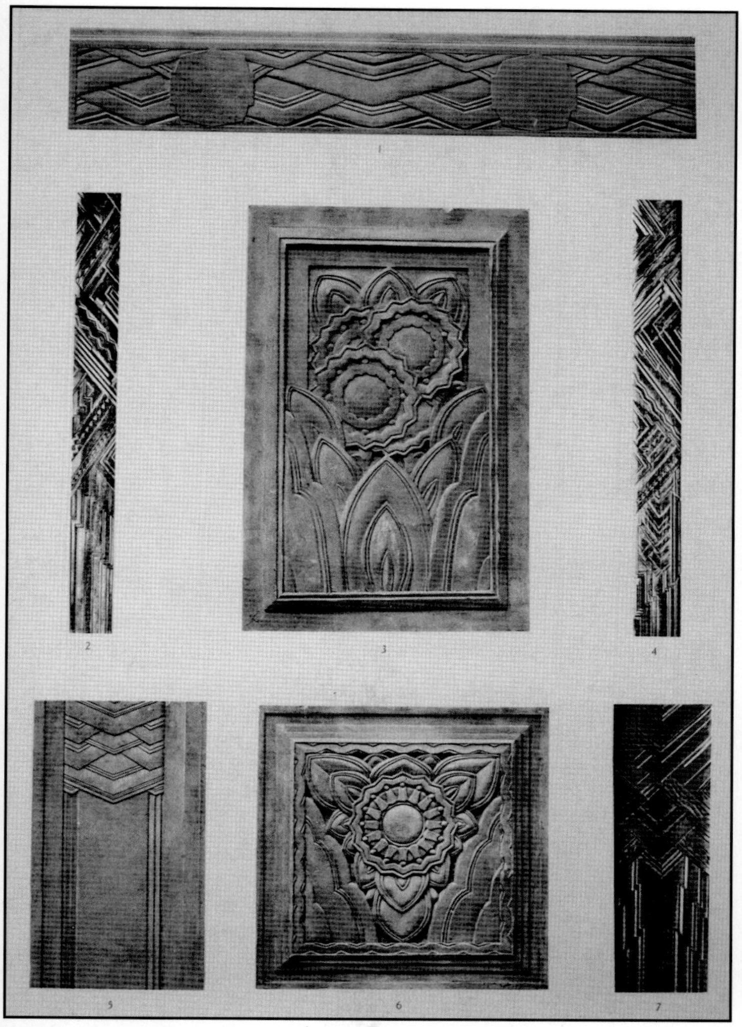

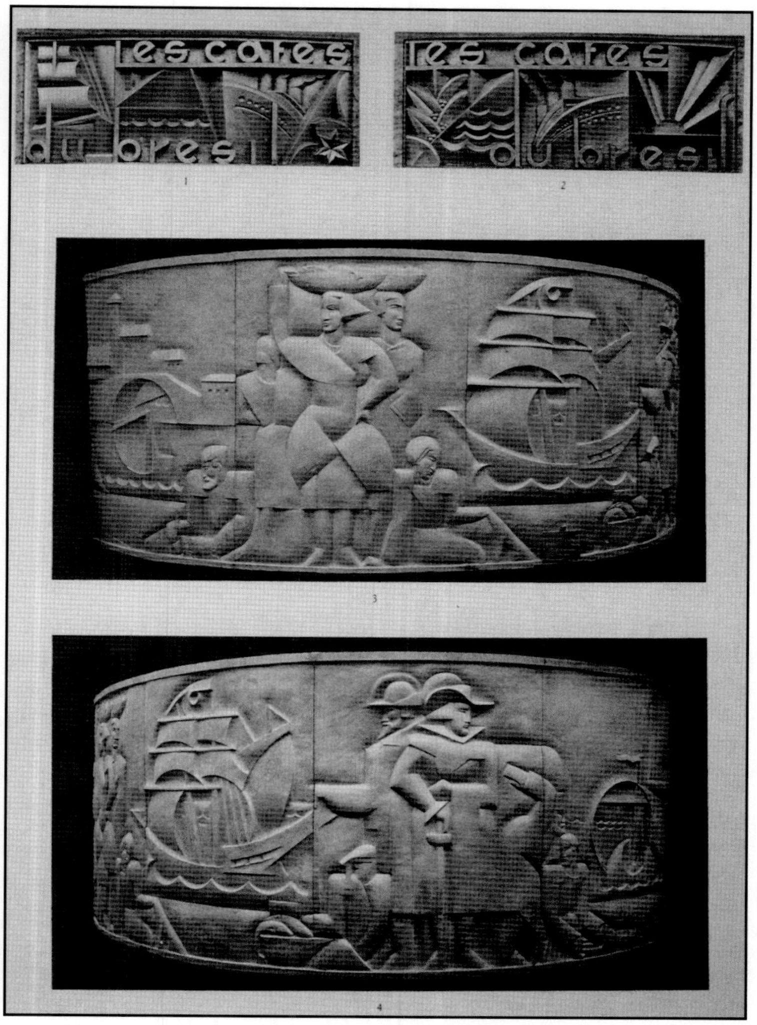
les cafes
du bresil
les cafes
du bresil

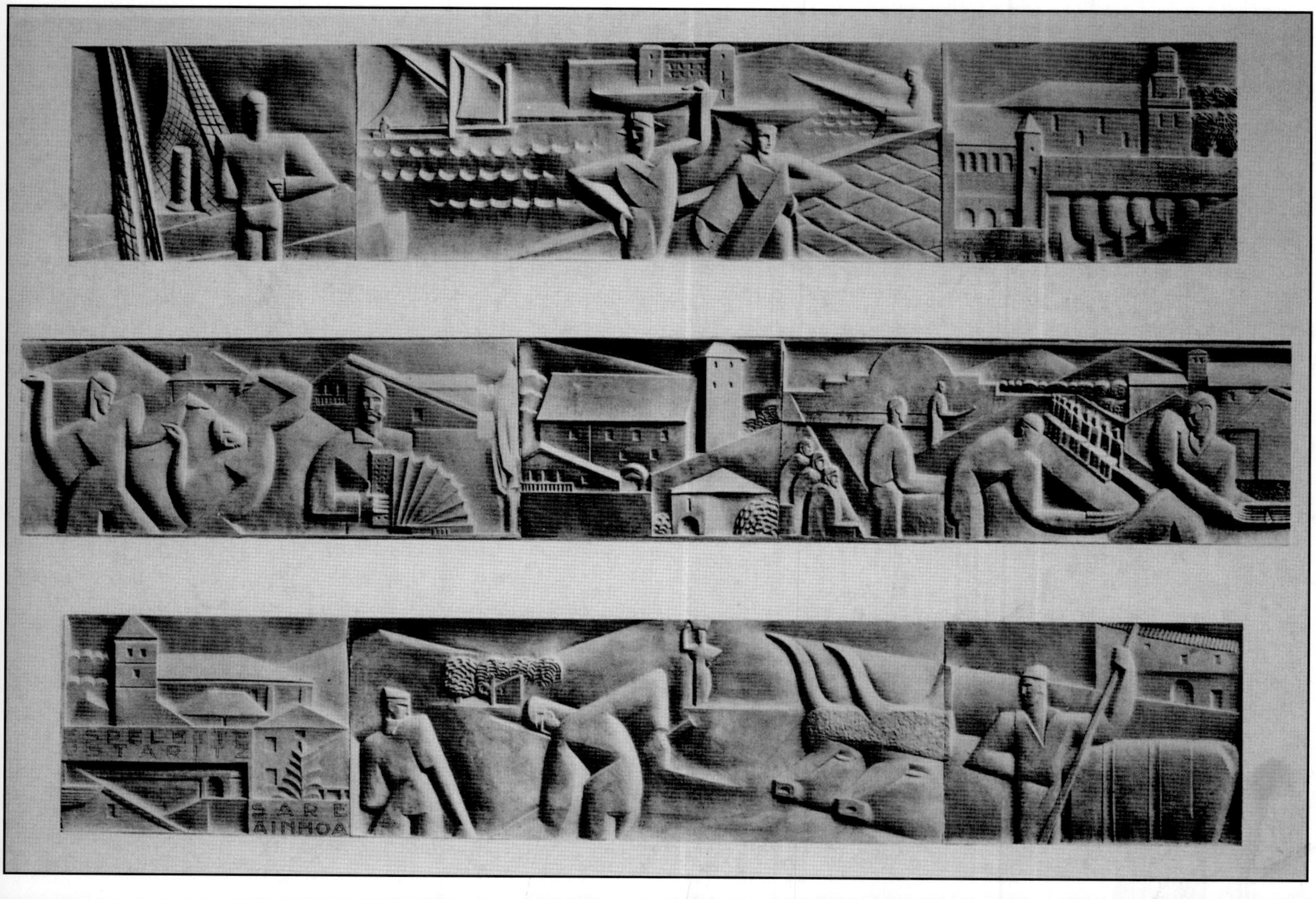
SARE
AINHOA

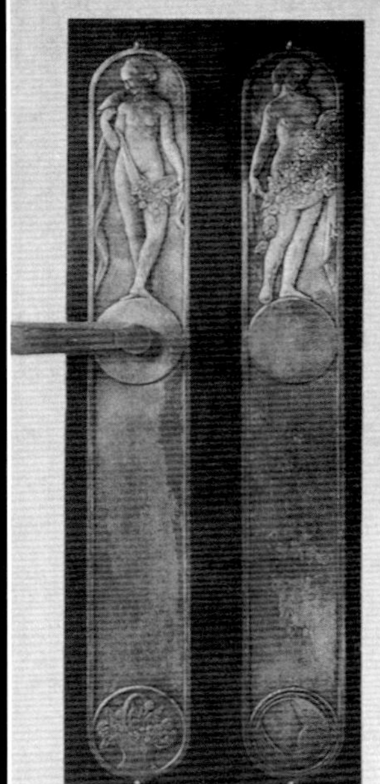

1

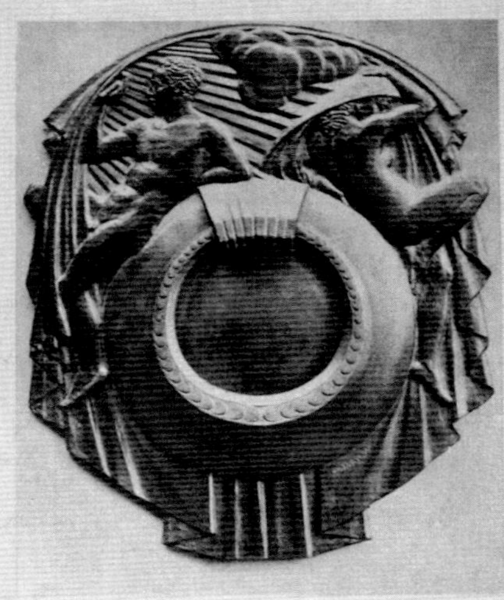

2

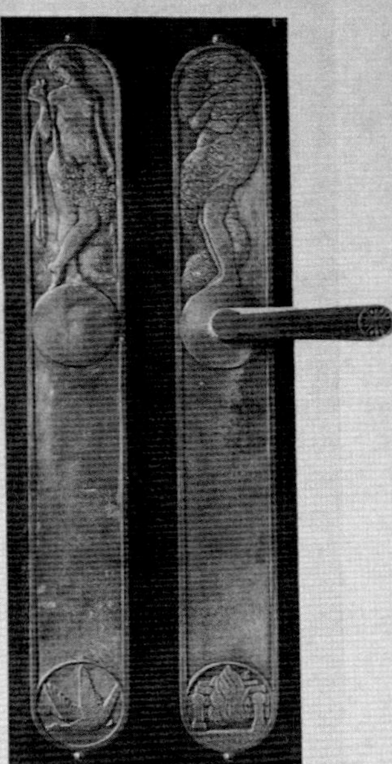

3

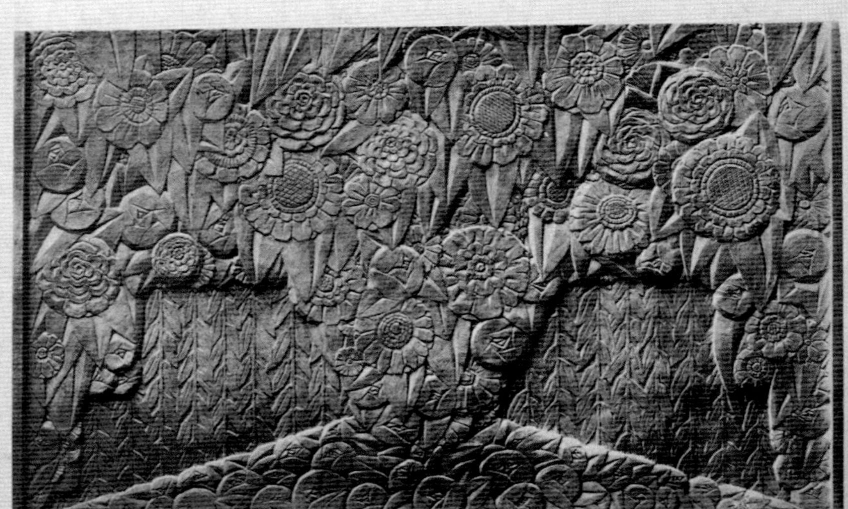

4

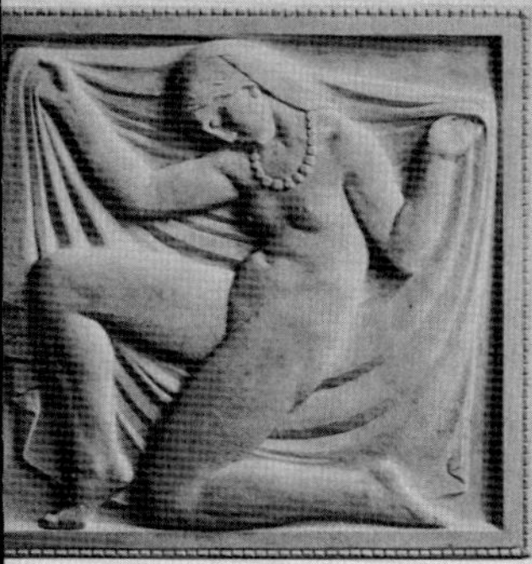
1

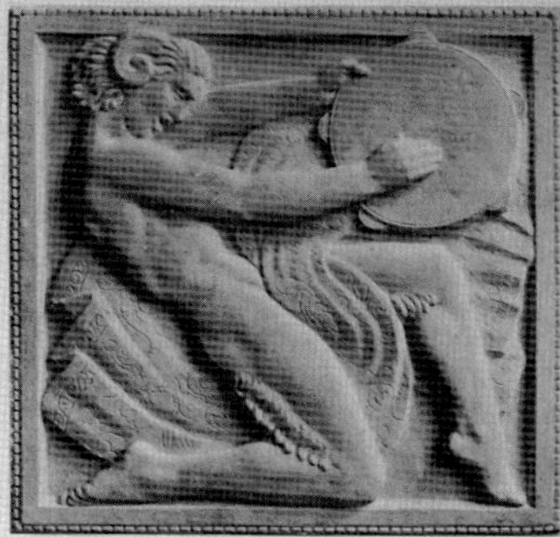
2

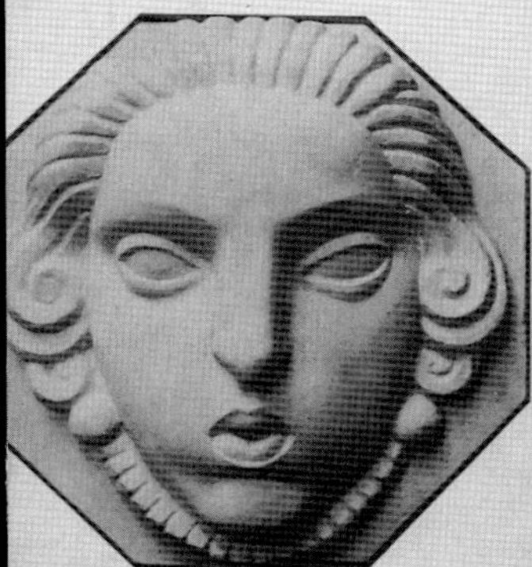
3

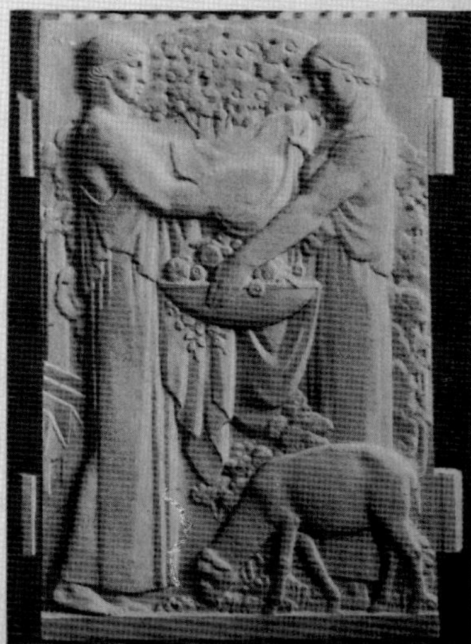
4

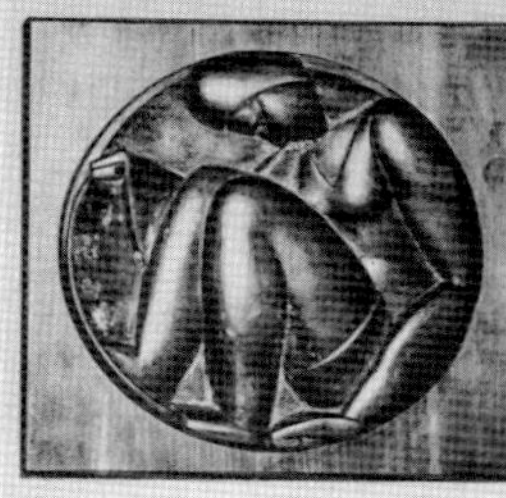
1

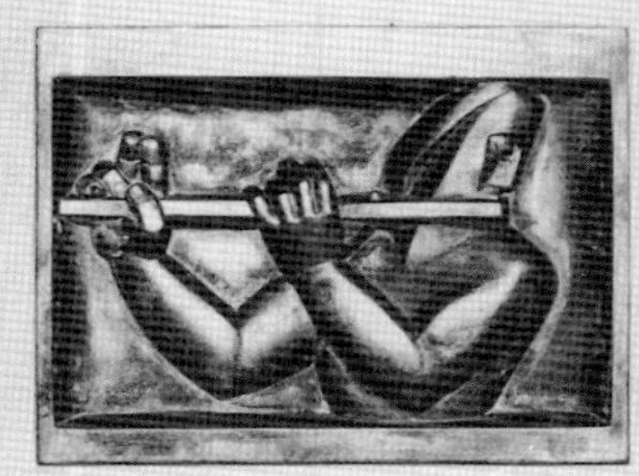
2

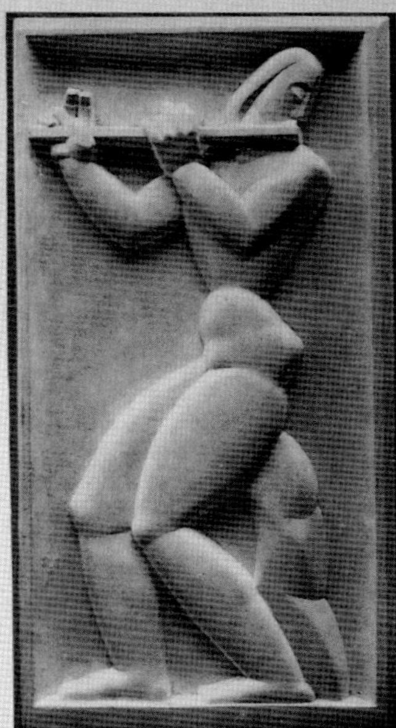
3

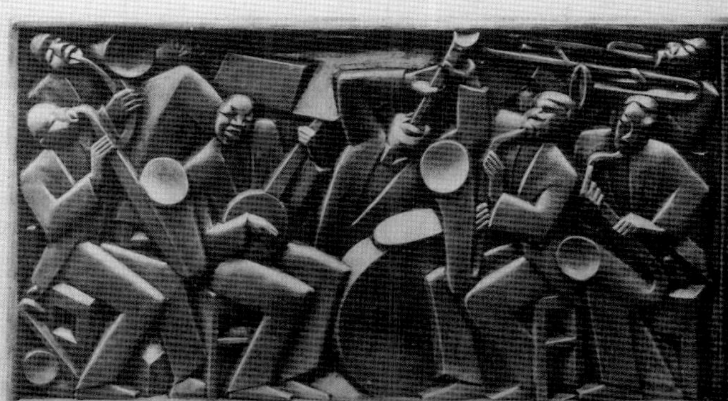
4

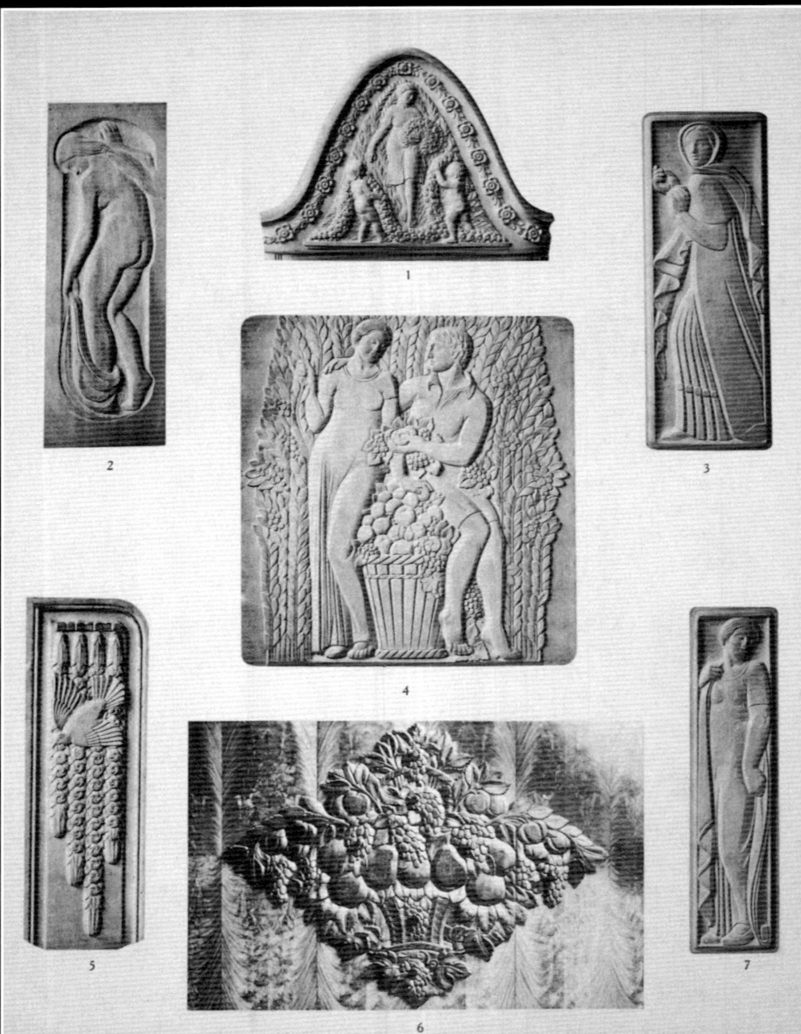
1
2
3
4
5
6
7

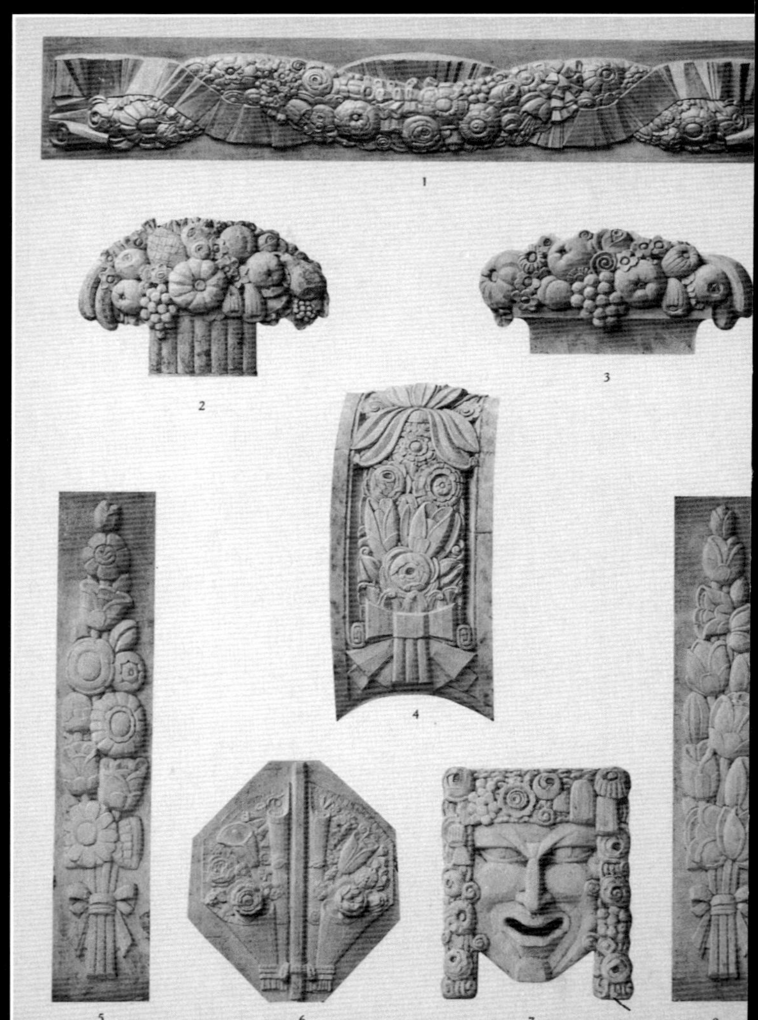
1
2
3
4
5
6
7
8

1

2

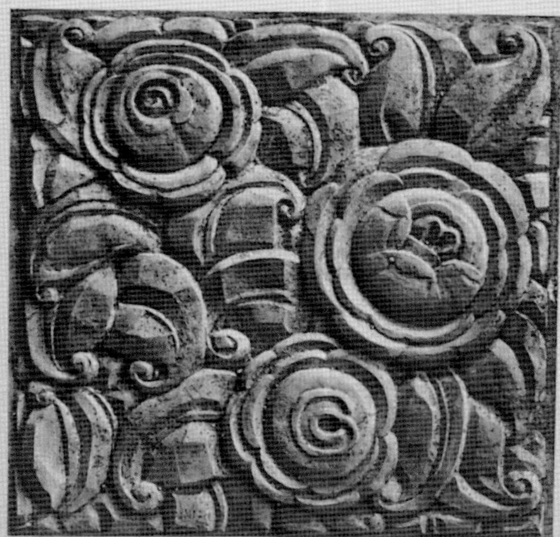

3

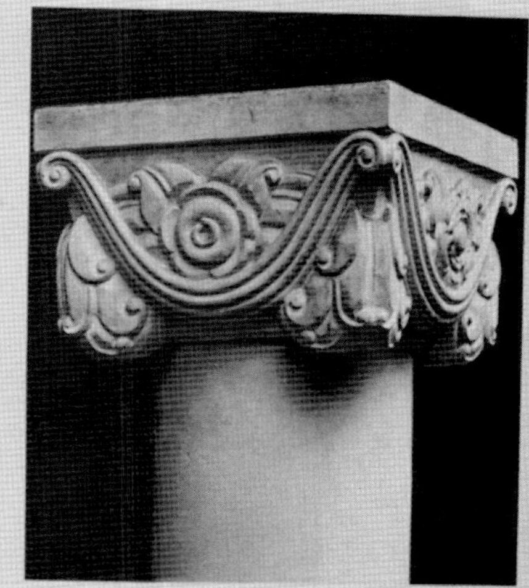

4

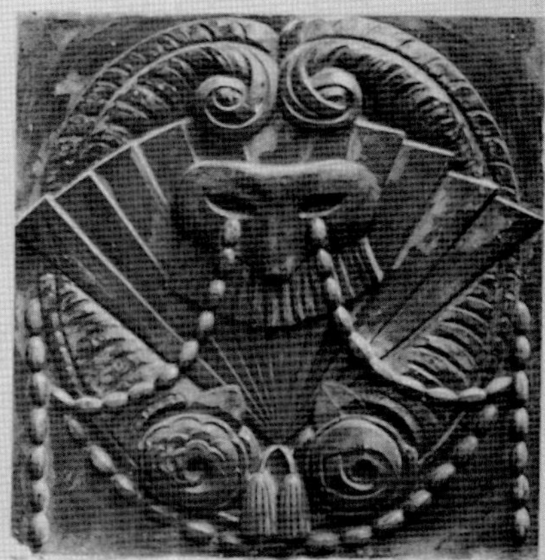

5

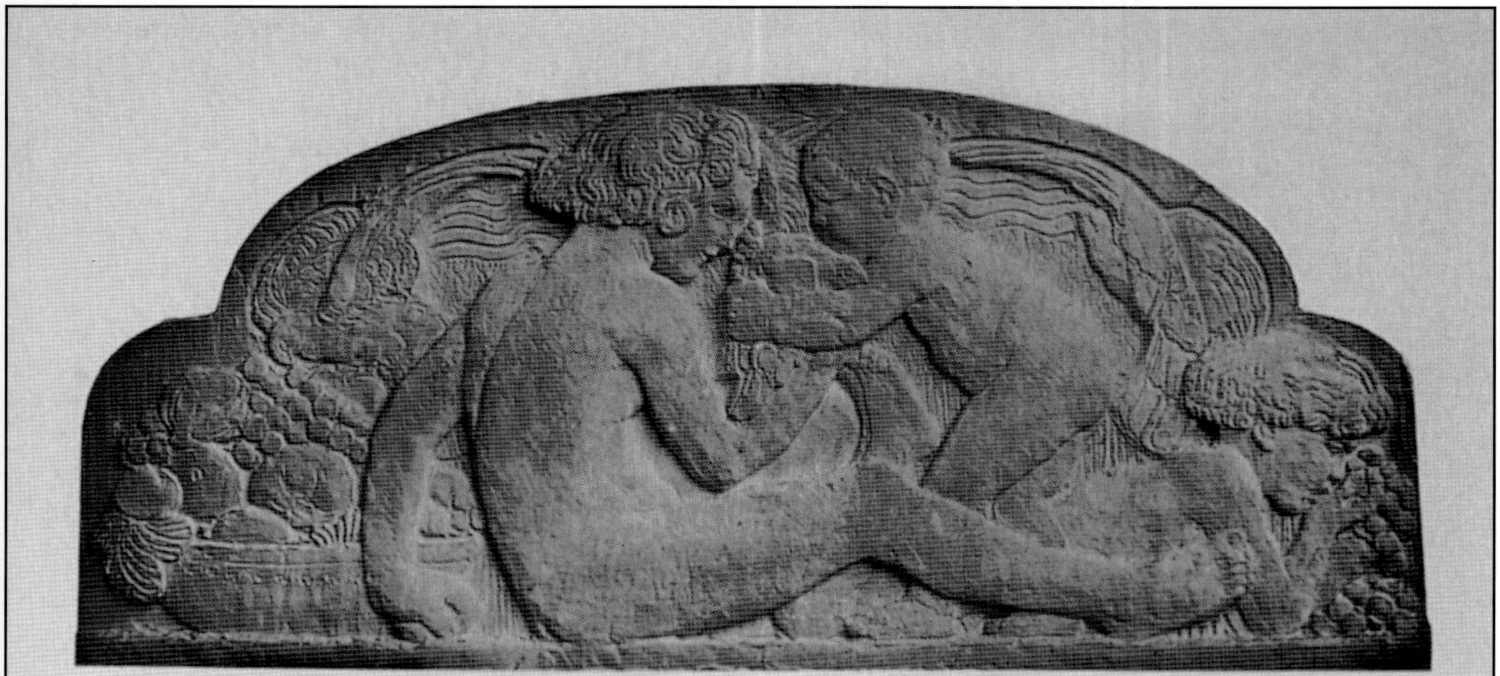

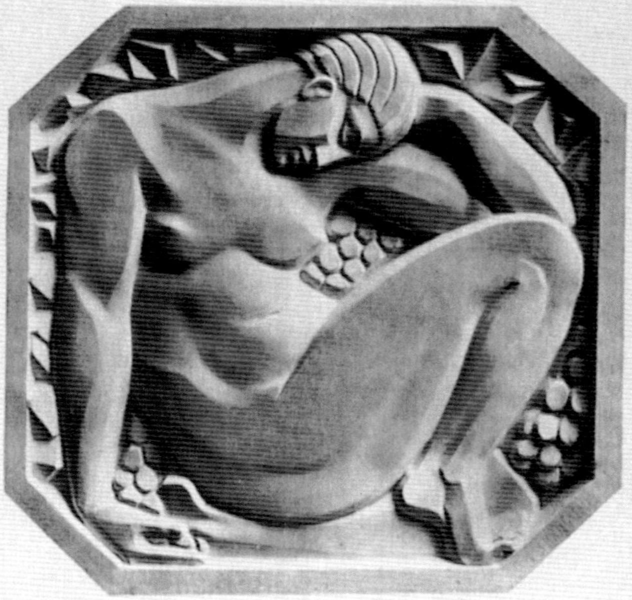

1

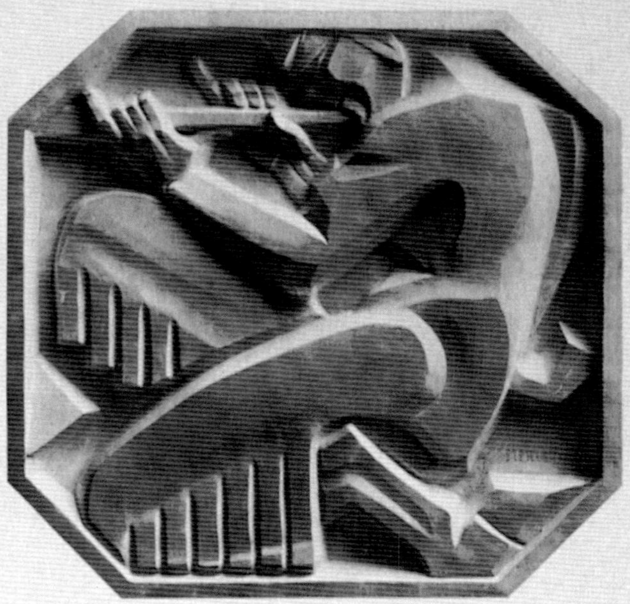

2

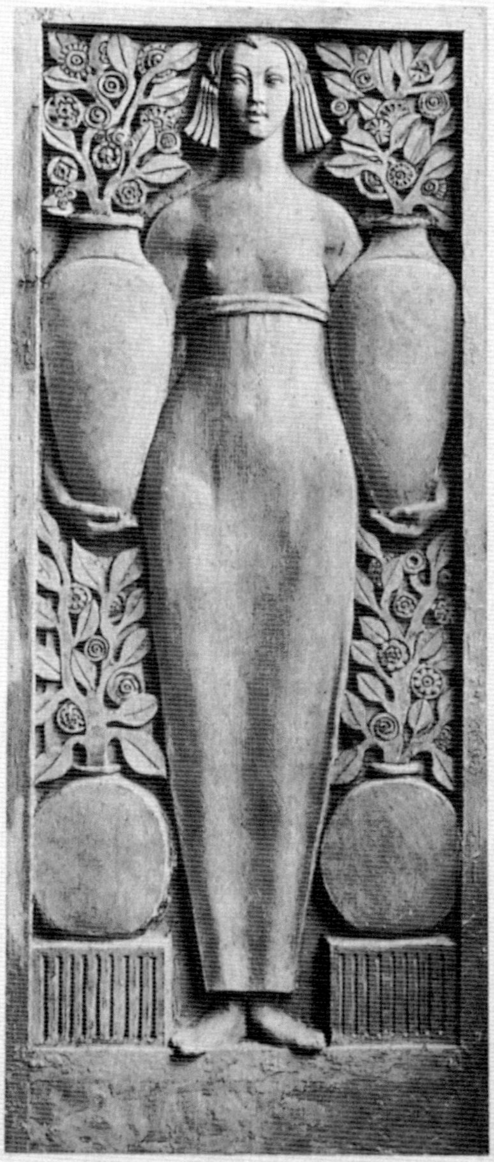

3

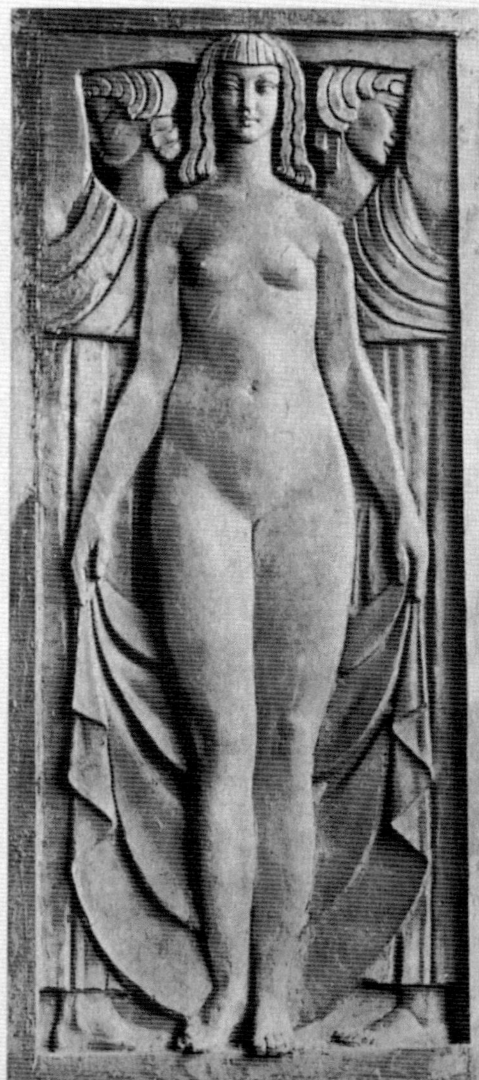

4

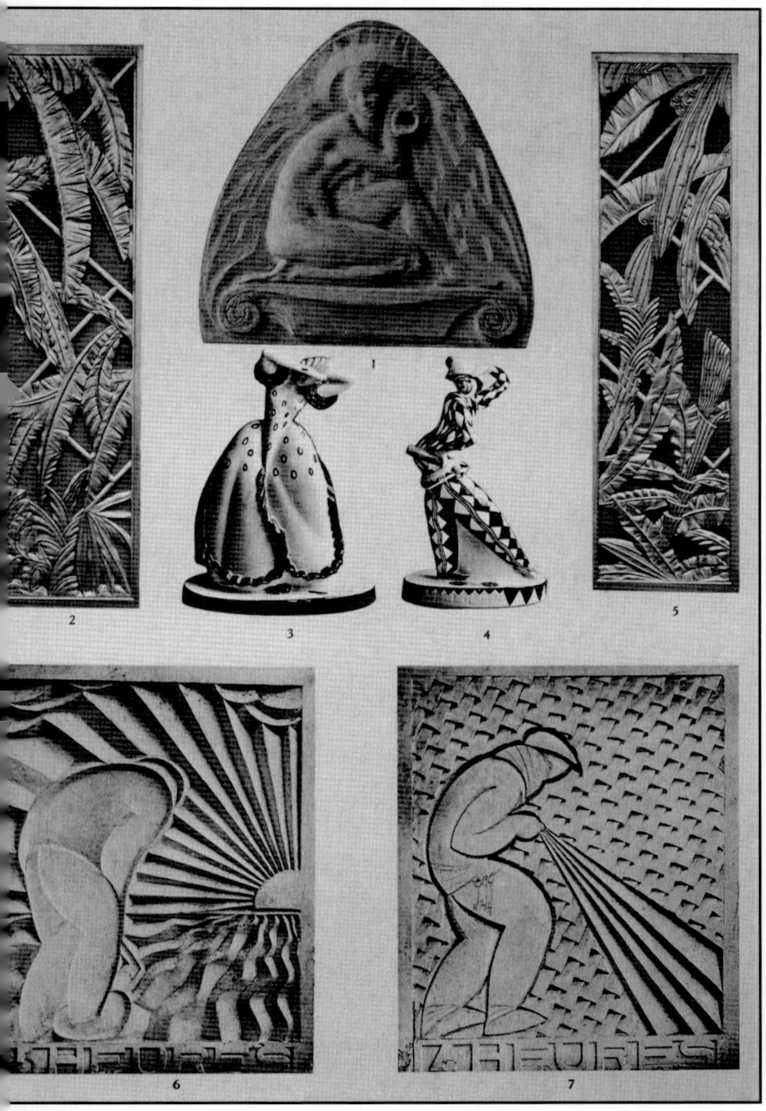

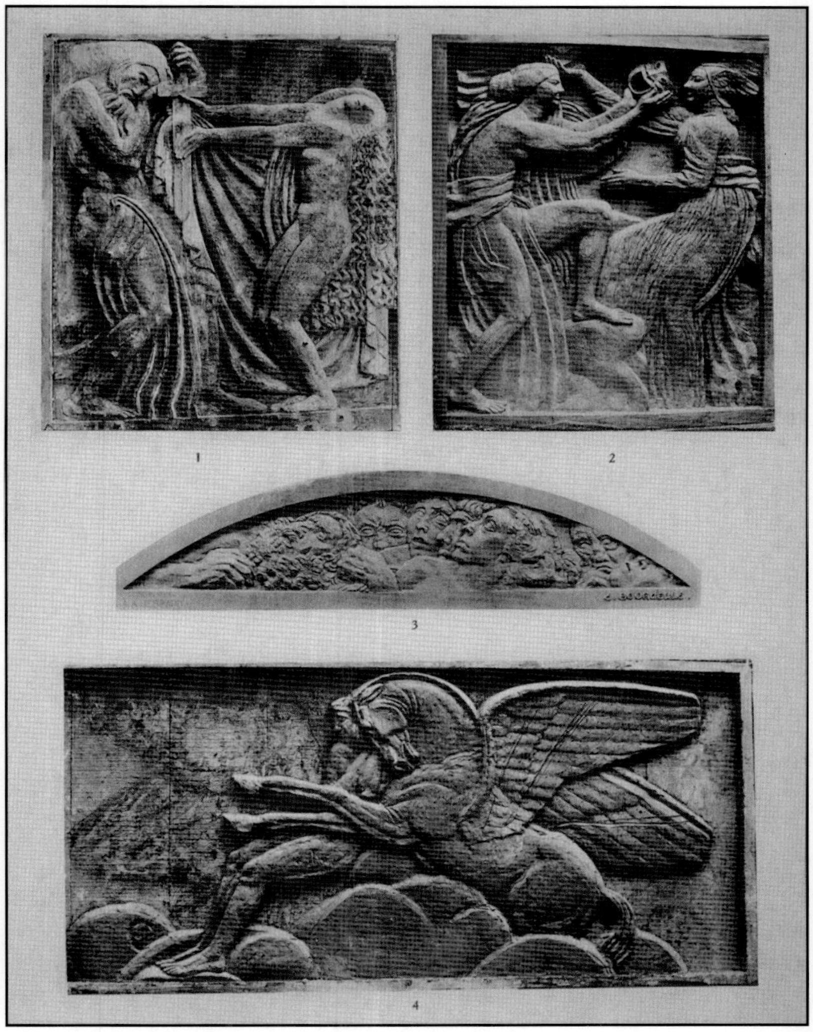

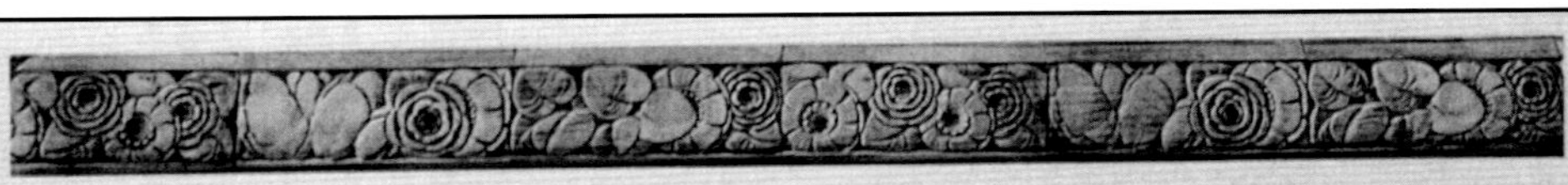

8

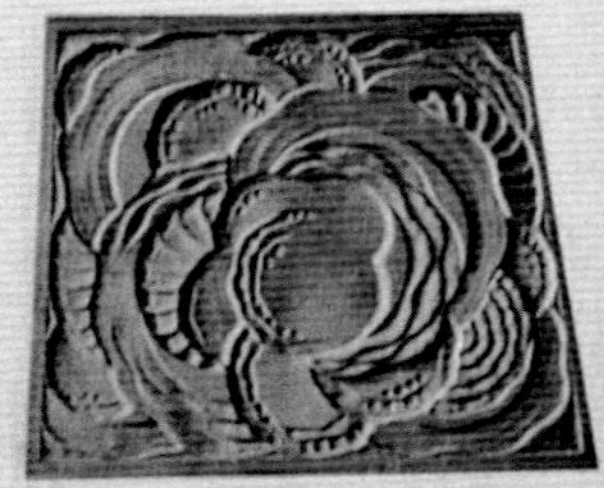

9

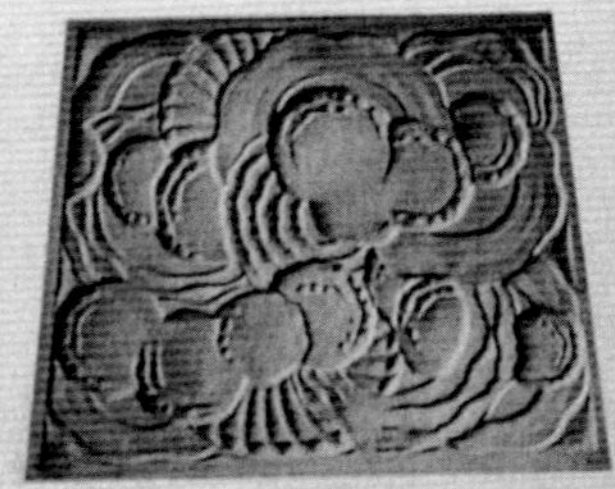

10

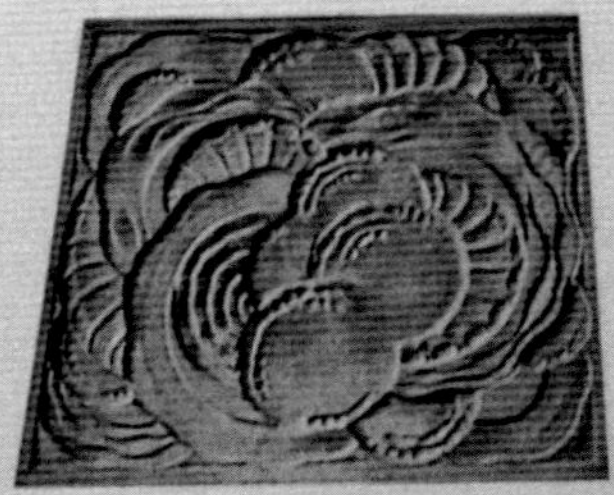

11

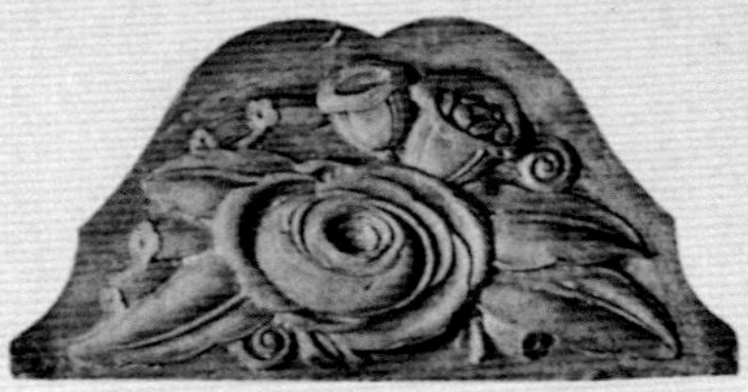

1

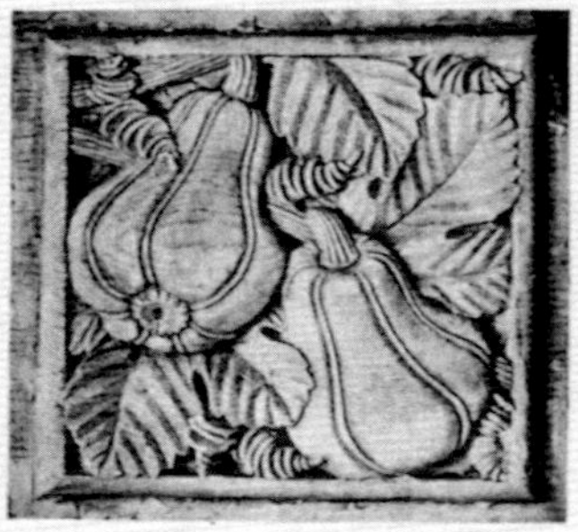

2

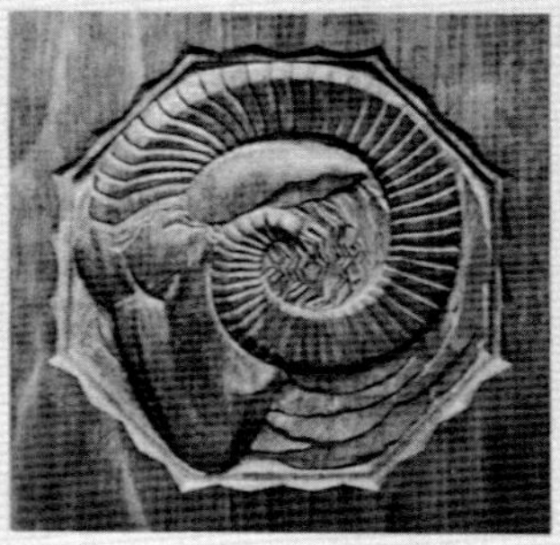

3

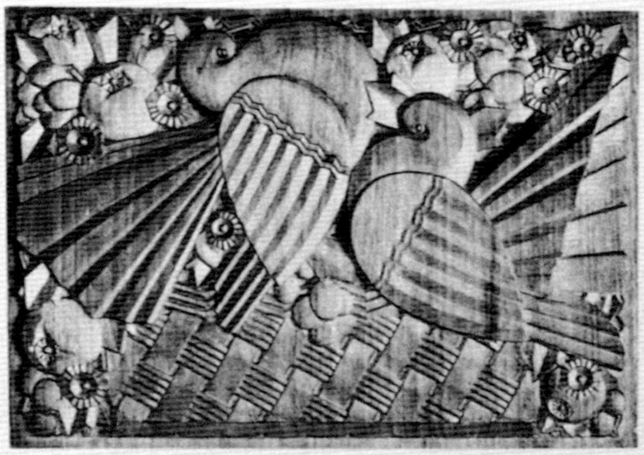

4

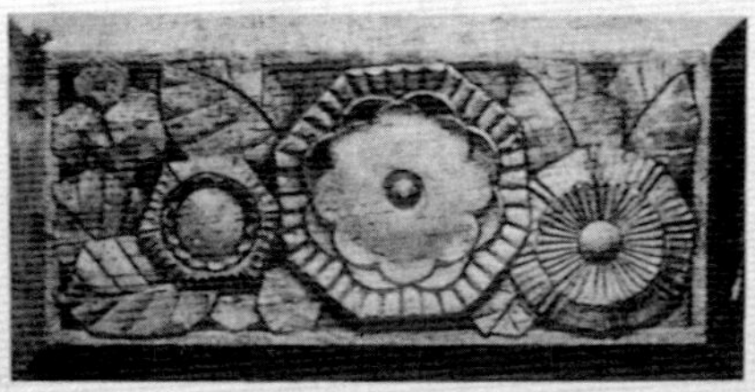

5

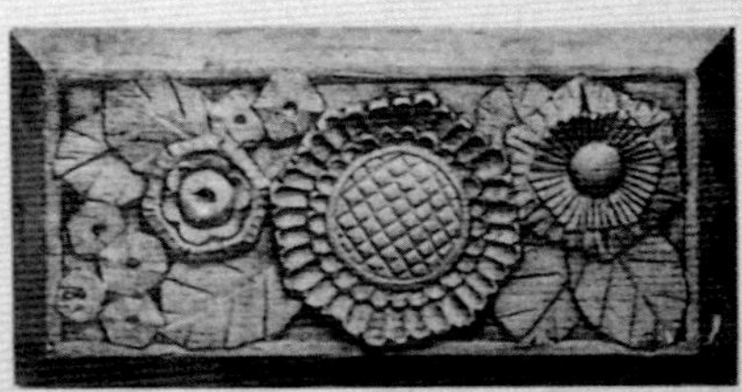

6

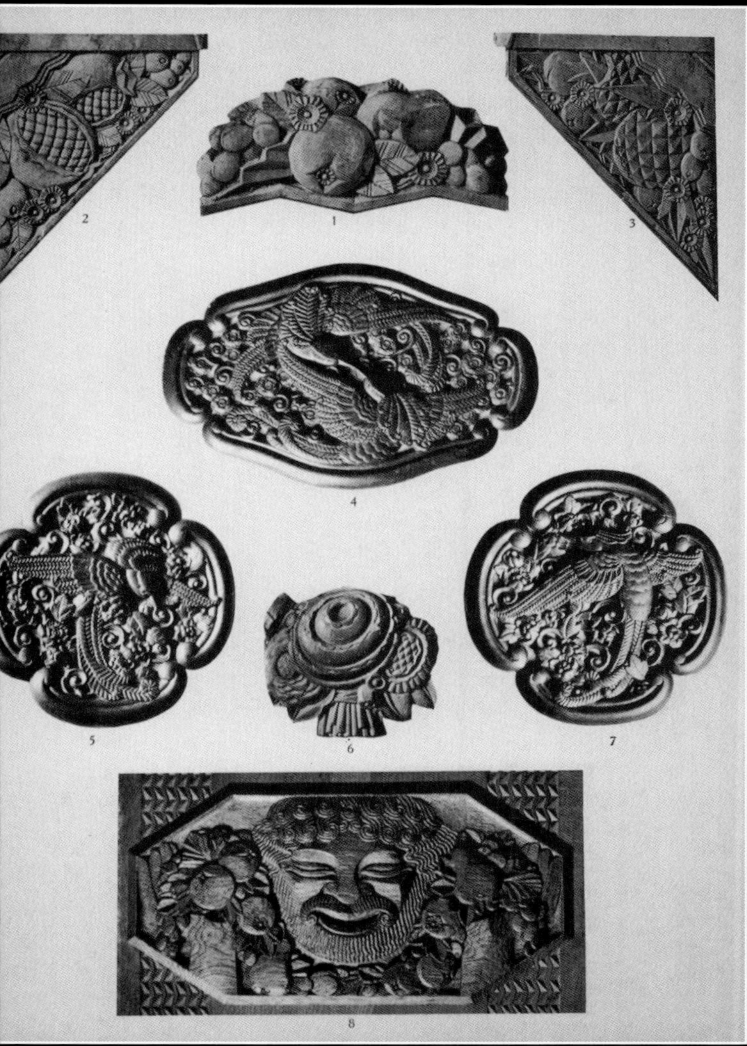

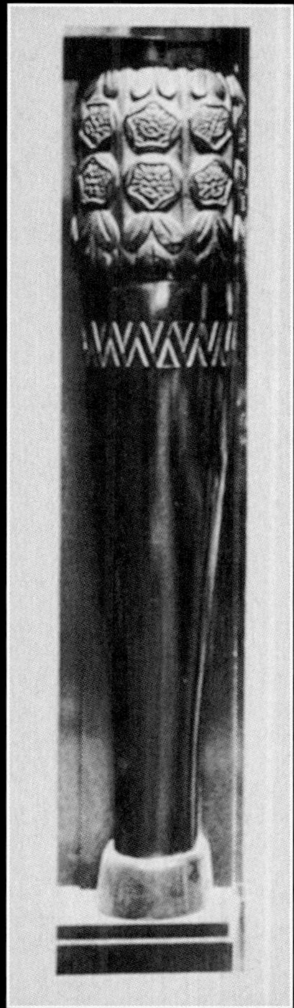

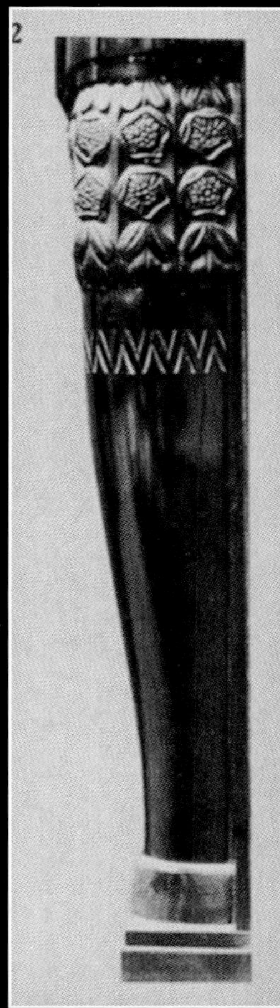

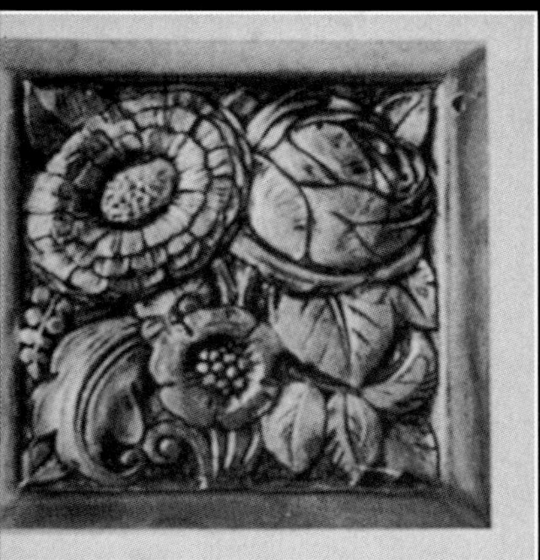

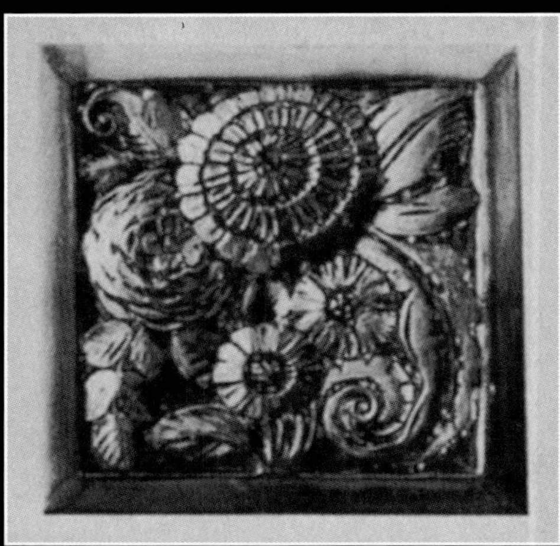

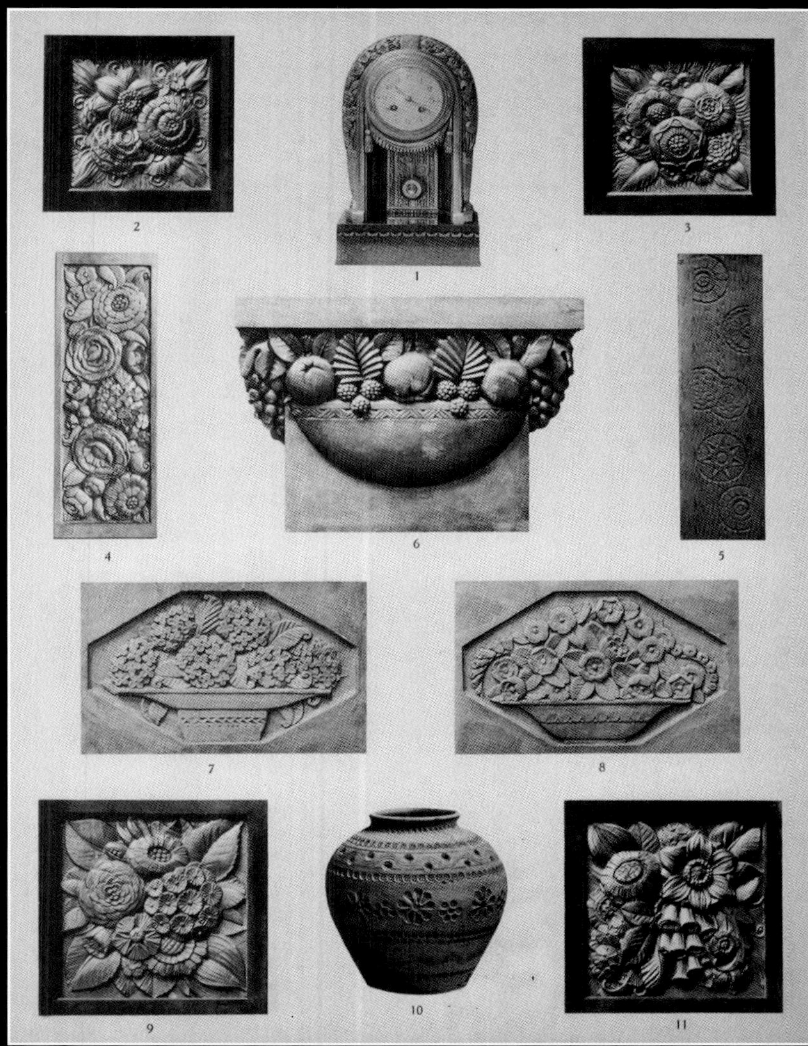

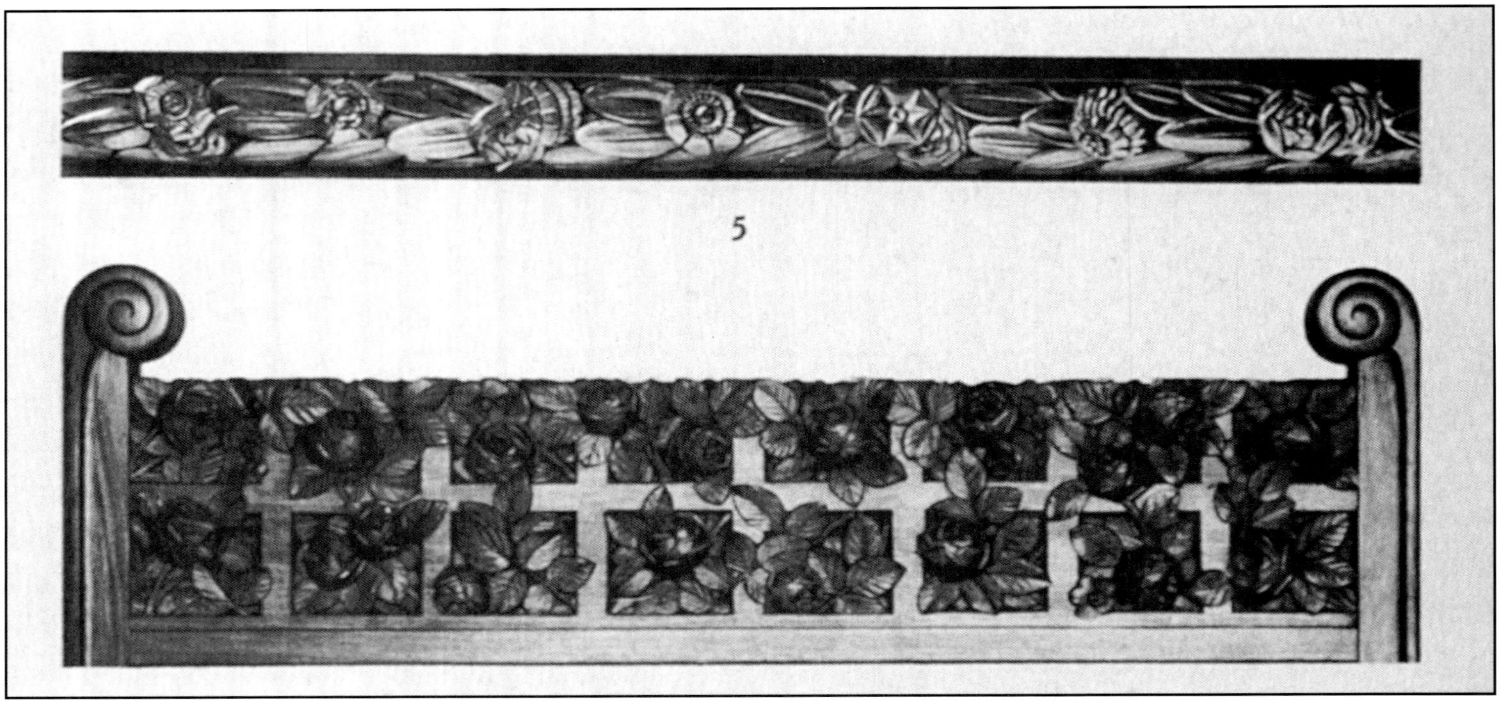
5

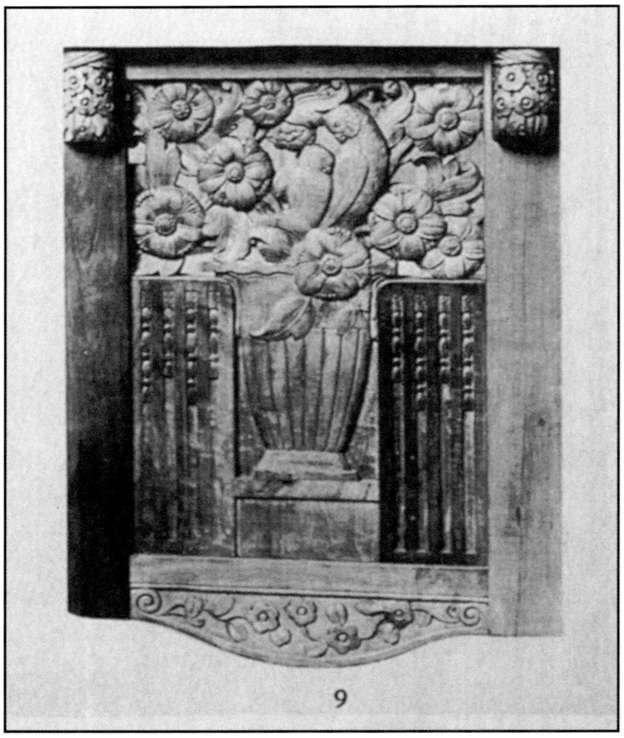
9

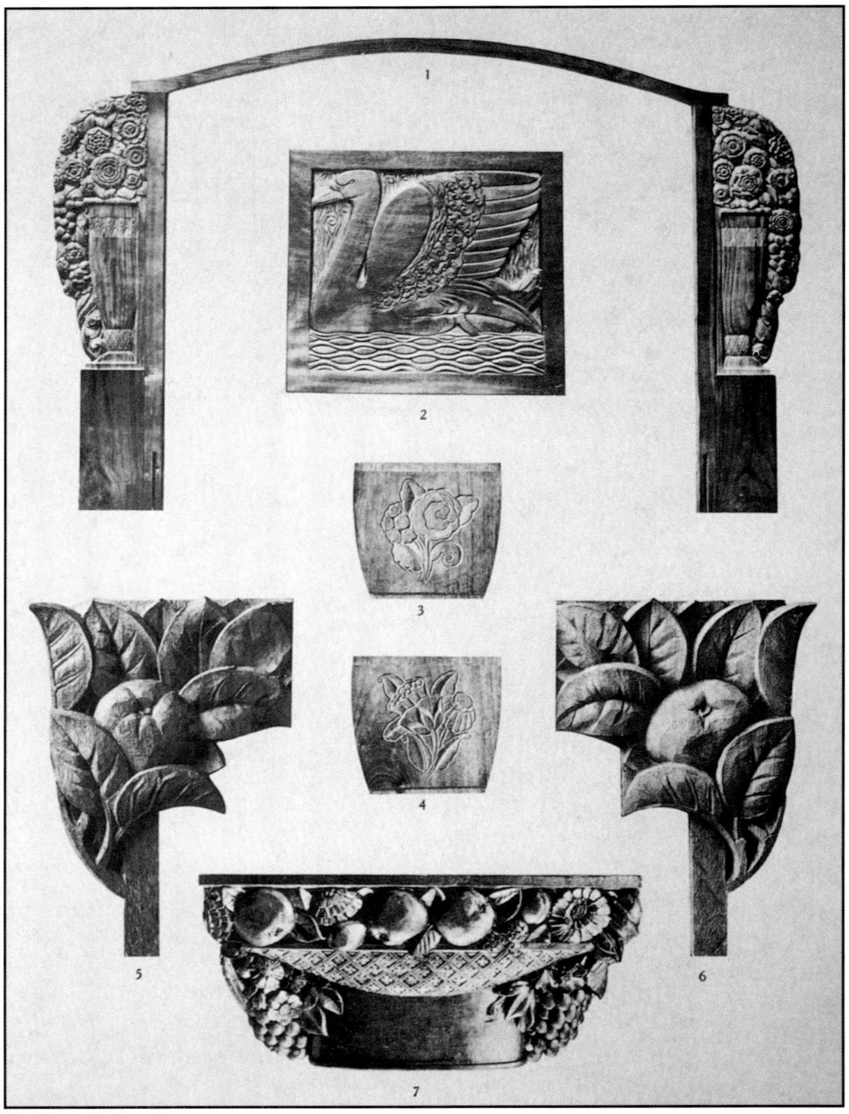
1
2
3
4
5
6
7

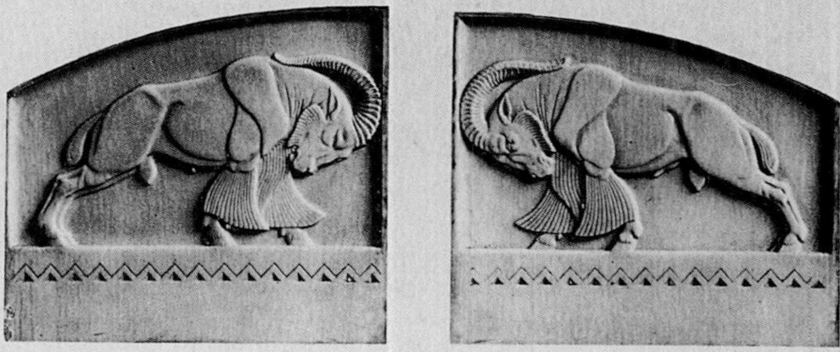

1

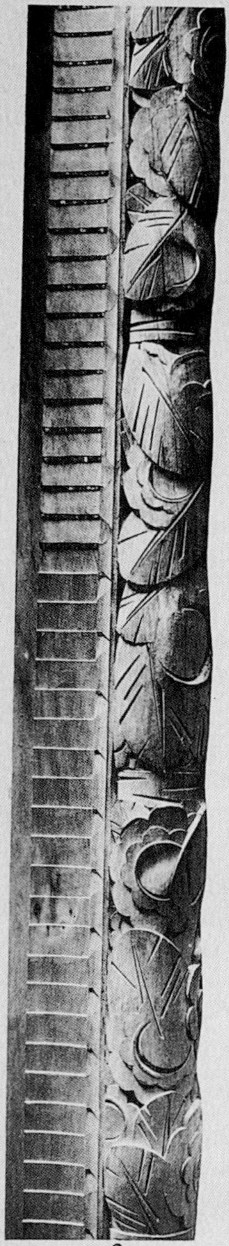

2

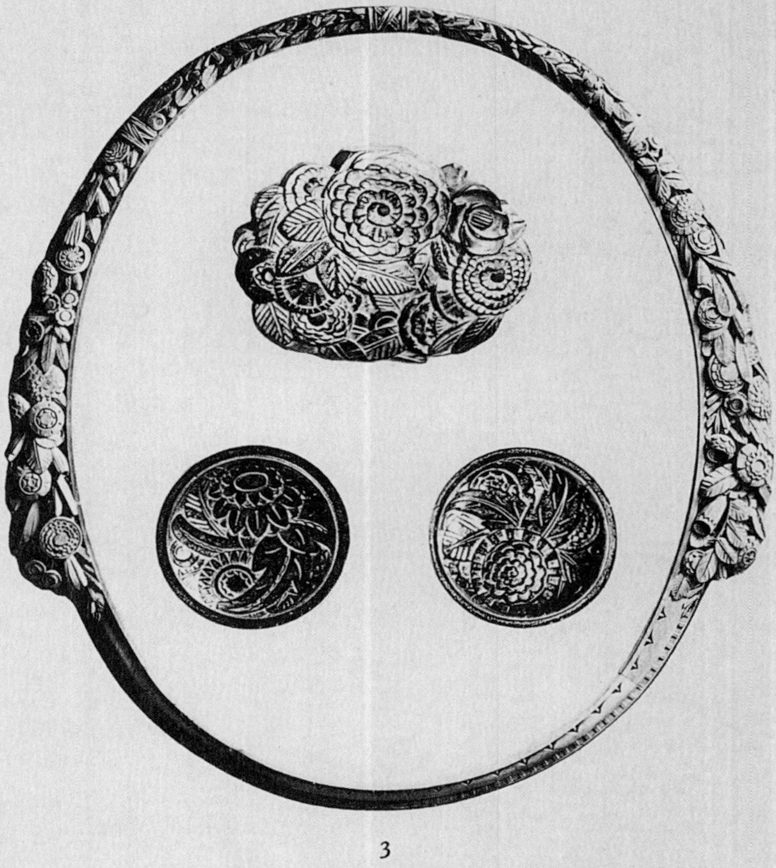

3

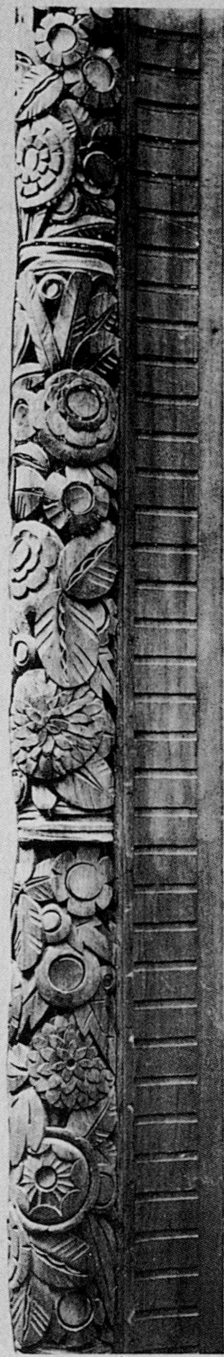

4

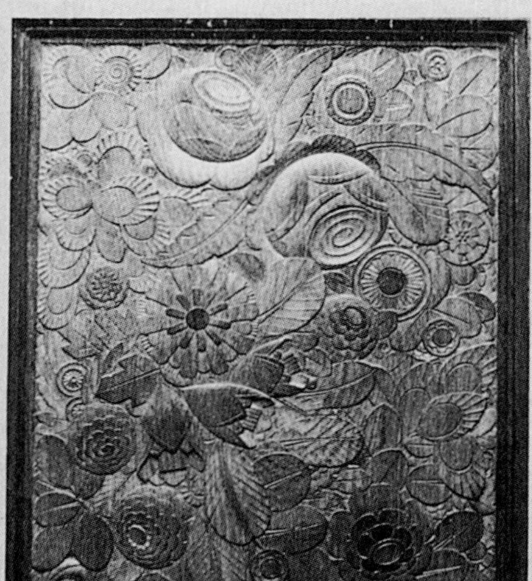

5

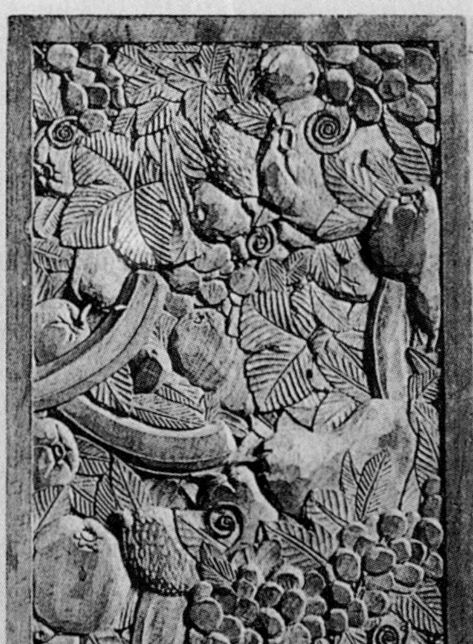

6

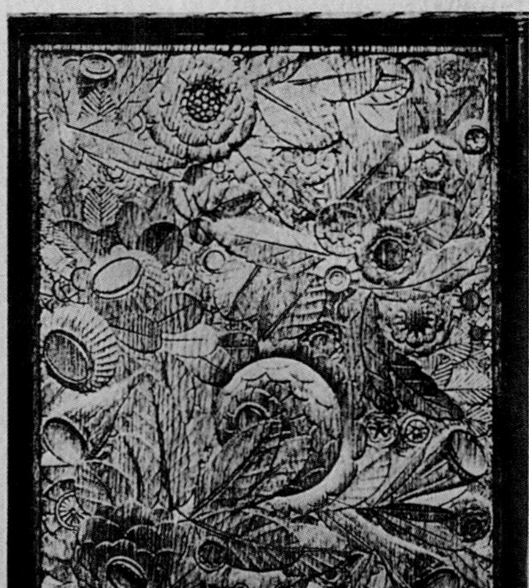

7

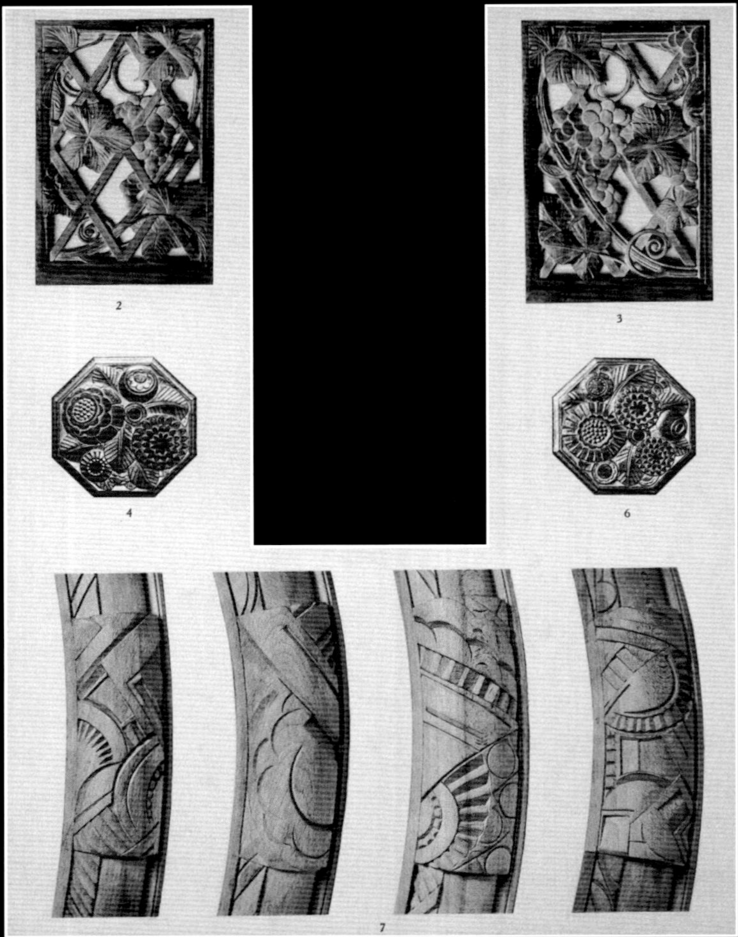
2
3
4
6
7

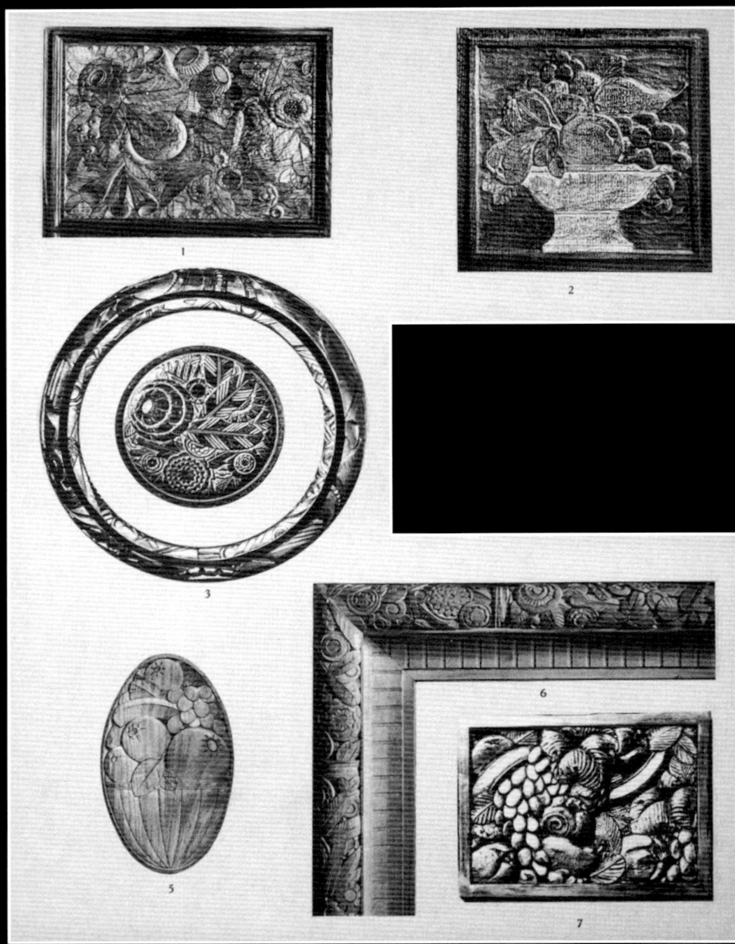
1
2
3
6
5
7

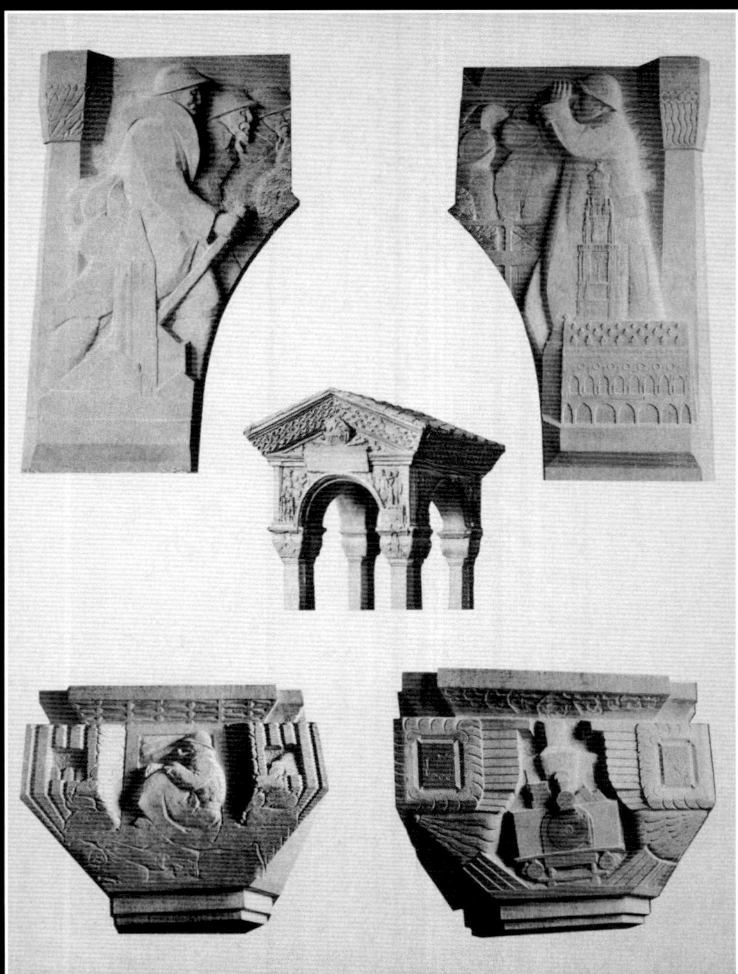

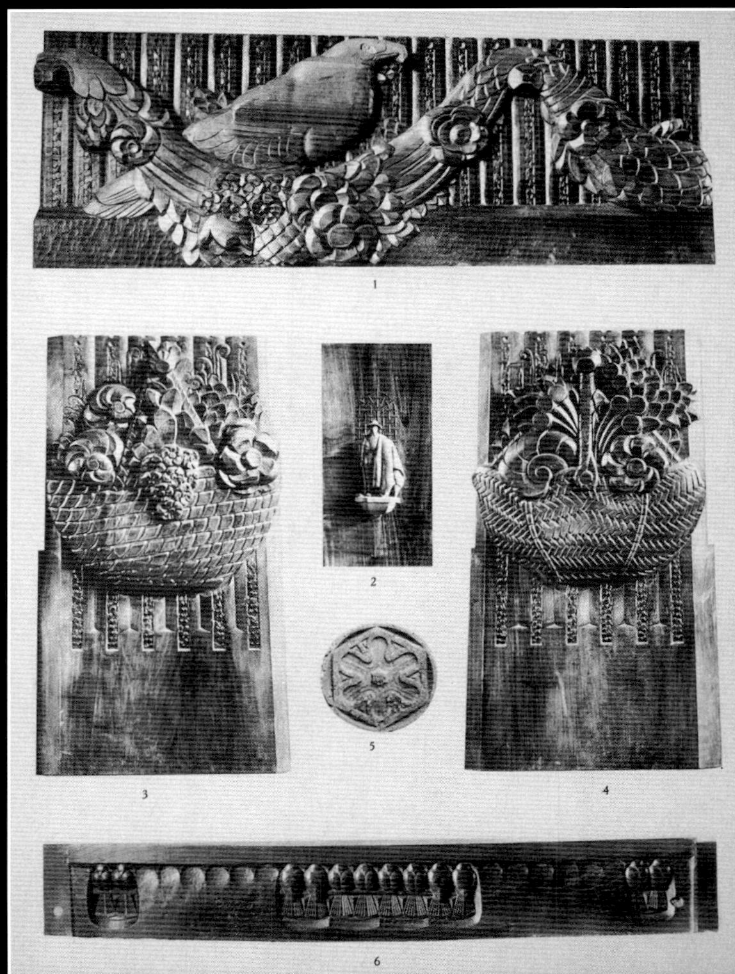
1
2
3
5
4
6

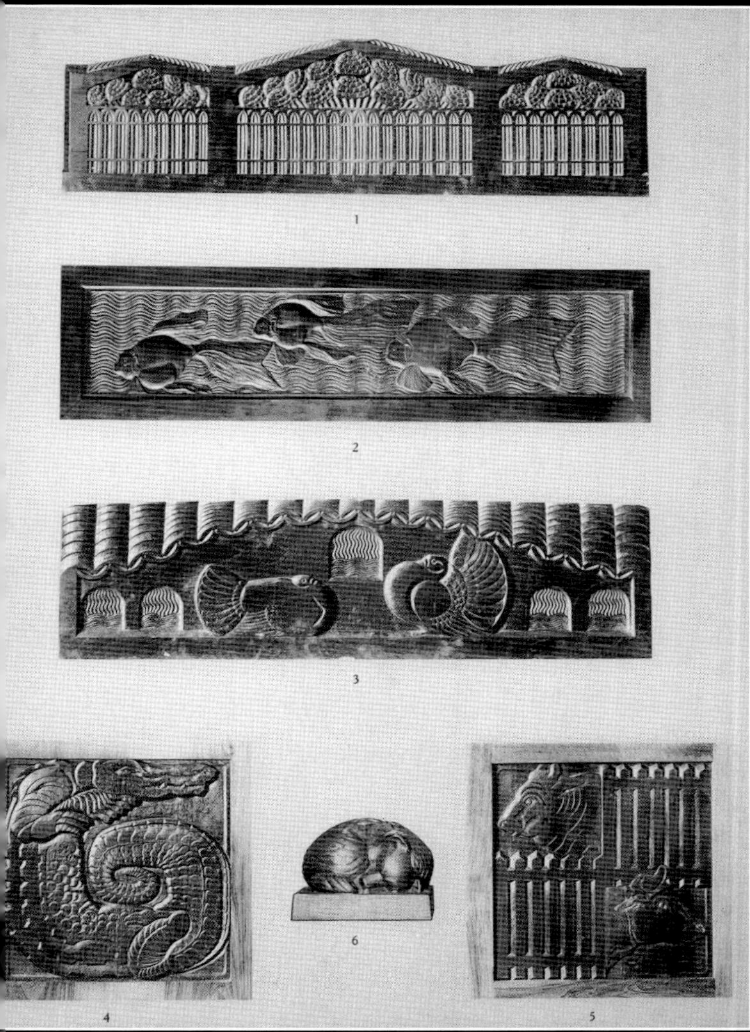
1
2
3
4
6
5

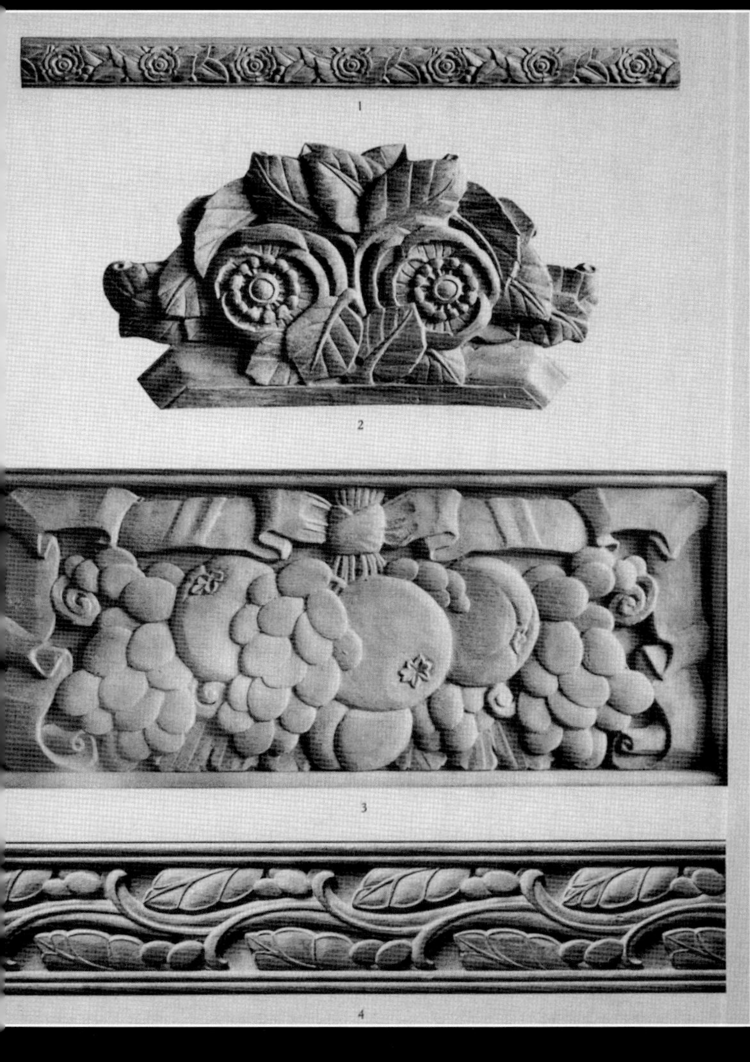
1
2
3
4

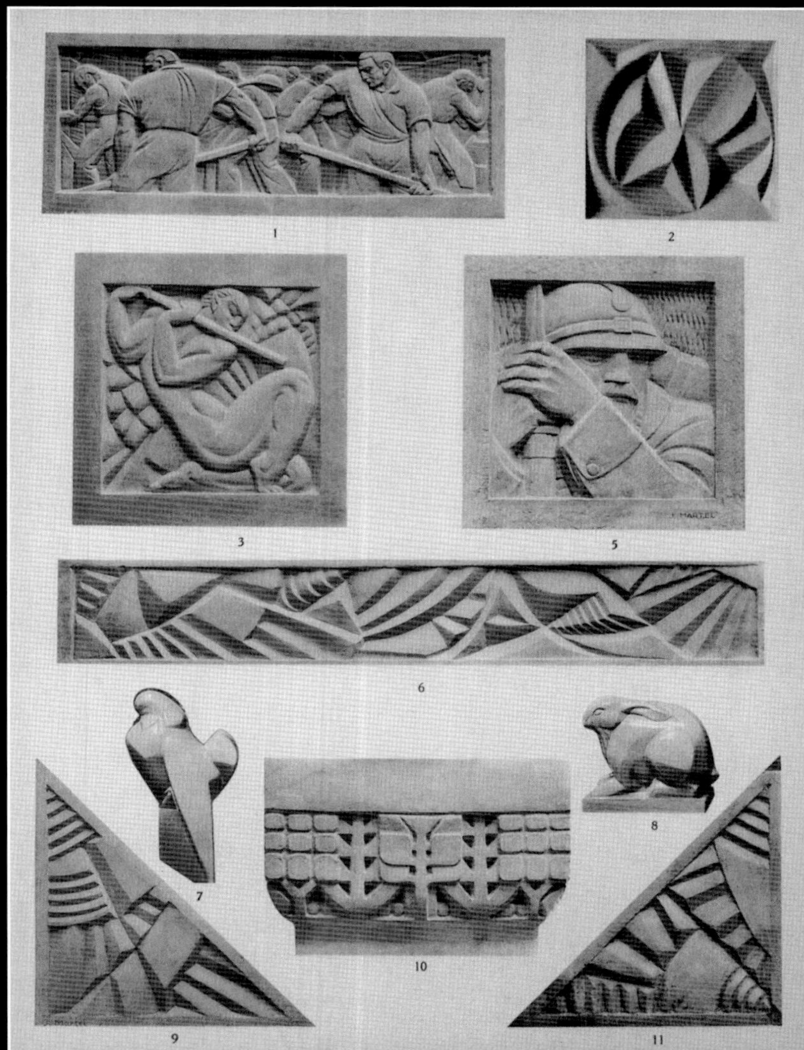
1
2
3
5
6
7
8
10
9
11

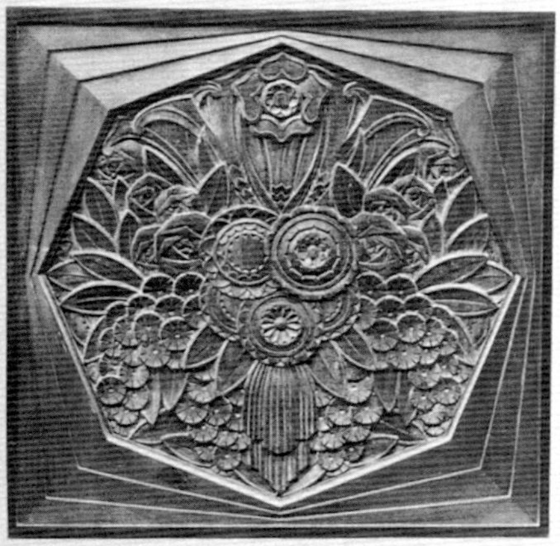

1

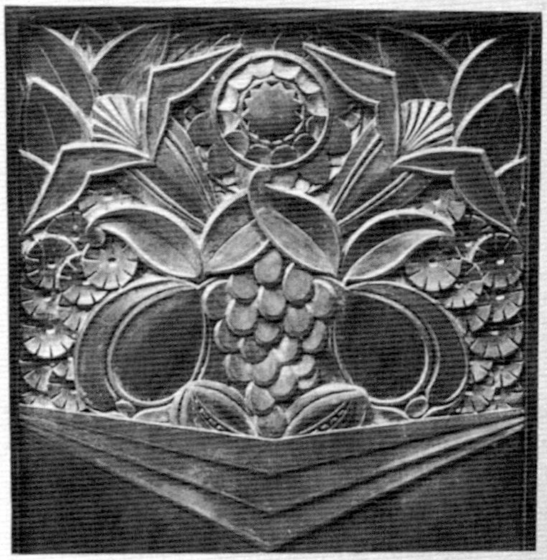

3

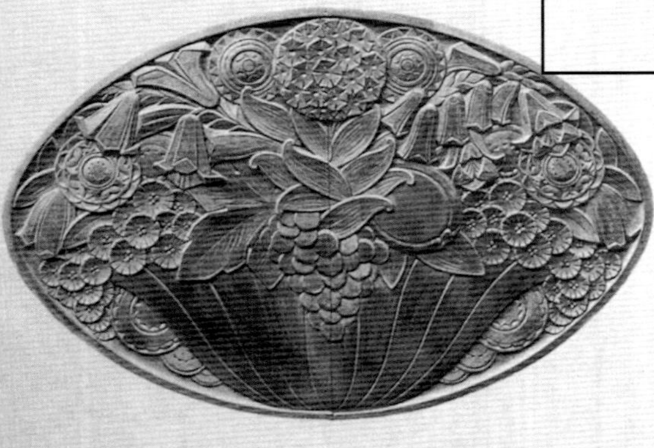

4

2

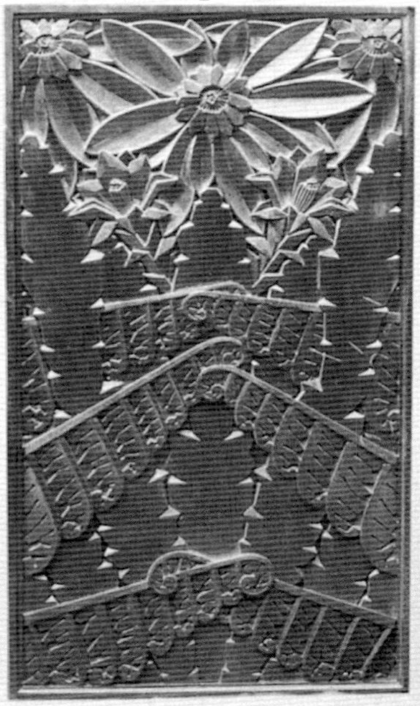

5

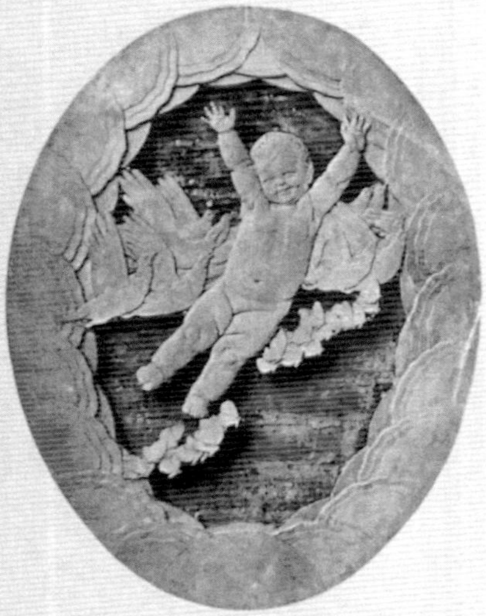

1

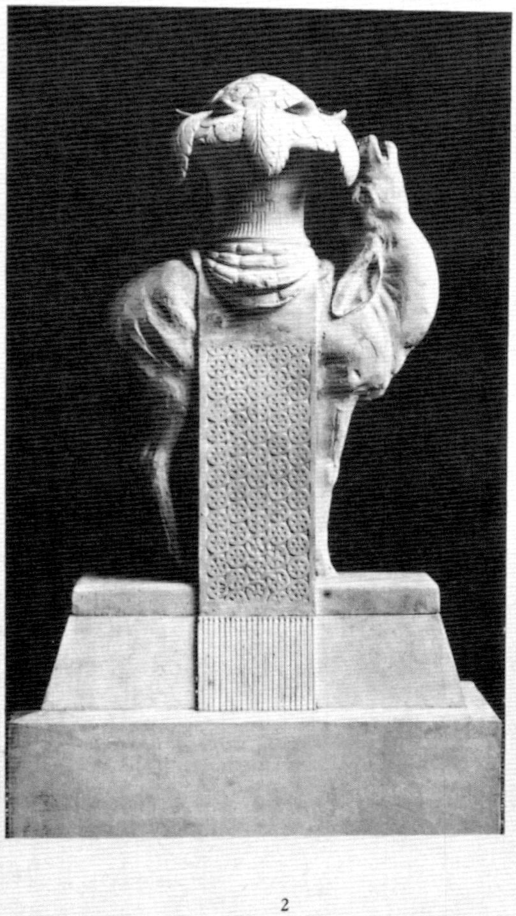

2

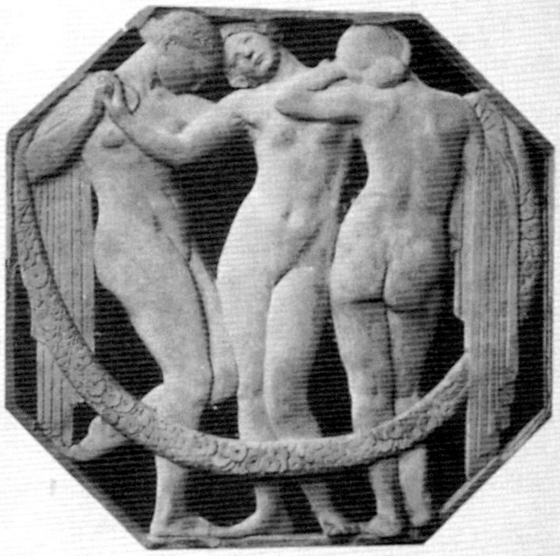

3

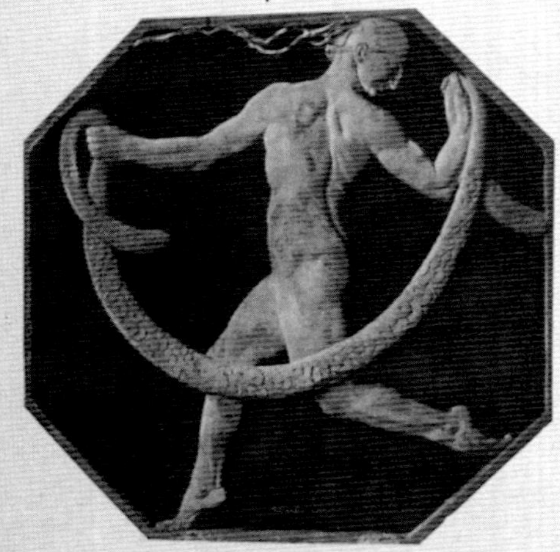

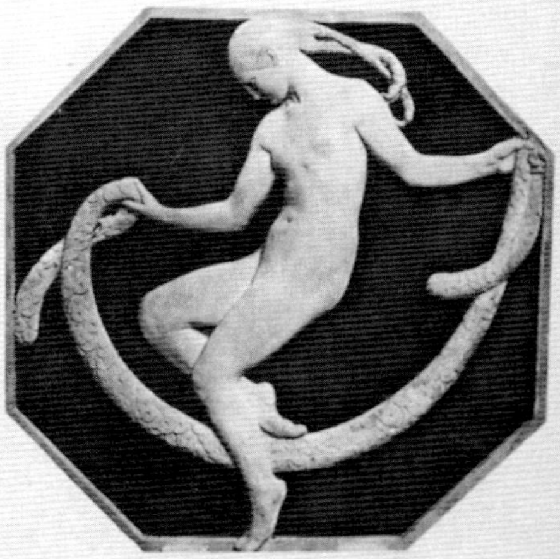

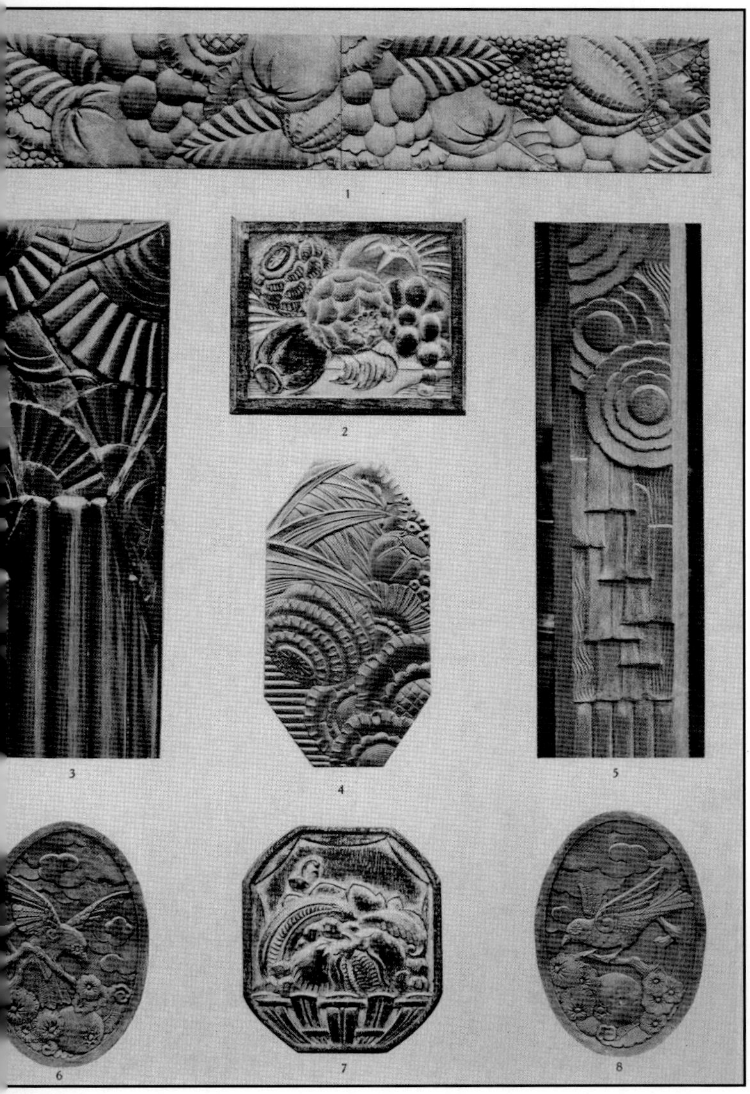

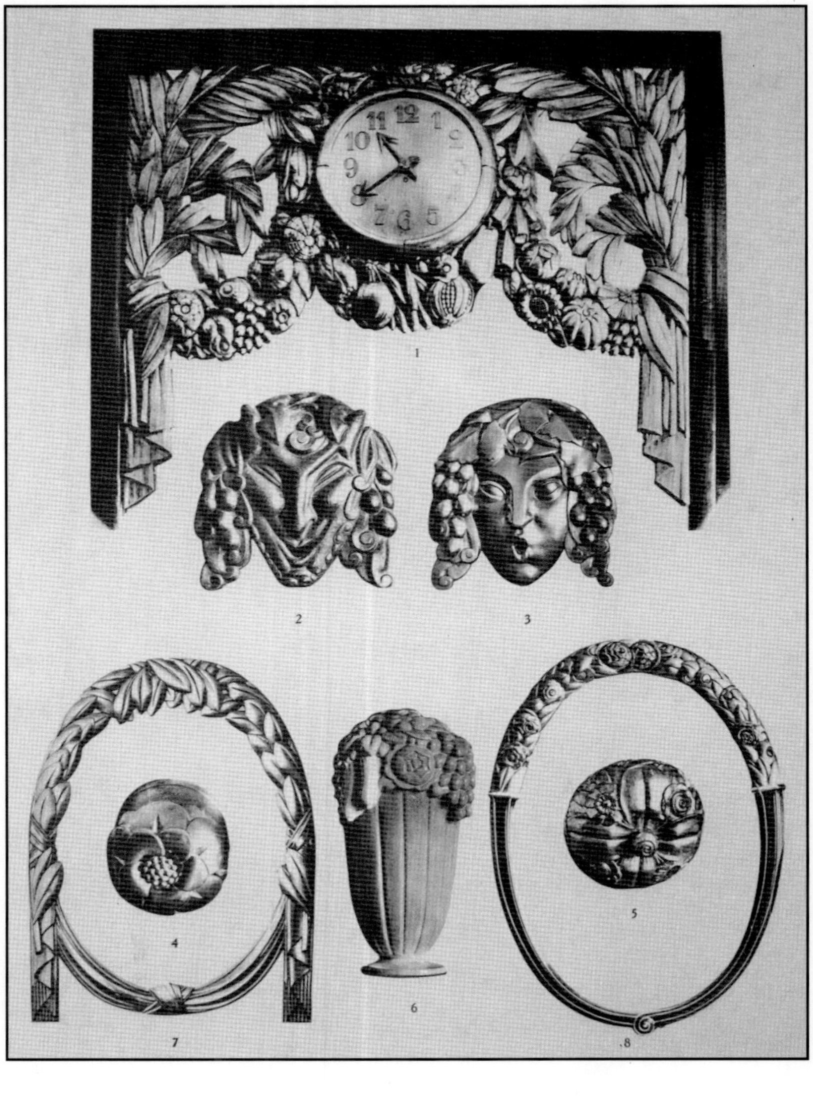

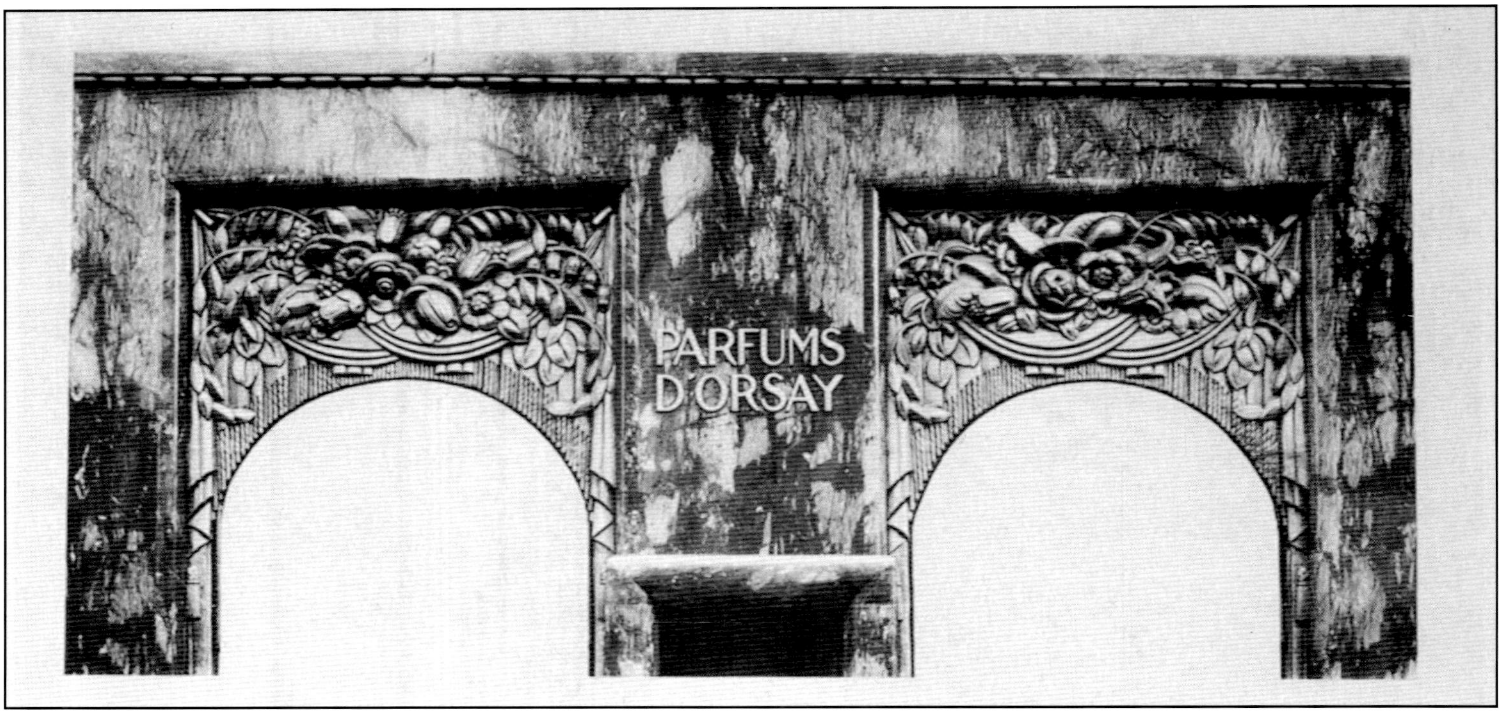
PARFUMS
D'ORSAY

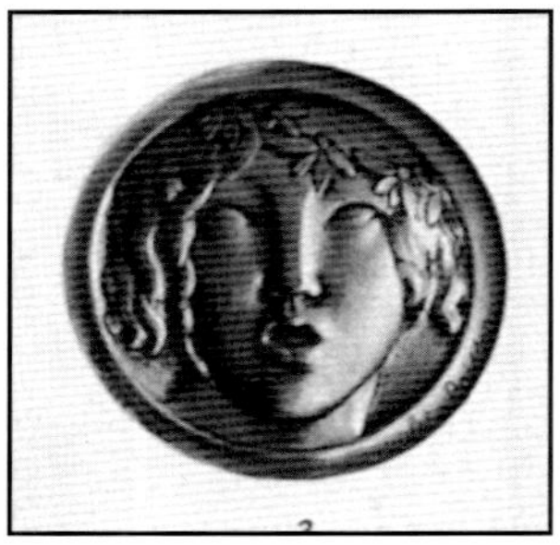

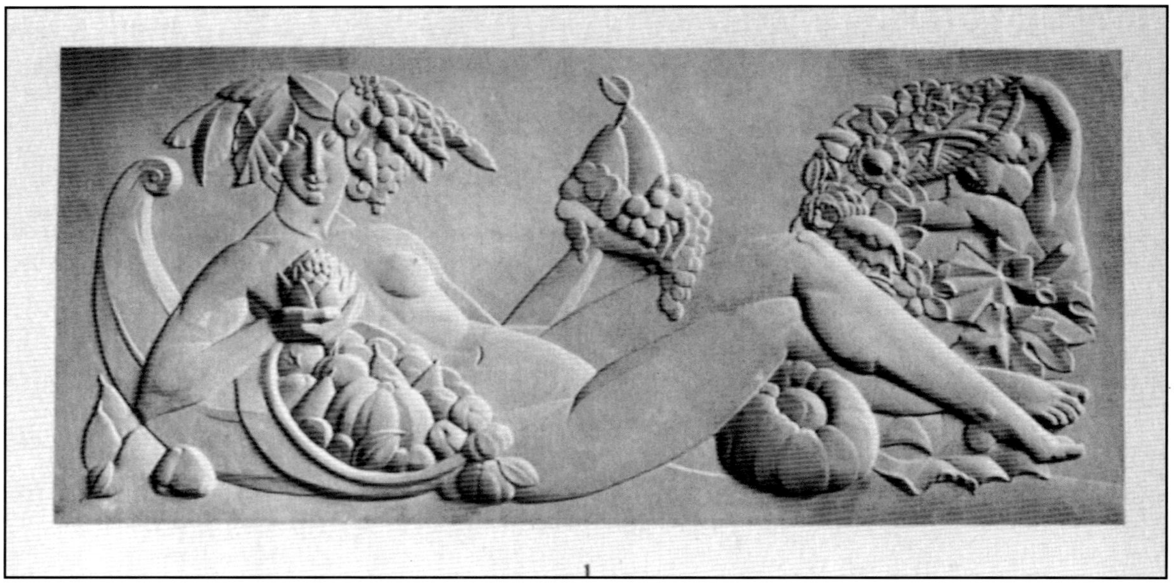

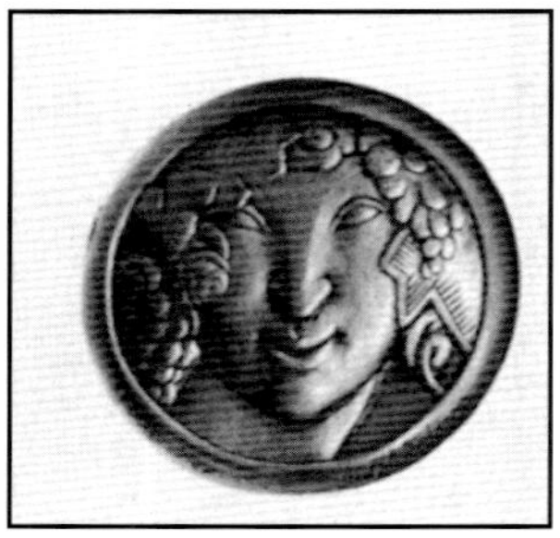

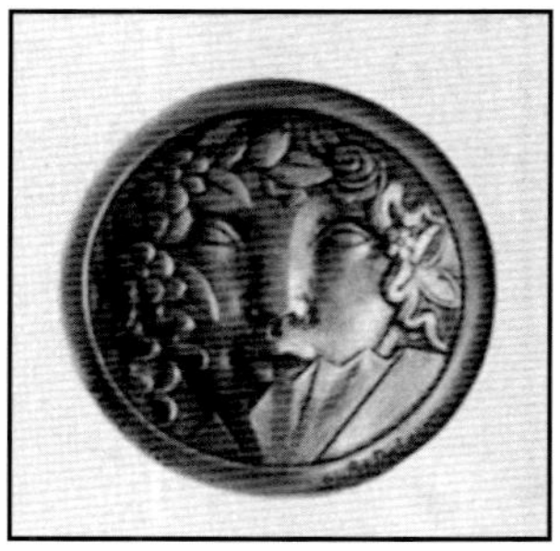

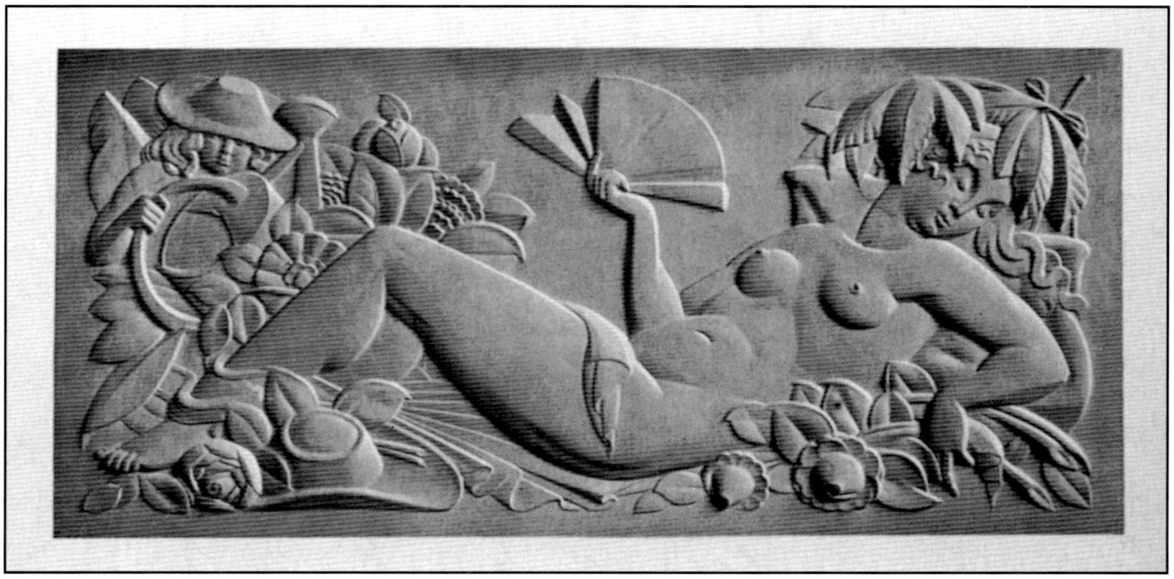

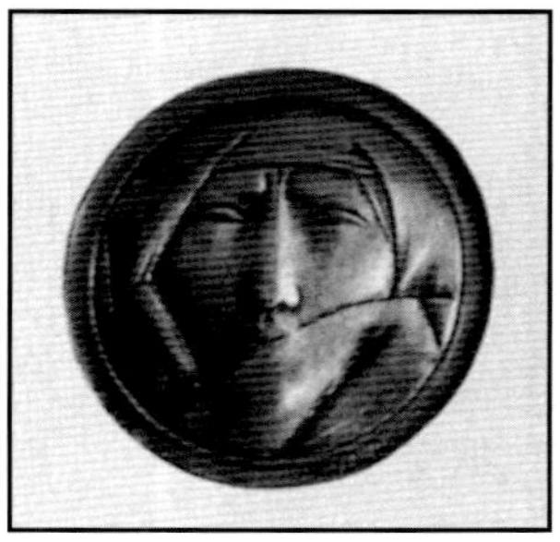

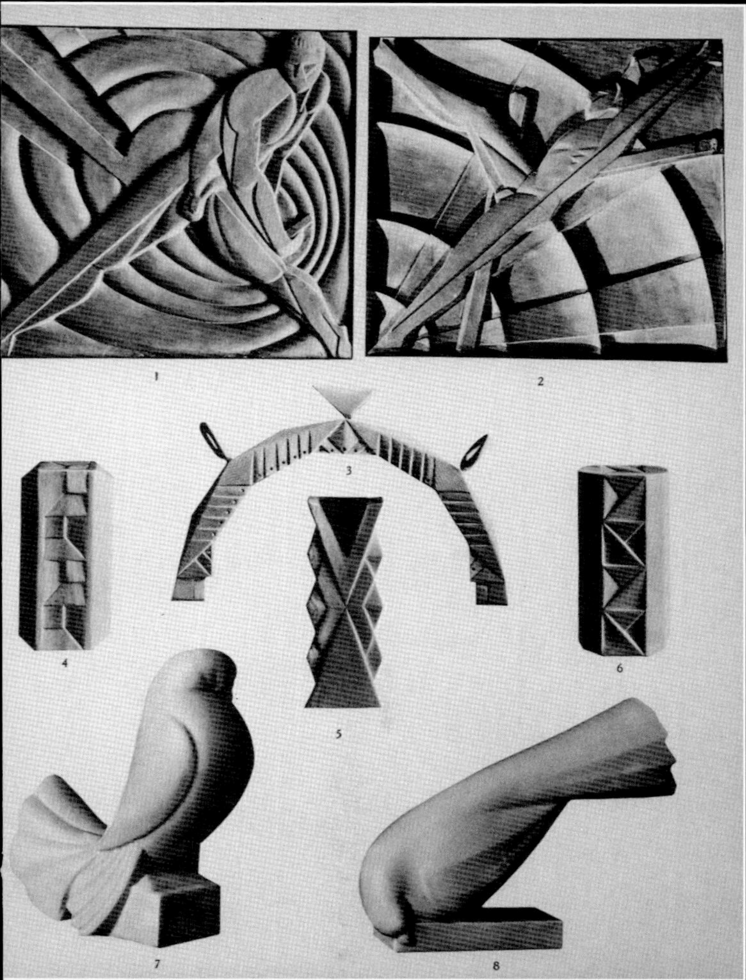

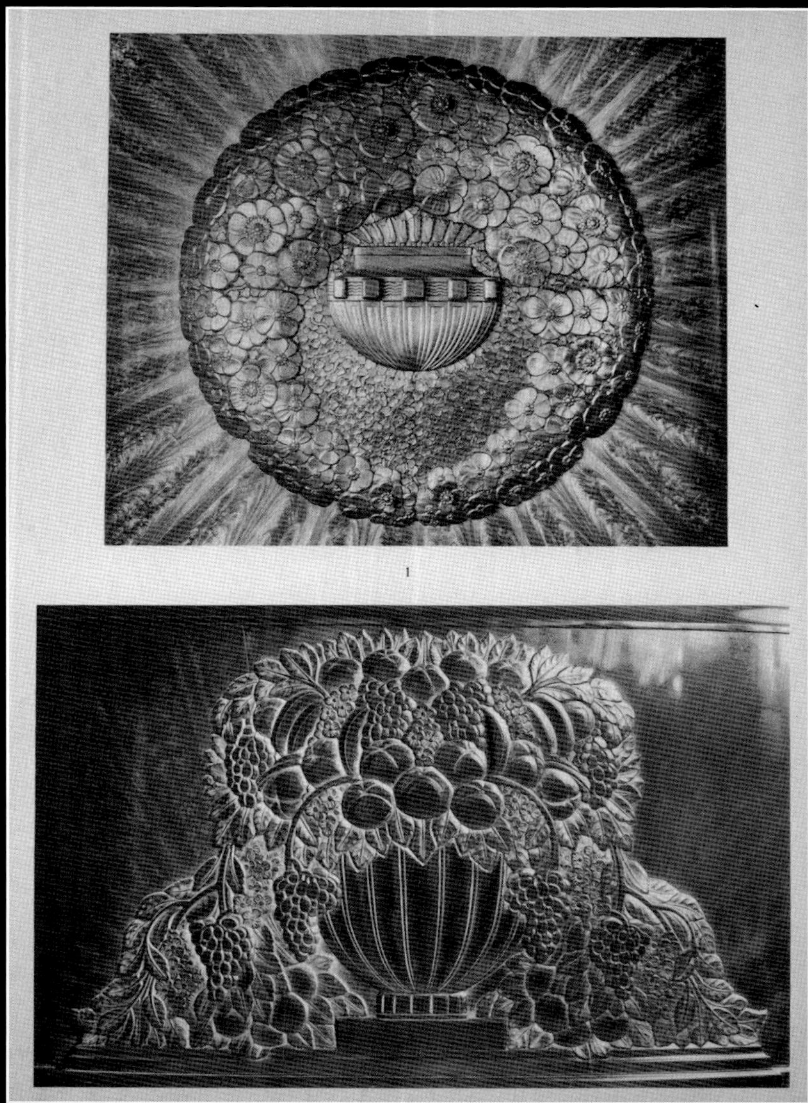

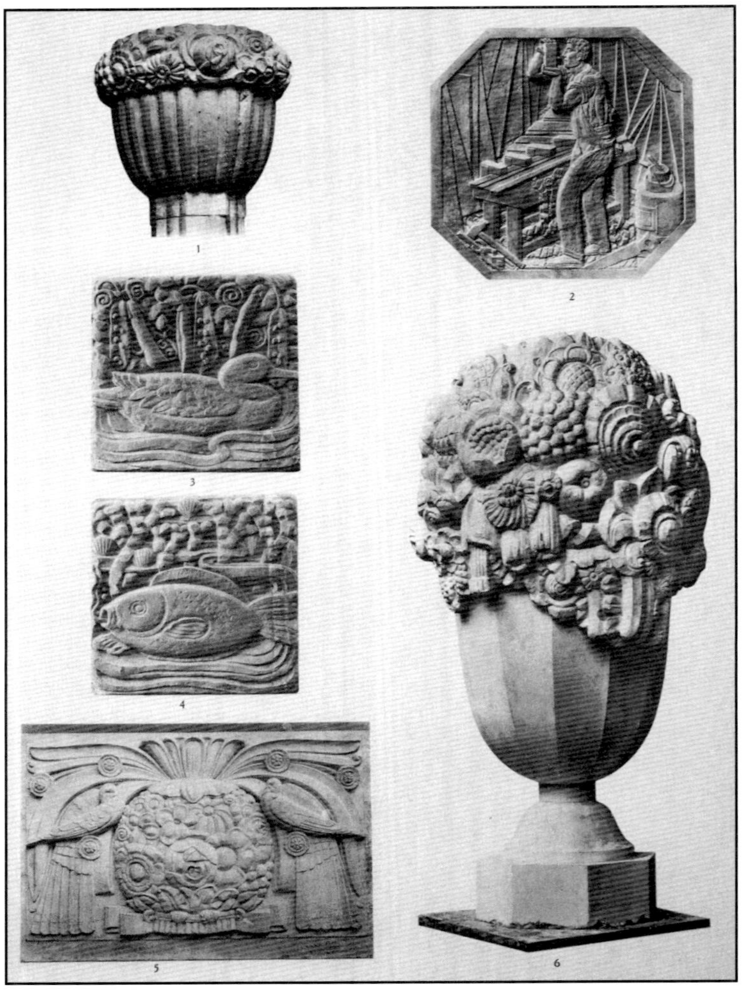

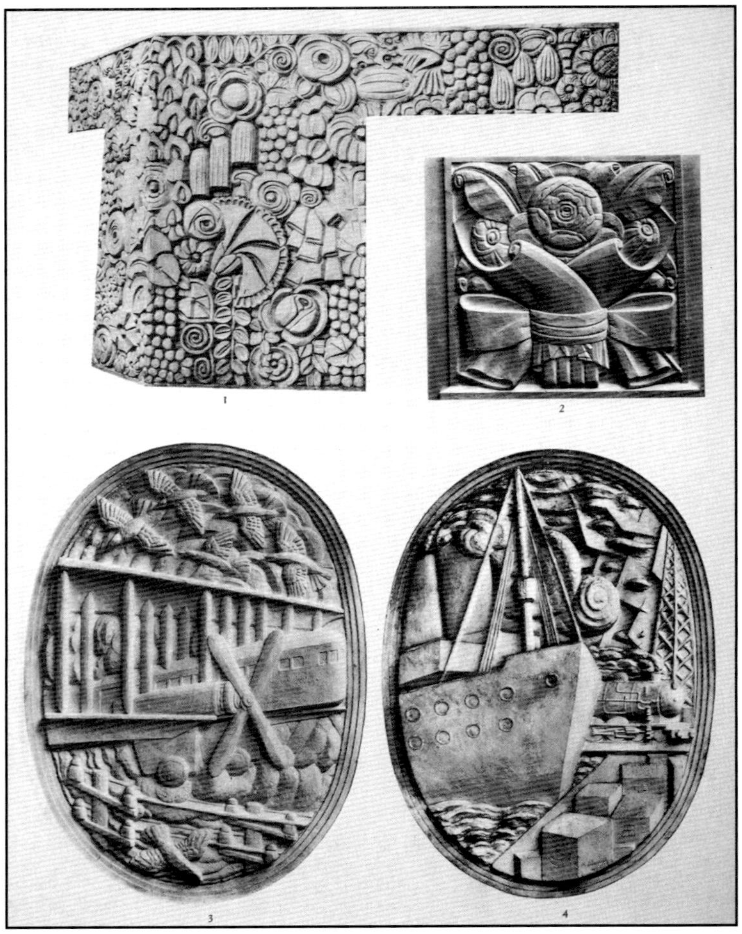

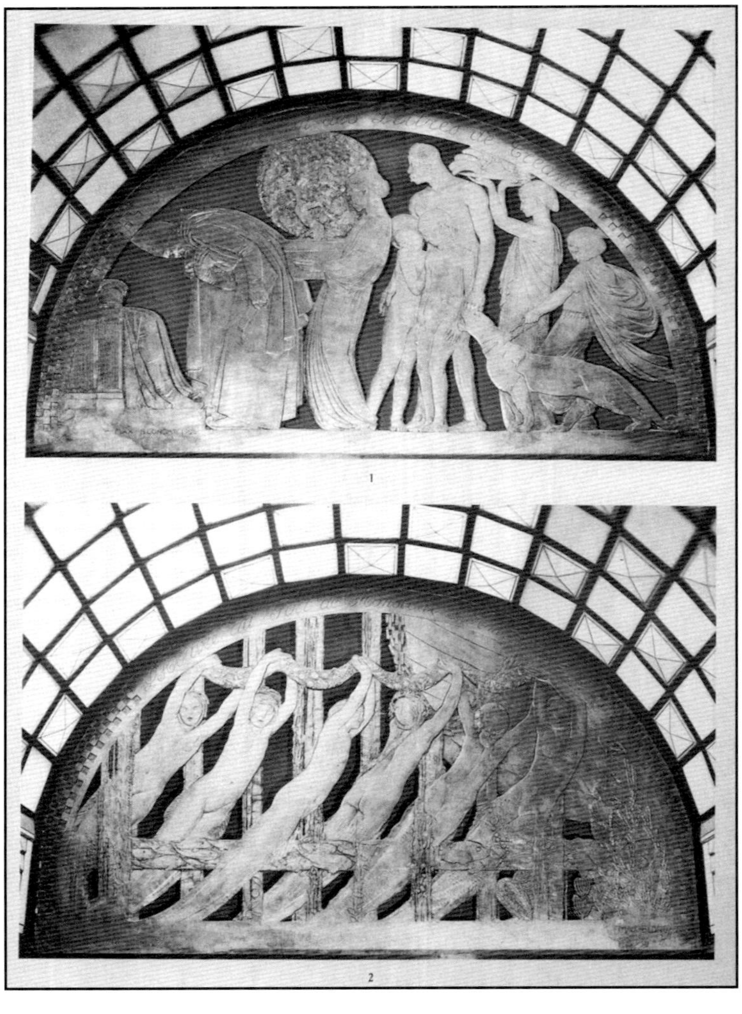

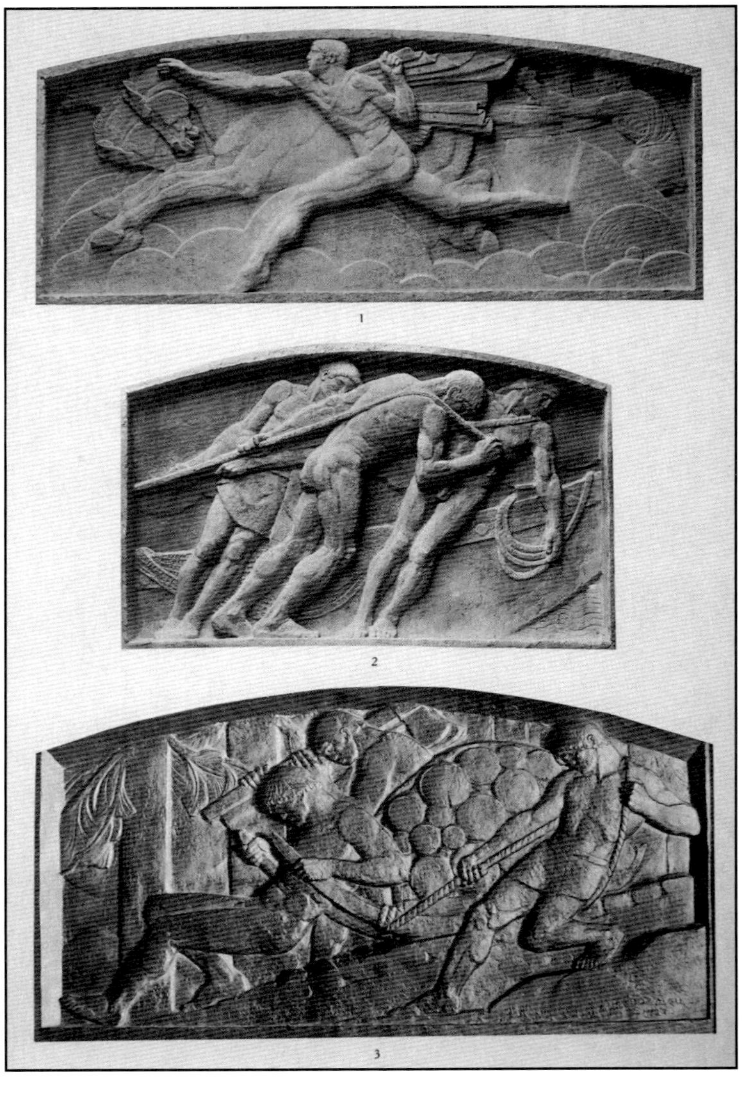

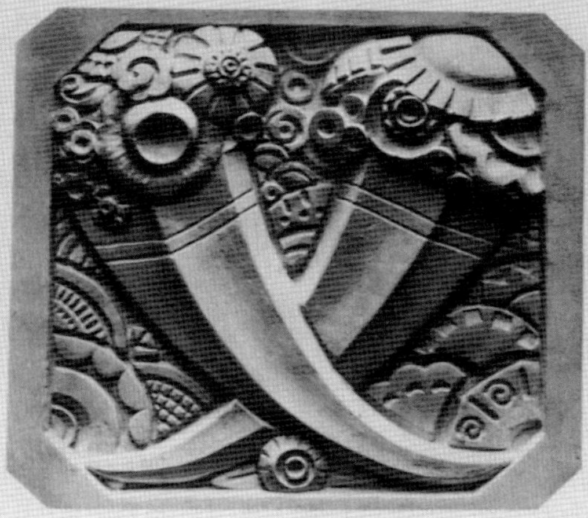

1

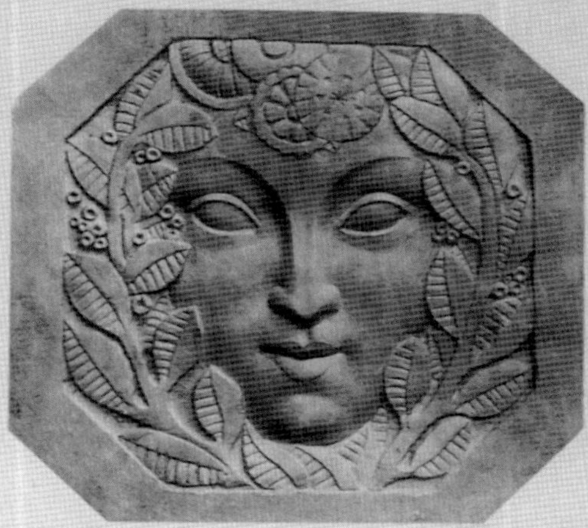

2

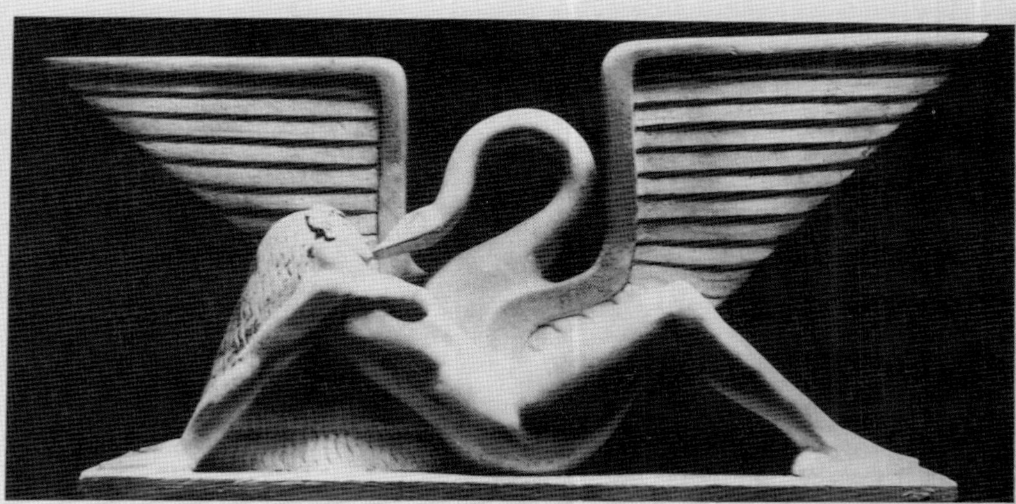

3

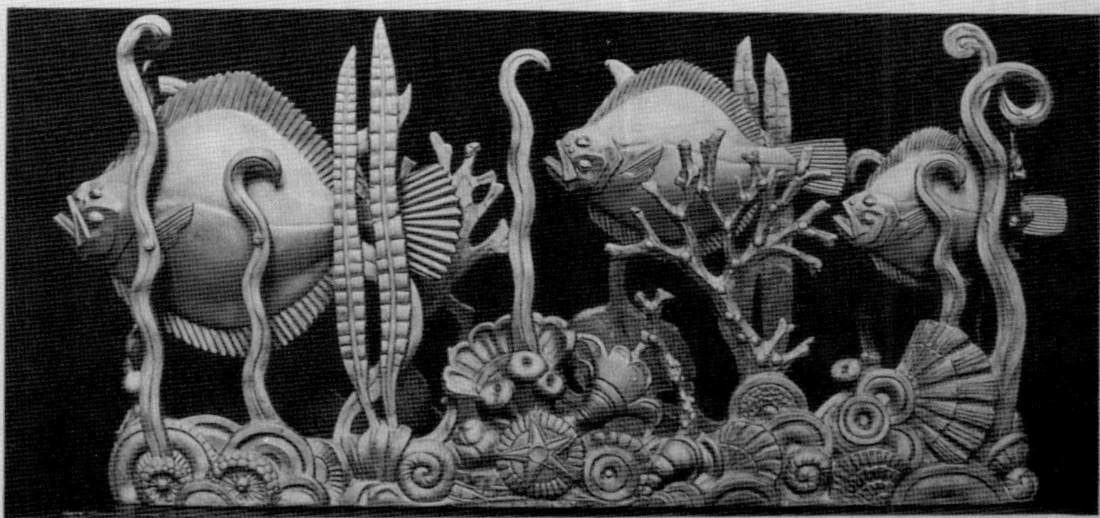

4

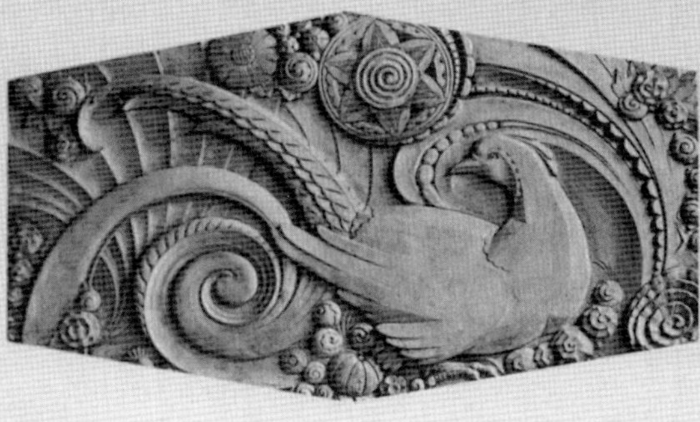

1

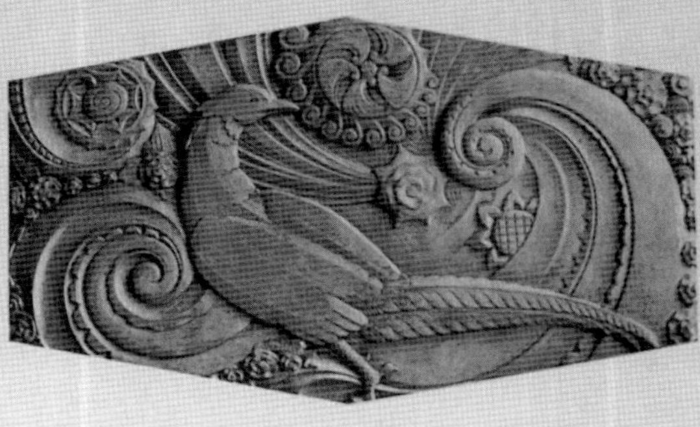

2

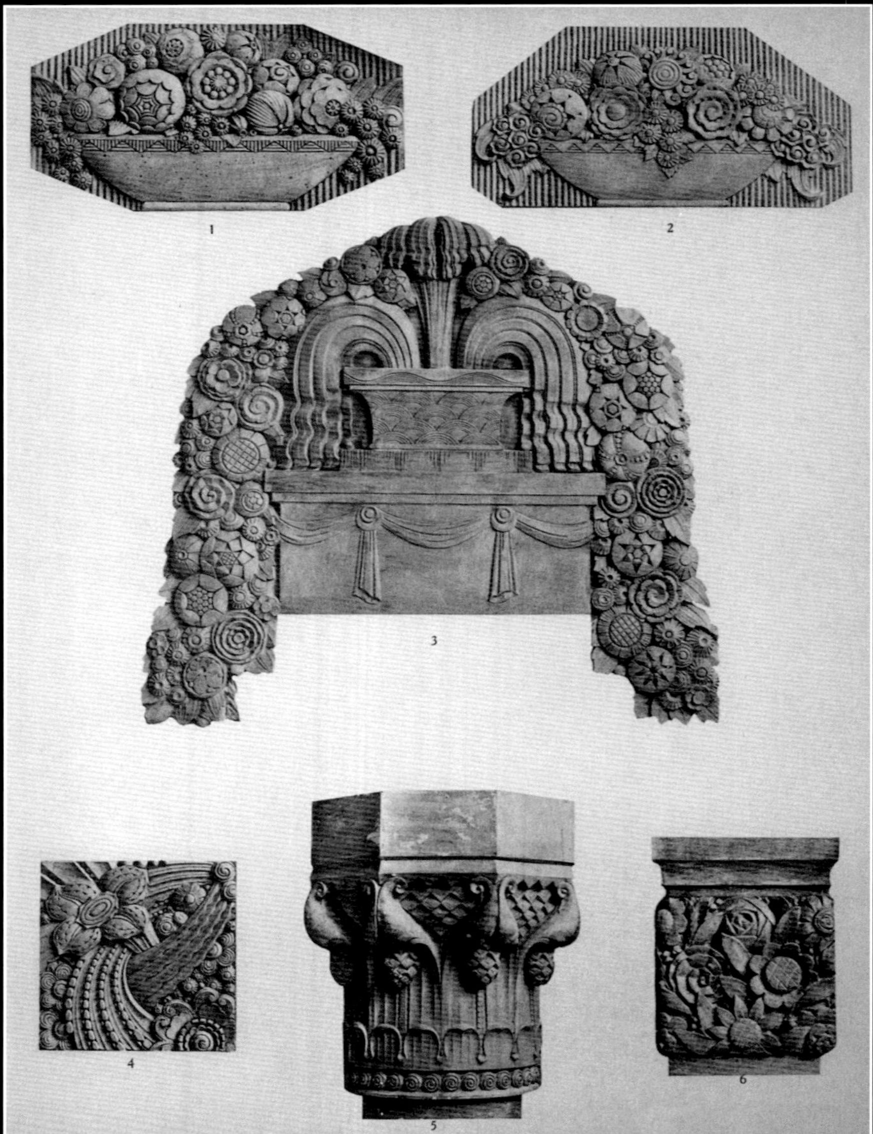
1
2
3
4
5
6

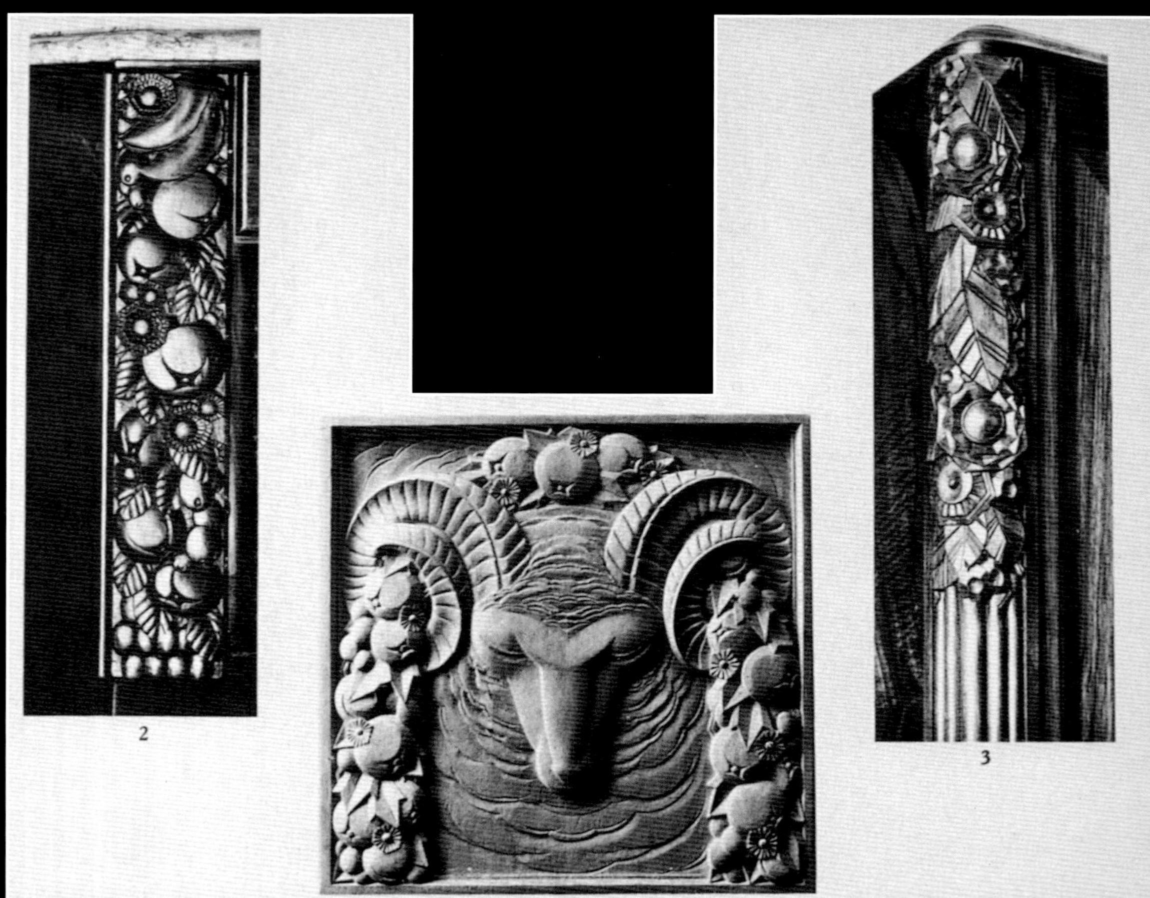
2
3
4

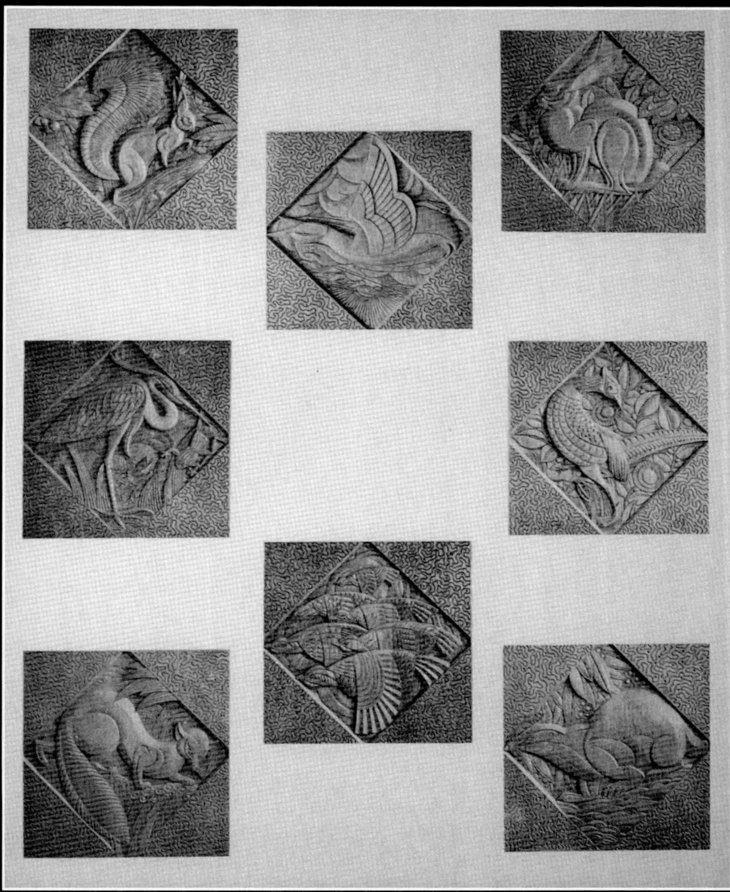

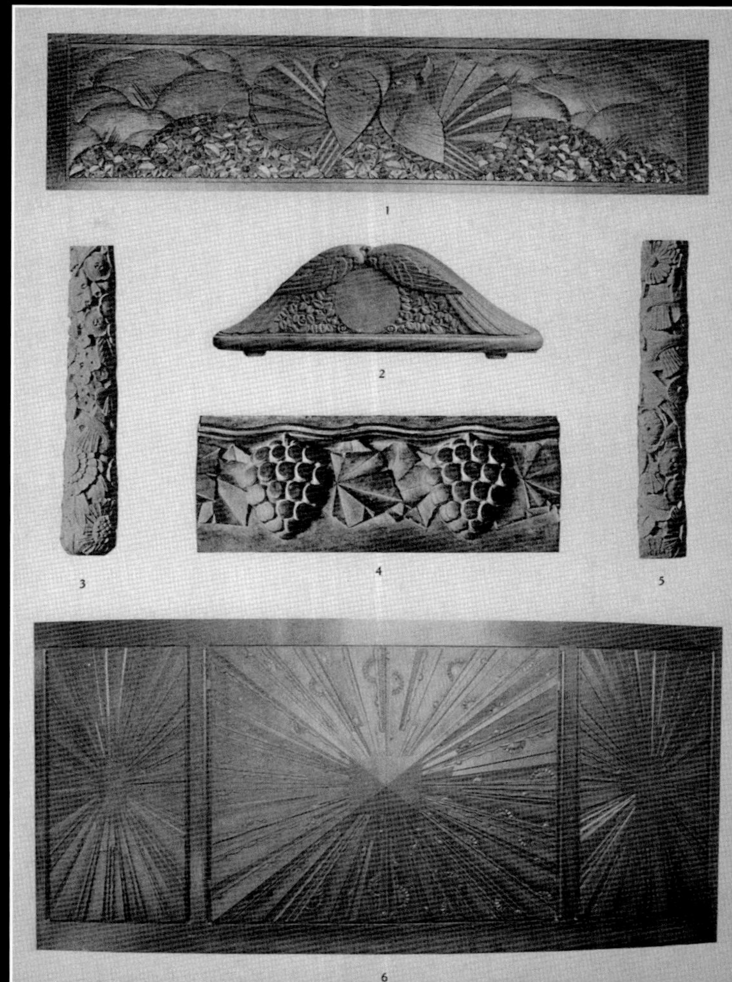
1
2
3
4
5
6

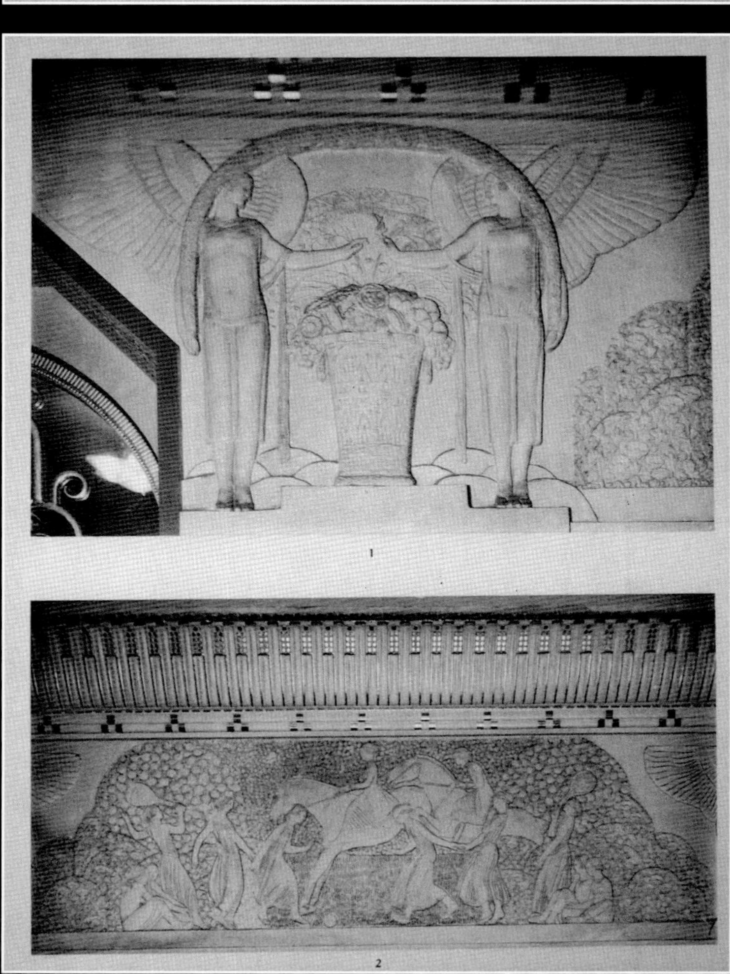
1
2

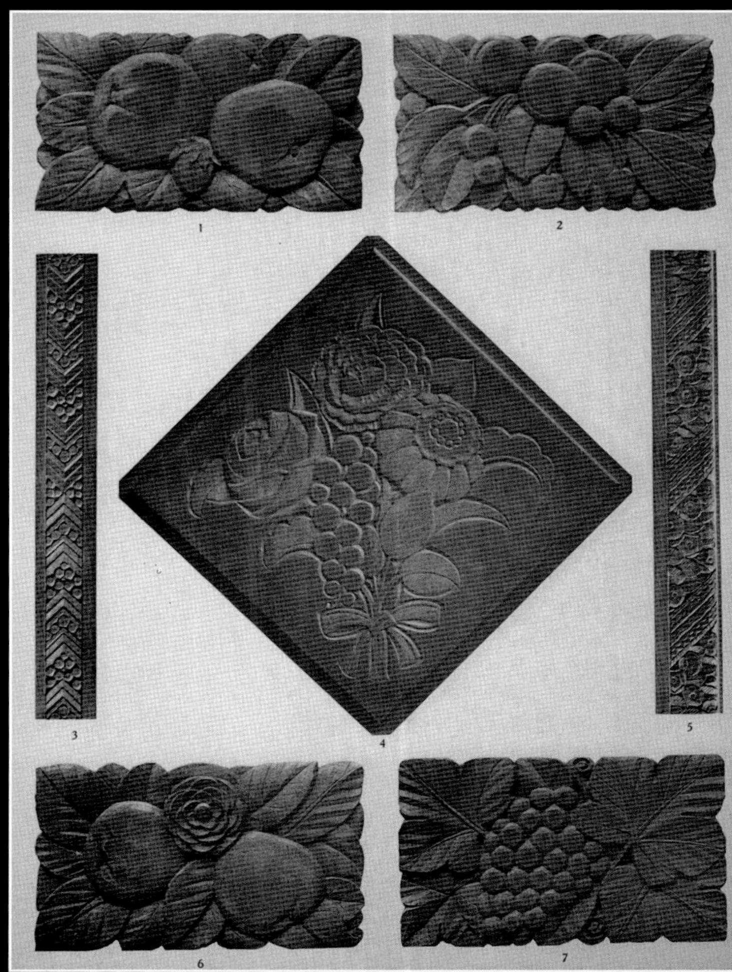
1
2
3
4
5
6
7

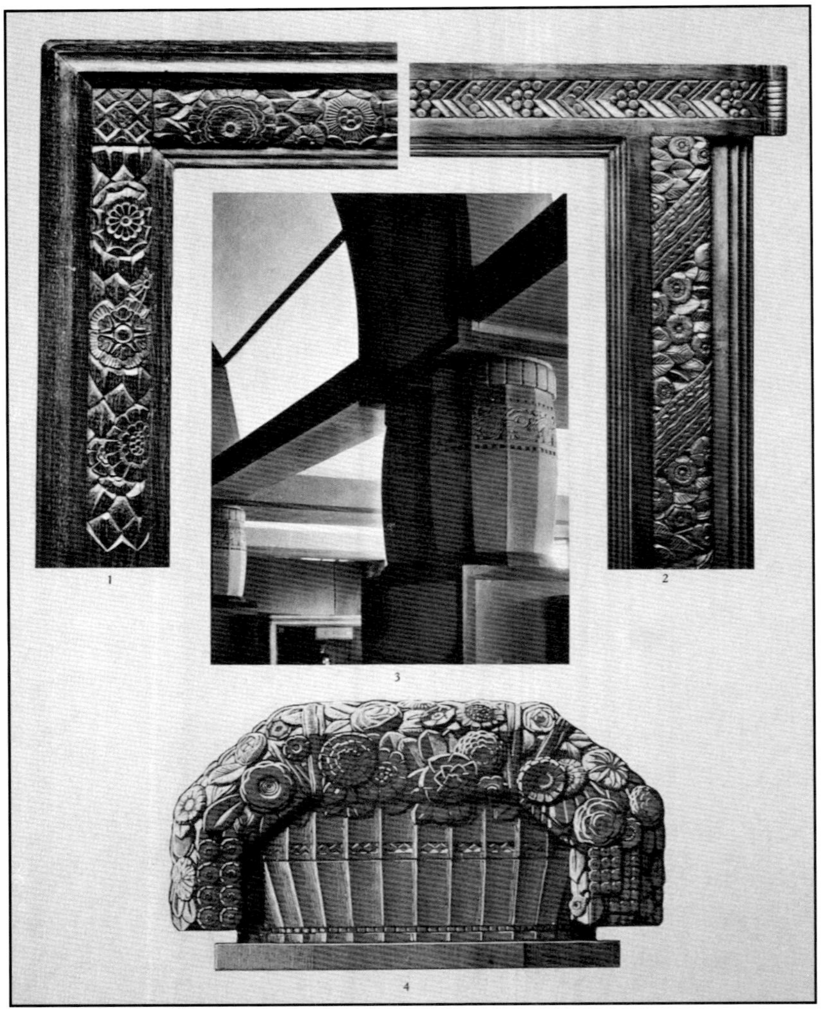

1 2 3 4

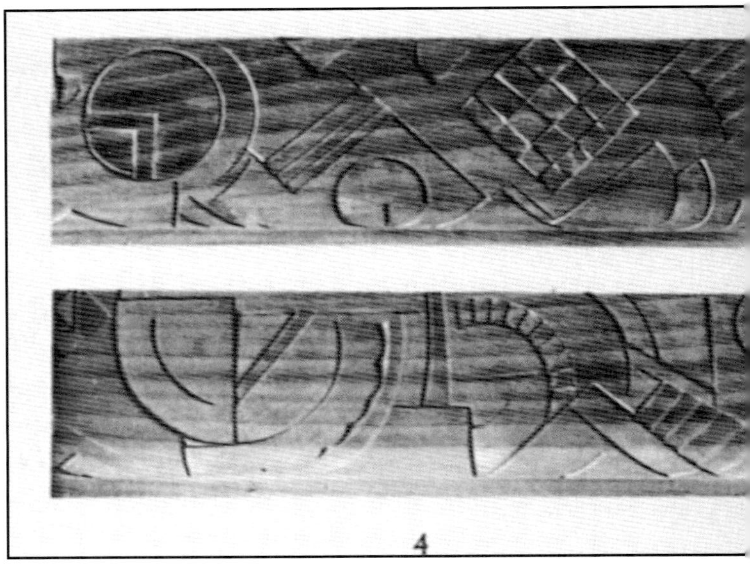

4

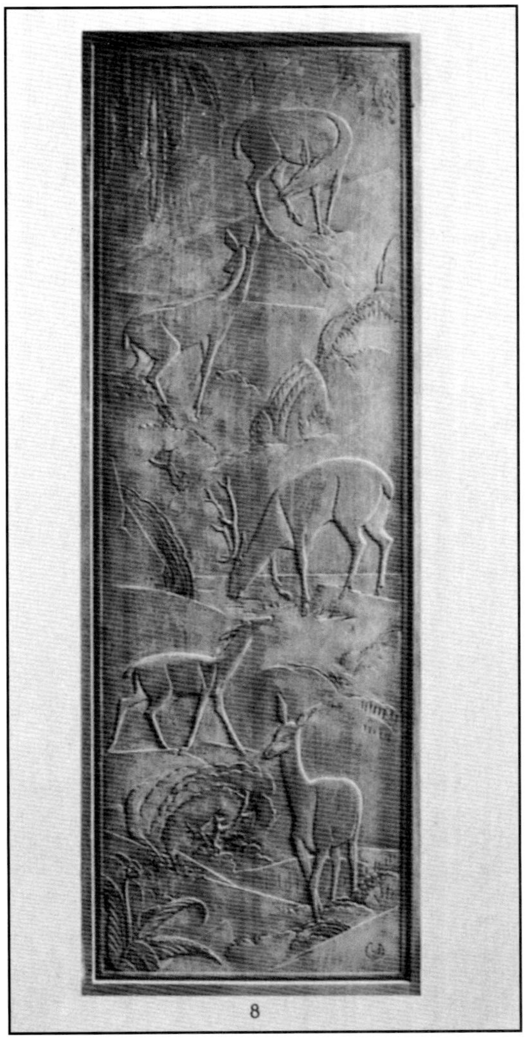

8

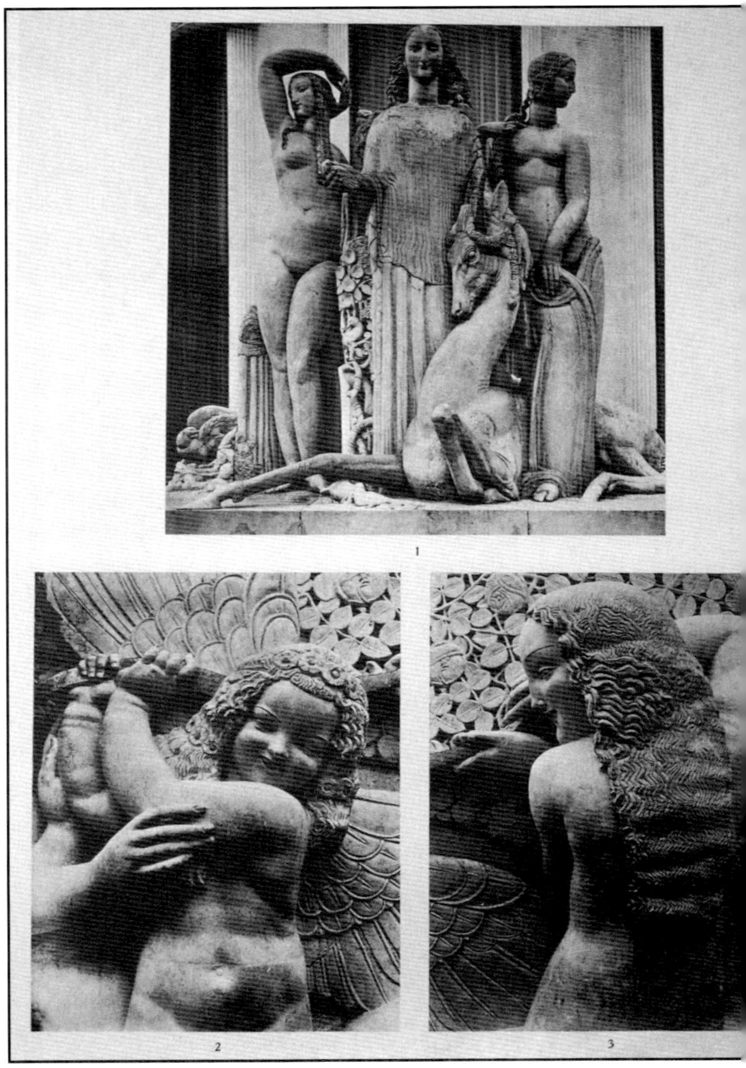

1 2 3

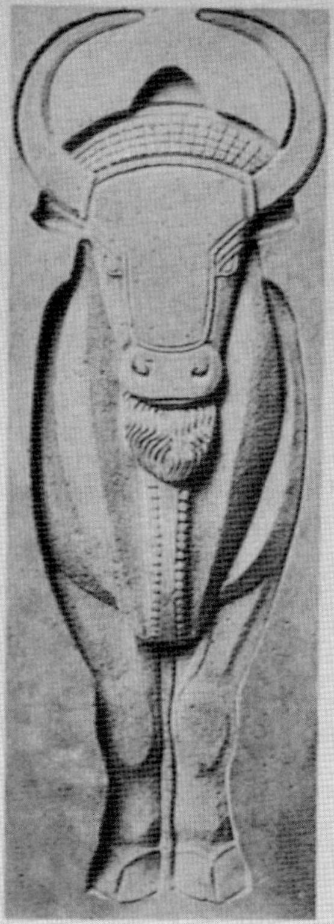

1

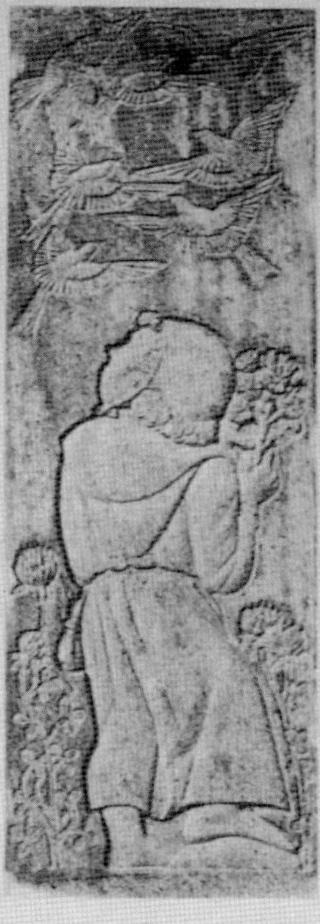

2

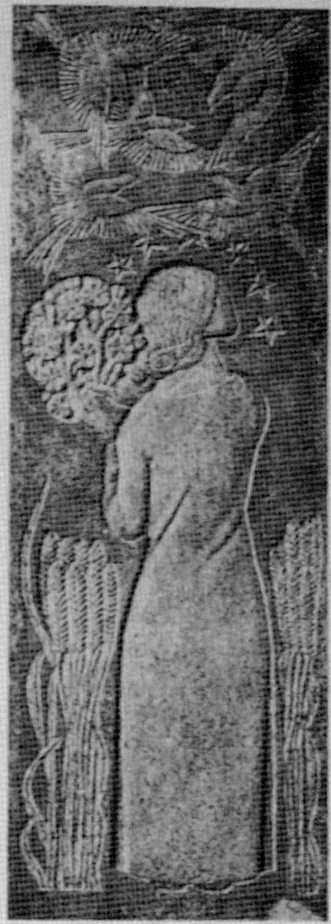

3

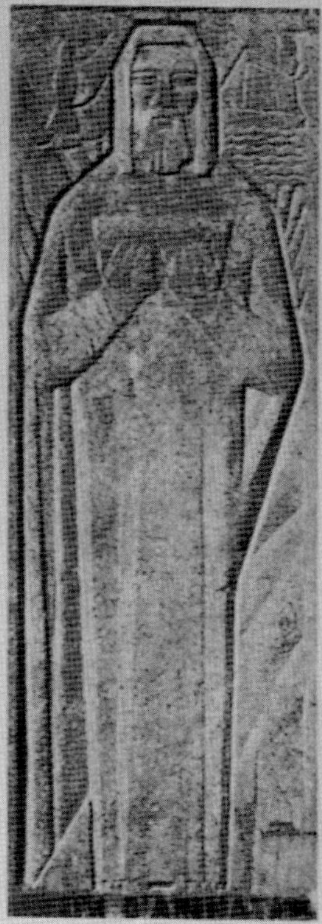

4

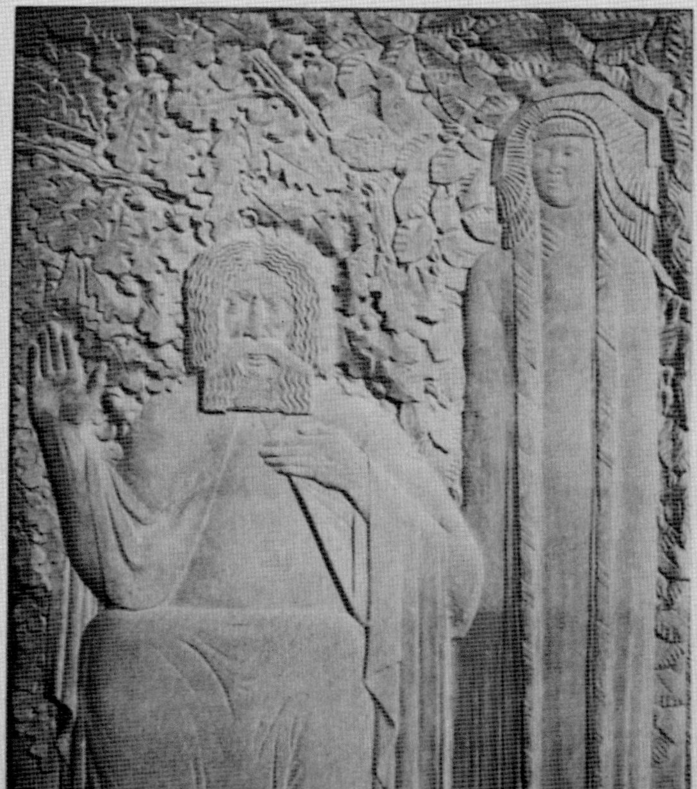

5

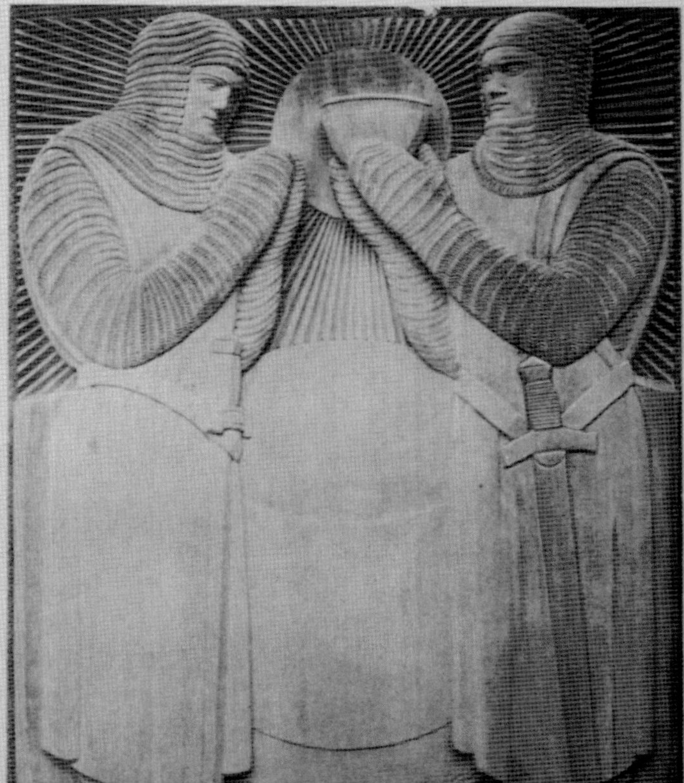

6

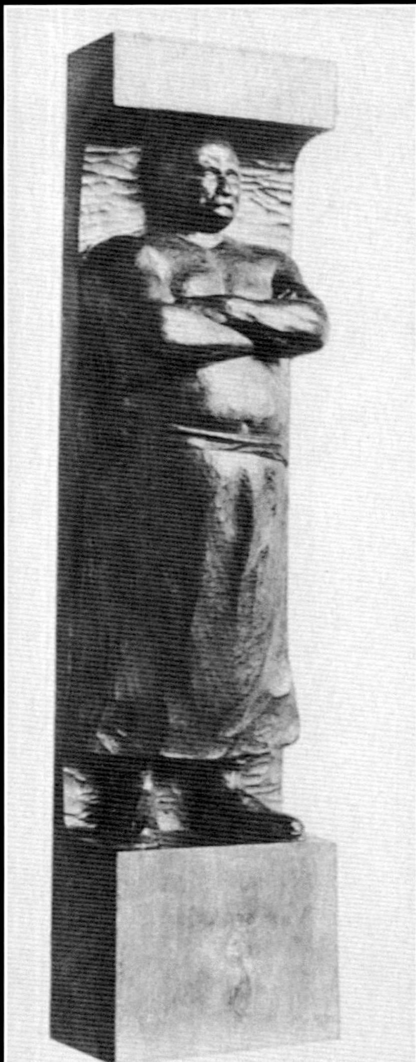

2

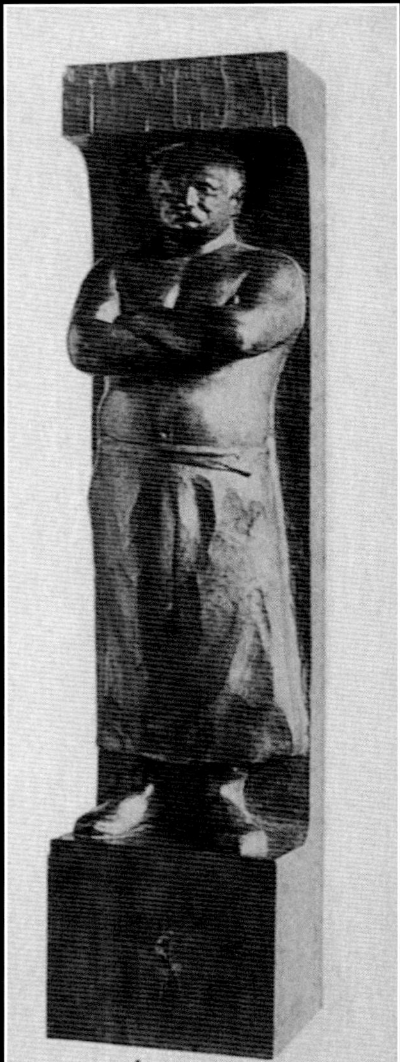

4

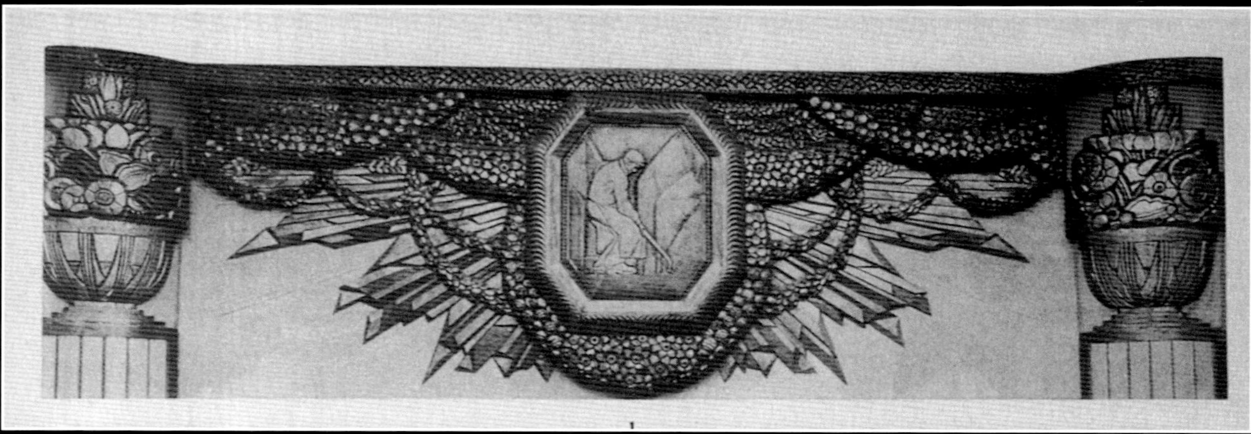

1

2 4

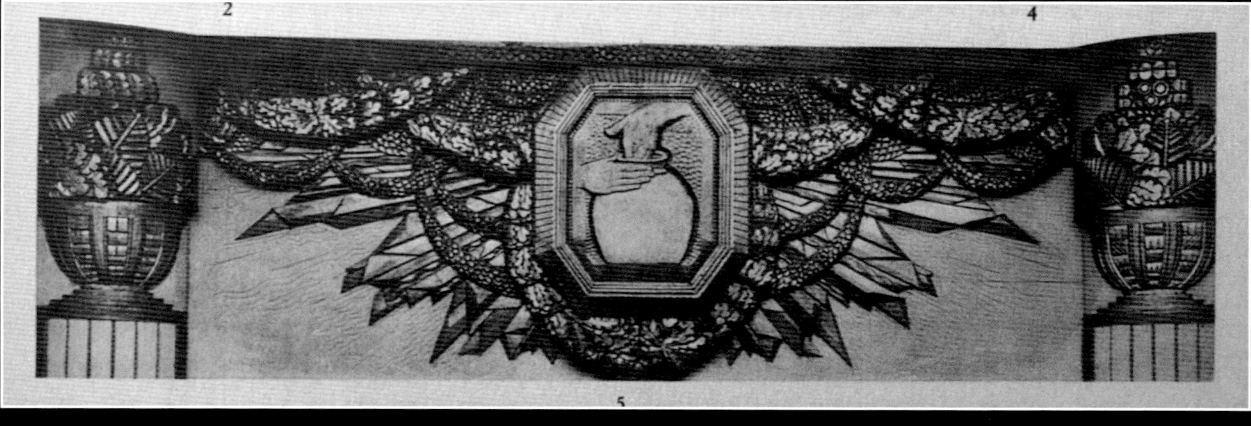

5

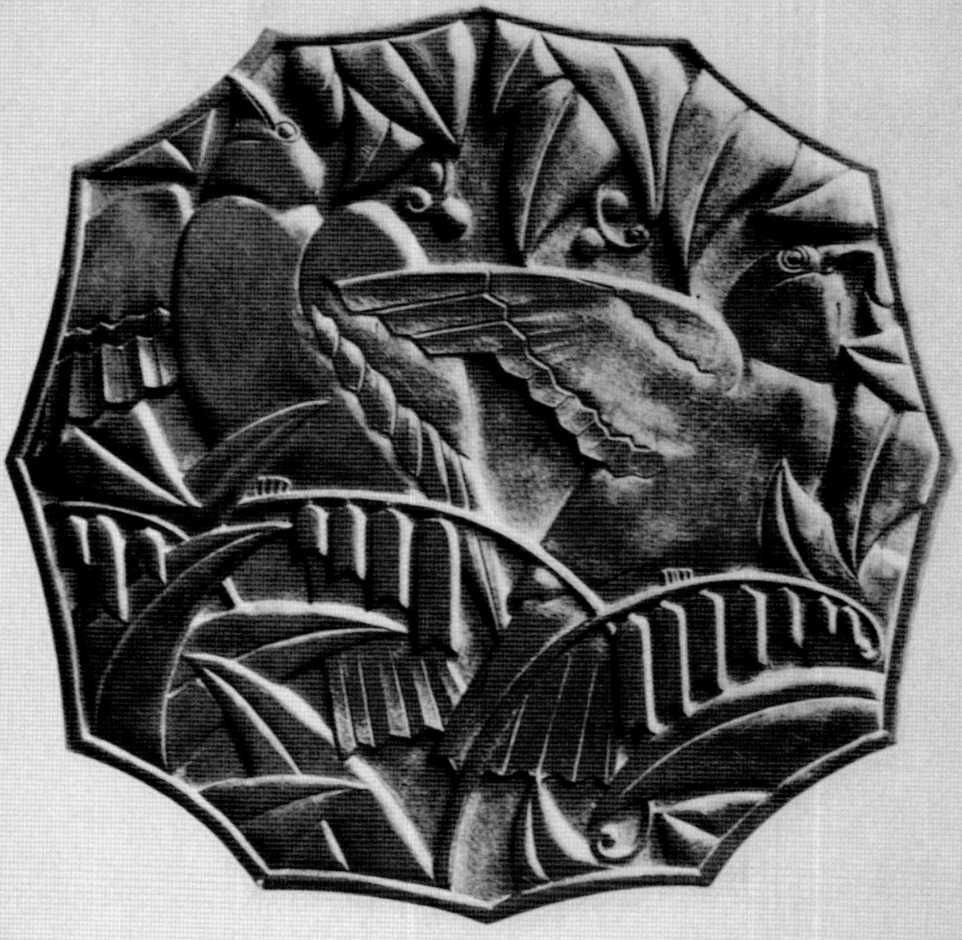

1

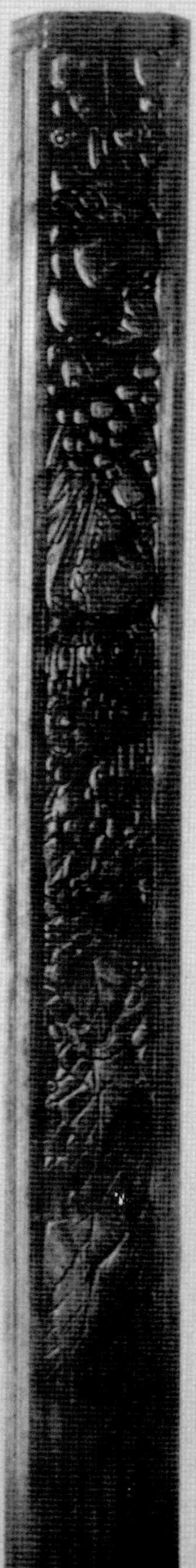

2

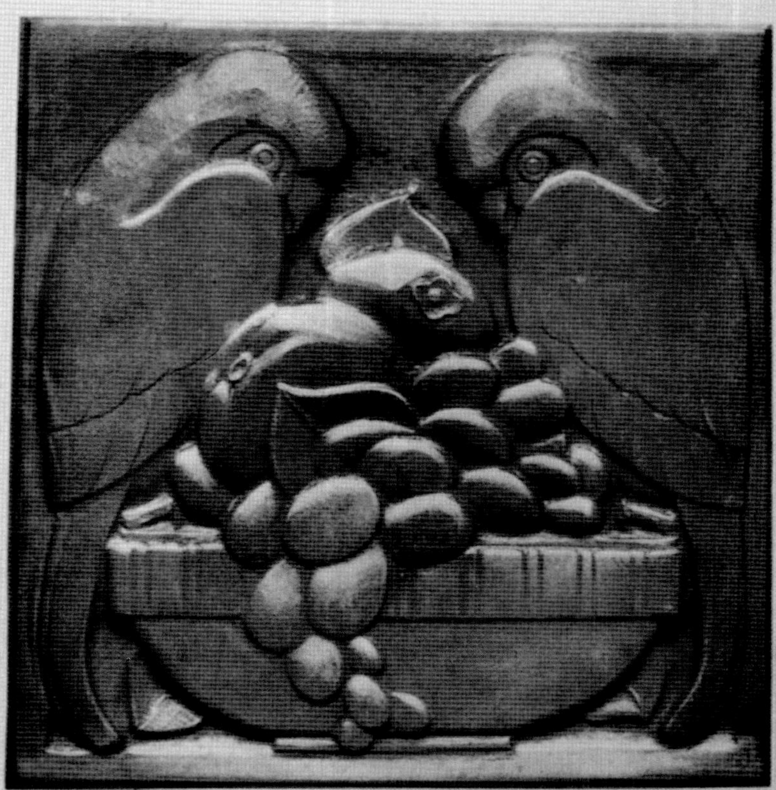

3

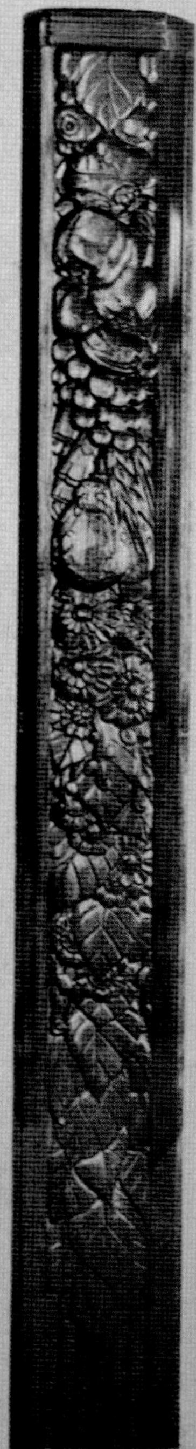

4

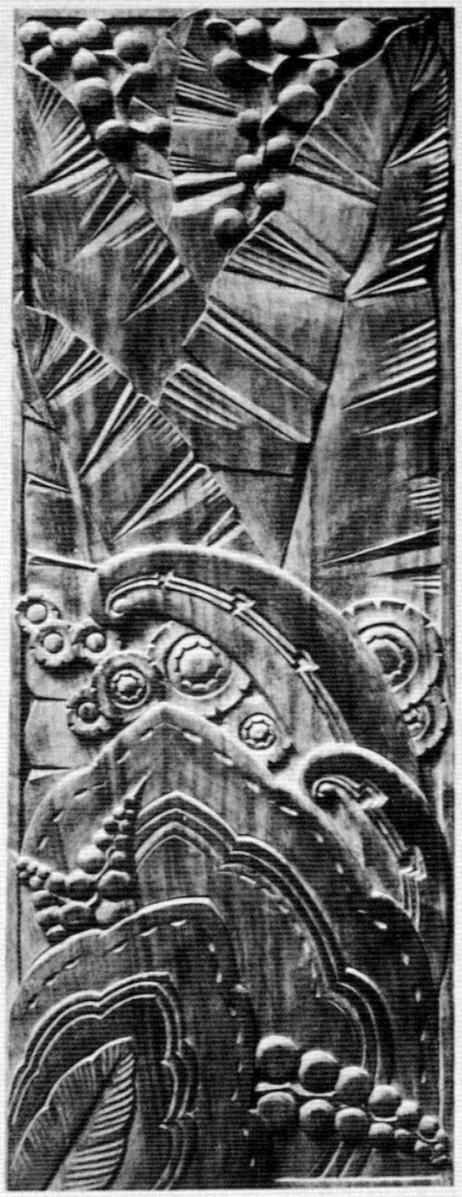

1

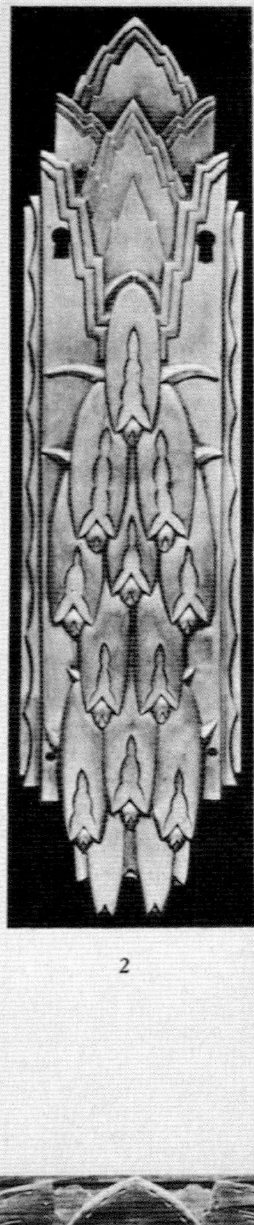

2

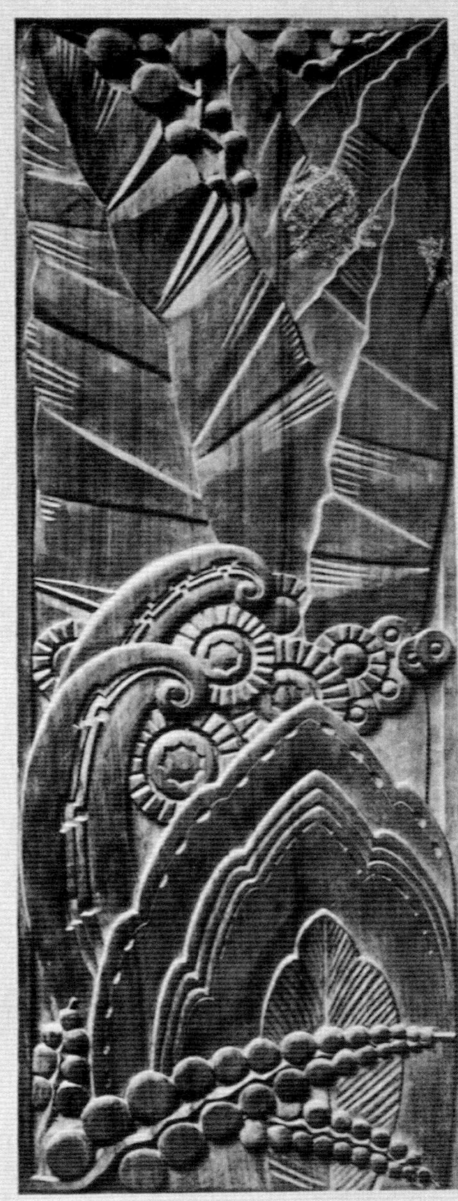

3

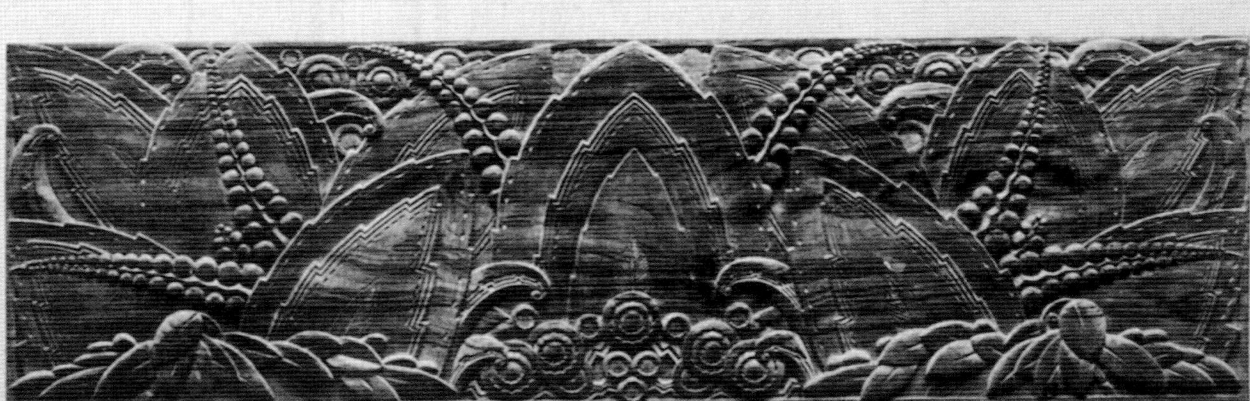

4

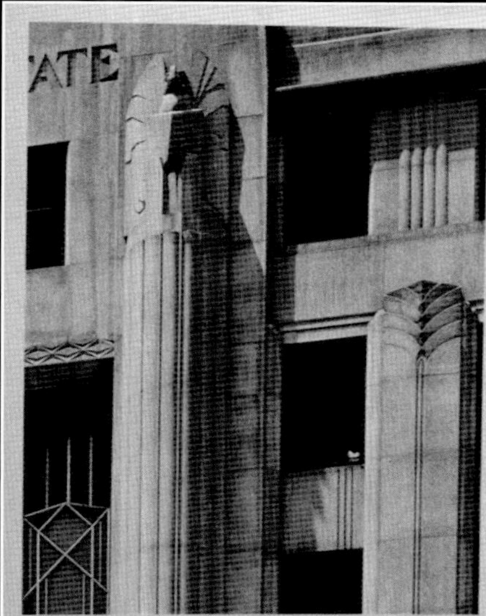

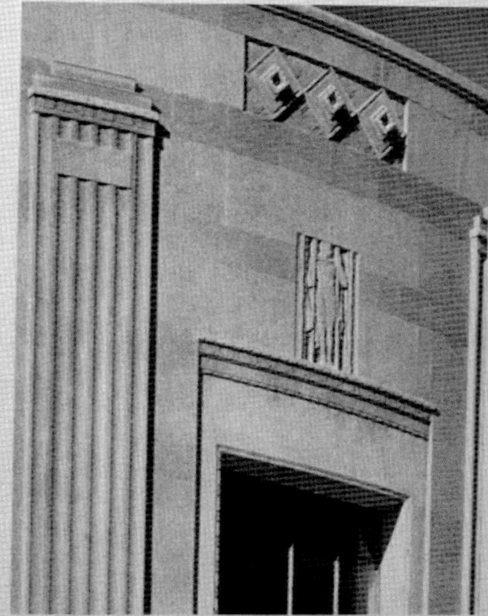

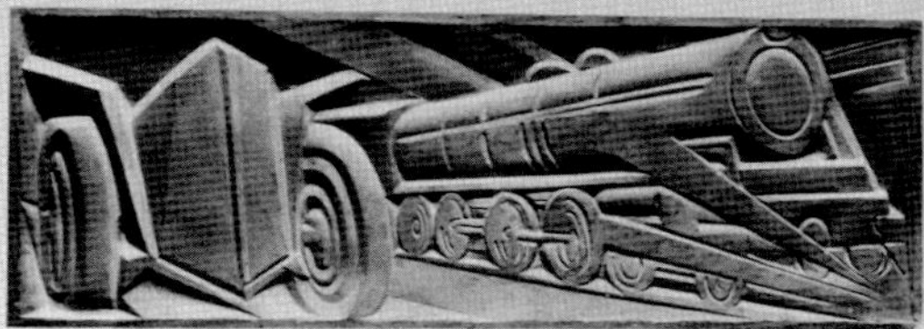

1

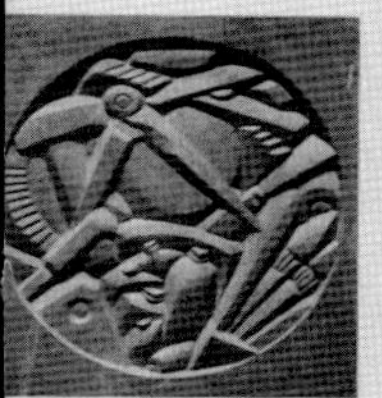

2

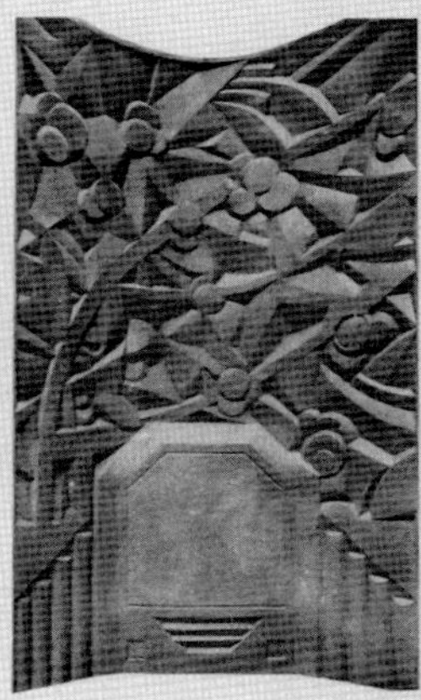

3

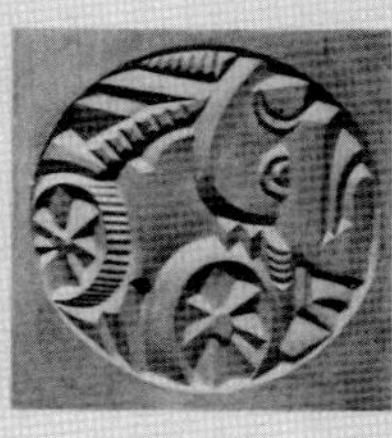

4

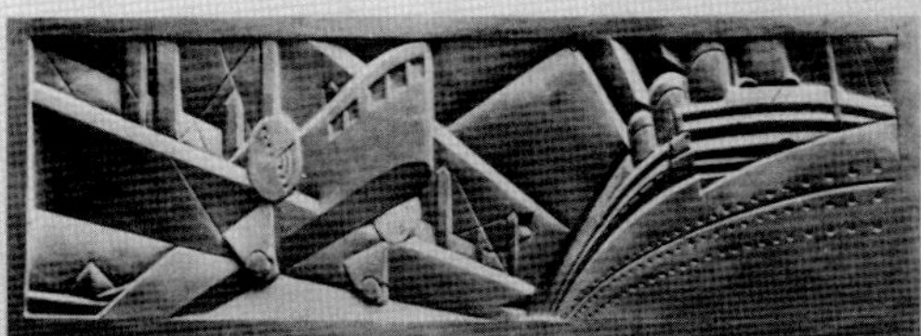

5

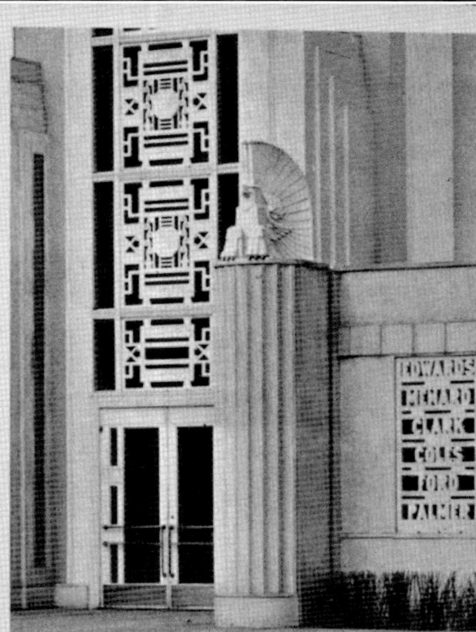

C. Herrick Hammond

Moise H. Goldstein *Nimmons, Carr & Wright*

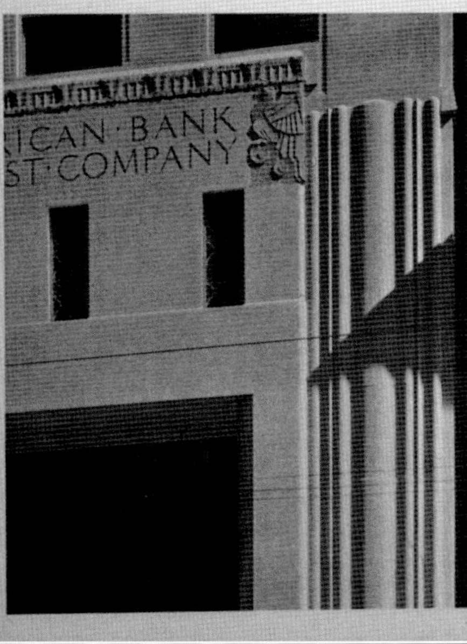

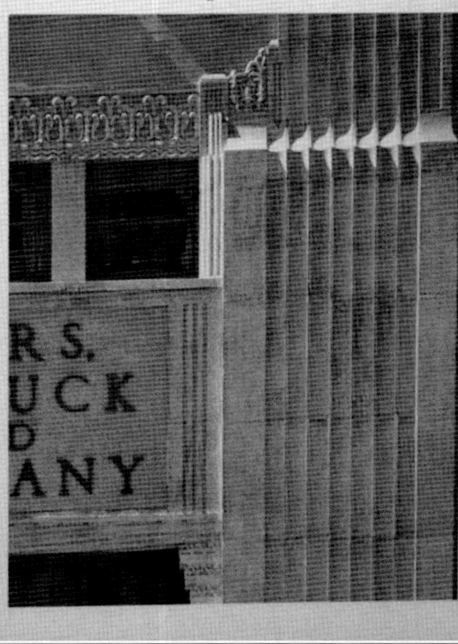

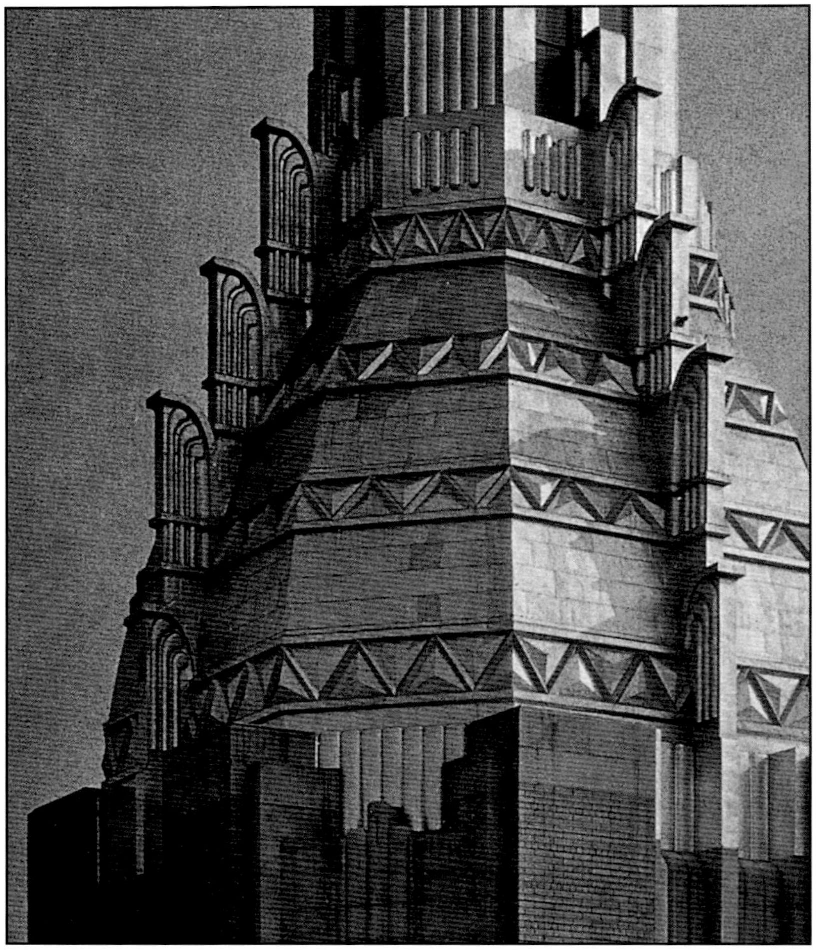

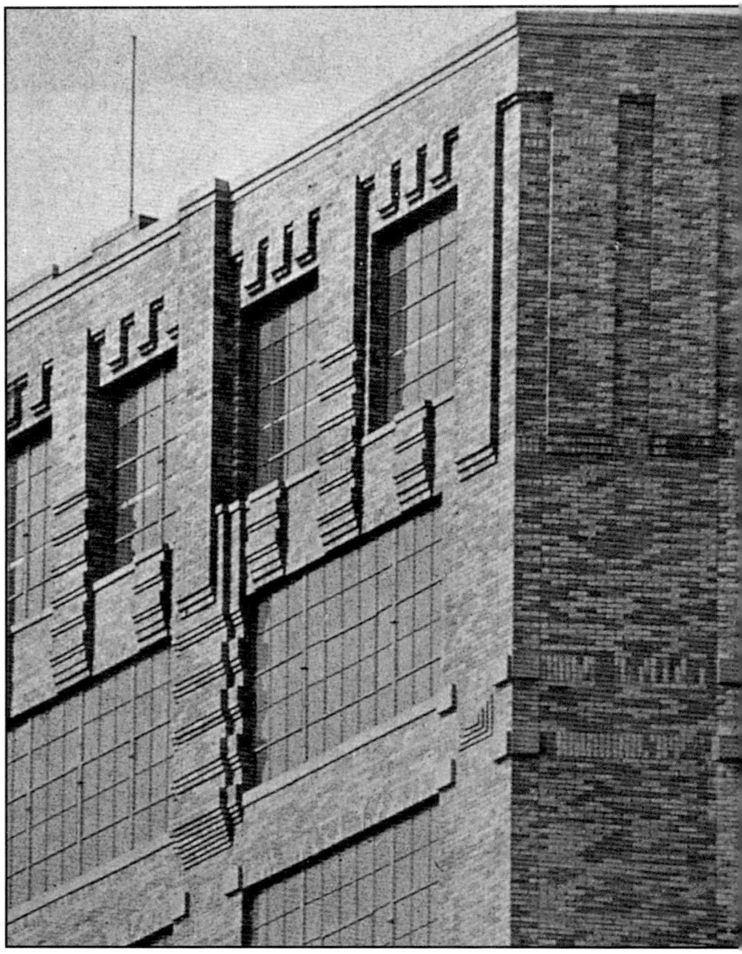

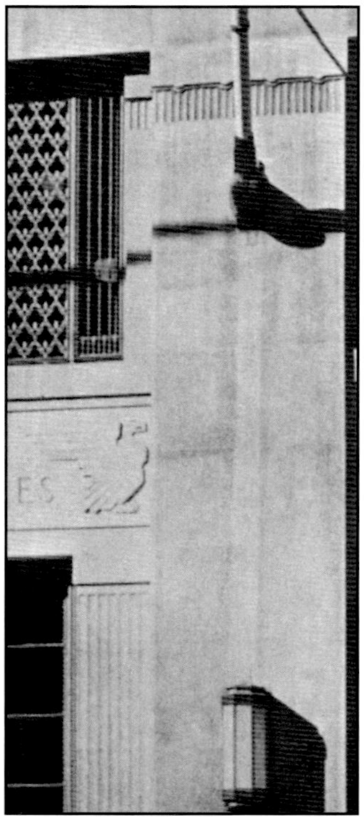

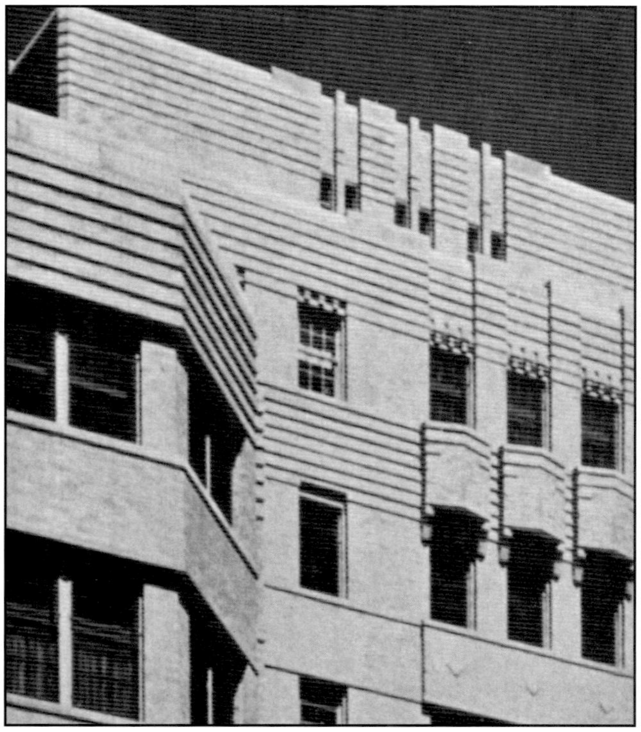

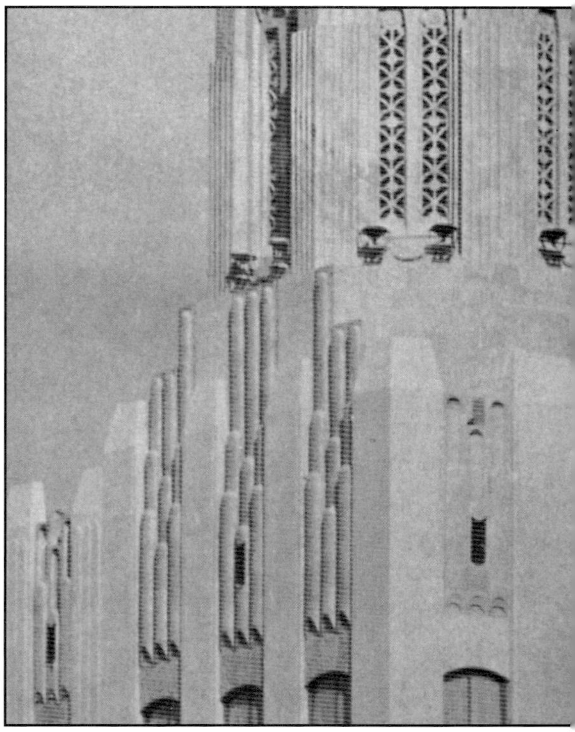

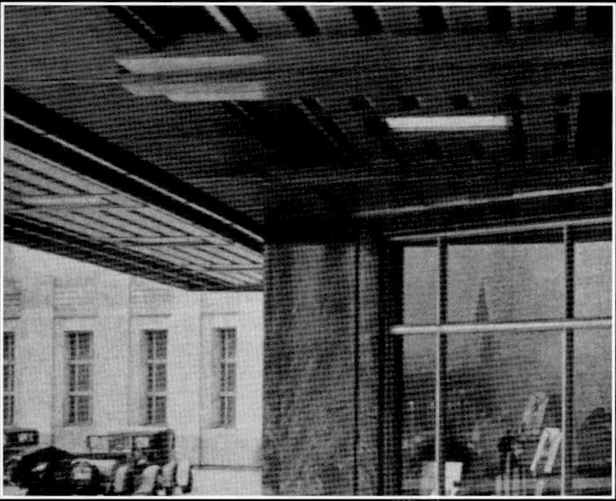

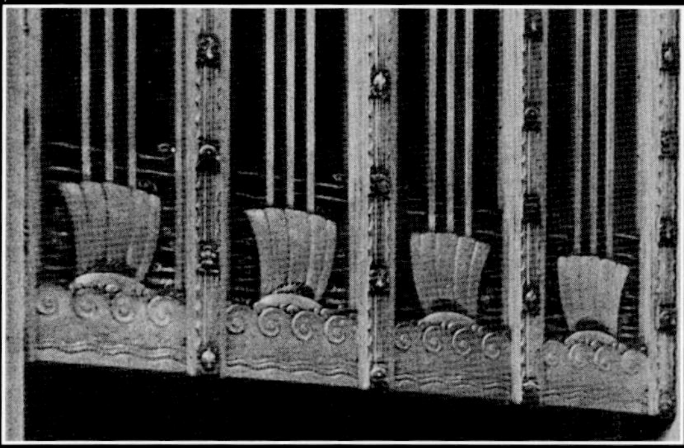

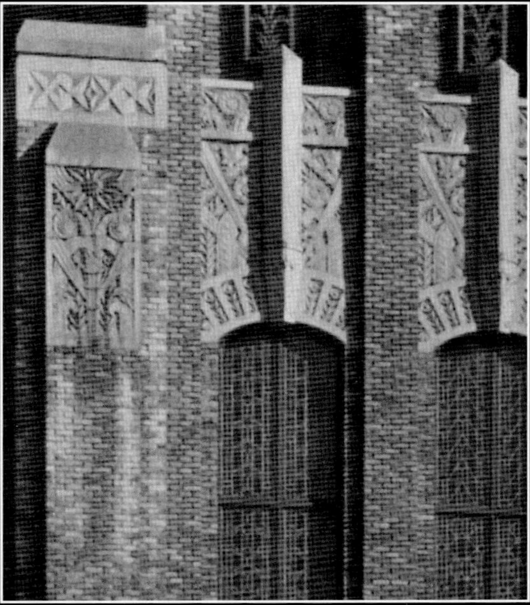

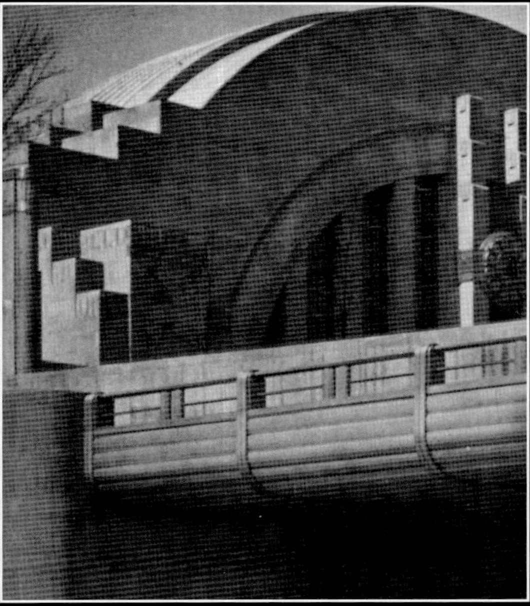

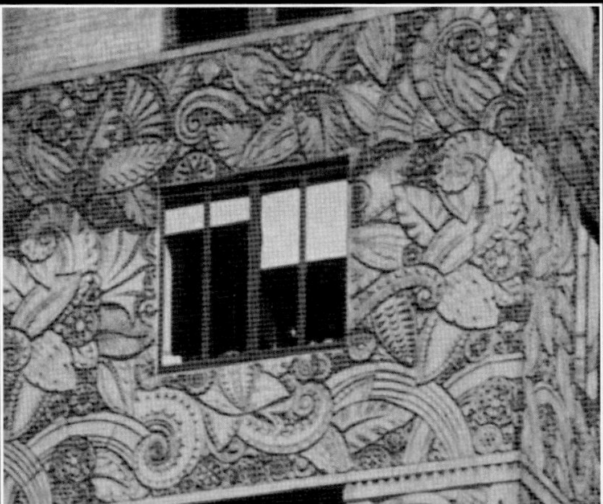

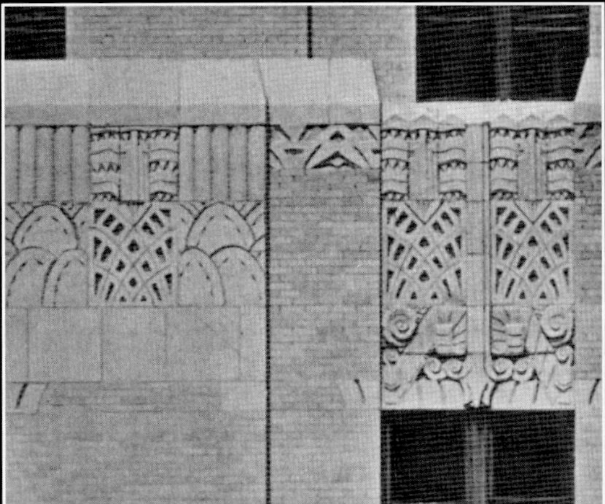

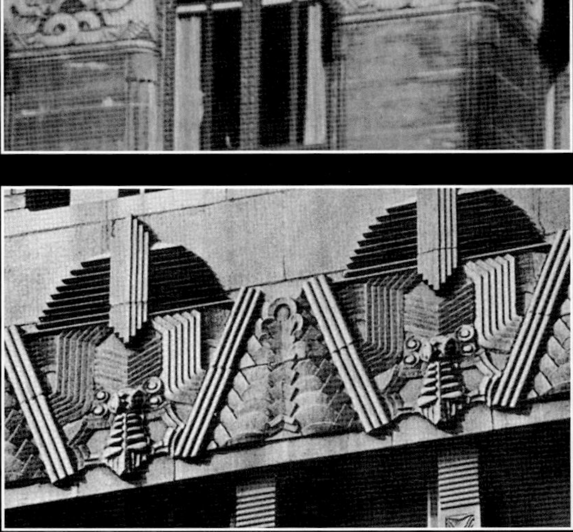

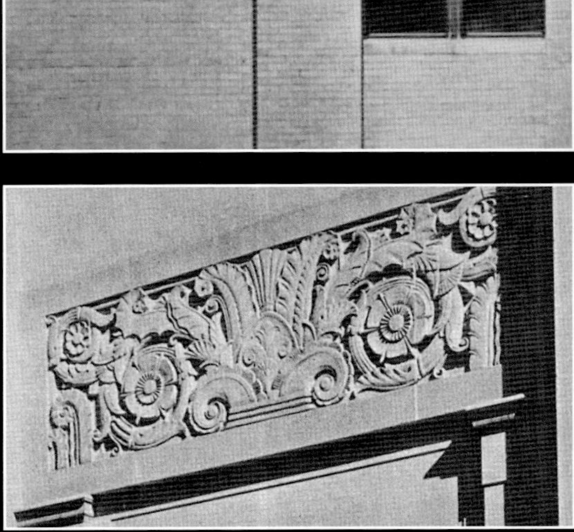

Acknowledgments

For the foresight of various collectors to carefully preserve the many catalogs, scrapbooks and portfolios over the years from which we were able to create this publication, we thank you. To the Anton Schroll & Co., Details D'Architecture Contemporaine Serie, Catalog of E. Borderel et Robert, La Ferronnerie Moderne Series, Nouvelles Devantures Agencements de Magasins, Ornamental Iron of Ye Iron in Des Moines, and all companies and publications that displayed these genious creations to the public. The iron-work and sculpture included were designed by artists and art directors such as R. Stubes, Henri Clouzot, René-Herbst, Herbert W. Hahn, and others from Europe and the United States from 1904 to 1933. Charles Moreau and other prominent editors displayed the artists' works to the world; we are now able to bring these designs back to inspire future generations.
Many thanks to Melissa Cardona and Pete Schiffer for their many hours of effort in editing and compiling these images.

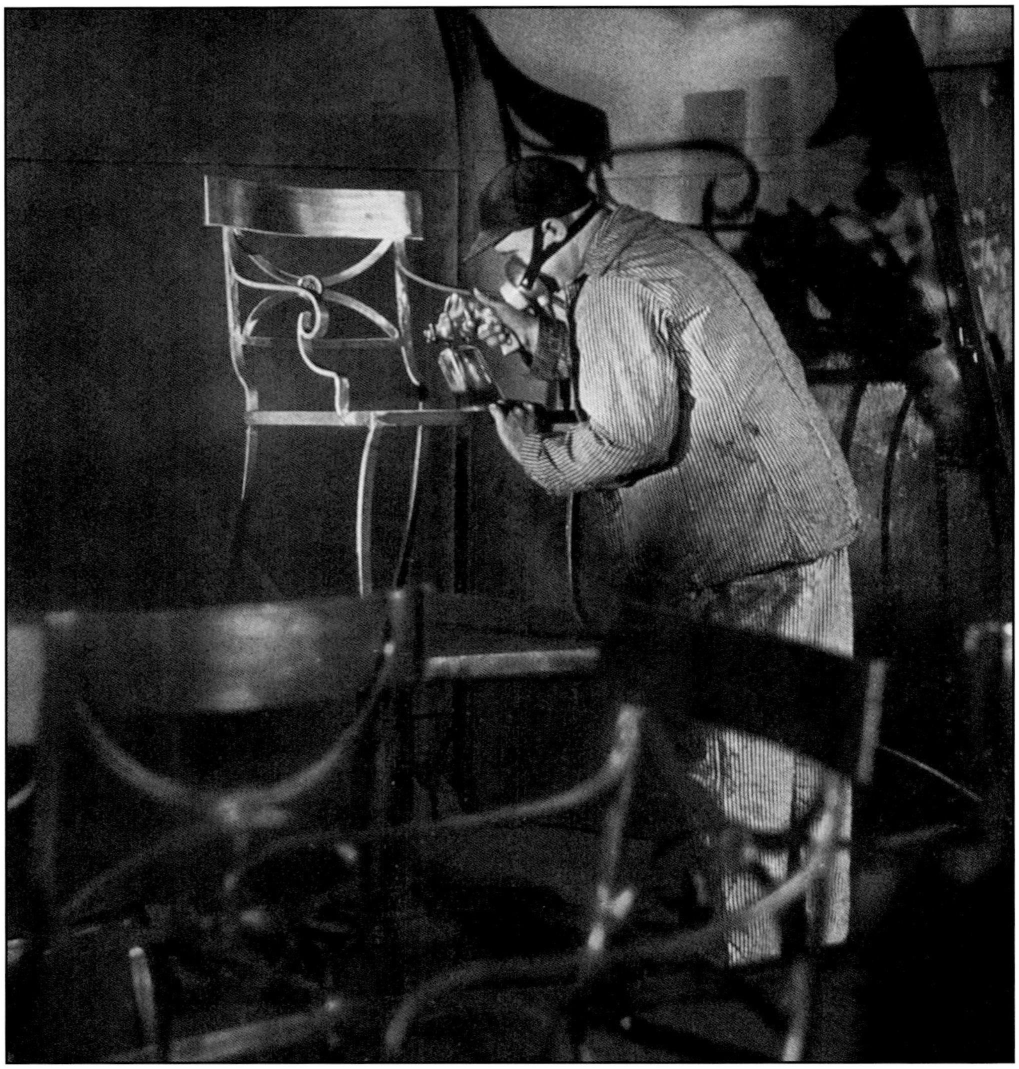

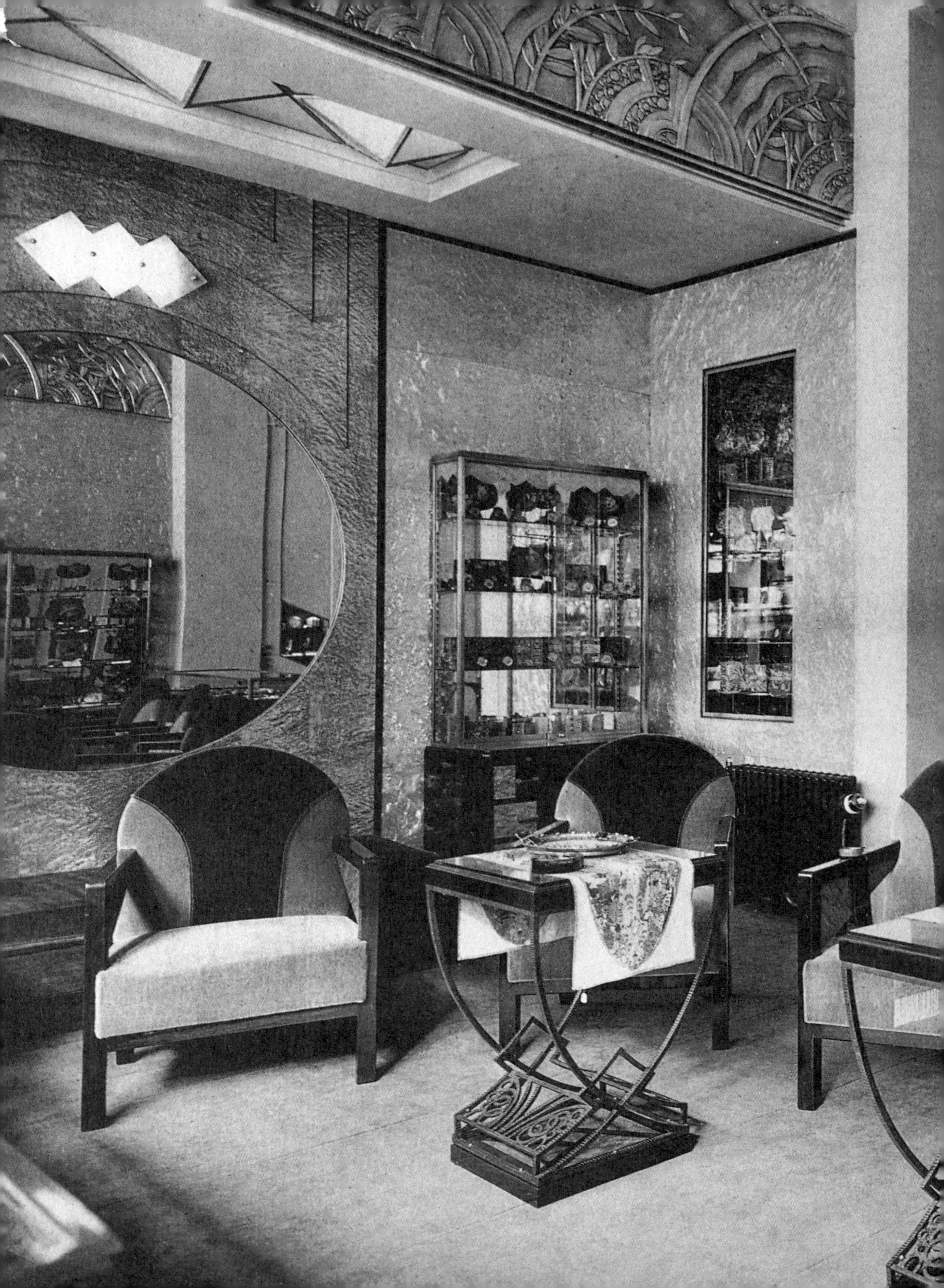